Neuropsychological Assessment
of Neuropsychiatric Disorders

Neuropsychological Assessment of Neuropsychiatric Disorders

edited by

IGOR GRANT, M.D., F.R.C.P.(C)

Professor of Psychiatry
University of California, San Diego, and
Assistant Chief of Psychiatry
San Diego Veterans Administration Medical Center
La Jolla, California

KENNETH M. ADAMS, PH.D., A.B.P.P.

Division Head
Division of Neuropsychology, and
Chief Psychologist, Senior Medical Staff
Henry Ford Hospital
Detroit, Michigan

New York   Oxford
OXFORD UNIVERSITY PRESS
1986

Oxford University Press

Oxford   New York   Toronto
Delhi   Bombay   Calcutta   Madras   Karachi
Petaling Jaya   Singapore   Hong Kong   Tokyo
Nairobi   Dar es Salaam   Cape Town
Melbourne   Auckland

and associated companies in
Beirut   Berlin   Ibadan   Nicosia

Copyright © 1986 by Oxford University Press, Inc.

Published by Oxford University Press, Inc.,
200 Madison Avenue, New York, New York 10016

LIBRARY OF CONGRESS CATALOGING IN PUBLICATION DATA
Main entry under title:
Neuropsychological assessment of neuropsychiatric disorders.
Includes bibliographies and index.
1. Mental illness—Diagnosis.   2. Nervous system—Diseases—Diagnosis.
3. Neuropsychological tests.   4. Neuropsychiatry.
I. Grant, Igor, 1942–   .   II. Adams, Kenneth M., 1948–   .
[DNLM: 1. Mental Disorders—diagnosis.   2. Nervous System Diseases—diagnosis.
3. Neuropsychological Tests. WM 145 N4945]
RC473.N48N47   1986   616.89′075   84-29629
ISBN 0-19-503545-3

Printing (last digit): 9 8 7 6 5 4 3 2 1

Printed in the United States of America

Preface

This book is devoted to advances in neuropsychology, the scientific discipline and clinical practice concerned with brain–behavior relationships. The growth of neuropsychology in the past quarter century has been nothing short of extraordinary. Publications in the field have risen from a handful annually in the 1950s to many hundreds of papers annually in the 1980s. New journals, devoted specifically to the field, have emerged; and one of the principal societies for exchange of neuropsychological information—The International Neuropsychological Society—has grown in the past decade from a few hundred psychologists and physicians to over 2,000 members as of this writing. This growth has been paralleled by increasing numbers of neuropsychological presentations at scientific meetings of psychologists, neurologists, neurolinguists, and psychiatrists. More remarkably, neuropsychological topics are becoming ever more commonplace in meetings of scientists concerned with other medical problems, for example, pulmonary physicians, diabetologists, nephrologists, cardiologists, oncologists, and specialists in infectious diseases.

The growth of neuropsychology has not been a happenstance; in medical sciences, it was fueled by research in basic neurosciences, advances in clinical neurosciences (neurology, neurosurgery, neuroradiology), the growth of biological psychiatry, and the redefinition of older notions of the "psychosomatic" interface. These developments were vitally shaped by the interactions of clinical, experimental, and developmental psychology.

The explosion of information in basic neuroscience need hardly be reviewed here. The structural and functional characterization of a large number of neurotransmitters, receptors, and their respective regulatory mechanisms; advances in molecular biology which are leading to an understanding of how genes control neural activity; progress in neuroanatomy, neurobiophysics, and computer assisted electrophysiology are all bringing us closer to bridging that leap of faith—that we will someday understand how molecular changes in the brain translate into thinking, feeling, and acting.

Clinical disciplines rooted in neuroscience have also experienced substantial advances, ranging from the mapping of the DNA marker linked to the gene of Huntington's disease to the discovery of an effective treatment for the dopamine deficiency of Parkinson's disease. If some component of that syndrome that we call schizophrenia is, indeed, related to excess mesolimbic dopamine activity, then it should be possible to relieve the symptoms of this disabling psychosis, as well. Perhaps some subset of the dementias of the elderly will be shown to be related to deficits in the cholinergic system. This could lead to effective pharmacological methods of enhancing the cholinergic circuits that remain intact.

The rate of scientific advance in the assessment, study, and remediation of brain-related cognitive and affective disorders has been rapid. Problems of basic identification of cerebral deficit have moved to more advanced issues of specificity, subtyping, and reversibility. This promise at both the basic and clinical levels has created a challenge for scientists and clinicians wishing to measure the product of brain function—its behavior—in as sensitive and specific a way as possible. We see the growth of neuropsychology as a response to this challenge, and much of the work contained in this book describes both methods of approach and specific results of application.

An increasing stimulus to neuropsychology is the gradual redefinition of traditional notions of "psychosomatics." Up to the early seventies, those concerned with the "mind–body" problem were principally psychiatrists and psychologists rooted in psychoanalytic epistemology. Allied with this were early efforts to identify a "borderland" between psychiatry and neurology on a speculative or subjective basis. More recently, behavioral and cognitive-behavioral notions have come to be applied to ever broader problems in medical psychology or "behavioral medicine." An equally important development however has been the desire of physicians from many different specialties to understand the impact of the diseases they were studying, and of the treatments they were delivering, on their patients' ability to think, remember, perceive—in a word, on their cognitive functions. This interest accounts for the increasing number of neuropsychological studies related to diseases such as chronic obstructive pulmonary disease (COPD), diabetes mellitus, hypertension, cancer and cancer chemotherapy, and, most recently, acquired immune deficiency disease (AIDS).

This book represents an attempt to capture this new ferment in neuropsychology. We have divided the book into two parts. Part One deals with some representative approaches to comprehensive neuropsychological assessment. We make no pretense of completely covering the many important approaches that exist; rather, we have selected a few that exemplify the richness of neuropsychological work today.

Part Two concerns itself with some applications of neuropsychology both in traditional clinical areas, i.e., neurology, neurosurgery, alcoholism—and also encompasses some of neuropsychology's newer interactions with psychiatry (e.g., in the areas of schizophrenia and the affective disorders), drug abuse, and general medical problems.

In editing this book, and in inviting our contributors, we have tried to appeal to a multidisciplinary audience. This we have done out of a conviction that one of neuropsychology's important roles in the future will be that of bridging our understanding of fundamental neurobiological phenomena and their expression in qualitative and quantitative aspects of information processing.

We wish to take this opportunity to thank our contributors for their thoughtful and thought-provoking chapters. We also thank the many individuals who assisted us with the practical work of putting this volume together. We acknowledge particularly the assistance of Robert Reed, Debi Taylor, Joanne McCoy, Janet Knauss, Dr. Linda Scharf, James Golowksi, Jill Rich, Melissa Azvara, Lucy Brysk, Anne Larson, and JoAnn Grant whose efforts included, but were not limited to, transcribing and proofreading the manuscript, checking references, assisting in the creation of subject, author, and test indexes, and general correspondence related to compilation of this volume. Special thanks are extended to Jeffrey House and Susan Meigs of Oxford University Press for their guidance and hard work on behalf of this volume. This work was also supported in part by the Medical Research Service of the Veterans Administration (award SA:325 to Dr. Grant), and by the Project and Human Rights Committee of Henry Ford Hospital (award R35679 to Dr. Adams).

I.G.
K.M.A.

Contents

Contributors

Kenneth M. Adams, Ph.D.
Division Head, Division of
Neuropsychology
Department of Psychiatry, and
Chief Psychologist, Senior Medical Staff
Henry Ford Hospital
Detroit, Michigan

Anne Dull Baird, Ph.D.
Senior Staff Psychologist
Division of Neuropsychology
Department of Psychiatry
Henry Ford Hospital
Detroit, Michigan

Francois Boller, M.D., Ph.D.
Professor of Neurology and Psychiatry
School of Medicine
University of Pittsburgh
Pittsburgh, Pennsylvania

Michael R. Bond, M.D., Ph.D., M.R.C.P.
(Glas), F.R.C.S. (Edin), M.R.C.Psych.
Professor and Head
Department of Psychological Medicine
University of Glasgow
Glasgow, Scotland

Jason Brandt, Ph.D.
Assistant Professor of Psychology
Johns Hopkins University and School
of Medicine
Baltimore, Maryland

Gregory G. Brown, Ph.D.
Senior Staff Psychologist
Division of Neuropsychology
Department of Psychiatry
Henry Ford Hospital
Detroit, Michigan

Nelson Butters, Ph.D.
Chief, Psychology Service
San Diego Veterans Administration
Medical Center
Professor of Psychiatry
University of California, San Diego
La Jolla, California

Eric D. Caine, M.D.
Associate Professor of Psychiatry and
Neurology
Director, Neuropsychiatry Program
University of Rochester
School of Medicine and Dentistry
Rochester, New York

Albert S. Carlin, Ph.D.
Associate Professor
Psychiatry and Behavioral Sciences
University of Washington
Seattle, Washington

Louis D. Costa, Ph.D.
Professor of Psychology and
Dean of Social Sciences
University of Victoria
Victoria, British Columbia
Canada

Elkhonon Goldberg, Ph.D.
Associate Professor
Albert Einstein College of Medicine
Director of Neuropsychology
Department of Psychiatry
Montefiore Medical Center
New York, New York

Gerald Goldstein, Ph.D.
Director, Neuropsychology Research
Program
Highland Drive Veterans Administration
Medical Center
Associate Professor of Psychiatry and
Psychology
University of Pittsburgh
Pittsburgh, Pennsylvania

Igor Grant, M.D., F.R.C.P.(C)
  Assistant Chief of Psychiatry
  San Diego Veterans Administration
    Medical Center
  Professor of Psychiatry
  University of California, San Diego
  La Jolla, California

Robert K. Heaton, Ph.D.
  Associate Professor
  Department of Psychiatry
  Director, Neuropsychology Laboratory
  University of Colorado School of
    Medicine
  Denver, Colorado

Nancy Hebben, Ph.D.
  Neurology Department, McClean
    Hospital
  Department of Psychiatry
  Harvard Medical School
  Boston, Massachusetts

Michael Joschko, Ph.D.
  Director of Psychology
  Queen Alexandra Hospital for Children
  Visiting Assistant Professor of Psychology
  University of Victoria
  Victoria, British Columbia
  Canada

Edith Kaplan, Ph.D.
  Director, Clinical Neuropsychological
    Services
  Boston Veterans Administration Medical
    Center
  Associate Professor of Neurology
    (Neuropsychology)
  Boston University School of Medicine
  Boston, Massachusetts

Alfred W. Kaszniak, Ph.D.
  Associate Professor
  Department of Psychiatry
  University of Arizona College of Medicine
  Tucson, Arizona

Nanci C. Keefe, M.A.
  Program Coordinator
  Alzheimer Research Program
  University of Pittsburgh
  Pittsburgh, Pennsylvania

Tor Løberg, Ph.D.
  Senior Lecturer in Neuropsychology
  Department of Clinical Neuropsychology
  University of Bergen
  Bergen, Norway

Charles G. Matthews, Ph.D.
  Professor of Neurology
  Director, Neuropsychology Laboratory
  University of Wisconsin Center for Health
    Sciences
  Madison, Wisconsin

Pat McKenna, Ph.D.
  Psychology Department
  The National Hospitals for Nervous
    Diseases
  London, England

William P. Milberg, Ph.D.
  GRECC Center, Boston
  Assistant Professor, Department of
    Psychiatry
  Harvard Medical School
  Boston, Massachusetts

Domenico Passafiume, Ph.D.
  Department of Psychology
  University of Rome
  Rome, Italy

Ralph M. Reitan, Ph.D.
  Director, Neuropsychology Laboratory
  Department of Psychology
  University of Arizona
  Tucson, Arizona

Byron P. Rourke, Ph.D.
  Professor, Department of Psychology
  University of Windsor
  Head, Department of Neuropsychology
  Windsor Western Hospital Centre
  Windsor, Ontario
  Canada

Diane L. Russell, M.A.
  Department of Psychology
  University of Windsor
  Windsor, Ontario
  Canada

Mark W. Shatz, Ph.D.
  Senior Staff Psychologist
  Division of Neuropsychology
  Director of Internship Training
  Department of Psychiatry
  Henry Ford Hospital
  Detroit, Michigan

Larry R. Squire, Ph.D.
  Research Career Scientist
  San Diego Veterans Administration
    Medical Center
  Professor of Psychiatry
  University of California, San Diego
  La Jolla, California

John D. Strang, Ph.D.
  Clinical Neuropsychologist
  Department of Neuropsychology
  Windsor Western Hospital Centre
  Windsor, Ontario
  Canada

Pamela J. Thompson, Ph.D.
  Department of Psychological Medicine
  The National Hospitals for Nervous
    Diseases
  London, England

Michael R. Trimble, M.R.C.P., F.R.C.P.
  Consultant Physician in Psychological
    Medicine
  The National Hospitals for Nervous
    Diseases
  Senior Lecturer in Behavioral Neurology

Institute of Neurology, University of
    London
  London, England

Elizabeth K. Warrington, Ph.D., Sc.D.
  Psychology Department
  The National Hospitals for Nervous
    Diseases
  London, England

Gerald C. Young, Ph.D.
  Department of Psychological Services
  St. Michael's Hospital
  Ontario Institute for Studies in Education
  University of Toronto
  Toronto, Ontario
  Canada

Allan Yozawitz, Ph.D.
  Director, Neuropsychology Unit
  Hutchings Psychiatric Center
  Assistant Professor, Department of
    Psychiatry
  State University of New York Upstate
    Medical Center
  Syracuse, New York

Neuropsychological Assessment
of Neuropsychiatric Disorders

1

Theoretical and Methodological Bases of the Halstead-Reitan Neuropsychological Test Battery

RALPH M. REITAN

Historical and Theoretical Background

Our general purpose in developing the Halstead-Reitan Neuropsychological test battery was to reflect reliably, validly, and completely the behavioral correlates of brain function. Obviously, this aim extends beyond our current achievements. As has been noted previously (Reitan, 1966a), insufficient information is presently available to develop a battery of tests that would reflect the full range of behavioral correlates of brain functions. Nevertheless, some information has been useful in making initial progress, including extensive knowledge of basic aspects of nervous system functioning and additional specific information regarding brain functioning. Thus, we have been able to make a reasonable start toward developing a fairly adequate neuropsychological test battery, taking into consideration (1) major theoretical factors that involve nervous system functioning, (2) the range and type of measurements that must be included, and (3) the measurement strategies that are required.

In determining what we are going to measure with a neuropsychological battery, we must first decide what the major categories of performance are that occur within the framework of nervous system functioning. In its most simple breakdown, it is obvious that receptive nervous system functions are involved (input from the environment), central processing functions are necessary, and expressive abilities or responses are needed (impact on the environment). The major emphasis of neuropsychological evaluation, contrasted with neurophysiological and some aspects of neurological examination, should be placed on the central processing functions that involve higher-level aspects of brain functions. Further, it is extremely important in a neuropsychological test battery to measure general as well as specific indicators of cerebral cortical functioning. The general indicators might provide an overall reflection of the biological integrity of the cerebral cortex, whereas the specific indicators might yield information regarding the differential functional characteristics of each cerebral hemisphere, as well as areas within each cerebral hemisphere. After deciding upon the types of measurements to be made, it is necessary to determine how to make the measurements themselves. Finally, consideration must be given to the measurement strategies to be used, or the complementary character of the various standardized experiments (psychological tests) proposed for inclusion. Prior experience has indicated that various approaches or strategies (level of performance, specific deficits or pathognomonic signs, patterns and relationships among the test results, and comparisons of functional efficiency of the two sides of the body as they are related to the contralateral cerebral hemispheres) are valid for assessing brain–behavior relationships. However, these approaches must be organized in accordance with the particular tests to be used and the range of measurements to be included. Thus, the Halstead-Reitan Neuropsychological Test Battery was developed to reflect the major components of nervous system functioning (input measurements, central processing, and output measurements), and the major areas of neuropsychological functioning reflected in human brain–behavior relationships. In terms of measurement strategies, the tests for the behavioral areas of cerebral cortical functioning had to be distributed among general and specific measurements and organized in such a way that the various methods of inference or strategic approaches would be adequately represented. Obviously, our approach in attempting to achieve this general aim was not simply to string together various types of psychological tests that we thought might be relevant to brain functioning. The aim was to develop a test battery that would reflect brain functions for the individual subject as contrasted with a test battery that represented only a series of measurements.

Using these guidelines it was possible to do some general planning about the nature of the test battery before deciding upon individual tests. Of course to implement such a general plan requires some knowledge of the behavioral correlates of cerebral lesions. Although Halstead and Reitan both observed individual patients with brain lesions and attempted to discern the fundamental kinds of abilities that need to be measured by a neuropsychological test battery, there can never be complete assurance that all types of deficits were observed. The tests that were initially included obviously represented informed guesses. Such guesses undoubtedly are highly important since the end result, even though validated through later experimental study, will represent no more than what originally was put in. Realizing that this was a weak point in the process of developing a neuropsychological test battery, and that there was no final basis for agreement among investigators in judging the adequacy of the content of the battery, it was apparent that another type of criterion was necessary. Halstead recognized this quite clearly from the beginning and insisted that the tests included in the battery be used to predict the condition of the brain of each subject who was examined. In this way one could empirically test the adequacy of the test battery's content as well as its organization. If it were possible to identify the relevant variables that would predict the biological condition of individual subjects' brains—one subject after another without failure—it would confirm on empirical grounds that the right tests had been included to represent higher-level aspects of brain functioning and that they were organized in such a way that they could be interpreted for the individual subject. In the early stages of the battery's development we did, in fact, encounter individual patients for whom results did not show any known abnormalities, even though independent neurological criteria distinctly showed brain damage. I recall having administered our test battery to a subject who I later learned from neurological surgeons had had his right anterior temporal lobe amputated, however it was not at all apparent in the test results. This finding, in its own right, clearly indicated that it was necessary either to add additional tests or to learn more about interpreting the existing tests with respect to the presence or absence of the right anterior temporal area. Eventually we solved the problem and now know quite well what the results from the battery relate to this particular area. It was possible to achieve this kind of progress only by evaluating a succession of subjects with various types of brain lesions, and the success of the battery, in this respect, has been clearly demonstrated (Reitan, 1964a). No other test battery, however, has been evaluated empirically with thousands of patients, tested one after another, to determine whether the battery included a sufficient range of measurements to reflect the deficits in each patient, regardless of the location of the lesion, the type of lesion, the duration of lesion, and other variables which, in total, make every brain unique. The conceptual plan first had to be in place before the many years of testing of thousands of individual patients, carefully and independently studied by neurosurgeons and neuropathologists, could be carried out.

Nervous System Functions

As an initial approach to the brain's functions, it is important to recognize that there are three general categories of nervous system function which occur regardless of the complexity of the organism's nervous system. First, it is necessary that the organism appreciate a stimulus from the outside environment and this, obviously, involves sensory perception. Secondly, it is necessary that the organism process this incoming information. Such analysis or understanding of the incoming information customarily is considered as brain functioning (or what has been referred to by many writers as the "black box"). Finally, if the behavioral cycle is completed, some type of response utilizing the effector system is necessary. Thus, the interaction of the organism with the outside environment requires input, central processing, and output. Various terms may be used to describe this cycle. The influence from the outside environment has been referred to as input, receptor function, or afferent processes, and involves the various senses. The motor aspect of the response cycle may be described as output, effector functioning, or expressive aspects of performance, and obviously involves muscular (and, to a lesser extent, glandular) functioning. Neuropsychological study of brain functioning, as mentioned earlier, would place the major emphasis upon central processing, or higher-level brain functions.

Before elaborating further, it may be worth describing this response cycle in its simplest form. A simple response cycle, which tends to deemphasize central processing, could be represented by the patellar tendon reflex. Briefly, it may be noted that this reflex first requires that a stimulus from the outside environment be delivered to the patellar tendon. Afferent input occurs through stretching of the quadriceps femoris muscle group. The afferent impulses are delivered via dendrites to the cell bodies which are located just outside the spinal cord. The impulses cross the cell body and are carried by the axons into the spinal cord where the first synapses occur. The impulses are transferred to neurons within the central nervous system and then to neurons that carry the impulse efferently through long axons back to the quadriceps femoris muscle. These impulses, stimulating the quadriceps femoris muscle, cause a contraction of the muscle. This contraction in turn causes movement of the lower leg because the quadriceps femoris inserts into the head of the tibia. The point of this brief recitation is to indicate that there are afferent, central, and efferent elements even in the most simple type of reflex action. Obviously, any neuropsychological test battery which attempts to evaluate the integrity of nervous system functioning must observe these three basic elements. We should note that these elements (input, central processing, and output) all occur within the organism, and belong to the organism rather than the external environment. The environment is a part of the system only insofar as the external stimulus is required to activate the cycle. Thus, any attempt to assess the integrity of this cycle, and its implications for the adaptive ability of the organism, must be concerned with all three elements. Thus, the input component might be adversely affected by impairment of sensory functions, the output component is subject to modification by the status of the muscles and glands, and the entire cycle involves nervous system function in conjunction with the rest of the body. It is necessary to take the adequacy of sensory and muscular functioning into account in evaluating the nervous system's role in mediating the behavioral cycle, but our major concern in developing a neuropsychological test battery is to measure the central processing component.

Content of the Halstead-Reitan Neuropsychological Test Battery

The adequate intactness of the sensory-perceptual (afferent or input) abilities of the human individual has been presumed in developing our test battery. Sensory psychologists and physiologists have often suggested that a very detailed assessment of sensory functions (visual tests, auditory measurements, etc.) be made to be sure that the stimuli are arriving properly at the brain. Such examinations could obviously be done, but they would be very time consuming. It is generally not necessary in neuropsychological testing to impose heavily upon the limits of the sensory systems, and the Halstead-Reitan Battery does not require extreme competence of the subject in this respect. It is probably safe to presume, in most instances, that the subject is able to see the fairly large stimulus figures and to hear the obvious sounds that are used. Thus, our test battery, in the main, has not focused on perception of minimal sensory stimuli. Instead, the sensory stimuli have been quite obvious and can be perceived adequately by most individuals if they have no obvious and pronounced sensory deficits. The motor or output requirements, however, may very well be limited by neuromuscular disease or disorder that involves the peripheral nervous system and effector organs. Thus, in individual instances it is sometimes necessary to consider the possibility that motor functions, rather than central processing abilities, are impaired and limiting an individual's response.

Sensory-perceptual functions are represented in the test battery by the Reitan-Kløve Sensory-Perceptual Examination and the Tactile Form Recognition Test. The Sensory-Perceptual Examination consists of tests of perception of double simultaneous tactile, auditory, and visual stimulation; measurements of tactile finger localization capabilities; and determination of ability in finger-tip number writing perception. The Tactile Form Recognition Test requires the subject to perceive through touch the shapes of various small objects. In each of these examinations the response component has been deliberately minimized. Thus, any deficits in performance, in all probability, represent sensory-perceptual input impairment rather than motor or response limitations. We should also note that these tests involve a central processing component (such as deciding which finger was touched). We built in this requirement deliberately in order to couple simple input tasks to their corresponding cerebral cortical areas. As a result, the tests make a more substantial contribution to evaluation of brain–behavior relationships than would tests that strictly evaluate sensory acuity.

Motor functions are evaluated using the Finger Oscillation Test, the test for Grip strength, and the Tactual Performance Test. The Finger Oscillation Test and the Grip Strength Test obviously have a minimal afferent component. Subjects are generally easily able to understand the simple verbal instructions involved, can follow these instructions, and perform the required motor response. Thus, these tests basically are measures of uncomplicated or "pure" motor performance. The Tactual Performance Test, on the other hand, involves sophisticated input considerations, very definite central processing requirements, and output performances as well. Comparisons of the results obtained on the pure motor measures, as contrasted with those obtained on the Tactual Performance Test, often provide significant information regarding primary motor deficiency as contrasted with impairment on a much more complex type of task.

The identification of the higher-level brain functions involved in central processing required observing and examining many persons with brain lesions. Ward Halstead began these observations and testing procedures. The conceptualization of their basic aspects owes much to his insights. Halstead had the good sense to actually observe persons with brain lesions and thus to gain some insight into the kinds of problems they experience. It was perfectly apparent that some persons with brain damage had resulting motor and sensory limitations. It was equally obvious, therefore, that a neuropsychological test battery must necessarily include at least some measures that reflected motor and sensory-perceptual skills in a rather basic way. However, Halstead had not fully understood the need to include systematic measures of this type. For example, he measured finger-tapping speed only with the preferred hand instead of measuring finger-tapping speed with both hands; he thereby failed to obtain comparative information regarding the two cerebral hemispheres. Nevertheless, he did realize that input and output considerations were necessary. The input (sensory or afferent) and the output (motor or efferent) components were, in fact, conceptualized by Halstead as the directional factor in his theory of biological intelligence (Halstead, 1947). This factor permitted interaction with the environment, the outside world having its influence on the brain through sensory avenues and the brain having its influence on the outside world through motor functions.

In terms of higher-level functions, Halstead's theory of biological intelligence included a central integrative field factor, which he viewed as representing the accumulated experience and background of the individual. In operational terms he tended to equate this factor with verbal intelligence. Our observations suggest that verbal abilities and language skills represent one of the four fundamental elements of the higher-level aspects of brain functions. In persons who have developed brain functions normally (as contrasted with persons who have sustained cerebral damage early in life), these abilities are usually subserved by the left cerebral hemisphere regardless of handedness. Nevertheless, a good deal of research suggests that damage to the brain during the developmental years will disrupt this relationship and, in addition, there is a tendency for persons who are left-handed to have a less complete association of verbal functions with the left cerebral hemisphere. Research evidence suggests that verbal abilities are related to the functional status of only a somewhat limited area within the left cerebral hemisphere, an area including the posterior-inferior frontal area, the temporal lobe, and adjacent parts of the parietal lobe (Penfield and Roberts, 1958). Thus, even though verbal functions are not represented throughout the cerebral cortex, they are a fundamental aspect of brain functions and must be included in any neuropsychological test battery.

The Halstead-Reitan Battery measures both simple and complex verbal functions. Even when complex verbal functions are relatively intact, brain lesions may disrupt basic aspects of both expressive and receptive language functions (Reitan, 1953). The Reitan-Indiana Aphasia Screening Test is used to evaluate simple language functions such as naming, spelling, reading, writing, and simple arithmetic computations. Somewhat more complicated verbal abilities are evaluated by the Halstead Speech-Sounds Perception Test. This test particularly emphasizes receptive aspects of verbal functions through both the auditory and visual avenues and is especially sensitive to the functional status of the left posterior temporal area. Additional representation of verbal abilities in the battery is obtained through the use of the verbal subtests of the Wechsler Adult Intelligence Scale. Several of the Wechsler verbal subtests have the disadvantage of failing to require any immediate problem-solving skills and essentially representing information accumulated by the individual before the examination. In this sense, they make limited immediate demands and do not stress the brain to a very great extent. Nevertheless, it is important to have such measures included in a neuropsychological test battery in order to obtain information about the verbal abilities the brain has developed over its lifetime, approximating the role of the central integrative field factor in Halstead's theory of biological intelligence.

Halstead had a very clear conceptualization of an abstraction factor in terms of brain functions. Research results (Reitan, 1955a; Doehring and Reitan, 1962) suggest that measures of abstraction abilities are among the most sensitive to any type of biological damage of the cerebral cortex. Of course, this is not a new idea. Kurt Goldstein over many years insisted that abstraction abilities were the most susceptible to impairment following damage to the brain (Goldstein and Sheerer, 1941). Our results suggest that abstraction abilities may be impaired by damage to any part of the cerebral cortex, although I have an impression that the anterior frontal areas may subserve this function to a somewhat greater extent than other areas of the cerebral cortex. Halstead (1947) felt that the anterior frontal areas of both cerebral hemispheres were much more important for this ability than my research has suggested. Nevertheless, I postulate that abstraction abilities represent the most important higher-level category of function. While verbal abilities, for example, are tremendously important, by themselves they may or may not carry a great deal of intellectual content. Halstead cited Binet in his differentiation of "verbal activity" and "verbal insight." This distinction was intended to identify the person who constantly engaged in verbal activity even though the verbal communication had little meaning as contrasted with the person whose verbal activity represented good abstraction and insight. Thus, in one sense the abstraction factor may be thought of as representing the individual's potential for use of other factors with meaningful insight and understanding. The principal instrument for measuring the abstraction factor is the Category Test, although we feel that the Trail Making Test (especially part B) also is an important contributor. The generality and importance of the abstraction factor may well be featured biologically by the fact that it is distributed throughout the cerebral cortex rather than being limited as a specialized function of one cerebral hemisphere or a particular area within a cerebral hemisphere. Generalized distribution of abstraction ability throughout the cerebral cortex may also be of significance in the interaction of abstraction with more specific abilities (such as language) that are represented more focally.

The third major area of higher-level brain function can be thought of as a visual-spatial factor. This function, of course, has become recognized as being related particularly to the integrity of the right cerebral hemisphere (Reitan, 1955a; Wheeler and Reitan, 1962). It is important to recognize that we live in a world of time and space as well as in a world of verbal communication. In fact, persons with impairment of visual-spatial abilities are often severely handicapped in terms of efficiency of functioning in a practical sense. The visual-spatial domain is represented in our test battery by the Wechsler Adult Intelligence Scale Performance subtests, the drawings required in the Aphasia test, and to an extent by parts A and B of the Trail Making Test.

Finally, there are other abilities that are required for adequate performance of nearly any psychological test and thus may be thought of as basic operational needs to achieve any degree of successful performance. These abilities facilitate efficient performance, and, in turn, are related to other brain functions. One of the required abilities could be called an alertness and concentration factor. If a person is not able to maintain alertness and a degree of concentration as he attempts to work on a problem, he is likely to make no progress. Since alertness and concentration are necessary for all kinds of problem-solving, it is important to include tests that evaluate the subject's attentiveness. Such tests should not be complicated and difficult, but should require the person to pay close attention over time to specific stimulus material. Two tests included in the battery that provide information of this kind are the Speech-sounds Perception and Rhythm Tests. Of course, it is possible that the subject may perform poorly on these tests because of a primary deficiency, but frequently one can discern from the results of the complete battery that the subject does have the basic abilities that would be required but fails because he has difficulty paying close attention.

Another factor, representing basic operational requirements for any degree of efficiency in performing, could be called a memory factor. Memory also is very pervasive, depending little on specific content. Readers are referred to Squire's comprehensive discussion of specific memory evaluation in Chapter 12, as well as to Brandt and Butters' review of Wernicke-Korsakoff memory pathology in Chapter 19. Memory is distributed throughout the full range of tests in our Battery and is probably particularly represented in the Category Test. However, any procedure that extends over time requires some degree of short-term memory inasmuch as the individual must remember the first part of the procedure and relate it to later parts. Our test battery is probably not as specifically represented in terms of the memory factor as it might be, and in individual cases it might be of value to include supplementary tests of memory for clinical evaluation (see Chapter 12). However, in addition to the Category Test, the memory factor is represented specifically by the memory and localization components of the Tactual Performance Test. Thus, the basic operational needs for expressing intellectual and cognitive functions are represented in the battery through measures of alertness and concentration as well as memory.

Although we have attempted to represent sensory-perceptual and motor functions, as well as the various areas involved in central processing, the battery has been criticized in some instances because we have not done adequate justice to the range of measurements required in each of the areas. In other words, critics feel that we should add additional tests. Others have commented that the battery is entirely too long—that 4–6 hours for administration extends far beyond reasonable limits for evaluating brain functions and that the battery should be reduced in size. (If the battery takes more than a day to administer to a subject with a normal energy level, the testing competence of the examiner must be questioned.) Considering the complexity of the relation between behavior and brain functions, my impression is that the various functions described above are not as thoroughly assessed by our battery as would be desirable. For example, motor functions are represented only by measuring finger-tapping speed, grip strength, and the more complex manipulatory, haptic, and problem-solving skills required by the Tactual Performance Test. When, for example, we described neuropsychological findings in patients with multiple sclerosis (Reitan, Reed, and Dyken, 1971), some neurologists reacted by saying that these tests were a grossly inadequate set of measures to reflect motor functions in multiple sclerosis as related to the brain and nervous system. These critics were absolutely right. Motor functions are much more complex than these particular tests can show. Thus, a more adequate neuropsychological test battery should be considerably more extensive in this area and, in fact, specialized batteries have been developed to fill this need, for example the Motor Steadiness Battery of Kløve and Matthews (described in Reitan and Davison, 1974).

Thus, if one needed to perform a more detailed evaluation of motor and sensory-perceptual functions, as might be the case in persons with multiple sclerosis, Parkinson's disease, or other diseases involving movement disorders, a more extensive battery should be used. However, we found that for routine neuropsychological evaluation the particular tests included in the Halstead-Reitan Battery provide useful and fairly adequate information regarding motor functioning.

With respect to sensory-perceptual functions, sensory psychologists and physiologists have, in some instances, been nearly aghast at the subbattery that we use in that area. They point out that we have failed even to perform tests of primary acuity in the visual and auditory areas, not to mention much more detailed examinations. In fact, Halstead did perform tests of both visual and auditory acuity in the early years of his laboratory. He also used von Frey hairs for testing tactile pressure sensitivity and collected data using graded weights in order to assess proprioceptive functions. While working in Halstead's laboratory, I also used these procedures. Both Halstead and I gradually gave up these tests, finding that they were routinely not helpful or necessary in providing data that was of clinical significance in the individual case. It is rare, for example, that a person has a visual form perception problem that is sufficiently severe to impair his ability to see the figures on the screen during the Category Test. In some instances we certainly find that the subject is impaired in his visual perception of the print used on the form for the Speech-Sounds

Perception Test. Usually, however, it is quite possible for the examiner to discern such sensory deficits, as well as obvious motor deficits, and to note these as conditions under which the test results were obtained and as factors that should be considered in clinical evaluation of the results.

There have also been criticisms of the inadequate representation of higher-level tests of central processing. While the verbal area is represented by the WAIS verbal subtests, the Speech-Sounds Perception Test, and the aphasia examination (providing a range from very simple verbal performances to more complex ones), we really do not have an adequate representation of problem-solving tests in this area. The Word Finding Test is a verbal problem-solving test that might be a valuable addition to the battery. Research results indicate that this test is extremely sensitive to heterogeneous brain damage (Reitan, 1972), to left cerebral damage, and even to damage in the right cerebral hemisphere. Apparently the left cerebral hemisphere is influenced both by the specific verbal requirements of the test as well as the required problem-solving skill, whereas the right cerebral hemisphere reflects the problem-solving component of the task.

Other areas involved in central processing are also rather meagerly represented in the battery. Many persons have complained that memory functions are not adequately tested. We do have some procedures, as noted above, specifically oriented toward memory, but it is possible that additional tests, devised particularly to measure memory, would add substantially to the effectiveness of the battery. My feeling is that memory is a basic operational function of the cerebral cortex and that we would actually need a subbattery to measure memory, with the content reflecting the major areas of central processing (abstraction, verbal function, and visual-spatial function). One would expect verbal memory to be dependent principally upon the left cerebral hemisphere, visual-spatial upon the right cerebral hemisphere, and memory in the area of reasoning, logical analysis, and abstraction to be broadly represented in the cerebral cortex. Furthermore, as discussed in Chapter 12, declarative memory ("remembering that") can be distinguished from procedural memory ("remembering how to"), these two forms probably having different neural substrates. Although I believe that many of our tests involve a memory component and that impaired memory in the individual patient is reflected in poor performances on many of them, some investigations utilizing the Halstead-Reitan Battery routinely augment it with immediate and delayed recall of prose passages and figures to provide a further sampling of verbal and nonverbal learning and recall (Grant et al., 1982; Prigatano et al., 1983). A general argument could be made, however, that the Halstead-Reitan Battery, in spite of being quite extensive, does not do *full* justice to any of the necessary areas in neuropsychological evaluation of the behavioral aspects of brain functions.

It must be noted at the same time, that the battery frequently is criticized for being too extensive and requiring too much time to administer. This complaint should be taken seriously and every effort should be made to use no more time than necessary to examine the behavioral correlates of brain functions. However, any person who expects to accomplish this complex task in 20 minutes, 40 minutes, or 60 minutes has little notion of the problem. The area of human brain–behavior relationships is inescapably complex. There have been entirely too many attempts in the past to oversimplify this area. It would be important to determine which tests provide overlapping information and on this basis to shorten the Battery. There have been attempts to do this but they have been quite simple-minded in their approach. For example, Golden (1976) decided that an adequate criterion for neuropsychological deficit was the Halstead Impairment Index, and he was able to learn that a few tests, taken in combination, yielded a relatively high coefficient of correlation with the impairment index. He published this information, suggesting that only a few tests were needed instead of the whole battery. Many psychologists accepted this recommendation, failing to see that it would, in effect, be a reversion to the oversimplified procedures that were in use years ago. In their desire to simplify the issue and save some time, they were willing to settle for a procedure that would do little more than classify humans into two categories—those with brain damage and those without. Obviously, it is necessary that even a general battery of tests used to evaluate brain–behavior relationships must be designed to attempt to develop an understanding of the behavioral correlates of brain functions, regardless of whether the brain is severely damaged, mildly damaged, or within the normal range. The examination should provide information regarding the unique aspects of ability structure for the individual subject as validly related to the biological status of the brain. Clinical assessment must be oriented toward developing an understanding of the individual rather than toward developing only a labeling capability. It is meaningful to label only if the label has some significance. The label of "brain damage" has little specific significance, considering the great variability among individuals who fall in this category. Thus, the development of a procedure which permits *only* identification of individuals for whom use of the label is appropriate is equivalent to name-calling, especially when the label has adverse connotations.

Reducing the length of the Halstead-Reitan Battery, or even developing a screening procedure, would have some real value if it could be done properly. The problem is essentially one of determining the sequence in which the tests should be given to generate the information necessary to answer the scientific question(s) that are being asked. Thus, if the question concerned the possible presence of a pathological area of damage, a few tests might be sufficient to answer it. On the other hand, if one wanted to obtain a thorough knowledge of brain–behavior relationships in each individual case, it might well be necessary to add additional tests to the ones included in the battery. These problems could be approached through formal research procedures, especially by those persons who have a complete battery and wish to learn the minimal number of tests necessary to provide a reasonably valid and accurate answer to specific questions. As with any screening process, it would be distinctly advantageous to screen for a well-defined and highly specific type of condition or situation. In studying persons with impaired, or even normal, brain functions however, it is often difficult to identify a single highly specific question or condition for which screening tests might be used.

Assessment Procedures

Psychological test data are usually evaluated with respect to level of performance—how well the subject (or group of subjects) performs. Most research studies and statistical analyses compare level of performance with relation to variability in reaching a conclusion as to whether or not a statistically significant difference is present. In fact, level of performance has permeated the thinking of psychologists and others to the extent that other methods of inference for evaluating psychological data frequently tend to be neglected almost entirely. In our studies of persons with brain injuries, we have learned that other approaches must also be used. We have noted and emphasized previously (Reitan, 1967a; 1974b) that in addition to level of performance in various content areas it is very helpful to obtain (1) data that can be evaluated in terms of whether the performance shows abnormal or pathological characteristics as contrasted with variations within the normal range; (2) data that can be evaluated in terms of relative or comparative levels of performance as the specific test results reflect the status of various areas of the cerebral cortex; and (3) data that can be used to compare differential performances of the individual on the right or left sides of the body, as these performances reflect the status of homologous areas within the contralateral cerebral hemisphere. Using several methods of inference permits one to draw conclusions that characterize the uniqueness of brain functions for the individual subject. To accomplish this, however, it is necessary that the tests included in the battery represent not only the areas of function described above but that they also meet the procedural requirements necessary to apply these various methods of inference. Thus, a meaningful neuropsychological test battery must be more than just a series of tests selected to represent the various areas thought to be important as behavioral correlates of brain functions. The tests must also be organized according to the various methods of inference and must complement each other to meet this methodological requirement.

Level of Performance

As noted above, many professionals tend to think only in terms of how well the subject has performed on a particular test. The presumption is that some tests may be sensitive to impairment of cerebral functions whereas others are not sensitive or are less sensitive. Thus, if a person performs poorly on a brain-sensitive test, the results presumably indicate the presence of brain damage.

This approach is regularly used in formal analysis of research data and is expressed in statistical probability terms that compare experimental and control groups. In a proper research design control groups are frequently composed so that any difference between the groups may be attributed to an identified independent variable rather than to other variables which could possibly have been responsible for the results. In evaluating an individual subject, however, it is difficult to apply such controls. One could note, for example, that a person was a college graduate and relatively young, and such information might influence the interpretation because of the expectation of a better than average performance. Nevertheless, any rigorous use of control information in individual interpretation is scarcely possible. Thus, for the individual subject, it is hazardous to postulate the level of performance that should be expected in order to presume that brain functions are within the range of normal variation.

Can one presume that certain tests are brain-sensitive and others not sensitive to brain functions and, on this basis, select a battery of brain-sensitive tests that should be performed adequately by all persons with normal brain functions? The problem with such a presumption is that it is very likely that some people have normal brain functions but fall in the lower part of the normal probability distribution and, as a result, perform relatively poorly even on tests that have been identified as being sensitive to brain functions. As for adopting a level of performance criterion, we can hardly presume that everyone who falls below a given percentile rank necessarily has an impaired, damaged, or defective brain. Equivalent variations within the upper end of the distribution might apply to individuals who were extremely gifted initially but who have sustained brain damage. Must we expect such persons to perform very poorly on certain tests? Might they not be impaired in comparison with premorbid levels even though they continue to be generally above average?

Such questions make it clear that an interpretation of neuropsychological data, based only on level of performance, can scarcely yield information that has specific meaning with respect to description of the brains of individual persons. I first realized that such problems existed when, in 1945, I examined a young physician who had sustained a depressed skull fracture in the right parietal area, had undergone surgical repair, and a contusion of the brain tissue was observed by the surgeon. This man clearly was brain-damaged, but on the measures I used at the time I could find no evidence of significant impairment. In fact, the subject performed much better than the average person on each of the tests I had administered. This man's complaints, however, suggested quite strongly that he had experienced significant impairment in comparison with his pre-injury capabilities. Even if I had been using an extensive battery of neuropsychological tests, covering the various areas included in our present battery, it is likely that this man would have performed relatively well in most areas (with the possible exception of the visual-spatial area). Nevertheless, he probably would have demonstrated definite deficits in his overall neuropsychological results, based on additional inferential methods that we have learned to use. The prospect that brain-related patterns or relationships among the test results may emerge for the individual subject, reflecting the functional integrity of various areas of the cerebral cortex, raises the possibility of another approach to the interpretation of neuropsychological test results.

Patterns and Relationships Among Test Results

The problem in my evaluation in 1945 of the physician with right parietal traumatic brain injury was that I did not know what category of psychological functioning might be impaired in association with an injury to the right parietal area of the brain. Obviously, an adequate neuropsychological test battery must include measurements that cover all functions of the cerebral cortex. The general procedure I have applied in trying to reach this goal has been to individually interpret neuropsychological data for thousands of subjects and to predict, on the basis of the test scores alone, the biological characteristics of the brain. Obviously, application of such a method requires knowledge of the differential functions of various areas of the cortex.

General differentiations between the left and right cerebral hemispheres have been established in terms of measurements of verbal abilities vs. visual-spatial abilities. (The third major category, abstraction, is particularly helpful because it shows evidence of impairment in most individual instances regardless of the cerebral hemisphere or the location of the lesion.) In addition to differentiating the lateralization of cerebral involvement, the test battery must also permit analysis of patterns and relationships that reflect more specific involvement within a cerebral hemisphere. For example, expressive aphasic deficits are commonly associated with damage to the anterior part of the language area in the left cerebral hemisphere, whereas prominent receptive deficits, particularly when they are auditory in nature, are associated with damage to the posterior part of the language area. As another example, dissociation of level of performance on the Picture Arrangement subtest of the Wechsler Scale as compared with the Block Design subtest provides a clue to focal involvement. A poor Picture Arrangement score is frequently associated with rather specific involvement of the right anterior temporal area (Reitan, 1955d; Meier and French, 1966) whereas Block Design is more specifically sensitive to the parietal, posterior temporal, and occipital areas of the right cerebral hemisphere. There are many "rules" of interpretation of relationships among results in the Halstead-Reitan Battery that have been verified in thousands of individual cases, and a very important aspect of knowledgable interpretation of neuropsychological test data is the evaluation of patterns and relationships among the test results as they reflect variations in the biological status of various parts of the individual's cerebral cortex. There are also definite patterns and variable relationships in a "normal" vs. "pathological" context. Frequently data related to level of performance, such as the Impairment index, are very helpful in this regard, and an integration must be accomplished between level of performance and patterns of test results as they relate to regional localization of deficit.

Pathognomonic Signs

Another approach that is often of value is one in which simple performances are assessed in terms of normal vs. pathological manifestations, which is similar to the approach used in many aspects of the medical examination and in clinical interpretation of electroencephalographic tracings. In neuropsychological evaluation it is probably best exemplified by Luria's approach (Christensen, 1975; see also Chapter 3), by the Boston process approach (see Chapter 4), and by the traditional interpretation of the Bender-Gestalt Test (Bender, 1956). The question asked is, "Is this performance abnormal (pathological)?", and it is not directly concerned with whether the individual has performed well or poorly, but instead with whether the response is characteristic of persons with cerebral damage. It is necessary to use very simple tasks to avoid complicating the interpretation with assessments of level of performance. As a result of using simple tasks, many persons (even with cerebral damage) may be able to perform without deficit. On the other hand, if deficits do occur the results can be very revealing and definitive of brain damage. An excellent example of this is the occurrence of specific dysphasic symptoms. If the person shows dysphasia, it does not make much difference what his verbal I.Q. or other scores might be. The patient still has a cerebral lesion, and very probably of the left rather than the right cerebral hemisphere. Another example of the "sign" approach is represented by the simple drawings that we ask the patient to produce. It is often possible to note specific deficits of the kind associated with right cerebral hemisphere lesions in these drawings, even when the general configuration of the drawing is fairly adequate. As with interpretations of EEG tracings, it is necessary to teach recognition of these kinds of deficiencies by example. Unfortunately, many neuropsychologists have not learned to differentiate the types of performances characterized by cerebral damage from instances only of poor drawing ability. The same problem occurs in differentiating dysphasic symptoms from poorly developed verbal skills.

A distinct limitation of the "sign" approach is that it produces a considerable number of false-negatives, since if a deficient performance is to be a genuine sign of brain damage, the task must necessarily be very simple so that any normal individual could be expected to perform satisfactorily. As a procedure based on normal vs. abnormal responses, the "sign" approach complements evaluations based on level of performance and patterns of test scores. When positive "signs" occur, the results may have unequivocal significance (Wheeler and Reitan, 1962).

Comparison of Performances of the Right and Left Sides of the Body

Another approach that has proved to be of great value in describing brain functions for individuals involves comparing performances on the right and left sides of the body. This approach exploits the anatomical organization of the nervous system. The pathways in the brain stem cross from one side to the other, relating performances of one side of the body to the status of the contralateral cerebral hemisphere. This generalization seems to hold very well even with respect to measures of auditory function, although conventional textbooks describe bilateral connections of this system. In other words, the hair cells in each cochlea (according to neuroanatomy texts) lead not only to the contralateral temporal lobe but also to the ipsilateral temporal lobe, at least in part. Nevertheless, in practice, the results of our sensory-perceptual testing procedures have a rather distinct and definite contralateral significance (except for the visual system). In the visual system, of course, receptor cells in each retina are represented on each side of the brain.

It was necessary to develop a subbattery of tests within the Halstead-Reitan Battery to represent comparisons of the two sides of the body and to obtain information regarding expected intraindividual differences. In testing finger-tapping speed, we have found the preferred hand to be about 10% faster than the nonpreferred hand. Another way of saying this is that the cerebral hemisphere across from the preferred hand is generally about 10% better at subserving finger-tapping speed than is the cerebral hemisphere across from the nonpreferred hand. The Tactual Performance Test is also evaluated in terms of comparative performances on the first (preferred hand) and second (nonpreferred hand) trials. Normal individuals customarily show about a one-third reduction in time on the second trial. Measurements of grip strength also show about a 10% greater reading with the preferred hand. However, we have noted no particular difference in the competence of the two sides of the body with respect to sensory-perceptual functions. In other words, we expect essentially comparable results on the two hands in tactile finger localization, finger-tip number writing perception, the imperception tests, and the Tactile Form Recognition Test. There is always a possibility that some type of peripheral involvement may complicate interpretations of right vs. left differences in performances, but if both motor and sensory-perceptual deficiencies occur on the same side of the body, the probability of the lesion being at the cerebral rather than peripheral level is much increased.

Use of these four methods of inference in a complementary manner permits detailed interpretation of results obtained on the individual subject. However, it was necessary to develop a measurement strategy that integrated these methods of inference with the same tests that covered the necessary areas of cerebral functions. We have achieved this to an extent at least, and this achievement represents a unique aspect of the Halstead-Reitan Neuropsychological Test Battery. Halstead had developed some ideas along these lines, as shown by the procedure he devised for the Tactual Performance Test. However, he had not clearly conceptualized the four methods of inference nor implemented them practically. For example, he obtained finger-tapping measurements only with the index finger of the preferred hand. In addition, he did not realize the importance of sensory-perceptual tests and it was necessary for Reitan and Kløve to develop the Sensory-Perceptual Examination in order

to fill out this aspect of the battery. He did not use a formal approach in eliciting pathognomonic signs nor did he have much information with respect to
patterns and relationships. In Halstead's laboratory he did not use the Wechsler Scale and thus was not able to obtain intraindividual comparisons of verbal
and performance intelligence levels. Nevertheless, he did have some preliminary ideas regarding each of these methods of inference and the various areas
of functioning under which appropriate tests could be subsumed.

General and Specific Indicators

Another requirement of an effective neuropsychological test battery is that it
include both general and specific indicators of cerebral cortical damage or
dysfunction. The general indicators are ones that show evidence of impairment regardless of location of cerebral damage and thus are essentially the
opposite, in an assessment approach, to the use of pathognomonic signs. General indicators assess the overall biological integrity of the cerebral hemispheres and represent an excellent starting point for analyzing results in individual subjects. Further, general indicators represent the types of functions
that characterize normal behavioral expressions of all cerebral cortical tissue
and, in this sense, may be considerably more important than the types of behavioral manifestations that are restricted or limited to specific areas of the
cerebral cortex. Many adaptive abilities of practical significance in everyday
life undoubtedly are not factorially pure but, instead, represent complex combinations of various abilities. In fact, to achieve a reasonable balance, it might
be important at the present time to emphasize the general characteristics of
cerebral cortical functioning since there has been such a pronounced tendency recently to concentrate on the differential or specialized functions of
the two cerebral hemispheres.

Analysis of our data has indicated that four measures are the most valid in
providing general indications of cerebral cortical functioning: the Impairment
Index, the Category Test, part B of the Trail Making Test, and the Localization component of the Tactual Performance Test (Reitan, 1955a; Wheeler,
Burke, and Reitan, 1963). The Impairment Index is remarkably sensitive to
brain lesions regardless of where they occur in the cerebral cortex. In fact, we
have learned through clinical experience that the Impairment Index cannot
be used very satisfactorily as an indicator of severity of cerebral dysfunction
because it is likely to show very distinct and definite impairment even with
relatively mild or discrete cerebral cortical lesions.

It is particularly interesting that the Category Test is a general indicator and
can show impairment regardless of location or type of lesion (Doehring and
Reitan, 1962). This observation suggests the biologically based importance of
abstraction and concept formation as a central feature of intellectual and cognitive skill. Part B of the Trail Making Test yields results that are basically
similar to these obtained with the Category Test (Reitan, 1955e; Reitan, 1958).

Although the Category Test and part B of the Trail Making Test can pick up impairment irrespective of the area of the brain which is involved, these tests may be somewhat more sensitive to anterior frontal lesions than lesions in other locations of the cerebral cortex.

The fourth general indicator is the Localization component of the Tactual Performance Test (Reitan, 1955a). This finding may possibly be a result of the procedure followed in eliciting the score. It should be remembered that the Localization component is a dependent score in that none of the figures can be given credit for localization unless they have already been identified in the drawing. Thus, the Memory score of the Tactual Performance Test represents a first order performance and credit for localizing figures is a second order performance in the sense that memory of the figure's shape must occur first. The Memory component of the Tactual Performance Test, although it shows a striking difference between groups with and without cerebral damage, is not as sensitive as the Localization component. A second-order measure of efficiency of brain functions (or a sequentially related type of judgment) seems to be an especially sensitive way of showing the deficiency of damaged brains. In any case, our data suggest that the Localization component is extremely sensitive to the effects of cerebral damage.

A fifth measure should also be mentioned because it has shown striking sensitivity—the Digit Symbol subtest of the Wechsler Scale. The Digit Symbol subtest appears to call upon functions of both the left and right cerebral hemispheres. The left hemisphere is stressed (or tested) by the requirement to deal with symbols whereas the right cerebral hemisphere is involved by the requirement of drawing various shapes. Both elements of the task are required to complete it and the subject also must work under pressure of time. These various components combine to produce a test that is generally sensitive to the condition of the cerebral cortex.

Specific indicators are necessary to gain an understanding of the functional condition of various areas of each cerebral hemisphere. Our identification of these indicators has depended principally upon three methods of inference—patterns and relationships, pathognomonic signs, and right vs. left comparisons. Level of performance, considered by itself, represents the normal probability distribution rather than providing much specific information about the biological condition of an individual's brain. Left hemisphere indicators in our battery are relatively weak with respect to patterns and relationships among higher-level aspects of performance (Heaton, Grant, Anthony, and Lehman, 1981). However, the Similarities subtest of the Wechsler Scale, as well as the Arithmetic subtest, sometimes appear to be rather specifically low, with relation to other Verbal subtests, in persons with left hemisphere lesions. This is also sometimes true of the Halstead Speech-Sounds Perception Test. When performance on the Speech-Sounds Perception Test is especially poor, compared with other types of verbal performances, one may suspect the possibility of a lesion in the posterior part of the left cerebral hemisphere and, perhaps, more specifically in the posterior temporal area. The Word Finding Test

(Reitan, 1972) appears to be much more sensitive to higher-level aspects of left cerebral functioning in the language area than is true for any of the Wechsler Verbal subtests. However, the Word Finding Test has not been formally included as part of the Halstead-Reitan Neuropsychological Test Battery. Verbal and language tests that actually involve immediate problem-solving skills in the language area are probably more sensitive to left cerebral functioning than measures that only require regurgitation of previously accumulated verbal knowledge. Results from the aphasia examination often are helpful in identifying impairment of left cerebral functions. However, the basic problem is that this procedure is represented by the "sign" approach and many persons, even those with left cerebral lesions, show no particular difficulties or deficits on these simple kinds of tasks. Nevertheless, the Wechsler Scale and the aphasia examination, in combination, often yield specific information about the status of the left cerebral hemisphere. Much additional information is derived from measures that permit performances on the two sides of the body to be compared, but these measures assess the status of both cerebral hemispheres and will be described below.

Two Wechsler subtests are good indicators of right hemisphere functioning. Picture Arrangement seems to be specifically sensitive to the status of the right anterior temporal lobe (Reitan, 1955d; Meier and French, 1966) and Block Design to more posteriorly located right hemispheric disturbances. Of course, judgment of deficiencies on these tests must be made within the context of other scores earned by the subject on the performance subtests of the Wechsler Scale. Localization of involvement within the posterior part of the right cerebral hemisphere is sometimes possible through evaluation of differential scores obtained on Picture Arrangement and Block Design.

We can also assess the right cerebral hemisphere using a "sign" approach, based upon the adequacy of the drawings from the aphasia examination. The criterion of the brain damage does not relate to artistic skill, but rather, to specific distortions of the spatial configurations involved. The square and the triangle are not particularly helpful figures because they are relatively simple and do not involve enough of a challenge to one's understanding and production of spatial configurations. The Greek cross has turned out to be an extremely useful figure because, though basically simple, it involves many turns and a number of dimensions. (I might note in this context that our experience with the Bender Gestalt Test is that the figures are somewhat complex and instead of representing the "sign" approach they clearly enter the area of drawing skill level of performance). It is difficult to describe verbally the specific characteristics of drawings that show right hemisphere deficiencies. These drawing deficits principally reflect distortion of spatial relationships and must be learned through experience by the individual neuropsychologist.

Comparisons of performances on the two sides of the body, using both motor and sensory-perceptual tasks, provide a great deal of information about each cerebral hemisphere and more specifically, areas within each cerebral hemisphere. We have never discovered any reliable specific indicators for anterior frontal involvement in either cerebral hemisphere. However, both finger-tapping speed and grip strength yield information about the posterior frontal (motor) areas. Of course, it is necessary to have determined hand preference in order to evaluate the differences on the two sides because the preferred hand is about 10% better than the nonpreferred hand in finger-tapping speed and grip strength.

The Tactual Performance Test also provides information regarding performances on the two sides of the body, with the first trial requiring more time than the second trial. Positive practice-effect results in a reduction of about one-third of the time from the first to second trial under normal circumstances, and a similar reduction from the second to third trial. The Tactual Performance Test requires both motor and tactile-perceptual abilities and, therefore, may be principally dependent on the middle part of the cerebral hemisphere. It should also be noted that this test is considerably more complex in its problem-solving requirements than either finger-tapping or grip strength.

The tests for double simultaneous sensory stimulation include tactile, auditory, and visual stimuli. While we have not discerned convincing evidence of the differential sensitivity of these tests to the parietal, auditory, and occipital areas, they probably do reflect some differential dependency. It is difficult to obtain specific information to validate the sensitivity of these tests to these three areas because these types of deficiencies are usually seen with destructive or progressive focal lesions, and few lesions are specifically restricted to either the parietal, temporal, or occipital areas. However, highly focal damage of the parietal area seems to produce tactile impairment, and auditory deficits are more closely related to temporal lobe damage. Our impression is that visual deficits may be related to lesions that more generally involve the posterior part of the hemisphere rather than centering to any degree on the occipital area alone. Of course, the damaged cerebral hemisphere is contralateral to the side of the body on which impairment of double simultaneous stimulation occurs.

The Tactile Form Recognition Test yields information regarding the integrity of the parietal areas. Kløve and Reitan devised this test because they recognized a need for an instrument that was not limited to any significant extent by motor function or verbal response capabilities but, instead, depended upon tactile recognition and differentiation of forms. Finger localization serves a similar purpose. We apply the stimulus to the distal end of the finger, recognizing that simulation at this point is more sensitive to the integrity of the cerebral cortex than is more proximal stimulation. Finger-tip number writing perception is a similar type of task, but it requires considerably more alertness and concentration, or perhaps even more general intelligence, than does finger localization (Fitzhugh, Fitzhugh, and Reitan, 1962b). In other words, a person might perform poorly on finger-tip number writing perception because of the more complex nature of the task, but differences between the error-rate on the two sides still have definite lateralizing significance. Finger localization and finger-tip number writing perception, as well as tactile form perception, all relate principally to the integrity of the contralateral parietal area.

It should be apparent at this point that the technical requirements of a neuropsychological test battery, in terms of assessment strategy, require using various methods of inference regarding brain–behavior relationships, as well as general and specific indicators. We have made an attempt to meet these requirements and, at the same time, to organize a battery of neuropsychological tests which covers the necessary areas of functioning. Thus, the overall battery is integrated in a rather complex manner, representing an organized and integrated battery of tests rather than only a continuous series of individual tests.

Validation Through Formal Research

While the plan for neuropsychological assessment outlined above may appear to be plausible and adequate, it means little unless it is actually shown to work. One way to demonstrate the validity of the battery is through formal, scientifically designed investigation. We shall not present a full review of the numerous research studies that have been published (Reitan, 1966b; Kløve, 1974), but it is important to know that a great deal of highly significant information has been generated.

The first step in these investigations was to test the battery's broad-range or broad-based effectiveness. The question is whether or not the battery is valid in identifying the effects of cerebral damage in one study after another, based on groups of subjects with and without cerebral damage, with many types of lesions and etiologies as well as varying control (comparison) groups, who have been tested in various locations by different investigators. A great number of positive reports of this nature have appeared in the literature over the years. (A partial listing would include Boll, Heaton, and Reitan, 1974; Chapman and Wolff, 1959; Doehring and Reitan, 1961a, 1961b; Fitzhugh, Fitzhugh, and Reitan, 1961, 1962a; Fitzhugh, Fitzhugh, and Reitan, 1960, 1965; Heaton et al., 1981; Heimburger and Reitan, 1961; Heimburger, DeMyer, and Reitan, 1964; Matthews, Shaw, and Kløve, 1966; Reed and Reitan, 1962, 1963a–c; Reitan, 1955a, 1955d, 1958, 1959a, 1959b, 1960, 1964a, 1970a, 1970b; Reitan and Boll, 1971; Reitan and Fitzhugh, 1971; Reitan, Reed, and Dyken, 1971; Ross and Reitan, 1955; Shure and Halstead, 1958; Vega and Parsons, 1967; Wheeler, Burke, and Reitan, 1963; and Wheeler and Reitan, 1962, 1963.)

Similar studies were necessary to evaluate the Wechsler Scales because of their role in conjunction with other tests in our method of evaluating brain–behavior relationships. Positive findings have been reported by Andersen, 1950; Doehring, Reitan, and Klove, 1961; Fitzhugh, Fitzhugh, and Reitan, 1962a; Kløve, 1959; Matthews and Reitan, 1964; Reed and Reitan, 1963b; Reitan, 1955c, 1960, 1964a, 1977a; Reitan and Fitzhugh, 1971; Wheeler, Burke, and Reitan, 1963; Wheeler and Reitan, 1963.

Many formal studies have similarly validated the sensitivity of the batteries for children. These include Boll and Reitan, 1972a–c; Finlayson and Reitan, 1976a, 1976b; Reed, Reitan, and Kløve, 1965; Reitan, 1970b, 1971a, 1971b, 1974a; Reitan and Heineman, 1968; Selz and Reitan, 1979a, 1979b; Townes, Reitan, and Trupin, 1978.

Another research approach has investigated the consistency of differential effects of left vs. right (lateralized) cerebral lesions. Although there has been a great deal of interest in this question, the original positive findings were reported using data from the Wechsler Scale (Anderson, 1950; Reitan, 1955c). Many other researchers have reported additional positive results (Doehring, Reitan, and Kløve, 1961; Fitzhugh, Fitzhugh, and Reitan, 1962a; Kløve and Reitan, 1958; Matthews and Reitan, 1964; Meier and French, 1966). Matarazzo (1972) and Kløve (1974) have summarized many of these findings. The general conclusion of these studies was that verbal intelligence is principally dependent upon the left cerebral hemisphere, whereas performance intelligence relates more closely to the biological condition of the right cerebral hemisphere. Many additional studies of lateralization effects have shown the validity of other tests from the Halstead-Reitan Battery in this respect, including Doehring and Reitan, 1961a, 1961b; Heimburger and Reitan, 1961; Heimburger, DeMyer, and Reitan, 1964; Kløve, 1959; Kløve and Reitan, 1958; Reitan, 1959a, 1959b, 1960, 1964a, 1964b; Wheeler, 1964; Wheeler and Reitan, 1963. The influence of posterior lesions within the left and right cerebral hemispheres has been studied in detail by Reitan (1964a).

A host of other variables has been studied with regard to the Halstead-Reitan Battery including the differential effects of acute vs. chronic cerebral damage (Fitzhugh, Fitzhugh, and Reitan, 1961, 1962a, 1962b, 1963); the influence of various types of disorders such as aphasia as shown by the battery (Doehring and Reitan, 1961b; Heimburger and Reitan, 1961; Reitan, 1960); emotional problems and their influence on cognitive deficits (Dikmen and Reitan, 1974a, 1974b, 1977a, 1977b; Fitzhugh, Fitzhugh, and Reitan, 1961; Reitan, 1970, 1977b); epilepsy (Reitan, 1977a); and sensory-perceptual losses related to intelligence (Fitzhugh, Fitzhugh, and Reitan, 1962b). Finally, a large number of specific conditions and types of neurological disorders have been explored individually, including cerebral vascular disease (Reitan, 1970a; Reitan and Fitzhugh, 1971); brain tumors (Hom and Reitan, 1982); multiple sclerosis (Ross and Reitan, 1955; Forsyth et al., 1971; Reitan, Reed and Dyken, 1971); Huntington's chorea (Boll, Heaton, and Reitan, 1974); craniocerebral trauma (Reitan, 1973; Dikmen and Reitan, 1976, 1977a, 1977b, 1978); alcoholism (Fitzhugh, Fitzhugh, and Reitan, 1960, 1965; see also Chapter 18); drug abuse (Grant et al., 1976; Grant et al., 1978; see also Chapter 20); mental retardation (Davis, Hamlett, and Reitan, 1966; Davis and Reitan, 1966, 1967; Matthews and Reitan, 1961, 1962, 1963; Reitan, 1967a); and aging effects (Fitzhugh, Fitzhugh, and Reitan, 1963, (1964; Reitan, 1955b, 1962, 1967b, 1970c; Reed and Reitan, 1962, 1963a; see also Chapter 6). These investigations not only have contributed knowledge about the conditions involved, but are indispensable in providing a background for valid clinical interpretations of individual test protocols.

Validation through Evaluation of Individual Subjects

The ultimate purpose of a neuropsychological test battery is to evaluate brain–behavior relationships in individual subjects. There are differing viewpoints regarding the best approach to use, but our battery has the advantages of being based upon a set of measures that taps the principal behavioral aspects of human brain functions (as tested with thousands of persons with brain disease or damage), is based on both intra- and interindividual comparisons (thus permitting comparisons of neuropsychological functions within the individual's own brain as well as with normative data), and was deliberately and explicitly organized to provide data relevant to interpretation of brain–behavior relationships for the individual person. My personal disappointments stem from instances where the breakdown of the method occurs at the endpoint—interpretation of the data by the individual neuropsychologist. There are still too many instances where neuropsychologists fail to understand the richness and complexity of brain–behavior relationships; this significantly limits the potential competence that could be achieved.

REFERENCES

Anderson, A. L. (1950). The effect of laterality localization of brain damage on Wechsler-Bellevue indices of deterioration. *J. Clin. Psychol., 6*, 191–194.
Bender, L. (1956). *Psychopathology of Children with Organic Brain Disorders.* Springfield, Illinois: Charles C. Thomas.
Boll, T. J., Heaton, R. K., and Reitan, R. M. (1974). Neuropsychological and emotional correlates of Huntington's Chorea. *J. Nerv. Ment. Dis., 158*, 61–69.
Boll, T. J., and Reitan, R. M. (1970a). Deficits in adaptive abilities in Parkinson's disease. Proceedings of the American Psychological Association, Washington, D.C.: APA.
Boll, T. J., and Reitan, R. M. (1970a). Psychological test results of subjects with known cerebral lesions and Parkinson's disease as compared with controls. *Percept. Motor Skills, 31*, 824.
Boll, T. J., and Reitan, R.M. (1972a). The comparative intercorrelations of brain-damaged and normal children on the Trail Making Test and the Wechsler-Bellevue Scale. *J. Clin. Psychol., 4*, 491–493.
Boll, T. J., and Reitan, R. M. (1972b). Motor and tactile-perceptual deficits in brain-damaged children. *Percept. Motor Skills, 34*, 343–350.
Boll, T. J., and Reitan, R. M. (1972c). Comparative ability interrelationships in normal and brain-damaged children. *J. Clin. Psychol., 28*, 152–156.
Chapman, L. F., and Wolff, H. G. (1959). The cerebral hemispheres and the highest integrative functions in man. *Arch. Neurol.,* 357–424.
Christensen, A.-L. (1975). *Luria's Neuropsychological Investigation.* New York: Spectrum Publications.
Davis, L. J., Hamlett, I., and Reitan, R. M. (1966). Relationships of conceptual ability and academic achievement to problem-solving and experiential backgrounds of retardates. *Percept. Motor Skills, 22*, 499–505.

Davis, J., and Reitan, R. M. (1966). Methodological note on the relationships between ability to copy a simple configuration and Wechsler Verbal and Performance IQ's. *Percept. Motor Skills, 22,* 281–282.

Davis, J., and Reitan, R. M. (1967). Dysphasia and constructional dyspraxia items and Wechsler Verbal and Performance IQ in retardates. *Am. J. Ment. Defic., 71,* 606–608.

Dikmen, S., and Reitan, R. M. (1974a). MMPI correlates of localized structural cerebral lesions. *Percept. Motor Skills, 39,* 831–840.

Dikmen, S., and Reitan, R. M. (1974b). Minnesota Multiphasic Personality Inventory correlates of dysphasic language disturbances. *J. Abnorm. Psychol., 83,* 675–679.

Dikmen, S., and Reitan, R. M. (1976). Psychological deficits and recovery of functions after head injury. *Trans. Am. Neurol. Assoc., 101,* 72–77.

Dikmen, S., and Reitan, R. M. (1977a). Emotional sequelae of head injury. *Ann. Neurol., 2,* 492–494.

Dikmen, S., and Reitan, R. M. (1977b). MMPI correlates of adaptive ability deficits in patients with brain lesions. *J. Nerv. Ment. Dis., 165,* 247–254.

Dikmen, S., and Reitan, R. M. (1978). Neuropsychological performances in post-traumatic epilepsy. *Epilepsia, 19,* 177–183.

Doehring, D. G., and Reitan, R. M. (1960). MMPI performance of aphasic and non-aphasic brain-damaged patients. *J. Clin. Psychol., 16,* 307–309.

Doehring, D. G., and Reitan, R. M. (1961a). Behavioral consequences of brain damage associated with homonymous visual field defects. *J. Comp. Physiol. Psychol., 54,* 489–492.

Doehring, D. G., and Reitan, R. M. (1961b). Certain language and nonlanguage disorders in brain-damaged patients with homonymous visual field defects. *AMA Arch. Neurol. Psychiat., 132,* 227–233.

Doehring, D. G., Reitan, R. M., and Kløve, H. (1961). Changes in pattern of intelligence test performance associated with homonymous visual field defects. *J. Nerv. Ment. Dis., 132,* 227–233.

Finlayson, M. A. J., and Reitan, R. M. (1976a). Tactual perceptual functioning in relation to intellectual, cognitive, and reading skills in younger and older normal children. *Dev. Med. Child Neurol., 18,* 442–446.

Finlayson, M. A. J., and Reitan, R. M. (1976b). Handedness in relation to measures of motor and tactile-perceptual functions in normal children. *Percept. Motor Skills, 43,* 475–481.

Fitzhugh, K. B., Fitzhugh, L. C., and Reitan, R. M. (1961). Psychological deficits in relation to acuteness of brain dysfunction. *J. Consult. Psychol., 25,* 61–66.

Fitzhugh, K. B., Fitzhugh, L. C., and Reitan, R. M. (1962a). Wechsler-Bellevue comparisons in groups with "chronic" and "current" lateralized and diffuse brain lesions. *J. Consult. Psychol., 26,* 306–310.

Fitzhugh, K. B., Fitzhugh, L. C., and Reitan, R. M. (1962c). The relationship of acuteness of organic brain dysfunction to Trail Making Test performances. *Percept. Motor Skills, 15,* 399–403.

Fitzhugh, K. B., Fitzhugh, L. C., and Reitan, R. M. (1963). Effects of "chronic" and "current" lateralized and non-lateralized cerebral lesions upon Trail Making Test performances. *J. Nerv. Ment. Dis., 137,* 82–87.

Fitzhugh, K. B., Fitzhugh, L. C., and Reitan, R. M. (1964). Influence of age upon measures of problem solving and experiential background in subjects with long-standing cerebral dysfunction. *J. Gerontol., 19,* 132–134.

Fitzhugh, L. C., Fitzhugh, K. B., and Reitan, R. M. (1960). Adaptive abilities and intellectual functioning in hospitalized alcoholics. *Quart. J. Studies on Alcohol, 21,* 414–423.

Fitzhugh, L. C., Fitzhugh, K. B., and Reitan, R. M. (1962b). Sensorimotor deficits of brain-damaged subjects in relation to intellectual level. *Percept. Motor Skills, 15,* 603–608.

Fitzhugh, L. C., Fitzhugh, K. B., and Reitan, R. M. (1965). Adaptive abilities and intellectual functioning of hospitalized alcoholics: Further considerations. *Quart. J. Studies on Alcohol, 26,* 402–411.

Forsyth, G. A., Gaddes, W. J., Reitan, R. M., and Tryk, H. E. (1971). Intellectual deficit in multiple sclerosis as indicated by psychological tests. *Res. Monograph No. 23*, Victoria, B. C., Canada: University of Victoria.

Golden, C. (1976). Identification of brain damage by an abbreviated form of the Halstead-Reitan Neuropsychological Battery. *J. Clin. Psychol., 4*, 821–826.

Goldstein, K., and Sheerer, M. (1941). Abstract and concrete behavior. *Psychol. Monographs, 53* (Whole No. 239).

Grant, I., Adams, K. M., Carlin, A. S., Rennick, P. M., Judd, L. L., and Schooff, K. (1978). The collaborative neuropsychological study of polydrug users. *Arch. General Psychiatr., 35*, 1063–1073.

Grant, I., Heaton, R. K., McSweeny, A. J., Adams, K. M., and Timms, R. M. (1982). Neuropsychological findings in hypoxemic chronic obstructive pulmonary disease. *Arch. Int. Med., 142*, 1470–1476.

Grant, I., Mohns, L., Miller, M., and Reitan, R. M. (1976). A neuropsychological study of polydrug users. *Arch. General Psychiatr., 33*, 973–978.

Halstead, W. C. (1947). *Brain and Intelligence: A Quantitative Study of the Frontal Lobes*. Chicago: University of Chicago Press.

Heaton, R. K., Grant, I., Anthony, W. Z., and Lehman, R. A. W. (1981). A comparison of clinical and automated interpretation of the Halstead-Reitan Battery. *J. Clin. Neuropsychol., 3*, 121–141.

Heimburger, R. F., DeMyer, W., and Reitan, R. M. (1964). Implications of Gerstmann's Syndrome. *J. Neurol., Neurosurg. Psychiat., 27*, 52–57.

Heimburger, R. F., and Reitan, R. M. (1961). Easily administered written test for lateralizing brain lesions. *J. Neurosurg., 18*, 301–312.

Hom, J., and Reitan, R. M. (1982). Effect of lateralized cerebral damage upon contralateral and ipsilateral performances. *J. Clin. Neuropsychol., 4*, 249–268.

Kløve, H. (1959). Relationship of differential electroencephalographic patterns to distribution of Wechsler-Bellevue scores. *Neurology, 9*, 871–876.

Kløve, H. (1974). Validation studies in adult clinical neuropsychology. In: R. M. Reitan and L. A. Davison, eds., *Clinical Neuropsychology: Current Status and Applications*. Washington, D.C.: V. H. Winston & Sons.

Kløve, H., and Reitan, R. M. (1958). The effect of dysphasic and spatial distortion on Wechsler-Bellevue results. *AMA Arch. Neurol. Psychiatr., 80*, 708–713.

Matarazzo, J. D. (1972). *Wechsler's Measurement and Appraisal of Adult Intelligence*. Baltimore: Williams & Wilkins.

Matthews, C. G., and Reitan, R. M. (1961). Comparison of abstraction ability in retardates and in patients with cerebral lesions. *Percept. Motor Skills, 13*, 327–333.

Matthews, C. G., and Reitan, R. M. (1962). Psychomotor abilities of retardates and patients with cerebral lesions. *Am. J. Ment. Deficiency, 66*, 607–612.

Matthews, C. G., and Reitan, R. M. (1963). Relationship of differential abstraction ability levels to psychological test performances in mentally retarded subjects. *Am. J. Ment. Deficiency, 68*, 235–244.

Matthews, C. G., and Reitan, R. M. (1964). Correlations of Wechsler-Bellevue rank orders of subtest means in lateralized and non-lateralized brain-damaged groups. *Percept. Motor Skills, 19*, 391–399.

Matthews, C. G., Shaw, D., and Kløve, H. (1966). Psychological test performances in neurological and "pseudoneurologic" subjects. *Cortex, 2*, 244–253.

Meier, M. J., and French, L. A. (1966). Longitudinal assessment of intellectual functioning following unilateral temporal lobectomy. *J. Clin. Psychol., 22*, 22–27.

Penfield, W., and Roberts, L. (1958). *Speech and Brain Mechanisms*. Princeton, N. J.: Princeton University Press.

Prigatano, G. P., Parsons, O., Wright, E., Levin, D. C., and Hawryluk, G. (1983). Neuropsychological test performance in mildly hypoxemic patients with chronic obstructive pulmonary disease. *J. Consult. Clin. Psychol., 51*, 108–116.

Reed, H. B. C., and Reitan, R. M. (1962). The significance of age in the performance of a complex psychomotor task by brain-damaged and non-brain-damaged subjects. *J. Gerontol., 17*, 193–196.

Reed, H. B. C., and Reitan, R. M. (1963a). A comparison of the effects of the normal aging process with the effects of organic brain damage on adaptive abilities. *J. Gerontol., 18*, 177–179.

Reed, H. B. C., and Reitan, R. M. (1963b). Intelligence test performances of brain-damaged subjects with lateralized motor deficits. *J. Consult. Psychol., 27*, 102–106.

Reed, H. B. C., and Reitan, R. M. (1963c). Changes in psychological test performances associated with the normal aging process. *J. Gerontol., 18*, 271–274.

Reed, J. C., and Reitan, R. M. (1969). Verbal and performance differences among brain-injured children with lateralized motor deficits. *Percept. Motor Skills, 29*, 747–752.

Reed, H. B. C., Reitan, R. M., and Kløve, H. (1965). The influence of cerebral lesions on psychological test performances of older children. *J. Consult. Psychol., 29*, 247–251.

Reitan, R. M. (1953). Intellectual functions in aphasic and non-aphasic brain-injured subjects. *Neurology, 3*, 202–212.

Reitan, R. M. (1955a). An investigation of the validity of Halstead's measures of biological intelligence. *AMA Arch. Neurol. Psychiatr., 73*, 28–35.

Reitan, R. M. (1955b). The distribution according to age of a psychologic measure dependent upon organic brain functions. *J. Gerontol., 10*, 338–340.

Reitan, R. M. (1955c). Certain differential effects of left and right cerebral lesions in human adults. *J. Comp. Physiol. Psychol., 48*, 474–477.

Reitan, R. M. (1955d). Discussion: Symposium on the temporal lobe. *Arch. Neurol. Psychiatr., 74*, 569–570.

Reitan, R. M. (1955e). The relation of the Trail Making Test to organic brain damage. *J. Consult. Psychol., 19*, 393–394.

Reitan, R. M. (1958). The validity of the Trail Making Test as an indicator of organic brain damage. *Percept. Motor Skills, 8*, 271–276.

Reitan, R. M. (1959a). The comparative effects of brain damage on the Halstead Impairment Index and the Wechsler-Bellevue Scale. *J. Clin. Psychol., 15*, 281–285.

Reitan, R. M. (1959b). *The Effects of Brain Lesions on Adaptive Abilities in Human Beings.* (Privately published.)

Reitan, R. M. (1960). The significance of dysphasia for intelligence and adaptive abilities. *J. Psychol., 50*, 355–376.

Reitan, R. M. (1962). The comparative psychological significance of aging in groups with and without organic brain damage. In: C. Tibbitts and W. Donahue, eds. *Social and Psychological Aspects of Aging.* New York: Columbia University Press, pp. 880–887.

Reitan, R. M. (1964a). Psychological deficits resulting from cerebral lesions in man. In: J. M. Warren and K. A. Akert, eds. *The Frontal Granular Cortex and Behavior.* New York: McGraw Hill.

Reitan, R. M. (1964b). Relationships between neurological and psychological variables and their implications for reading instruction. In: K. A. Robinson, ed. *Meeting Individual Differences in Reading.* Chicago: University of Chicago Press.

Reitan, R. M. (1966a). Problems and prospects in studying the psychological correlates of brain lesions. *Cortex, 2*, 127–154.

Reitan, R. M. (1966b). A research program on the psychological effects of brain lesions in human beings. In: N. R. Ellis, ed., *International Review of Research in Mental Retardation*, vol. 1. New York: Academic Press, pp. 153–218.

Reitan, R. M. (1967a). Psychological assessment of deficits associated with brain lesions in subjects with normal and subnormal intelligence. In: J. L. Khanna, ed., *Brain Damage and Mental Retardation: A Psychological Evaluation.* Springfield, Illinois: Charles C. Thomas.

Reitan, R. M. (1967b). Psychological changes associated with aging and with cerebral damage. *Mayo Clinic Proc., 42*, 653–673.

Reitan, R. M. (1970a). Objective behavioral assessment in diagnosis and prediction. Presentation 15. In: A. L. Benton, ed., *Behavioral Change in Cerebrovascular Disease*. New York: Harper & Row, pp. 155–165.

Reitan, R. M. (1970b). Sensorimotor functions, intelligence and cognition, and emotional status in subjects with cerebral lesions. *Percept. Motor Skills, 31,* 275–284.

Reitan, R. M. (1970c). Measurement of psychological changes in aging. *Duke University Council on Aging and Human Development, Proceedings of Seminars.* Durham: Duke University.

Reitan, R. M. (1971a). Sensorimotor functions in brain-damaged and normal children of early school age. *Percept. Motor Skills, 33,* 655–664.

Reitan, R. M. (1971b). Trail Making Test results for normal and brain damaged children. *Percept. Motor Skills, 33,* 575–581.

Reitan, R. M. (1972). Verbal problem solving as related to cerebral damage. *Percept. Motor Skills, 34,* 515–524.

Reitan, R. M. (1973). Psychological testing after craniocerebral injury. In: J. R. Youmans, ed., *Neurological Surgery*, vol. II. Philadelphia: W. B. Saunders, pp. 1040–1048.

Reitan, R. M. (1974a). Psychological effects of cerebral lesions in children of early school age. In: R. M. Reitan and L. A. Davison, eds., *Clinical Neuropsychology: Current Status and Applications*. Washington, D. C.: V. H. Winston & Sons, pp. 53–90.

Reitan, R. M. (1974b). Methodological problems in clinical neuropsychology. In: R. M. Reitan and L. A. Davison, eds., *Clinical Neuropsychology: Current Status and Applications*. Washington, D. C.: V. H. Winston & Sons, pp. 19–46.

Reitan, R. M. (1977a). Psychological testing of epileptic patients. In: P. J. Vinken and G. W. Bruyn, eds., *Handbook of Clinical Neurology: The Epilepsies*, vol. XV. Amsterdam: North Holland Publishing Company, pp. 559–575.

Reitan, R. M. (1977b). Neuropsychological concepts and psychiatric diagnosis. In: V. M. Rakoff, H. C. Stancer, and H. B. Kedward, eds., *Psychiatric Diagnosis*. New York: Brunner/Mazel, pp. 42–68.

Reitan, R. M., and Boll, T. J. (1971). Intellectual and cognitive functions in Parkinson's disease. *J. Consult. Clin. Psychol., 37,* 364–469.

Reitan, R. M., and Boll, T. J. (1973). Neuropsychological correlates of minimal brain dysfunction. In: Annals of the New York Academy of Sciences, *Conference on Minimal Brain Dysfunction*. New York: New York Academy of Sciences, pp. 65–88.

Reitan, R. M., and Davison, L. A., eds. (1974). *Clinical Neuropsychology: Current Status and Applications*. Washington, D.C.: V. H. Winston & Sons.

Reitan, R. M., and Fitzhugh, K. B. (1971). Behavioral deficits in groups with cerebral vascular lesions. *J. Consult. Clin. Psychol., 37,* 215–223.

Reitan, R. M., and Heineman, C. (1968). Interactions of neurological deficits and emotional disturbances in children. In: J. Hellmuth, ed., *Learning Disorders*, vol. III. Seattle, Washington: Special Child Publications, pp. 93–135.

Reitan, R. M., Reed, J. C., and Dyken, M. L. (1971). Cognitive, psychomotor, and motor correlates of multiple sclerosis. *J. Nerv. Ment. Dis., 153,* 218–224.

Ross, A. T., and Reitan, R. M. (1955). Intellectual and affective functions in multiple sclerosis: A quantitative study. *AMA Arch. Neurol. Psychiatr., 73,* 663–677.

Selz, M., and Reitan, R. M. (1979a). Comparative test performance of normal, learning disabled, and brain-damaged older children. *J. Nerv. Ment. Dis., 167,* 298–302.

Selz, M., and Reitan, R. M. (1979b). Rules for neuropsychological diagnosis: Classification of brain function in older children. *J. Clin. Consult. Psychol., 47,* 258–264.

Shure, G. D., and Halstead, W. C. (1958). Cerebral localization of intellectual processes. *Psychol. Monographs, 72* (12, Whole No. 465).

Townes, B. D., Reitan, R. M., and Trupin, E. W. (1978) Concept formation ability in brain-damaged and normal children. *Academic Therapy, 13,* 517–526.

Vega, A., Jr., and Parsons, O. A. (1967). Cross-validation of the Halstead-Reitan tests for brain damage. *J. Consult. Psychol., 31,* 619–625.

Wheeler, L. (1964). Complex behavioral indices weighted by linear discriminant functions for the prediction of cerebral damage. *Percept. Motor Skills, 19,* 907–923.

Wheeler, L., Burke, C. J., and Reitan, R. M. (1963). An application of discriminant functions to the problem of predicting brain damage using behavioral variables. *Percept. Motor Skills, 16,* (Monograph Suppl.) 417–440.

Wheeler, L., and Reitan, R. M. (1962). The presence and laterality of brain damage predicted from responses to a short Aphasia Screening Test. *Percept. Motor Skills, 15,* 783–799.

Wheeler, L., and Reitan, R. M. (1963). Discriminant functions applied to the problem of predicting cerebral damage from behavior tests: A cross validation study. *Percept. Motor Skills, 16,* 681–701.

2

The Analytical Approach
to Neuropsychological Assessment

PAT MCKENNA / ELIZABETH K. WARRINGTON

The major advances in neurology at the turn of the century were followed by a developmental period which lasted until the late 1950s when clinicians no longer felt forced to concede that the brain was characterized by homogeneity of function. Remnants of equipotentialist thinking can still be found, but they are confined to minor aspects of organization such as the controversy over whether or not rudimentary language can be coaxed from the nondominant hemisphere in patients who have sustained near-total damage to the dominant hemisphere. Other areas of investigation, which still give a certain degree of credence to this idea, are those of functional organization in left-handed subjects and patients who have sustained early brain damage. For the most part, however, neurologists and psychologists agree about the broad functional specialization and localization along the dimensions of language, perception, memory and movement.

Beyond this point, however, any further investigation encounters diverse schools of thought, a proliferation of documented syndromes of cognitive disorders, and an unwieldy empirical literature without, more often than not, any clear theoretical basis, and certainly not one that is shared throughout the field. This state of the science clearly limits the contribution of neuropsychologists to the diagnosis, assessment, and treatment of patients, since the efficiency of clinical tools must ultimately depend on the progress of research. Indeed, Yates (1954) and Piercy (1959) very clearly described the frustration of being a clinician at this stage of development and could lament the lack of an adequate theory of brain function and the concomitant limitations of clinical tests.

The present climate is far more optimistic—developments in neuropsychological research are accelerating, and we are now attempting to incorporate the new levels of understanding into an expanding battery of more efficient and specific tests of brain function. These developments have resulted from a method that combines traditional neurological observation with the modern empiricism of cognitive psychology, which we claim overcomes the very real barrier posed by notions of equipotentiality.

Until recently, clinical tests fell into one of two categories. First, experimental psychologists provided formal tests based on global facets of cognitive behavior along gross dimensions such as aptitudes and intelligence. These tests were really measures of behavioral skills—the final orchestrated result of many different cognitive functions. They were originally intended for, and far better suited to, group studies within the normal population. Second, a "hunch" led the more innovative clinicians to improvise test stimuli to collect samples of behavior which inferred more skill-specific difficulties in particular patients. This latter approach underlies the anecdotal evidence of neurologists which, though providing new insights, could not progress without formal tests to validate and replicate results. Our method is a synthesis of both the empirical and intuitive styles and is one which started to evolve in the late 1950s and still continues to do so. In this chapter we attempt to describe how this methodology has affected the theoretical orientation, research techniques, and clinical tests of our department and finally their application to the assessment of neorological and neuropsychiatric patients.

Theoretical Orientation

Evidence is rapidly accumulating to show that the organization of cognitive functions is more complex than has hitherto been supposed. Beyond the first sensory levels of analysis, the cumulative evidence for higher stages of information processing has not revealed any parallel processing between the hemispheres but instead increasingly points to their independent organization and specialization. This appears to be particularly applicable to the temporal and parietal lobes, those areas subserving functions with which we have made most progress. The focus of this research has been memory (short-term, semantic, and event), perception, and reading and writing, and how these skills interrelate. The benefits of a commitment to the theory of cerebral specialization are already evident in the analysis of complex neurological syndromes. For example, constructional apraxia, most commonly observed in a patient's inability to draw, is often described as arising from either left or right hemisphere damage. It now seems clear that such deficits arising as a result of right hemisphere damage are secondary to impaired space perception, which precludes the ability to draw, whereas left hemisphere lesions give rise to the primary praxis deficit, the inability to carry out purposive voluntary movements (Warrington, 1969).

Some of the most persuasive evidence for hemisphere specialization comes from the relationship between perception and meaning. We have found that the post-Rolandic regions of the right hemisphere appear to be critical for visuospatial and perceptual analysis, whereas the post-Rolandic regions of the left hemisphere are implicated in the semantic analysis of perceptual input. Furthermore, if one accepts this differentiation of modalities in semantic analysis, certain controversies are resolved. For example, word comprehension is generally acknowledged to be a predominantly left hemisphere function, but the visual equivalent, object recognition or comprehension, is often denied, ignored, or implicitly attributed to the right hemisphere. This state of affairs provides enormous scope for clinicians and researchers alike to communicate at cross purposes and, like the apraxia example above, it illustrates the conceptual and terminological confusion that often serves to fuel and perpetuate controversies in the literature.

The degree and complexity of specialization of brain functioning are even more striking when one investigates a particular cognitive system. The following sections outline some of the evidence for delineation of complex behaviors into systems and their subsystems in an attempt to illustrate that the complex phenomena in brain-damaged patients can be analyzed in terms of a greater degree of functional specialization than had hitherto been supposed.

A major consequence of this theoretical orientation has been a reappraisal of the role of traditional neurological syndromes—which tend to be clusters of commonly occurring symptoms in neurological patients, as a basis for research. However, this basis of classification may reflect no more than the facts of anatomy, such as the distribution of the arterial system, and may contribute little to the understanding of the cerebral organization of the components of complex skills. The commonly adopted strategy of comparing Broca and Wernicke aphasics is a clear example. The traditional syndromes of language breakdown are now seen to fractionate. For example, we have found conduction aphasia to be a double deficit of at least two partially unrelated functions—articulation and short term memory. The already quoted example of constructional apraxia is a further example of the multi-component nature of a traditional neurological syndrome and while it is understandable how neurologists came to give the same label to such fundamentally different deficits, there is little justification for neuropsychologists perpetuating the confusion. A syndrome should now be function-based rather than symptom-based and should serve to elucidate the nature of a neurobehavioral system or one of its subsystems.

In summary, it is our experience that cognitive functions can best be studied and understood by an information processing approach to the analysis of a complex skill into its functional components and subcomponents. This approach has resulted in a commitment to a theory of differentiation and localization between and within cognitive functions that overrides notions of equipotentiality.

Research Methods and Testing Materials

The three stages in our research are, first, using a single case study to observe and document properties of a neurological syndrome or cognitive deficit; second, validating the significant findings in appropriate clinical groups to test their pragmatic strength in terms of frequency of occurrence, detectability, and their localization value; third, harnessing the results of these validation studies to new tests that have greater specificity and sensitivity for diagnosis and assessment, our ultimate aim being to provide an exhaustive battery of function-specific and subfunction-specific tests.

Shallice (1979) has provided a full discussion of the single case study approach, but for the purpose of this chapter suffice it to say that given a patient with an observed deficit that appears to be selective (to a system or subsystem) and is consistent and quantifiably significant, then a series of exhaustive experiments can be prepared and repeated to specify the nature and extent of the deficit. One important aspect of single case study methodology is the notion of dissociation. For example, given a patient who has a specific difficulty in reading abstract words as opposed to concrete ones (Shallice and Warrington, 1975), the conclusion that concrete and abstract words are organized separately requires a prediction that it is equally possible to observe the reverse deficit such that a patient cannot read concrete words but can read abstract words (Warrington, 1981a). Thus, for any particular hypothesis of functional organization, it is possible to draw up a table of predictions of double or even triple dissociations. Without the use of single case studies, it would be impossible, or extremely difficult, to progress in mapping out the organization of cognitive skills.

The second, or intermediate, stage in our research is, when appropriate, to prepare a series of tests based on the results of a single case study for a group study to provide information on lateralization, localization, and frequency of the observation in the clinical population. For example, having discovered single incidents of material specific deficits of perception (Whiteley and Warrington, 1977), a consecutive series of patients with right hemisphere lesions were tested using the same stimulus materials to determine the frequency of these dissociations (Warrington, 1982a).

The third stage aims to standardize tests which have been successfully validated in order to provide more appropriate tools for clinical use in the diagnosis and assessment of cognitive deficits. We are now attempting to standardize tests of literacy, memory, perception, naming, and reasoning all of which have evolved from our more analytical research investigations.

Clinical Testing of Cognitive Functions

Intelligence and General Factors

Despite our increasing awareness of and sensitivity to the individual variation in strengths and weaknesses of different cognitive skills, it is undoubtedly the case that patients can still usefully be screened according to general level of intellectual ability. Though age affects many skills to their detriment, an individual's intelligence level remains constant in relation to his age group. Furthermore, in any given individual, levels of performance on different aspects of cognitive behavior will tend to be more similar than not. In common with most clinicians in Britain and the United States we use the concept of I.Q. as measured by the Wechsler Adult Intelligence Scale (WAIS) for a preliminary overview of the patient (Wechsler, 1955, 1981). Though it is an example of subtests which are sampling patterns of skills rather than specific functions, it is able to give a rough guide to some of the more commonly occurring syndromes. The Progressive Matrices—a test of abstract problem-solving using nonverbal stimulus materials—is also useful in this regard (Raven, 1960).

At this general level of clinical assessment, the overriding and growing problem is to detect an incipient decline in intellectual powers over and above the aging process and often in the presence of depression. Our efforts to provide some indication of premorbid level of functioning have resulted in a formula based on the Schonell reading test, which can predict optimal level of functioning up to I.Q. 115, and in the National Adult Reading Test (NART), which has a higher ceiling of I.Q. 125 (Nelson and McKenna, 1975; Nelson, 1982). These tests were made viable in the first instance on the findings that reading vocabulary is I.Q.-related (reinforcing the point made above that performances on different tests tend to be correlated) and that reading is one of the most resistant skills in any process of intellectual decline. The NART resulted from research on dyslexic syndromes that showed word knowledge to be essential for reading irregularly spelled words.

Visual Perception

We are often so preoccupied with the complexity of meaning that it renders us insensitive to our remarkable (and probably more perfected) skill in organizing our visual world. This is in spite of there being a comparable, if not greater, area of brain subserving visual function. Our evidence indicates that the perceptual systems are capable of equating diverse percepts of a single stimulus-object and of categorizing visual stimuli *before,* and independently of, any investment of meaning in the percept. Should this appear paradoxical, it is only because of a common-sense bias towards semantics as the essential criterion of intelligent behavior. Our evidence points to two distinct stages of visual perception prior to semantic analysis, and individual case studies show dissociations between and within all three stages.

Before implicating a deficit at the level of categorical perception, it is necessary to establish that visual analysis is intact. It is known that lesions of the primary and secondary visual cortex give rise to, in the first place, impaired brightness and acuity discrimination and in the second, deficits of color, contour, and location. Visual disorientation, sufficiently marked to be a handicap in everyday life, is invariably associated with bilateral lesions. However, more detailed investigation has revealed unilateral visual disorientation in both the right or left half field of vision in patients with a lesion in the contralateral hemisphere (Cole, Schutta, and Warrington, 1962). This also appears to be the case for color imperception (Albert, Reches, and Silverberg, 1975). The inference from such observations is that the functions of the secondary visual cortex, as is the case for the primary visual cortex, maintain a retinotopic organization. Thus, there appears to be no lateralization at this stage of visual analysis, and the identification of such deficits with 'free' vision indicates bilateral dysfunction.

The more complex processes of the second stage of perceptual analysis appear to be functions lateralized to the right hemisphere. Two major systems have been identified—that subserving space perception and that subserving form perception. The overriding conclusion from research to date is that these two classes of deficit are dissociated. Furthermore, recent findings suggest that each of these may fractionate into subcomponents.

SPACE PERCEPTION. The concept of space perception implies more than the location of a single point in space; it implies the integration of successive or simultaneous stimuli in a spatial schema. The essential principle guiding our methods of testing for spatial disorders is that the involvement of other cognitive skills be minimized, in particular, praxis skills, including drawing. The test we have found most useful is that of position discrimination (the subject is merely required to say which figure has the dot *exactly* in the center), and the ability to perform it has been shown to be selectively impaired in patients with right parietal lesions (Taylor and Warrington, 1973). Further observations suggest there may be two components of this syndrome—the ability to discriminate position and a dissociable defect in the more abstract facility of spatial imaging. In this regard, we are exploring the use of the Stanford-Binet cube analysis test and tests requiring spatial rotation.

FORM PERCEPTION. This stage of visual perceptual analysis—postsensory but presemantic—is difficult to conceptualize and is best introduced by the research findings that led to it being postulated. First, we have shown that although some patients were able to identify and name prototypical views of common objects, they were significantly impaired in identifying the same object from an unfamiliar orientation or less typical view (Warrington and Taylor, 1973). In a further experiment, it was shown that when a prototypical view was paired with a less usual view, patients with a right parietal lesion were unable to judge whether the two had the same *physical* identity (Warrington and Taylor, 1978). It was on the basis of these studies that an unusual-view photograph test was devised. Furthermore, it has been shown in both individual case and group studies that patients with unilateral lesions of the left hemisphere resulting in impaired semantic processing can do these tests relatively normally (e.g., Warrington, 1975; Warrington and Taylor, 1978) though they may not know what the object is.

Further tests, based on similar principles of departure from the prototype use other visual stimuli such as letters and faces. In addition to providing a more comprehensive measure of form perception, discrepancies in performance of some individuals alerted us to the possibility of further fractionation of this perceptual function, namely, the material selectivity of perceptual categorization. Comparing perception of objects, faces, letters, and buildings in fifty patients with right hemisphere lesions, we have observed 9 of the possible 12 single dissociations and 3 of the possible 6 double dissociations (Warrington, 1982a). Again, these deficits are all held to be at a postsensory presemantic stage of processing. This formulation clarified the boundary between presemantic perceptual processing lateralized to the right hemisphere and those left hemisphere systems that achieve meaning.

The Semantic System

The function of the semantic system is to process percepts in order to achieve meaning. It is not a reasoning system, but a store of concepts, perhaps analogous to a thesaurus or encyclopedia. In the domain of nonverbal knowledge systems in man, the visual modality is by far the most important. Extensive knowledge of the visual world is a very early acquisition and almost certainly precedes verbal knowledge. However, language, par excellence, illustrates a system subserving meaning. Our approach to investigating and assessing the verbal semantic system has been to focus on single word comprehension, thus mirroring an early manifestation of language acquisition.

Our evidence to date suggests that there can be a double dissociation between deficits of visual and verbal knowledge, indicating that the semantic system fractionates into at least two independent modality-specific systems and that they are both associated with damage to the posterior dominant hemisphere. This conclusion is based on evidence from (1) patients with intact recognition of the visual representation of a concept but not its verbal representation (verbal agnosia); (2) patients with the mirror image deficit, i.e., the recognition of the verbal representation of a concept but not is visual representation (visual agnosia); and (3) recent studies of patients in whom both verbal and visual representations of a concept are intact but a disconnection between the two systems (optic aphasia) can be demonstrated (Lhermitte and Beauvois, 1973).

Within these two domains, the predominant recurrent findings are category specificity and a hierarchical organization. These findings derive from two lines of investigation. The first draws on evidence of the pattern of loss of conceptual knowledge in patients with agnosic deficits. It has been shown that supraordinate information is often relatively preserved. The order of loss of conceptual knowledge appears to be constant going from the particular to the general. Thus, a canary can be identified as living, animal, and a bird but not as yellow, small, and a pet. These effects have been demonstrated for visual as well as verbal knowledge and for comprehension of the written as well as the spoken word (Warrington and Shallice, 1979). Secondly, our investigations suggest that the selective impairment of particular semantic categories in naming and comprehension tasks occur much more commonly than has hitherto been supposed. It has long been accepted in the neurological literature that selective anomias for objects, symbols, colors and body parts can occur, and our own growing evidence from individual case studies would add proper names (with further subdivision of people and place names), animate, inanimate, concrete, and abstract dimensions (Warrington, 1981b). We would interpret these data in terms of the categorical organization of the semantic knowledge systems. Unpublished evidence for further subdivisions within these categories is available, and ongoing group studies on patients with left hemisphere pathology are providing feedback on the incidence in our clinical population of category-specific impairment.

We have studied the organization of semantic memory for the most part as observed in agnosic, dysphasic, and dyslexic patients but there is every reason to suppose that our formulations apply to other classes of conceptual knowledge. For example, we have observed a patient with a highly specific acalculia whereby the arithmetical facts of addition, subtraction, division, and multiplication were no longer accessible to him though he continued to display a superior facility with mathematical reasoning. It was argued that arithmetical facts are a further independent category of our knowledge systems (Warrington, 1982b).

In summary, it is held that there are modality-specific semantic systems that are hieararchically and categorically organized. Our understanding of these systems is too incomplete as yet to do other than speculate on the range of modality-specific subsystems and categories and on their interaction with episodic memory, reasoning, and linguistics. However, the disproportionate difficulty in later life of learning new "facts" and skills compared with the recall of ongoing "events" would possibly be explained in maturational terms by the capacity of the semantic system reaching its asymptote by the time adulthood is reached.

The clinical relevance of our findings is twofold. First, at a conceptual level it has enabled us to differentiate and delineate a deficit of semantic processing as opposed to sensory or perceptual processing, which can confidently be diagnosed as having pathology in the posterior dominant hemisphere. Secondly, new tests have been developed based on our findings. A test of arithmetical facts has been finalized for clinical use following the discovery of selective impairment of this ability in the patient described above, and a single word comprehension task has been validated in patients with unilateral cerebral lesions. The findings of this investigation (Coughlan and Warrington, 1978) are now being developed to form the basis of a graded difficulty word comprehension task. Though a formal clinical battery of visual semantic tests is not available, there are numerous tasks used in research reports to probe modality and category effects. For example, the differentiation of a deficit at the level of perceptual processing and semantic processing entirely within the visual domain can be tested by comparing the patient's ability to match photographs of objects by physical and functional identity (Warrington and Taylor, 1978). This combination of standardized clinical tests and research techniques can thus provide an extensive array of methods with which to explore semantic deficits.

Literacy

Neurologists have long since identified two major syndromes of reading disorders: dyslexia with dysgraphia and dyslexia without dysgraphia. The value of this distinction was to acknowledge some independence of the reading and writing skills, but they did not succeed in developing this taxonomy further. More recently, there has been a renewed interest in this area. Patients with unique reading and writing difficulties have been investigated using experimental methods and a detailed analysis of their deficits is yielding a coherent perspective of the organization of these skills.

With regard to reading, it has been suggested that acquired dyslexia can arise from 'peripheral' or 'central' deficits. Peripheral dyslexias share the property of failing to achieve a visual word-form (the integrity of the pattern or gestalt provided by the written word, or part thereof) at a purely visual level of analysis. These include (1) neglect dyslexia, characterized by letter substitutions at the beginning of words (Kinsbourne and Warrington, 1962), (2) attentional dyslexia, which can easily be tested for by comparing the ability to read single lettters and arrays of letters (Shallice and Warrington, 1977), and (3) word-form or spelling dyslexia, characterized by letter by letter reading resulting in a greater difficulty reading words written in script than in print (Warrington and Shallice, 1979). It is not yet clear whether these difficulties reflect general properties of the perceptual system or are specific to the reading system.

Central dyslexias describe an inability to derive meaning from the written word given intact visual analysis of it. There is little disagreement in the present literature that there appear to be two main reading routes—the phonological and the sèmantic. These are the inevitable inferences from characteristics of two classes of acquired dyslexias. In the first type, there is a complete, or near complete dependence on the use of phonology for reading. Thus, the patient can read regular words (those which use commonly occurring grapheme-phoneme correspondences) but is unable to read irregular words: the greater the deviation from the regular phoneme-grapheme correspondence the greater the difficulty in reading. In these patients, in whom the direct semantic route is inoperative, the characteristics of the phonological route are open to inspection. Though some patients in this category can apply only the most regular grapheme-phoneme rules, others show a much more versatile facility, which leads us to believe that the properties of the phonological processing are more extensive than at first thought, such patients being able to use irregular rules to some extent (Shallice, Warrington, and McCarthy, 1983).

In the second type, there is an inability to use phonology. Patients are able to read real words but cannot begin to read nonsense words. In the extreme case, they are unable to sound single letters or pronounce two letter combinations. This type of dyslexic has a relatively (sometimes completely) intact semantic route, such that the visual word-form has direct access to verbal semantic systems. The properties and characteristics of the semantic route can be investigated in patients in whom the phonological route is inoperative and there has been partial damage to the semantic route. For example, category-specificity has been observed or indeed may be commonly the case. Furthermore, this class of dyslexic patient has been further subdivided into those having an 'access' deficit and a 'storage' deficit (Shallice and Warrington, 1980).

Following these advances in research on dyslexia, data have emerged from investigations on dysgraphic patients, which show a similar organization for writing. A single case study of a patient who could not write irregular words but could write phonologically regular words, whether real or nonsense words, has been reported (Beauvois and Derouesne, 1979). Evidence for a double dissociation between the inferred phonological and direct routes to writing has now been found. Shallice (1981) has reported a patient who could write real words and letter names but could neither write nonsense syllables nor letter sounds.

A graded difficulty irregular word reading test is already available for clinical purposes, as described earlier, and a comparable graded difficulty irregular spelling test is being standardized. The assessment of nonsense word reading and writing together with these two standard tests is sufficient to identify the majority of acquired central dyslexic syndromes in the neurological population.

Language

For theoretical purposes, experimental psychologists have found it profitable to differentiate syntax and semantics in research on language. Certainly our own experience would lend support to the notion that these are dissociable aspects of language. Syntax, however, is the area we have least explored since our efforts to date have been concentrated on single word comprehension. However, for diagnosis and assessment, our strategy is very similar to our assessment of other cognitive skills. Since most of the available tests of dysphasia are insufficiently sensitive to detect minor degrees of deficit in the general neurological population, our aim has been to develop a battery of graded difficulty language tests.

A series of tests based on a group study of patients with unilateral lesions has provided a preliminary test battery of selected language skills. To some extent, this battery illustrates our methodological approach in that it attempts to test various unitary functions which it seems reasonable to assume are implicated in word comprehension and usage. This approach represents a departure from the traditional taxonomic basis of language batteries that are tuned to the symptomatology of the classic neurological syndromes such as Broca's and Wernicke's. Thus the battery includes tests for word perception, word comprehension, word retrieval, and word articulation.

Though some of these tests are modified versions of existing ones, such as the Peabody and Token tests, most of them are new. The hard core tests, and indeed the ones we have found most useful, attempt to distinguish between visual and verbal presentation and between word comprehension and word retrieval. From the point of view of localization, it has been demonstrated that certain of these tests, i.e., word retrieval and comprehension, have localizing value—temporal lobe structures are implicated—while others have merely lateralizing value.

The usefulness of these tests motivated the development of a graded difficulty naming test. Like the reading and spelling tests described above it has the added advantage of taking into account a person's general intellectual level in clinical assessment (McKenna and Warrington, 1983).

Our preliminary research findings suggest that word frequency and word length are important variables for speech production and that the degree of meaningfulness and transitional probabilities are the crucial parameters for verbal repetition. From detailed investigation of patients with conduction aphasia we have developed new graded difficulty tests of speech production and verbal repetition (the two components of the syndrome) (McCarthy and Warrington, 1984).

As yet our range of standardized and graded difficulty tests is far from comprehensive. The most obvious shortcoming is that we have limited our analysis of language skills to single words which, of course, we appreciate would hardly be accepted as an adequate assessment of language functions.

Event Memory

Psychologists and lay people alike often use the concepts of knowing and remembering interchangeably. A further area of confusion is provided by the phenomenon of repeating, which is also implicated in common-sense ideas of "being able to remember." Among psychologists, both experimental and clinical, short-term memory is now generally acknowledged to be an independent and dissociable system that can be conceptualized as a limited capacity system that 'holds' auditory verbal information for very short time durations. More controversial is the relationship between "knowing" and "remembering." Indeed, many psychologists argue that the difference is one of degree and that the same cognitive systems subserve, for example, "knowing" a word and "remembering" who telephoned yesterday. However, evidence is now emerging that supports the view that memory for facts and memory for events are independent systems that can be selectively impaired. The amnesic syndrome is characterized by an almost total inability to recall or recognize autobiographical events either before or since the onset of their illness, yet amnesics' memory for other classes of knowledge can be on a par with normal subjects and they can score normally on tests of intelligence. The complementary syndrome, the impairment of semantic systems, or of memory for facts, has been observed in patients in whom memory for past and present events is relatively well preserved. We have now documented triple dissociations between these three systems: short-term memory, memory for facts (semantics), and memory for events. In this section we discuss only the investigation and assessment of event memory.

Event memory appears to be an independent system with unique properties for mapping ongoing experiences on to an individual schema of events. Contrary to the commonly held assumption that memory for remote events is less vulnerable compared to memory for recent events, Warrington and Sanders (1971) showed that although memory for events (tested either by recall or recognition) declined with age in normal subjects, there was no greater vulnerability of memory for recent as compared to remote events in any age group. Similarly, no sparing of remote memories in amnesic patients could be demonstrated (Sanders and Warrington, 1971). Furthermore, after closed head injuries the severity of the anterograde deficit roughly correlates with the severity of the retrograde deficit (Schachter and Crovitz, 1977). We would interpret this evidence as indicating that a unitary memory system subserves both recent and remote events, and consequently the assessment of new learning and retention over short recall intervals is appropriate and sufficient to document event memory impairment. This strategy has the additional advantage that artifacts such as differences in the salience of past experiences, interference during recall intervals and differences in rehearsal activity can be avoided.

Numerous investigations have established the occurrence of modality-specific memory deficits. Since the classic studies of Milner (1966) it is widely accepted that verbal memory deficits are associated with unilateral lesions of the left hemisphere and nonverbal memory deficits with the right hemisphere. Our aim was to develop a test for specific investigation of event memory which would incorporate the verbal/nonverbal dichotomy. A recognition paradigm was chosen in preference to recall since the former task appears to be much less influenced by affective disorders and by the normal aging process; in addition, identical procedures can be used for the separate assessment of verbal and nonverbal material. Consequently, a forced two-choice recognition memory test for fifty common words and fifty unknown faces [previously described by Warrington (1974) in the context of the analysis of the amnesic syndrome] has been standardized. The normalized scores provide a quantitative measure of performance that can be compared directly with other measures of cognitive skills. Validation studies have been successful in so far as a right hemisphere group was shown to be impaired on the face recognition memory test but not on the word recognition test. By contrast the left hemisphere group, although mildly impaired on the face recognition, had a clearcut deficit on the word recognition test. Perhaps of greater relevance for the majority of assessment problems was the fact that the test was sufficiently sensitive to detect memory deficits in patients with only a mild degree of atrophy. Thus, the findings of a number of investigations have led to the development of a test with the discriminative power to detect minor degrees of modality specific memory deficits (Warrington, 1984).

Further characteristics of the event memory system have emerged from investigations of the "pure amnesic syndrome"—a very severe yet circumscribed memory impairment. It has become increasingly apparent that the amnesic memory deficit is not so absolute nor so dense as either clinical impressions or conventional memory test results would suggest. For example, strikingly different results are obtained when retention is tested by cueing recall and prompting learning; retention scores can be normal or near normal and learning can occur albeit more slowly than for the normal subject (Warrington and Weiskrantz, 1968; 1970). These observations have led to the development of two memory tests to attempt to differentiate cortical and subcortical memory deficits. First, retention of words tested by a yes/no recognition procedure is compared with retention tested by cueing recall with the first three letters of the word. A discrepancy in the level of performance on these two tasks (cued recall superior to recognition memory) we interpret to indicate a subcortical amnesia and validation studies (in progress) should indicate the generality and robustness of this pattern of test scores. Secondly, perceptual learning is tested by giving repeated trials to identify fragmented visual stimuli. Two versions of this test, incomplete word learning and incomplete picture learning, have been adapted from the original technique used to investigate retention in amnesic patients. Our aim in validating these memory tests is to achieve a test that would be useful not only in assessment, but also for differential diagnosis. Preliminary results suggest that there are three patterns of response to this task indicating cortical impairment, subcortical impairment, and nonorganic impairment.

Our approach to the assessment of memory deficits illustrates the three stages of investigation we initially outlined. Analytic research studies led to group studies that in turn have led to the development of standardized tests that can be used in a much broader population of neurological and neuropsychiatric patients.

Reasoning and Behavior

We cannot claim to have made any progress in furthering the understanding of reasoning processes, which neuropsychologists find the most baffling and elusive phenomena to study. It is not unusual for a patient recovering from frontal lobe treatment to be sent home with no discernible deficit only to be readmitted a few weeks later with a history of job incompetence or other atypical behavior. Again, performance on formal tests of cognitive function can be normal. Even more frustrating is for the clinician to assess the patient's behavior subjectively as somewhat "odd" but be unable to be more specific. Blanket terms such as "inappropriate", "apathetic", "impulsive" or even "disinhibited" behavior give no clue to what psychological process is implicated. Nevertheless, it is clear that the frontal lobes play a major if little understood part in the orchestration of our cognitive systems (and affect, though this is beyond the scope of the present chapter).

At a theoretical level, neuropsychological research has clarified to some extent which cognitive operations can be eliminated from the reasoning process. For example, our investigations of a patient with acalculia suggest that the core deficit was accessing the "facts" of arithmetic, i.e., given that the sum $3 + 2$ is comprehended, the solution 5 can be accessed directly, computation being unnecessary (though this presumably need not be the case during acquisition). Indeed, the generally accepted finding that frontal patients can perform relatively well on intelligence tests that follow the format of the WAIS may well be due to its loading on stable, well-practiced cognitive skills, which it seems clear are subserved by post-Rolandic regions of the cerebral hemispheres. We concur with the generally held view that impairment of reasoning abilities in such patients may only emerge with tests, such as the progressive matrices, that require relatively novel cognitive strategies.

Following this principle of novel manipulations in problem-solving behavior, the Cognitive Estimates test was developed (Shallice and Evans, 1978), which requires the subject to manipulate data and deduce an approximation to an answer he does not actually know. For instance, the example given to the patient for demonstration purposes is "what is the height of a double decker bus?" We have found this test to be very useful in diagnosing frontal pathology. Sometimes even a single answer can give a definitive diagnosis, as when a patient produces a ridiculous answer (e.g., 1000 feet as the height of a double decker bus) and with encouragement will only modify it slightly.

However, at this stage of our understanding, our battery is composed of pragmatically validated materials [e.g., Weigl Sorting Test (Weigl, 1941), Wisconsin Card Sorting (Berg, 1948), Stroop Test (Stroop, 1935)] for localization purposes and cannot as yet provide a functional breakdown of the processes which make up reasoning. Further research into different aspects of 'novel' manipulation in problem-solving is being done using the methodology of group studies. It is hoped that the more analytical focus of these frontal lobe research studies will result in a battery of tests that will have greater clinical application than any now available.

Differential Diagnosis

Most, but not all, of our research efforts are concentrated on the neurological patient population, which has provided a most beneficial, if oblique, approach to differential diagnosis in the neuropsychiatric patient group. The fundamental problem posed by this group is to distinguish between impairment of an organic nature and impairment of a functional nature. The most obvious indication is a mismatch between subjective complaints and objective performance. A further indication lies in the recurrent theme in all areas of our research, that cognitive systems not only fractionate but they do so along dimensions that do not necessarily follow common-sense ideas of what constitutes a function. Unless a patient is aware of the 'rules' of breakdown, he cannot produce the correct pattern of disability other than on an organic basis. Thus it becomes more and more possible, with our increasing understanding of cognitive organization, to differentiate between organic and functional elements of a symptom.

Most referrals which touch on this problem request a differential diagnosis between depression and dementia, organic or functional memory loss and investigation of general complaints of intellectual inefficiency. One test of memory described earlier has proved particularly useful and illustrates the mismatch of common sense and the 'rules' of cognitive breakdown, namely perceptual learning. This task makes small demands on memory resources for it has been shown that patients with dementia and patients with the amnesic syndrome are able to learn and to retain over relatively long time delays. A gross impairment on this learning task can be accepted as a strong indication of nonorganic factors. Similarly, intact performance on this test effectively eliminates a memory disorder. A further example from the amnesic syndrome that has very direct application to this differential diagnosis is the generally accepted 'rule' that the degree of anterograde amnesia is highly correlated with the degree of retrograde amnesia. Thus patients who present with a severe anterograde amnesia but no retrograde amnesia do not conform to any known organic pattern (Pratt, 1977).

An occasionally observed mismatch is the patient who is alert and able to perform relatively normally in a day to day situation but obtains test scores compatible with a gross degree of intellectual failure. More commonly, the mismatch is the reverse, namely, patients and their relatives complain of failing intellectual and memory skills, which even after exhaustive testing cannot be demonstrated objectively. In the area of word retrieval skills, a failure to show the very robust frequency effects either of accuracy or latency would be very strong indication for nonorganic factors.

Sometimes the reverse situation occurs, when our knowledge of a cognitive system confirms that an apparently bizarre or non-common-sense symptom could indeed have an organic basis. For example, individual case studies suggest that infrequently there may be a treble dissociation in the deficits associated with the secondary visual cortices, namely visual analysis of contour, color, and location. Visual disorientation, the inability to locate in space is a particularly handicapping syndrome which together with normal acuity may suggest a mismatch when in fact none exists.

Conclusion

We have outlined an approach to neuropsychological assessment which has been developing since the 1950s, when an impasse had been reached in the understanding and measurement of cognitive impairment. In 1954, Yates claimed that "a purely empirical approach is unlikely to yield satisfactory results, nor is an approach based on a theory which has not been adequately tested experimentally." Our strategy attempts to use the findings of analytical research either from single case or group studies in a clinical situation by devising more specific tests of cognitive function. Thus we are committed in the first instance to research aimed at furthering the understanding of cognitive functions (albeit still at an embryonic stage of development) and secondly to improved clinical tests based on this knowledge. We have cited investigations which, for the most part, have originated at the National Hospital, Queen Square, to illustrate our approach. However, the procedures that we have developed and are developing still in no way override our use of other tools and techniques available; they are merely intended to supplement them. Indeed, we are of the opinion that a flexible and eclectic approach is essential for the assessment of the neuropsychological and neuropsychiatric patient.

ACKNOWLEDGMENTS

We are most grateful to Dr. P. C. Gautier Smith for his advice in the preparation of this manuscript.

REFERENCES

Albert, M. L., Reches, A., and Silverberg, R. (1975). Hemianopic color blindness. *J. Neurol., Neurosurg. Psychiat.*, *38*, 546–549.

Beauvois, M. F. and Derouesne, J. (1979) Phological alexia: Three dissociations. *J. Neurol., Neurosurg. Psychiat.*, *42*, 1115–1124.

Berg, E. A. (1948) A simple objective technique for measuring flexibility in thinking. *J. General Psychol.*, *39*, 15–22.

Cole, M., Schutta, H. S., and Warrington, E. K. (1962). Visual disorientation in homonymous half-fields. *Neurology*, *12*, 257–263.

Coughlan, A. K., and Warrington, E. K. (1978). Word-comprehension and word retrieval in patients with localized cerebral lesions. *Brain*, *101*, 163–185.

Kinsbourne, M., and Warrington, E. K. (1962). A variety of reading disabilities associated with right hemisphere lesions. *J. Neurol., Neurosurg. Psychiatr.*, *25*, 339–344.

Lhermitte, F., and Beauvois, M. F. (1973). A visual speech disconnection syndrome: Report of a case with optic aphasia, agnosia, alexia and color agnosia. *Brain*, *96*, 695–714.

McCarthy, R., and Warrington, E. K. (1984). A two-route model of speech production: Evidence from aphasia. *Brain*, *107*, 463–485.

McKenna, P., and Warrington, E. K. (1983). *Graded Naming Test Manual.* Windsor, England: NFER-Nelson Publishing Company, Ltd.

Milner, B. (1966). Amnesia following operation on the temporal lobes. In: C.W.M. Whitty and O. L. Zangwill, Eds., *Amnesia.* London: Butterworths, pp.109–133.

Nelson, H. E. (1982) *The National Adult Reading Test Manual.* Windsor, England: The NFER-Nelson Publishing Co., Ltd.

Nelson, H. E., and McKenna, P. (1975). The use of current reading ability in the assessment of dementia. *Br. J. Soc. Clin. Psychol.*, *14*, 259–267.

Piercy, M. (1959). Testing for intellectual impairment—Some comments on the tests and testers. *J. Mental Sci.*, 489–495.

Pratt, R. T. C. (1977). Psychogenic loss of memory. In: C.W.M. Whitty and O. L. Zangwill, Eds., *Amnesia*, 2d ed. London: Butterworths, pp. 224–232.

Raven, J. C. (1960). *Guide to the Standard Progressive Matrices.* London: H. K. Lewis.

Sanders, H. I., and Warrington, E. K. (1971). Memory for remote events in amnesia patients. *Brain*, *94*, 616–668.

Schacter, D. L., and Crovitz, H. F. (1977). Memory function after closed head injury: A review of the quantitative research. *Cortex*, *13*, 150–176.

Shallice, T. (1979). Case study approach in neuropsychological research. *J. Clin. Neuropsychol.*, *1*, 183–211.

Shallice, T. (1981). Phonological agraphia and the lexical route in writing. *Brain*, *1–4*, 413–429.

Shallice, T., and Evans, M. E. (1978). The involvement of the frontal lobes in cognitive estimation. *Cortex, 14,* 294–303.

Shallice, T., and Warrington, E. K. (1975). Word recognition in a phonemic dyslexic patient. *Quart. J. Exp. Psychol., 27,* 187–199.

Shallice, T., and Warrington, E. K. (1977). The possible role of selective attention in acquired dyslexia. *Neuropsychologia, 15,* 31–41.

Shallice, T., and Warrington, E. K. (1980). Single and multiple component central dyslexic syndromes. In: M. Coltheart, K. E. Patterson, and J. C. Marshall, eds., *Deep Dyslexia.* London: Routledge & Kegan Paul, pp. 119–145.

Shallice, T., Warrington, E. K., and McCarthy, R. (1983). Reading without semantics. *Quart. J. Exp. Psychol., 35a,* 111–138.

Stroop, J. R. (1935). Studies of interference in serial verbal reactions. *J. Exp. Psych., 18,* 643–662.

Taylor, A. M., and Warrington, E. K. (1973). Visual discrimination in patients with localized cerebral lesions. *Cortex, 9,* 82–93.

Warrington, E. K. (1969). Constructional apraxia. In: P. J. Vinken and G. W. Bruyn, eds., *Handbook of Clinical Neurology,* vol. 4. Amsterdam: Elsevier North-Holland, pp. 67–83.

Warrington, E. K. (1974). Deficient recognition memory in organic amnesia. *Cortex, 10,* 289–291.

Warrington, E. K. (1975). The selective impairment of semantic memory. *Quart. J. Exp. Psychol., 27,* 635–657.

Warrington, E. K. (1981a). Concrete word dyslexia. *Br. J. Psychol., 72,* 175–196.

Warrington, E. K. (1981b). Neuropsychological studies of verbal semantic systems. *Phil. Trans. R. Soc. Lon. B., 295,* 411–423.

Warrington, E. K. (1982a). Neuropsychological studies of object recognition. *Phil. Trans. R. Soc. Lon. B., 298,* 15–33.

Warrington, E. K. (1982b). The fractionation of arithmetical skills. A single case study. *Quart. J. Exp. Psychol., 344,* 31–51.

Warrington, E. K. (1984). *Manual for recognition memory tests.* NFER-Nelson Publishing Company Ltd., Windsor, England.

Warrington, E. K., and Sanders, H. I. (1971). The fate of old memories. *Quart J. Exp. Psychol., 23,* 432–442.

Warrington, E. K., and Shallice, T. (1979). Semantic access dyslexia. *Brain, 102,* 43–63.

Warrington, E. K., and Shallice, T. (1980). Word-form dyslexia. *Brain, 103,* 99–112.

Warrington, E. K., and Taylor, A. M. (1973). The contribution of the right parietal lobe to object recognition. *Cortex, 9,* 152–164.

Warrington, E. K., and Taylor, A. M. (1978). Two categorical stages of object recognition. *Perception, 7,* 695–705.

Warrington, E. K., and Weiskrantz, L. (1968). New method of testing long-term retention with special reference to amnesic patients. *Nature, 277,* 972–974.

Warrington, E. K., & Weiskrantz, L. (1970). Amnesia: Consolidation or retrieval? *Nature, 228,* 628–630.

Wechsler, D. (1955). *The Wechsler Adult Intelligence Scale: Manual.* New York: Psychological Corporation.

Wechsler, D. (1981). *WAIS-R Manual: The Wechsler Adult Intelligence Scale-Revised.* New York: Harcourt Brace Jovanovich.

Weigl, E. (1941). On the psychology of so-called processes of abstraction. *J. Abnormal Soc. Psychol., 36,* 3–33.

Whiteley, A. M., and Warrington, E. K. (1977). Prosopagnosia: A clinical, psychological and anatomical study of 3 patients. *J. Neurol., Neurosurg. Psychiat., 40,* 395–403.

Yates, A. (1954). The validity of some psychological tests of brain damage. *Psychol. Bull., 51,* 4.

3

Qualitative Indices in Neuropsychological Assessment: An Extension of Luria's Approach to Executive Deficit Following Prefrontal Lesions

ELKHONON GOLDBERG / LOUIS D. COSTA

The use of qualitative indices in psychological assessment has been a subject of controversy for some time. While some empiricists might maintain that quantification is the *sine qua non* of science, we believe that this is an overly simplistic position. We would argue that quantification is a desirable end of most scientific inquiry and technical application, but that most meaningful quantification in psychology occurs only after sufficient observation and theory building.

Behavior can be defined as the overtly observable action of muscles, exocrine glands, and their products (e.g., speaking, walking, sweating). This conceptualization of behavior defines responses as aspects of the behavior of interest to the psychologist. Thus, systematic observation of behavior involves selecting from the totality of such behavior significant facets which are measureable and scorable. In neuropsychological assessment the stimuli for eliciting responses (e.g., WAIS blocks) and the methods for recording observations in the form of test scores are, in theory at least, standardized. Scores derived from common tests may be used directly to make clinical decisions (e.g., Costa et al., 1963) or they may be interpreted as measuring constructs (e.g., verbal, motor, spatial abilities) thought relevant for neuropsychological assessment. The validity of such constructs, for theory and for clinical decision making, is often evaluated quantitatively.

The behavior that generates scorable responses is, however, far richer and more varied than any scoring system will allow. Strategic approaches to Block Design or Object Assembly tasks which may indeed characterize patients with different lesion loci (Kaplan, 1980) are not accommodated by the scoring procedures outlined in the WAIS Manual (Kaplan, 1980; Chapter 4). Thought disorder is sometimes noted in patients' responses to WAIS verbal subtest items but is not scored. It is not our contention that such behaviors cannot be scored—certainly they can. But they can be scored only after they are identified through observational techniques that are qualitative in nature.

The same argument can be applied to the process of clinical inference. Given a referral question involving differential diagnosis between dementia and depression or neurological involvement vs. schizophrenia, a typical clinician will have a variety of aids in diagnosis. He will commonly have quantitative data from a battery of neuropsychological and personality tests. Performance on each test, individually or in combination, can be compared to the performance of those in appropriate normative groups. In addition, the clinician may well have available medical, educational and social history data. He may interview the patient, and/or relatives, and he may actually see the patient perform on the neuropsychological test battery. Much of these data available to the clinician are not ordinarily quantified. The patient may refuse eye contact, be self-referential, explain a delusion, manifest a catastrophic reaction, show visual inattention, become evasive when asked questions about the recent past. He can exhibit a variety of behaviors from which the clinician routinely infers his clinical state.

It is certainly possible to attempt diagnosis entirely derived from scorable test data. In this case, two options are open to the clinician: (1) analysis of the test scores using empirically derived weightings or decision-making rules (e.g., Adams, 1975; Russell, Neuringer, and Goldstein, 1970; Chapter 5), with or without the use of a computer; (2) subjective, *qualitative* weighting of test scores on the basis of prior clinical experience.

The latter approach is certainly more common and often, in addition to perusing test score patterns (e.g., see Reitan, Chapter 1), the clinician integrates facts and observations adduced through history taking, reviewing medical and school records, and a clinical interview. While it is certainly desirable that the data gathered from these sources be quantified and objectified, diagnostic decision-making in neuropsychological and neuropsychiatric contexts is presently a far from objective process. In our opinion, far more qualitative analysis must occur both at the level of behavioral observation and at the level of clinical inference before it will be possible to teach computers to provide meaningful characterizations of neuropsychiatric patients.

The present chapter focusses on qualitative approaches to the analysis of patient *behavior*. It does not deal with clinical inference. We explore, in some detail, two types of behavior often observed in patients with frontal lobe disorders—perseveration and "memory-like" deficits. We then relate these phenomena to similar phenomena observed in chronic schizophrenic patients and speculate about possible reasons for the similarity. Our purpose is to *illustrate* the potential utility of qualitative approaches to neuropsychological analysis as a means of identifying meaningful constructs which, when better understood, can be adequately quantified. No attempt is made to inventory or examine the broad range of qualitative observations that have been reported by other investigators, some of which are discussed in Chapters 1, 2, 4, and 12.

Perseverative Behavior

In investigating qualitative aspects of deficit the main concerns are to ensure that behavioral constructs can be specified in the most unambiguous and replicable ways and to ensure an easy way of eliciting data relevant to them. This imposes constraints on the nature of the tasks and phenomena which can be considered.

The analysis of perseveration has traditionally afforded the most scrutinizable material for evaluating an executive deficit (Luria, 1980; Tow, 1955). Perseverative deficit, if present, can be quite ubiquitous in the patient's performance across tasks (Goldberg and Tucker, 1979; Luria, 1980), but various tasks afford various degrees of precision in identifying the defective level of functioning on the basis of observed perseverative behavior.

Luria developed a variety of techniques for eliciting perseveration in tasks which require a sequence of drawings in rapid alternation following verbal instructions. When this technique is applied and the elicited perseverations analyzed, it appears that various types of phenomena, each indicative of a breakdown on a particular level of the cognitive hierarchy, are observed.

The following discussion is based on an investigation of 19 postoperative patients with neurological impairment (four trauma, three vascular, 12 tumor) referrable to frontal lobe damage. The subjects were inpatients at the Bourdenko Institute of Neurosurgery in Moscow, and were native Russian speakers. The nature of this sample is described in more detail elsewhere (Goldberg and Tucker, 1979). The purpose of this discussion is to consider this diverse body of data and discuss the possibilities of using it to assess the hierarchic characteristics of an executive deficit and the levels of its manifestation. Phenomenologically, two general types of motor perseveration can be observed.

Hyperkinesia-like Motor Perseveration

By hyperkinesia-like motor perseveration we mean exactly what was described by Luria (1980): an inability to terminate the execution of elementary movements which resembles hyperkinesia. As does Luria, we treat it as a homogeneous type. According to Luria, this type of perseveration follows anterior subcortical lesions with basal ganglia involvement. [Examples of this type can be seen in patient's drawings of circles on page 298 (Fig. 83) and page 303 (Fig. 88) in Luria (1980)].

Higher-Order Cortical Perseveration

In other types of perseveration, individual motor acts do not suffer, nor does the patient experience difficulty terminating elementary motor components of the task. However, he cannot shift completely from one motor task to another. Consequently, one may observe fragments of several motor sequences combined in a single behavior. According to Luria (1980) and Lebedinsky (1966), such perseveration follows bilateral prefrontal lesions that do not involve the basal ganglia. Luria treats these as the second internally homogeneous type.

Closer analysis reveals, however, that these perseverations neither constitute a single internally homogeneous type, nor are they all strictly speaking "motor". The following specific subtypes were delineated.

PERSEVERATION OF ELEMENTS. This phenomenon is represented in Fig. 1(a) and (b). No hyperkinetic effect is observable. The patient can draw accurately the figure, a cross, but when instructed to draw a circle, and then a square, he continues to draw a cross within each figure. Many of the patients merged fragments of figures or whole figures in this way.

PERSEVERATION OF FEATURES. This phenomenon is represented in Fig. 1(c) and (d). Here, no graphical fragments have been confused. Rather, the perseverations seem to involve more generalized confusions: the "closeness" vs. "openness" of the figures for instance, or the number of their elementary components, regardless of the specific graphic natures of these components. This type of perseveration has been discussed in greater detail elsewhere (Goldberg & Tucker, 1979). Here it will suffice to say that this type of perseveration appears to involve general spatial characteristics describing the prototype concepts of various classes of figures (the class of crosses vs. the class of circles, etc.) rather than actual motor or graphical sequences corresponding to their realization.

PERSEVERATION OF ACTIVITIES. This phenomenon is represented in Fig. 1(e) and (f). In producing (e), the patient was instructed to draw a circle, a square, and a triangle, and then to write a sentence (which did not include the names of any geometric figures). None of these tasks revealed perseverations. However, when subsequently instructed to draw geometric figures, the correct forms were accompanied by letters. These are the terminal letters of the Russian names of the corresponding shapes. (The Russian word for circle is **КРУГ** ; for square it is **КВАДРАТ** ; for triangle it is **ТРЕУГОЛЬНИК** .)

Perseverations between different categories of stimuli can be identified in (f). The patient first drew geometric figures and then performed simple arithmetical computations. Neither activity revealed perseverations. When subsequently instructed to draw geometric figures, however, the patient started to replace them by mathematical symbols. As was evident in the situation previously described, this inaccurate production was not random. A multiplication sign " × " appeared instead of a cross, with the perceptual similarity being apparent. Similarly, the two subsequent replacements can be naturally interpreted semantically.

Unlike the previously described types of perseveration, these can hardly be explained in terms of confusion between graphical elements or distortion of figures based on more generalized aspects of individual items. Rather, these manifestations seem to reflect confusion between whole semantic categories.

It is clear that not all of the above described perseverations are "motor". Only hyperkinesia-like perseverations and the perseveration of elements can

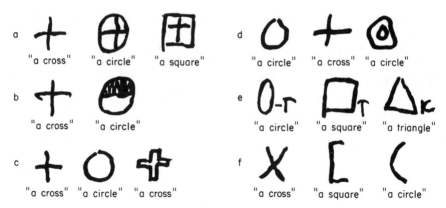

Fig. 1. Types of perseveration. (a,b) Perseveration of elements, (c,d) perseveration of features, (e,f) perseveration of activities. (a), (b), (e), and (f) are from patient K. who suffered head trauma with prefrontal site of impact and fracture of the frontal bone. The operation consisted of removal of the fractured bone and resection of the frontal poles. Pronounced symptoms of convexital and mediobasal frontal dysfunctions were observed. The experimental data were obtained 2 weeks to 3½ months after the operation. In (f), the patient's choice of items in a wrong semantic category was facilitated by the similarity of verbal labels. The Russian term for *bracket* translates as "square bracket"; for *parenthesis* it translates as "circle bracket." Figures 1(c) and (d) are from patient S. who had a cystic tumor of the third ventricle. The operation consisted of the removal of the cyst, with the approach through the premotor zone and the body of the third ventricle. Postoperative edema was observed, with the prevailing dysfunction of deep and medial areas of the premotor zone and ventral areas of the brain stem. The data were obtained 8 to 12 days after the operation. [Reprinted by permission from E. Goldberg and D. Tucker (1979). Motor perseveration and long-term memory for visual forms. *J. Clin. Neuropsychol., 1,* 273–288.]

readily be seen to occur primarily as deficits in motor activity. What then, are the aspects of processing reflected in the remaining types of perseveration? We shall discuss all of these phenomena, attempting to place them within the context of a hierarchy of stages involved in the execution of cognitive task.

For a set of cognitive operations, two requirements ought to be met in order to hypothesize a hierarchic interaction among the operations. First, the cognitive operations must lend themselves to being organized sequentially so that the content of any operation $i+1$ is dependent upon the output of operation i. Second, the earlier stages of the process should involve more generalized representations of the desired output of the task than the later ones. Whereas the output of one level of a cognitive hierarchy contains all the information about the output of the antecedent level, the opposite is not true. In other words, there must be a homomorphic relation between the contents of the two sequential cognitive operations for those operations to be considered hierarchically organized.

The various types of perseveration exhibited by the patients described above reflect deficits at different levels of cognitive hierarchy. *Perseveration of activities,* Fig. 1(e), (f), seems to involve confusion between semantic categories, such as mathematical symbols and geometric figures, or pictorial and linguistic representations. In these cases, retrieval of the most appropriate item from an inappropriate memory location occurs. *Perseveration of features,* Fig. 1(c), (d), seems to reflect a confusion of the generalized spatial characteristics of individual items within a given category, in this case that of geometric figures. *Perseveration of elements,* Fig. 1(a), (b), involves unification of components of specific graphic sequences each of which corresponds to a different individual item. Finally, *hyperkinesia-like perseveration* involves loss of motor control over the realization of individual graphic components, specifically the inability to terminate elementary movements.

If one reconstructs the normal cognitive operations whose impairment leads to the aforementioned perseverations, a sequential relation among them is evident. First, the general category of information must be addressed (perseveration of *activities*). Second, the engram describing the appropriate type of figure must be accessed (perseveration of *features*). Third, the specific metrics must be imposed on the engram and it has to be converted into a motor sequence (perseveration of *elements*). Lastly, specific muscle groups must be innervated for the execution of each of the specific motor components of the sequence (*hyperkinesia-like* perseveration). These four types of cognitive operations involved in a task meet the requirements of sequentiality, and constitute distinct stages of processing.

The second requirement, a descending generality of representation generated on each successive level, also appears to have been met. When comparing the motor stage output (*hyperkinesia-like* perseveration) with its antecedent level (perseveration of *elements*), there is a loss of information about a specific muscle innervation. Thus, this penultimate level of representation could as easily generate an action involving other motor systems as one involving the hands. When moving from this level (perseverations of *elements*) to its antecedent perseverations of *features,* there is a loss of specific metric information. This level of representation could generate a number of specific instances of a given figure. When moving from this level (perseverations of *features*) to the earliest level reflected in our data (perseverations of *activities*), there is a loss of information regarding the individual item to be retrieved or generated from long-term memory. only information of the semantic class to which the target item belongs is retained.

Although the cognitive operations that presumably underlie the presented types of motor perseveration can be arranged hierarchically, it remains to be established that such a heirarchy describes normal processing. Should this be the case, various types of motor perseveration would correspond to breakdowns at specific levels of the hierarchy. While the interpretation is hypothetical, it is supported by the following considerations. First, there is no apparent memory impairment in the patients for the items used in the experiment. In control procedures they were able to draw, name, and identify individual stimuli. Perservation emerged only in the context of rapid alternation of the tasks. It is likely, therefore, that these deficits are limited to the executive domain.

Second, the question then emerges whether these executive deficits reflect the features of impaired normal organization or individual features of the pathology involved. The latter possibility appears to be unlikely. In all the cases in which more than one type of perseveration was present, during early postoperative stages (whatever the combination of perseverations), the process of recovery was invariably the one predicted by the hierarchic model. Higher-order perseverations recovered later than did the lower-order perseverations. That the same types of perseverations occur across a wide variety of pathological conditions also speaks for the hierarchical model as a reconstruction of normal organization (Goldberg and Tucker, 1979, pp. 278–279).

This set of illustrations has been provided to suggest that patients with anterior lesions show perseverations that can be understood in the framework of a hierarchic model of executive function which contains both motor and cognitive features, thus relating motor perseverations to the executive aspects of hierarchic retrieval from long-term semantic memory.

The larger issue of the relationship between the perseveratory processes and specific focal lesions is left open. It is clear that lesions of various foci within the frontal lobes can lead to perseverations. Our study, however, was not an adequate basis for clearcut double dissociation of different types of perseverations and different loci of lesions within the frontal lobes. Luria (1980) maintains that, when the prefrontal areas are affected, virtually every behavior can be subject to perseveration. Cases have been reported, however, in which perseverations were consequent to posterior lesions. Hecaen et al. (1956) have described perseverations of writing following parieto-temporo-occipital lesions of the minor hemisphere. Critchley (1964) and Lhermitte and Beauvois (1973) suggested that perseveration of naming can be part of associative visual agnosia following lesions of the occipital areas of the dominant hemisphere. Buckingham, Whitaker, and Whitaker (1979) have reported linguistic perseverations consequent to left parietal and left temporo-parietal lesions. Irigaray (1967) and Sjogren, Sjogren, and Lindgren (1952) have described linguistic perseveration in diffuse conditions (dementia). Goldstein (1975) maintained that perseverations are a secondary phenomenon reflecting a catastrophic response to potential failure and therefore of little focal significance.

It appears that to make definitive statements regarding the focal significance of perseverations, the phenomenology of perseverations will first have to be refined. It is possible that specific kinds of perseverations are associated with different lesion locations (not necessarily anterior), whereas, massive frontal lesions make the deficit omnipresent.

Deficits of Mnestic Behavior

Although the executive deficits characteristic of prefrontal pathology can be most explicitly demonstrated on tasks involving explicit sequential motor output, they are indeed ubiquitous and can be observed in tasks which are strictly ideational and do not entail an explicit manual component, for instance, memory tasks.

Performance on tasks involving memory is conspicuously deficient following prefrontal damage, which has led to the supposition that the frontal lobes contain "mechanisms of memory." The argument in favor of this hypothesis relied on the fact that after the removal of the frontal lobes, animals were unable to execute delayed responses, while the ability for immediate responses remained intact (Jacobsen, 1935).

However, Pribram (1961), Weiskrantz, Mihailavic, and Gross (1960), and Konorski and Lawicka (1964), have demonstrated that, in addition to the above phenomena, the experimental animals displayed distractability toward irrelevant ongoing stimuli and that the balance of excitation and inhibition of the behavioral stereotypes proved to be severely damaged. If the flow of ongoing irrelevant stimulation was reduced, or the excitability of the nervous system was diminished pharmacologically, then the "mnestic" deficits in the experimental animals disappeared. These data led to a reconsideration of the view that the frontal lobes were the "seat of memory."

A similar reconsideration of human studies took place. The experiments of Luria (1976) and Tsvetkova (1966) have demonstrated that following prefrontal lesions the very structure of mnestic activity suffers, rather than the more elementary aspects of storage and/or retrieval *per se:* The mnestic processes lose their purpose-oriented, hierarchical organization.

We will illustrate this general point by analyzing the story recall of a patient with a bilateral trauma of the frontal lobes with subsequent removal of the fractured frontal bone and resection of both frontal poles.

Story Recall after Prefrontal Lesions

The story "A Hen and Golden Eggs" reads as follows: "A man owned a hen that was laying golden eggs. The man was greedy and wanted to get more gold at once. He killed the hen and cut it open hoping to find a lot of gold inside, but there was none." After an oral presentation of the story, the patient's recall was as follows:

A man was living with a hen . . . . or rather the man was the hen's owner. She was producing gold. . . . The man . . . the owner . . . wanted more gold at once . . . so he cut the hen into pieces but there was no gold. . . . No gold at all . . . he cuts the hen more, . . . no gold . . . the hen remains empty. . . . So he searches again and again. . . . No gold . . . he searches all around . . . in all places. The search is going on with a tape recorder . . . they are looking here and there, nothing new around. They leave the tape recorder turned on, something is twisting there . . . what the hell are they recording there . . . some digits . . . 0, 2, 3, 0 . . . so, they are recording all these digits . . . not very many of them . . . that's why all the other digits were recorded . . . turned out to be not very many of them either . . . so, everything was recorded . . . and I'll tell you what . . . there were only 5–6 digits there . . . *(Experimenter: Have you finished?)* Not yet, I'll finish soon . . . so, there were only 5–6 digits there. . . . When they took the bus #5 and went along the Lefortoff Drive . . . so, you get there and transfer to bus #5 *(Experimenter: You better finish!)* Not yet! Wait a moment! So you take bus #5 and get to the Bauman Square . . . From the Bauman

Square you go further on . . . further on. Here you take off . . . and again you take bus #5. . . . I'll make it precise . . . so you take off . . . and take bus #5 . . . and you get to cafeteria . . . number 5 point 6. . . . *(monologue continues)*.

The story "A Lion and a Mouse" reads as follows: "A lion was asleep and a mouse was running around making noises. The lion woke up, got very angry, caught the mouse and was about to eat him up, but then he decided to be kind and let the mouse go. A few days later, hunters caught the lion and tied him to a tree with ropes. The mouse learned about it, ran down, gnawed the ropes and set the lion free." After the story was read to the patient, his recall was as follows:

So the lion made friends with the mouse. The mouse was caught by the lion. He wanted to strangle him but then let him go. The mouse started dancing around him, singing songs and was released. After that the mouse was accepted in his house by . . . lions, various animals. After that he was released, so to say he hadn't been captured, it was like if he were captured but he was still free. But after that he was completely re-leased and was walking free. So, he was released by the lion completely, after the lion listened to him, and he was released to all the four directions. He didn't run away and remained to live in his cave, then the lion caught him once again, some time later . . . I don't remember it quite exactly. So, he caught him, and released again. Now the mouse got out of there to his moor *(Russian slang for a secure place)*, to his railroad station. The mouse goes further and further and tells about his railroad station . . . and there is another mouse and the third one at the station. . . . So the mouse opens the door to this. . . . What's his name? Hullo! Hullo! How are you doing? Okay, more or less. . . . All set. Glad to find you. . . . I have an apartment . . . and a house . . . and a room. The bigger mouse asks the small one: How are you doing? How is it going? So it was all right, I had a lot of friends. They often meet . . . but the friendship broke apart, so you tell him that I'm sorry for those short rendezvous. . . . Or you don't tell any-thing." *(The story ends with the two friends drinking beer in a railroad station bar)*.

It is clear that both storage and retrieval of the first story by the patient was, by and large, adequate, since the initial segment of the patient's monologue contains most of its content virtually undistorted. It was reasonably adequate for the first half of the second story as well, as manifested by the initial seg-ment of the patient's second monologue.

The remaining portions of both monologues, however, were grossly irrele-vant to the actual stories. In response to the instructions to recall a short story, the subject builds up a lengthy monologue, which sometimes continues for 40–60 minutes. Beginning with an authentic fragment of the original story, he then starts to deviate from it until there is no resemblance at all between the original story and the content of the patient's monologue. The patient, how-ever, goes on and on. Even when urged by the experimenter to stop, he an-swers, "Not yet. Wait a minute." and continues to develop his monologue. The inability to terminate an activity once it has begun can be observed in frontal subjects in many behaviors, such as writing and drawing. It is inertia in re-verse. Often, this reverse inertia goes together with the real inertia. It is very difficult to coax the subject to initiate recall. In response to the instructions to tell the story, he responds, "I've told it already," or, "There was nothing in this story." However, when he eventually starts, he cannot stop. This leads one to believe that "real" inertia and the inertia of interminability of action are two manifestations of one and the same deficit.

The subject's verbal production obviously is not governed by the text engram in the subject's memory, since both the engram of the text and its availability for retrieval are relatively intact, as demonstrated before, while the discrepancy between the patient's monologue and original story is quite profound.

The question then arises, what is the mechanism behind the patient's ability to "manufacture" a lengthy monologue of the kind described above in response to a short story?

Perseverations are an obvious factor. Indeed, the patient's monologue is ridden with them. However, they cannot account for the "creativity" of the subject's monologues. At best, perseverations can account for the least productive aspects: repetition of a few verbal or thematic cliches. But the subject's monologues are not entirely repetitive. They obviously have some development: new events are introduced, which lead to the inclusion of still other new events, etc. A long chain of events is "invented" by the subject in the most bizarre combinations.

The phenomenon of "field-dependent behavior" is commonly observed in frontal patients. As a rule this term is used to describe frontal patients' tendency to react to every stimulus that occurs in their sensory field instead of accomplishing the behavioral task. The monologues' structure is somewhat reminiscent of this behavior. By "verbal field-dependent behavior" we mean the subject's inability to follow the task of communication at hand (recalling a story, describing a picture) without being distracted by whatever current stimuli happen to appear in the subject's physical surroundings or in his "context-free" associative field. These stimuli—events or statements—then become incorporated into the subject's monologue, causing the discourse to veer off in another direction.

Analysis of "prefrontal monologues" has revealed at least four types of mechanisms that can provoke the inclusion of "field associations" into the subject's monologue:

(1) INTRUSIONS BY EXTERNAL STIMULI. Objects or activities in the patient's sensory field can inappropriately find their way into the response. The inclusion of the tape recorder in the first monologues (during which one of the authors was taping the patient) is an example.

Another example of this kind of external intrusion is provided by the patient's recall of the story "A Daw and the Pigeons." The story reads as follows: "A daw (jackdaw) learned that pigeons were fed very well. So the daw dyed herself white and flew to the pigeons. The pigeons accepted her and the daw began to live among them. But one day the daw cried out the way daws do and the pigeons realized that she was an imposter and chased her away. The daw tried to join other daws but was not accepted by them either, because she was white."

The patient responded: "Pigeons were well-fed, and the daw envied them. So she flew to the dove-cote. But the net was too thick, so she couldn't even pull her head through it" *(points to the net that guards his bed)*.

(2) THE PATIENT'S OWN CONDITION IS ATTRIBUTED TO THE PROTAGONISTS OF THE STORY. In reproducing the story "A Daw and the Pigeons," another patient projected his own verbal exhaustion:

A daw, or rather a pigeon, or rather a daw learned the daw language, flew to her pigeons and told them that she learned to speak the daw language. She went on talking, some time passed, and a pigeon asks a daw; 'where did you learn to speak this way, how could you make it? How long can you talk this way?' And the daw answers that she can talk a year, two, probably three—and that's it. . . . I'm telling you all precisely . . . they ask the daw, how could you learn to talk this way. . . . So, they ask this daw, how long can you talk? And the daw answers that she can talk a year, two, well, three at most and that's it. A year passes, two, three, the daw gets exhausted, she doesn't know what else to say. A year passes, two, three . . . the daw's vocabulary gets exhausted. . . . *(a long perseveration followed)*.

(3) VERBAL OUT-OF-THE-GIVEN CONTEXT ASSOCIATIONS. Still another patient reproduced the story "A Daw and Pigeons" in the following way:

So the daw flew back to the daws, but they did not accept her either. Then she flew to her . . . little fledgelings . . . brought them food . . . to the nest . . . looked at them . . . then looked into the mirror . . . and the girl Daw . . . and she started dancing around the mirror . . . because she was pretty . . . it was the girls' silk that was pretty . . . so she looked at her . . . wedding dress *(the monologue continues)*.

The daw turns into a girl Daw. In Russian, the word (galka) means the name of a bird and also is a female first name.

(4) OUT-OF-CONTEXT SITUATIONAL ASSOCIATIONS TO THE ITEMS OF THE DISCOURSE. The patient's introduction of "bus route 5" in the first monologue about the "Hen and Golden Eggs" illustrates this type of intrusion. Having made an inappropriate association from "5–6 digits" to "bus #5" the patient then moved tangentially to a description (which was in itself accurate) of the route of bus #5.

Another example is afforded by a patient's recall of the story "A Lion and a Mouse."

Hunter caught the Lion . . . and tied him to the tree . . . mouse came and untied him . . . so, the lion is free. . . . Now, the hunter caught the lion again. . . . So, they are in trouble . . . they got together once . . . and another time . . . there is nothing good . . . they got together once again . . . everyone got together . . . and they discuss how to save the hostage-lion . . . and the mouse tells them: 'Don't you run away . . .' *(a person with a white coat enters the room)* . . . The doctor will come . . . and prescribe what to do.

While "the doctor" exemplifies the intrusion of a physical object from the subject's visual field into the monologue, the subsequent statement is, apparently, the beginning of tangential thinking concerning a common event associated with a doctor (prescription).

Thus, at least four types of intrusions can influence the behavior of frontal patients. Only one of them, the first one, is "localized" in the external field; the other three, in one way or another, belong to his internal representation and the last two apparently are "localized" in his long-term memory. Had it been possible to examine the effect of the last two types of intrusions by themselves, it would have provided a unique method of analyzing the "metrics" of inner representation of knowledge in the subject's semantic memory.

It is not the purpose of this discussion to ascertain the degree of impairment of storage and retrieval *per se* in prefrontal pathology. The foregoing analysis should make it clear, however, that regardless of the condition of storage and retrieval, an entirely different type of deficit contributes to the grossly distorted performance of frontal patients on the tasks of verbal recall. This deficit is executive in nature, and can be best described as an inability to subordinate selectively the process of retrieval to the task at hand. Instead, the process of recall takes on the quality of a chain of free associations which are not subjected to "editing" by either the context of the task or the context of the specific material to be recalled.

Executive Deficits in Schizophrenia and Frontal Lobe Disease

The above-described phenomenology associated with structural damage to the prefrontal areas is similar to certain aspects of cognitive deficits seen in schizophrenic patients, both with respect to perseverations and, particularly, with respect to the structure of "unedited" associative processes. Thus, mechanism (2) is analogous to projection, mechanism (3) may be the lexical equivalent of clang association, and mechanism (4) is similar to tangentiality or even loose association.

In fact, with the possible exception of temporal lobe epilepsy, it is frontal lobe dysfunction more than any other (relatively) focal neurological condition which can be confused diagnostically with schizophrenia (in particular, with what was referred to in the past as hebephrenia). Note how the following response elicited by one of the authors in testing a thirty-year-old male patient with a diagnosis of chronic schizophrenia resembles the prefrontal monologues described earlier.

Examiner: "What is the thing to do if you find an envelope in the street that is sealed, addressed and has a new stamp?"
Patient: "I found such an envelope once, it was on West Farms Road, across the street from the Zoo. So I went into the Zoo and saw the lions and the tigers. . . . . Then I went home and made spaghetti."

In considering the possible relationship of frontal lobe pathology to schizophrenia, at least five possibilities come to mind. (1) The two are unrelated, except at a phenomenological level; in the global cognitive breakdown implicit in schizophrenia, the executive deficit is the most likely one to be observed simply because processes at the highest level of organization tend to be the first to show degradation in the face of noxious influences of whatever cause, as long as they produce a diffuse dysfunction of the brain. This would constitute a trivial "tip of the iceberg" explanation. (2) In certain cases of schizophrenia there is indeed structural brain damage which is most pronounced in the frontal lobes. (3) There is a predominantly frontal lesion in schizophrenia, but it is chemical rather than structural in nature. Indeed, it is known that dopamine, which has been implicated in schizophrenia, shows the greatest preponderance in the frontal cortex and basal forebrain. (4) The observed "frontal" signs in schizophrenic patients are secondary to long-term treatment with neuroleptics. Perseveration and cognitive inertia could reflect supersensitivity of mesolimbic/mesocortical dopaminergic receptors just as tardive dyskinesia is thought to represent supersensitivity of nigrostriatal dopamine receptors. This is unlikely to be the whole answer, since executive deficits were described in schizophrenia before the advent of neuroleptics. (5) Certain types of lesions outside the frontal lobes per se can simulate a "frontal" symptom-picture. Indeed, such a situation has been observed, associated with a ventral tegmental lesion in the mesencephalon. This lesion probably had a selective effect on ventrally distributed branches of the ascending reticular activating system (Goldberg et al., 1982).

At the present time we still do not have unequivocal neuropathologic, neuroradiologic, or electrophysiologic confirmation of brain disease in schizophrenia, nor specifically of frontal lobe pathology in this disorder. Since Goldstein deals with this issue at length in Chapter 8, we only refer to some of the key studies here.

Recent reports of CT studies of various schizophrenic populations have suggested that perhaps up to half of schizophrenics have some degree of ventricular enlargement or sulcal widening (Adams et al., 1984; Andreasen et al., 1982). Yet with one exception (Golden et al., 1981), they failed to reveal a frontal preponderance of such lesions (Johnstone et al., 1978; Weinberger et al., 1979a, 1979b). Recent electrophysiological (Heath, 1977; Sem-Jacobsen et al., 1956; Stevens, 1977), metabolic (Buchsbaum et al., 1982; Farkas et al., 1980); and blood flow (Ingvar, 1976; Mathew et al., 1981) findings have implicated frontal lobes in the schizophrenic disorder; yet by their very nature these studies cannot distinguish between possibilities (2)–(5) outlined above.

All these considerations notwithstanding, it will be clear to clinicians experienced with schizophrenic patients and those with "dry" structural prefrontal lesions that the two clinical pictures are not the same, in spite of the fact that their performance on a limited number of tests sensitive to the executive deficit might appear similar. Furthermore, in some forms of schizophrenia and frontal disease executive control should, on theoretical grounds, be affected

Table 1. Comparison of clinical features of fronto-orbital syndrome and schizophrenia

	Fronto-orbital syndrome	Paranoid schizophrenia
Personality	Friendly, happy-go-lucky	Hostile, paranoid
Prevalent mood	Euphoric	Blunted affect
Libido	Sexually disinhibited Seek immediate gratification	Anhedonic
Associative processes	"Ultra-stable" perseveratory	Unstable associations
Direction of thought disorder	Field-dependent by delusion	Organized

in opposite rather than in identical directions. Paranoid schizophrenia and the fronto-orbital syndrome (lesions of the fronto-basal and fronto-orbital cortex) are cases in point. In the former, hyperfunction of the mesolimbic dopamine pathways has been proposed. The latter, on the other hand, entails destruction of the cortical areas that are the main targets of mesolimbic dopamine projections, thus presumably producing hypofunction of cortical dopamine. Complicating matters even more are some recent studies which indicate that the fronto-orbital clinical picture can be caused by lesion in the ventral tegmental area of mesencephalon (the source of mesolimbic dopamine neurons projecting to the fronto-orbital areas) even in the absence of a frontal lesion (Oades, 1982; Goldberg et al., 1982; Simon, Scatton, and LeMoal, 1980).

The clinical pictures of paranoid schizophrenia and the fronto-orbital syndrome are summarized in Table 1.

It will be seen that although the same dimensions of cognition and emotion are disturbed in the two conditions, they appear to be affected in opposite rather than identical ways. These considerations stress the fact that mere documentation of the presence of executive deficits is not sufficient to make a diagnosis nor to specify the precise qualitative features of a particular condition.

Summary

We have presented a detailed examination of perseverative behavior to exemplify the possibilities inherent in a systematic qualitative approach to the analysis of patient behavior. This qualitative approach owes a particular debt to the work of Luria, but the general utility of this strategy certainly has been recognized by other leading investigators, beginning with Hughlings Jackson.

The value of this approach is affirmed by McKenna and Warrington (Chapter 2) and Milberg et al. (Chapter 4), who describe the fundamental role played by detailed qualitative analysis of behavior in the evolution of research and clinical practice at the National Hospital and the Boston V.A., respectively.

Discussions of memory pathology in Chapter 12 and 19 further exemplify these principles.

According to the specific model which we chose, deficit of executive control is seen as deficit of hierarchic organization of behavior (Miller, Pribram, and Galanter, 1960). Furthermore, to the extent that deficient hierarchic organization is implicit in frontal lobe syndrome and in schizophrenia, the nature of the deficits is fundamentally different in at least one respect. In the case of prefrontal pathology due to a distinct neurological condition (tumor, aneurysm, head trauma), the breakdown of hierarchic organization of behavior is superimposed on a premorbidly fully formed, completed pattern of hierarchic organization; what is observed is genuinely a breakdown. At least in certain forms of schizophrenia, on the other hand, it seems possible that the whole course of cognitive development, most likely long before the first overt psychotic manifestation, is affected. In this case, therefore, one should talk about maldevelopment of the hierarchic organization of behavior rather than the breakdown of one that was once intact. Put another way, the "depth of deficit" is presumed to be greater in schizophrenia than in focal prefrontal pathology of later onset. This could account for some of the qualitative differences in cognitive function in the two conditions. At the same time, before the assessment of executive deficits can be used meaningfully in neuropsychiatric diagnosis, the phenomenology of executive deficits requires much more precise definition.

REFERENCES

Adams, K. M. (1975). Automated clinical interpretation of the neuropsychological test battery: An ability based approach. *Dis. Abst. Int.*, *35*, 6085B (University Microfilms No. 75-13, 289).
Adams, K. M., Jacisin, J. J., Brown, G. G., Boulos, R. S., and Silk, S. D. (1984). Neurobehavioral deficit and computed tomographic abnormalities in three samples of schizophrenic patients. *Percept. Motor Skills, 59*, 115–119.
Andreasen, N. C., Smith, M. R., Jacoby, C. J., Dennert, J. W., & Olsen, S. A. (1982). Ventricular enlargement in schizophrenia. Definition and prevalence. *Am. J. Psychiatr., 139*, 292–296.
Buchsbaum, M. S., Ingvar, D. H., Kessler, R., Waters, R. N., Cappalletti, J., van Kammen, D. P., King, A. C., Johnson, J. L., Manning, R. G., Flynn, R. W., Mann, L. S., Bunney, W. E., and Sokoloff, L. (1982). Cerebral glucography with emission tomography. Use in normal subjects and in patients with schizophrenia. *Arch. General Psychiat., 39*, 251–259.
Buckingham, H. W., Whitaker, H., and Whitaker, H. A. (1979). On linguistic perseverations. In: H. Whitaker, Ed., *Studies in Neurolinguistics*, vol. 4. New York: Academic Press.
Costa, L. D., Vaughan, H. G., Jr., Levita, E., and Farber, N. (1963). Purdue Pegboard as the predictor of the presence and laterality of cerebral disease. *J. Consulting Psychol., 27*, 133–137.
Critchley, M. M. (1964). The problem of visual agnosia. *J. Neurol. Sci., 1*, 274–290.
Farkas, T., Reivich, M., Alavi, A., Greenberg, J. H., Fowler, J. S., MacGregor, R. R., Christman, D. R., and Wolf, A. P. (1980). The application of ^{18}F-deoxy-2-fluoro-D-glucose and position emission tomography in the study of psychiatric conditions. In: J. V. Pas-

sonneau, R. A. Hawkins, W. D. Lust, et al., eds., *Cerebral metabolism and neural functions*. Baltimore: Williams and Wilkins.

Goldberg, E., Mattis, S., Hughes, J., and Antin, S. (1982, June). Frontal syndrome without a frontal lesion: A case study. Presented at the meeting of the International Neuropsychological Society, Deauville, France, 1982.

Goldberg, E., and Tucker, D. (1979). Motor perseverations and long-term memory for visual forms. *J. Clin. Neuropsychol., 4*, 273–288.

Golden, C. J., Graber, B., Coffman, J., Berg, R. A., Newlin, D. B., and Bloch, S. (1981). Structural brain deficits in schizophrenia: Identification by computed tomographic scan density measurement. *Arch. General Psychiat., 38*, 1014–1017.

Goldstein, K. (1975). Functional disturbances in brain damage. In: S. Arieti, ed., *American Handbook of Psychiatry*, vol. 2. New York: Basic Books.

Heath, R. G. (1977). Subcortical brain function correlates of psychopathology and epilepsy. In: C. Shagass, S. Gerson, and A. J. Friedhoff, eds., *Psychopathology and Brain Dysfunction*. New York: Raven Press.

Hecaen, H., Penfield, W., Bertrand, C., and Malmo, R. (1956). The syndrome of apractognosia due to lesions of the minor cerebral hemisphere. *Arch. Neurol. Psychiatr., 75*, 400–434.

Ingvar, D. H. (1976). Functional landscape of the dominant hemisphere. *Brain Res., 107*, 181–197.

Irigaray, L. (1967). Approach psycholinguistique de langage des dements. *Neuropsychologia, 5*, 25–52.

Jacobsen, C. F. (1935). Function of frontal association area in primates. *Arch. Neurol. Psychiatr., 33*, 558.

Johnstone, E. C., Crow, T. J., Frith, C. D., Stevens, M., Kreel, L., and Husband, J. (1978). The dementia of dementia praecox. *Acta Psychiatr. Scand., 57*, 305–324.

Kaplan, E. (1980, February). Qualitative neuropsychological assessment of adult brain-injured patients. Presented at the meeting of the International Neuropsychological Society, San Francisco, 1980.

Konorski, J., and Lawicka, W. (1964). Analysis of errors by prefrontal animals in the delayed response test. In: I. M. Warren and K. Akert, eds., *The Frontal Granular Cortex and Behavior*. New York: McGraw-Hill.

Lebedinsky, V. V. (1966). Execution of symmetric and asymmetric programs in patients with frontal lesions. In: A. R. Luria and E. D. Homskaya, eds., *Frontal Lobes and Regulation of Psychological Processes*. Moscow: Moscow University Press.

Lhermitte, F. and Beauvois, M. F. (1973). A visual-speech disconnection syndrome—Report of a case with optic aphasia, agnostic alexia and color agnosia. *Brain, 96*, 695–714.

Luria, A. R. (1976). *Neuropsychology of memory*. Washington. D. C.: Winston, Press.

Luria, A. R. (1980). *Higher cortical functions in man*, 2d ed. New York: Basic Books.

Malmo, R. B. (1942). Interference factors in delayed response in monkeys. *J. Neurophysiol., 5*.

Mathew, R. J., Meyer, J. S., Francis, D. J., Schoolar, J. C., Weinman, M., and Mortel, K. F. (1981). Regional blood flow in schizophrenia: A preliminary report. *Am. J. Psychiat., 138*, 112–113.

Miller, G. A., Pribram, K. H., and Galanter, E. (1960). *Plans and the Organization of Behavior*. New York: Holt.

Oades, R. D. (1982). Search strategies on a holeboard are impaired in rats with ventral tegmental damage: Animal model for test of thought disorders. *Bio. Psychiat., 2*, 243–258.

Russell, E. W., Neuringer, C., and Goldstein, G. (1970). *Assessment of Brain damage: A Neuropsychological Key Approach*. New York: Wiley Interscience.

Pribram, K. H. (1961). A further analysis of the behavior deficit that follows injury to the primate frontal cortex. *J. Exp. Neurol., 3*, 432–466.

Sem-Jacobsen, C. W., Patersen, M. C., Dodge, H. W., Lynge, H. N., Nazarte, J. A., and Holman, C. B. (1956). Intra-cerebral electrographic study of 93 psychotic patients. *Acta Psychiatr. Scand., Suppl. 106*, 222–226.

Simon, H., Scatton, B., and LeMoal, M. (1980). Dopaminergic A10 neurones are involved in cognitive functions. *Nature, 286,* 150–151.

Sjogren, T., Sjogren, H., and Lindgren, A. G. H. (1952). Morbus Alzheimer and Morbus Pick. A genetic, clinical and pathoanatomical study. *Acta Psychiatr. Neurol. Scand., Suppl.* 52.

Stevens, J. R. (1977). All that spikes is not fits. In: C. Shagass, S. Gershon & A. J. Friedhoff, eds. *Psychopathology and Brain Dysfunction,* New York: Raven Press.

Tow, P. M. (1955). *Personality Changes Following Frontal Leucotomy.* Oxford: Oxford University Press.

Tsvetkova, L. S. (1966). Disturbance of the analysis of texts in patients with frontal lobe lesions. In: A. R. Luria and E. D. Homskaya, eds. *The Frontal Lobes and Regulation of Psychological Processes.* Moscow: Moscow University Press.

Weinberger, D. R., Torrey, E. F., Neophytides, A. N., and Wyatt, R. J. (1979a). Lateral cerebral ventricular enlargement in chronic schizophrenia. *Arch. General Psychiatr., 36,* 735–739.

Weinberger, D. R., Torrey, E. F., Neophytides, A. N., and Wyatt, R. J. (1979b). Structural abnormalities in the cerebral cortex of chronic schizophrenia patients. *Arch. General Psychiatr., 36,* 935–939.

Weiskrantz, L., Mihailavic, L., and Gross, C. (1960). Stimulation of frontal cortex and delayed alternation performance in the monkey. *Science, 131.*

4

The Boston Process Approach
to Neuropsychological Assessment

WILLIAM P. MILBERG / NANCY HEBBEN / EDITH KAPLAN

In the last decade the practice of clinical neuropsychology has progressed rapidly. Initially, it involved either a series of specialized techniques known only to a few or a perfunctory acknowledgement of "organicity" based on "pathognomonic signs" evident in a battery of psychometric tests. At present, it is a widely respected specialty of clinical assessment based on a growing body of research. To its credit, the American tradition of clinical neuropsychology is supported by a bulwark of empirical clinical research that has focused on directly relating test scores to central nervous system (CNS) damage. It is now possible for an experienced clinician to use a series of test scores reliably to determine the presence or absence of brain damage in nonpsychiatric patients and somewhat less reliably to localize and establish the etiology of this damage.

Unfortunately, most of the assessment techniques used in clinical neuropsychology evolved with little regard for the developments in experimental, cognitive, and developmental psychology, experimental neuropsychology, and the clinical science of behavioral neurology. The historical separateness of clinical and experimental psychological science has been lamented by many (e.g., Cronbach, 1957), but it could be argued that in no discipline is this separateness more obvious than in the practice of clinical neuropsychology.

For example, many of the assessment techniques require the clinician to use norms (Reitan and Davison, 1974), keys (Russell, Neuringer, and Goldstein, 1970) and patterns of scores (Golden, 1981), while little emphasis is given to the cognitive functions these scores summarize, the way the patient attained these scores, the preserved functions the scores reflect, or the way in which these scores relate to the patient's daily life and rehabilitation program.

The Boston Process Approach is based on a desire to understand the qualitative nature of the behavior assessed by clinical psychometric instruments, a desire to reconcile descriptive richness with reliability and quantitative evidence of validity, and a desire to relate the behavior assessed to the conceptual framework of experimental neuropsychology.

Development of the Boston Process Approach

The Boston Process Approach had its origins in the efforts of one of the authors (E. K.) to apply Heinz Werner's distinction between "process and achievement" in development (Werner, 1937) to understanding the dissolution of function in patients with brain damage. The early studies focused on apraxia. It was observed that the loss of voluntary movement to command was not a unitary phenomenon, and that the clinical subtypes of motor, ideomotor, and ideational apraxia were understood best when one actually observed the incorrect attempts of patients to follow simple commands.

The quality of the patients' responses differed depending on the size and location of their lesion. Some patients would be unresponsive to certain commands; others attempted to follow the command with a primitive, undifferentiated version of the response, such as using a body part as the object; and still others used well-differentiated but irrelevant responses, such as brushing their teeth when they were asked to comb their hair. These early observations permitted precise description of the clinical phenomena and provided important data for understanding the development of motor behavior and the localization of lesions.

A similar strategy was then applied to analyzing the process by which patients pass or fail various Wechsler Adult Intelligence Scale (WAIS) (Wechsler, 1955) and Wechsler Memory Scale (WMS) (Wechsler, 1945) subtests, as well as a number of other commonly employed clinical measures.

Other tests developed with the "process" approach in mind included a test to measure parietal lobe functions and the Boston Diagnostic Aphasia Examination (Goodglass and Kaplan, 1972), a test that allows the precise characterization of the breakdown of language function in patients with aphasia using a series of finely-grained quantitative scales. As the Boston group and other investigators developed new and better tests to measure brain function, they were adapted and integrated into the collection of core and satellite tests now used clinically as part of the Boston Process Approach.

If one were to examine the literature from the last 10 to 20 years in clinical psychology journals one would find that many of the tests originally intended as tests of personality (e.g., Rorschach Test), cognitive development (e.g., Bender-Gestalt Test), and cognitive function (e.g., Wechsler Memory Scale; Standard Progressive Matrices; Seguin-Goddard Formboard) for the clinical psychologist were also sensitive to brain damage in both adults and children.

A number of principles have been formulated to account for tests that appear to differentiate patients with dysfunction from those without brain dysfunction (Russell, 1981). These include the principles of "complexity" and "fluidity." Complex functions are those composed of a number of simpler subelements; fluid functions are those requiring the native intellectual ability of an individual. Fluid intellectual functions are distinguished from crystallized intellectual functions, the latter being well-learned abilities that are dependent on training and cultural experience. The tests most sensitive to brain damage are those that measure complex and fluid functions. Unfortunately, although tests of complex functions can be used to measure specific cognitive domains (e.g., abstraction), most are not sufficiently differentiated to allow the clinician to specify what component of intellectual competence is impaired or what cognitive strategies the patient used to solve specific problems.

Modern experimental psychology has demonstrated that each general category of human cognitive function is made up of many subcomponents (Neisser, 1967) and that as information is processed it appears to pass through numerous, distinct subroutines. These subroutines are not necessarily used rigidly by every individual in the same way, and there is variation that naturally occurs in the selection and sequencing of these subcomponents. Subjects vary in their use of the underlying cognitive components, and thus they may be said to differ in their cognitive style (Hunt, 1983), skill (Neisser, Novick and Lager, 1963), or general level of intellect (Hunt, 1983; Sternberg, 1980).

Unfortunately, many of the paradigms of experimental psychology have had limited utility in the clinical setting. The major difficulty has been the relative insensitivity of many experimental procedures to the effects of brain lesions.

Although some of the experimental techniques might not be useful on their own, the Boston group believed that they held promise in enhancing existing clinical neuropsychological procedures. With this in mind, they gradually combined tests that had been proven valid in the clinical discrimination of patients with and without brain damage, with tests that purported to measure narrow specifiable cognitive functions. They also performed careful systematic observations of the problem-solving strategies used by patients (i.e., the way they successfully solved or failed to solve each problem presented to them). The resulting method allowed both a quantitative assessment of a patient's performance and a dynamic serial "picture" of the information processing style that each patient used.

Description of the Process Approach

General Procedures

Although the Boston Process Approach uses a core set of tests for most patients, it cannot accurately be characterized as a "battery approach" because the technique can be used to assess the pattern of preserved and impaired functions despite the particular tests used. In addition to the core tests, several "satellite tests" are used to clarify particular problem areas and to confirm the clinical hypotheses developed from early observations of the patient. The satellite tests may consist of standardized tests or a set of tasks specifically designed for each patient. The only limits to the procedures that are employed (beyond the patient's tolerance and limitations) are the examiner's knowledge of available tests of cognitive function and his ingenuity in creating new measures for particular deficit areas (e.g., Milberg et al., 1979). Of the patients

Table 1. A representative sample of the tests used in the Boston Process Approach to neuropsychological assessment

Intellectual and Conceptual Functions	
Wechsler Adult Intelligence Scale-Revised[a]	Wechsler, 1981
Standard Progressive Matrices	Raven, 1960
Shipley Institute of Living Scale	Shipley, 1940
Wisconsin Card Sorting Test	Grant and Berg, 1948
Proverbs Test	Gorham, 1956
Memory Functions	
Wechsler Memory Scale[a]	Wechsler, 1945
Rey Auditory Verbal Learning Test[a]	Rey, 1964
Rey-Osterrieth Complex Figure[a]	Osterrieth and Rey, 1944
Benton Visual Recognition Test (Multiple Choice Form)	Benton, 1950
Consonant Trigrams Test	Butters and Grady, 1977
Cowboy Story Reading Memory Test	Talland, 1965
Corsi Blocks	Milner, 1971
Language Functions	
Narrative Writing Sample	Goodglass and Kaplan, 1972
Tests of Verbal Fluency (Word List Generation)	Thurstone, 1938
Visuo-perceptual Functions	
Cow and Circle Experimental Test	Palmer and Kaplan, note 2
Automobile Puzzle	Wechsler, 1974
Parietal Lobe Battery	Goodglass and Kaplan, 1972
Hooper Visual Organization Test	Hooper, 1958
Academic Skills	
Wide Range Achievement Test	Jastak and Jastak, 1978
Self-Control and Motor Functions	
Porteus Maze Test	Porteus, 1965
Stroop Color-Word Interference Test	Stroop, 1935
Luria Three-Step Motor Program	Christensen, 1975
Finger Tapping	Halstead, 1947

[a]These tests include procedural modifications.

seen clinically over the last 5 years at the Veterans Administration Medical Center in Boston, 90% were given a selection from the basic core set of tests shown in Table 1.

It has been necessary to modify many original test measures to facilitate the collection of data about individual cognitive strategies. In each case, however, an attempt was made to make modifications that did not interfere with the standard administration of the tests. Thus, one can still obtain reliable and generalizable test scores referable to available normative data because most of the modifications involved techniques of data collection rather than changes in the test procedures themselves. For example, we keep a verbatim account of a patient's answers in verbal tasks and a detailed account of a patient's performance on visuo-spatial tasks. In some cases, such as on the Block Design subtest on the WAIS, keeping a record of a patient's performance can be tricky, taking a great deal of practice and experience.

We also emphasize "testing the limits" whenever possible. Patients with neuropsychological disorders can meet the criterion for discontinuing a subtest and still be able to answer more difficult items not yet administered. This occurs because brain damage often disrupts but does not cleanly destroy a function; instead patients are forced to use new, less efficient strategies that produce an inconsistent performance. Information can be preserved but not be reliably accessible (Milberg and Blumstein, 1981). This can be tested only by asking patients to respond to questions beyond the established point of failure and by simplifying response demands.

In addition, certain forms of damage may produce a loss of the ability to initiate a response rather than a loss of the actual function tested (see Chapter 3). In these instances it is critical to push beyond consistent "I don't know" responses, and minimal responses of one-or-two-word elliptical phrases. Test questions must be repeated and patients must be encouraged to try again and try harder. Testing the limits and special encouragement are critical when it appears that a patient's premorbid level of functioning should have produced a better performance. When done at the end of a subtest this encouragement can occur without substantially affecting the reliability of a test score.

Another procedural modification involves time limits. In most cases, when a patient is near a solution as the time limit approaches he is allowed additional time to complete the problem at hand. Response slowing often accompanies brain damage, and its effects on test performance need to be examined separately from the actual loss of information-processing ability. A patient who consistently fails because of inertia in the initiation of a response (Goldberg and Costa, Chapter 3), or because he works too slowly must be distinguished from a patient who cannot complete problems no matter how much time is given. Allowing more time may also identify patients who actually perform more poorly if allowed additional time after their initial response. A record of response latencies is critical so that performance on timed tests can be compared to performance on untimed tasks. This comparison allows one to distinguish general slowing from slowness related to the specific demands of a particular test.

Specific Test Modifications

Other procedural modifications involve adding new components to published tests so that the functions of interest are measured more comprehensively. These additions will be described here but, because of space limitations, only two of the most commonly used tests—the Wechsler Adult Intelligence Scale—Revised (WAIS-R) (Wechsler, 1981) and the Wechsler Memory Scale—are described. Following a description of our revised test procedures we will give examples of the variety of data that can be collected with these techniques, and how these data can be used to answer clinical neuropsychological questions. It should be kept in mind that, though its description is limited here to two tests, the method can be used on all neuropsychological tests.

BOSTON MODIFICATION OF THE WAIS-R (KAPLAN AND MORRIS, 1985). In general, fewer modifications have been made to the administration of the verbal subtests than to the administration of the performance subtests. This is so because it is difficult to engineer modifications that make the covert process underlying verbal problem-solving accessible within the context of standard test administration.

Overall, the verbal subtests represent an opportunity to analyze the form and content of a patient's speech. On any verbal test it is important to look for basic language difficulties such as anomia, dysarthria, dysprosody, agrammatism, press of speech, perseveration, and word-finding problems as evidenced in paraphasias, as well as tendencies to be circumstantial and tangential. In addition, the verbal subtests require a patient to comprehend orally presented information and then to produce an oral response.

Both the verbal and performance subtests can be examined for scatter because the items within each subtest are ordered in levels of increasing difficulty. Patients from different clinical populations can have the same total subtest score, but differing amounts of scatter within their protocol require different interpretations of performance.

Information: The information subtest samples knowledge gained as part of a standard elementary and high school education. A pattern of failure on easy items and success on more difficult items on this subtest suggests retrieval difficulties. Poor performance which is not due to difficulties in language production usually stems from difficulty retrieving information from long-term memory. Retrieval difficulties may arise because the information was never learned, because overlearned information was not available, or because of a deficit recalling information from one of the specific content areas represented (e.g., numerical information, geography, science, literature, and civics). The latter difficulty is most often observed in patients with functional rather than brain-related dysfunction. In addition, some conditions such as temporal lobe epilepsy may result in a specific impairment of this subtest (Milberg et al., 1980).

Comprehension: This subtest addresses a patient's ability to interpret orally presented information. A patient's answers can reveal thinking disorders such as concreteness, perseveration, and disturbed associations. This subtest also can show specific deficits in a patient's knowledge of the various areas represented: personal and social behavior, general knowledge, and social obligations.

Arithmetic: This subtest measures the patient's ability to perform computations mentally, and thus a variety of factors which may impair performance must be controlled. Patients with a short attention span, for example, are given on the completion of the subtest a visual presentation of the auditorily presented verbal problems they failed; in this way deficits in the ability to organize the problem and solve it can be separated from memory problems. If a patient still cannot adequately execute the problem mentally, paper and pencil are provided to assess the patient's ability to transform the verbal problem into a mathematical representation and to evaluate his more fundamental computational skills. In addition, by examining the patient's written formulation, errors due to misalignment can be distinguished from those secondary to impairment in arithmetic functions *per se*, and from difficulties in ordering the series of operations.

Incorrect answers in this subtest are analyzed to learn how a specific answer was derived. A typical error includes the use of numbers without consideration of the content of the problem. This error occurs when a patient is impulsive or becomes stimulus-bound and attempts to simplify a multi-step problem, or when he is distracted by the numbers themselves at the expense of the computation required.

Similarities: This test requires the patient to form a superordinant category relating pairs of words. The kind of errors a patient makes will vary. His answers might be concrete or he might only be able to provide definitions for each word but not be able to integrate the pairs. He might provide an answer related to only one word in the pairs or describe differences between the words, while ignoring the task of finding similarities.

Digit Span: In this subtest we consider it especially important to record the patient's response verbatim. Although we discontinue the subtest after failure of both trials of any series, if a patient is able to recall all of the digits, but in the wrong order, we administer the next series. Because the patient's "span of apprehension," or the number of digits recalled, is separate from the process of making errors in the order of recall, two different scores for both forward and backward recall are available for this subtest: the patient's span with correct order of recall and the patient's span regardless of order. We also note if the patient "chunked" digits by repeating in sets of 2 or 3 digits or multiple unit integers. The record also indicates impulsive performances, such as patients beginning a series before the examiner is finished or repeating the digits at a very rapid rate.

Although the WAIS manual gives equal weight to the number of strings successfully repeated forward and backward in computing the digit span scaled score, we have found that there is a dissociation between the capacity to repeat forward and backward in patients with brain dysfunction. Repeating digits forward seems to require only the capacity to briefly hold several bits of simple information in short-term memory. The elementary nature of this process is underscored by the fact that patients with severe amnesia can have normal or even hypernormal digit spans (Butters and Cermak, 1980). Repeating digits backward requires some cognitive processing of the information. This may be achieved by rehearsing the string of digits again and again, or by transforming the auditorily presented information to a "visual" representation, and then successively "reading" the digits backwards. The former strategy is heavily reliant on repetition and is susceptible to interference and perseveration within and between strings. The latter requires flexible movement between modalities. In either event digit span backward is more sensitive to brain dysfunction than digit span forward. In general, digit span forward is usually equal to or better than digit span backward. With some patients, however, it is not uncommon to find their backward span to be longer than their forward span because they perceive that the former is a more demanding task and thus requires a mobilization of energy and active engagement in the task.

Vocabulary: This subtest, like Information and Comprehension, taps a patient's established fund of knowledge and is highly related to educational, socioeconomic, and occupational experience. It is generally considered the best single measure of "general intelligence" and is least affected by CNS insult except for lesions directly involving the cortical and subcortical language zones. The standard administration of this test calls for the examiner to point to each word listed on a card while saying each word aloud. Due to the many visual and attentional disorders in patients with CNS dysfunction, we also have available a printed version with enlarged words to help focus patients who become distracted when a word is embedded in a list of other words.

Numerous types of errors can occur in this subtest. One is defining a word with its polar opposite. This is frequently seen in patients with developmental learning disabilities.

Patients may also be distracted by the phonetic or perceptual properties of words and provide associative responses. A tendency to perseverate may be seen in the presence of the same introduction to each response by a patient. In addition, although a patient can be credited with one of the two score points for responses which use examples to define the word, such responses can reveal CNS dysfunction when they reflect an inability to pull away from the stimulus.

Digit Symbol: We administer this subtest in the usual manner, except that as the patient proceeds with the task, the examiner places marks on another form every 30 seconds to indicate the patient's progress. This allows an analysis of changes over time in the rate of transcription, changes which can signal fatigue or practice effects. After the 90-second time limit expires the examiner allows the patient to continue until he has completed at least three full lines of the form. This equalizes patient experience with the symbols used in the subtest. If the patient is proficient enough, however, to complete more than three lines of the form within 90 seconds, then he is stopped at 90 seconds. At the end of three complete lines, the key and first three lines are completely covered and the patient is asked to fill in the last row without reference to the key. After this the final row is covered and the patient is instructed to write in any order in the margin all the symbols he can remember.

The measurement of paired and free recall of the symbols permits examination of the amount of incidental learning which has taken place during the subtest.

We find it important to examine the actual symbols produced by the patient. Are they rotated, flipped upside down, or transformed into perceptually similar letters? Are the characters produced by the patient micro- or macrographic? Does the patient use the box as part of the symbol, that is, is the patient "pulled" to the stimulus box? Does the patient consistently make incorrect substitutions, or skip spaces or lines of the task? All these attributes help define the patient's cognitive difficulties and may aid in localizing pathology. For example, we have observed that the systematic inversion of symbols to form alphabetic characters (e.g., ∨ for ∧ or ⊤ for ⊥) may be associated with pathology of the dorsolateral surface of the right frontal lobe, whereas a patient is more likely to become "stimulus bound" with bilateral frontal lobe pathology.

One major change in the Digit Symbol subtest is an addition called Digit Symbol Copy which is administered after the standard subtest. This version is like the original except that symbols in the key are paired with other symbols, not numbers. The patient transcribes each symbol to its place beneath the appropriate symbol, and 30-second intervals are marked until all the lines are completed. This version allows the dissociation of motor speed in the patient's performance from the process of learning the symbols. This is especially important with older patients because motor slowing can confound interpretation of the test score.

Picture Completion: This subtest requires visual discrimination and verbal labeling of (or discrete pointing to) the essential missing component in meaningful visual stimuli. Failures on specific items can be related to any number of factors. A patient's perception of the stimulus item may be impaired due to primary visual problems, or visual or secondary visuo-organizational problems. Complete misidentification of the stimulus may occur in patients with visual agnosia. A patient may have difficulty identifying missing embedded features but no difficulty when the important feature belongs to the contour. A patient may have difficulty with items requiring inferences about symmetry, inferences based on the knowledge of the object, or inferences based on knowledge of natural events. Finally, he may have difficulty making a hierarchy of the missing details.

Block Design: Valuable information can be gained by observing the strategy the patient uses in his constructions on this subtest, so we record the exact process a patient goes through in completing a design. We note (1) the quadrant in which the patient began his construction; (2) the side of the design the patient completed first; (3) whether the patient worked in the normally favored directions for a right hander (left to right and top to bottom); (4) whether the patient rotated the blocks in place or in space; (5) whether the patient broke the 2×2 or 3×3 matrix configurations on the way to solution; (6) whether the patient produced a mirror image or an up-down reversal of the actual design as his final product; and (7) whether the patient perseverated a design across items. Later in this chapter the strategy of "breaking the configuration" (see point 5 above) will be addressed in more detail.

Picture Arrangement: Visual perception, integration and memory of details, and serial ordering are all important for success in this subtest. As with the Picture Completion subtest, the examiner must be sensitive to visual field and visuo-spatial neglect deficits. The cards may have to be placed in a vertical column in front of the patient to minimize such effects.

After the subtest is completed, we ask the patient to tell the story for each sequence as he sees it. Several consequences may result. (1) the patient may provide the appropriate story to a correctly sequenced series; (2) he may provide the correct story for a disordered arrangement; or (3) he may provide neither the correct story nor the correct sequence of cards. The verbal account following each arrangement permits a closer analysis of the underlying problems in an incorrect arrangement. For some patients giving a verbal account will bring into focus illogical elements in their arrangements and may guide them to a correct rearrangement. The verbal account may also reveal misperceptions of detail, lack of appreciation of spatial relationships, or overattention to details which results in the inability to perceive similarities across pictures.

By allowing a patient to work past the specified time limits on this subtest, his capacity to comprehend and complete the task in spite of motor slowing or scanning deficits can be evaluated.

Again, we observe the process by which a patient arranges the cards. Some patients may study the cards and preplan their arrangement. Other patients may arrange them impulsively, and still other patients may require the visual feedback of their productions as they arrange the cards, study them, and then rearrange them.

Errors may occur for a variety of reasons. A patient may not move cards from their original location because of a poor strategy or because of attentional deficits. The former suggests a strategy characterized by inertia which is often seen in patients with frontal lobe dysfunction (see the detailed consideration of frontal lobe syndrome by Goldberg and Costa, Chapter 3); the latter suggests a strategy more often seen in posterior damage. A patient may fail because of inattention to detail, or focus on irrelevant details. A patient may misunderstand the task and attempt to align the visual elements within the cards or he may separate the cards into subgroups based on similar features.

Object Assembly: Three additional puzzles have been added to the four standard puzzles in this subtest in order to elucidate the effect of certain stimulus parameters such as the presence or absence of internal detail on solutions. As in the Block Design subtest, the actual process employed by the patient to solve each puzzle is recorded. The Automobile puzzle from the Wechsler Intelligence Scale for Children—Revised (WISC-R) (Wechsler, 1974) has been added to permit a comparison between the puzzles that rely heavily for solution on edge alignment information (i.e., Hand and Elephant).

Two other experimental puzzles, the Circle and the Cow (Palmer and Kaplan, 1985) have been added to demonstrate patients' reliance on one of these two strategies to the exclusion of the other. The Circle can only be solved by using contour information, whereas the Cow, constructed so that each juncture is an identical arc, cannot be solved by using contour information and demands instead a piece-by-piece analysis. Patients who rely too heavily on contour information will fail to solve the Cow, and patients who are unable to appreciate the relationship between pieces will fail to solve the Circle.

WECHSLER MEMORY SCALE. A number of additional subtests and procedural modifications have been added to make this test a more complete assessment of a patient's ability to learn and recall new verbal and visuo-spatial information.

General Information and Orientation: A number of items based on autobiographical information have been added to these two subtests so that recall of personal, current, and old information can be assessed more fully.

Mental Control: Two items which have been found to be useful in the characterization and localization of retrieval deficits (Coltheart, Hull and Slater, 1975) have been added to this subtest. After reciting the alphabet patients are asked to name all the letters of the alphabet that rhyme with the word "tree" and then to name all the letters of the alphabet that contain a curve when printed as a capital letter. These two items provide specific information about a patient's ability to retrieve information from memory based on specific auditory or visual physical characteristics.

Logical Memory: Two changes have been made to this subtest. First, in addition to the standard immediate recall condition, a 20-minute delayed recall condition has been added. Patients with adequate attentional and rote memory abilities may do well when initially recall the information, but may show severe deficits on delayed recall. Impairment after a delay may be due to inadequate retrieval strategies or defective storage abilities.

Second, in addition to the two auditorily presented paragraphs, a third paragraph (viz., the Cowboy Story: Talland, 1965), which must be read aloud and retained by the patient, is presented and tested for recall immediately and after a 20-minute delay. This additional paragraph allows examination of complaints from patients about an inability to retain information that has been read.

Beyond quantifying how much information is learned and recalled, we also take note of qualitative features of the responses, such as impoverishment, confabulation, disorganization, and confusion of details across stories.

Associative Learning: Three major modifications have been made to this subtest. First, immediately after the third standard trial, "backward retrieval" is measured. The order of each pair of words is reversed, and patient are presented with the second word of the pair and asked to recall the first. Second, 20 minutes later free uncued recall of the pairs is assessed. Third, following this, the first word of each pair is provided as a cue and paired recall is measured once again. As in the Logical Memory subtest, these recall conditions allow deficits in immediate recall to be examined separately from those in delayed recall. Patient responses on this task may reflect internal and external intrusions, perseveration, or a simple inability to learn new information.

Visual Reproduction: This subtest was revised to include two conditions. First, the patient is required to copy the geometric designs following the immediate recall condition. Second, he is asked to reproduce the designs again 20 minutes later. The copy condition provides an opportunity to assess a patient's visuo-perceptual analysis of the designs. The delayed recall condition assesses changes in recall following an added exposure to the designs. Using a flow chart we record the manner in which the patient produces each design. Such analysis can provide information about brain dysfunction, as will be discussed in greater detail later in this chapter. In addition, we note the type of errors a patient makes. Recall can be characterized by impoverishment, simplification and distortion of details, disorganization, and confusion between designs.

Using the Process Approach to Localize Lesions

The modifications of testing and data-recording procedures specific to the Boston Process Approach that allow the clinician to obtain a dynamic record of a patient's problem-solving strategy were described above. In this section we will show how the specific strategic information that can be collected with the process approach can be useful in the analysis of brain and behavior relationships and in the prediction of behavior outside of the clinical laboratory. For purposes of this discussion we will concentrate on several broad categories of cognitive strategies that can be observed across many different measures.

Featural vs. Contextual Priority

Most tasks that are useful in assessing brain damage consist of a series of elements or basic stimuli arranged together within a spatial, temporal, or conceptual framework. One important strategic variable, therefore, is the extent to which patients give priority to processing low-level detail or "featural" information vs. higher-level configural, or contextual, information (viz., Schmeck and Grove, 1979, for related literature from experimental and educational psychology).

This dichotomy of information, featural on one hand and contextual on the other, can be used to characterize both verbal and visuo-spatial information within each of the sensory modalities. For example, words and their basic phrase structure within a sentence can be thought of as the basic elements or features important in linguistic analysis. Phrases are put together into sentences and sentences are put together into a conceptually focused paragraph to create a higher-level context or organization. Aside from simple phonemes and acoustic energy transitions the word or phrase seems to represent the first major point at which the basic units of language can be isolated from their use in expressing organized thought.

Similarly, a photograph of a street scene can be broken down into low-level categorical units of perception, such as cars, people, or litter, and then organized into relational information placing these disparate elements into a larger conceptual or spatial unit.

To successfully interpret most test material requires the use and integration of both featural and contextual information. Brain damage produces a lawful

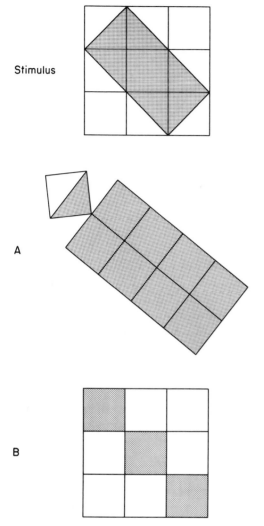

Stimulus

A

B

Fig. 1. Two examples of informational strategies pursued by patients in solving complex tasks.

fractionation of a patient's ability to use both types of information simultaneously. Furthermore, the type of information processing given priority is related to the laterality and location of a patient's lesion. Specifically, patients with damage to the left hemisphere are more likely to use a strategy favoring contextual information, whereas patients with damage to the right hemisphere are more likely to give priority to featural information.

We can infer the type of informational strategy favored by a patient from many of the tasks described earlier. For example, a patient may in the course of assembling a block design shaped like a diagonal rectangle within a square (see Fig. 1) align pairs of solid blocks to form a diagonal rectangle without regard for the 3×3 matrix in which it is placed (Fig. 1a).

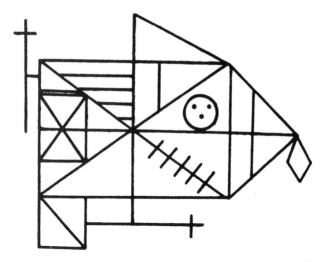

Fig. 2. The Rey-Osterreith Complex Figure (Osterreith and Rey, 1944).

This is an example of a patient giving attentional priority to the internal features of the design without regard for the configuration. Another patient may assemble the same design by retaining the 3×3 shape but drastically simplifying the diagonal rectangle into a line of three solid red blocks (Fig. 1b). In this case the patient is giving attentional priority to the configuration with little regard for the accuracy of the internal features. Similar performance strategies have been found in analyses of block design performance in normal subjects (Royer, 1967; Haeberle, 1982) though not with the rigidity or consistency found in patients with pathology of the CNS. Normal performance is typically characterized by the integration of featural and configural information, whereas pathological performance is characterized by their dissociation. Thus, normal subjects will rarely neglect one source of information completely, while using the other.

Using featural information to the exclusion of contextual information can also be seen on the Rey-Osterreith Complex Figure (Osterreith and Rey, 1944). By keeping a flow chart of the patient's method of copying or recalling the Rey Figure (see Fig. 2) evidence about the strategy used by a patient can be obtained. The Rey-Osterreith Figure includes smaller rectangles, squares, and other details placed within and around it.

A normal strategy for copying this complex design makes use of the obvious organizational features, such as the large rectangle and the large diagonal, to organize and guide performance. Some patients will copy the design as if they were using a random scan path, adding small line segments until their final design resembles the original. Such a painstaking performance can be taken as evidence of a featural priority strategy in the perceptual organization of the design.

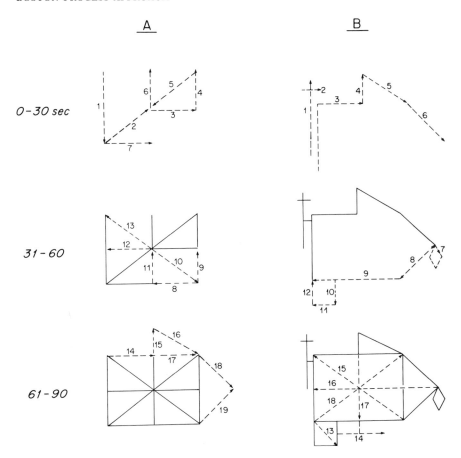

Fig. 3. Two examples of performance strategies by patients on the Rey-Osterreith Complex Figure.

Other patients may approach the task of copying the design by producing the entire extreme outline but omitting smaller features. This approach is evidence of a strategy of contextual priority. Additional evidence for the emphasis of one or the other of these strategies can often be seen in the patient's recall of the design after a delay. A patient who is overly dependent on featural information may show a performance like that seen in the left column of Fig. 3, whereas a patient who directs his attention primarily to configural information may show a production like that seen in the right column of Fig. 3.

Occasionally, patients will actually retrieve featural information independently of the spatial context in which it originally appeared. For example, a patient may recall one of the designs from the Visual Reproduction subtest of the WMS when asked to recall the Rey-Osterreith Complex Figure or he may recombine features from two different designs into one.

Similar deficits in a balance between featural and contextual priorities can be seen in verbal tasks. A patient may show evidence of featural priority when recalling the Logical Memory stories from the WMS. He may recall many of the correct items from the original stories but in an incorrect order along with additional irrelevant information based on his own associations to the stories or to other stories presented in the course of testing.

For example, when recalling the second story from the WMS (Form 1) a patient with a lesion in the right frontal lobe may respond: "15 passengers were rescued and the purser was on board." In this case, the patient has recombined elements from the two stories into one. Anna Thompson, a character in the first story, was robbed of fifteen dollars and a purse was made up to compensate her for her loss. This patient has borrowed the elements of 15 and purse from that story and added them to the second story. A patient may also show evidence of configural or contextual priority when recalling the stories. In that case he would be able to explain the general theme of the story, but he would rely too heavily on paraphrases and he would be unable to recall specific details.

The dimension of featural vs. configural priority is useful in predicting behavior outside the clinical laboratory. For example, patients who show an inability to process contextual information despite a preserved ability to process featural information are often found to be handicapped in situations that require an ability to spontaneously organize and direct one's own behavior. This inability to organize personal behavior along with an impaired ability to detect organization and to interpret complex arrays of information greatly diminishes large scale goal-directed behavior. These deficits are subtle, but often manifested in tasks that require responsibility and self-direction.

Thus, the business executive who favors a strategy of "featural" priority after a head injury may begin to experience difficulty in his job because he is unable to make long-range decisions, give consistent orders, and complete complex assignments. Despite this, he may still have an intimate knowledge of the workings of his business, he may still be able to function in a minor advisory capacity, and he may still be able to perform more circumscribed tasks requiring less long-term planning. It is not unusual for this loss of sensitivity to the overall organization and cohesion of information to have a profound negative effect on social and personal adjustment.

Patients who have retained their ability to process configural or contextual information but who suffer from a diminished ability to process the "fine details" of their world, on the other hand, may be inefficient and even forgetful, but in many cases will still be able to make accurate long-range decisions, and to relate to others in a consistent appropriate fashion. Patients who have recovered from aphasia often show this latter pattern of deficits.

Professionals who have sustained a head injury which resulted in aphasia may often return to work even though they still have difficulty processing featural information. These patients will be less efficient and need more time to accomplish tasks that they once accomplished easily. Of course, their deficits are likely to be most pronounced in areas requiring verbal competence. Thus, the analysis of strategy can be useful in developing rehabilitation programs.

Hemispatial Priority

Though not strictly a cognitive strategy, the direction in which patients deploy attention in analyzing and solving spatial problems, and the accuracy with which they are able to use information presented visually to the left and right side of space, is an important source of data concerning the integrity of the brain.

It is well known that visual system lesions posterior to the optic chiasm and in the occipital lobe result in visual field losses contralateral to the side of the lesion (Carpenter, 1972). In addition, lesions that occur in the anterior dorsolateral portion of the occipital lobe or in the parietal cortex may result in neglect of or inattention to the side of space contralateral to the lesion (Heilman, 1979). Subtle manifestations of "neglect" or "inattention" may be observed in a patient's attempt to solve various spatial problems even though the full-blown clinical syndrome is not present.

For example, right-handed adults tend to begin scanning spatial problems on the left side of space, although over the course of many problems they may shift from beginning on one side of the stimulus to beginning on the other. In contrast, patients with lesions of the right hemisphere will characteristically scan from right-to-left on spatial problems, whereas patients with lesions of the left hemisphere will often use a stereotyped left-to-right strategy.

The latter case can be distinguished from a strong normal tendency to scan from left-to-right because in addition to using an inflexible left-to-right scanning approach to problems a patient with a lesion in the left hemisphere will tend to make more errors and to be slower processing information in the field contralateral to his lesion. Hence, patients with lesions in the left hemisphere will often have difficulty completing the right side of a design or they will omit details from the right side of a design. Adults without brain lesions may show a strong preference for working from left to right on spatial problems but will not tend to make more errors in one particular field.

Other Specific Strategies

The observation of the informational and spatial priorities that a patient uses can be made across materials, modalities, and functions. These are only two of the many possible process variables that have been isolated. They were presented here because of their pervasiveness and ease of observation. Specific cognitive functions, such as memory, praxis, and language, have special sets of process variables related to each of them, and this information has been detailed in other sections of this book (see Chapters 2, 12, and 19), and elsewhere (Butters and Cermak, 1975; Goodglass and Kaplan, 1972).

Strengths and Weaknesses of the Process Approach

Improved Sensitivity

This method of qualitative analysis affords several advantages over other approaches to the assessment of the neuropsychological sequelae of brain damage. For the purposes of diagnosis, it is as valid for the detection and localization of cortical lesions as other widely used methods (i.e., Halstead-Reitan: Reitan and Davison, 1974; Luria-Nebraska: Golden, 1981). Trained neuropsychologists using the procedures described herein report agreement with radiological evidence in at least 90% of their cases. In some instances, the qualitative data are inconsistent with the quantitative data (i.e., test scores). For example, a patient who works quickly may be able to overcome his use of pathological, haphazard strategies and achieve a normal test score, so his test score will not reflect impairment. In cases like this, the hit rate using the qualitative analysis method is superior to the hit rate from methods that do not take qualitative information into account. A similar conclusion was reached by Heaton et al. (1981) when they demonstrated that clinicians who rated Halstead-Reitan results had better success in correctly classifying brain damaged cases than did a psychometric formula approach rooted heavily in level of performance. Heaton et al. (1981) believed that the clinicians' superiority was related to their ability to supplement test scores with consideration of the qualitative and configural features of their data.

Clinical Relevance

The greatest strength of this method may be its usefulness in treatment planning and its relevance to patients' daily lives. Qualitative analysis provides the most precise delineation of function available, and allows the relative strengths and weaknesses of each patient to become obvious in a "face valid" manner.

Resistance to Practice Effect

This method also shares with other methods the advantages of repeatability and comparability across testing intervals (Glosser, Kaplan, and LoVerme, 1982). Although strategic variables are to some extent more difficult to quantify, they are less susceptible to the practice and repetition effects which can confound interpretation of test scores. This makes qualitative data more useful than test scores alone in the assessment of recovery. Using both qualitative and quantitative data assures the reliable estimate of change that can be evaluated normatively from test scores combined with an estimate of the effects of change independent of the effects of practice.

Effects of Aging

Aging systematically alters neuropsychological test performance, as discussed in Chapter 6. Aging also affects strategic variables, changes which have been discussed in detail by Albert and Kaplan (1980). In brief, it appears that normal aging produces strategic changes akin to those observed among some patients with frontal system disorder, including cognitive slowing and loss of ability to process configural information.

The process approach permits relatively easy differentiation of aging from specific asymmetric neuropathologies, such as left frontal or right frontal disease. It is less effective in sorting out aging from mild generalized cerebral disorder, as occurs in very early dementia. In common with other approaches (e.g., see Chapters 1 and 2) we base our differentiation partly on estimates of premorbid functioning by considering demographic indices (Wilson et al., 1979; Karzmark, Heaton, Grant & Matthews, 1984), and performance on tests relatively resistant to the effects of brain damage. We also pay attention to memory impairment which exceeds that to be expected with the benign senescent forgetfulness of normal aging, and to strategic pathologies reflecting frontal lobe dysfunction which are more severe than one ordinarily encounters in the elderly. Regrettably, our normative work is not yet sufficiently advanced to propose specific rules or norms to aid in this important distinction.

Effects of Education

Once again, test performance changes in relation to education are considered in detail in a later section of this book (see Chapter 6). Regarding qualitative information, people who are 50 to 60 years old and who have completed at least ninth grade show little difference in strategy from individuals who have completed high school and college on most tasks involving visuo-spatial information. Amount of education does not appear to produce strategic differences in scanning, stimulus selectivity, and contextual or featural sensitivity. Verbal skills, naturally, are more sensitive to the effects of education.

Nonetheless, through the combined use of qualitative and quantitative information the effects of education can be differentiated from changes in cognitive function due to brain disease. Likewise, culture and bilingualism also have an effect on various verbal skills, but the effects of these factors on test performance can also be distinguished from those of acquired brain injury through the combined use of qualitative and quantitative data.

Sensory Motor Handicaps

Our method emphasizes separating strategic differences from generalized slowing. Being slow must be distinguished from being slowed-up by the difficulty of the task (Welford, 1977). Peripheral handicaps often make it difficult to work quickly, but by observing the strategy used by a disabled patient on verbal and visuo-spatial tasks one can distinguish the defects due to peripheral injury from those due to cognitive dysfunction.

Psychopathology

Differentiating severe psychopathology from dysfunction related to neurologic processes is one of the most difficult tasks for the neuropsychologist. Patients with severe psychopathology sometimes perform on neuropsychological tests like patients with confirmed lesions of the CNS.

From our observation, chronic schizophrenics often have naming problems, difficulties analyzing details in visuo-spatial tasks, and difficulty maintaining attention, deficits which we associate with left hemisphere pathology (see also Goldberg and Costa's discussion of executive deficits in schizophrenics Chapter 3, and Goldstein's full review of the neuropsychology of schizophrenia, Chapter 8). Patients with severe depression sometimes resemble patients with right hemisphere pathology and, in particular, right frontal lobe dysfunction. These patients can have difficulty analyzing contextual information relative to a preserved ability to use details. In addition, they can have difficulty with visuo-spatial memory, although their memory for verbal materials is relatively intact in terms of recalling details (see further discussion of the neuropsychology of depression and pseudodementia by Caine, Chapter 10).

Summary

The Boston Process Approach has, over the years, developed a systematic method for assessing qualitative neuropsychological information which, taken in concert with more traditional test performance data, adds sensitivity and meaning to neuropsychological assessment. We have discussed two strategic elements—featural vs. contextual priority and hemispatial priority—to illustrate the possibilities of our approach. As the method we have described is refined both in our laboratory and by other investigators, we foresee that it will help move neuropsychological assessment beyond a reliable cataloging of deficits toward an understanding of the underlying processes. With such an understanding neuropsychology will be in a better position to assist in the more important task of treatment panning and rehabilitation.

ACKNOWLEDGMENTS

The authors would like to thank the VA Medical Service for the support of this chapter. We are indebted to Virginia Marquard for secretarial assistance, and to Leonard Poon and Barbara Segarra for their help in the preparation of the manuscript.

REFERENCES

Albert, M. S. and Kaplan, E. (1980). Organic implications of neuropsychological deficits in the elderly. In: L. W. Poon, J. L. Fozard, L. S. Cermak, D. Arenberg, and L. W.

Thompson, eds., *New Directions in Memory and Aging.* Hillsdale, N.J.: Lawrence Erlbaum Associates, Inc., pp. 403–432.

Arthur, G. A. (1947). *A point scale of performance tests.* Revised Form II. New York: Psychological Corporation.

Bender, L. A. (1938). A visual motor gestalt test and its clinical use. *American Orthopsychiatric Association Research Monographs,* No. 3.

Benton, A. L. (1950). A multiple choice type of visual retention test. *Arch. Neurol. Psychiat., 64,* 699–707.

Butters, N. and Cermak, L. S. (1975). Some analyses of amnesia syndrome in brain damaged patients. In: K. Pribram and R. Isaacson, eds., *The Hippocampus.* New York: Plenum Press, pp. 377–409.

Butters, N. and Cermak, L. S. (1980). *The alcoholic Korsakoffs syndrome: An information processing approach to amnesia.* New York: Academic Press.

Butters, N. and Grady, M. (1977). Effects of predistractor delays on the short-term memory performance of patients with Korsakoffs and Huntington's Disease. *Neuropsychologia, 13,* 701–705.

Carpenter, M. D. (1972). *Core text of neuroanatomy.* Baltimore: Williams and Williams.

Christensen, A. L. (1975). *Luria's neuropsychological investigation: Text, manual, and test cards.* New York: Spectrum.

Coltheart, M., Hull, E., and Slater, D. (1975). Sex differences in imagery and reading. *Nature, 253,* 438–440.

Cronbach, L. J. (1957). The two disciplines of scientific psychology. *Am. Psychol., 12,* 671–684.

Glosser, G., Kaplan, E., and LoVerme, S. (1982). Longitudinal neuropsychological report of aphasia following left subcortical hemorrhage. *Brain Lang., 15,* 95–116.

Golden, C. J. (1981). A standardized version of Luria's neuropsychological tests. In: S. J. Filskov and T. J. Boll, eds., *Handbook of Clinical Neuropsychology.* New York: John Wiley & Sons, pp. 608–642.

Goodglass, H., and Kaplan, E. (1972). *The Assessment of Aphasia and Related Disorders.* Philadelphia: Lea & Febinger.

Gorham, D. R. (1956). *Proverbs Test.* Missoula: Psychological Test Specialists.

Grant, D. A., and Berg, E. A. (1948). A behavioral analysis of degree of reinforcement and ease of shifting to new responses in a Weigl-type card sorting program. *J. Exp. Psychol., 38,* 404–411.

Haeberle, K. C. (1982, March). *Multidimensional scaling of block design patterns.* Presented at the 53rd Annual Meeting of the EPA, Baltimore, Maryland.

Halstead, W. C. (1947). *Brain and Intelligence: Quantitative Study of the Frontal Lobes.* Chicago: University of Chicago Press.

Heaton, R. K., Grant, I., Anthony, W. Z., and Lehman, R. A. W. (1981). A comparison of clinical and automated interpretation of the Halstead-Reitan Battery. *J. Clin. Neuropsych., 3,* 121–141.

Heilman, K. M. (1979). Neglect and related disorders. In: K. M. Heilman & C. Valenstein, eds., *Clinical Neuropsychology.* New York: Oxford University Press, pp. 268–307.

Hooper, H. E. (1958). *The Hooper Visual Organization test Manual.* Los Angeles: Western Psychological Service.

Hunt, E. (1983). On the nature of intelligence. *Science, 129,* 141–146.

Jastak, J. F., and Jastak, S. R. (1978). *The wide range achievement test manual (revised).* Los Angeles: Western Psychological Services.

Kaplan, E. and Morris, R. (1985) Boston modification of the WAIS-R. Unpublished.

Karzmark, P., Heaton, R. K., Grant, I., and Matthews, C. G. (1984). Use of demographic variables to predict full scale IQ and level of performance on the Halstead-Reitan Battery. *J. Consult. Clin. Psychol., 52,* 663–665.

Milberg, W., and Blumstein, S. E. (1981). Lexical decisions and aphasia: Evidence for semantic processing. *Brain Lang., 14,* 371–385.

Milberg, W., Cummings, J., Goodglass, H., and Kaplan, E. (1979). Case report: A global sequential processing disorder following head injury: A possible role for the right hemisphere in serial order behavior. *J. Clin. Neuropsych., 1* (3), 213–225.

Milberg, W., Greiffenstein, M., Lewis, R., and Rourke, D. (1980). Differentiation of temporal lobe and generalized seizure patients with the WAIS. *J. Consult. Clin. Psych., 48,* 39–42.

Milner, B. (1971). Interhemispheric differences in the localization of psychological processes in man. *Br. Med. Bull., 27,* 272–277.

Neisser, U. (1967). *Cognitive Psychology.* New York: Appleton.

Neisser, U., Novick, R., and Lagar, R. (1963). Searching for ten targets simultaneously. *Perceptual and Motor Skills, 17,* 955–961.

Osterreith, P., and Rey, A. (1944). Le test de copie d'une figure complexe. *Arch. Psychologie, 30,* 206–356.

Palmer, P. and Kaplan, E. (1985) *The cow and circle experimental test.* Unpublished test. Available from E. Kaplan.

Porteus, S. D. (1965). *Porteus Maze Test.* Palo Alto: Pacific Books.

Raven, J. C. (1960). *Guide to the Standard Progressive Matrices.* London: H. K. Lewis.

Reitan, R. M., and Davison, L. A. (1974). *Clinical Neuropsychology: Current Status and Applications.* New York: Winston/Wiley, 1974.

Rey, A. (1964). *L'Examen Clinique en Psychologie.* Paris: Presses Universitaires de France.

Rorschach, H. (1942). *Psychodiagnostics: A Diagnostic Test Based on Perception,* P. Lemkau and B Kronenberg, trans. Berne: Huber, U.S. Dist: Grune & Stratton.

Royer, F. L. (1967). Information processing in the Block Design Task. *Intelligence, 1,* 23–50.

Russell, E. W. (1981, June). Some principles of psychometric neuropsychology and the Halstead-Reitan battery. *Perspectives in V.A. Neuropsychology and Rehabilitation: Proceedings of the Mental Health and Behavioral Sciences Service Conference.* Salt Lake City, Utah.

Russell, E. W., Neuringer, C., and Goldstein, G. (1970). *Assessment of Brain Damage: A Neuropsychological Key Approach.* New York: John Wiley & Sons.

Schmeck, R. R., and Grove, E. (1979). Academic achievement and individual differences in learning processes. *Appl. Psychol. Measurement, 3,* 43–49.

Shipley, W. C. (1940). A self-administering scale for measuring intellectual impairment and deterioration. *J. Psychol., 9,* 371–377.

Sternberg, R. J. (1980). Sketch of a componential subtheory of human intelligence. *Behav. Brain Sci., 3,* 573–614.

Stroop, J. R. (1935). Studies of interference in serial verbal reactions. *J. Exp. Psychol., 18,* 643–662.

Talland, G. A. (1965). *Deranged Memory.* New York: Academic Press.

Thurstone, L. L. (1938). *Primary Mental Abilities.* Chicago: University of Chicago Press.

Wechsler, D. A. (1945). A standardized memory scale for clinical use. *J. Psychol., 19,* 87–95.

Wechsler, D. A. (1955). *Wechsler Adult Intelligence Scale.* New York: Psychological Corporation.

Wechsler, D. A. (1974). *Wechsler Intelligence Scale for Children-Revised.* New York: Psychological Corporation.

Wechsler, D. A. (1981). *Wechsler Adult Intelligence Scale-Revised.* New York: Psychological Corporation.

Welford, A. T. (1977). Causes of slowing of performance with age. *Interdisciplinary Topics in Gerontology, 11,* 43–45.

Werner, H. (1937). Process and achievement: A basic problem of education and developmental psychology. *Harvard Ed. Rev., 7,* 353–368.

Wilson, R. S., Rosenbaum, G., Brown, G., and Grisell, J. (1979). An index of premorbid intelligence. *J. Consult. Clin. Psychol., 46,* 1554–1555.

5

The Role of the Computer in Neuropsychological Assessment

KENNETH M. ADAMS / GREGORY G. BROWN

From Clinician to Computer to Clinician

Regardless of one's theoretical orientation or approach to the practice of clinical neuropsychology, it is essential that the clinician ultimately specify the procedures to be used to evaluate a patient's performance. This becomes especially important in neuropsychiatric disorders, where an evaluation may have a variety of purposes (e.g., diagnosis, baseline evaluation for treatment, measurement of drug effect). The neuropsychological assessment for these varying purposes requires careful selection of tasks and consideration of how specific effects will be identified among other sources of variance in or explanation of the patient's data.

It is our contention that the specification of how patients are measured and how their performances are to be evaluated are unavoidable steps which any neuropsychological methodology must take to be considered viable. This standard of public definition of procedure to the rest of the scientific community is a minimal one. It is an achievable one as well, in our opinion. Qualitative as well as quantitative procedures can be used in the neuropsychological examination, and the methods for evaluating these procedures can be defined as well. There is no essential inconsistency or contradiction in collecting both qualitative and quantitative data, provided that both modes of evaluation are held to the same scientific standard of public specification of procedures (Adams, 1980a, 1980b).

At this point, it is logical to introduce the computer as a powerful tool to assist in the task of collecting, reducing, and analyzing neuropsychological results, which facilitates the process of definition and specification described above. The computer can only do what it is programmed to do, and in this sense is limited by the comprehensiveness and accuracy of the programmed instructions it receives. It makes no decisions that are not provided in its rules, and if computations or classifications turn out to be incorrect, one must look to the programmer's faulty logic.

At the presence stage of development of clinical neuropsychology, our knowledge of various problems that require evaluation will not permit complete and effective specification of clinical interpretation rules for the computer. However, there is really no reason not to attempt to develop computer assisted assessment and interpretation. There is every reason to believe that neuropsychological methods will continue to improve, and their precise operational definition and testing using the computer will hasten improvement.

The expert neuropsychologist always should be in control of the computer and its products. Computer calculations or descriptions of clinical questions about patients always require professional review in ethical practice; and such outputs will always be studied by astute neuropsychologists seeking to improve the computer algorithm. In effect, the process started by the clinician eventually returns full circle.

Yet, in a wider sense, how have computers been used in clinical neuropsychology to date? What models for neuropsychological assessment and interpretation have been used and with what results? We turn next to a consideration of these questions.

Some General Principles

At present, computing applications can be seen as a function of two parameters: (1) the computer size and scale, and (2) the type of information processing required.

The number of individual uses and their complexity are dependent upon the type of computer and its availability. Some of the representative computing tasks in neuropsychology may be common to many assessment service settings.

Computing Applications

Administrative Uses

Administrative applications usually include such tasks as patient census, patient scheduling, billing, and word processing. However, other functions such as building scientific databases, evaluating referral patterns, monitoring followup appointments, and writing administrative reports can be performed on any type of computer—mainframes, minicomputers, and microcomputers. This last task should be an especially helpful one, given the time busy professionals spend writing memoranda to bureaucrats to justify their clinical activities. Software exists for many of these administrative uses, ranging from dBase for microcomputer, database management to mainframe routines such as RPG for report writing. A consultation with local experts in business computing usually will provide good ideas.

Patient Testing

Programs to administer psychological tests, tasks, and inventories are being written, published, and sold at a very fast rate. The limited interactive capability of most mainframes and the distributed computing arrangements in minicomputers have been barriers to the development of truly interactive programs. However, the advent of easily programmable microcomputers has removed these obstacles. Neuropsychologists and programmers are busy developing computerized routines to administer cognitive, perceptual, and motor tests. Questionnaires such as the Minnesota Multi-phasic Personality Inventory (MMPI) have long been easily programmed for computers. More recently, microcomputers with color graphic capabilities, voice synthesizers, graphic tablets, and response transducers of all types have made nearly any neuropsychological test potentially translatable into computer commands for automated administration.

This is not a totally unproblematic development, though. Administering tests by computer changes the nature of the tests and, of course, influences the patient's perception of the procedure. This, in turn, actually reduces the tests' clinical usefulness when patients' motivation, response style, sensory handicaps, etc., enter into the assessment.

Indeed, currently available programs sold along with proprietary computers for test administration are uniformly less effective or useful than their promoters suggest. Those impressed by such wares at professional conventions would do well to consider all the conditions under which the test administration program will be used before purchase.

Intermediate Clinical Analysis ("Number Crunching")

Intermediate clinical analysis—the use of automata to count, record, score or calculate various parameters of patient performance for the clinician's study—is in many ways the least developed application and has the greatest promise. It may take diverse forms such as calculating I.Q.'s, comparing a recorded performance against extensive norms, and analyzing aspects of performance beyond the power of raw observation (e.g., Wisconsin Card Sorting Indices). These programs do not supplant the need for the clinician's ability but extend the power of the scoring and comparative analysis arising from the assessment.

It appears that programs that do this type of analysis can reside on any of the three types of computer, with the exception of those that require considerable interactive capability with the devices in the laboratory. Computer programs to detect timing, motor response, speech, etc., are best written for microcomputers.

The "number crunching" function is the capability to perform calculations needed for higher order mathematical analysis or commonly employed statistical tests for research purposes. Programs for these applications have long resided in large mainframe computers. The most complex of routines will continue to be best maintained there. However, more common statistical packages (e.g., BMDP, SPSS) and most mathematical programming tools are now available in microcomputer forms.

Expert Report Writer/Interpretation Programs

The "expert" application of computers in medical settings is their use in the scoring, analysis, and interpretation of psychological tests. Because the theoretical issues of psychological approach and computer design of such programs are central to clinical neuropsychological assessment, we will consider in detail the currently available programs. A variety of tests are used in medical psychology to assess intelligence, achievement, cognition, language, motor performance, sensation, perception, personality, and other behavior. Psychological assessment and its interpretation play an important role in diagnosis, preoperative baseline measurement, treatment planning, quality of life assessment, and the documentation of treatment gains or problems.

The qualitative and quantitative information emerging from neuropsychological assessment and testing is the evidence on which the clinician bases his clinical predictions. It is the process of data inspection, evaluation, weighting, and interpretation which invites computer modeling and possible automation to reduce the amount of professional staff time involved and to increase the reliability of repetitive tasks.

Moreover, a substantial body of scientific evidence (Goldberg, 1968; Meehl 1954; Meehl, 1973; Rich, 1983; Sawyer, 1966; and Wiggins, 1973) suggests that defined clinical classification tasks can be executed more reliably and rapidly by a computer than by expert clinical judges, regardless of their experience or time investment. This particular finding obtains, not because of any inherent superiority of computers, but because the computer program executes its decision rules with utter reliability, and without distractions, hunches, or "second guesses."

Some Approaches to Computer Classification or Diagnosis in Neuropsychology

Three major approaches have been used to construct computer programs for behavioral classification of cerebral dysfunction: a taxonomic "key" approach, a geographic/geometric probability approach, and two methods which attempt to recreate the cognitive activity of the clinician. Each has distinctive advantages and liabilities.

Taxonomic Approaches to Computer Classification

The "key" method in biology for identifying and naming species is the use of a taxonomic manual (Russell, Neuringer, and Goldstein, 1970). The use of the manual is not a system of classification in and of itself, but a means of placing an individual specimen within a classification scheme that already has been constructed. Classification consists in grouping species according to their characteristics; that is, a class or category consists of members who all have the same characteristics. The *key* uses the characteristics of a species to locate the class or category to which the species belongs. The key should identify the classification or name of an unknown specimen by using characteristics of the organism.

Beyond this, the topic of taxonomy in botany and zoology becomes more complex than is useful to describe in this context. Differing forms of taxonomy (e.g., indented vs. parallel) and varying systems make this seemingly dry enterprise a lively practical challenge.

For the student of medical computing, the applicability of the key should be obvious. Given a number of diseases or problems with discrete characteristics or interrelated symptoms, it should be possible to construct computer programs which follow their own key.

This presumes that the computer program can be constructed to include objective decision rules or "characters" which will allow the user to enter raw data and obtain results. Two problems which can occur result from (1) any lack of clarity in the key's criteria, and (2) any difficulty in clearcut decision rules concerning the disposition of a case—or, put another way, cases in which the degree of "fit" to a syndrome ideal is imperfect.

This method and these problems are well illustrated in a neuropsychological key program developed by several neuropsychologists (Russell, Neuringer, and Goldstein, 1970). They based their key on experience and expectancy concerning the performance of patients on tests of intelligence, achievement, learning/cognition, sensation/perception, and motor skills. Moreover, they focused their key on the absolute numerical scores or level of performance on the tests—rather than on the pattern of scores, special signs or other more elaborate methods of clinical inference.

Their key included several subprograms for (1) the identification of brain-damaged performances, (2) the likely localization of the cerebral problem, and (3) the momentum or process of the lesion (i.e., active vs. static). In initial studies, the key produced a significant degree of agreement with good clinical judges (Russell, Neuringer, and Goldstein, 1970). Cross-validation studies have confirmed these initial findings (Goldstein and Shelly, 1982; Anthony, Heaton, and Lehman, 1980), but the generalizability of the program to other settings may still be in question. Results on this aspect of the key program are presented below.

Geometric/Geographic Approaches

The key or taxonomic programs just described focus on rules for identifying a specimen or case within a pre-existing classificatory or diagnostic framework. In contrast, the geometric/geographic type of approach attempts to develop a "goodness of fit" for an individual case or specimen against some mathematical or graphic standard.

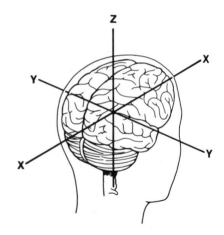

Fig. 1. A three-dimensional Cartesian coordinate system on which relationships between obtained and ideal cases may be superimposed in geometric/geographic approaches.

More specifically, this approach can be applied to brain-behavior relationships. Results from known *index or ideal* cases of brain damage or dysfunction can be programmed into a computer. In the case of the brain, the relative relation of the array of test results in relation to the three spatial coordinates of the brain (X,Y,Z) can be stored for reference. This can be seen in Fig. 1.

One neuropsychological program (Swiercinsky, 1978) used an approximation of this method to compare new cases against three-dimensional ideal which served as a standard. In an ideal program, each case could be mathematically compared by calculating a correlation coefficient between the standard index case and the unidentified one. Figure 2 illustrates this idea in rough form.

This method could be further refined using various statistics for "goodness of fit" between new unknown cases and identified standard ones whose brain-behavior significance is clear. Further sophistication would result from the introduction of a probablistic model for such fitting.

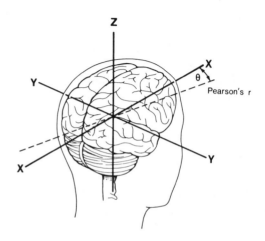

Fig. 2. An example of a correlation between variables and axes displayed on a Cartesian coordinate system.

The disadvantage of such systems rests in their advanced mathematical conception of the nervous system. In many instances, these "smart" calculation schemes—many of which could incorporate stunning graphic displays—are "dumb" with respect to fundamental problems and variability within any attempt to use such schemes for clinical and behavioral purposes. In the cognate area of clinical electrophysiology, this was certainly the case when very sophisticated systems were used to analyze evoked potentials or EEG spectra (Duffy, 1982; John et al., 1977). Such programs use incredibly powerful technology to verify incredibly simple features—done readily using simpler means and without computer hoopla. Other applications attempt to extract information from sinusoidal brain waves whose relation to behavior must be seen as controversial (John et al., 1977).

Attempts to Simulate the Cognitive Activity of the Clinician

Research on the process of clinical judgment has indicated that man-made reconstructions of the cognitive activity of the clinician should imitate as closely as possible the style and content of the clinician. In this respect, the computer program would be a "paramorphic representation" of this process, mirroring the clinician's activity. This particular point of view has a place in the wider and developing field of artificial intelligence. Put another way, the logic in such programs is derived directly from expert clinicians.

Two programs have been developed that attempt to simulate the clinician's activity. One program (Finkelstein, 1976), entitled BRAIN I, incorporates the four major ways in which neuropsychological clinicians examine test scores and results. The computer program looks at (1) *level of performance,* the absolute elevation and dispersion of individual test scores in relation to normative expectancies and within patient scatter of scores; (2) *left-right comparisons,* the direct comparison of sensory, perceptual, and motor performances presented or executed by the two sides of the body; (3) *pathognomonic signs,* special features or very poor single performances or specific clusters of test scores pointing clearly to the existence of discrete disorders (e.g., Broca's aphasia); and (4) *differential patterns,* larger arrays of profiles or score performances which are predictive of disease or disordered effects based upon previous research or experience.

These four methods are applicable to other areas of psychology and medicine and are incorporated in computer decision rules that result in computer-generated statements about the existence of the behavioral effects of cerebral dysfunction. Predictions are made concerning the locus, lateralization, and process of the suspected disease or disorder.

Given these ways of approaching the data, the ideal computer program for a clinician's study of relevant issues in the neuropsychological assessment would provide information in each of the intersecting cells seen in Fig. 3.

Close as this program is to the clinician's thinking, it ignores an essential component of the clinician's thought in the analysis of brain-behavior rela-

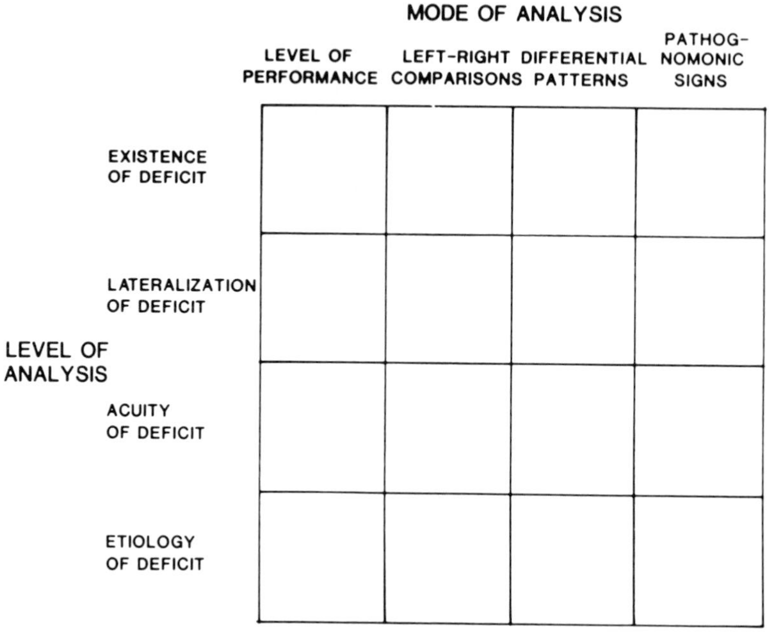

Fig. 3. Modes of analysis and issues to address in the assessment of the individual case.

tionships. This component rests in the specification of psychological *abilities* (e.g., short-term memory, abstraction, etc.) to be used in the model of the clinical reasoning process. That is, the translation from test score to cerebral dysfunction is a complex one—involving the clinician's assumptions about the relation between brain and behavior. While it may be inviting to omit this step as a shorthand in writing the computer program, such a tactic will fail to identify the scientific basis of the brain-behavior inference process. In turn, this will render the program developer less able to identify faulty *behavioral* assumptions and to improve program accuracy.

This lack of psychological ability specification is addressed by the Adams' Revised Program (ARP), another "expert" program which seeks to simulate the clinician's activity (Adams, 1975). It consists of logical-sequential statements which make interpretations about psychological abilities based upon comparison of certain subsets of test scores on an individual case. Patterns of *behavioral* performance are analyzed by the computer in search of abilities which may be suspect in relation to their known cerebral substrate.

This approach is different from some of the others described above in that it relies more upon the psychological aspects of test scores to arrive at predictions concerning cerebral status. The analytical scheme assumes that many psychological test scores are multidetermined and complex. A test complex enough to capture specific errors or inefficiency of the brain injured patient may also be multifactorial—involving attention, memory, or other high level skills unrelated to the ability measured by the task but essential for the task's completion. Even "simple" clinical tests of memory, seen in mental status examinations, can involve a number or component skills.

A Practical Test

Are there differences in the accuracy of the expert program approaches described above? We attempted to compare three of these programs: the Key method, BRAIN I, and ARP. These are the best available examples of the approaches to automated interpretation discussed in this chapter. Thirty older, right-handed patients (mean age, 60.7 years, S.D., 7.0 years) of average socioeconomic status and education (mean education, 11.6 years; S.D., 3.2 years) were carefully selected from HFH patients having transient ischemic attacks with clear lesion causation and confirmation. These patients were carefully screened to rule out secondary risk factors (e.g., excessive alcohol consumption, diabetic retinopathy) as well as for more frank pre-existing neurological disorder (e.g., head injury, etc.). Complete neuropsychological examinations were obtained on all patients and the results entered into each of the computer programs.

Some Results

The three computer systems were compared using the subject pool described above; results for determining the *presence* of brain damage in brain damaged individuals are shown in Fig. 4. The ARP was 92% correct for left hemisphere cases, followed by 67% correct response for BRAIN I, and 58% correct responses for the Key approach. For right hemisphere cases, BRAIN I identified 82%, followed by 73% for ARP. The Key determined some 45% correctly. Finally, both BRAIN I and the ARP were 86% correct in determining diffuse damage cases, and the Key Approach was 71% accurate for diffuse cases. Overall, ARP was correct for 82% of the cases, BRAIN I was correct for 75% of the cases, and the Key Approach was correct for 65% of the cases.

Figure 5 reveals that the Key Approach was accurate in determining *lateralization* for 14% of the left hemisphere cases, while BRAIN I identified 63% and the ARP 27%. In right hemisphere cases, a 20% rate was achieved by the Key, no hits were achieved by BRAIN I, and ARP identified 29%. For diffuse cases, the Key hit 60%, BRAIN I identified 50%, and the ARP identified 57%. Overall, the Key identified laterality in 29% of the cases, while BRAIN I and the ARP both accurately identified laterality in 38% of the predictions.

Some Conclusions about Automated Interpretation

Our results indicated that all three computer programs are inadequate as comprehensive neuropsychological "experts." While accurate decisions may be made concerning the presence of cerebral dysfunction, these results are in

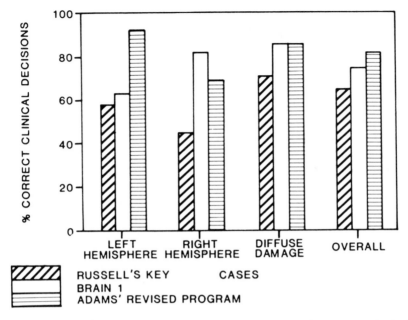

Fig. 4. The diagnostic accuracy of three automated interpretation programs in the identification of cerebral dysfunction in a sample of impaired patients.

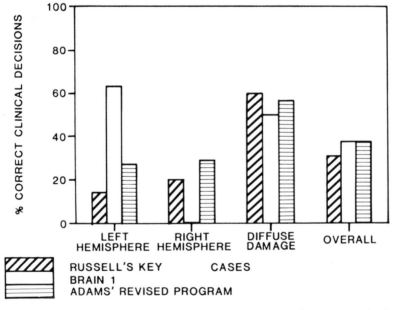

Fig. 5. The diagnostic accuracy of three automated interpretation programs in the identification of lesion lateralization in a sample of impaired patients.

agreement with others (Heaton et al., 1981) in that more subtle distinctions concerning lateralization are not made consistently by each of the present generations of algorithms in use.

The clinical value of any of these programs must be seen as limited. Each of the programs was offered by their authors as an experimental endeavor needing development. It is nonetheless interesting that the three programs produce comparable results using very different theoretical approaches. The Key is a quasi-taxonomic program, BRAIN I a comprehensive interpretative system modeling four proven modes of clinical neuropsychological inference, and ARP is an ability-based program dependent upon psychological constructs.

Various subtleties in lesion location, type, and severity might have served to handicap the computer programs. As Smith (1981) points out, these factors will often render hard and fast rules for lateralization and localization invalid. Expert programs in the future must attempt to tackle the interactions among these three variables and account for differences in the time course of the various classes of neurologic diseases.

The present set of results does not address the issue of "clinical vs. actuarial" judgment. Indeed, no study comparing current computerized interpretation systems and clinician reports can be represented as such a comparison. Actuarial methods imply reference to properly developed tables based upon experience and updated continuously to reflect change. No current method does this, and thus no strictly actuarial exemplar exists for comparison with the clinician in any area of medical computing.

While in need of development, these programs represent attempts to perform clinical decisions by set rules. Each program represents a different approach and objective; as many others could be conceived from obvious models or departure points in clinical neuropsychology. Future programs are likely to be more elegant. Yet, it may not be the case that programs need be more "sophisticated" to work. Rather, one may only need to successively eliminate unproductive rules and build in a feedback loop so that the program actually trains itself via re-entry of data and update of the data base from each case.

Some Closing Thoughts

Neuropsychological assessment can be facilitated by the thoughtful incorporation of computers to perform certain of its component tasks. Computers will not organize our professional lives, test our patients, do our research, or write our clinical reports. Rather, computers can be programmed to do mundane, time-consuming, extremely precise, and monotonous jobs far better than people. This will occur because the computer is likely to be more reliable in its performance—if it is given precise and unambiguous sequential instructions.

Several of the approaches to neuropsychology described in part I can be facilitated by computer usage. The approach described by Reitan (Chapter 1) has already been initially tested with respect to clinical interpretation. Others could benefit as well (e.g., manipulating stimulus features in the perseverative behavior investigation described in Chapter 3, by using color cathode ray tube (CRT) displays and graphics tablets).

Special problems of a neuropsychiatric nature described in part II (Chapters 6–20) can be better studied with the computer as well. Drug effects, attentional mechanisms, memory performance, and a variety of problems important in the assessment of patient problems are clearly more carefully measured using automated methods.

Finally, the degree to which the computer is integrated into neuropsychological assessment will depend greatly upon the type of work one does and the level of thought which accompanies its incorporation. Those interested in the use of computers in their clinical, teaching and research activities are well advised to investigate the realities first-hand.

REFERENCES

Adams, K. M. (1980a). In search of Luria's battery: A false start. *J. Consult. Clin. Psychol., 48,* 511–516.

Adams, K. M. (1980b). An end of innocence for behavioral neurology? Adams replies. *J. Consult. Clin. Psychol., 48,* 522–524.

Adams, K. M. (1975). Automated clinical interpretation of the neuropsychological test battery: An ability based approach (Doctoral dissertation, Wayne State University, 1974). Diss. Abstr. Int., 35, 6085B. (University Microfilms No. 75-13, 289).

Anthony, W. Z., Heaton, R. K., and Lehman, R. A. W. (1980). An attempt to cross-validate two actuarial systems for neuropsychological test interpretation. *J. Consult. Clin. Psychol., 48,* 317–326.

Duffy, F. H. (1982). Topographic display of evoked potentials: Clinical applications of brain electrical activity mapping (BEAM). *Ann. N.Y. Acad. Sci., 388,* 183–196.

Finkelstein, J. N. (1976). BRAIN: A computer program for interpretation of the Halstead-Reitan Neuropsychological Test Battery (Doctoral dissertation, Columbia University). Diss. Abstr. Int., 37, 5349B. (University Microfilms No. 77-8, 8864).

Goldberg, L. (1968). Simple models or simple processes? Some research on clinical judgments. *Am. Psychol., 23,* 483–496.

Goldstein, G., and Shelly, C. (1982). A further attempt to cross-validate the Russell, Neuringer, and Goldstein Neuropsychological Keys. *J. Consult. Clin. Psychol., 50,* 721–728.

Heaton, R. K., Grant, I., Anthony, W. Z., and Lehman, R. A. W. (1981). A comparison of clinical and automated interpretation of the Halstead-Reitan Battery. *J. Clin. Neuropsychol., 3,* 121–141.

John, E. R., Karmel, B. Z., Corning. W. C., Easton, P., Brown, D., Ahn, H., John, M., Harmony, T., Prichep, L., Toro, A., Gerson, I., Bartlett, F., Thatcher, R., Kaye, H., Valdes, E., and Schwartz, E. (1977). Neurometrics. *Science, 196,* 1393–1410.

Meehl, P. E. (1954). *Clinical vs. Statistical Predicton.* Minneapolis: University of Minnesota Press.

Meehl, P. E. (1973) *Psychodiagnosis: Selected Papers.* Minneapolis: University of Minnesota Press.

Rich, E. (1983). *Artificial Intelligence.* New York: McGraw-Hill.

Russell, E. W., Neuringer, C., and Goldstein, G. (1970). *Assessment of Brain Damage: A Neuropsychological Key Approach.* New York: Wiley-Interscience.

Sawyer, J. (1966). Measurement and prediction, clinical and statistical. *Psychol. Bull., 66,* 178–200.

Smith, A. (1981). Principles underlying human brain functions in neuropsychological sequelae of different neuropathological processes. In: S. Filskov and T. Boll, eds., *Handbook of Clinical Neuropsychology*. New York: Wiley.

Swiercinsky, D. (1978). Computerized SAINT: System for analysis and interpretation of neuropsychological tests. Presented at the annual meeting of the American Psychological Association, Toronto.

Wiggins, J. (1973). *Personality and Prediction: Principles of Personality Assessment*. Reading, Massachusetts: Addison-Wesley.

6

Differences in Neuropsychological Test Performance Associated with Age, Education, and Sex

ROBERT K. HEATON / IGOR GRANT / CHARLES G. MATTHEWS

It is well known that performances on neuropsychological tests are significantly related to the subject's ages, education and, for a few tests, sex (Parsons and Prigatano, 1978). The influence of demographic factors is even more apparent for neurologically normal individuals than for those who have cerebral disorders (Finlayson, Johnson, and Reitan, 1977; Reitan, 1955; Vega and Parsons, 1967). Thus, a common problem in clinical neuropsychological assessment is to determine whether a given set of test results is within normal limits, for example, for a 60-year-old with a grade-school education, or whether the results suggest brain pathology. Unfortunately, most tests have only a single set of norms that do not include any adjustment for the demographic characteristics of the individual being considered. Even for those tests that do have some data available concerning age and/or education effects, information concerning the effects of such factors in combination is lacking.

In this chapter we will examine the results of a large group of normal subjects on the WAIS and Halstead-Reitan Battery, considering in detail the relationships between test performances and demographic variables. First, however, a brief review of previous research will provide some perspective on these findings and will focus attention on several key issues.

Demographic Influences on WAIS Performance

Of the instruments considered in this chapter, by far the most is known about the WAIS with regard to the relationships between demographic factors and test performance (Matarazzo, 1972). The original WAIS standardization sample and subsequent cross-sectional findings reflect lower average performances for each successive age group tested after their mid-thirties. The correlations between age and total scores on the Performance and Verbal subtests are $-.53$ and $-.27$, respectively. These correlations reflect the fact that different abilities change at different rates, the "classic pattern" being that verbal skills and stored information hold up best while perceptual-integrative and psychomotor skills decline the most with advancing age (Botwinick, 1967).

The above *pattern* of age-related changes in intellectual functioning has been found in both cross-sectional and longitudinal studies of the WAIS. However, these two kinds of studies have differed in their conclusions about the *amount* of change that occurs. Longitudinal studies appear to underestimate age-related change because of a selective dropout of less able subjects over time, and possibly also because of practice effects occurring with repeated exposures to the same test. Cross-sectional studies by contrast, have tended to overestimate age effects by confounding these with educational/cultural differences among groups of subjects from different generations or "cohorts" (Botwinick, 1977). (Cohorts are groups of subjects who were born and entered as given culture at approximately the same time.) Since performance on the WAIS is even more correlated with educational attainment than with age (rs with WAIS total scores = .70 for education vs. − .42 for age), it is unfair to compare young subject groups with older less educated ones (Matarazzo, 1972). On the other hand, equating older and younger samples for education may reduce the representativeness of one or both samples because the norm for education has increased over time. Nevertheless, although a given education level may not be truly equivalent for different age-cohorts, it is clear that age and education should be considered together when evaluating WAIS results.

Demographic Influences on Halstead-Reitan Test Performance

There have been several studies relating age and/or education to the performance of neurologically normal subjects on Halstead's tests and the Trailmaking Test from the current Halstead-Reitan Battery (HRB) (Reitan and Davison, 1974). However, other tests that are typically given with the HRB have not been considered (Aphasia Screening Exam, Spatial Relations, Sensory-Perceptual Exam, Tactile Form Recognition Test, Hand Dynamometer, Grooved Pegboard). Also, no previous study of the HRB has tested a large sample of older subjects (over 60 years old) with varying educational backgrounds.

Performances on most of the individual tests in the HRB have shown significant negative relationships with age (Reitan, 1955, 1957; Vega and Parsons, 1967). Reitan (1955) warned that after the age of 45 many normals score in Halstead's brain-damaged range on the Impairment Index. More recently, Price, Fein and Feinberg (1980) studied a group of 49 retired school teachers (mean age, 72 years) and found that most of them scored in the impaired range according to the standard norms on the HRB. However, there was considerable variability in the number of subjects misclassified as brain-damaged by the different tests (range, 18%–90%), and on a prorated Average Impairment Rating approximately 44% of subjects in this elderly sample scored in the normal range for younger people. Thus, "impaired" performance on the HRB appears to occur with most but not all normal elderly subjects, and age-related deficits are more pronounced on some tests than on others. Reed and Reitan (1963) compared 29 measures from the HRB and Wechsler-Bellevue Intelligence Scale in terms of the degrees to which they discriminated an older from a younger subject group. The tests that showed the greatest age effects were characterized as most dependent upon "immediate adaptive ability," and in general are the same tests that tend to be most sensitive to cerebral lesions (e.g., Category Test, Tactual Performance Test).

There has been less research concerning the relationship between educational attainment and HRB performance. Vega and Parsons (1967) administered the Halstead tests to 50 medical-surgical controls, and found significant positive correlations between years of education and adequacy of performance on five of the seven test measures. Although some measures were more strongly related to age and some to education, correlations of equal magnitude were obtained between the Halstead Impairment Index and both age $(r = -.57)$ and education $(r = .56)$. Finlayson et al. (1977) compared HRB performances of normals at three educational levels $(ns = 17)$. Significant education effects were found on the Category Test, Trailmaking Test, Speech-Sounds Perception Test, and Seashore Rhythm Test, but not on the Tactual Performance Test or Finger Tapping Test.

A question addressed in several previous studies is whether the rate of age-related cognitive decline is related to subjects' initial level of functioning or socioeconomic status (education, occupation). In reviewing this literature, Botwinick (1967) noted that cross-sectional studies have provided some inconsistent evidence that subjects with lower initial ability and lower occupations show greater age-related impairment on some tests. The available longitudinal studies do not support this hypothesis. However, these studies are limited by the use of a restricted range of tests over relatively brief age ranges, and by the above-mentioned selective attrition of initially less able subjects (Botwinick, 1967). Birren and Morrison (1961) found no significant age-by-education interaction effects using data from the WAIS standardization sample, but the possibility of such interactions has not been studied with the HRB.

Research comparing males and females on ability tests has found no difference in general intelligence, although there do appear to be sex differences in a few specific ability areas (see reviews by Buffery and Gray, 1972 and Maccoby and Jacklin, 1974). Males have tended to do better on tests that involve manipulating spatial relationships, quantitative skills, and physical strength, whereas females have shown an advantage on tests of certain verbal abilities. Sex differences on the WAIS subtests tend to be inconsequential because Wechsler omitted or counterbalanced items that favored the males or females in his standardization sample (Matarazzo, 1972). We are aware of no previous research that has explored sex differences on the HRB. Russell, Neuringer and Goldstein (1970) did provide separate norms for males and females on the Finger Tapping Test, but they were based upon clinical estimates rather than empirical findings. The Hand Dynamometer is the only other test in the expanded HRB that is known to show sex differences; i.e., males have greater grip strength (Clement, 1974).

Questions Remaining Unanswered

The above review suggests several questions that will be addressed in the present chapter. First, how do performances on the various tests in the battery relate to age and education when high and low values of these demographic factors are adequately represented in the subject sample? Which tests are more sensitive to age effects and which appear to be more dependent upon educational attainment? Are there any significant age-by-education interaction effects on tests in the battery and, if so, are they consistent with the hypothesis that better-educated groups show less age-related decline in neuropsychological functioning? How well or how poorly do the standard HRB norms work for groups of normal subjects at different age and education levels? Finally, which tests in the battery show significant sex differences, and are these differences large enough to necessitate developing separate norms for males and females?

Halstead-Reitan Normative Data Pool

To address these questions we merged results of neuropsychological testing of groups of normal controls accumulated at our respective laboratories into a Halstead-Reitan Normative Data Pool.

Subjects

Our subjects consisted of all normal controls for whom there was complete test data available at the neuropsychology laboratories of the University of Colorado ($N = 207$), University of California at San Diego ($N = 181$), and University of Wisconsin ($N = 165$) Medical Schools. None of the subjects had any history of neurological illness, significant head trauma, or substance abuse. There were 356 males and 197 females. Forty (7.2%) were left-handed and 513 were right-handed. Their ages ranged from 15 to 81 years, with a mean of 39.3 (S.D. = 17.5) years. Their years of education ranged from zero (no formal education) to 20 (M.D./Ph.D.), with a mean of 13.3 (S.D. = 3.4) years.

Some planned analyses called for evaluating age and education effects across broad ranges of these variables, as well as assessing age-by-education interaction effects. For these analyses subjects were divided into three age categories (<40 years, 40–59 years, ≥60 years) and three education categories (<12 years, 12–15 years, ≥16 years). Respectively, the total ns for the three age categories are 319, 134, and 100, for the three education categories were 132, 249, and 172. The ns for the nine age/education subgroups were over 25 in all cells except the high age/high education category ($N = 17$).

In order to assess sex differences in neuropsychological test performance, males and females were individually matched within five years in age and within two years in education. This resulted in 177 matched pairs. The mean ages of the two groups were virtually identical (36.6 for males, 36.7 for females), as were the means for education (13.2 for males, 13.1 for females).

Neuropsychological Testing

All subjects were tested by trained technicians, and all were rated as having put forth adequate effort on their evaluations. The tests given were the Wechsler Adult Intelligence Scale (WAIS; Wechsler, 1955) and an expanded Halstead-Reitan Battery (HRB). The latter battery has been described elsewhere (Reitan and Davison, 1974), and included the Category Test, Tactual Performance Test (Time, Memory and Location components), Seashore Rhythm Test, Speech-Sounds Perception Test, Aphasia Screening Exam, Trailmaking Test, Spatial Relations Assessment, Sensory-Perceptual Exam, Tactile Form Recognition Test, Finger Tapping Test, Hand Dynamometer, and Grooved Pegboard Test.

The scores used for the WAIS subtests were regular scaled scores (not age-corrected). The Russell et al. (1970) scoring system was used for the Aphasia Screening Exam, Spatial Relations, Sensory-Perceptual Exam and Average Impairment Rating. In addition, the cutoff scores provided in the Russell et al. (1970) book were used to determine how many subjects in the different age and education categories were correctly classified as normal by the Average Impairment Rating and each of its component test measures.

Results

The first step in assessing age and education effects was to compute product-moment correlations with each test variable. Previously it had been determined that partialling out either age or education did not significantly affect correlations between test scores and the other demographic variable.

AGE EFFECTS. Statistically significant ($p<.05$) correlations were obtained between age and all test variables except WAIS Vocabulary and the Hand Dynamometer. However, some small and clinically trivial correlations were "significant" because of the large n. All correlations were in the direction of poorer performances being associated with older age. Figure 1 shows for each test measure the percent of variance accounted for by age (i.e., R^2).

Among the Wechsler subtests, substantial age effects are apparent on Digit Symbol and Picture Arrangement, whereas age showed little or no relationship with performance on Vocabulary, Information and Comprehension. The rank order of correlations between age and scores on the various Wechsler subtests is virtually identical to rankings reported in other studies of the WAIS (Botwinick, 1967, p. 9).

In the right side of Figure 1 it is apparent that performances on several

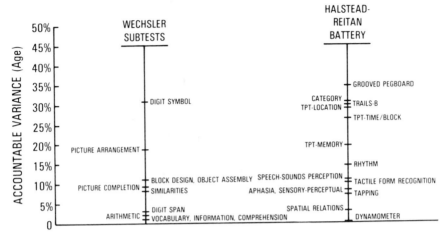

Fig. 1. Percentage of test variance accounted for by age.

HRB tests are strongly related to age. This is particularly true for measures of psychomotor speed, conceptual ability, flexibility of thinking, and incidental memory. On the other hand, scores on HRB tests of language skills and simple sensory and motor abilities show relatively weak associations with age.

EDUCATION EFFECTS. Statistically significant correlations were obtained between education and scores on all WAIS and HRB test measures. All correlations, even those involving measures of simple motor and sensory functions, showed better test performance being associated with higher previous educational attainment. Figure 2 shows the percent variance in each test measure accounted for by education (i.e., R^2).

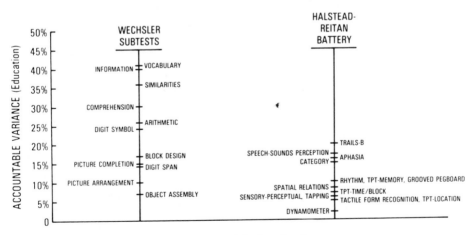

Fig. 2. Percentage of test variance accounted for by education.

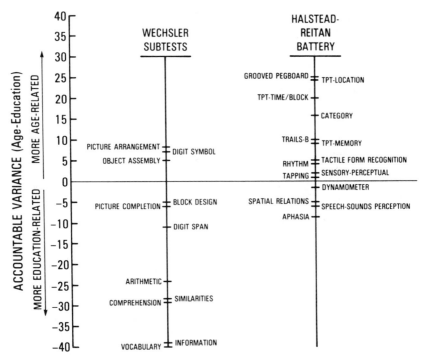

Fig. 3. Difference in percentage of test variance accounted for by age vs. education (i.e., age variance minus education variance).

As expected, and in contrast to the results shown previously for age, education level is most strongly related to scores on the WAIS Verbal subtests. Education tends to be less related to scores on the HRB, but within the latter battery the highest correlations are with tests of language skills, conceptual ability, and cognitive flexibility.

TESTS SHOWING GREATEST AGE OR EDUCATION SENSITIVITY. Figure 3 shows for each test measure the difference between the amount of variance accounted for by age versus education. Tests listed above the middle horizontal line are more age-related and those below the line are more education-related. In general, WAIS subtests tend to fall below the line and most HRB tests are above it. Also, not surprisingly, within both batteries tests of verbal skills and past accumulated knowledge are more education-related, whereas nonverbal tests of psychomotor speed and/or new problem solving are more age-related.

THE INTERACTION BETWEEN AGE AND EDUCATION. Table 1 presents the test score means for the three age groups and three education groups defined above, and summarizes the results of the 3×3 ANOVAs performed on all test measures. Inspection of the group means across age and education levels reveals consistent advantages for younger groups and better educated groups. The ANOVAs produced age and education main effects that are in agreement with the results of the correlation analyses discussed above; that is, the tests previously found to be more age-related or more education-related are similarly classified by these analyses. In addition, there are several significant age-by-education interaction effects. These occurred on both HRB summary measures as well as on certain individual tests in the WAIS and HRB.

As noted above, the previous literature contains several speculations and a few empirical findings regarding possible interactions between subjects' baseline characteristics and their age-related decline in neuropsychological functioning. Based upon these reports, we might look for three possible patterns of age-by-education interaction effects in our data: (1) subjects with most education show less age-related impairment; (2) subjects in the lowest education group show more age-related impairment; and (3) a "regression toward the mean" occurs, with less difference being seen between older groups at different education levels than between younger groups at different education levels (similar to the pattern found in a WAIS longitudinal study by Eisdorfer and Wilke, 1973). It should be noted that these three patterns are not mutually exclusive; in fact, the data on several test variables are consistent with pattern (1) and/or (2) across the first two age levels, but fit pattern (3) between the second and third age levels.

To explore the possible patterns of interaction effects, mean test scores of subgroups at each education level were plotted across the three age levels (see Figs. 4 through 9). It is tempting to consider this type of graph to be a cross-sectional view of how groups at each education level may change with advancing age. However, it must be recognized that these curves do not reflect *change* in any direct sense, as each point on the graph reflects the performance of a separate group that was tested only once.

Before considering test variables that have significant age-by-education interaction effects, we plotted the results on two variables that are known to show little change in older age groups. Figure 4 summarizes the data for our nine age/education subgroups on the WAIS Vocabulary and Information subtests. The curves for each education level fit the expected pattern of no significant age-related decrease in test performance. Furthermore, the comparability of the three age subgroups within education levels suggest that the subgroups are fairly well matched in terms of previously-learned information, or "crystallized" intelligence (Cattell, 1963; Horn and Cattell, 1966).

Figure 5 plots the mean scores of these same subgroups on two WAIS subtests that have significant age-by-education interaction effects. On Picture Arrangement (Fig. 5a), the results across the first two age levels suggest more age-related impairment for the least educated subgroup (i.e., the subgroup with less than 12 years of education that is in the 40–59 year age category). This is consistent with pattern (2) above. For the Block Design subtest (Fig. 5b), the curves across the first two age levels are more consistent with pattern (1); that

Table 1. Summary of age, education, and age-education interaction effects for WAIS subtests and Halstead-Reitan Battery

	Means for age subgroups			Age main effects	Means for education subgroups			Education main effects	Age by education interactions
	<40 years (N=319)	40–59 years (N=134)	60+ years (N=100)	F	<12 years (N=132)	12–15 years (N=249)	16+ years (N=172)	F	F
Wechsler Subtests (scaled scores)									
Information	12.2	12.2	11.0	n.s.	10.1	11.5	14.1	111.0[b]	n.s.
Comprehension	12.8	12.6	11.7	n.s.	10.4	12.2	14.7	83.3[b]	2.6[d]
Arithmetic	11.9	11.9	10.5	n.s.	9.7	11.5	13.4	54.7[b]	n.s.
Similarities	12.5	11.5	10.2	11.9[b]	9.7	11.6	13.9	94.6[b]	n.s.
Digit Span	11.5	10.8	9.9	3.6[d]	10.0	10.9	12.4	24.4[b]	n.s.
Vocabulary	12.2	12.3	11.3	n.s.	9.7	11.7	14.3	148.2[b]	n.s.
Digit Symbol	12.0	9.8	7.4	93.4[b]	8.2	10.7	12.5	57.0[b]	n.s.
Picture Completion	12.0	10.5	9.1	14.9[b]	9.2	10.8	11.4	23.0[b]	2.8[d]
Block Design	11.8	11.3	8.9	29.2[b]	9.6	11.1	12.4	25.4[b]	2.6[d]
Picture Arrangement	10.7	9.8	7.5	50.7[b]	8.6	10.0	10.7	9.8[b]	4.1[c]
Object Assembly	11.2	10.7	8.7	22.8[b]	9.5	10.7	11.5	8.4[b]	n.s.
Halstead-Reitan Battery									
Halstead Impairment Index	0.18	0.32	0.64	146.6[b]	0.48	0.27	0.19	23.2[b]	4.6[b]
Average Impairment Rating	0.75	1.07	1.76	172.1[b]	1.45	0.97	0.73	48.7[b]	2.9[d]
Category Test (errors)	29.3	42.6	66.4	92.8[b]	53.8	38.6	28.9	19.9[b]	4.0[c]
Trailmaking-B (sec)	58.5	78.3	116.8	81.8[b]	102.2	69.7	57.9	29.9[b]	3.7[c]
TPT-Total Time (min/blk)	0.39	0.50	0.85	82.8[b]	0.64	0.47	0.43	n.s.	n.s.
TPT-Memory	8.1	7.5	6.2	49.7[b]	6.9	7.7	8.0	7.8[b]	3.8[d]
TPT-Location	5.3	4.0	2.0	88.9[b]	3.6	4.4	5.0	n.s.	3.0[d]
Seashore Rhythm (correct)	26.9	26.1	23.8	27.6[b]	24.6	26.4	27.0	11.4[b]	n.s.
Speech-Sounds Perception (errors)	4.3	5.0	8.4	22.7[b]	7.3	5.3	3.5	17.0[b]	3.0[d]
Aphasia (errors)	2.9	3.7	5.9	9.7[b]	6.0	3.5	2.1	24.2[b]	n.s.
Spatial Relations (errors)	2.6	2.6	3.2	6.0[c]	3.2	2.7	2.4	11.1[b]	n.s.
Sensory-Perceptual (errors)	3.5	3.9	8.3	20.9[b]	7.0	4.1	3.0	9.4[b]	n.s.
Tactile Form Recognition (sec)	18.0	20.8	23.8	20.5[b]	21.9	19.8	17.9	5.2[c]	n.s.
Tapping Dominant Hand[a]	53.6	52.8	47.9	12.0[b]	48.7	53.3	53.7	9.3[b]	n.s.

	<40 years	40–59 years	60+ years		<12 years	12–15 years	16+ years		
Tapping Nondominant Hand[a]	48.8	47.5	43.5	10.4[b]	44.0	48.1	49.0	9.2[b]	n.s.
Dynamometer Dominant Hand (kg)[a]	51.4	51.7	44.3	10.2[b]	47.1	51.1	51.5	n.s.	n.s.
Dynamometer Nondominant Hand (kg)[a]	47.8	46.8	40.5	11.0[b]	43.4	47.1	47.1	n.s.	n.s.
Pegboard Dominant Hand (sec)	61.1	68.1	85.1	95.0[b]	74.6	66.0	62.3	6.2[c]	n.s.
Pegboard Nondominant Hand (sec)	65.7	74.7	90.0	76.9[b]	79.3	71.3	67.6	3.5[d]	n.s.

[a] Results reported on Tapping and Dynamometer are only for males because there were large sex differences; the Ns for the six respective age and education subgroups are 190, 95, 71, 90, 166, 100.

[b] p < .001 [c] p < .01 [d] p < .05

Table 2. Percent of subjects in six age and education subgroups who are classified as normal by Russell et al. (1970) criteria

	Age subgroups			Education subgroups			Total (N = 553)
	<40 years (N = 319)	40–59 years (N = 134)	60+ years (N = 100)	<12 years (N = 132)	12–15 years (N = 249)	16+ years (N = 172)	
Average impairment rating	96.9	84.3	39.0	58.3	90.0	93.0	83.4
Category Test	89.0	70.2	31.0	49.2	76.7	89.0	74.0
Trailmaking-B	91.5	74.6	33.0	54.6	79.9	89.5	76.9
TPT-Total Time	87.5	69.4	23.0	53.7	75.9	78.5	71.4
TPT-Memory	97.8	90.3	69.0	78.8	93.2	96.5	90.8
TPT-Location	65.5	41.8	9.0	35.6	49.0	61.1	49.5
Seashore Rhythm	84.3	75.4	52.0	61.2	77.5	85.5	76.3
Speech-Sounds Perception	89.6	82.1	55.0	66.7	80.7	94.2	81.5
Aphasia Exam	86.5	81.3	68.0	66.7	81.9	93.6	81.9
Spatial Relations	81.8	86.6	75.0	73.5	81.5	88.4	81.7
Sensory-Perceptual Exam	95.6	94.8	79.0	84.1	93.6	97.1	92.4
Tapping, Worse Hand (Males)	75.8	66.0	33.8	41.1	72.3	73.0	64.6
Tapping, Worse Hand (Females)	53.5	28.2	13.8	21.4	42.2	55.6	42.6
Digit Symbol	91.5	75.4	42.0	51.5	82.7	93.6	78.7

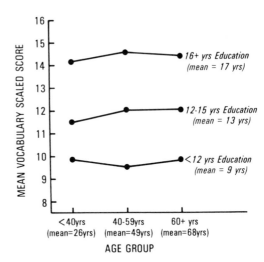

Fig. 4a. Results of groups in nine age/education categories on WAIS Vocabulary test.

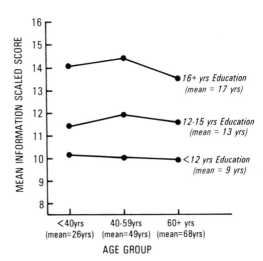

Fig. 4b. Results of groups in nine age/education categories on WAIS Information test.

is, they suggest less age-related impairment for the subgroup with 16+ years of education. On both of these subtests, however, the curves from the second to the third age level fit pattern (3) (less difference between education subgroups at the older age level).

For HRB measures it is possible to consider not only subgroup mean scores, as before, but also the percent of subjects in each age/education category who performed "normally" according to the standard test score cutoffs that were developed with younger subjects. Thus, the remaining figures will contain two graphs for the same variable: subgroup mean scores will be plotted on the left (part A), whereas the percent of subjects retaining normal abilities (by younger standards) will be plotted on the right (part B).

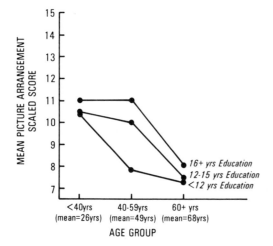

Fig. 5a. Results of groups in nine age/education categories on WAIS Picture Arrangement.

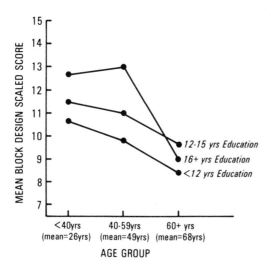

Fig. 5b. Results of groups in nine age/education categories on WAIS Block Design.

Figures 6 and 7 display this information for the two HRB summary scores. For both the Halstead Impairment Index and the Average Impairment Rating, high scores reflect greater impairment. Of course, high scores on part B of each figure (showing percent normal subjects) indicate *less* impairment. Except for this difference in scaling, the patterns shown by the two kinds of graphs are very similar. However, the plots of percent subjects classified as normal show the significant age-by-education interaction effects even more dramatically. For each summary measure, pattern (2) is apparent between the first two age levels (less educated subjects having more age-related impairment), whereas the curves between the second and third age level fit pattern (3) (less difference between education subgroups at the older age level).

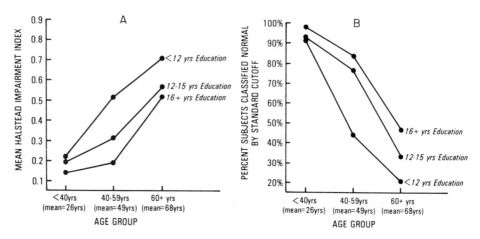

Fig. 6. (a) Results of groups in nine age/education categories on Halstead Impairment Index. (b) Results of groups in nine age/education categories: percentage classified as normal by Halstead Impairment Index.

The last two figures show the same information for two tests in the HRB, the Category Test, and the Trailmaking Test. Again the curves fit pattern (2) between the first two age levels and pattern (3) between the second and third age level.

The graphs to the right in Figs. 6 through 9 (i.e., part B) all show that the standard cutoff scores for these test measures are adequate for all education subgroups at the first age level. At the second age level the cutoffs misclassify only a few more normal subjects in the two higher education categories, but misclassify the majority of subjects in the lower education subgroup. Finally, although a significant *minority* of subjects in the oldest subgroups still performed at a level that would be considered normal for a young adult, it is apparent that the standard cutoffs are not appropriate as norms for older subjects.

Table 2 shows the adequacy of the standard HRB cutoff scores for the total subject group, and also for subjects at our three age levels and three education levels. In general, the norms for most test measures appear to be adequate at the lower age levels and upper education levels. However, on HRB measures that have significant age-by-education interaction effects, Figures 6 through 9 indicate that most middle-aged normal subjects who failed to complete high school will be misclassified as having impaired brain function. Also, although there are important differences among individual test measures listed in Table 2, the standard cutoffs for most HRB tests appear to misclassify too many normals in the lowest education and highest age levels. Our data further suggest that the Russell et al. (1970) standards for TPT-Location and the Finger Tapping Test are too stringent in general, even for young subjects who have completed high school or college. Finally, the clinically derived sex cor-

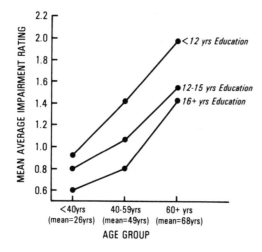

Fig. 7a. Results of groups in nine age/education categories: mean average impairment rating.

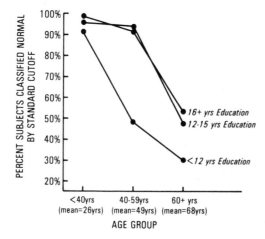

Fig. 7b. Results of groups in nine age/education categories: percentage classified as normal by average impairment rating.

rection on the Finger Tapping Test is not sufficient and should be made more lenient for females.

SEX EFFECTS. T-tests for paired samples were used to compare results of our matched male and female groups on all WAIS and HRB measures. There was virtually no difference between these groups on any WAIS I.Q. value or HRB summary score. Thus, the males and females were comparable with respect to general intelligence and overall neuropsychological functioning. However, statistically significant differences were obtained on a few of the individual tests in the battery. As expected, the males did much better ($p < .001$) with each hand on tests of motor speed (Finger Tapping Test) and grip strength (Hand Dynamometer). On Finger Tapping and respective dominant-hand and non-dominant-hand means were 51.6 and 46.9 for males, and 46.4 and 42.7 for

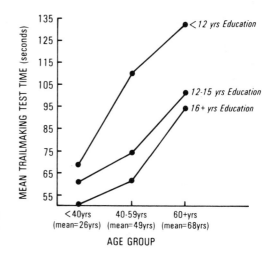

Fig. 8a. Results of groups in nine age/education categories on Trail-making Test (part B).

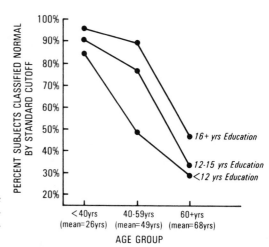

Fig. 8b. Results of groups in nine age/education categories: percentage classified as normal by Trail-making Test (part B).

females. On the Hand Dynamometer these means were 44.5 and 35.1 for males, and 40.9 and 32.3 for females. Significant differences also occurred on the Tactual Performance Test and the Aphasia Screening Exam; these were not anticipated, but are consistent with the general psychological literature on sex differences in normals. Males did significantly better ($p < .05$) on the TPT-Total Time score (13.5 minutes, vs. 15.6 minutes for females). However, the females showed a significant advantage ($p < .001$) on the Aphasia Screening Exam; their mean error score was 2.7, vs. 4.0 for males. Finally, there was a statistically significant ($p < .05$) but clinically trivial difference on the WAIS Comprehension subtest (mean scores were 12.7 for females and 12.1 for males).

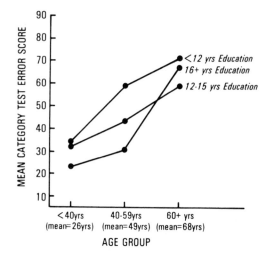

Fig. 9a. Results of groups in nine age/education categories on Halstead Category Test.

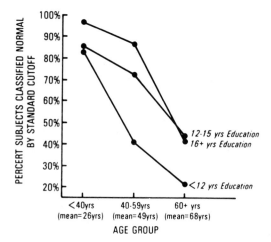

Fig. 9b. Results of groups in nine age/education categories: percentage classified as normal on Halstead Category Test.

Implications

The relationships we found between age and the various test measures are consistent with previously reported results for the WAIS and Halstead tests. Among the WAIS subtests, Digit Symbol and Picture Arrangement consistently show the strongest correlations with age (Botwinick, 1967). These are complex tests requiring efficiency in perceptual-motor activities, new learning, and conceptualization of social cause–effect or part–whole relationships. Of the Halstead instruments, performance on the Category Test of new concept formation was most age-related in our study as well as in studies by Vega and Parsons (1967) and Reed and Reitan (1963). The latter authors also rated the

Category Test as being the one most dependent upon "immediate adaptive ability," and in neuropsychological studies this typically has been the most sensitive HRB test to cerebral dysfunction. It is interesting to note that the Category Test is untimed and is not dependent upon speed of response. TPT-Location performance (a measure of incidental memory) also is untimed, and the other HRB measures that are most age-related require significant cognitive and perceptual-motor ability as well as speed (i.e., Trailmaking Test, TPT-Time, Grooved Pegboard). On the other hand, the most "pure" measures of motor speed and perceptual ability in the HRB are among the *least* age-related tests (Finger Tapping Test, Sensory-Perceptual Exam). Doppelt and Wallace (1955) found also that age differences on the WAIS were not due to the speed factor, as the older subjects still did significantly worse when they were examined without time limits.

Considering the entire group of tests in our study, by far the most education-related scores were on the Wechsler Verbal subtests (excluding Digit Span). These tests depend heavily on past accumulated knowledge and tend to be least sensitive to effects of normal aging and cerebral dysfunction. By contrast, the HRB tests require little previously acquired knowledge, and all measures on this battery show relatively modest relationships with education (Fig. 2). As in the previous studies of the Halstead tests, TPT and Finger Tapping performance showed particularly weak relationships with education level. This was also true of the added tests of elementary motor and sensory skills (Hand Dynamometer, Tactile Form Recognition, Sensory-Perceptual Exam).

Our findings regarding tests that are more age-related vs. education-related are consistent with the distinctions Cattell and Horn (1966) have made between "fluid" vs. "crystallized" intelligence. Crystallized intelligence is measured by tests of knowledge and skills that were acquired in previous learning experiences. Examples of such instruments are the WAIS Vocabulary and Information subtests. According to the theory, crystallized intelligence develops rapidly during the first 20 years of life and then levels off; subsequently it remains relatively stable for decades, although it may rise slightly due to the individual's continuing learning experiences. By contrast, fluid intelligence is considered most dependent upon biological factors, and more specifically upon the development and continued integrity of the central nervous system. This form of intelligence is measured by tasks requiring learning, conceptual, and problem-solving operations within the context of novel situations (i.e., situations in which stored knowledge and previously acquired skills are of little use). Speed of response and spatial "visualization" skills may be required in certain tests of fluid intelligence, but are not integral parts of this ability factor; in fact, these are considered separate ability factors (Horn and Cattell, 1966). The concept of fluid intelligence is similar to Halstead's (1951) description of "biological intelligence," which his test battery was designed to measure. Good examples of fluid intelligence tests in our battery are the Category Test, the TPT, and the WAIS Performance subtests. According to the theory and data presented by Horn and Cattell (1966), fluid intelligence develops due to biological maturation and reaches its peak in the late teens or early 20s. Then this form of intelligence is expected to decline at a rate that is dependent upon various accumulating insults to the CNS that occur during the life span of the individual. Horn and Cattell do not attribute deterioration in fluid intelligence to age *per se*, but to the effects of illness and injuries that tend to be more prevalent in older than in younger groups. Hence, the correlations found between age and fluid intelligence are sizeable but do not approach unity, and it is possible for healthy older *individuals* to show very little decline in cognitive functioning.

Several research findings are consistent with the view that decline in fluid intelligence is caused by CNS changes that are more prevalent in older subject groups but not due to age per se. A recent cross-sectional study of elderly retirement community residents found that age was significantly related to both neuropsychological performance and the degree of cerebral atrophy demonstrated on CT scans; in each age group, however, there was considerable variability in brain atrophy and test performance. Furthermore, the CT scan results made some contribution, independently of age, to the prediction of cognitive impairment in these subjects (Earnest et al., 1979). The Duke longitudinal study found that worsening WAIS performance in older subjects was associated with high blood pressure, chronic illness (generally considered), slowing of the EEG, and decreased cerebral blood flow. Considering the latter findings, Wang (1973, p. 105) concluded ". . . that intellectual function of healthy elderly persons in the community is dependent to a great extent on the status of their brain(s)."

Our results on several test measures suggest different patterns of age-related cognitive decline for subject groups having different educational levels (Figs. 5 through 9). Groups at the lowest education level (mean, 9 years) gave evidence of greater cognitive decline between the young and middle-age periods. However, the better-educated groups tended to "catch up" by the later age period, then showing levels of impairment that were not much different from the group with least education. The pattern observed across our first two age levels is consistent with some early cross-sectional findings (Botwinick, 1967), but not with the WAIS findings of the Duke longitudinal study (Eisdorfer and Wilke, 1973). The latter study found evidence of "regression toward the mean"; i.e., greater decline in WAIS performance by subjects with higher baseline I.Q.s. It is interesting to note, however, that all subjects in the Duke project were over 60 years old, and that our cross-sectional data also would be consistent with such "regression" at the 60+ age level. It is only at the middle age level that our better educated subjects showed less age-related impairment. And again, these age-by-education interaction effects in the present study occurred only on certain test measures (HRB summary scores and some individual tests, mostly of the fluid intelligence variety).

There are several possible explanations of why the age-by-education interaction effects might occur. First, subjects with lower education and lower socioeconomic status may tend to have less optimal health care. This could result in a higher prevalence during middle age of health problems that might compromise brain function (e.g., high blood pressure). It might also be that people in the higher education groups tended to have more adequate brains to begin with, and as a consequence were more able to keep functioning at a relatively high level despite the same absolute losses in CNS efficiency. Both of the foregoing speculations would have some difficulty explaining the greater age-related cognitive impairment shown by our higher education subgroups between the second and third age levels (i.e., their "regression toward the mean"). A third possible explanation is that subjects in the lower education subgroups tend to have less intellectually stimulating jobs and general life styles, so that their fluid intelligence declines faster because of disuse. For the same reason the better educated subjects might then "catch up" during their retirement years. This is an attractive hypothesis because it suggests the possibility of using intellectually stimulating activities to help sustain fluid intelligence in old age.

Although it is most unlikely that any single explanation can account for different patterns of age-related decline among groups of people, the above factors (and others) might combine to produce the kind of age-by-education interaction effects we observed. In any event, our results suggest that the outcome of research concerning such interaction effects is affected by the age ranges studied as well as the kinds of subjects and tests that are used.

Before leaving the discussion of age-effects and age-by-education interaction effects on test performance, it is again noted that our data are cross-sectional in nature. They demonstrate age-related (or age-cohort) differences in abilities, but perhaps not age-related *changes* in abilities. It is generally accepted that longitudinal studies are needed to establish that changes have occurred. On the other hand, there are two considerations that bear on the degree to which the age-effects in our study reflect generational differences vs. age-related changes in abilities. One has been mentioned in the Results section above: all three age subgroups at each of our education levels had similar scores on the WAIS Vocabulary and Information subtests. Thus, there does not appear to be any difference among age-cohorts in crystallized intelligence. It seems reasonable to assume that generational differences would be more likely to affect crystallized intelligence (being more dependent upon cultural and educational experiences) than fluid intelligence. Yet it was tests of fluid intelligence that showed the greatest age-effects and age-by-education interaction effects. A second point bearing on the interpretation of the present results is that ours is not the first cross-sectional study of age-effects on the Wechsler and Halstead tests; similar differences were found between younger and older groups that were tested at least 20 years ago (Reitan, 1955; Reed and Reitan, 1963; Wechsler, 1955). If these repeatedly observed differences in test performances were generational differences that were only coincidentally related to age, then this would mean that each successive generation has had substantially better cognitive functioning. This does not seem plausible in general, and is especially unlikely to have occurred for fluid intelligence and not crystallized intelligence (again, tests of the latter abilities have shown little or no age-effect in cross-sectional studies). Also, clinical experience indicates that the same HRB norms for younger people have been appropriate for decades, suggesting that fluid abilities have not tested substantially better in successive generations.

For the above reasons it seems likely to us that the age-effects found in this and other cross-sectional studies of the HRB primarily reflect true change in most subjects' abilities with advancing age. Even if this is wrong, however, and the findings actually represent innate or culturally based differences among successive generations, it would be important to understand these differences so that they could be considered in clinical neuropsychological assessment.

Summary

A single set of HRB norms cannot be used for subjects at different age and education levels. Most test measures show significant age and education effects, so both factors must be considered when determining whether an individual's performance was normal or abnormal.

Our results on most HRB tests do not suggest that separate norms are required for males and females. However, more lenient norms must be used for females on the Finger Tapping Test and Hand Dynamometer. Also, smaller corrections for sex may be justified on the Time component of the Tactual Performance Test (perhaps a two minute advantage for females) and the Aphasia Screening Exam (a one or two point advantage for males).

REFERENCES

Birren, J. E., and Morrison, D. F. (1961). Analysis of WAIS subtests in relation to age and education. *J. Gerontol. 16*, 363–369.
Botwinick, J. (1967). *Cognitive Processes in Maturity and Old Age.* New York: Springer Publishing Co., Inc.
Botwinick, J. (1977). Intellectual abilities. In J. E. Birren and K. W. Schaie, eds., *Handbook of the Psychology of Aging.* New York: Van Nostrand Reinhold Co., pp. 123–157.
Buffery, A. W. H., and Gray, J. A. (1972). Sex differences in the development of spatial and linguistic skills. In: C. Ounsted and D. C. Taylor, eds., *Gender Differences: Their Ontogency and Significance.* Baltimore: Williams & Wilkins.
Cattell, R. B. (1963). Theory of fluid and crystallized intelligence: A critical experiment. *J. Ed. Psychol. 54,* 1–22.
Clement, F. J. (1974). Longitudinal and cross-sectional assessments of age changes in physical strength as related to sex, social class, and mental ability. *J. Gerontol. 29,* 423–429.
Doppelt, J. E., and Wallace, W. L. (1955). Standardization of the Wechsler Adult Intelligence Scale for older persons. *Journal of Abnormal and Social Psychology, 51,* 312–330.
Earnest, M. P., Heaton, R. K., Wilkinson, W. E., and Manke, W. F. (1979). Cortical atrophy, ventricular enlargement and intellectual impairment in the aged. *Neurology, 29,* 1138–1143.
Eisdorfer, C., and Wilke, F. (1973). Intellectual changes with advancing age. In: L. E. Jarvik,

C. Eisdorfer, and J. E. Blum, eds., *Intellectual Functioning in Adults*. New York: Springer Publishing Company, pp. 21–29.

Finlayson, M. A. J., Johnson, K. A., and Reitan, R. M. (1977). Relationship of level of education to neuropsychological measures in brain-damaged and non-brain-damaged adults. *J. Consult. Clin. Psychol. 45*, 536–542.

Halstead, W. C. (1951). Biological intelligence. *J. Personality, 20*, 118–130.

Horn, J. L., and Cattell, R. B. (1966). Age differences in primary mental ability factors. *J. Gerontol. 21*, 210–220.

Maccoby, E. E., and Jacklin, C. N. (1974). *The Psychology of Sex Differences*. Stanford, California: Stanford University Press.

Matarazzo, J. D. (1972). *Wechsler's Measurement and Appraisal of Adult Intelligence*. Baltimore: Williams & Wilkins.

Parsons, O. A., and Prigatano, G. P. (1978). Methodological considerations in clinical neuropsychological research. *J. Consult. Clin. Psychol., 46*, 608–619.

Price, L. J., Fein, G., and Feinberg, I. (1980). Neuropsychological assessment of cognitive functioning in the elderly. In: L. W. Poon, ed., *Aging in the 1980s: Psychological Issues*. Washington, D.C.: American Psychological Association, pp. 78–85.

Reed, H. B. C., Jr., and Reitan, R. M. (1963). Changes in psychological test performance associated with the normal aging process. *J. Gerontol. 18*, 271–274.

Reitan, R. M. (1957). Differential reaction of various psychological tests to age. In: *Fourth Congress of the International Association of Gerontology*. Tito Mattioli, Fidenza, 4, 158–165.

Reitan, R. M. (1955). The distribution according to age of a psychologic measure dependent upon organic brain functions. *J. Gerontol. 10*, 338–340.

Reitan, R. M., and Davison, L. A., eds. (1974). *Clinical Neuropsychology: Current Status and Applications*. New York: Wiley & Sons.

Russell, E. W., Neuringer, C., and Goldstein, G. (1970). *Assessment of Brain Damage: A Neuropsychological Key Approach*. New York: Wiley-Interscience.

Vega, A., Jr., and Parsons, O. A. (1967). Cross-validation of the Halstead-Reitan tests for brain damage. *J. Consult. Clin. Psychol., 31*, 619–623.

Wang, H. S. (1973). Cerebral correlates of intellectual function in senescence. In: L. E. Jarvik, C. Eisdorfer, and J. E. Blum, eds. *Intellectual Functioning in Adults*. New York: Springer Publishing Company, pp. 95–106.

Wechsler, D. (1955). *Manual for the Wechsler Adult Intelligence Scale*. New York: Psychological Corporation.

7

Applied Neuropsychology in a Psychiatric Center

ALLAN YOZAWITZ

A Central Diagnostic Problem

Modern researchers have been studying the association between psychiatric behavior and brain dysfunction for more than a century (Goldstein, 1978; Mirsky, 1969; Vaughan, 1978). However, few of the research findings to date have been translated into practical means for the effective diagnosis and treatment of psychiatric disorders. Why has the available evidence concerning the cerebral substrate of psychiatric disorders not been put to clinical use?

Perhaps one explanation may be traced to the restrictive nature of professional specialization. Typically, none of the traditional mental health practitioners (psychiatrists, psychologists, or neurologists) have had sufficient grounding in cross-disciplinary knowledge to permit the translation of brain-behavior research into clinical practice. The emergence of neuropsychology as a clinical profession within the past two decades has partially solved this specialization problem, and created new ones.

Clinical neuropsychology developed originally within the medical hospital setting and found its niche within traditional (neurosurgery and neurology) services. To the extent that psychiatric patients continued to be referred to these clinical neuroscience services, the practice remained traditional (i.e., to rule out the presence of neurological disorder). If the patient did not meet established criteria for neurological impairment, the disposition was for conventional treatment by the referring psychiatrist. If neuropsychological instruments could be applied to improve the detection of the neurologically impaired among psychiatric patients—it was thought—differential diagnoses might be provided more efficiently and differential treatment might also ensue.

It is within this clinical context that numerous neuropsychological studies of psychiatric patients were conducted (see reviews by Heaton, Baade, and Johnson, 1978; Malec, 1978). These studies focused on the ability of a given instrument or battery to make the "neurological vs. psychiatric" discrimination. Unfortunately, tests that were sensitive to a wide range of neurobehavioral limitations were equally sensitive to motivational limitations on performance.

Reliance upon simple "level of performance" norms for brain damaged populations was a primitive criterion, at best, for the identification of cerebral dysfunction. The price that was paid for the seeming efficiency of "brain damage" detection was an unwanted and sizable number of false positive classifications for psychiatric patients. While reductions in the overall hit rate of an instrument or battery could be realized by adjusting cutoff points downward, the proportion of false-positive classifications due to motivational variables would not be reduced (Watson et al. 1968). This would suggest that no amount of norm revision could improve the specificity of selection in this simple method.

Many of the studies using this "level of performance" approach found moderate to severe degrees of neuropsychological dysfunction for their groups of psychiatric patients (Klonoff, Fibiger, and Hutton, 1970; Lacks et al., 1970; Taylor, Abrams, and Gaztanaga, 1975). This led some investigators to conclude that their psychiatric patients were neurologically impaired, with a global and diffuse cerebral deficit that was indistinguishable from chronic brain damage.

Actually, the concept of neuropathologically-based disease as the substrate of psychiatric disorder is a notion that was popularized in the last century, and was perhaps best expressed by Griesinger in 1845 (reprinted 1965) that mental diseases are by definition brain diseases. The widest application of this concept could allow one to accept modern findings of diffuse brain disease in psychiatric patients as consistent with a Kraeplinian formulation of dementia praecox (Johnstone et al., 1978).

These findings were not uncontested. Other researchers, using different diagnostic and inclusion criteria could find no difference between the neuropsychological performance of psychiatric patients and neurologically intact controls (Barnes and Lucas, 1974; Golden, 1977; Goldstein and Shelly, 1972; Levine and Feirstein, 1972; Small et al., 1972). These data also have found philosophical support by their consistency with psychoanalytic (Sullivan, 1953) and ecological (Kohn, 1968; Proshansky, Nelson-Shulman, and Kaminoff, 1978) conceptualizations of psychopathology.

Neither type of result encouraged the application of clinical neuropsychological skills in a psychiatric setting. If psychiatric patients had either global and diffuse neuropathology or none at all, there would be little need for rigorous neuropsychological assessment or intervention. It is therefore not surprising that the neuropsychologist's role in some mental health systems has been limited. The clinical neuropsychology service in psychiatric institutions has been the exception, rather than the rule. Yet recent developments have given the neuropsychologist a new and more intellectually interesting set of challenges. It is to these that we now turn.

Evolution of the Neuropsychologist's Contemporary Role in Psychiatric Settings

Technological advances such as the advent of the CT scan have refined the nature of the question that the neuropsychologist must address. The neuropsychologist's role has become less of a lesion detector and more of a neurobehavioral descriptor of functional strengths and weaknesses. Commensurate with this changing emphasis, clinical neuropsychological methods sensitive to subtle symptom differentiation were developed (Luria, 1966). Several investigators took this approach to the evaluation of psychiatric patients (Cox and Ludwig, 1979; Flor-Henry and Yeudall, 1979; Fuller Torrey, 1980; Taylor, Redfield, and Abrams, 1981), and found that it was possible to identify *focalized*, syndrome-specific deficits in psychiatric patients.

Yet there were problems. Skeptics could rightfully argue that the cognitive, perceptual, and motor performance of psychiatric patients would be seriously compromised by motivational variables (Clark, Brown, and Rutschmann, 1967) and psychotropic medication (Hartlage, 1965; Grant et al., 1978; Klonoff et al., 1970) that are central features of the disorders seen in most psychiatric settings. Moreover, even if such influences were not important, how meaningful would the detection of subtle neuropsychological dysfunction be to the treatment of these patients? To explore these questions, we next present the background, methods and results of a representative neuropsychological program.

A Representative Approach to the Problem

The possiblities for neuropsychology in its contemporary role in psychiatry, described above, appear to be great. If the specific strengths and weaknesses of patients can be determined apart from their psychodiagnostic classification, much can be done to replace prejudicial "stock therapies" with individualized treatment approaches.

The Hutchings Psychiatric Center is an acute care facility of the New York State Department of Mental Health and is affiliated with the SUNY Upstate Medical Center in Syracuse. Its neuropsychology service was founded in 1977. The clinical objectives of the service were to provide staff with assistance in detecting and evaluating functional neurological impairment, to assess adaptive functioning in response to neuropathology, to systematically analyze behavioral strengths and weaknesses of function, and to assist in formulating rehabilitative strategy. Using a flexible approach to neuropsychological assessment (see Chapter 4), the service has provided comprehensive evaluations of brainbehavior relationships for selected individuals who were referred from any of the in-patient or out-patient units of the psychiatric center.

The flexible approach permitted us to side-step issues that had typically confounded the neuropsychological evaluation of psychiatric patients. Specifically, we were able to (1) avoid relying upon the level of patient performance by focusing upon pathognomonic signs of cerebral dysfunction to identify meaningful syndromes; (2) employ "on line" hypothesis testing to verify clinical assumptions through concurrent validation with overlapping measures of neuropsychological performance; and (3) abandon the simplistic dichotomy between organic and nonorganic classifications in favor of descriptive syndrome analysis (see Chapter 3).

Since it began to operate, the clinical neuropsychology service has identified a surprisingly large number of psychiatric patients with neuropsychological dysfunction. It must be cautioned that although we have found a high percentage of neuropsychological disorder among *referrals* from a "functional" population, the biased nature of our *referred* sample did not permit us to reach conclusions about the incidence or prevalence of neuropsychological disorder in a psychiatric population. Instead, the purpose here is to convey an appreciation for the diversity of neuropsychological disorder that exists within a "functional" population and to illustrate the patterns of performance that are encountered in a referral service of this kind.

A Retrospective Analysis

We undertook a *post hoc* analysis of 100 consecutive referrals to our service to determine the patterns of neuropsychological dysfunction and psychopathology. Six of these patients received only brief screening evaluations because the severity of their psychopathology precluded more extensive testing, or a review of the referral question and supporting documentation (including his-

Table 1. Identifying data for 94 psychiatric patients

Age			Race		
Mean	S.D.	Range	Black	American Indian	White
32.79	18.27	8–73	13%	1%	86%

Chronicity			
Median number of hospitalizations[a]	Range	Patients with two or fewer hospitalizations	
1.4	0–15	Outpatients without any hospitalizations	27%
		Patients with only one hospitalization[a]	24%
		Patients with two hospitalizations[a]	14%
		Total	65%

[a] Including present.

Table 2. Comparison of diagnostic categories

DSM II Nomenclature	Hospital diagnoses	
	Yearly hospital population (N = 2625)	Referred sample (N = 94)
Schizophrenia	32%	29%
Organic brain syndrome	6%	18%
Affective disorder	11%	14%
Personality disorder	11%	7%
Mental retardation	2%	7%
Behavior disorder of adolescence	—	6%
Transient situational disturbance	19%	6%
Neuroses	18%	5%
Drug abuse	—	3%
Paranoid state	—	1%
Diagnosis deferred	—	2%

tory and clinical reports) did not warrant additional evaluation. The remaining 94 psychiatric patients constituted our sample. The identifying characteristics of this group are presented in Table 1.[1] Although there was a wide range of age and chronicity among the patients, our sample was fairly young and nonchronic. Fifty-nine percent were in-patients and 41% were out-patients. The sex distribution was 62% male and 38% female.

While we cannot be certain how representative this referred sample was of a psychiatric population, there was surprising concordance between the distribution of psychiatric diagnoses in the sample and in the total yearly hospital population (see Table 2). There was only a 3% difference for the major psychiatric diagnoses of schizophrenia and affective disorder between the two groups.

Semi-structured psychiatric interviews with the patients in our sample were the basis for project diagnoses using research diagnostic criteria (RDC) (Spitzer, Endicott, and Robins, 1978) (see Table 3). Comparison of our hospital psychiatrists' diagnoses to RDC diagnoses revealed that hospital psychiatrists had a much broader concept of schizophrenia and a much narrower concept of affective disorder. Hospital psychiatrists applied the diagnosis of schizophrenia 21% more readily and they used the diagnosis of affective disorder 30% less often than had been suggested by semi-structured interviewing and RDC

Table 3. Project psychiatric classification

Not interviewed	Nondisclosure	Affective	Schizophrenic	Personality disorder
21%	16%	44%	8%	11%

criteria. This diagnostic discrepancy between hospital and project diagnoses was similar to that reported in the Cross National US–UK Diagnostic Project of admissions to public mental hospitals and thus suggests that the psychiatric disability of our group was not unique (Cooper, et al., 1969; Pope and Lipinski, 1978).

The neuropsychological functioning of all patients was clinically assessed on the basis of historical and available medical data and measures of current cognitive, perceptual, and motor performance. Although the nature of the presenting problem determined which measures of assessment were employed, several common measures were used in this sample. This permitted us to standardize the performance of our patients across these measures, which included the Wechsler Intelligence Scales (Wechsler, 1955, 1974), Raven Coloured Progressive Matrices (Raven, 1962), Benton Visual Retention Test (Benton, 1974), Buschke List Learning Test[2] (Buschke, 1973), Purdue Pegboard Test of Manual Dexterity (Costa et al., 1963; Tiffin, 1968), Wepman Auditory Discrimination Test (Wepman, 1973), Spreen-Benton Token Test and Sentence Repetition Test (Spreen and Benton, 1977), Wide Range Achievement Test (WRAT) (Jastak, Bijou, and Jastak, 1965), and somatosensory tests of resolution, sequencing, and double simultaneous perception[3] (Boll, 1981; Fink, Green, and Bender, 1952; Kinsbourne and Warrington, 1962).

We then compared objective profiles of patients' neuropsychological functioning with clinically based neuropsychological classifications. Figure 1 contrasts the uniformly inferior performance of all neuropsychologically diagnosed psychiatric patients with a performance baseline of psychiatric patients without collateral neuropsychological diagnoses. Had we limited our investigation to this step, we would have identified one group of unimpaired patients who performed no differently than would be expected for neurologically intact individuals and another group of mildly impaired patients who demonstrated a global and diffuse performance deficit that could engender the label of "mild organicity." We went on, however, to group the clinical diagnoses into nine categories (developmental perceptual disorder, frontal lobe dysfunction, seizure disorder, nutritional disorder, secondary language disorder, sequela of head trauma, secondary visual-spatial disorder, drug toxicity, and executive-motor disorder).[4]

The most common diagnostic category, identified in nearly half (46%) of all patients with neuropsychological disorders,[5] was developmental perceptual disorder (defined according to the operational criteria of DSM III). The neuropsychological performance of this group differed from that of patients without diagnoses of neuropsychological disorder and or with nondevelopmental neuropsychological disorders. The developmental perceptual disorder group performed poorer than either of the comparison groups on the Wechsler Verbal I.Q. Test and all three subtests of the Wide Range Achievement Test[6] (see Fig. 2). While the developmental disorder group evidenced impaired performance for other language and visual-spatial measures, their per-

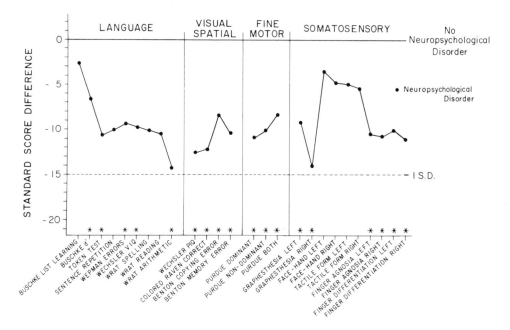

Fig. 1. A performance profile across 26 measures for 74 patients with neuropsychological diagnoses referenced to 20 patients without neuropsychological diagnoses. Asterisks indicate two-tailed t comparisons with $p \leq .05$.

formance was not unique from other neuropsychologically impaired patients with nondevelopmental disorders. Interestingly, the developmental group's fine motor and somatosensory functioning was relatively unimpaired.

In an effort to further describe the developmental group, we subdivided it into two groups of nearly equal size of patients with developmental language and developmental visual-spatial disorder[7] (Fig. 3). Comparison of these two groups and the group of psychiatric patients for whom no neuropsychological disorder was identified revealed that the developmental language disorder group was the most academically impaired.[8]

Measures significantly discriminating the language disorder group from the other two groups were the Token Test, Sentence Repetition Test, and the spelling and reading subtests of the Wide Range Achievement Test. Multiple comparisons further revealed that the language disorder group was characterized by significantly poorer Wepman, verbal I.Q., Raven, and WRAT arithmetic scores than the group without neuropsychological disorder. Compared to the same baseline of psychiatric patients without neuropsychological disorder, the visual-spatial group was characterized by significantly fewer nondominant hand Purdue Pegboard placements and poorer performance I.Q. While dominant hand performance was not significantly impaired for the language

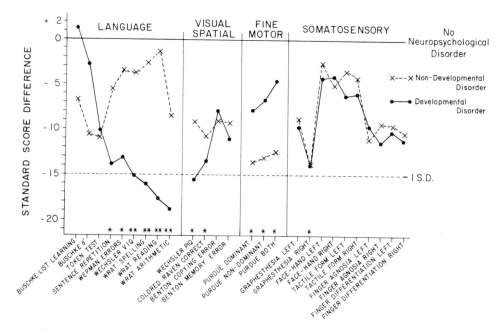

Fig. 2. Referenced to 20 patients without neuropsychological diagnoses, a performance profile of 34 patients with developmental disorder is compared to a performance profile of 40 patients with nondevelopmental disorder. Scheffé multiple comparisons with $p < .05$ are denoted by single asterisks for single discriminations between the group without neuropsychological diagnoses and either of the comparison groups. Double asterisks denote double discriminations between the developmental group and each of the other groups.

disordered group, it is interesting to note that it was inferior to nondominant hand performance. This observation, while not of any statistical consequence, nevertheless provided concurrent clinical validity for this neuropsychological taxonomy.

Since neuropsychological diagnoses were based, in part, upon a review of historical information, we sought to identify the historical items that were most often associated with the classification of developmental perceptual disorder. We identified up to six risk factors per patient and grouped them into 12 categories (Table 4).

Risk factors that significantly distinguished patients with developmental perceptual disorders from those with other neuropsychological disorders and those without neuropsychological disorder were the absence of acute deteriorative functioning and the presence of greater environmental deprivation, indices of childhood behavioral disorder, and indices of congenital and genetic disorder (Fig. 4).

Subdividing the developmental group into language and visual-spatial disorder groups revealed that the risk factor of childhood behavioral disorder

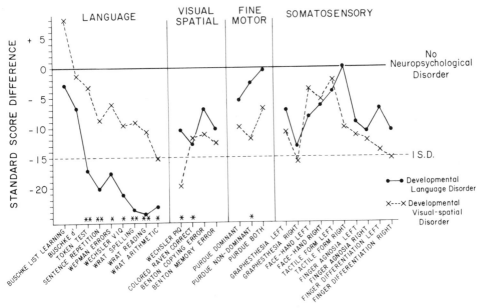

Fig. 3. Referenced to 20 patients without neuropsychological diagnoses, a performance profile of 14 patients with developmental language disorder is compared to a performance profile of 13 patients with developmental visual-spatial disorder. Scheffé multiple comparisons with $p < .05$ are denoted by single asterisks for single discriminations between the group without neuropsychological diagnoses and either of the comparison groups. Double asterisks denote double discriminations between the developmental language group and each of the other groups.

distinguished the visual-spatial group, while the risk factor of congenital and genetic disorder distinguished the language group from patients without neuropsychological disorder (Fig. 5). Thus, we observed that the developmental language disorder group frequently appeared mentally deficient according to historical documentation, while the visual-spatial disorder group frequently appeared to be learning disabled on historical review. Unlike other psychiatric patients with or without neuropsychological disorders, neither developmental disorder group experienced any recent decline in functioning.

The clinical advantages of investigating the quantitative and qualitative features of psychiatric patients' performance should be clear. Through syndrome classification, based upon a functional understanding of cerebral organization, we have identified a group of individuals with developmental perceptual dysfunction that may represent an etiologically distinct group of psychiatric patients (see Gurland, 1972). More importantly, we characterized this group as demonstrating a coherent academic disability that could be amenable to rehabilitation. The developmentally dysfunctional patients were further resolvable into neurologically meaningful subgroups that may have more

Table 4. Risk factors

Categories	Items	Frequency	Patients (N)
Deteriorative functioning	Memory impairment	26	
	Confusion	11	
	Behavioral and cognitive changes	8	
	Sleep pattern change	3	36
	Diminished functioning	2	
	Recent work dysfunction	2	
	Wandering	1	
	Disorganization	1	
Early childhood behavior	Learning disability	15	
	Specialized classes	13	
	Poor academic performance	11	
	Developmental lags	11	37
	Hyperactivity	3	
	Chronic behavior problems	2	
	State school resident	1	
	Enuresis, encopresis	1	
General medical history	Acute infection	8	
	Hypertension	5	
	Major surgery	5	
	Coma	4	
	Diabetes	3	
	Hypothyroidism	2	21
	Asthma	2	
	Coronary insufficiency	2	
	Cancer	1	
	Kidney dysfunction	1	
	Jaundice	1	
	Parathyroid adenoma	1	
Behavioral evidence of neuropathology	Dysarthria	4	
	Language comprehension difficulty	4	
	Postural asymmetry	4	
	Parkinsonism	3	
	Perseverative behavior	3	
	Seizure disorder history	3	
	Abnormal reflexes	3	
	Diagnosis of stroke	3	
	Muscular weakness	3	
	Disorientation	2	
	Gait disturbance	2	
	Hand tremor	2	35
	Diagnosis of cerebral palsy	2	
	Left sided numbness	2	
	Numbness of extremities	1	
	Dysphasic symptoms	1	
	Altered olfactory & gustatory sensations	1	

Categories	Items	Frequency	Patients (N)
Behavioral evidence of neuropathology	Facial numbness	1	
	Expressive language disorder	1	
	Muscle atrophy	1	
	Convulsions	1	
	Transient loss of speech	1	
	Diminished direction sense	1	
	Gilles de la Tourette Syndrome	1	
Early childhood medical history	Perinatal injury	13	
	Anoxia	5	
	Premature birth	5	
	Early craniocerbral trauma	3	
	Early high fevers	3	28
	Hypernatremia	1	
	Intrauterine anoxia	1	
	Spinal meningitis	1	
	Sydenham's chorea	1	
Drug abuse	Alcoholism	13	
	Drug abuse	12	
	Glue intoxication	1	24
	Drug toxicity	1	
	Drug overdose	1	
Speculative behavioral evidence of neuro-pathology	Headache	7	
	Limited verbal interaction	2	
	Speech problem	2	
	Difficulty controlling drowsiness	1	
	Blackouts	1	
	Altered consciousness	1	
	Diplopia	1	18
	Hyperacousis	1	
	Long response latencies	1	
	Syncopal episodes	1	
	Suspected childhood seizures	1	
	Auditory and visual hallucinations	1	
	Muscular rigidity	1	
Physiological evidence of neuropathology	Craniocerebral trauma	12	
	History of EEG abnormalities	6	
	Craniectomy	3	
	Skull fractures	3	
	Cerebral edema	1	
	Left fronto-temporal intracerebral hematoma	1	23
	Right holohemispheric subdural hematoma	1	
	Abnormal cerebral flow study	1	
	Left parieto-temporal skull fracture with hematoma	1	
	Hyperostosis frontalis internal	1	

Table 4. Risk factors *(continued)*

Categories	Items	Frequency	Patients (N)
Congenital and genetic	Moderate to severe mental retardation	9	16
	Borderline mental retardation	3	
	Primary dyslexia	3	
	Congenital abnormalities	3	
	Abnormal chromosomal analysis	2	
	Microcephaly	2	
	Turner's Syndrome	1	
Environmental	Inadequate nutrition	3	9
	History of experiencing abuse in childhood	3	
	History of experiencing maternal deprivation	3	
	Absence of formal schooling	1	
Episodic behavior	Impulsivity	4	17
	Temper outbursts	3	
	Sudden onset of violent behavior	3	
	Destructive acts	2	
	Impulsive suicidal behavior	2	
	History of assaultiveness	2	
	History of impulsive sexuality	2	
	Chronic and impulsive destructiveness	1	
Speculative physiological evidence of neuropathology	Falls with suspected craniocerebral trauma	8	14
	ECT	6	
	Suspected neonatal neurosurgery	1	
	Suspected congenital hydrocephalus	1	

functional relevance to treatment. It is conceivable that differential strategies of cognitive rehabilitation (Gianutsos, 1980) could be applied to these groups to improve their educational, vocational, communication, and living skills.

An often cited reservation about the potential application of clinical neuropsychological assessment in psychiatric populations has been the notion that the cognitive, perceptual, and motor performance of psychiatric patients would be obscured by motivational variables and psychotropic medication. It is clear from these data that neither psychotropic medication or motivational variables have compromised syndrome-specific neuropsychological resolution in these psychiatric patients.

To affirm this conclusion, patients were split into nearly equal size groups with and without medication. There were no differences in comparative neuropsychological performance on any measures[9] (Fig. 6). Not only was patient

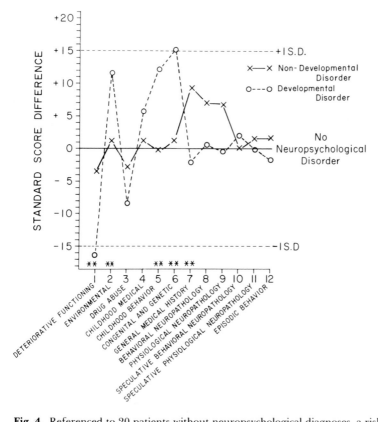

Fig. 4. Referenced to 20 patients without neuropsychological diagnoses, a risk factor profile of 34 patients with developmental disorder is compared to a risk factor profile of 40 patients with nondevelopmental disorder. Scheffé multiple comparisons with $p < .05$ are denoted by double asterisks, indicating discrimination between the developmental and nondevelopmental groups.

performance not differentially impaired by medication, there was reason to suspect improved functioning for patients who were receiving medication[10] (see Gruzelier and Hammond, 1978; Hymowitz and Spohn, 1980; Spohn, Lacoursiere, Thompson and Coyne, 1977). While only 12% of nonmedicated patients were neuropsychologically intact, the corresponding percentage for medicated patients was nearly triple (Fig. 7).

If motivational variables had affected patient performance, we might have expected to find inconsistencies both across and within meaningful categories of performance (that is, for language, visual-spatial, fine motor, and somatosensory measures). To the contrary, syndrome-specific patterns of neuropsychological disability were evident for these clusters of performance, demonstrating a certain face-validity for our a priori determined performance categories. To assess the consistency of patient performance across these cat-

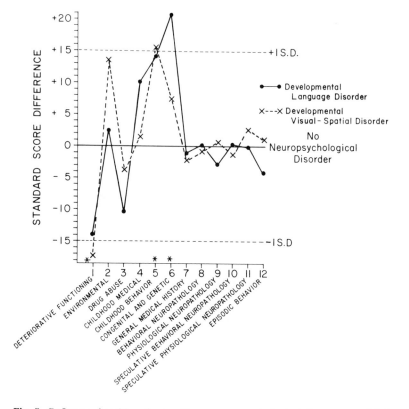

Fig. 5. Referenced to 20 patients without neuropsychological diagnoses, a risk factor profile of 14 patients with developmental language disorder is compared to a risk factor profile of 13 patients with developmental visual-spatial disorder. Scheffé multiple comparisons with $p < .05$ are denoted by asterisks.

egories, we determined Pearson correlations of the verbal–performance I.Q. differences for each subject vs. the Z score average for all other language measures minus the Z score average for all other visual-spatial and somatosensory measures. The highly significant outcome suggested excellent consistency across measures for these patients ($r = .48$, $p < .001$).

The ability to identify developmental perceptual disorder patients among a "functional" population suggests that our flexible approach to neuropsychological assessment may be fruitfully applied in a psychiatric setting. Despite relatively poorer patient performance, syndrome-specific patterns of performance may be identified that can lead to a greater understanding of patients' strengths and weaknesses. It is inappropriate on the basis of these data to infer that learning disabled patients constitute a substantial proportion of the psychiatric population. Indeed, Rourke and his associates (Chapter 11) have

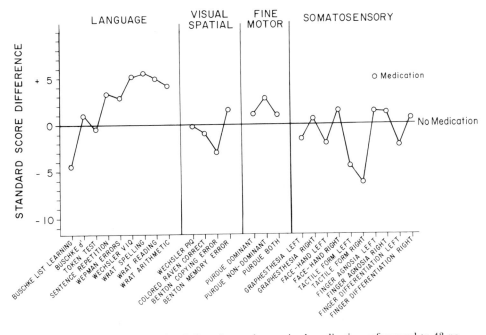

Fig. 6. A performance profile of 47 patients who received medication referenced to 43 patients who were medication free. Two-tailed t tests did not reach the .05 probability level for any of the 26 comparisons.

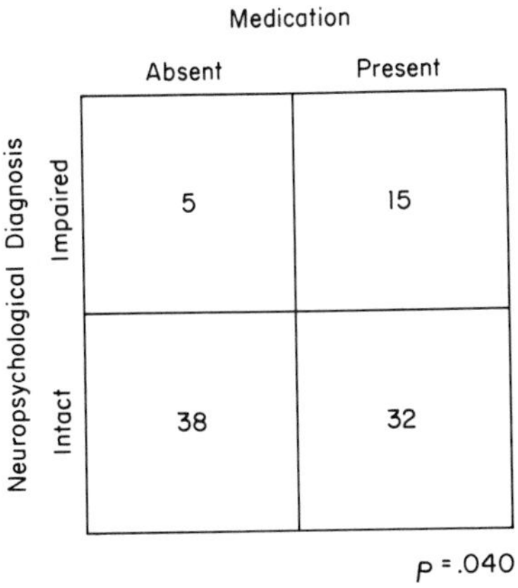

Medication

	Absent	Present
Impaired	5	15
Intact	38	32

Neuropsychological Diagnosis

$p = .040$

Fig. 7. Chi-square analysis for 47 medicated and 43 nonmedicated patients split with respect to neuropsychological diagnosis.

very carefully shown that the conditions under which learning disorder result in adult psychiatric disorder are complex and not general at all.

Nevertheless, there are indications in the literature (Bellak, 1979; Cox and Ludwig, 1979; Cantwell, Baker, and Mattison, 1979, 1980; Fish, 1977; Quitkin, Rifkin, and Klein, 1976; Werner and Smith, 1979) that neurologic soft signs and language disorders, in particular, may be etiologically associated with psychiatric disorder. These observations deserve more careful inquiry.

Investigators in other areas have proposed diathesis-stress models (Meehl, 1962) in an attempt to explain how stress may precipitate psychiatric episodes through the mediation of environmental demands upon a less than capable organism (Shields, 1978). Developmental perceptual disorders may constitute a diathesis by rendering the individual less flexible in coping with the considerable demands of our technological environment. That is, the patient's responses or repertoire may be limited as a characteristic of the disorder, which would make the person highly vulnerable to emotional stress. In the face of adaptational demands, ineffective or inappropriate responses are made because of the limitations of the disorder. In fact, this is exactly what Rourke et al. (Chapter 11) describe in Group 3 patients. Moreover, considering that affective disorders have been perceived as a neuroendocrine consequence of profound stress, it may be meaningful that our patient sample was mostly reclassified, upon careful diagnostic assessment, as affectively disordered (see Barchas and Freedman, 1963; Bliss and Zwanziger, 1966; Carroll, Curtis, and Mendels, 1976; Cassens, Roffman, Kuruc, Orsulak, and Schildkraut, 1980).

Some Future Research Directions and a Framework for Care

If one accepts the diathesis-stress model as a heuristic tool for predicting approaches to *treatment,* the absence of reported interventions attempting to remediate the presumed neurogenic diathesis becomes apparent. There are chemotherapeutic strategies that attempt to diminish the stress reaction (see Iversen, 1980; van Praag and Verhoeven, 1981) and there are strategies to reduce the environmental demands on the individual (Mosher and Keith, 1980; Jones, 1953), but there has been little attempt at direct cognitive/academic intervention (Cox and Leventhal, 1978).

The few attempts that have focused upon developing skills in psychiatric patients have shown it to be the most effective intervention strategy for long-term psychiatric outcome (Anthony and Margules, 1974; Vitalo and Ross, 1979). These results, however, based upon recidivism and employment statistics, are still far from optimal (Anthony, Cohen, and Vitalo, 1978; Stern and Minkoff, 1979). One explanation for this limitation may be that there is typically inadequate identification and development of those skills likely to produce the most favorable outcome for each patient.

To ensure that tasks are appropriate with respect to rehabilitation outcome, their selection should consider neuropsychological constraints upon adaptive functioning. Incorporating neuropsychological evaluations into the rehabilitation process could separate patients more meaningfully into homogeneous groups of cognitive disability (see Shakow, 1962, p. 3). A detailed proposal of how this might be accomplished is presented schematically in Fig. 8.

The program outlined in Figure 8 combines a comprehensive neurodiagnostic assessment with intensive psychiatric and medical evaluation to determine a biologically relevant course of rehabilitation strategy for each patient. Patients would initially receive a comprehensive psychiatric screening including neurological (Andersson, 1970; Cole, 1978), neuropsychological, medical, and serological evaluation (Cutting, 1980; Hall et al., 1978; Koranyi, 1979). This would require the collaboration of a psychiatrist, neurologist, neuropsychologist, and internist. Psychiatric screening would include a brief assessment of historical and current behavior pathology, with a record review, and an abbreviated semi-structured interview. The neurological screening would include a sleep-deprived EEG in addition to clinically assessing motor, sensory, and perceptual function. The neuropsychological screening would evaluate language, memory, conceptual, academic, attentional, and visuo-constructive functioning. The medical assessment would include a physical examination, electrocardiogram, and serological screening consisting of a 34-panel automated blood chemistry analysis, CBC, and routine urinalysis (see Hall et al., 1980).

Depending upon the outcome of this interdisciplinary screening, some patients would be directly referred for medical treatment to an acute care medical facility, others would be directly referred to an inpatient unit for intensive management of their acute psychiatric symptoms, and others would enter the first stage of the cognitive rehabilitation program (Gianutsos, 1980; Powell, 1981). It is at this point that the patient would receive a more comprehensive neuropsychological evaluation of his or her rehabilitation potential, which would include a detailed assessment of conceptual, language, visual-spatial, and motor abilities. If it is determined that intensive cognitive remediation in any of these four basic areas is required, the patient would enter one or more specialized training modules. These programs, staffed by speech pathologists, learning disabilities specialists, and physical therapists, would give intensive individualized training in the area of disability by using strengths to subserve adaptive functioning (Diller, 1971; LeVere, 1980). It should be pointed out that to minimize boredom and frustration, patients may be operating in more than one module and in more than one program level at the same time. Nevertheless, there is a general linear progression of training that should be followed within each program level to ensure that basic competency is attained (Diller and Gordon, 1981).

At each stage of intervention each patient's progress is continually assessed. In response to this feedback, decisions are made to guide the patient through more advanced levels of training. Patients who have demonstrated competence in the four basic areas of cognitive training receive more detailed academic evaluation followed by specific training in reading, spelling, and arith-

Fig. 8. Schematic proposal for incorporating neuropsychological evaluation and cognitive rehabilitation into a comprehensive mental health care system.

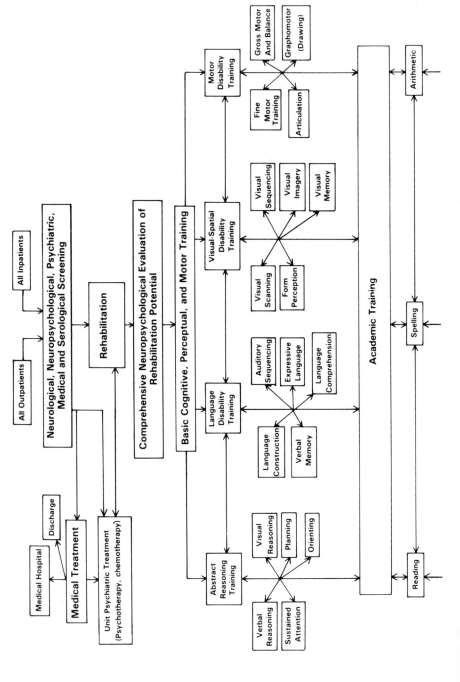

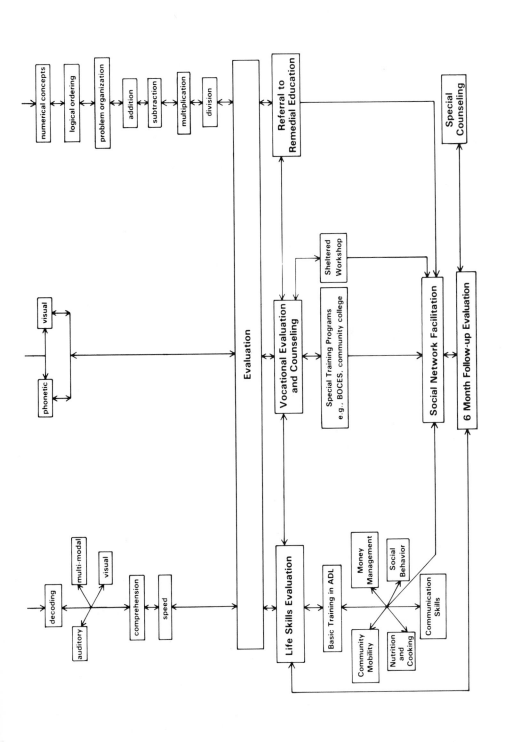

metic. Based upon their specific needs, patients may enter a module of training in activities of daily living, occupational training, or sheltered workshop activity. It may also be possible for an individual to be referred for further academic training to independent educational institutions within the community. Irrespective of disposition, all patients would enter a social network where they would receive counseling and followup evaluations at 6-month intervals to assess their capacity to continue to function independently (Marsh, Glick, and Zigler, 1981).

While such a program is utopian, most mental health centers do have the capacity to reallocate their resources to meet many of these objectives. At Hutchings Psychiatric Center, we are actively involved in testing this model as an alternative strategy for mental health treatment. We will be assessing the value of these cognitive interventions for consecutively admitted psychiatric patients in the short-term, for its affect upon the attainment of academic, vocational, and social skills, and in the long-term, for the persistence of these benefits in affecting post-treatment outcome in the community at 6-month intervals (Anthony and Farkas, 1982).

The rehabilitation approach that has been outlined here, while providing an alternative to contemporary approaches to the treatment of psychiatric disorder, is not without precedent. More than seventy years ago Adolph Meyer outlined his conception of an ideal mental health center (Meyer, 1913). He described a highly specialized diagnostic and treatment center that would carry on an interdisciplinary and well-integrated program of prevention, treatment, and aftercare for psychiatric disorders. Meyer emphasized the importance of a cross-disciplinary training base for mental health professionals to develop a theoretical model of mental health diagnosis and treatment based upon both psychiatric and neurological expertise. His model stressed the complexity of psychiatric disorder as an integration of biological and environmental forces that contributed to a patient's clinical presentation.

The basic objective of Meyer's psychobiological therapy was to help individuals make the best adaptation possible, given their constitutional resources and the demands of society. Recognition of each patient's assets as well as their liabilities was critical to the therapeutic approach:

We must get away from the idea that one examines only for some all-inclusive asylum diseases like dementia praecox and manic-depressive insanity and paresis. One examines primarily for the range of personal capacity to help in an examination and to cooperate in any plan for treatment, that is, assets as shown in plain life problems and successes and failures. If there are any failures, one determines whether there are any toxic or infectious intruders, any disorders of the internal organs and their functions, any neurologic disorders (including the suprasegmental as well as the segmental symptoms); and finally any disorders of behavior or of mental reactions, not in the abstract but in terms of what the patient does with the jobs, with the family, and with other people, and with his own worries, and feelings, and notions and moods, the thoughts he cannot throw off, the memory and judgment, and the speech and writing, and the management of his eliminative functions and sleep and appetite. One does not fish merely for a few so-called "frontal lobe symptoms. (Meyer, 1922, p. 6)

Modern discussants of psychiatric illness would be hard pressed to provide a better statement of the tasks before those attempting to treat patients. Psychiatric illness is a complex amalgam of multiple biologic and environmental variables that influence prognosis and treatment outcome. To the extent that a poor premorbid state (characterized by developmental perceptual disorders that reduce resourcefulness and coping strategies) contributes to a patient's chronic presentation, strategies that can isolate these variables from the current episode should be of therapeutic importance. The proposed model for rehabilitation attempts to separate and treat those constitutional (premorbid) variables apart from the acute psychiatric behavior that has brought the patient to clinical attention. As Zubin (1965, 1980a) has pointed out, it is these constitutional variables that perpetuate the notion of psychiatric disorder as a chronic entity and have "given schizophrenia a bad name" (Zubin, 1980b).

Perhaps the evolution of clinical neuropsychology into a distinct service, with demonstrable utility for the diagnosis and potential treatment of psychiatric disorder, is an indicator that the time has arrived for an interdisciplinary rehabilitation program similar to the ideal mental health center envisioned by Meyer in the early years of this century.

ACKNOWLEDGMENT

The author wishes to express appreciation to Mr. Steve Reiter who played a vital role in this investigation, to Dr. Alan Miley who aided in statistical analysis, and to Drs. Louis Costa and Lois Stack for their scholarly advice.

REFERENCES

American Psychiatric Association, Committee on Nomenclature and Statistics. (1980). *Diagnostic and statistical manual of mental disorders*, 3rd ed. New York: American Psychiatric Association.

Andersson, P. G. (1970). Intracranial tumors in a psychiatric autopsy material. *Acta Psychiatr. Scand., 46,* 213–224.

Anthony, W. A., Cohen, M. R., and Vitalo, R. (1978). The measurement of rehabilitation outcome. *Schizophrenia Bull., 4,* 365–383.

Anthony, W. A., and Farkas, M. (1982). A client outcome planning model for assessing psychiatric rehabilitation interventions. *Schizophrenia Bull., 8,* 13–38.

Anthony, W. A., and Margules, A. (1974). Toward improving the efficacy of psychiatric rehabilitation: A skills training approach. *Rehab. Psychol., 21,* 101–105.

Barchas, J., and Freedman, D. (1963). Brain amines: Response to physiological stress. *Biochem. Pharmacol., 12,* 1232–1235.

Barnes, G., and Lucas, G. J. (1974). Cerebral dysfunction vs. psychogenesis in the Halstead-Reitan tests. *J. Nerv. Ment. Dis., 158,* 50–60.

Bellak, L. (1979). Schizophrenic syndrome related to minimal brain dysfunction: A possible neurologic subgroup. *Schizophrenia Bull., 5,* 480–489.

Benton, A. L. (1974). *The Revised Visual Retention Test*, 4th ed. New York: Psychological Corporation.

Bliss, E., and Zwanziger, J. (1966). Brain amines and emotional stress. *J. Psychiat. Res., 4,* 189–198.

Boll, T. J. (1981). The Halstead-Reitan neuropsychology battery. In: S. B. Filskov and T. J. Boll, eds., *Handbook of Clinical Neuropsychology*. New York: Wiley.

Buschke, H. (1973). Selective reminding for analysis of memory and learning. *J. Verbal Learning Verbal Behavior, 12,* 543–550.

Carroll, B. J., Curtis, G. C., and Mendels, J. (1976). Neuroendocrine regulation in depression I. Limbic system-adrenocortical dysfunction. *Arch. General Psychiat., 33,* 1039–1044.

Cassens, G., Roffman, M., Kuruc, A., Orsulak, P. J., and Schildkraut, J. J. (1980). Alterations in brain norepinephrine metabolism induced by environmental stimuli previously paired with inescapable shock. *Science, 209,* 1138–1140.

Cole, G. (1978). Intracranial space-occupying masses in mental hospital patients: Necropsy study. *J. Neurol., Neurosurg. Psychiat., 41,* 730–736.

Cantwell, D. P., Baker, L., and Mattison, R. E. (1979). The prevalence of psychiatric disorder in children with speech and language disorder. An epidemiologic study. *J. Am. Acad. Child Psychiat., 18,* 450–461.

Cantwell, D. P., Baker, L., and Mattison, R. E. (1980). Psychiatric disorders in children with speech and language retardation. *Arch. General Psychiat., 37,* 423–426.

Clark, W. C., Brown, J. C., and Rutschmann, J. (1967). Flicker sensitivity and response bias in psychiatric patients and normal subjects. *J. Abnormal Psychol., 72,* 35–42.

Cooper, J. E., Kendell, R. E., Gurland, B. J., Sartorius, N., and Farkas, T. (1969). Cross-national study of diagnosis of the mental disorders: Some results from the first comparative investigation. *Amer. J. Psychiat., (Suppl.), 125,* 21–29.

Coren, S., and Porac, C. (1977). Fifty centuries of right-handedness: The historical record. *Science, 198,* 631–632.

Costa, L. D., Vaughan, H. G., Jr., Levita, E., and Farber, N. (1963). The Purdue Pegboard as a predictor of the presence and laterality of cerebral lesions. *J. Consult. Psychol., 27,* 133–137.

Cox, M. D., and Leventhal, D. B. (1978). A multivariate analysis and modification of preattentive, perceptual dysfunction in schizophrenia. *J. Nerv. Ment. Dis., 166,* 709–718.

Cox, S. M., and Ludwig, A. M. (1979). Neurological soft signs and psychopathology. *J. Nerv. Ment. Dis., 167,* 161–165.

Cutting, J. (1980). Physical illness and psychosis. *Br. J. Psychiatry, 136,* 109–119.

Diller, L. (1971). Cognitive and motor aspects of handicapping conditions in the neurologically impaired. In: W. S. Neff, ed., *Rehabilitation Psychology.* Washington: American Psychological Association, Inc.

Diller, L., and Gordon, W. A. (1981). Interventions for cognitive deficits in brain-injured adults. *J. Consult. Clin. Psychol., 49,* 822–834.

Fink, M., Green, M., and Bender, M. B. (1952). The face-hand test as a diagnostic sign of organic mental syndrome. *Neurology, 2,* 46–58.

Fish, B. (1977). Neurobiologic antecedents of schizophrenia in children: Evidence for an inherited, congenital neurointegrative defect. *Arch. General Psychiat., 34,* 1297–1313.

Flor-Henry, P., and Yeudall, L. T. (1979). Neuropsychological investigation of schizophrenia and manic-depressive psychoses. In: J. Gruzelier and P. Flor-Henry, eds., *Hemisphere Asymmetries of Function in Psychopathology.* Amsterdam: Elsevier/North Holland Biomedical Press.

Fuller Torrey, E. (1980). Neurological abnormalities in schizophrenic patients. *Biol. Psychiat., 15,* 381–388.

Gianutsos, R. (1980). What is cognitive rehabilitation? *J. Rehab., 23,* 37–39.

Golden, C. J. (1977). Validity of the Halstead-Reitan neuropsychological battery in a mixed psychiatric and brain-injured population. *J. Consult. Clin. Psychol., 45,* 1043–1051.

Goldstein, G. (1978). Cognitive and perceptual differences between schizophrenics and organics. *Schizophrenia Bull., 4,* 161–185.

Goldstein, G., and Shelly, C. H. (1972). Statistical and normative studies of the Halstead neuropsychological test battery relevant to a neuropsychiatric hospital setting. *Perceptual and Motor Skills, 34,* 603–620.

Grant, I., Adams, K. M., Carlin, A. S., Rennick, P. M., Judd, L. L., and Schooff, K. (1978).

The collaborative neuropsychological study of polydrug users. *Arch. General Psychiat.,* 35, 1063–1074.

Griesinger, W. (1965). *Mental Pathology and Therapeutics.* New York: Hafner Press.

Gruzelier, J. H., and Hammond, N. V. (1978). The effect of chlorpromazine upon psycho-physiological, endocrine and information processing measures in schizophrenia. *J. Psychiat. Res., 14,* 167–182.

Gur, R. E. (1977). Motoric laterality imbalance in schizophrenia: A possible concomitant of left hemisphere dysfunction. *Arch. General Psychiat., 34,* 33–37.

Gurland, B. (1972). A flexible approach to psychiatric classification. In: M. Hammer, K. Salzinger, and S. Sutton, eds., *Psychopathology.* New York: John Wiley and Sons.

Hall, R. C. W., Gardner, E. R., Stickney, S. K., LeCann, A. F., and Popkin, M. K. (1980). Physical illness manifesting as psychiatric disease II. Analysis of a state hospital inpatient population. *Arch. General Psychiat., 37,* 989–995.

Hall, R. C. W., Popkin, M. K., Devaul, R. A., Faillace, L. A., and Stickney, S. K. (1978). Physical illness presenting as psychiatric disease. *Arch. General Psychiat., 35,* 1315–1320.

Hartlage, L. C. (1965). Effects of chlorpromazine on learning. *Psychol. Bull., 64,* 235–245.

Heaton, R. K., Baade, L. E., and Johnson, K. L. (1978). Neuropsychological test results associated with psychiatric disorders in adults. *Psychol. Bull., 85,* 141–162.

Hymowitz, P., and Spohn, H. (1980). The effects of antipsychotic medication on the linguistic ability of schizophrenics. *J. Nerv. Ment. Dis., 168,* 287–296.

Iversen, S. D. (1980). Brain chemistry and behaviour. *Psychol. Med., 10,* 527–539.

Jastak, J., Bijou, S. W., and Jastak, S. R. (1965). *Wide Range Achievement Test.* Wilmington, Delaware: Guidance Associates.

Johnstone, E. C., Crow, T. C., Frith, C. D., Stevens, M., Kreel, L., and Husband, J. (1978). The dementia of dementia praecox. *Acta Psychiat. Scand., 57,* 305–324.

Jones, M. (1953). *The Therapeutic Community.* New York: Basic Books.

Kinsbourne, M., and Warrington, E. K. (1962). A study of finger agnosia. *Brain, 85,* 47–66.

Klonoff, H., Fibiger, C. H., and Hutton, G. H. (1970). Neuropsychological patterns in chronic schizophrenia. *J. Nerv. Ment. Dis., 150,* 291–300.

Kohn, M. L. (1968). Social class and schizophrenia: A critical review. In: D. Rosenthal and S. S. Kety, eds., *Transmission of Schizophrenia.* London: Pergamon Press.

Koranyi, E. K. (1979). Morbidity and rate of undiagnosed physical illness in a psychiatric clinic population. *Arch. General Psychiat., 36,* 414–419.

Lacks, P. B., Colbert, J., Harrow, M., and Levine, J. (1970). Further evidence concerning the diagnostic accuracy of the Halstead organic test battery. *J. Clin. Psychol., 28,* 480–481.

LeVere, T. E. (1980). Recovery of function after brain damage: A theory of the behavioral deficit. *Physiol. Psychol., 8,* 297–308.

Levine, J., and Feirstein, A. (1972). Differences in test performance between brain-damaged, schizophrenic, and medical patients. *J. Consult. Clin. Psychol., 39,* 508–511.

Lishman, W. A., and McMeekan, E. R. L. (1976). Hand preference in psychiatric patients. *Br. J. Psychiat., 129,* 158–166.

Luria, A. R. (1966). *Higher Cortical Functions in Man.* New York: Basic Books.

Malec, J. (1978). Neuropsychological assessment of schizophrenia versus brain damage: A review. *J. Nerv. Ment. Dis., 166,* 507–516.

Marsh, A., Glick, M., and Zigler, E. (1981). Premorbid social competence and the revolving door phenomenon in psychiatric hospitalization. *J. Nerv. Ment. Dis., 169,* 315–319.

Meehl, P. E. (1962). Schizotaxia, schizotypy, schizophrenia. *Am. Psychol., 17,* 827–838.

Meyer, A. (1913). The aims of a psychiatric clinic. *Transactions of the Seventeenth International Congress of Medicine* (part 1, section 12). (In E. E. Winters, ed., *The Collected Papers of Adolf Meyer,* vol. 2. Baltimore: Johns Hopkins Press, 1951).

Meyer, A. (1922). Interrelations of the domain of neuropsychiatry. President's address read at the forty-eighth annual meeting of the American Neurological Association, Washington, D.C., May 1922. (In E. E. Winters, ed., *The Collected Papers of Adolf Meyer,* vol. 1. Baltimore: Johns Hopkins Press, 1950).

Mirsky, A. F. (1969). Neuropsychological bases of schizophrenia. *Ann. Rev. Psychol., 20,* 321–348.

Mosher, L. R., and Keith, S. J. (1980). Psychosocial treatment: Individual, group, family, and community support approaches. *Schizophrenia Bull., 6,* 10–40.

Nasrallah, H. A., Keelor, K., Van Schroeder, C., and McCalley-Whitters, M. (1981). Motoric lateralization in schizophrenic males. *Am. J. Psychiat., 138,* 1114–1115.

Pope, H. G., and Lipinski, J. F. (1978). Diagnosis in schizophrenia and manic-depressive illness. *Arch. General Psychiat., 35,* 811–828.

Powell, G. E. (1981). *Brain Function Therapy.* London: Gower Publishing Company.

Proshansky, H., Nelson-Shulman, Y., and Kaminoff, R. (1978). The role of physical settings in life crisis experiences. In: I. Sarason and C. Spielberger, eds., *Stress and Anxiety,* vol. 6. New York: John Wiley and Sons.

Quitkin, F., Rifkin, A., and Klein, D. F. (1976). Neurologic soft signs in schizophrenia and character disorders. *Arch. General Psychiat., 33,* 845–853.

Raven, J. C. (1962). *Coloured Progressive Matrices.* New York: Psychological Corporation.

Shakow, D. (1962). Segmental set. A theory of the formal psychological deficit in schizophrenia. *Arch. General Psychiat., 6,* 1–17.

Shields, J. (1978). Genetics. In: J. K. Wing, ed., *Schizophrenia: Towards a New Synthesis.* London: Academic Press.

Small, I. F., Small, J. G., Milstein, V., and Moore, J. E. (1972). Neuropsychological observations with psychosis and somatic treatment. *J. Nerv. Ment. Dis., 155,* 6–13.

Spitzer, R. L., Endicott, J., and Robins, E. (1978). Research Diagnostic Criteria. Rationale and reliability. *Arch. General Psychiat., 35,* 773–782.

Spohn, H. E., Lacoursiere, R. B., Thompson, K., and Coyne, L. (1977). Phenothiazine effect on psychological and psychophysiological dysfunction in chronic schizophrenics. *Arch. General Psychiat., 34,* 633–644.

Spreen, O., and Benton, A. L. (1977). *Neurosensory Center Comprehensive Examination for Aphasia.* Victoria, British Columbia: University of Victoria, Department of Psychology, Neuropsychology Laboratory.

Spreen, O., and Gaddes, W. H. (1969). Developmental norms for 15 neuropsychological tests age 6 to 15. *Cortex, 5,* 171–191.

Stern, R., and Minkoff, K. (1979). Paradoxes in programming for chronic patients in a community clinic. *Hosp. Community Psychiat., 30,* 613–617.

Sullivan, H. S. (1953). *The Interpersonal Theory of Psychiatry.* New York: W. W. Norton.

Taylor, M. A., Abrams, R., and Gaztanaga, P. (1975). Manic-depressive illness and schizophrenia: A partial validation of research diagnostic criteria utilizing neuropsychological testing. *Comp. Psychiat., 16,* 91–96.

Taylor, M. A., Redfield, J., and Abrams, R. (1981). Neuropsychological dysfunction in schizophrenia and affective disease. *Biol. Psychiat., 16,* 467–478.

Tiffin, J. (1968). *Purdue pegboard.* Chicago: Science Research Associates.

van Praag, H. M., and Verhoeven, M. A. (1981). Endorphin research in schizophrenic psychoses. *Comp. Psychiat., 22,* 135–146.

Vaughan, H. G., Jr. (1978). Toward a neurophysiology of schizophrenia. *J. Psychiat. Res., 14,* 129–154.

Vitalo, R. L., and Ross, C. (1979). The differential effects of skill training and chemotherapy in serving the chronically mentally ill. In: W. Anthony, ed., *The Principles of Psychiatric Rehabilitation.* Baltimore: University Park Press.

Watson, C., Thomas, R., Anderson, D., and Felling, J. (1968). Differentiation of organics from schizophrenics at two chronicity levels by use of the Reitan-Halstead organic test battery. *J. Consult. Clin. Psychol., 32,* 679–684.

Wechsler, D. (1955). *Wechsler Adult Intelligence Scale.* New York: Psychological Corporation.

Wechsler, D. (1974). *Wechsler Intelligence Scale for Children—Revised.* New York: Psychological Corporation.

Wepman, J. M. (1973). *Auditory Discrimination Test.* Chicago: Language Research Associates.

Werner, E. E., and Smith, R. S. (1979). An epidemiologic perspective on some antecedents and consequences of childhood mental health problems and learning disabilities. A report from the Kauai longitudinal study. *J. Am. Acad. Child Psychiat.*, 18, 292–306.

Zubin, J. (1965). Psychopathology and the social sciences. In: O. Klineberg and R. Christie, eds., *Perspectives in Social Psychology*. New York: Holt, Rinehart and Winston.

Zubin, J. (1980a). Chronic schizophrenia from the standpoint of vulnerability. In: C. Baxter and T. Melnechuk, eds., *Perspectives in Schizophrenia Research*. New York: Raven Press.

Zubin, J. (1980b). *Schizophrenia in the 80's*. Paper presented at the Department of Psychiatry, Upstate Medical Center, Syracuse, May, 1980.

NOTES

1. Most patients (88%) indicated right hand preference upon clinical assessment with the lateral dominance examination described by Spreen and Gaddes (1969); 8% indicated left hand preference, 2% indicated mixed preference, and 1% was unknown. These percentages corresponded to normal expectancies (Coren and Porac, 1977; Lishman and McMeekan, 1976) and did not support some observations of increased left handedness in psychiatric patients (Gur, 1977; Nasrallah et al., 1981).

2. We used the categorized word list of 10 articles of clothing for adults and 10 animal names for children. Two indices of performance were studied. One, a measure of consistent recall, was the count (on the sixth trial) of words that would be recalled on all subsequent trials. The other, a recognition measure, evaluated the detection (proportion of hits to false positive identifications) of 10 target words embedded among 10 distractor words of the same category.

3. Five somatosensory measures were employed. (1) Our finger differentiation index was the total error score for the in-between and two-point-finger tests described by Kinsbourne and Warrington (1962). (2) Our finger agnosia index was the error score of the tactile finger localization test, which is an allied procedure of the Halstead-Reitan neuropsychological test battery. (3) Our tactile form index was the error score of the tactile form recognition test, also an allied procedure of the Halstead-Reitan neuropsychological test battery. (4) Our face-hand index was the error score on a 20-trial test of double simultaneous tactile perception described by Fink et al. (1952). Individuals, seated and facing the examiner with eyes closed, were touched lightly on either or both sides of their face, on either or both hands, and on one side of their face together with the same or opposite-side hand (10 conditions). (5) Our graphesthesia index was the error score of the fingertip number writing perception test, which is another allied procedure of the Halstead-Reitan neuropsychological test battery. Our administration was slightly different in that numbers were traced in noninverted orientation, while individuals faced their palms with eyes closed. Four trials were obtained for each finger and each palm, resulting in 24 trials for each hand.

4. These categories represented only *primary* diagnoses and were mutually exclusive. Patients with neuropsychological disorders were distributed as follows: developmental perceptual disorder (39%), frontal lobe dysfunction (20%), seizure disorder (12%), nutritional disorder (7%), secondary language disorder (5%), sequela of head trauma (5%), secondary visual-spatial disorder (4%), drug toxicity (3%), and executive-motor disorder (4%).

5. This was based upon a combination of primary and secondary neuropsychological diagnoses.

6. Although the developmental perceptual disorder group was younger ($\bar{x} = 20.4$) than the group with nondevelopmental disorder ($\bar{x} = 41.3$) and the group without neuropsychological disorder ($\bar{x} = 36.8$) ($p = .01$), age should not have differentially affected these groups' performance on these measures. Wechsler and Wide Range Achievement Test scores were converted into age-corrected standard scores, based upon each test's published norms, prior to being standardized in our sample.

7. Seven developmental disorder patients could not be classified within either of these categories. Moreover, there was insufficient descriptive homogeneity among them to suggest the creation of a third group.

8. The visual-spatial and language disorder groups did not differ from each other in age, number of admissions, psychiatric diagnosis, years of education, or sexual composition.

9. Four patients, two for whom medication status was uncertain and two who were treated with only a minor tranquilizer (Valium), were excluded from this analysis. Of the 47 patients receiving psychotropic medication, 31 received only antipsychotics, 6 received only mood-active drugs, and 10 received combinations of antipsychotics and mood-active drugs. The 43 nonmedicated patients, some of whom had never been medicated, were without medication at the time of testing. As might be expected, patients receiving psychotropic medication were more chronic (i.e., had more inpatient admissions, $p<.05$) than nonmedicated patients.

10. There were no positive correlations between individual mg/kg dosage levels (*re* estimated equivalent dosage of chlorpromazine) and any neuropsychological measures. Instead, a negative correlation existed for three neuropsychological measures (Wepman, finger agnosia, and finger differentiation tests), suggesting an inverse relationship between dosage and performance levels. Additionally, our neuropsychologically diagnosed group received significantly less medication than our group without neuropsychological disorder ($p<.05$). Our developmental group also had the lowest mean mg/kg dosage of the groups to which they were compared ($p=.05$). There was no difference in mean dosage between the visual-spatial and language disorder groups.

8

The Neuropsychology of Schizophrenia

GERALD GOLDSTEIN

What Is Schizophrenia?

To many clinicians, the term schizophrenia has become controversial because it has been applied to a wide variety of conditions that apparently have little in common. Individuals described as "schizophrenic" may exhibit a diversity of behaviors that reflect not only the wide variability inherent in the disorder itself, but also the influence of a number of factors extraneous to it. Notable among them are the long-term effects of institutionalization, the short and long-term effects of various somatic treatments and a wide range of behaviors associated with what has been termed "impression management" (Price, 1972; Watson, 1972). Research over the past several decades has raised numerous questions about the reliability, and in some cases, the validity of psychiatric diagnosis. Indeed, the most recent *Diagnostic and Statistical Manual of Mental Disorders* (DSM III) has taken note of these difficulties, and provides a more specific definition of schizophrenia than was commonly applied within American psychiatry. At least in part, these problems arise from the fact that there are as yet no definitive diagnostic markers for schizophrenia—biological or otherwise—and we continue to depend upon clinical phenomenology to identify it.

Let us briefly review the DSM-III diagnostic criteria for schizophrenia. In order to make the diagnosis, six criteria must be met: (1) The patient must have certain critical symptoms: bizarre delusions; auditory hallucinations; incoherence; and blunted, flat or inappropriate affect or catatonic behavior. (2) There must be evidence of deterioration from a previous level of function. (3) The signs of illness must persist for at least 6 consecutive months of the individual's life. (4) If the patient also has a major affective disorder, it must have developed after the psychotic symptoms and must be brief in duration relative to them. (5) The onset of the disorder must occur before age 45. (6) The condition may not be due to an organic mental disorder or mental retardation, as defined elsewhere in DSM-III. Most significantly, schizophrenic disorders are distinguished from schizophreniform disorders, in which the duration of illness is less than 6 consecutive months; schizoaffective disorders, in which the clinician cannot distinguish between schizophrenia and an affective disorder; and various organic mental disorders that may resemble schizophrenia, notably, illnesses associated with abuse of amphetamine or phencyclidine. Various structured interviewing procedures and diagnostic criteria have been devised to assure maximal reliability of psychiatric diagnosis (Feighner et al., 1972; Helzer et al., 1981; Spitzer, Endicott, and Robins, 1978), and many researchers and clinicians make use of these schedules and criteria in their assessment related work.

DSM-III takes a descriptive approach, characterizing schizophrenia in the phenomenological terms summarized above. This strategy is appropriate for many of the psychiatric disorders, clearly including schizophrenia, because their pathogenesis and etiology remain essentially unknown. Within this descriptive framework, investigators of schizophrenia have also found it useful to apply Hughlings Jackson's (1932) distinction between positive and negative symptoms. In psychopathology, the negative symptoms are the signs of deficit in the cognitive or affective sphere such as blunted affect or intellectual impairment, while the positive symptoms are identifiable phenomena such as delusions and hallucinations. During the acute phase of schizophrenic disorders, the positive symptoms tend to become more pronounced, while during the more quiescent phases, the patient tends to demonstrate mainly the negative symptoms. Thus, the schizophrenic patient, when not in an episode of illness, may be emotionally flat and withdrawn, but may not demonstrate florid psychotic behavior such as using bizarre language or hearing voices. As we will see later, neuropsychology may have more to offer regarding the negative symptoms than the positive ones.

A major unresolved issue concerning schizophrenia has to do with its course. At first, schizophrenia was commonly regarded as a slowly deteriorating illness, and in fact it was originally called "dementia praecox" (premature dementia). It is no longer thought to be a progressive dementia, if one defines that condition in terms of slowly advancing deterioration of intellectual function. Long-term observation of schizophrenic patients suggests that most do not become demented at all, but stay the same or even get better sometimes. There may be a type of schizophrenia in which deterioration does in fact occur over the years, but it appears to be a relatively rare form of the disorder. According to the "vulnerability theory" of Zubin and Spring (1977), schizophrenia is not a deteriorative disorder, but an episodic one. Individuals who from genetic or acquired factors are particularly susceptible to life stress may experience episodes involving behaviors that would be characterized as schizophrenic. However, these episodes are generally time-limited and the individual returns to his or her premorbid level. It has been reported that when these individuals are not going through episodes, they are indistinguishable from the rest of the community (Bleuler, 1978; Zubin, Magaziner, and Steinhauer, 1983). Many clinicians would now agree that a large portion of their schizophrenic patients experience episodes or acute exacerbations of illness intermixed with more quiescent periods.

Thus, in answer to the question "What is schizophrenia?" we have the descriptive definition of DSM III, and the commonly accepted view that it is a partially genetic, partially acquired disorder marked by intermingled episodes of disorganized behavior and quiescent phases. During the episodes both positive and negative symptoms may be present, but at other times only the negative symptoms may be noted. The former view that schizophrenia is a degenerative disease of the brain has been largely discarded, although there is accumulating evidence that at least some schizophrenics have characteristic anomalies of brain function and structure.

Clinical Neuropsychological Assessment of Schizophrenia

The Early Years

Some years ago, I reviewed the early attempts made within psychology to describe the various cognitive and perceptual deficits commonly found in schizophrenics and to determine how the nature of these deficits differed from what is seen among patients with structural brain lesions (Goldstein, 1978). Malec (1978) and Heaton, Baade, and Johnson (1978) have written similar review articles, and we all reached essentially the same conclusions. While the early years produced exciting and innovative conceptions of schizophrenic thinking and of the differences between thinking in schizophrenics and brain-damaged individuals, the studies were severely handicapped by various technical and theoretical difficulties, making it hard to interpret in the light of contemporary knowledge and research methods. Modern clinical neuropsychology no longer makes a simplistic distinction between "organic" and "schizophrenic" patients. Furthermore, it is probably fair to say that many psychopathologists now prefer structured psychiatric interviews to either objective or projective tests as the instruments of choice for psychiatric diagnoses. This accounts for the use of such procedures as the Schedule for Affective Disorders and Schizophrenia (SADS) (Spitzer and Endicott, 1973), and the Renard Diagnostic Interview (Helzer et al., 1981). The Diagnostic Interview Schedule (DIS) (Robins et al., 1981) is also quite commonly used to establish diagnoses for research purposes and in some cases for clinical applications. Clinical neuropsychological tests are not used to diagnose schizophrenia, and their application to differential diagnosis between schizophrenia and structural brain damage has become controversial. Thus, the early years during which we tried to tell if a patient was schizophrenic or brain-damaged by looking at the Bender-Gestalt drawings or performance on the Rorschach test are behind us.

Nevertheless, it may be imprudent to reject completely some of the earlier conceptions of the neuropsychology of schizophrenia that have stood the test of time. For example, it is still recognized that schizophrenics typically have difficulties with complex cognitive tasks, and that K. Goldstein's theories concerning impairment of the "abstract attitude" were correct in principle (Goldstein, 1939; 1959). Numerous studies performed in recent years (e.g., Watson et al., 1968) have attested to the difficulties schizophrenics have with conceptual tasks. Contemporary theory, however, has gone one step further and raised the question of why they do so poorly. Many researchers now feel that the apparent conceptual deficits of the schizophrenic patient may well be a matter of failure to attend to the task, often because of interfering ideation, in combination with motivational lag (Sutton, 1973). The problem of attention in schizophrenia has received extensive study, with particular emphasis on the reaction time experiment (Zubin, 1975); however, while schizophrenics do have attentional deficits, it is clear they also have many other neuropsychological disturbances. Indeed, Chapman and Chapman (1973) have described this phenomenon as the "general deficit syndrome". The apparent generality of deficit has raised questions regarding the specificity, clinical correlates, and predictive validity (in terms of treatment outcome or natural history) of neuropsychological strategies in schizophrenia. Before reviewing some recent work, let us consider the central challenges faced by neuropsychological research in this disorder.

Some Challenges for Clinical Neuropsychology

Since the pathogenesis and etiology of schizophrenia remain unknown, the neuropsychologist is in a somewhat different position than when he examines brain-damaged patients. With brain-damaged patients, there are generally marker cases in which the area and nature of some structural lesion are well described, or the etiology of the disorder in question is relatively well understood. Thus, much of the clinical neuropsychological literature is based on the detailed study of patients with well-documented brain lesions.

In the case of schizophrenia, one's neuropsychology has to be based on the theoretical conception of the disorder that one holds. The vulnerability model implies that the neuropsychological assessment of an individual will yield different patterns depending on whether he is experiencing an episode. If one accepts this view, longitudinal testing should provide a variable picture of diminished and improved function. If schizophrenia is a degenerative disease, one would expect testing to reveal slowly progressive change for the worse.

To add to the complexity, the vulnerability model makes a distinction between vulnerability markers and episode markers. The episode markers may involve both positive and negative symptoms, while the vulnerability markers may be only or mainly negative symptoms. Both types can be present if the patient is in the midst of an episode, but only the vulnerability markers when the patient is not having an episode. It is also possible that some of the vulnerability markers may be seen to some extent in unaffected family members of the patient (Zubin and Steinhauer, 1981). One challenge for neuropsychology, then, is to determine which model of schizophrenia is most consistent with what is known and discovered about brain-behavior relationships in this disorder.

The clinical phenomenology of schizophrenia is characterized by bizarre behavior and sometimes unintelligible language, delusions and hallucinations, and a series of affective and personality characteristics such as withdrawal, affective blunting and apathy. The standard neuropsychological tests measure formal cognitive processes, perceptual and motor skills, memory, visual-spatial skills, and related functions. While schizophrenics frequently do poorly on these tests, their performance is not linked in any apparent way with the clinical phenomenology. Kietzman, Spring, and Zubin (1980) comment on such neuropsychological studies as follows: "Often those studies seem rather arid and removed from meaningful contexts in the lives of psychiatric patients. In fact, one often wonders why those investigations were ever begun, since they seem to reveal deviant responses far removed from those presented as the patient's chief complaint. It is the authors' premise here that the deviant responses patients display in laboratory testing underlie some of the symptoms they present clinically" (p. 334). Thus, a second challenge for neuropsychology is to relate the performance patterns seen on neuropsychological tests to the actual nature of schizophrenia as it is manifested. If this challenge is not met, then what is found in the test performance of schizophrenics may be merely epiphenomena related to failures of attention, motivation, and comprehension of instructions. We will have learned little about the disorder itself.

Neuropsychological assessment, like other forms of assessment and diagnostic evaluation, is ideally linked to treatment. Thus, the assessment should provide suggestions for planning rehabilitation or other forms of amelioration of a disabling disorder. In the case of rehabilitation oriented neuropsychological evaluation, an effort is made to identify the patient's deficits and preserved abilities, generally in an attempt to use the remaining assets to aid in compensating for those skills no longer available. As Luria (1963) puts it, the attempt is made to replace a destroyed link in a functional system with an intact link.

These links between assessment and treatment have not been constructed for schizophrenia. The customary pharmacological and behavioral management of schizophrenic patients tends to bear little relationship to the results of the neuropsychological testing, even though such testing might have been done. Instead, schizophrenic patients generally are referred for neuropsychological testing because the referring clinician seeks advice concerning the existence of other disorders, notably structural brain diseases, that would contraindicate the use of conventional somatic therapies. Thus, a third challenge is to make neuropsychological assessment more relevant to the treatment of schizophrenia. Failure to meet this challenge could call into question the role of neuropsychologists in psychiatric settings, except perhaps to rule out structural brain disorders in patients known to be schizophrenic or for whom the diagnosis is unclear. With the advent of sophisticated brain imaging techniques even this role can soon become redundant.

Perhaps the ultimate challenge for neuropsychology is to make a significant contribution to the discovery of the etiology and pathogenesis of schizophrenia. While the syndrome is relatively easily recognized clinically, and while much is known about biological correlates of the disorder, its cause remains unknown. There is a great deal of evidence (Mirsky, 1969) to suggest, however, that it is, at least in certain respects, a neuropsychological disorder. That is, most authorities would agree that there is something aberrant about the central nervous system of schizophrenics, but we do not quite know what it is. The use of techniques derived from information theory (Kietzman, Spring, and Zubin, 1980) can be helpful in tracing events through various stages in the central nervous system and to identify deviances from normal information processing. Even given this, neuropsychologists still need to know the biological bases, be they primarily structural or neuropsychological, of such deviances.

Recent Neuropsychological Studies of Schizophrenia

In this section, I will consider how neuropsychological investigation has responded to the challenges outlined above. First, we will consider the matter of whether or not neuropsychological tests can diagnose schizophrenia. In other words, is there a pattern of neuropsychological test performance that distinguishes the schizophrenic patient from members of other diagnostic groups within both the psychiatric and neurologic realms? While neuropsychological tests generally do not evaluate, nor do they attempt to systematically elicit, such positive symptoms as delusions and hallucinations, they do assess many of the negative symptoms, particularly in the cognitive and perceptual domains. I might add, parenthetically, here that some neuropsychologists feel that the question is an unfair one, since the standard neuropsychological tests, at least, were not designed or intended to be used for the assessment of schizophrenic patients. Nevertheless, there is by now abundant evidence that there is a neuropsychology of schizophrenia, and if that is the case, then neuropsychologists should have some capability of assessing schizophrenic patients. Second, there is a long tradition, at least going back to the Greystone Psychosurgery studies (Mettler, 1949) of using neuropsychological tests to evaluate schizophrenic patients and in diagnostic assessments to determine whether the patient is schizophrenic or structurally brain damaged (Goldstein, 1978). One cannot at this point "apologize" for several decades of research directed toward solving this problem, much of which was unproductive, by claiming that the tests were not designed for the purpose in the first place.

In commenting on the diagnostic utility of neuropsychology in schizophrenia, the conclusions reached by Heaton and Crowley (1981) following an extensive survey of the relevant literature seem a fitting place to start. They found that neuropsychological tests failed to discriminate between patients with "functional" and "organic" disorders when chronic/process schizophrenics were included in the "functional" group, but succeeded when they were not included. Second, neuropsychological tests had great difficulty identifying known neurological conditions in schizophrenic patients primarily because chronic/process schizophrenics performed like brain-damaged patients on neuropsychological tests even without known lesions. These findings are troublesome, since the modern nosology of schizophrenia tends to restrict that diagnosis primarily to persons who would have been considered "process" in earlier studies (for example, DSM III requires a 6-month duration of illness, and omits the older term "acute schizophrenia").

The St. Cloud Studies and Their Legacy

Heaton and Crowley's (1981) conclusions were forcefully thrust upon the professional community by a group of investigations conducted at the St. Cloud VA Hospital, all of which concluded that the Halstead-Reitan neuropsychological test battery failed to discriminate between schizophrenic and brain-damaged patients regardless of whether the schizophrenics were "acute" or "chronic" (Watson et al., 1968). This study was criticized for various methodological errors, notably failure to provide adequate neurological assessments of the schizophrenic subjects (Levine, 1974; Levine and Feirstein, 1972). However, subsequent studies with better documented cases (Chelune et al., 1979; Goldstein, 1977) reached essentially the same conclusions and, in retrospect, it appears that the St. Cloud group was essentially correct in their conclusion that the Halstead-Reitan battery does not generate performance patterns that can discriminate between brain-damaged and schizophrenic patients. At the same time, the principle that schizophrenics had neuropsychological deficit was finally established, and the existence of a neuropsychology of schizophrenia has been strongly supported by those studies; specifically, schizophrenic patients characteristically performed poorly on perceptual and cognitive tests which demanded complex information processing, maintenance of attention, and exercise of rapid psychomotor speed. While much of this was known already, the St. Cloud studies underscored the fact that commonly used neuropsychological tests are sensitive to the influence of these now well-known characteristics of schizophrenic patients. Whether or not these characteristics are purely "behavioral" phenomena or the result of impaired brain function will be considered in a later section of this chapter. However, one perhaps oversimplified response to the St. Cloud studies was that schizophrenics are indistinguishable from brain-damaged patients on neuropsychological tests because they, too, are brain damaged.

One proposed solution to the problem of failure to discriminate application of multivariate statistics. The use of powerful tools such as discriminant analysis might reveal performance patterns not observable through the application of univariate statistics or even clinical judgement. This attempt was not particularly successful either, particularly because while the optimizing power of these methods yielded some initially promising results, cross-validations based on applying the discriminant functions from the original studies to new data were generally unsuccessful (Goldstein, 1977). Thus, in my view, no one has been able to successfully derive a characteristic performance pattern on standard neuropsychological tests that is specific to schizophrenia.

If it is correct that schizophrenic patients demonstrate many of the same cognitive and perceptual deficits seen in patients with structural brain damage, what is the cause? One line of reasoning, echoing Werner's (1937) distinction between process and achievement has assumed that while the brain-damaged patient cannot do well on these tests, the schizophrenic patient *will* not do well. Thus, investigators have looked at many factors that might influence cognitive performance among schizophrenic patients, such as fear of failure (Webb, 1955) or disclosure (Shimkunas, 1972); interpersonal threat (Cameron, 1938a,b, 1944; Whiteman, 1954); intrusive ideation (Whiteman, 1954); distractability (Chapman, 1956a,b); and related motivational and stress associated considerations. Interestingly enough, it is often assumed, but not demonstrated, that patients with structural brain damage are not subject to these various influences, but rather simply fail to perform certain tasks on the basis of the capacity deficits associated with the brain disorder itself.

Other factors, beyond some specific "schizophrenic brain disorder", which can impair neuropsychological performance, include coexisting or complicating illnesses, the effects of institutionalization, length-chronicity of schizophrenia, and iatrogenic factors. In regard to the first point, many schizophrenics living out of institutional settings tend to neglect themselves, running a higher risk of nutritional and infectious disorders (Torrey and Peterson, 1976). There are subpopulations of schizophrenics who are alcoholics and substance abusers or who have other psychiatric disorders (Alterman, Erdlen, and Murphy, 1981). As Loberg points out in Chapter 18 and Carlin in Chapter 20, neuropsychological deficit is associated with alcoholism and drug abuse. Such observations, beyond highlighting some possible confounding influences, raise questions about the accuracy and reliability of traditional clinical diagnoses, and bespeak the importance of utilizing strict and reliable criteria for diagnosing schizophrenia. The Research Diagnostic Criteria (RDC) (Spitzer, Endicott, and Robins, 1978), based on a structured interview, are one example of a useful approach.

A second risk commonly associated with schizophrenia is long-term institutionalization. Institutionalization is thought to dull cognitive processes, thereby producing impairment on tests. For example, Goldstein and Halperin (1977) were able to show that length of institutionalization was a more powerful neuropsychological test discriminator than paranoid-nonparanoid status or presence or absence of a structural lesion superimposed on the schizophrenia (i.e., brain-damaged vs. non-brain-damaged schizophrenics).

The issue of the possible neuropsychological effects of somatic treatments for schizophrenia has recently been reviewed by Heaton and Crowley (1981). Neuroleptics can produce powerful extrapyradmidal effects, and their use has speculatively been related to the emergence of tardive dyskinesia, a movement disorder which is frequently irreversible. This problem is particularly pertinent for neuropsychologists because of their extensive use of tests of motor dexterity and speed. In addition to motor system effects, neuroleptic drugs may also affect vision and level of arousal, particularly during the early stage of treatment. Nor are the effects uniformly negative. For example, Spohn and associates have demonstrated that treated schizophrenics had improved attention and (possibly) abstraction when compared to untreated patients (Spohn et al., 1977). On the other hand, long-term use of neuroleptics might be associated with neuropsychological deficit. In their polydrug studies, Grant and associates found a relationship between cumulative exposure to antipsychotics and impairment in a small group of younger schizophrenics. It was not clear whether drugs were causal, or merely reflected a more refractory form of schizophrenia which was characterized by pre-existing deficit (Grant et al., 1978).

The other somatic treatments—ECT and psychosurgery—are discussed more fully in Chapters 10, 12, and 13. These treatments are not commonly used for schizophrenia.

To summarize the points made so far, the manifestation of deficits on standard neuropsychological tests might reflect some combination of the effects of the disorder itself, the influence of current treatment and treatment history, the possible influence of living for a long time in an institutional setting, the possible effects of disorders other than schizophrenia and, if one accepts the vulnerability model, the state of the disorder, particularly with regard to whether the patient is in or out of an episode. With regard to the latter point, most neuropsychological research with schizophrenic patients has implicitly viewed the disorder as a steady-state condition, thereby making the (perhaps) incorrect assumption that the patient's performance on one occasion somehow reflects some stable aspect of his condition. While some studies have looked at the effects of treatment on performance (see Heaton and Crowley, 1981, for a review), there has been little consideration of the well-known variability of the schizophrenic patient and, perhaps more significantly, the distinction between state and trait characteristics. It may be that in some cases test performance reflects transitory states not stable traits.

I began this discussion with a consideration of the St. Cloud studies, which demonstrated a rather well accepted phenomenon—substantial impairment among schizophrenics on standard neuropsychological tests. However, considering the implications of these studies has introduced many complexities. How then do we proceed to develop a neuropsychology of schizophrenia? There are both practical and theoretical difficulties. The major practical difficulty is that there are very few drug-free, noninstitutionalized schizophrenics in the world today. Therefore, the ideal subject would appear to be the "first break" patient who has never been hospitalized or on medication. The problem here, other than identifying the first episode, is that such patients are difficult to evaluate and may not cooperate with the standard neuropsychological tests. Even if they are cooperative, the bizarre nature of their positive symptoms can compromise interpretation of the test results. Perhaps the next best solution is to withdraw the stabilized patient from medication to do the evaluation, or alternatively, to use patients who have voluntarily stopped taking their medicine. The practical problems here are that it is often difficult to convince clinicians and administrators to withdraw patients from medication and correspondingly difficult to delay reinstatement of medication in patients who chose to stop using it, particularly if symptoms are starting to recur. A practical solution to several of these problems is to establish a clinical research unit in which nursing and other professional staff are trained to monitor patients carefully and to deal with the problems associated with drug withdrawal. Indeed, increasing our knowledge in this difficult area would require studies of carefully diagnosed patients evaluated under conditions that take into account medication status as well as other conditions that could influence performance on behavioral measures.

The Luria-Nebraska Studies

Purisch, Golden, and Hammeke (1978) reported that an objective battery based on a variety of Luria's procedures, now called the Luria-Nebraska Neuropsychological Battery (LNNB), discriminated effectively between chronic schizophrenic and brain injured patients. A discriminant analysis utilizing 14 summary measures derived from this battery yielded 88% correct classifications. Thus, we appear to have a standard neuropsychological test battery that produces results that stand in sharp contrast to what was found for the Halstead-Reitan battery by the St. Cloud group and others. The finding that seems most important is that schizophrenic patients performed significantly better than the brain-injured patients on all but four of the summary measures: Rhythm, Impressive (Receptive) Speech, Memory, and Intellectual Processes. Basically, the authors concluded that while brain injury produces deficits on both simple and complex tasks, schizophrenia only produces deficits on complex tasks. In later investigations it was found that chronicity of disorder and length of hospitalization had no effect on LNNB scores (Lewis et al., 1979) and that there are statistically significant correlations in young schizophrenics between various LNNB-derived measures and cerebral ventricular size as assessed by CT scan (Golden et al., 1980). The former finding contradicts Goldstein and Halperin's (1977) finding that Halstead-Reitan results are influenced by length of hospitalization in chronic schizophrenic patients. In an attempted replication of the Purisch et al. (1978) study, Shelly and Goldstein (1983) found that while the schizophrenic patients in their study obtained approximately the same profile on the LNNB as in the original study, the degree of discrimination between brain damaged and schizophrenic patients was not as high. It was suggested that the discrepancy resulted from differences in the level of impairment in the brain-damaged groups in the two studies.

Numerous substantive and methodological criticisms of Luria's neuropsychology and the Luria-Nebraska battery have been published (Adams, 1980; Crosson and Warren, 1982; Delis and Kaplan, 1982; Reitan, 1976; Spiers, 1981) to which the reader is referred. Here, we will only consider the potential contributions the LNNB can make to the neuropsychology of schizophrenia. First, we may ask what new information and methodological advances were gained from the series of studies reviewed above. Clearly, the failure to discriminate between brain damaged and schizophrenic patients on the Rhythm, Receptive Speech, Memory, and Intellectual Processes scales is another affirmation of the difficulties schizophrenics typically have with complex tasks involving sustained attention, abstract reasoning, and ability to function under distracting conditions. Perhaps more interesting is the fact that they performed better than brain damaged patients on several of the summary measures, thereby providing us with some objective tests on which the performance level obtained by chronic schizophrenic patients is not indistinguishable from what is found with brain damaged patients. However, as Shelly and Goldstein (1983) have suggested, and as I have pointed out before in a general way (Goldstein, 1978), findings of this type may be somewhat artifactual since similarities and differences between diagnostic groups can be altered by varying levels of impairment in one or more of the groups being compared. It should be noted that the schizophrenics' performance levels on the discriminating scales were not distinguishable from normal performance; they were simply distinguishable from mean scores obtained by a group of brain damaged patients. The fact that these scores were not in the normal range was confirmed by Lewis et al. (1979). The most important finding was that highly comparable LNNB profiles for chronic schizophrenic patients were found in two independent studies (Purisch, Golden, and Hammeke, 1978; Shelly and Goldstein, 1983). These profiles are presented in Fig. 1. It remains to be seen however, whether the profile is specific to schizophrenia, and indeed, if it has any differential diagnostic significance at all.

Schizophrenia: "Front vs. Back," "Right vs. Left," and "Top vs. Bottom"

The search for the "schizophrenic lesion" has taken us on a journey throughout the central nervous system, and in fact, into areas outside of the CNS such as the endocrine system. Here we will only consider evidence for localization obtained from behavioral indices, notably but not exclusively neuropsychological tests. Let us begin with Moniz's important dictum about schizophrenia, as cited by Freeman (1959). "In accordance with the theory which we have developed, one conclusion is derived: to cure these patients we must destroy the more or less fixed arrangements of cellular connections that exist in the brain, and particularly those which are related to the frontal lobes." (*op. cit.*, p. 1521). Freeman himself goes on to say, "The frontal lobe is the prime location for operations to relieve mental disorders." (*op. cit.*, p. 1522). Clearly, the relationship between the frontal lobes and schizophrenia was tied in with the idea of treatment by surgery, but the important point to be considered here is that there appears to have been some evidence for the relationship between frontal lobe function and schizophrenia. This relationship is congruent with views of K. Goldstein (1959) and his followers concerning the im-

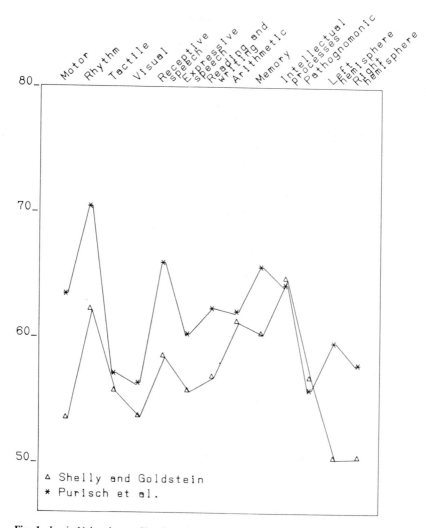

Fig. 1. Luria-Nebraska profiles for schizophrenic patients in Purisch, Hammeke and Golden, and Shelly and Goldstein studies.

portance of the frontal lobes for abstraction. Clinically, we tend to relate the cognition of the schizophrenic to that of the patient with a frontal lobe lesion in regard to abstraction, planning, regulation of behavior and judgement. While in recent years evidence for frontal lobe dysfunction in schizophrenics has come from measures of cerebral metabolism (Buchsbaum and Ingvar, 1982), there have been very few recent advances in the behavioral realm, aside from the many studies of post-frontal-lobotomy patients (Pribram, 1971; Walsh, 1978; see also Chapter 13). However, in these studies, observed results tend to be attributed more to the consequences of the surgery than to the mental disorder that led to its occurrence. As a conclusion, it would probably be fair to say that while the schizophrenic patient may exhibit many of the same behaviors seen in patients with frontal lobe lesions, there is no compelling evidence that Moniz was correct in implicating the frontal lobes as the anatomic locus for the pathogenesis of schizophrenia. It is, however, interesting to note that when schizophrenics are not active or interacting (i.e., at rest with pads over the eyes and in a quiet room) they show an abnormal pattern of cerebral activity, as measured by either regional cerebral blood flow (rCBF) or position emission tomography (PET). That is, they do not show the normal "hyperfrontal pattern" with relatively high flow in areas anterior to the Sylvian and Rolandic fissures, and relatively low flow posteriorly. Indeed, the reverse pattern is often found in schizophrenic patients (Buchsbaum and Ingvar, 1982). Thus, many schizophrenics do not do what normal people do when they are at rest, but the significance of this phenomenon in the etiology or pathogenesis of schizophrenia is unclear. Ingvar (1980) speculated that the high flow in the posterior regions may relate to abnormal perceptual experiences while the low flow in the frontal lobes may have to do with lack of synthesis of goal-related behavior, giving rise to lack of response to the environment.

While the PET scan and rCBF studies have restored some degree of interest in frontal lobe function in schizophrenia, the preponderance of neuropsychological interest in recent years has clearly been in the area of cerebral hemisphere asymmetries. The beginning of this interest is generally attributed to Flor-Henry (Flor-Henry, 1969; Flor-Henry and Yeudall, 1979) who noted several resemblances between schizophrenic behavior and the behavior of individuals with temporal lobe epilepsy—specifically temporal lobe epilepsy with a left hemisphere focus. These early observations ultimately led to what is by now a major hypothesis (if not an accepted belief in some quarters) that schizophrenia is associated with a yet to be delineated deficit involving the left cerebral hemisphere. The literature supporting this view has been reviewed several times (Alpert and Martz, 1977; Gruzelier and Flor-Henry, 1979; Nasrallah, 1982) and will not be covered in detail here. In general, however, the hypothesis is supported by electrophysiological (Shagass et al., 1979), neuropsychological (Flor-Henry and Yeudall, 1979; Gruzelier and Hammond, 1976) and to some extent neurochemical (Myslobodsky, Mintz, and Tomer, 1979) data, but not by anatomic evidence. In other words, when one looks at left hemisphere function, there seems to be extensive evidence for abnormality among schizophrenic patients; but when one looks at the left hemisphere structure, with the help of brain imaging or postmortem anatomic examinations, there are no variations specifically involving the left hemisphere (Andreasen 1982; Andreasen et al., 1982). There are clearly CT scan abnormalities in some schizophrenic patients, but they are not generally lateralized (Weinberger and Wyatt, 1982).

There are several theories about the nature of the left hemispheric dysfunction. One major theory, based primarily on Gur's (1978) work utilizing tachistoscopic hemifield stimulation and studies of lateral eye movement, is that schizophrenics overactivate the dysfunctional hemisphere. Schizophrenics were found to relatively dysfunctional in the right hemifield on a tachistoscopic task, and they demonstrated more rightward eye movements than did nonschizophrenics when answering questions. Putting these findings together, it was concluded that they tended to overactivate the very hemisphere that was dysfunctional.

A second theory postulated that schizophrenia is a type of disconnection syndrome in which there is impaired communication between the two hemispheres. This theory, developed by Beaumont and Dimond (1973), is based on studies contrasting ipsilateral and cross-lateral transfer of information. For example, Green (1978) reported that schizophrenics had greater than normal difficulty relearning a tactile task previously learned by the opposite hand.

A third theory postulates the presence of left temporal-limbic dysfunction and is based on psychophysiological data largely involving the galvanic skin response. This work was done mainly by Gruzelier and his group (Gruzelier, 1979). The found that some schizophrenics demonstrated an electrodermal asymmetry, with higher amplitude right-handed responses. Gruzelier took this as an indicator of impaired contralateral inhibition, but the neurology of electrodermal activity is complex and somewhat unsettled. Indeed, in reviewing his own work and that of others, Gruzelier (1979) recently wrote "at this stage, caution is necessary when interpreting both the direction of the influence (excitatory or inhibitory), and the hemisphere involved in the central influences on bilateral electrodermal activity." (p. 155).

The work of Gruzelier and his colleagues leads us naturally into a consideration of the "top vs. bottom" dimension. It is thought by some that schizophrenia does not involve the cerebral cortex directly, but rather a set of subcortical structures known as the limbic system. The limbic system has long been thought to be important in the mediation of emotion. Since the time of psychosurgery research there was great interest in subcortical structures, notably the connections between the frontal lobes and thalamic nuclei. Patients with limbic system lesions can develop schizophrenialike symptoms—hallucinations, ideas of reference, and catatonia (Gruzelier, 1979). However, with the exception of Gruzelier's work, there are no other neuropsychological studies addressing subcortical or limbic disturbance. This dearth of research is unfortunate since a subcortical localization is compatible with the most widely accepted neurochemical theory of schizophrenia—the dopamine hypothesis (Henn, 1982). Stevens (1982) suggests that disturbance is most likely to be found in dopaminergic pathways involving the amygdala and hippocampus.

The search for the "schizophrenic lesion" has not ended, but, as we have seen, over the years neuropsychological research has implicated a wide variety of structures and systems. In my view, there are two important problems at the present stage of this research. First, information obtained using different methods is not providing a consistent picture. Data from brain imaging suggest generalized neuronal depletion (enlarged ventricles bilaterally), or an abnormal pattern of cerebral metabolism along the anterior–posterior axis. Much of the behavioral evidence, on the other hand, suggests that the difficulty is along the lateral axis—left hemisphere dysfunction, in particular. The neurochemical and neuropharmacological data are largely supportive of a subcortical localization. While these three points of view are not necessarily mutually exclusive, they have yet to be integrated into a comprehensive statement concerning etiology and pathogenesis. The second problem is how to relate the neurological findings and the clinical phenomenology of schizophrenia. So far, attempts to bridge this gap have been largely speculative, based on reasoning by analogy. At present, we still know of no neurological or neuropsychological correlate of a delusion, hallucination, or idea of reference.

The Schizophrenic Brain

A book has recently been published with the intriguing title *"Schizophrenia as a Brain Disease"* (Henn and Nasrallah, 1982). As most of us know, scientists and clinicians have been looking at schizophrenic brains for many years, either through imaging techniques or at autopsy, but nothing obvious has "popped out" as characteristic of the disorder. Indeed, the gross anatomic appearance of the schizophrenic brain is generally quite normal. Perhaps one of the most intriguing and puzzling aspects of schizophrenia is this discrepancy between the bizarre and deviant behavior of the schizophrenic during life and the normal appearance of the central nervous system after death. What has changed during recent years is technology, and so we now have the opportunity to look at schizophrenic brains in the living individual and after death in ways that until recently were not possible. Thus, it is hoped that these new technologies will help discover the basic biological nature of the disorder. In this section, I will review briefly some of the emerging findings, and attempt to relate them to behavioral data.

Morphology and Neuropathology

Essentially every study that has used the CT scan with schizophrenic patients has found that a certain number of them have abnormalities. The major abnormality is atrophy, usually in the form of ventricular enlargement (Weinberger and Wyatt, 1982). The review article by Weinberger and Wyatt *(op. cit.)* cites 15 such studies. It seems quite clear that there is a substantial incidence of cerebral atrophy among schizophrenics, although it must be emphasized that most schizophrenics have normal CT scans. Thus, it is unlikely that this finding relates to pathogenesis or etiology in any general way. However, it may well explain to some extent the substantial deficits that many schizophrenics demonstrate on neuropsychological tests. There have been several studies that produced various levels of correlation between the degree of atrophy and the neuropsychological deficit (Adams et al., 1984; Donnelly et al., 1980; Golden et al., 1980; Reider et al., 1979). These correlations were found for both the

Halstead-Reitan and Luria-Nebraska batteries, suggesting that the obtained relationships apply to a wide variety of types of neuropsychological impairment, or alternatively, to the general deficit syndrome. It also seems clear that the schizophrenic with atrophy differs in many respects from those without atrophy. As a general statement, Weinberger and Wyatt (1982) suggest that all of these differences are associated with poorer prognosis for the group with atrophy.

Autopsy studies of schizophrenics have produced a variety of findings, but nothing consistent. These include significant depletion of neurons and myelin, gliosis, and certain specific findings such as a particularly large amount of neuronal depletion and myelin degeneration in the globus pallidus of catatonic patients (Stevens, 1982). In a way, the neuropathological and CT scan findings are both consistent with "premature aging"—the view that many of the pathological changes normally found in the brains of elderly individuals are found in schizophrenics during young adulthood and middle age. It has also been suggested that some of the findings are consistent with an infectious etiology (Torrey and Peterson, 1976); but even if this were so, it would still be unclear if infection causes schizophrenia, or if schizophrenics are more likely to become infected because of some basic immune system disturbance linked to the pathogenic process, or because of poor self care and nutrition.

Neurophysiology

The results of routine EEG procedures using scalp electrodes are that schizophrenics have a somewhat higher prevalence of abnormal EEGs than the normal population—in some series as high as 35% (Hill, 1956; Itil, 1977; Stevens, 1982). However, when more sophisticated procedures are used, certain characteristic abnormal findings begin to appear. For example, Flor-Henry and Yeudall (1979) reported an abnormal power distribution in the 20–35 Hz band in the left temporal region of unmedicated schizophrenics. Some studies have revealed that schizophrenics tend to have low amplitude irregular beta waves with relative reduction of alpha (Itil, 1977). Activated EEG studies (i.e. with subjects premedicated) have also yielded interesting results. For example, Gibbs and Gibbs (1963) found "mitten patterns" in the sleep EEGs of psychotic patients after administration of barbiturates far more frequently than was the case for normals. Itil (1964) found differences between schizophrenics' and depressives' sleep patterns following administration of thiopenthal.

The literature on evoked potentials (Zubin, Kietzman, and Steinhauer, *in press*) is also extensive, probably the most interesting aspect of it having to do with the analysis of information processing. One of the more significant findings is that schizophrenic patients fail to develop a normal appearing P300 component of the wave form during information processing (Levit, Sutton, and Zubin, 1973). The P300 component is thought to be related to decision making. This finding has been replicated in several laboratories, but there is an impression among workers in the field that it may be more of an episode than a vulnerability marker since the P300 tends to normalize following effective treatment. One group working with evoked potentials has also discovered some interesting phenomena when looking at the P300 component in combination with pupillometry (Steinhauer and Zubin, 1982). Basically, schizophrenics tend toward diminution of the P300 component plus absence of the degree of pupillary dilation seen in normals (Steinhauer, Hakerem, and Spring, 1979; Steinhauer and Zubin, 1982).

Cerebral Metabolism

In recent years, two major techniques have been developed that are capable of evaluating brain activity or cerebral metabolism—regional cerebral blood flow, and positron emission tomography. The technology for both of these techniques is quite complex, and they are currently available in very few settings. However, it is particularly interesting to note that both of them arrive at essentially the same conclusion regarding an anomaly in the cerebral metabolism of schizophrenics. In the case of the blood flow studies, while it is normal to have a relatively high flow frontally and a low flow posteriorly when at rest, the reverse relationship is found with schizophrenics. Correspondingly, in the case of the PET scan, it is normal to show a higher glucose uptake in the frontal than in the occipital cortex. This relationship is reversed in schizophrenics (Buchsbaum and Ingvar, 1982).

Conclusions

Whether or not schizophrenia is a brain disease, there clearly appear to be numerous anomalies of brain function and structure. As a rule, however, the majority of schizophrenic patients tend not to show these anomalies. Thus, for example, most schizophrenics have a normal EEG and CT scan. It is not clear from the current literature what proportion of schizophrenics have the P300 anomaly discussed above, or the hypofrontal pattern found on PET scans and regional cerebral blood flow measures. Thus, the findings do not converge on a general theory of pathogenesis or etiology. The findings *do* underscore the heterogeneous nature of schizophrenia, and point to the need to develop consistent typologies based on reliable criterion information.

Current Status and Future Prospects in the Neuropsychology of Schizophrenia

Following what in hindsight was a false start involving an overly empirical attempt to use neuropsychological tests to separate "schizophrenic" from "brain damaged" patients, certain neuropsychologists have developed a more technical and specific interest in schizophrenia itself, and are looking at it in terms of brain–behavior relationships. Probably the most active followers of this course are now engaged in the laterality and CT scan studies described above, with growing interest in cerebral blood flow (Ingvar, 1980). However, while the hemisphere asymmetry, metabolic and evoked potential findings are undoubtedly quite important, what I find most striking is that in almost all cases, not all of the schizophrenic patients studied, during life or after death, show the deviation or abnormality under investigation. While it might have been argued in the past that patients who did not demonstrate the phenomenon under scrutiny were not really schizophrenics but had some other disorder, the advent of rigorous diagnostic criteria based on structured interviewing techniques in combination with advances in brain imaging have made this possibility increasingly less likely. It seems more likely that while there are some commonalities emcompassing all of schizophrenia, there are, nevertheless, important subtypes that remain to be fully described. For example, Crow et al. (1982) have presented evidence for two distinct syndromes within schizophrenia. This dichotomy can be described along several dimensions, the crucial ones being a predominance of positive or negative symptoms, a normal or abnormal CT scan, and good or poor response to neuroleptic medication. What we can call type I are the individuals with mainly negative (deficit) symptoms, abnormal CT scans, and poor drug response, with type II being the opposite. In general, the long term prognosis seems to be poorer for type I than for type II schizophrenics.

If one accepts this basic premise, then the neuropsychological findings can be viewed within that context. The type I patient has observable structural brain disease and so can be expected to have those neuropsychological deficits generally associated with neuronal depletion. This group may be more appropriately described by the old term "dementia praecox". The hemisphere asymmetry findings are not as easy to interpret along these lines. However, Magaro (1978) has reported data that suggest that paranoid patients, rather than showing a left hemisphere deficit, actually prefer to process information with their left hemispheres. If one assumes that paranoid patients would generally show a preponderance of positive symptoms (e.g. delusions, hallucinations) then they may, as a group, tend to fall more into the type II than the type I category. Thus, the patients with left hemisphere deficiencies may be primarily type I patients. Correspondingly, Gruzelier (1979) reports that predominance of right handed electrodermal activity was more prevalent in institutionalized, chronic patients who were poor drug responders. Crow et al. (1982) suggest that the underlying pathological process in type I schizophrenia is cell loss and structural changes of a type that is observable with the CT scan. Type II, on the other hand, has a different pathogenesis, possibly associated with an increase in dopamine receptors. With regard to the type I structural changes, their etiology is unknown, but could be consistent with several theoretical mechanisms, viral infection or early life brain injury among them.

While I have offered plausible neuropsychological explanations for the negative symptoms of schizophrenia, what can be said about the positive symptoms? It has been speculated that the positive symptomatology may wax and wane with changes in dopamine uptake, but the underlying mechanisms for the phenomena remain unclear. It is possible that some aspects of positive symptomatology are explainable on the basis of underlying cognitive deficits with known cerebral correlates. Horenstein (1970), in another context, has also provided us with many pertinent clinical examples of how psychotic-appearing symptoms such as visual illusions, are readily explainable on the basis of identified structural brain disease. This question has probably been most carefully studied with regard to the relationships between schizophrenic language and aphasia (Andreasen, 1982; Gerson, Benson, and Frazier, 1977). Since the cerebral correlates of aphasia are reasonably well understood, and since they involve mainly the left hemisphere, it would be very important to know whether the characteristics of schizophrenic language are in fact aphasic. Unfortunately, there is no consensus concerning the answer to this question.

Neuropsychologists are increasingly interacting with investigators interested in information processing approaches to clinical phenomena. With regard to schizophrenia, there is some evidence that there is a deficit in early sensory integration in the information processing chain (Zubin, et al., *in press*) while others have provided support for the view that the deficit is more central, and involves defects at the level of information transfer between the two cerebral hemispheres (Beaumont and Dimond, 1973). The notion that something goes awry between stimulus and response in the schizophrenic, and that the nature of the deficit can be elucidated using informational approaches is an appealing one, but it now appears that the findings are considerably influenced by the specifics of the experimental program. Thus, while Collins (1972) infers defects in an early sensory stage, based on a visual persistence study, and Gur (1978) makes the same inference on the basis of a tachistoscopic study, Green, Glass, and O'Callaghan (1979) postulate that the difficulty lies at the point at which information must be transferred from one cerebral hemisphere to another, on the basis of their studies of intermanual transfer. Thus, we appear to be a long way from unequivocally identifying the actual level at which information processing goes awry in the schizophrenic, and even further away from identifying a cerebral correlate. However, the notion that the difficulty is at the level of the corpus callosum and that the schizophrenic bears some resemblance to a "split-brain" patient is an intriguing and eminently testable hypothesis, perhaps utilizing some of the procedures developed by Sperry and his various coworkers (Gazzaniga, 1970). It is clearly also possible that some defect in early processing has implications for what happens further upstream.

In contrast to information processing techniques, traditional neuropsychology has employed multivariate statistics or some form of qualitative analysis in attempts to identify a profile or pattern that characterizes the schizophrenic patient and distinguishes between schizophrenia and other forms of psychopathology. This method of qualitative or quantitative syndrome analysis has been quite effective historically in clinical neuropsychology; it has provided, as an example, a useful means of classifying the aphasias (Goodglass and Kaplan, 1972). Perhaps it has been less effective in the case of schizophrenia because it typically did not take into account the notion of the two syndromes discussed above. I suggest that the neuropsychological profile of the type I patient would be essentially indistinguishable from that of the patient with mild or early dementia associated with structural brain disease. It is difficult to predict a pattern for type II patients since they may do poorly on neuropsychological tests not because of structural brain damage but because of the attentional, motivational and attitudinal considerations discussed above. Clinically, I have seen a wide range of performance levels among schizophrenic patients—from essentially normal neuropsychological test performance to extremely impaired performance. Thus, while one might expect to find a characteristic "dementia-like" profile among type I schizophrenics, one can anticipate a great deal of variability among type II schizophrenics.

In view of these considerations, I would summarize the current status of the field in the following manner. The standard clinical neuropsychological tests generally do not discriminate well between brain damaged and schizophrenic patients, but reasons for failure to discriminate are becoming increasingly clarified. First, radiological and neuropathological evidence indicates that there is a group of schizophrenics that demonstrate frank neuronal depletion. Second, there is suggestive, but not yet definitive, evidence of some form of chemical or structural disorder involving the left hemisphere. It is not clear that the standard neuropsychological tests can distinguish between the postulated two schizophrenic syndromes, since patients with either syndrome may do poorly in a general way on these tests, but perhaps for different reasons. We know of no pattern or specific information processing deficit that can distinguish between the two subtypes at the moment. However, CT scan data and success/failure of response to neuroleptics might aid in making the delineation. Perhaps one conclusion that can be drawn is that the standard neuropsychological tests are sensitive to structural brain damage, as indicated by the high correlations found between atrophy and test performance, even in schizophrenic patients. However, they are not sensitive to schizophrenia; that is they do not appear to discriminate well between functional impairment associated with structural loss or damage and functional impairment associated with attitudinal, attentional and motivational considerations. Perhaps this distinction can only be made through unobtrusive measures or, as Sutton (1973) has suggested, utilizing measures over which the subject has no control (e.g. psychophysiological indices of information processing) or for which the patient's performance is better than normal. The latter type of measure, if found, can be a powerful tool in dealing with the general deficit syndrome problem or the inference that the patient did not perform well because of emotional or motivational considerations.

One might wish to make a distinction between neuropsychological assessment of schizophrenic patients and the neuropsychology of schizophrenia. The former matter remains beset with problems because it is often difficult to identify structural brain damage in schizophrenic patients, and to discriminate between schizophrenic and brain damaged patients with the standard, commonly used neuropsychologigal tests. Referral questions regarding ruling out of structural damage in schizophrenics and "functional vs. organic" differential diagnosis therefore remain difficult to answer. With regard to the neuropsychology of schizophrenia, there has been substantial progress during recent years, and a great deal has been learned about functional and structural aspects of the schizophrenic's central nervous system. The CT and PET scan, and regional cerebral blood flow studies are obviously of great importance potentially, as is the material on hemisphere asymmetries. The distinction between the two types of schizophrenia would appear to be of great heuristic value, particularly from the standpoint of neuropsychology. The search goes on for definitive markers of schizophrenia in the genetic, neurochemical and behavioral spheres particularly, and more definitive answers to our diagnostic problems must await their discovery.

REFERENCES

Adams, K .M. (1980). In search of Luria's battery: A false start. *Percept. Motor Skills, 59*, 115–119.
Adams, K. M., Jacisin, J., Brown, G. G., and Boulos, R. (1984). Neurobehavioral and CT deficit in schizophrenics. *Percept. Motor Skills, 59*, 115–119.
Alpert, M., and Martz M. J., Jr. (1977). Cognitive views of schizophrenia in the light of recent studies of brain asymmetry. In: C. Shagass, S. Gershon, and A. J. Friedhoff, eds. *Psychopathology and Brain Dysfunction*. New York: Raven Press, pp. 1–13.
Alterman, A. I., Erdlen, F. E., and Murphy, E. (1981). Alcohol abuse in the psychiatric population. *Addictive Behav., 6*, 69–73.
Andreasen, N. C. (1982). The relationship between schizophrenic language and the aphasias. In: F. A. Henn and H. A. Nasrallah, eds. *Schizophrenia as a Brain Disease*. New York: Oxford University Press, pp. 99–111.
Andreasen, N. C., Dennert, J. W., Olsen, S. A., and Damasio, A. R. (1982). Hemispheric asymmetries and schizophrenia. *Am. J. Psychiat., 139*, 427–430.
Andreasen, N. C., Smith, M. R., Jacoby, C. G., Dennert, J. W., and Olsen, S. A. (1982). Ventricular enlargement in schizophrenia: Definition and prevalance. *Am. J. Psychiat., 139*, 292–296.
Beaumont, J. F., and Dimond, S. J. (1973). Brain disconnection and schizophrenia. *Br. J. Psychiat., 123*, 661–662.
Bleuler, M. (1978). *The Schizophrenic Disorders: Long-term Patient and Family Studies*, trans. S. M. Clemens. New Haven: Yale University Press.
Buchsbaum, M. S., and Ingvar, D. H. (1982). New visions of the schizophrenics brain: Regional differences in electrophysiology, blood flow, and cerebral glucose use. In: F. A. Henn and H. A. Nasrallah, eds. *Schizophrenia as a Brain Disease*. New York: Oxford University Press, pp. 235–252.
Cameron, N. (1938a). Reasoning, regression and communication in schizophrenics. *Psychol. Monogr., 50*, 1–33.
Cameron, N. (1938b). A study of thinking in senile deterioration and schizophrenic disoganization. *Am. J. Psychol., 51*, 650–664.
Cameron, N. (1944). Experimental analysis of schizophrenic thinking. In: J. S. Kasanin, ed., *Language and Thought in Schizophrenia*. Berkeley: University of California Press, pp. 50–64.

Chapman, L. J. (1956a). Distractibility in the conceptual performance of schizophrenics. *J. Abnorm. Soc. Psychol.*, *53*, 286–291.

Chapman, L. J. (1956b). The role of type of distractor in the concrete conceptual performance of schizophrenics. *J. Personality*, *25*, 130–141.

Chapman, L. J., and Chapman, J. P., eds. (1973). *Disordered Thought in Schizophrenia.* New York: Appleton-Century-Crofts.

Chelune, G. J., Heaton, R. K., Lehman, R. A., and Robinson, S. (1979). Level versus pattern of neuropsychological performance among schizophrenic and diffusely brain damaged patients. *J. Consult. Clin. Psychol.*, *47*, 155–163.

Collins, P. (1972). Reaction time measures of visual temporal integration in schizophrenic patients, other psychiatric patients, and normal subjects. Unpublished doctoral dissertation, Columbia University.

Crosson, B., and Warren, R. L. (1982). Use of the Luria-Nebraska neuropsychological battery in aphasia: A conceptual critique. *J. Consult. Clin. Psychol.*, *50*, 22–31.

Crow, T. J., Cross, A. J., Johnstone, E. C., and Owen, F. (1982). Two syndromes in schizophrenia and their pathogenesis. In: F. A. Henn and H. A. Nasrallah, eds., *Schizophrenia as a Brain Disease.* New York: Oxford Press, pp. 196–234.

Delis, D. C., and Kaplan, E. (1982). The assessment of aphasia with the Luria-Nebraska neuropsychological battery: A case critique. *J. Consult. Clin. Psychol.*, *50*, 32–39.

Donnelly, E. F., Weinberger, D. R., Waldman, I. N., and Wyatt, R. J. (1980). Cognitive impairment associated with morphological brain abnormalities on computed tomography in chronic schizophrenic patients. *J. Nerv. Ment. Dis.*, *168*, 305–308.

Feighner, J., Robins, E., Guze, S. B., Woodruff, R. A., Winocur, G., and Munoz, R. (1972). Diagnostic criteria for use in psychiatric research. *Arch. General Psychiatr.*, *26*, 57–63.

Flor-Henry, P. (1969). Psychoses and temporal lobe epilepsy; a controlled investigation. *Epilepsia*, *10*, 363–395.

Flor-Henry, P., and Yeudall, L. T. (1979). Neurospsychological investigation of schizophrenia and manic-depressive psychoses. In: J. Gruzelier and P. Flor-Henry, eds., *Hemisphere Asymmetries of Function in Psychopathology.* Amsterdam: Elsevier/North Holland, pp. 341–362.

Freeman, W. (1959). Psychosurgery. In: S. Arieti, ed., *American Handbook of Psychiatry*, vol II. New York: Basic Books.

Gazzaniga, M. S. (1970). *The Bisected Brain.* New York: Appleton-Century-Crofts.

Gerson, S. N., Benson, F., and Frazier, S. H. (1977). Diagnosis: Schizophrenia versus posterior aphasia. *Am. J. Psychiatr.*, *134*, 966–969.

Gibbs, F. A., and Gibbs, E. L. (1963). The mitten pattern. An electroencephalographic abnormality correlating with psychosis. *J. Neuropsychiatr.*, *5*, 6–13.

Golden, C. J., Moses, J. A., Zelazowski, R., Graber, B., Zatz, L. M., Horvath, T. B., and Berger, P. A. (1980). Cerebral ventricular size and neuropsychological impairment in young chronic schizophrenics. *Arch. Gen. Psychiatr.*, *37*, 619–623.

Goldstein, G. (1977, February). *The use of multivariate analysis in neuropsychological assessment of schizophrenia and brain damage.* Presented at the Contributions of Clinical Neuropsychology to Psychiatry Symposium, Ann. Int. Neuropsychol. Soc. Meet., Sante Fe.

Goldstein, G. (1978). Cognitive and perceptual differences between schizophrenics and organics. *Schizophrenia Bull.*, *4*, 160–185.

Goldstein, G., and Halperin, K. M. (1977). Neuropsychological differences among subtypes of schizophrenia. *J. Abnor. Psychol.*, *86*, 36–40.

Goldstein, K. (1939). *The Organism.* New York: American Book.

Goldstein, K. (1959). Functional disturbances in brain damage. In: S. Arieti, ed., *American Handbook of Psychiatry*, vol. I. New York: Basic Books, pp. 770–794.

Goodglass, H., and Kaplan, E. (1972). *The Assessment of Aphasia and Related Disorders.* Philadelphia: Lea & Febiger.

Grant, I., Adams, K. M., Carlin, A. S., Rennick, P. M., Judd, L. L., Schooff, K., and Reed,

R. (1978). Organic impairment in polydrug users: Risk factors. *Am. J. Psychiatr., 135,* 178–184.

Green, P. (1978). Defective interhemispheric transfer in schizophrenia. *J. Abnorm. Psychol., 87,* 472–480.

Green, P., Glass, A., and O'Callaghan, M. A. J., (1979). Some implications of abnormal hemisphere interaction in schizophrenia. In: J. Gruzelier and P. Flor-Henry, eds. *Hemisphere Asymmetries of Function in Psychopathology.* Amsterdam: Elsevier/North Holland, pp. 431–448.

Gruzelier, J. (1979). Lateral asymmetries in electrodermal activity and psychosis. In J. Gruzelier and P. Flor-Henry, eds. *Hemisphere Asymmetries of Function in Psychopathology.* Amsterdam: Elsevier/North Holland, pp. 149–168.

Gruzelier, J., and Flor-Henry, P., eds. (1979). *Hemisphere Asymmetries of Function in Psychopathology.* Amsterdam: Elsevier/North Holland.

Gruzelier, J., and Hammond, N. (1976). Schizophrenia: A dominant hemisphere temporal-limbic disorder. *Res. Commun. Psychol., Psychiatr. Behavior, 1,* 33–72.

Gur, R. E. (1978). Left hemisphere dysfunction and left hemisphere overactivation in schizophrenia. *J. Abnor. Psychol., 87,* 226–238.

Heaton, R. K., Baade, L. E., and Johnson, K. L. (1978). Neuropsychological test results associated with psychiatric disorders in adults. *Psychol. Bull., 85,* 141–162.

Heaton, R. K., and Crowley, T. J. (1981). Effects of psychiatric disorders and their somomatic treatments on neuropsychological test results. In: S. B. Filskov and T. J. Boll, eds. *Handbook of Clinical Neuropsychology.* New York: Wiley-Interscience, pp. 481–525.

Helzer, J., Robins, L., Croughan, J., and Welner, A. (1981). Renard Diagnostic Interview. *Arch. Gen. Psychiatr., 38,* 393–398.

Henn, F. A. (1982). Dopamine: A role in psychosis or schizophrenia. In: F. Henn and H. A. Nasrallah, eds. *Schizophrenia as a Brain Disease.* New York: Oxford University Press, pp. 176–195.

Henn, F. A., and Nasrallah, H. A., eds. (1982). *Schizophrenia as a Brain Disease.* New York: Oxford University Press.

Hill, D. (1956). *Electroencephalography.* London: MacDonald.

Horenstein, S. (1970). Presentation 17: Effect of cerebrovascular disease on personality and emotionality. In: A. L. Benton, ed. *Behavioral Change in Cerebrovascular Disease.* New York: Harper and Row, pp. 171–194.

Ingvar, D. (1980). Regional cerebral blood flow and psychopathology. In: J. O. Cole and J. E. Barrett, eds., *Psychopathology in the Aged.* New York: Raven Press, pp. 73–80.

Itil, T. M. (1964). Elektroencephalographische Studien Bei Psychosen und Psychotropen Medikamenten. Ahmet Sait Mathaas: Istanbul.

Itil, T. M. (1977). Qualitative and quantitative EEG findings in schizophrenia. *Schizophrenia Bull, 3,* 61–79.

Jackson, J. H. (1932). *Selected writings of John Hughlings Jackson,* ed. J. Taylor. London: Hedder & Stoughton.

Kietzman, M. L., Spring, B., and Zubin, J. (1980). Perception, cognition and attention. In: H. I. Kaplan, A. M. Freedman, and B. J. Sadock, eds. *Comprehensive Textbook of Psychiatry,* vol. I. Baltimore: Williams & Wilkins, pp. 334–371.

Kietzman, M. L., Sutton, S., and Zubin, J. (1975). *Experimental Approaches to Psychopathology.* New York: Academic Press.

Levine, J. (1974). Differences between organic and schizophrenic groups on the Halstead-Reitan battery; a reply to Watson. *J. Consult. Clin. Psychol., 42,* 134–135.

Levine, J., and Feirstein, A. (1972). Differences in test performance between brain-damaged, schizophrenic and medical patients. *J. Consult. Clin. Psychol., 39,* 508–511.

Levit, A. L., Sutton, S., and Zubin, J. (1973). Evoked potential correlates of information processing in psychiatric patients. *Psychol. Med., 3,* 487–494.

Lewis, G., Golden, C. J., Purisch, A. D., and Hammeke, T. A. (1979). The effects of chronicity of disorder and length of hospitalization on the standardized version of Luria's neuropsychological battery in a schizophrenic population. *Clin. Neuropsychol., 1*, 13–18.

Luria, A. R. (1963). *Restoration of Function after Brain Injury*, trans. B. Haigh. New York: The Macmillan Company.

Magaro, P. A. (1978, August). *Information processing and hemispheric specialization in sch : ophrenia and paranoia*. Presented at the American Psychological Association Conv ntion, Toronto.

Malec, J. (1978). Neuropsychological assessment of schizophrenia *versus* brain damag :: A review. *J. Nerv. Ment. Dis., 166*, 507–516.

Mettler, F. A., ed. (1949). *Selective Partial Ablation of the Frontal Cortex*. New York: Hoeber.

Mirsky, A. (1969). Neuropsychological bases of schizophrenia. *Ann. Rev. Psychol., 20*, 321–348.

Myslobodsky, M., Mintz, M., and Tomer, R. (1979). Asymmetric reactivity of the brain and components of hemispheric imbalance. In: J. Gruzelier and P. Flor-Henry, eds., *Hemisphere Asymmetries of Function in Psychopathology*. Amsterdam: Elsevier/North Holland, pp. 125–148.

Nasrallah, H. A. (1982). Laterality and hemispheric dysfunction in schizophrenia. In: F. A. Henn and H. A. Nasrallah, eds., *Schizophrenia as a Brain Disease*. New York: Oxford University Press, pp. 273–294.

Pribram, K. H. (1971). *Languages of the Brain*. Englewood Cliffs, New Jersey: Prentice-Hall, Inc.

Price, R. H. (1972). Psychological deficit versus impression management in schizophrenic word association performance. *J. Abnorm. Psychol., 79*, 132–137.

Purisch, A. D., Golden, C. J., and Hammeke, T. A. (1978). Discrimination of schizophrenic and brain-injured patients by a standardized version of Luria's neuropsychological tests. *J. Consult. Clin. Psychol., 46*, 1266–1273.

Reider, R. O., Donnelly, E. F., Herdt, J. R., and Waldman, I. N. (1979). Sulcal prominence in young chronic schizophrenic patients: CT scan findings associated with impairment on neuropsychological tests. *Psychiatr. Res., 1*, 1–8.

Reitan, R. M. (1976). Neuropsychology: The vulgarization Luria always wanted. *Contemporary Psychol., 21*, 737–738.

Robins, S. L., Helzer, J., Croughan, N. A., and Ratcliff, K. (1981). National Institute of Mental Health Diagnostic Interview Schedule. *Arch. Gen. Psychiatr., 38*, 381–389.

Shagass, C., Roemer, R. A., Straumanis, J. J., and Amadeo, M. (1979). Evoked potential evidence of lateralized hemispheric dysfunction in the psychoses. In: J. Gruzelier and P. Flor-Henry, eds. *Hemisphere Asymmetries of Function in Psychopathology*. Amsterdam: Elsevier/North Holland, pp. 293–316.

Shelly, C., and Goldstein, G. (1983). Discrimination of chronic schizophrenia and brain damage with the Luria-Nebraska battery: A partially successful replication. Clin. Neuropsychol., 5, 82–85.

Shimkunas, A. M. (1972). Demand for intimate self-disclosure and pathological verbalizations in schizophrenia. *J. Abnorm. Psychol., 80*, 197–205.

Spiers, P. A. (1981). Have they come to praise Luria or to bury him?: The Luria-Nebraska battery controversy. *J. Consult. Clin. Psychol., 49*, 331–341.

Spitzer, R. L., and Endicott, J. (1973). *Schedule for Affective Disorders and Schizophrenia (SADS)*. New York: Biometrics Research Branch, New York State Department of Mental Hygiene.

Spitzer, P., Endicott, J., and Robins, E. (1978). Research diagnostic criteria: Rationale and reliability. *Arch. Gen. Psychiatr., 35*, 773–782.

Spohn, H. E., Lacoursiere, R. B., Thompson, K., and Coyne, L. (1977). Phenothiazine effects on psychological and physiological dysfunction in chronic schizophrenics. *Arch. Gen. Psychiatr., 34*, 633–644.

Steinhauer, S., Hakerem, G., and Spring, B. (1979). The pupillary response as a potential indicator of schizophrenia. *Psychopharmacol. Bull., 15,* 44–45.

Steinhauer, S., and Zubin, J. (1982). Vulnerability to schizophrenia: Information processing in the pupil and event-related potential. In: I. Hanin and E. Usdin, eds., *Biological Markers in Psychiatry and Neurology.* Oxford: Pergammon Press, pp. 371–385.

Stevens, J. R. (1982). Neurology and neuropathology of schizophrenia. In: F. A. Henn and A. H. Nasrallah, eds. *Schizophrenia as a Brain Disease.* New York: Oxford University Press, pp. 112–147.

Sutton, S. (1973). Fact and artifact in the psychology of schizophrenia. In: M. Hammer, K. Salzinger, and S. Sutton, eds. *Psychopathology: Contributions from the Biological, Behavioral and Social Sciences.* New York: Wiley, pp. 197–213.

Torrey, E. F., and Peterson, M. R. (1976). The viral hypothesis of schizophrenia. *Schizophrenia Bull., 2,* 136–146.

Walsh, K. W. (1978). *Neuropsychology: A Clinical Approach.* Edinburgh: Churchill Livingstone.

Watson, C. G., (1972). Roles of impression management in the interview, self-report, and cognitive behavior of schizophrenics. *J. Consult. Clin., 38,* 452–456.

Watson, C. G., Thomas, R. W., Andersen, D., and Felling, J. (1968). Differentiation of organics from schizophrenics at two chronicity levels by use of the Reitan-Halstead organic test battery. *J. Consult. Clin. Psychol., 32,* 679–684.

Webb, W. W. (1955). Conceptual ability of schizophrenics as a function of threat of failure. *J. Abnorm. Soc. Psychol., 50,* 221–224.

Weinberger, D. R., and Wyatt, R. J. (1982). Brain morphology in schizophrenia: *In vivo* studies. In: F. A. Henn & H. A. Nasrallah, eds., *Schizophrenia as a Brain Disease.* New York: Oxford University Press, pp. 148–175.

Werner, H. (1937). Process and achievement. *Harvard Ed. Rev., 7,* 353–368.

Whiteman, M. (1954). The performance of schizophrenics on social concepts. *J. Abnorm. Soc. Psychol., 49,* 266–271.

Zubin, J. (1975). Problem of attention in schizophrenia. In: M. Kietzman, S. Sutton, and J. Zubin, eds. *Experimental Approaches to Psychopathology.* New York: Academic Press, pp. 139–166.

Zubin, J., Kietzman, M. L., and Steinhauer, S. R. *(in press).* Psychological foundations of psychiatry. In: M. Shepherd, ed., *Handbook of Psychiatry,* vol 5. Cambridge: Cambridge University Press.

Zubin, J., Magaziner, J., and Steinhauer, S. R. (1983). The metamorphosis of schizophrenia: From chronicity to vulnerability. *Psychol. Med., 13,* 551–571.

Zubin, J., and Spring, B. J. (1977). Vulnerability-a new view of schizophrenia. *J. Abnorm. Psychol., 86,* 103–126.

Zubin, J., and Steinhauer, S. (1981). How to break the logjam in schizophrenia: A look beyound genetics. *J. Nerv. Ment. Dis., 169,* 477–492.

9

The Neuropsychology of Dementia

ALFRED W. KASZNIAK

The Syndrome of Dementia

The third edition of the Diagnostic and Statistical Manual of Mental Disorders (American Psychiatric Association, 1980, p. 107) defines the essential feature of dementia as a "loss of intellectual abilities of sufficient severity to interfere with social or occupational functioning." Diagnostic criteria include memory impairment and at least one of the following: (1) impairment of abstract thinking (e.g., inability to find similarities and differences between related words, concrete interpretation of proverbs), (2) impaired judgement, (3) other disturbance of higher cortical function (e.g., aphasia, agnosia, constructional apraxia), and (4) personality change (alteration or accentuation of premorbid traits). In addition, the patient must be free of evidence of clouded consciousness and must present evidence of a specific organic factor judged to be etiologically related, or have such a factor presumed through reasonable exclusion of conditions other than organic mental disorders.

The syndrome of dementia can have many different causes. Psychiatric disorders (particularly depression) may also present as "psuedodementia" (Hutton, 1980; Roth, 1980; Wells, 1977). The importance of accurate differential diagnosis in dementia is underscored by the fact that several of these causes are potentially reversible (Cummings et al., 1980). Across several different studies (e.g., Delaney, 1982; Garcia et al, 1981; Fox, Topel and Huckman, 1975a; Freeman, 1976); a range of from 10% to over 20% of cases with apparent dementia were found to have treatable causes (see review by Hutton, 1980).

Following the now classic studies of Tomlinson and associates (1968, 1970), several groups of investigators have confirmed Alzheimer's disease to be the pathology in the majority of cases of dementia—at least those presenting in old age (see recent reviews by Roth, 1980; Terry and Davies, 1980; Terry and Katzman, 1983; Tomlinson, 1982). Across the available neuropathologic studies, Alzheimer's disease has been found to account for between 50% to 70% of older patients with dementia seen in psychiatric practice. An additional 15% to 25% are found to have multiple infarctions of the brain, either alone or in combination with Alzheimer's disease. The present chapter will consequently focus upon dementia of the Alzheimer type (DAT) and multi-infarct dementia (MID) (Hachinski, Lassen, and Marshall, 1974). Other causes of dementia will be briefly discussed, although DAT and MID will remain the central focus in our review of neuropsychological research in dementia. In all of what follows, the term "dementia" will be used to refer to the clinical syndrome, when pathologic specification is not known or not intended.

Diagnosis

At present, the diagnosis of dementia relies heavily upon clinical examination, neuropsychological testing, CT scanning, and certain laboratory procedures (Roth, 1980). Accumulating empirical evidence indicates that dementia—particularly DAT—typically does not come to professional attention until several years after the apparent illness onset (Pfeffer, in press; Roth, 1980). Once the dementia has progressed several years into its course, thorough history taking (preferably from a reliable family member close to the patient), careful clinical mental status examination (e.g., Folstein and McHugh, 1978), and application of various psychological assessment instruments (e.g., Fleiss et al., 1976; Kendrick and Post, 1967; Roth and Hopkins, 1953; Trier, 1966) are reasonably successful in differentiating the demented patient from healthy members of his or her age cohort, as well as from patients with disorders other than dementia (e.g., depression). However, difficulty in diagnosis does occur when (1) the dementia is early in its course (and therefore mild), (2) the clinician confuses signs and symptoms of dementia with those of other disorders, or (3) a patient without an organic mental disorder presents with significant cognitive deficit (i.e., pseudodementia).

Research concerning accuracy in the clinical diagnosis of dementia supports the impression that such diagnostic difficulty is of significant proportion. Ron and colleagues (1979) obtained 5–15 year follow-up on 51 patients discharged from the Bethlehem Royal and Maudsley Hospitals with a firm diagnosis of presenile dementia. All were below the age of 65 at time of diagnosis, and none showed evidence of cerebrovascular disease, severe head injury, space-occupying lesion, intracranial infection, metabolic or endocrine disorder, alcoholism or drug addiction. All patients were hospitalized between 1963 and 1972. At follow-up study in 1977, 33 patients had died, and 18 were still alive. At follow-up, neurological, psychiatric, and psychological test examinations were conducted. From this data, the original diagnosis of presenile dementia was confirmed in 35 cases (69%), and rejected in 16 (31%). Twelve of this latter group were alive and four had died. Of the 16 cases in which the diagnosis of dementia was rejected, retrospective diagnoses of affective illness were made in eight patients, paranoid psychosis in one, schizophrenic disorder in one, Parkinson's disease in three, nonprogressive brain damage of uncertain etiology in two, and "transient acute organic reaction with marked affective symptoms" in one. Comparable data on misdiagnosis was reported by Garcia et al. (1981) from their study of 100 older patients referred to a specialized outpatient dementia clinic. Twenty-six were found to be not demented. Of these, 15 were diagnosed as depressed, seven as having other miscellaneous neuropsychiatric disorders, and four as being normal. Thus, misdiagnosis of dementia appears to be common, with differentiation from depression posing the greatest difficulty.

Factors contributing to the difficulty of differentiating dementia from depression in old age, as well as approaches to improving diagnosis, have been reviewed in detail elsewhere (e.g., Kaszniak and Allender, 1985; Roth, 1980; Shore et al., 1983), and will therefore only be summarized here. First, intellectual functioning does show some deterioration, albeit mild, with normal aging (Botwinick, 1977; Willis and Baltes, 1980), which can be mistaken for early indicators of dementia. Second, depression is frequently accompanied by cognitive difficulty (McAllister, 1981; W. R. Miller, 1975), particularly in older persons (Donnely, et al., 1980). In some patients this cognitive difficulty reaches sufficient proportion to warrant the term pseudodementia (Caine, 1981; McAllister, 1983). Third, signs and symptoms of neurologic disorder accompanied by dementia (e.g., Alzheimer's, Huntington's and Parkinson's diseases) may have some overlap with those of depression (Kaszniak et al., 1981; Miller, 1980), and depression may occur as a complication in these disorders (Caine and Shoulson, 1983; Mayeux, 1982; McAllister and Price, 1982; Reifler et al., 1982). Finally, there are age-related changes in the central nervous system which are reflected in the results of clinical neurologic, psychologic, electrophysiologic, neuroradiologic and neuropharmacologic assessment techniques (see Kaszniak, Sadeh, and Stern, 1985), complicating interpretation.

Clinical Presentation

The first step in diagnosis is the identification of signs and symptoms which raise the suspicion of dementia. While patients who are several years into the course of dementia typically present easily recognized memory and other cognitive deficits in clinical examination, as well as a clear history of progressive intellectual deterioration, identification of earlier cases is more difficult. Unfortunately, there is a lack of prospective empirical data on the characterization of the earliest features of dementia, and one must rely upon information gained from clinical anecdotal and family member reports. The course of deterioration in DAT is typically gradually deteriorative, rather than occurring in discrete "stages." However it is useful to reconstruct, from anecdotal sources, a series of "snap-shots" or "phases" of the clinical course. Based upon such reconstruction, investigators at the New York University Geriatric Study and Treatment Program (Schneck et al., 1982) have suggested three phases in the progression of DAT. In the earliest phase (termed the "forgetfulness phase"), there is primarily subjective cognitive deficit, with the patient, and occasionally other close family members, noticing increasing forgetfulness, often accompanied by anxiety. At this phase, differentiation from the memory changes of normal aging (Hartley et al., 1980) is difficult or impossible. Katzman (1981) cautions that, with increasing public and professional awareness of Alzheimer's disease, there may be a growing tendency to confuse "benign senescent forgetfulness" (Kral, 1962) with senile dementia. Important distinctions involve the progressive nature of the memory impairment in DAT, as well as its severity being sufficient to interfere with work and/or social functioning. Katzman (1981) provides the following example: "If an older person forgets the name of one of the guests at a granddaughter's wedding—that is normal aging; if the wedding itself is forgotten—that is dementia." (p. 62).

The next stage, termed the "confusional phase" by Schneck et al. (1982), is characterized by particularly severe deficit in memory for recent events, difficulty in orientation and concentration, and subtle language deficits (e.g., word-finding difficulty) despite generally intact vocabulary and syntax. At this phase, the patient more clearly fits the diagnostic criteria for dementia set forth in the DSM-III. The third phase, termed the "dementia phase," is characterized by severe disorientation, abnormalities of language, perception and praxis, and behavioral problems, including motor restlessness, wandering, and psychotic symptoms (e.g., paranoid ideation, delusions, hallucinations) in some patients. It is at this phase that somatic and neurologic abnormalities (e.g., incontinence, abnormal reflexes) are most likely to appear.

In addition to the cognitive deficits of DAT, personality and emotional changes occur with disease progression. Personality may become ". . . a caricature of its worst features, and undesirable traits such as meanness, tactlessness, impulsiveness, hypochondriasis, disinhibition of sexually deviant conduct formerly held in check . . ." (Roth, 1980), p. 211) Such behavior is often the most distressing aspect of a patient's dementia for other family members (Rabins et al., 1982). Social judgement may become progressively impaired, with decreasing concern for others and narrowing of interest. As already discussed, depression may accompany DAT. Based on clinical observation, some authors (e.g., Busse, 1975; Pfeiffer, 1977) have suggested depressive symptoms to be most common in the earlier stages of dementia, while others (Demuth and Rand, 1980) have observed depression in patients with severe dementia. Similarly, some empirical studies (e.g., Reifler et al., 1982) have found the rate of coexisting depression to decrease with greater severity of dementia, while others (Kaszniak et al., 1981) have failed to find a relationship between severity of depressive symptoms and severity of cognitive impairment. It would thus appear most prudent to anticipate the possible occurence of depressive symptoms at any point in the course of dementia.

The clinical course of other dementias may be quite different from that seen in DAT. In MID, clinical features are believed to be secondary to the accumulation of abrupt vascular episodes ("strokes"). Consequently, the onset of dementia in MID is typically abrupt, with a stepwise course of deterioration, focal neurological signs and symptoms, a history consistent with cerebrovascular accident (CVA), and a history or presence of hypertension (Hachinski et al., 1974). Hachinski et al. have included these features in a clinical rating scale which provides a summary "ischemic score." Rosen et al. (1980), using a modification of this ischemic score, were able to correctly differentiate five Alzheimer's from 11 MID or mixed MID and DAT cases (defined by post-mortem neuropathologic criteria). Ladurner et al. (1982), studying clinical features associated with dementia in 71 patients with ischemic stroke, found hypertension, bilateral neurologic signs/symptoms, bilateral infarcts on CT scan (or generalized atrophy in combination with an infarct) to differentiate those patients with dementia from those without. Some caution needs to be exercised by the clinician in evaluating the presence of focal signs and symptoms. Sluss et al., (1982) reported focal signs to occur both in their cases diagnosed as MID ($N = 13$), and in those diagnosed as DAT ($N = 27$). They caution that it is important to consider the developmental sequence and the total clinical context of the disorder in evaluating focal signs.

Space does not permit a review of the clinical presentation of dementia in other disorders (e.g., Huntington's and Parkinson's diseases, space-occupying lesions, CNS infection), and the reader is referred to available recent reviews (Chase et al., 1979; Hutton, 1980; Mayeux, 1982; Roth, 1980). Clinical presentation in pseudodementia is discussed in chapter 10 of this volume, and elsewhere (Kaszniak, Sadah, and Stern, 1985).

Laboratory Procedures in Diagnosis

CT SCANNING. Since its introduction (Ambrose, 1973; Hounsfield, 1973), CT scanning has had particular value in evaluating dementia, given its sensitivity to a variety of focal structural lesions. However, its diagnostic utility in helping to differentiate DAT or MID patients from normally aging or depressed older persons remains in doubt (see Fox et al., 1979; Wells and Duncan, 1977).

Initially, there was enthusiasm concerning the potential role of CT scan visualization in the diagnosis and prognosis of dementia (e.g., Fox et al., 1975b). However, subsequent research has considerably dempened this enthusiasm (see reviews by Bird, 1982; deLeon and George, 1983). Although DAT patients, as a group, show greater ventricular and sucal enlargement than age-matched control subjects, there is considerable group overlap (e.g., Wilson et al., 1982). The CT scan of a moderately demented patient not infrequently shows only minimal ventricular and sulcal enlargement. Conversely, ventricular enlargement is seen in normal adult aging. By the eighth decade, there is an increase of approximately 15% in ventricular size (e.g., Barron et al. 1976; Yamaura et al., 1980). Although more difficult to measure, increased width of cortical sulci has also been shown to be age-associated (Jacoby, Levy, and Dawson, 1980). Despite some degree of correlation between cognitive deficit in DAT and CT scan measures of ventricular and sulcal size (e.g., Kaszniak et al., 1979), such measures thus do not appear to be reliable now for either diagnostic or prognostic (Kaszniak et al., 1978) purposes. Correlations between CT scan and neuropsychological measures will be discussed later in this chapter.

CT scanning also has limitations in diagnosing MID and some focal lesions producing dementia. Radue et al. (1978) reported on the CT scan results in 50 patients with "primary neuronal degeneration" (presumably DAT) and 26 patients with MID, based on Hachinski's ischemia score and substantiated by cerebral blood flow measurements. Compared to those with DAT, the MID patients showed fewer visible cortical sulci, and more frequent focal ventricular enlargement, unequal size of Sylvian fissures, and focal areas of low CT density. However, CT scanning by itself was able to make a diagnosis of MID in only approximately 20% of the patients. Roberts et al., (1978), based on their study of CT in vascular and nonvascular dementia, also concluded that, while CT scanning can be of benefit if infarcts are clearly demonstrable, it is not helpful in the majority of cases. A final note of caution is sounded by Jacobson and Farmer (1979) in their report of CT scanning of three older patients with a history of dementia for 2–6 months. The CT scans of each showed "hypernormal" brain parenchyma (in comparison to age-expectation), with the appearance of small and symetrical ventricles and minimal sulci. Further investigation showed each to have a bilateral subdural hematoma which was isodense with brain parenchyma, and hence not visible on CT scanning.

Newer approaches to the analysis of CT scan data, such as that based on tissue density measurement (e.g., Naeser et al., 1980) have been suggested (Bird, 1982; deLeon and George, 1983) as holding promise in the diagnosis and prognosis of dementia. However, recently reported failures to find CT scan density measure differences between DAT and healthy age-matched individuals (e.g., Wilson et al., 1982) argues for caution in *any* present clinical application of such measures.

ELECTROENCEPHALOGRAPHY. The electroencephalogram (EEG) can be useful in the diagnosis of dementia (Hutton, 1980; Sim, 1979), given knowledge of its limitations, and caution exercised in interpretation. A factor to be considered in interpretation is that of normal age-changes. The EEG alpha frequency slows with increasing age, changing from approximately 10 cycles per second (Hz) in middle age to 9.5 Hz at age 70, 9 Hz at age 80, and 8.5 Hz after age 90 (Drechsler, 1978; Hughes and Cayafa, 1977). The cause of this slowing is not clear, and it appears to have little clinical importance. In addition, it is not unusual to find slow, irregular theta activity recorded from one or both temporal regions in the normal older individual (Busse et al., 1956). This does not necessarily reflect any underlying disorder, and in the absence of independent evidence of disease to account for it, it should be considered a normal variant.

A more diffuse distribution of theta activity, or slowing into the delta range is typically indicative of central nervous system disease. Although drug effects and systemic disease can produce such slowing, diffuse EEG slowing is most frequently seen in dementia in older age, and is most associated with the plaque and tangle formation, ventricular dilatation, and cortical atrophy characteristic of Alzheimer's disease (Müller and Schwartz, 1978). In addition, the degree of EEG slowing is positively correlated with the severity of cognitive impairment in DAT (e.g., Johannesson et al., 1979; Kaszniak et al. 1979), and is somewhat predictive of 1-year survival (Kaszniak et al., 1978). While such data supports the utility of the EEG in diagnosis of DAT, it should be noted that DAT patients early in the course of dementia may show normal or only mildly abnormal EEGs (Sim, 1979). Recent innovations in the analysis of EEG frequency data, such as the topographic measurement of EEG coherence, may hold additional diagnostic promise (O'Connor et al., 1979), provided that adequate age-appropriate normative data can be developed.

The EEG has less diagnostic value in assessing MID patients. Müller and Schwartz (1978) found that brain infarcts may produce no EEG abnormalities if they are small and/or remote from the cortical surface. When lesions were large and close to the cortex, persistent EEG asymmetries were seen. Similarly, Johannesson et al. (1979) found that the EEG was often normal or only slightly abnormal in their 24 patients with dementia secondary to cerebrovascular lesions.

Diagnostic utility of the EEG in other dementia etiologies is variable. The EEG in Creutzfeldt-Jakob disease shows progressive slowing and disorganization of background activity, with development of periodic sharp wave discharges or other abnormalities (e.g., Burger et al., 1972; Johannesson et al., 1979).

Recently, interest has developed in the possible diagnostic application of measures of brain electrical activity temporally related to specifiable sensory stimuli, termed "event-related potentials" (ERPs). Normal adult aging appears to have only minimal effect on early components of the ERP, while later components show increased latencies in older groups, whether visual (Celesia and Daly, 1977), auditory (Goodin et al., 1978) or somatosensory (Desmedt and Cheron, 1980) ERPs are examined. However, considerable individual variability is seen; ERP studies in older adults have produced mixed results. There appears to be various sources of potential ERP artifact (see reviews by Hansch et al., 1980; Pfefferbaum et al., 1982).

OTHER LABORATORY PROCEDURES. While an extensive discussion of the rationale and interpretation of the various laboratory procedures required to identify dementias with treatable etiologies is beyond the scope of this chapter, some mention must be made of the typical battery of laboratory studies. Those most often recommended (Hutton, 1980; Wells, 1977) include: (1) Blood tests (complete blood count, serological test for syphilis, SMA-12, T^3 and T^4, vitamin B^{12} and folate levels, and serum bromide, barbiturate, or other drug assay if appropriate); (2) urine analysis for heavy metals, if clinically indicated; (3) urinalysis; (4) CSF analysis (total cells, protein, glucose, VDRL, India ink, and cultures for fungi and bacteria); (5) chest x-ray; and (6) CT scan and EEG (discussed above). Other procedures (e.g., cerebral angiography, nuclear brain scans) may also be indicated on the basis of clinical and other laboratory data.

Given the difficulty, discussed above, of differentiating dementia from pseudodementia, recent interest has focused upon the possible diagnostic use of a "pharmacologic challenge," such as the dexamethasone suppression test (DST) to differentiate depression from dementia in old age. Despite encouraging anecdotal reports (e.g., McAllister et al., 1982), others have found DAT patients to be as likely to show abnormal DST results as depressed patients (Raskind et al., 1982; Spar and Gerner, 1982).

Although not presently sufficiently developed to permit widespread clinical application, newer techniques exist which hold some diagnostic promise. The first of these is cerebral blood flow (CBF) measurement, employing inhalation of redioactively labeled xenon. Reduction in grey matter flow has been demonstrated in DAT patients, compared to age-matched control subjects (Yamaguchi et al., 1980), and CBF may prove useful in differentiating depression from DAT, MID, and Pick's disease (Gustafson, Risberg, and Silverskjold, 1981). Correlations between CBF and neuropsychological measures will be discussed later in this chapter.

Positron emission tomography (PET) is another radiologic procedure which may eventually prove useful in diagnosing dementia. It allows tomographic measurement and visualization of regional cerebral metabolism, which has been shown to be sensitive to brain activity during various perceptual and cognitive processes (e.g., Mazziotta et al., 1982). Much of the excitement concerning its possible diagnostic application in dementia derives from recent observations that PET measures do not appear to change with normal aging, but do demonstrate cerebral metabolism decrease in DAT (deLeon et al., 1983; Friedland et al., 1983). PET scanning may prove useful in differentiating various dementia etiologies (Benson, 1982; Benson and Cummings, 1982); but the equipment is available at very few centers, and remains plagued by several technical difficulties in its use and interpretation.

A final note should be made of the possibility of future diagnostic application of nuclear magnetic resonance (NMR) imaging (James et al., 1982), which has been shown to yield extremely detailed visualization of intracranial structure, is sensitive to the molecular composition of tissue, and may have fewer practical limitations than PET scanning. Moreover, its potential for the direct study of metabolism is of great value in research on cerebral activity.

Pathologic Anatomy and Biochemistry

Alois Alzheimer, in 1907, employed newly available silver stains to examine the brain of a 51-year-old man who had died with a progressive dementia, and first described the neuritic plaques and neurofibrillary tangles of what is now termed Alzheimer's disease. Alzheimer's disease has been traditionally defined as a presenile dementia, with onset before age 65. However, there is now general agreement among neurologists and pathologists that light microscopic appearance and ultrastructural aspects of the neurofibrillary tangle and neuritic plaque are the same in patients with onset below age 65 as in those with later onset (senile dementia) (Terry and Katzman, 1983). The term "senile dementia of the Alzheimer type" (SDAT) is now used for the clinico-pathologic entity with onset over age 65. The DSM-III uses the term "primary degenerative dementia, senile onset," rather than SDAT, in recognition of the difficulty of clinically differentiating dementias due to Alzheimer's from those due to Pick's disease.

Despite the apparent pathologic identity of SDAT and "presenile dementia of the Alzheimer type" (PSDAT) (termed "primary degenerative dementia, presenile onset," in DSM-III), the continuing differentiation of patients by age of onset reflects the current controversy over three issues: (1) age-specific incidence (a continuous distribution would argue for a single disease entity, while a bimodal distribution, with peaks, for example in the late 50s and late 80s, would argue for two varieties) (Grufferman, 1978); (2) possible hereditary differences (greater familiar aggregation in earlier onset cases) (Harris, 1982; Heston et al., 1981); and (3) possible histologic differences (patients with fewer locus coeruleus neurons at autopsy have been found to be younger and more severely demented during life) (Bondareff, Mountjoy, and Roth, 1982).

Neuritic plaques and neurofibrillary tangles also occur in normal aging. Neuritic plaques appear in the neocortex of up to 80% of all brains by the ninth decade, and neurofibrillary tangles in the hippocampus in over 90% (Terry and Katzman, 1983). There are, however, two features that distinguish dementia from normal aging. First, the number of neuritic plaques in the neocortex and neurofibrillary tangles in the hippocampi is much higher in demented than in nondemented individuals. Second, neurofibrillary tangles in the neocortex occur almost exclusively in the brains of patients who were demented during life, and not in normal elderly brains (Terry and Katzman, 1983). Further, there is some evidence that suggests a threshold effect. Tomlinson, Blessed, and Roth (1968, 1970), in their study of a hospital sample of healthy, functionally ill, and demented patients, found a mean plaque count of 11/mircoscopic field to separate most of those who had been demented in life from those who were not. Large concentrations of neuritic plaques and neurofibrillary tangles in these patients were also found to have a high correlation with severity of dementia during life. Recently, study of the ultrastructure and biochemistry of neurofibrillary tangles and neuritic plaques has been vigorously pursued for clues to the etiology of DAT.

While widespread and symetrical, plaques and tangles are not uniformly distributed in the brains of DAT patients. The hippocampus and adjacent structures are particularly severely affected, and cortical involvement is most marked in the temporal and frontal lobes, somewhat less in parieto-occipital gyri, and least in inferior frontal and inferior occipital gyri (Tomlinson, 1977). Primary sensory and motor areas appear to be relatively spared. Even within the hippocampus itself, a topographic pattern of neurofibrillary tangle formation is found (Ball, 1978).

The brainstem and other subcortical structures are said to be typically spared in DAT (Tomlinson, 1977), although there are reports (e.g., Ishii, 1966) of neurofibrillary tangles in hindbrain monaminergic neurons, which may be of interest because of possible associations between Alzheimer's and Parkinson's diseases.

In addition to the classic neuritic plaques and neurofibrillary tangles of Alzheimer's disease, there are other pathologic features. Since the earliest neuropathologic descriptions, brain atrophy has been thought to be characteristic of the disease. However, the degree of brain atrophy is quite variable among patients, whether one examines it with CT scanning during life (Kaszniak et al., 1979), or by whole brain weight at postmortem study (Terry et al., 1981). In the study by Terry et al. (1981), the SDAT brains were found to average 1050 g, approximately 100 g (9%) less than age-matched normal cases. While the difference was statistically significant ($p < 0.05$), marked individual variability was observed. The shrinkage of brain in SDAT appeared due to shrinkage of cerebral white matter, rather than significantly reduced cortical ribbon. Reduced gyral white matter and centrum ovale, and thinned massa intermedia, seem to be the cause of the characteristic appearance of widened sulci and enlarged lateral and third ventricles seen on gross examination of SDAT brain. Although typically quite diffuse when present, the cerebral atrophy in SDAT is often most prominent in the frontal lobes and in the region of the hippocampus. The parietal and temporal lobes are often involved, but the occipital poles and paracentral region may be relatively spared. The basal ganglia, thalamus, midbrain and brainstem appear relatively normal on gross examination (Terry and Katzman, 1983). The cerebellum, while slightly atrophic in comparison to brains of younger individuals, is the same as healthy age-matched individuals' cerebella (Koller et al., 1981).

Terry et al. (1981) also documented a loss of cortical neurons in SDAT, to an extent greater than that accompanying normal aging. Not only was the number of cortical neurons decreased in SDAT, but their configuration was also altered, in a pattern similar to that seen in normal aging. The changes included altered shape of pyramidal cell bodies and a loss of dendrites.

Recently, reports of select areas of loss of magnocellular neurons of the basal forebrain, within the substantia innominata, have generated considerable interest (Whitehouse et al., 1982). Nissl-stained sections through the major portion of the nucleus basalis of Meynert showed a highly consistent and marked decrease in neuronal density and absolute cell number in five Alzheimer's disease patients, compared with five age-matched patient's brains who were not demented in life. No consistent differences in cell density were found in adjacent structures contained within sections such as the hypothalamus or dorsal globus palladus. The importance of this observation is that the nucleus basalis appears to be the site of origination of cell bodies of acetylcholine-releasing neurons innervating wide-spread areas of cerebral cortex and hippocampal formations (see Coyle, Price, and DeLong, 1983). As will be discussed below, there is persuasive evidence of impaired cholinergic neurotransmission in DAT, which appears to have an important role in cognitive functions, particularly memory. Further, these same investigators have more recently shown cholinergic innervation to be important in the evolution of neuritic plaques. Their research (see Coyle, Price, and DeLong, 1983) has suggested that acetylcholinesterase (AChE)-rich dystrophic neurites, presumed to be derived from nucleus basalis neurons, are an early component of neuritic plaque, and that loss of these neurites is associated with the formation of older, "burned-out" plaques and reduction in cortical AChE activity.

While the above pathologic characteristics of SDAT and PSDAT have received the greatest attention, other features also exist, including (1) amyloid angiopathy (amyloid infiltration of the vascular walls in the leptomeninges or cortex itself), seen in many, but not all SDAT cases; (2) granulovacuolar change (small, dark, basophilic granules lying in a clear vacuole within the cytoplasm of hippocampal pyramidal cells); and (3) Hirano bodies (eosinophilic rods in longitudinal section, lying in or near the cytoplasm of hippocampal pyramidal cells).

There is now general agreement (Bartus et al., 1982; Coyle, Price, and DeLong, 1983; Terry and Katzman, 1983) that deficiency of acetylcholine (ACh) is the most important neurotransmitter abnormality in Alzheimer's disease. The brains of SDAT and PSDAT patients show a marked decrease in cerebral choline acetyltransferase (ChAT) activity, in comparison to the brains of age-matched patients without dementia in life (Bowen et al., 1976; Davies and Maloney, 1976; Perry et al., 1977), a feature not characteristic of the brains of MID or depressed patients (Perry et al., 1977). Since these initial observations, decreased ChAT in DAT has been frequently documented, and ChAT deficiency has been correlated with cognitive dysfunction (Perry et al., 1978; Fuld et al., 1982). However, concentrations of muscarinic cholinergic receptors, as identified by QNB-binding, have been found to be normal in DAT (Davies and Verth, 1977; Perry et al., 1977), encouraging attempts to pharmacologically enhance Ach activity, as a possible treatment strategy. Aside from somatostatin (Davies, 1979), no other neurotransmitters have been consistently shown to be deficient in DAT.

The dementia of MID, as its name suggests, is thought to be due to an accumulation of multiple cerebral infarcts. Research has indicated that most cerebral infarcts are caused by thromboembolism from the heart and extracranial arteries, with only a minority of cases showing cerebral softenings due to thrombosis of cerebral vessels (Hachinski et al., 1974). According to Escourolle and Poirier (1973, pp. 83–109), the brain changes in patients with old ischemic strokes consist of a ragged-edged cystic cavity within the distribution of a particular artery. Lacunar strokes appear as smaller cystic cavities (typically 2–10 mm), occurring most often in the pons, thalamus, lenticular nuclei, caudate nuclei, and internal capsule. In the studies of Tomlinson, Blessed, and Roth (1968, 1970), the volume of cerebral softening (or infarction), measured in a 1-cm coronal brain section, significantly correlated with a measure of severity of dementia during life. A threshold phenomenon was found, similar to that observed in relating neuritic plaques to dementia in their Alzheimer's cases: dementia was rare when less than 50 cc of total infarction was present, but almost invariable with infarction above this volume. In brains with evidence of both multiple infarctions and Alzheimer's changes, the two pathologic processes appear to make additive contributions to the severity of dementia.

Epidemiology

Estimates of the prevalence of dementia among the elderly, based on several studies carried out primarily in northern Europe (Mortimer et al., 1981; Pfeffer, in press) have ranged from 1.3% to 6.2% of persons over 65 years of age, for severe dementia, and from 2.6% to 15.4% for those with milder dementia. Differences in diagnostic criteria, methods and intensity of case-finding, and age distributions of the populations studied appear to account for the variability between studies. The prevalence of dementia appears to be age-associated, with a four to sevenfold increase from ages 70–79 to ages greater than 80. Because of the very low prevalence of dementing illness in persons below age 60 (and the consequent necessity of a very large sample needed to obtain accurate estimates), data on dementia prevalence below age 60 are lacking.

By combining data from the Tomlinson et al. (1970) clinicopathologic study with an average taken from the community studies of dementia prevalence discussed above, the prevalence of SDAT can be estimated to be approximately 25/1000 of the population of persons over age 65 (Mortimer et al., 1981, p. 10). Similar calculations suggest that MID accounts for a prevalence of 9 cases/1000, and combined MID/SDAT for 9 cases/1000. The remaining possible etiologies would account for less than 10/1000. Since the Tomlinson study's series of cases was taken from patients who were institutionalized, and the distribution of etiologies among institutionalized and community-dwelling dementia patients may differ, these estimates need to be interpreted and applied cautiously.

Estimates of the annual incidence of SDAT and MID among persons over age 65 has ranged from 1.4% to 2.7% in community studies. There is some data to suggest that incidence may increase with age until approximately age 75, when it then levels off (Larsson et al., 1963), despite the continuing increase of prevalence with older age. There is also evidence indicating that the severity of neurofibrillary tangle formation in the hippocampus levels off in the ninth decade of life (e.g., Matsuyama and Nakamura, 1978). While not compelling, such evidence suggests the possibility that changes in incidence rate may not entirely account for the increase in prevalent cases among the oldest age groups. DAT patients with earlier age of onset appear to survive longer than those with later onset. However, the excess mortality (in comparison to age peers) associated with organic brain syndromes decreases with age of onset (Larsson et al., 1963; Wang, 1978). Mortimer et al. (1981) suggest that this might explain the apparent discrepancy between dementia incidence and prevalence by age.

While excess mortality varies with age of onset and diagnosis, overall, dementia patients have approximately one-third the life expectancy of nondemented age-matched individuals (Go et al., 1978). Based upon available prevalence and mortality data, Katzman (1976) has suggested that SDAT is the fourth or fifth most common cause of death in later life, although it is not the proximate cause listed on death certificates. Proximate causes of death among SDAT patients are similar to those of nondemented adults of comparable age and sex (e.g., pneumonia, cardiac disease, neoplasm, urinary tract infection), except there is an excess number of deaths due to pneumonia (Nielsen et al., 1977).

There is continuing debate concerning whether or not there is any sex differential in the incidence or prevalence of SDAT. At present, there is insufficient data concerning variation in dementia incidence or prevalence by other personal characteristics (e.g., race, birth order, place or time) (Mortimer et al. 1981).

It has been estimated that 60% to 80% of nursing home admissions are due to dementia, with total nursing home costs in the United States projected to rise from 21 billion dollars in 1981 to 75 billion in 1990. Such economic impact is one additional indicator of the magnitude of the public health problem posed by dementia.

Treatment

While there is no proven effective treatment for DAT, the observations of cholinergic deficiency, as noted above, have encouraged several clinical trials that have attempted to manipulate aspects of cholinergic neurotransmission. Bartus et al., (1982) have reviewed these studies, and concluded that the attempts to increase available ACh by providing precursors (i.e., choline, lecithin) have been disappointing. However, studies in which the breakdown of ACh has been limited by supplying an anticholinesterase (i.e., physostigmine) have been somewhat more encouraging. While this research has not led to an effective treatment for DAT, it has suggested that cholinergic manipulation, particularly that which has the greatest probability of affecting the postsynaptic receptor site, may eventually provide a palliative treatment, once an effective, safe, and practical drug can be found. This line of research will continue to depend heavily upon neuropsychological assessment of memory and other cognitive functions as measures of treatment effectiveness. Such assessment has been done in most previous studies, and has proven useful in demonstrating treatment effects in disorders for which apparent dementia is secondary to reversible systemic illness (e.g., Reynolds et al., 1981). Research on the reliability and validity of neuropsychological assessment procedures in dementia will be reviewed here. Later, issues specifically relevant to the application of neuropsychological measures in evaluating treatment effects will be discussed.

Neuropsychological Assessment

Mental Status Examination

A clinical mental status examination and thorough history typically reveal the syndrome of dementia once the patient is several years into the course of a dementing illness. However, the clinician must be cautious that his expectations for cognitive functioning in the elderly are not inappropriate. Intellectual functioning (Botwinick, 1977), learning and memory (Hartley et al., 1980), psychomotor speed (Birren et al., 1980), and sensory/perceptual functioning (Corso, 1981) all show age-related changes in adulthood. Consequently, the use of mental status examination protocols with age-appropriate standardization is important. The present discussion will focus only on the most frequently used instruments for which adequate information concerning reliability and validity is available.

The Geriatric Mental Status Interview (GMS), developed by Gurland et al., (1976), is one of the more comprehensive mental status examinations available. The GMS is a semistructured interview technique which can be administered by a trained interviewer in typically less than an hour. Between 100 and 200 questions, concerning dimensions such as cognitive functioning (including specific tests of orientation and memory), affective state, behavioral symptoms, and somatic concerns are asked, resulting in ratings on 500 items. Based upon data from both the United States and United Kingdom (Gurland et al., 1976), 21 factors have been found to characterize these 500 ratings. Normative data is available for each of these factors. Interrater reliability is acceptable (Gurland et al. 1976), although items based on patient self-report and specific tests of memory and orientation yield higher agreement than observations of the patient's expression, speech pattern, and spontaneous behavior. Valid discrimination of dementia from functional psychiatric disorders (including depression) has been demonstrated for the GMS (Fleiss et al., 1976; Gurland and Toner, 1983).

The GMS has been expanded and incorporated into the Comprehensive Assessment and Referral Evaluation (CARE), which covers psychiatric, medical, nutritional, economic, and social problems. The items of the CARE that are most relevant to the assessment of dementia demonstrate high interrater reliability (Gurland et al., 1977–78). Two relatively short CARE scales, for assessing cognitive impairment and depression respectively, together misclassified only 2% of a sample of 107 depressed and 31 demented older persons (Gurland et al., 1982).

While these and other (e.g., Pfeiffer, 1976; Fillenbaum and Smyer, 1981; Lawton et al., 1982) comprehensive interview protocols for assessing mental status and other important dimensions, appear to provide reliable and valid diagnostic information, they are relatively lengthy to administer and require specific training. Brief, specific mental status examination protocols are available for examining patients with known or suspected dementia. One example is the orientation and memory examination of Blessed, Tomlinson, and Roth (1968), which the authors have shown correlates well with the average number of neuritic plaques observed at postmortem microscopic examination of cerebral grey matter. Fuld (1978) has created a 33-item modification of this instrument, appropriate for examining patients in the United States. Test-retest reliability of 0.96 was found for this modified test, in 17 patients (both demented and nondemented) reexamined after three weeks (Fuld, 1978). In addition, scores of eight or more errors on this test differentiated community dwelling ($N = 54$) from nursing home resident ($N = 500$) elderly (Fuld, 1978). Follow-up evaluation of the nursing home sample revealed error scores to correlate well ($r = 0.59$) with neuritic plaque count in the cortex, while 1-year follow-up of the community sample showed that five to eight errors at first examination were predictive of deterioration into the dementia range of scores (Fuld, 1982a).

Another of the more popular brief mental status screening protocols is the Mini-Mental State (MMS) examination of Folstein, Folstein, and McHugh (1975). Adequate test-retest reliability, valid discrimination of demented from depressed (with and without accompanying cognitive impairment) from normal older persons, and significant correlations with Wechsler Adult Intelligence Scale (WAIS) (Wechsler, 1958) I.Q. score have been demonstrated (Folstein et al, 1975; Folstein and McHugh, 1978). Recent research has shown specific MMS items to correlate with age and education, and false-positive errors in diagnosing dementia are more frequent for older, less educated patients (Anthony et al., 1982), arguing against exclusive diagnostic reliance upon the MMS. This same caution, of course, should be exercised with the use of similar mental status screening instruments, such as the Mental Status Questionnaire (MSQ) (Kahn et al., 1960), the Short Portable Mental Status Questionnaire (SPMSQ) (Pfeiffer, 1975) (see Brink et al., 1978; Haglund and Schuckit, 1976), or those contained within the GMS and CARE.

Instruments such as the Blessed et al. (1968) protocol, MMS, MSQ and SPMSQ have the advantage of being brief and easy to administer. Further, brief mental status screening instruments can be administered to more severely demented patients who may not be examinable with more complex psychometric instruments, thus allowing repeat examination over several years of the patient's illness (e.g., Wilson and Kaszniak, in press). However, these advantages also result in unacceptably high false-negative errors for patients early in the course of dementia (Pfeffer et al., 1981; Wilson and Kaszniak, in press). Some (e.g., Pfeffer et al., 1981) have addressed this problem by combining brief mental status screening measures (i.e., MMS) with performance-based psychometric instruments. This results in markedly improved sensitivity, but at the cost of some decrease in specificity (Pfeffer et al., 1981).

Dementia Rating Scales

Another approach to this problem is to construct an examination protocol that has some of the brevity and ease of administration of brief mental status screening instruments, yet samples a more comprehensive range of cognitive functions using both interview questions and direct performance measures. One of the more widely used examples of such an instrument is the Mattis Dementia Rating Scale (MDRS) (Mattis, 1976). Items of the MDRS are grouped into five areas, designed to assess attention, initiation and perseveration, construction, conceptualization, and memory. Scores from all five areas are also summed to provide a general index of dementia severity (maximum total score = 142). Extremely high test-retest reliability (.97) has been reported for a group of 30 PSDAT patients (Coblentz et al., 1973), and impressive split-half reliability (.90) was found for a sample of 25 older (65–94 years of age) institutionalized demented patients (Gardner et al., 1981). Correlation between the MDRS and WAIS full scale I.Q. was reported as .75 for a group of 20 patients with presenile dementia of mixed etiology (primarily PSDAT) (Coblentz et al., 1973). Relatively high correlation between the MDRS and other psychometric instruments (e.g., WAIS vocabulary subtest, Benton Visual Retention Test) has also been reported for a sample of 85 normal elderly (Montgomery and Costa, 1983). Normal elderly subjects have generally been found to score at or near the ceiling score of the MDRS (Coblentz et al., 1973; Montgomery and Costa, 1983), while our own experience, and that of others (e.g., Gardner et al., 1981) indicates that institutionalized demented patients almost always score below 100. Various clinicians (e.g., Albert, 1981) anecdotally report the MDRS to be useful in evaluating the mild to moderately demented DAT patient, and a recent study (Vitaliano et al., 1984) found MDRS scores (with the exception of the "attention" items) to differ significantly between healthy elderly and mildly demented DAT patients living in the community. Further, this same study found that MDRS item scores were predictive of independent measures of functional competence in their DAT patients.

Hersch (1979) has expanded and modified the scoring (weighting items based on their empirically determined relative difficulty) of the MDRS. Based on data from 90 psychogeriatric in-patients, he found high internal consistency for the scale as a whole; valid discrimination of demented from nondemented in-patients; good correlation with an independent rating-scale completed by ward staff; and a significant decline in the scores of dementia patients retested after 6 and 12 month intervals.

Since DAT, MID, and several other dementias progressively deteriorate there is a need for instruments that can be repeatedly administered throughout the course of dementia. As noted above, some of the briefer mental status examination protocols, and possibly the MDRS, appear able to fill this need. Observation-based rating scales are a useful addition to such instruments since they typically do not necessitate patient cooperation, and often provide ratings of behavioral features observed later in the course of dementia. An example of a rating scale, developed specifically to evaluate various "stages" throughout the course of dementia, is the Global Deterioration Scale of Primary Degenerative Dementia (GDS) (Reisberg et al., 1982). It defines seven stages in the course of dementia, with well-specified observational criteria. While reliability data is not available yet—Levin and Peters (1982) report preliminary support for interrater reliability—GDS ratings do correlate well with various independent psychometric measures of cognitive impairment, as well as with CT and PET measures in DAT patients. While further characterization of the psychometric properties of the GDS is needed (e.g., reliability; age, sex, education, and cultural influences), it is a promising approach to the difficult task of classification of dementia severity (see Levin and Peters, 1982). Such classification is necessary in order to compare research based on different DAT or other dementia patient samples.

In addition to the type of rating scale represented by the GDS, there is a need for observation-based rating scales that can be completed by persons familiar with the patient's behavior in his/her residential environment (whether community, hospital, or nursing home). Reviews of such instruments, appropriate for use with impaired older patients, are available (Kaszniak and Allender, 1985; Robinson, 1979; Salzman et al., 1972).

Comprehensive Neuropsychological Assessment

While mental status examination protocols and dementia rating scales play an important role in diagnostic assessment and patient follow-up, they are often inadequate alone. Typically, they are relatively insensitive to very mild dementia, and they lack sufficient specificity to separate various disorders presenting as dementia. Consequently, neuropsychologists who are experienced in assessing older patients suspected of having dementia recommend the use of more extensive neuropsychological assessment batteries. While there is some variability in the specific tests neuropsychologists include in a recommended battery, most agree on the need to sample a range of cognitive functions, including general intelligence, memory, attention, language, perception, and praxis. In the following subsections, our knowledge concerning the diagnostic utility of representative instruments for such assessment will be surveyed. The use of neuropsychological assessment instruments in the examining older patients requires the consideration of some special issues, and the reader is directed to available reviews (e.g., Albert, 1981; Heaton, Chapter 6; Kaszniak and Allender, 1985; Klisz, 1978).

Assessment of Intelligence

Since impairment in intellectual functioning is one of the defining features of dementia, most neuropsychologists include formal intelligence testing in their assessment battery. The most frequently used instrument is the Wechsler Adult Intelligence Scale (WAIS) (Wechsler, 1958), or its revised version (WAIS-R) (Wechsler, 1981). Of ten studies reviewed by Miller (1977), only one failed to find average I.Q.s below the expected population mean of 100, and those testing control groups always found the dementia group to show lower scores. While the Wechsler tests thus appear to validly reflect the intellectual impairment of dementia, there is greater variability in subtest scores of demented, compared to healthy elderly, and overlap of respective score distributions (see Miller, 1977a, pp. 35–36).

One attempt to improve the accuracy of the WAIS in the diagnosis of dementia is to employ procedures that estimate intellectual decline. Wechsler's (1958) deterioration index uses several of the WAIS subtests showing least decline with age as indicators of premorbid levels, with other subtests, more sensitive to the effects of age, as measures of present levels. Such approaches are problematic in that they assume the manifestations of dementia to be similar to those of normal aging; and the results of validation studies employing such deterioration indices generally have not been encouraging (see Miller, 1981b, pp. 126–127). An alternative approach is to estimate premorbid intelligence by applying an equation differentially weighting age, sex, race, years of formal education, and occupation. The application of such a formula, based upon such a regression has been supported in a recent validation study (Wilson et al., 1979). However, given the variation in I.Q. among people with comparable educational and occupational backgrounds, caution needs to be exercised in the clinical application of this estimation equation.

In addition to the above studies of the sensitivity of the WAIS to dementia, other studies have investigated the possibility of WAIS subtest pattern specificity differentiating various causes of dementia (e.g., DAT, MID, pseudodementia).

One of the more frequent diagnostic problems the clinical neuropsychologist faces is the differentiation of dementia from pseudodementia. Pseudodementia can occur in various syndromes, including hysterical disorders and schizophrenia, although depresive illness appears to be the most frequent cause. Various investigations have documented the presence of cognitive deficit in depression (see reviews by McAllister, 1981; W. R Miller, 1975), and older depressed patients may be more likely to show such deficits (Donnelly et al., 1980).

Little convincing data on the validity of the WAIS for depression-dementia differential diagnosis exists (Crookes, 1974). Whitehead (1973), comparing elderly depressed patients with those with diffuse brain damage, found the brain-damaged patients scored at generally lower levels on the WAIS. However, there was no evidence that the *patterns* of scores were related to diagnosis. Thus, it would appear that attempting to differentiate depression from dementia must be done with considerable caution. In my experience, an examination of WAIS score patterns or levels alone is not very helpful in differentiating dementia from depressive pseudodementia. However, the observation of a qualitative feature in intelligence test performance may be helpful. I, as well as other authors (e.g., Wells, 1979) have noted that the pseudodementia patient will frequently give "don't know" answers in response to intelligence test items, while the dementia patient gives fewer such responses and often makes several "near miss" errors or is obviously guessing.

Several attempts have also been made to determine the utility of the WAIS in differentiating DAT from MID. Perez et al. (1975) reported a 74% accuracy of classification of DAT, MID, and vertebrobasilar insufficiency (VBI) with dementia patients, via a discriminant analysis of WAIS subtests. While successful cross-validation has been reported (Perez et al., 1976), clinical application does not appear to be warranted. In both studies reported by Perez and colleagues, the DAT patients were more educated than the MID patients. Further, the DAT patients were, overall, more severely impaired than the MID group. Such education and dementia severity confounds invalidate the discriminant analysis results. Brinkman (1983) analyzed WAIS I.Q. and subtest scores of 20 MID and 16 DAT patients matched for age, education, and dementia severity, and failed to find any significant differences.

Fuld (1982b) has suggested that, while WAIS I.Q. or individual subtests may not effectively differentiate DAT from other dementia patients, the relationship between WAIS subtests might. She presented a formula for such analysis of WAIS subtests. Brinkman and Braun (1984), comparing 39 MID and 23 DAT patients, found 13 of the DAT and only 2 of the MID patients to present with Fuld's WAIS profile. This profile was unrelated to age, sex or overall impairment severity.

Memory Assessment

In addition to loss of intellectual ability, memory impairment is another necessary feature for the diagnosis of dementia. Neither most mental status examination protocols nor the WAIS provide sufficiently sensitive or comprehensive memory evaluation.

The instrument most frequently employed to clinically assess memory is the Wechsler Memory Scale (WMS) (Wechsler, 1945). The WMS has been frequently criticized (e.g., Erickson, 1978; Erickson & Scott, 1977). Prigatano (1978) has summarized the weaknesses of the WMS as follows: (1) absence of scaled or standard scores for individual subtests; (2) problems in scoring the Logical Memory subtest (a task involving immediate recall of short spoken stories); (3) lack of adequate norms for the sexes and for various age groups, based on large, representative samples; (4) lack of sufficient information on test-retest reliability of Memory Quotient (MQ) scores for normal individuals; (5) lack of data concerning the distribution of WAIS full scale I.Q. minus WMS MQ scores (particularly for persons with superior I.Q. scores); and (6) the need for re-standardization of the MQ scores with WAIS (or preferably WAIS-R) full scale I.Q. Albert (1981) adds to these criticisms the confounding of perceptual and constructional skills with nonverbal memory (in the Visual Reproduction subtest), and the omission of delayed recall assessment.

Despite these difficulties, the WMS continues to be widely used, and several of the above criticisms have been addressed by recent improvements in the WMS. Russell (1975) has provided a revision of the WMS in which both immediate and delayed recall of both verbal (Logical Memory Passages) and nonverbal (Visual Reproduction subtest) abilities are assessed. When specific scoring conventions are adopted, the revised WMS demonstrates good interrater reliability (Power et al., 1979). Alternate form reliability (comparing form

I and form II) for the revised WMS has been found adequate for immediate recall on both subtests, but less adequate for delayed recall, and inadequate for percentage retained scores (McCarty et al., 1980).

The revised WMS has been shown to validly differentiate demented from age, sex, and education-matched normal groups (Logue and Wyrick, 1979), and the WMS subtests appear helpful in differentiating elderly psychiatric patients with functional disorders from those with a variety of organic brain syndromes (Gilleard, 1980). Recently, (Brinkman et al., 1983) the revised WMS was shown to validly differentiate carefully diagnosed DAT patients from age and education-matched healthy elderly persons. However, a bimodal distribution of percent retained (delayed recall/immediate recall) scores was noted in the patient group, but not in the control group, suggesting the possibility of subgroups of DAT patients. Perez et al. (1975) reported that the subtests of the original WMS accurately discriminate between DAT, MID, and vertebrobasilar insufficiency with dementia patients. However, as discussed above regarding WAIS scores, differences among the groups in education and dementia severity confound interpretation of results.

Clinical interpretation of WMS and revised WMS scores depends upon the application of age-appropriate norms. Given the increasingly large body of research demonstrating differences between younger and older adults in both qualitative and quantitative aspects of memory and learning processes (see review by Hartley, Harker, and Walsh, 1980), it is not surprising that both cross-sectional and longitudinal data show an age-related decline in WMS performance (McCarty et al., 1982). Recently, Haaland et al. (1983) revised the WMS norms for ages 65 through over 80 years. While such normative data has been badly needed, these norms should be cautiously applied. The volunteer subjects composing the normative sample were better educated than is typical for the general population of these ages. Number of years of formal education has a significant correlation with older individuals' WMS performance (Bak and Green, 1981). Further, the magnitude of this correlation may independently account for as much of the variance in WMS subtest scores as do relationships with age, degree of cerebral atrophy (by CT scan), and EEG slowing in older patients suspected of dementia (Kaszniak et al., 1979).

One further caution must be made about attempting to clinically interpret any observed differences between verbal ("semantic") and nonverbal ("figural") initial or delayed recall scores on the revised WMS. One approach to interpretation, perhaps particularly tempting to clinical neuropsychologists, would associate such differences with asymmetric status of particular hemispheric structures (semantic scores more affected by left hemispheric damage, and figural scores by right hemispheric damage). Although there is some support for the validity of such an interpretation of the revised WMS when used with younger adult patients (Russell, 1975), several factors argue against this interpretation for older patients. First, there may be differences in the factor structure of the WMS for older adults (Dye, 1982). Such alteration in factor structure would suggest that the processes contributing to WMS performance change with age. Second there is data to indicate that adult age effects are stronger for the figural than for the semantic subtests (Bak and Green, 1981). Finally, as Albert (1981) and Rosen (1983) remind us, perceptual, constructional, and nonverbal memory skills are confounded in the figural subtest of the revised WMS. Both authors suggest including conditions of copying and matching of visual reproductions, although normative data for such procedures does not yet exist.

While the WMS is the most widely used memory assessment instrument, there are others which appear promising in the evaluation of dementia. The Benton Revised Visual Retention Test (BVRT-R) (Benton, 1974) is a figural retention task often employed in neuropsychological assessment. As with the figural subtests of the revised WMS, aging appears to markedly affect performance (Arenberg, 1978), and normative data appropriate to the age of the patient being examined (Benton et al., 1981) should be used.

The Guild Memory Test (GMT) (Crook, Gilbert, and Ferris, 1980) is another instrument that employs immediate and delayed recall of paragraphs and paired-word associates, and recall of visuospatial designs. Normative data for older individuals is available, and GMT performance is significantly correlated with WMS subtest performance (Crook et al., 1980). Another task developed by this group of investigators, the Misplaced Objects Task (Crook, Ferris, and McCarthy, 1979), employs a board with a drawing of the cross-section of a furnished seven-room house. Ten magnetized vinyl shapes of objects that are often misplaced (e.g., keys) have to be identified and placed on the board to show where in the home they would be kept. Following removal of the board for an interval, the patient is asked to replace the objects in their original position. Using this task, Crook et al. (1979) have demonstrated valid differentiation of intact and impaired memory functioning. Its high face validity, and the possibility that it therefore would elicit greater patient cooperation, encourages the further development of this task, particularly for use with moderately to severely demented patients.

Another recently developed instrument that is promising for more demented patients is the Fuld Object Memory Evaluation (Fuld, 1980, 1981). Using a modification of the Buschke and Fuld (1974) procedure of selective reminding, it allows for differential evaluation of storage and retrieval memory processes from within a single testing session. The test also evaluates the subject's ability to retrieve words rapidly from familiar semantic categories. It "guarantees" that stimulus processing of information will occur by presenting ten common objects in a bag, having the subject identify and describe each object by touch, and afterwards, visually identify them, with the examiner correcting any identification errors. This procedure limits visual and auditory impairments common in the elderly, as well as naming difficulties, which are frequently observed in dementia patients. Following a 60-second distraction (semantic category naming task), recall is assessed, over five consecutive recall trials (with selective reminding of items omitted), allowing separate estimates of storage and retrieval processes. Fuld (1980) has reported good internal reliability (coefficient alpha = 0.84), and storage scores were correlated 0.72 with retention after three weeks, for a sample of nursing home residents. Further, Fuld demonstrated significant differences on the test, comparing moderately impaired and unimpaired elderly nursing home residents [grouped on the basis of independent mental status examination scores (Blessed et al., 1968)]. Finally, intrusion errors on this test have been shown to be correlated with ChAT levels and neuritic plaque counts in the brain tissue of autopsied nursing home residents (Fuld et al., 1982). Norms for the Fuld Object Memory Evaluation are available for community-active, as well as nursing-home-residing 70 and 80 year olds (Fuld, 1980).

Finally, note should be taken of the recently developed New York University Memory Test (Osborne, et al., 1982; Randt et al., 1980), which allows immediate and delayed recall (at 10 seconds, 3 minutes, and 24 hours) assessment for objects, words, short stories and pictures (as well as providing selective reminding and incidental learning procedures). Five equivalent alternate forms are available, facilitating longitudinal study and application to treatment evaluation. Normative data is available on 300 subjects (grouped by decade from 20 to 80 years), and the instrument has been shown to differentiate normal from memory-impaired elderly subjects (Osborne, et al., 1982). If future research continues to support the reliability and validity of this test battery, it may prove to be an excellent instrument for the detailed evaluation of various memory processes in persons with mild to moderate memory loss, including patients in the early stages of dementia.

Assessment of Other Cognitive Processes

While intellectual and memory assessment can occupy the largest portion of the neuropsychological assessment of patients suspected of dementia, other procedures should also be included in any comprehensive evaluation.

The most frequently employed procedures for evaluating attention are the auditory digit span (as contained within the WAIS and WMS, as well as other test batteries) and the visual letter (Talland and Schwab, 1964) or digit (Lewis and Kupke, 1977) cancellation task. Digit span, although relatively unaffected by normal aging (e.g., Gilbert and Levee, 1971; Kaszniak, Garron and Fox, 1979), becomes increasingly impaired over time in DAT (Storandt et al., in press). Digit span has also been shown to be negatively correlated with CT scan measures of cerebral atrophy (Kaszniak, Garron, and Fox, 1979) and degree of EEG slowing (Kaszniak, Garron, Fox, et al., 1979) in otherwise healthy older patients suspected of dementia. Digit or letter cancellation tasks, although having less adequate age-norms than digit span, also reveal progressive impairment in longitudinal study of DAT patients (Storandt et al., in press).

Abstract thinking ability is most frequently evaluated by examining WAIS Similarities and Comprehension ("proverbs" items) subtests. Other procedures for evaluating abstraction ability and cognitive flexibility, such as the Wisconsin Card Sorting Test (Berg, 1948) are available, but adequate norms for older age groups are not widely available, and its specific validity in assessing dementia remains to be empirically demonstrated. The present author has found the Picture Absurdities subtest of the Stanford-Binet Intelligence Scale (Terman and Merrill, 1973) to be useful as an index of the patient's ability to make judgements about the appropriateness of actions shown in a particular setting (provided that visual perceptual functioning is not severely impaired). Performance on this measure has been shown to be related to electroencepalographic and clinical features in at least two studies (Kaszniak et al., 1978; Kaszniak et al., 1979).

Constructional ability is most frequently examined by the Block Design subtest of the WAIS or by various drawing tasks. Studies have consistently demonstrated Block Design impairment, inability to copy two-dimensional geometric forms, and significantly more errors in drawing the Bender-Gestalt (Bender, 1938) geometric figures (Bender, 1938; Danziger and Storandt, 1982; Miller, 1977a).

Clinical observers (e.g., Schneck et al., 1982) have noted a variety of perceptual deficits in DAT and other dementia patients, which are particularly frequent as dementia severity increases. Eslinger and Benton (1983) compared a group of 40 dementia patients of mixed etiology to 40 age, sex and education-matched normal volunteers, employing the Benton Facial Recognition Test (Benton and Van Allen, 1968) and the Benton Line Orientation Test (Benton, Varney and Hamsher, 1978). Large and significant differences emerged on both tests in the comparison of the dementia and matched normal groups, supporting the validity of these instruments in assessing dementia. Further, dissociations in performance on the two tests were common for the dementia patients, but rare for the normals, suggesting that dementia may manifest in differential perceptual deterioration. Normative data is available on these tests for subjects aged 65 to 84 years (grouped by five-year intervals) Benton et al., 1981).

An evaluation of language functioning is also important in the comprehensive neuropsychological assessment of dementia. Word finding difficulty and confrontation-naming deficit have long been recognized (e.g., Critchley, 1964) as common in dementia. While these are not the only aspects of language that are impaired in dementia (see Bayles, 1984; Bayles et al., 1982), they have been the most frequently assessed aspects in neuropsychological examination protocols. The Boston Naming Test (Kaplan, Goodglass, and Weintraub, 1978) produces significantly more naming errors in DAT, compared to age and education-matched normal subjects (Martin and Fedio, 1983). Similarly, object and body-part naming subtests of the Boston Diagnostic Aphasia Examination (Goodglass and Kaplan, 1972) are performed more poorly by DAT than by age and education matched controls (Wilson et al., 1981). However, it should be noted that similar naming deficits may not occur in some other dementing illnesses (e.g., Huntington's and Parkinson's diseases), at least when the dementia is only of mild to moderate severity (Bayles and Tomoeda, 1983). The Boston Naming Test and the Boston Diagnostic Aphasia Examination have the advantage, in comparison to other standardized language measures, of there being published normative data (grouped by age and education level) for adults aged 25 through 85 years (Borod, Goodglass, and Kaplan, 1980).

Spontaneous word-finding difficulty has typically been evaluated by various "fluency" measures, such as the word finding and phrase length ratings of conversational speech and the animal naming subtest of the Boston Diagnostic Aphasia Examination, or the fluency measure of the Mattis Dementia Rating Scale. Such measures of fluency (or productive naming) demonstrate DAT patients to be impaired in comparison to matched controls (Martin and Fedio, 1983; Weingartner et al., 1981; Wilson et al., 1981), with such impairment generally being more severe than that observed for confrontation naming (Wilson et al., 1981).

Before completing this review of neuropsychological assessment in dementia, some mention must be made of the application of "batteries," such as the Halstead-Reitan (Reitan and Davison, 1974). While the Halstead-Reitan Battery has been employed in the study of dementia (e.g., Jenkyn et al., 1977), the difficulty level of several of its subtests may argue against its general application, except, perhaps, when dementia is mild. Normative data for this particular battery is available (Chapter 6; Reitan, 1979).

The battery constructed by Christensen (1979) to operationalize Luria's approach to neuropsychological examination has recently been applied to the study of DAT patients, and the initial data indicates that it is able to differentiate moderate from severely demented patients (Sulkava and Amberla, 1982). More information is needed to confirm its reliability and validity. This battery lacks normative data for older age groups, which prohibits its clinical application at present.

Neuropsychological Research in Dementia

As reviewed above, neuropsychological procedures have been shown to make a reliable and valid contribution to diagnostic assessment in dementia. Of equal importance is the role played by neuropsychological research in helping to understand the nature and correlates of cognitive impairment in dementia. Recent reviews of research concerned with the nature of memory (Fozard, in press; Miller, 1977a, 1981a; Morley et al., 1980), language (Bayles, 1984), and other cognitive deficits (Miller, 1977a, 1981a) in dementia have been published. The present chapter will focus upon select research on memory deficit, in order to illustrate the approach and contributions of neuropsychological investigation in this area.

The Nature of Memory Deficit in Dementia

Most, although not all, of the research concerned with characterizing the nature of memory deficit in dementia has employed an information processing approach. This approach (see Estes, 1978; Fozard, in press; Kaszniak, et al., in press), considers the individual to be an active participant in the learning and decision making process, and assumes that a response can be partitioned into theoretical stages or components. By manipulating various aspects of stimulus input and response choices, characteristics of the individual's "central processor" can be inferred by observing the quality and pattern of his response. The most frequently employed theoretical model of information processing in memory posits several different stages or storage capacites (sensory, primary, secondary and tertiary memory), and various processes (encoding, storage and retrieval) involved in moving information in and out of these capacities.

SENSORY MEMORY. Sensory memory is conceptualized as a preattentive and very unstable information registration system, which is modality-specific. "Iconic memory" (Sperling, 1963) is the term used to describe this system within the visual modality. Miller (1977b) published the report of a preliminary study of iconic memory in PSDAT patients. However, both Miller (1981a) and the present author have subsequently found that the backward masking, as well as conceptually similar experimental paradigms for evaluating sensory memory, are very difficult to execute with dementia patients (largely because of the patients' problems understanding instructions and task demands). Consequently, it is unlikely that such paradigms will provide us with reliable information concerning the status of sensory memory in dementia.

PRIMARY MEMORY. The next hypothetical stage in the sequential processing of information in memory has been termed "primary" or "short-term" memory (Waugh and Norman, 1965), which seems to serve the purpose of acquiring and briefly retaining new information. Storage capacity is very limited, so items are briefly held, then are displaced by new items and permanently lost. Rehearsal of items, however, enables various coding processes to occur, which store the items in "secondary" or "long-term" memory (theoretically, a relatively permanent repository, with unlimited capacity).

The procedure most frequently used to study primary memory is the forward digit span, as contained within the WAIS and WMS and described above. Word span (employing words rather than digits) and block span tasks (the subject is required to tap spatially arranged blocks in the sequence indicated by the examiner) demonstrate similar impairment in DAT (Corkin, 1982; Miller, 1973).

Another task traditionally employed to examine primary memory is the Brown (1958) or Peterson and Peterson (1959) technique, in which either three words or a consonant trigram (CCC) is presented. Recall is then tested either immediately, or following various delay intervals (typically 1–18 seconds) that are filled with distracting cognitive activity (e.g., counting backwards by twos). Since the distracting activity is presumed to prevent rehearsal, any decrease in recall with increasing distraction interval is taken to reflect a loss of information from primary memory. Using this procedure with DAT patients, Corkin (1982) found no difference between dementia and control subjects in immediate recall, but found impairment in dementia with increasing distraction intervals. Performance was also found to be negatively correlated with ADL impairment. While it has been questioned whether the Brown-Peterson technique reflects primary memory processes (Baddely, 1976), results with this procedure applied to DAT are similar to those obtained with span tasks.

Still another task which has been used to examine primary memory in dementia is based upon free recall. In this procedure, the subject is serially presented a supra-span list of words, and instructed to recall as many words as possible (in any order) immediately following the last presented word. When probability of recall is ploted against the serial position in which the word was presented, normal individuals demonstrate a U-shaped curve, in which the first few words and the last few words of the list are recalled better than the words presented in the middle of the list. Following Glanzer and Cunitz (1966), the relatively good recall of words from the end of the list has been interpreted as reflecting short-term or primary memory. Words recalled from the beginning of the list are presumed to reflect material which has passed (through rehearsal and other active encoding processes) into secondary or long-term storage.

Miller (1971) was the first to report free recall serial position data comparing PSDAT and matched-control subjects. While control subjects demonstrated the expected U-shaped curve, the dementia patients, in comparison, had poorer recall across all serial word positions. Words from the end of the list (primary memory component) were recalled more poorly by the PSDAT patients, although the group difference was even more marked for words from the beginning of the list (secondary memory component). These results are consistent with a reduced primary memory capacity and/or efficiency in PSDAT (interpretation of the markedly reduced secondary memory component of the serial-position curve in PSDAT will be discussed below). Using a similar verbal free recall procedure, Kaszniak, Wilson, and Fox (1981) obtained the same evidence of reduced primary memory in both PSDAT and SDAT patients, compared to age-matched controls.

The interpretation that the "recency effect" (relatively good recall of words which were presented at the end of the list) in the serial position curve reflects primary memory, and the "primacy effect" (relatively good recall of words from the beginning of the list) reflects secondary memory, has been criticized. Baddley (1976) has questioned whether the recency effect results from a retrieval strategy that uses serial position as a cue, rather than reflecting primary memory. Tulving and Colotla (1970) described a procedure for evaluating free recall data which takes into account both serial-list-position of word presentation and serial order of word recall. In this procedure, each word which is recalled within six or less intervening word presentations and recall productions is assigned to primary memory. All other recalled words are assigned to secondary memory. The Tulving and Colotla (1970) procedure for deriving primary and secondary memory scores from free recall data has found considerable empirical support in experimental investigations of normal memory functioning (Watkins, 1974), as well as in neuropsychological studies of amnesia (Moscovitch, 1982). Employing this scoring procedure, Wilson et al. (1983a) found primary memory to be impaired in DAT patients (relative to matched healthy controls), and further showed that the size of the patients' primary memory deficit increased linearly with increasing number of items between presentation and recall. Longitudinal study of these same DAT patients and control subjects, with annual reexamination over a three-year period, demonstrated the primary memory score to deteriorate over time for the DAT, but not for the control subjects (Wilson and Kaszniak, in press).

In summary, while no single experimental procedure for defining primary memory has escaped theoretical debate concerning its validity, all of the procedures have shown impairment in DAT. Collectively, the research suggests that impairment of primary memory is mild early in the course of dementia, and increases over time and with greater general severity of dementia. It is of interest to note that the impairment of primary memory in DAT contrasts with the findings of a lack of normal aging effects upon primary memory (see reviews by Craik, 1977; Fozard, in press; Poon, in press), and relative preservation of primary memory in amnesic patients whose cerebral damage is limited to medial temporal areas (Corkin, 1982; Drachman and Arbit, 1965; Miller, 1973; Warrington, 1982).

SECONDARY MEMORY. "Secondary" or "Long-term" memory is conceptualized as a relatively permanent repository of newly learned information, with theoretically unlimted capacity. With rehearsal and various active encoding processes (see Craik, 1979), information held in primary memory enters into secondary memory. Research concerned with secondary memory in dementia has employed a wide variety of tasks in which stimulus material, encoding processes, duration of storage, and aspects of retrieval have been systematically manipulated in order to understand the nature of memory impairment in dementia.

Recall of material presented in verbal learning tasks has been considered to reflect at least some secondary memory, since the word lists that have been used have been longer than presumed primary memory capacity. In a verbal list learning task (repeat presentation of ten words representing common items found on shopping lists) in which number of trials to accurate recall is the dependent variable, SDAT patients were shown to be impaired relative to matched controls (McCarthy et al., 1981). Additional evidence of impairment in delayed recall and recognition memory testing further suggested that the SDAT patients' impairment involved aspects of storage and retrieval processes. Studies employing verbal supra-span list learning tasks, in which accuracy of recall of lists of progressively longer length is assessed (Miller, 1973), and those employing a paired-associate learning paradigm report impairment in DAT (Barbizet and Cany, 1969; Caird et al., 1962; Corkin, 1982; Danziger and Storandt, 1982; Inglis, 1959; Inglis and Caird, 1963; Kaszniak, Garron, and Fox, 1979; Rosen and Mohs, 1982; Wilson et al., 1982). Paired-associate learning for geometric forms shows impairment similar to that seen with verbal paired-associate learning tasks in DAT (Corkin, 1982). For DAT patients, level of performance in verbal paired-associate learning has been shown to be negatively correlated with the degree of cerebral atrophy seen on CT scan (deLeon et al., 1980; Kaszniak, et al., 1979), and with severity of EEG slowing (Johannesson et al., 1979; Kaszniak et at., 1979). Further, studies of regional cerebral blood flow distribution (e.g., Hagberg, 1978; Hagberg and Ingvar, 1976) in presenile dementia patients (of mixed neuropathology at autopsy examination) have found verbal paired-associate learning impairment to be most associated with left temporal lobe blood flow reductions. This suggests that secondary memory deficit (as indexed by paired-associate learning) in dementia is particularly related to abnormal functioning of the same brain regions known to be affected in certain amnesic disorders (e.g., Milner, 1971).

Recall of verbal textual material (e.g., short stories) is another task thought to involve predominantly secondary memory, which has been employed in the study of dementia. Compared to matched controls, DAT patients demonstrate impairment in immediate recall of spoken short stories and show the same negative correlations with the degree of cerebral atrophy and EEG slowing, as was described above for paired-associate learning. When recall of short stories is tested both immediately after presentation, as well as after a delay interval (during which the patient engages in other cognitive activity), DAT patients show a lower percentage of retention than matched controls (Brinkman et al., 1983; Logue & Wyrick, 1979).

It is of particular interest to note in one study using the Tulving and Colotla (1970) procedure, that primary and secondary memory scores were found to be independent in the healthy elderly control group, but were significantly correlated in the DAT group (Wilson et al., 1983). This observation, together with the fact that the size of the patients' primary memory deficit increased linearly with increasing items between presentation and attempted recall, argues that the secondary memory deficit in DAT is at least partially due to impaired primary memory. Other investigators (Miller, 1971; Diesfeldt, 1978) employing the free recall/serial position paradigm with DAT patients have come to the same conclusion.

Also consistent with this view is data concerning proactive interference (previously learned information interfering with recall of more recent material) in DAT. Wilson et al. (1983) examined proactive interference by measuring both decline in secondary memory recall across four consecutive list presentations (Underwood, 1957) and number of prior-list-item intrusions (words from a previous list produced during the the subjects attempt to recall a subsequent list). While the control group showed the expected linear decline in secondary memory recall over lists, the DAT patients did not. Further, the patients showed fewer prior list intrusions than the controls (patient intrusion errors were predominantly extra-list). Thus, DAT patients appear to lack any substantial proactive interference effect. This is in contrast with the pattern observed in alcoholic Korsakoff's amnesia, in which there is increased susceptibility to proactive interference (Cermak and Butters, 1972). Both the lack of evidence of proactive interference and the marked impairment of secondary memory recall in DAT may reflect initial processing failure.

Recognition memory paradigms have provided additional insight into the mechanisms of secondary memory impairment in DAT. Such paradigms involve the forced choice recognition of mixed target and distractor stimuli (typically words, but other stimuli have also been employed) following target stimuli presentation. An advantage of recognition memory tasks is that they allow variables to be examined (e.g., response bias) that are not easily evaluated in free recall tasks, and, by virtue of being "easier" than free recall, are not as prone to basement effects in examining more severely demented patients (see Wilson and Kaszniak, in press).

Recognition memory has been shown to be impaired in DAT, employing both verbal and nonverbal stimuli. The application of signal detection analysis (Marcer, 1979; Swets, 1973) to verbal and facial recognition memory performance of DAT patients (Wilson, Kaszniak et al, 1982) indicates that the deficit is due to a problem in the memory discrimination of target from distractor stimuli, rather than to any response bias. Edgar Miller (1975, 1978) had proposed that this recognition memory deficit is predominantly (although not exclusively) one of retrieval, since it worsens as the number of recognition alternatives increases and improves when testing employs a partial information rather than uncued recognition procedure. However, it has been shown that both of these findings can be reproduced in normal individuals if the retention interval (length of time between stimuli exposure and retention testing) is increased so that normal performance is in a range similar to that seen in immediate recognition testing of dementia patients (Mayes and Meudell, 1981; Meudell and Mayes, 1981). Thus, it is possible that poor initial encoding of information into secondary memory could account for the recognition memory deficit in DAT.

Several recent observations support this interpretation. First, verbal, but not facial, recognition memory performance in DAT is negatively correlated with the severity of language impairment (as measured by a summary index of performance on the Boston Diagnostic Aphasia Examination) (Wilson, Kaszniak et al, 1982). This suggests that linguistic deficits limit verbal encoding in DAT and make a specific contribution to verbal, but not nonverbal recognition memory impairment. Second, manipulation of depth of processing (Craik & Tulving, 1975) of verbal stimuli (by asking orienting questions prior to presentation of each stimulus word, which focus the subject upon either phonemic or semantic aspects of the word) has less of an effect upon the verbal recognition memory performance of DAT patients than on that of matched controls (Corkin, 1982; Wilson, Kaszniak, Bacon, Fox & Kelly, 1982). Similarly, DAT patients appear to have relatively more difficulty making use of verbal imagery in free recall (see Pavio, 1971) than matched controls (Kasz-

THE NEUROPSYCHOLOGY OF DEMENTIA

niak, Wilson & Fox, 1981). These observations again support the hypothesis of defective encoding of information as contributing to the secondary memory deficit of DAT.

A more direct examination of the hypothesis that encoding deficits contribute to the impaired recognition memory performance of DAT patients was provided by Wilson, Bacon, Kramer, Fox & Kaszniak (1983). In normal individuals, recognition memory for rare words is superior to that for common words (Kinsbourne & George, 1974; Poon & Fozard, 1980, Shepard, 1967). The rare word advantage in hit rates on recognition memory tasks is thought to be a function of incremental integration, dependent upon active attention to and analysis of the the stimulus words as they are presented. Wilson, et. al. (1983b) reasoned, therefore, that analysis of the word frequency effect would provide another way of examining the efficiency of encoding operations in DAT. Consistent with their hypothesis, and with previous research concerning encoding operations, the DAT patients failed to show the normal rare word advantage in their hit rate, despite the fact that they showed a normal tendency to false alarm to common words. In a second experiment recognition memory of normal subjects was examined both immediately after word list presentation, and after a delay of one week when it is aproximately equal to that of the DAT patients. Recognition memory performance of these normal individuals at the one week delay showed no attenuation of the rare word advantage, arguing that the DAT patient data could not be explained simply as the result of poor retention or as an artifact of the difficulty of the memory test (Wilson, Bacon, Kramer, Fox & Kaszniak, 1983).

In addition to deficits in encoding along semantic and verbal imagery dimensions, DAT patients have recently been shown to be deficient in ability to use visual context (relationships among pictured figures and objects) as an aid in pictorial secondary memory (Butters, Albert, Sax, Miliotis, Nagode & Sterste, 1983). Further, illustrating the heterogeneity of the dementias, Huntington's disease patients were able to utilize verbal mediators (stories linking figures to background scenes) for circumventing their pictorial memory deficit, while DAT patients were not.

In summary, the available evidence confirms that there is a severe deficit in DAT patients' secondary memory, with memory for both verbal and nonverbal material affected. The deficit in primary memory documented for these patients appears to contribute to the severity of the secondary memory deficit, perhaps by limiting the amount of information available to be processed into secondary memory. While the possiblity of secondary memory retrieval deficits in DAT cannot be excluded, recent research supports the hypothesis that failure to encode contextual, featural, and intrastructural elements of to-be-remembered information contributes markedly. While secondary memory is impaired in normal aging, amnesic disorders, and in other dementias (e.g., Huntington's disease), recent research demonstrates the nature of such impairment to differ from that of DAT patients. In general, the secondary memory impairment of DAT appears more severe, more pervasive (affecting all types of stimuli and all types of processes which have been studied), and more affected by other deficits (e.g., primary memory, linguistic encoding), than that of other conditions showing secondary memory deficit.

TERTIARY MEMORY. Tertiary or remote memory is recall of information acquired in the distant past. Clincial observation of dementia patients has suggested that such memory might be spared, as patients often seem able to recall childhood or other remote events despite severe deficit in recall of recent events. Interpretation of such clinical observations is problematic, in that the remote events recalled not only occurred in the more distant past, but also are frequently of greater emotional siginficance or have been more frequently rehearsed than recent events. Wilson, Kaszniak, and Fox (1981) attempted to systematically investigate remote memory in DAT. Remote memory was assessed with the procedure constructed by Albert and her coworkers (Albert et al., 1979) to examine the temporal gradient of remote memory deficit in alcoholic Korsakoff's amnesia. The procedure involves two tests of memory for persons and events that became famous between 1930 and 1975 (equated for difficulty of recall). Wilson, Kaszniak, and Fox (1981) found DAT patients to be significantly impaired, relative to matched controls, on these tests. The DAT patients showed a relatively consistent recall deficit over the time period examined (i.e., persons and events that became famous between 1930 and 1975), unlike the retrograde gradient which has been found to characterize the remote memory deficit of Korsakoff's patients. Albert et al. (1981) have observed a similar remote memory deficit, without retrograde gradient, in demented Huntington's disease patients. Thus, dementia in DAT and Huntington's disease appears to include impairment in retrieval of remotely acquired information, without relative sparing of presumably oldest memories.

EPISODIC VERSUS SEMANTIC MEMORY. Tulving (1972) has drawn the distinction between "episodic memory", which is "memory for personal experiences and their temporal relations," and "semantic memory," which is "a system for receiving, retaining and transmitting information about meaning of words, concepts and classification of concepts" (Tulving, 1972, pp. 401–402). Most of the memory research reviewed above involves episodic memory. However, semantic memory tasks, such as those involving productive or confrontation naming also reveal deficit in DAT (e.g., Bayles and Tomoeda, 1983; Kirshner et al., 1984; Martin and Fedio, 1983; Wilson et al., 1981). It has therefore been suggested (Martin and Fedio, 1983) that DAT may lead to a disruption in semantic knowledge, most characterized by a difficulty in differentiating between items within the same semantic category. This difficulty may also contribute to the encoding deficit in episodic secondary memory functioning of DAT patients (Weingartner et al., 1981).

AUTOMATIC VERSUS EFFORTFUL PROCESSING IN MEMORY. Hasher and Zacks (1979) have distinguished automatic memory processing from effortful memory processing, the later of which involves active, effortful encoding of new information. This distinction has proven useful in interpreting the results of studies of various amnesic syndromes (see Hirst, 1982). Recent evidence (Weingartner et al., 1982) indicates that DAT patients are impaired in both effortful and automatic memory processes.

DECLARATIVE VERSUS PROCEDURAL KNOWLEDGE. Another distinction, which has helped in interpretating studies of amnesic disorders, is that of declarative and procedural knowledge (Squire, 1982). Declarative knowledge is information based on specific items or data, while procedural knowledge is information based on rules or procedures (Squire, 1982, p. 259). When amnesic patients (including those with Korsakoff's syndrome, damage to the dorsal thalamus, and patients receiving electroconvulsive treatment) are asked to read sets of words that are reversed by a mirror, they improve their skill at a normal rate (over three days of practice) and retain the skill at a normal level (three months later). However, they continue to show a profound amnesia for the specific words they had read, as well as for other aspects of the testing situation (Cohen and Squire, 1980).

Gordon (1984) has provided some preliminary data concerning the procedural memory of a single DAT patient. While patients with right or left temporal lobectomies (with varying degrees of hippocampal resection) demonstrated preserved repetition effects with word reading (interpreted as indicative of preserved procedural memory), the DAT patient showed no such effect. Thus, while confirmation of this observation with a larger series of DAT patients is necessary, this single case study suggests that both declarative and procedural memory may be affected in DAT. Further experiments along this line would be of considerable interest, since it has been hypothesized that neural systems subserving procedural learning may be different, and phylogenetically more primitive, than those subserving declarative learning (Squire, 1982, p. 260).

Summary and Directions for Future Research

The research reviewed within this chapter documents the important role neuropsychological assessment plays in both diagnosis and efforts to better understand the nature of cognitive impairment in dementia. While caution must be excercised in interpreting neuropsychological assessment results in diagnosis, such assessment is of paramount importance, particularly when the dementia is relatively mild. Comparisons of DAT patients with matched controls, comparisons between patients with various types of dementia, and studies of relationship to neurobiologic measures all support the validity of neuropsychologic assessment procedures in the evaluation of dementia.

Neuropsychological research concerning the nature of memory deficit in dementia has also made important contributions to our understanding of these disorders, particularly DAT. While various amnesic disorders appear to affect relatively specific aspects of memory processing, DAT appears characterized by deficit in all aspects of memory studied thus far. This is important in evaluating attempts to correlate measures of memory in DAT with measures of regional brain anatomy from CT scans, or measures of regional brain physiology, such as those obtained from positron emmission tomography, regional cerebral blood flow, or evoked response.

Both PET and CBF have suggested particularly marked hypometabolism in the temporal lobes of DAT patients. This corresponds with pathologic evidence of marked accumulation of neuritic plaques and neurofibrillary tangles as well as gross atrophy in the hippocampi of DAT patients. Verbal secondary memory deficit in dementia has been found to be most associated with left temporal lobe CBF reductions. Further, recent PET studies have revealed lateral asymmetry in hemispheric metabolism to be common in DAT, with the pattern of neuropsychological deficits corresponding, in expected directions, to the lateralization of hypometabolism (Koss et al., 1984). All of these findings have encouraged the search for regional brain anatomic and physiologic correlates of specific patterns of cognitive deficit which vary among DAT patients. However, given the number of mnemonic and other cognitive processes impaired in DAT, and the contributions which deficits in one process make to deficits in other processes, it is likely that correlations between cognitive and regional cerebral anatomic and physiologic measures will be enormously complex, and will require more detailed assessment of cognitive processess than has thus far been the case. Similar considerations apply to evaluating the effects of treatment, such as pharmacologic manipulation of cholinergic neurotransmission, upon memory measures. Some of the apparently contradictory results in this area may be due to variability, between studies, in the degree to which cognitive deficits, other than in the specific memory processes studied, are present and affecting performance on the dependent measure.

Another area in which more research is needed involves direct comparisons of the memory and other cognitive deficits of dementing illness with those seen in amnesic disorders and with cognitive changes in normal aging. Through such comparisons, viewing DAT and other dementias as "experiments of nature," a better understanding of both the nature of dementing illness and the nature of brain–behavior relationships should be gained. The application of information-processing based procedures for the evaluation of memory, particularly those requiring sophisticated computerized task administration may have limitations in the study of dementia. While such approaches have proven quite valuable in the study of normal memory, aging (e.g. Bacon, Wilson, and Kaszniak, 1982), and other neurologic disorders (e.g., Wilson et al., 1980), the severity of the cognitive impairment in dementia may place limits upon obtaining reliable and valid data, except, perhaps, for those patients very early in the course of their disease. Careful attention to stimulus presentation and response complexity dimensions will certainly be necessary in such research.

There remain many unanswered questions concerning the heterogeneity of neuropsychological presentations of the dementias. Certainly, different dementing illnesses demonstrate differences in the nature and pattern of their cognitive deficits (e.g., Butters et al., 1983). Even within a given dementing illness, such as DAT, there appears to be heterogeneity in patterns of cognitive deficit and correlated neurobiologic measures. The present review has treated studies of PSDAT and SDAT similarly, following the similarity of neuropathologic presentation (Terry and Katzman, 1983) of these disorders. However, there is debate concerning the neuropsychologic identity of PSDAT and SDAT. Some investigators (e.g., Sulkava and Amberla, 1982) find no difference between PSDAT and SDAT patients in either severity or pattern of neuropsychologic test deficit, while others (e.g., Loring and Largen, 1984; Seltzer and Sherwin, 1983) do find such differences. At this point, it is important for investigators to preserve the ability to analyze data differentially by age of dementia onset. A major problem in all studies comparing different dementing illnesses, or different subgroups within a disorder (as well as attempts to review and integrate research), is that dementia is a progressive syndrome: Until quite recently, few studies attempted to systematically characterize the "stage" or severity of dementia and to equate for severity across groups being compared.

At present, there are very few available longitudinal studies of dementia. Such research is critical in evaluating whether different levels and patterns of neuropsychological and/or neurobiological assessment results have validity in predicting differential rate or pattern of deterioration, or treatment response. Such research would also be of great importance in helping to better understand the changing nature of brain–behavior relationships throughout the course of dementing illness.

A final area of needed research is the nature of relationships between neuropsychological assessment measures and performance outside the laboratory situation (e.g., Baddeley, Sunderland, and Harris, 1982). Such information would be an important contribution to the management of dementia patients and the design of psychosocial and environmental interventions (see Lawton, 1980).

While much remains to be learned about the neuropsychology of dementia, the vigor of research over the past few years, and the progress of our understanding are considerable reasons for encouragement.

ACKNOWLEDGMENT

Preparation of this manuscript was partially supported by DHHS grant AG00905, and a grant from the University of Arizona Long-Term Care Gerontology Center. The author wishes to thank James Allender, M. A., for his assistance in the literature search.

REFERENCES

Ajuriaguerra, J. de, and Tissot, R. (1968). Some aspects of psycho-neurologic disintegration in senile dementia. In: C. Muller and L. Ciompi, eds., *Senile Dementia*. Switzerland: Huber, pp. 69–79.

Albert, M. S. (1981). Geriatric neuropsychology. *J. Consult. Clin. Psychol., 49,* 835–850.

Albert, M. S., Butters, N., and Brandt, J. (1981). Patterns of remote memory in amnesic and demented patients. *Arch. Neurol., 38,* 495–500.

Albert, M. S., Butters, N., and Levin, J. (1979). Temporal gradients in the retrograde amnesia of patients with alcoholic Korsakoff's disease. *Arch. Neurol., 36,* 211–216.

Alzheimer, A. (1907). Uber eigenartige Krankereits falle des spateran alters. *Allegemeine Zeitschrift fur Psychiatrie, 64,* 146–148.

Ambrose, J. (1973). Computerized transverse axial scanning (tomography): Part 2. Clincial application. *Br. J. Radiol., 46,* 1023–1047.

American Psychiatric Association (1980). *Diagnostic and Statistical Manual of Mental Disorders,* 3d ed. Washington, D.C.: American Psychiatric Association.

Anders, T. R., and Fozard, J. L. (1973). Effects of age upon retrieval from primary and secondary memory. *Dev. Psychol., 9,* 411–415.

Anthony, J. C., LeResche, L., Nraz, V., von Korff, M. R., and Folstein, M. F. (1982). Limits of the 'Mini-Mental State' as a screening test for dementia and delirium among hospital patients. *Psychol. Med., 12,* 397–408.

Arenberg, D. (1978). Differences and changes with age in the Benton Visual Retention Test. *J. Gerontol., 33,* 534–540.

Bacon, L. D., Wilson, R. S., and Kaszniak, A. W. (1982). Age differences in memory scanning? *Percept. Motor Skills, 55,* 499–504.

Baddeley, A. D. (1976). *The Psychology of Memory.* New York: Basic Books.

Baddeley, A., Sunderland, A., and Harris, J. (1982). How well do laboratory-based psychological tests predict patients' performance outside the laboratory? In: S. Corkin, K. L. Davis, J. H. Growdon, E. Usdin, and R. L. Wurtman, eds., *Aging, vol. 19, Alzheimer's Disease: A Report of Progress* New York: Raven, pp. 141–148.

Bak, J. S., and Greene, R. L. (1981). A review of the performance of aged adults on various Wechsler Memory Scale subtests. *J. Clin. Psychol., 37,* 186–188.

Ball, M. J. (1978). Topographic distribution of neurofibrillary tangles and granulovacuolar degeneration in hippocampal cortex of aging and demented patients. A quantitative study. *Acta Neuropathol., 42,* 73–80.

Barbizet, J., and Cany, E. (1969). A psychometric study of various memory deficits associated with cerebral lesions. In: G. A. Talland and N. C. Waugh, eds., *The Pathology of Memory* New York: Academic Press, pp. 49–64.

Barron, S. A., Jacobs, L., and Kinkel, W. R. (1976). Changes in size of normal lateral ventricles during aging, demonstrated by computerized tomography. *Neurology, 26,* 1011–1013.

Bartus, R. T., Dean, R. L., Beer, B., and Lippa, A. S. (1982). The cholinergic hypothesis of geriatric memory dysfunction. *Science, 217,* 408–417.

Bayles, K. A. (1984). Language and dementia. In: A. Holland, ed., *Language Disorders in Adults* San Diego: College-Hill, pp. 209–244.

Bayles, K. A., Boon, D. R., Kaszniak, A. W., and Stern, L. Z. (1982). Language impairment in dementia. *Arizona Med., 39,* 308–311.

Bayles, K. A., and Tomoeda, C. K. (1983). Confrontation naming impairment in dementia. *Brain and Language, 19,* 98–114.

Bender, L. A. (1938). *A Visual-Motor Gestalt Test and its Clinical Use.* New York: American Orthopsychiatric Association.

Benson, D. F. (1982). The use of positron emission scanning techniques in the diagnosis of Alzheimer's disease. In: S. Corkin, K. L. Davis, J. H. Growdon, E. Usdin, and R. L. Wurtman, eds., *Aging,* vol. 19, *Alzheimer's Disease: A Report of Progress* New York: Raven, pp. 79–82.

Benson, D. F., and Cummings, J. L. (1982). Angular gyrus syndrome simulating Alzheimer's disease. *Arch. Neurol., 39,* 616–620.

Benton, A. L. (1974). *Revised Visual Retention Test: Clinical and Experimental Application,* 4th ed. New York: The Psychological Corporation.

Benton, A. L., Eslinger, P. J., and Demasio, A. R. (1981). Normative observations on neuropsychological test performances in old age. *J. Clin. Neuropsychol., 3,* 33–42.

Benton, A. L., and Van Allen, M. W. (1968). Impairment in facial recognition in patients with cerebral disease. *Cortex, 4,* 344–358.

Benton, A. L., Varney, N. R., and Hamsher, K. (1978). Visuospatial judgement: a clinical test. *Arch. Neurol., 35,* 364–367.

Berg, E. A. (1948). A simple objective test for measuring flexibility in thinking. *J. General Psychol., 39,* 15–22.

Bienenfeld, D., and Hartford, J. T. (1982). Pseudodementia in an elderly woman with schizophrenia. *Am. J. Psychiat., 139,* 114–115.

Bird, J. M. (1982). Computerized tomography, atrophy and dementia: a review. *Prog. Neurobiol., 19,* 91–115.

Birren, J. E., Woods, A. M., and Williams, M. V. (1980). Behavioral slowing with age: Causes, organization and consequences. In: L. W. Poon, ed., *Aging in the 1980s: Psychological Issues,* Washington, D.C.: American Psychological Association, pp. 293–308.

Blessed, G., Tomlinson, B. E., and Roth, M. (1968). The association between quantitative measures of dementia and of senile change in the cerebral grey matter of elderly subjects. *J. Psychiat., 114,* 797–811.

Bondareff, W., Mountjoy, C. Q., and Roth, M. (1982). Loss of neurons of origin of the adrenergic projection to cerebral cortex (nucleus locus coeruleus) in senile dementia. *Neurology, 32,* 164–168.

Borod, J. C., Goodglass, H., and Kaplan, E. (1980). Normative data on the Boston Diagnostic Aphasia Examination, Parietal Lobe Battery, and the Boston Naming Test. *J. Clin. Neuropsychol., 2,* 209–215.

Botwinick, J. (1977). Intellectual abilities. In: J. E. Birren and K. W. Schaie, eds., *Handbook of the Psychology of Aging,* New York: Van Nostrand Reinhold, pp. 580–605.

Bowen, D. M., Smith, C. B., White, P., and Davison, A. N. (1976). Neurotransmitter-related enzymes and indices of hypoxia in senile dementia and other abiotrophies. *Brain, 99,* 459–496.

Brink, T. L, Capri, D., DeNeeve, V., Janakes, C., and Oliveira, C. (1978). Senile confusion: Limitations of assessment by the face-hand test, mental status questionnaire, and staff ratings. *J. Am. Geriatrics Soc., 26,* 380–382.

Brinkman, S. D. (1983). Neuropsychological differences between Alzheimer's disease and multiinfarct dementia. Presented at the Talland Memorial Conference on Clincial Memory Assessment of Older Adults, Wakefield, Massachusetts.

Brinkman, S. D., and Braun, P. (1984). Classification of dementia patients by a WAIS profile related to central cholinergic deficiencies. *J. Clin. Neuropsychol., 6,* 393–400.

Brinkman, S. D., Largen, J. W., Gerganoff, S., and Pomara, N. (1983). Russell's revised Memory Scale in the evaluation of dementia. *J. Clin. Psychol., 39,* 989–993.

Brown, J. (1958). Some tests of the decay theory of immediate memory. *Quart. J. Exp. Psychol., 10,* 12–21.

Brust, J. C. M. (1983). Dementia and cerebrovascular disease. In: R. Mayeux and W. G. Rosen, eds., *The Dementias,* New York: Raven, pp. 131–147.

Burger, L. J., Rowan, A. J., and Goldenshon, E. S. (1972). Creutzfeld-Jakob disease: an electroencephalographic study. *Arch. Neurol., 26,* 428–432.

Buschke, H., and Fuld, P. A. (1974). Evaluating storage, retention and retrieval in disordered memory and learning. *Neurology, 24,* 1019–1025.

Busse, E. W. (1975). Aging and psychiatric diseases of late life. In: S. Aireti, ed., *American Handbook of Psychiatry,* 2d ed., vol. IV: *Organic Disorders and Psychosomatic Medicine,* New York: Basic Books, pp. 67–89.

Busse, E. W., Barnes, R. H., Friedman, E. L., and Kelty, E. J. (1956). Psychological functioning of aged individuals with normal and abnormal electroencephalograms: I. A study of non-hospital community volunteers. *J. Nerv. Ment. Dis., 124,* 135–141.

Butters, N. (1984). The clinical aspects of memory disorders: contributions from experimental studies of amnesia and dementia. *J. Clin. Neuropsychol., 6,* 17–36.

Butters, N., Albert, M. S., Sax, D. S., Miliotis, P., Nagode, J., and Sterste, A. (1983). The effect of verbal mediators on the pictorial memory of brain-damaged patients. *Neuropsychol., 21,* 307–323.

Caine, E. D. (1981). Pseudodementia: current concepts and future directions. *Arch. General Psychiat., 38,* 1359–1364.

Caine, E. D., and Shoulson, I. (1983). Psychiatric syndromes in Hungtington's Disease. *Am. J. Psychiat., 140,* 728–733.

Caird, W. K., Sanderson, R. E., and Inglis, J. (1962). Cross validation of a learning test for use with elderly psychiatric patients. *J. Mental Sci., 108,* 368–370.

Celesia, G. G., and Daly, R. F. (1977). Effects of aging on visual evoked responses. *Arch. Neurol., 34,* 403–407.

Cermak, L. S., and Butters, N. (1972). The role of interference and encoding in the short-term memory deficits of Korsakoff patients. *Neuropsychol., 10,* 89–96.

Chase, T. N., Wexler, N. S., and Barbeau, A., eds. (1979). *Advances in Neurology,* vol. 23, *Huntington's Disease.* New York: Raven.

Christensen, A. L. (1979). *Luria's Neuropsychological Investigation. Text* 2d ed. Copenhagen: Munksgaard.

Coblentz, J. M. Mattis, S., Zingesser, L. H., Kassoff, S. S., Wisniewski, H. M., and Katzman, R. (1973). Presenile dementia: Clinical devaluation of cerebrospinal fluid dynamics. *Arch. Neurol., 29,* 299–308.

Cohen, N. J., and Squire, L. R. (1980). Preserved learning and retention of pattern analyzing skill in amnesia: dissociation of knowing how and knowing that. *Science, 210,* 207–209.

Corkin, S. (1982). Some relationships between global amnesias and the memory impairments in Alzheimer's disease. In: S. Corkin, K. L. Davis, J. H. Growdon, E. Usdin, and R. L. Wurtmen, eds., *Aging,* vol. 19, *Alzheimer's Disease: A Report of Progress* New York: Raven, pp. 149–164.

Corso, J. F. (1981). *Aging Sensory Systems and Perception.* New York: Praeger.

Coyle, J. T., Price, D. L., and DeLong, M. R. (1983). Alzheimer's disease: a disorder of cortical cholinergic innervation. *Science, 219,* 1184–1219.

Craik, F. I. M. (1977). Age differences in human memory. In: J. E. Birren and K. W. Schaie, eds., *Handbook of the Psychology of Aging,* New York: Van Nostrand Reinhold, pp. 384–420.

Craik, F. I. M. (1979). Human memory. *Ann. Rev. Psychol., 30,* 63–102.

Craik, F. I. M., and Tulving, E. (1975). Depth of processing and the retention of words in episodic memory. *J. Exp. Psychol.: General, 104,* 268–294.

Critchley, M. (1964). The neurology of psychotic speech. *Br. J. Psychiatr., 110,* 353–364.

Crook, T., Ferris, S., and McCarthy, M. (1979). The misplaced-objects task: a brief test for memory dysfunction in the aged. *J. Am. Geriatrics Soc., 27,* 284–287.

Crook, T., Ferris, S., McCarthy, M., and Rae, D. (1980). Utility of digit recall tasks for assessing memory in the aged. *J. Consult. Clin. Psychol., 48,* 228–233.

Crook, T., Gilbert, J. G., and Ferris, S. (1980). Operationalizing memory impairment for elderly persons: The Guild Memory Test. *Psychol. Reports, 47,* 1315–1318.

Crookes, T. G. (1974). Indices of early dementia on WAIS. *Psychol. Reports, 34,* 734.

Crystal, H. A., Horoupian, D. S., Katzman, R., and Jotkowitz, S. (1982). Biopsy-Proved Alzheimer disease presenting as a right parietal lobe syndrome. *Ann. Neurol., 12,* 186–188.

Cummings, J., Benson, D. F., and LoVerme, S. (1980). Reversible dementia: illustrative cases, definition and review. *J. Am. Med. Assoc., 243,* 2434–2439.

Danziger, W. L., and Storandt, M. (1982, November). Psychometric performance of healthy and demented older adults: a one-year follow-up. Presented at the Annual Meeting of the Gerontological Society of America, Boston, Massachusetts.

Davies, P. (1979). Neurotransmitter-related enzymes in senile dementia of the Alzheimer type. *Brain Res., 171,* 319–327.

Davies, P., and Maloney, A. J. F. (1976). Selective loss of central cholinergic neurons in Alzheimer's disease. *Lancet, 2,* 1403.

Davies, P., and Verth, A. H. (1977). Regional distribution of the muscarinic acetylcholine receptor in normal and Alzheimer's type dementia brain. *Brain Res., 138,* 385–392.

Delaney, P. (1982). Dementia: the search for treatable causes. *Southern Med. J., 75,* 707–709.

deLeon, M. J., Ferris, S. H., George, A. E., Christman, D. R., Fowler, J. S., Gentes, C., Reisberg, B., Gee, B., Emmerich, M., Yoshiharu, Y., Brodie, J., Kricheff, I. I., and Wold, A. P. (1983). Positron emission tomographic studies of aging and Alzheimer disease. *Am. J. Neuroradiol., 4,* 568–571.

deLeon, M. J., Ferris, S. H., George, A. E., Reisberg, B. Kricheff, I. I. and Gershon, S. (1980). Computed tomography evaluations of brain-behavior relationships in senile dementia of the Alzheimer's type. *Neurobiol. Aging, 1,* 69–79.

deLeon, M. J., and George, A. E. (1983). Computed tomography in aging and senile dementia of the Alzheimer type. In: R. Mayeux and W. G. Rosen, eds., *The Dementias,* New York: Raven, pp. 103–122.

Demuth, G. W., and Rand, B. S. (1980). Atypical major depression in a patient with severe primary degenerative dementia. *Am. J. Psychiat., 137,* 1609–1610.

Desmedt, J. E., and Cheron, G. (1980). Somatosensory evoked potentials to finger stimulation in healthy octogenerians and in young adults: Wave forms, scalp topography and transit times of parietal and frontal component. *Electroencephalogr. Clin. Neurophysiol., 50,* 404–425.

Diesfeldt, H. F. A. (1978). The distinction between long-term and short-term memory in senile dementia: an analysis of free recall and delayed recognition. *Neuropsychologia, 16,* 115–119.

Donnelly, E. F., Waldman, I. N., Murphy, D. L., Wyatt, R. J., and Goodwin, F. K. (1980). Primary affective disorder: thought disorder in depression. *J. Abnorm. Psychol., 89,* 315–319.

Drachman, D. A., and Arbit, J. (1965). Memory and the hippocampal complex. *Arch. Neurol., 15,* 52–61.

Drachman, D. A., and Leavitt, J. (1974). Human memory and the cholinergic system: a relationship to aging? *Arch. Neurol., 30,* 113–121.

Drechsler, F. (1978). *Quantitative analysis of neurophysiological processes of the aging CNS. J. Neurol., 218,* 197–213.

Dye, C. J. (1982). Factor structure of the Wechsler Memory Scale in an older adult population. *J. Clin. Psychol., 38,* 163–166.

Erickson, R. C. (1978). Problems in the clinical assessment of memory. *Exp. Aging Res., 4,* 255–272.

Erickson, R. C., and Scott, M. L. (1977). Clinical memory testing: a review. *Psychol. Bull., 84,* 1130–1149.

Eslinger, P. J., and Benton, A. L. (1983). Visuoperceptual performances in aging and dementia: clinical and theoreticcl implications. *J. Clin. Neuropsychol., 5,* 213–220.

Escourolle, R., and Poirier, J. (1973). *Manual of Basic Neuropathology.* Philadelphia: W. B. Saunders.

Estes, W. K. (1978). The information-processing approach to cognition: A confluence of metaphors and methods. In: W. K. Estes, ed., *Handbook of Learning and Cognitive Processes:* vol. 5, *Human Information Processing,* New York: Wiley, pp. 1–18.

Fillenbaum, G. G., and Smyer, M. (1981). The development, validity and reliability of the OARS multidimensional functional assessment questionnaire. *J. Gerontol., 36,* 428–434.

Fleiss J., Gurland, B., and Des Roche, P. (1976). Distinctions between organic brain syndrome and functional psychiatric disorders based on the Geriatric Mental State interview. *Int. J. Aging Human Dev. 7*, 323–330.

Folstein, M. F., Folstein S. E., and McHugh, P. R. (1975). "Mini-Mental State": A practical method for grading the cognitive state of outpatients for the clinician. *J. Psychiat. Res., 12*, 189–198.

Folstein, M. F., and McHugh, P. R. (1978). Dementia syndrome of depression. In R. Katzman, R. D. Terry, and K. L. Bick, eds., *Alzheimer's Disease: Senile Dementia and Related Disorders*, New York: Raven, pp. 87–93.

Fox, J. H., Kaszniak, A. W., and Huckman, M. (1979). Computerized tomographic scanning not very helpful in dementia. *New Eng. J. Med., 300*, 437.

Fox, J. H., Topel, J. L., and Huckman, M. S. (1975a). Dementia in the elderly—a search for treatable illness. *J. Gerontol., 30*, 557–564.

Fox, J. H., Topel, J. L., and Huckman, M. S. (1975b). The use of computerized tomography in the diagnosis of senile dementia. *J. Neurol. Neurosurg. Psychiat., 38*, 948–953.

Fozard, J. (in press). Normal and pathological age differences in memory. In: J. H. Brocklehurst, ed., *Textbook of Geriatric Medicine and Gerontology*, 3rd ed., London: Churchill-Livingstone.

Freeman, F. R. (1976). Evaluation of patients with progressive intellectual deterioration. *Arch. Neurol., 33*, 658–659.

Friedland, R. P. Budinger, T. F., Ganz, E., Yano, Y., Mathis, C. A., Koss, B., Ober, B. A., Huesman, R. H., and Derenzo, S. E. (1983). Regional cerebral metabolic alterations in dementia of Alzheimer type: positron emission tomography with [^{18}F] Flurodeoxyglucose. *J. Comp. Assisted Tomogr., 7*, 590–598.

Friedland, R. P., Koss, B., Thompkins-Ober, B. A., Budinger, T. F., Ganz, E., and Yano, Y. (1983, February). Neuropsychological correlates of regional cerebral metabolic alterations in Alzheimer-type dementia. Presented at the Annual Meeting of the International Neuropsychological Society, Mexico City, Mexico.

Fuld, P. A. (1978). Psychological testing in the differential diagnosis of the dementias. In: R. Katzman, R. D. Terry, and K. L. Bick, eds., *Alzheimer's Disease: Senile Dementia and Related Disorders*, New York: Raven, pp. 185–193.

Fuld, P. A. (1980). Guaranteed stimulus-processing in the evaluation of memory and learning. *Cortex, 16*, 255–271.

Fuld, P. A. (1981). *The Fuld Object Memory Evaluation*. Stoelting Instrument Co., 1350 S. Kostner Avenue, Chicago, Illinois.

Fuld, P. (1982a, November). Mental status examination of 80 year olds—what is normal? Presented at the Annual Scientific Meeting of the Gerontological Society of America, Boston, Massachusetts.

Fuld, P. A. (1982b). Behavioral signs of cholinergic deficiency in Alzheimer dementia. In: S. Corkin, K. L. Davis, J. H. Growdon, E. Usdin, and R. L. Wurtman, eds., *Alzheimer's Disease: A Report of Progress Aging*, vol. 19 New York: Raven, pp. 193–196.

Fuld, P. A., Katzman, R. Davies, P., and Terry R. D. (1982). Intrusions as a sign of Alzheimer dementia. Chemical and pathological verification. *Ann. Neurol., 11*, 155–159.

Garcia C. A., Reding, M. J., and Blass, J. P. (1981). Overdiagnosis of dementia. *J. Am. Geriatrics Soc., 29*, 407–410.

Gardner, R., Oliver-Munoz, S., Fisher, L., and Empting, L. (1981). Mattis Dementia Rating Scale: Internal reliability study using a diffusely impaired population. *J. Clin. Neuropsychol., 3*, 271–275.

Gilbert, J. G., and Levee, R. F. (1971). Patterns of declining memory. *J. Gerontol., 26*, 70–75.

Gilleard, C. J. (1980). Wechsler memory scale performance of elderly psychiatric patients. *J. Clin. Psychol., 36*, 958–960.

Glanzer, M., and Cunitz, A. R. (1966). Two storage mechanisms in free recall. *J. Verbal Learning Verbal Behav., 5*, 351–360.

Go, R. C. P., Todorov, A. B., Elston, R. C., and Constantinidis, J. (1978). The milignancy of dementias. *Ann. Neurol., 3*, 559–561.

Goodin, D. S., Squires, K. C., Henderson, B. H., and Starr, A. (1978). Age related variations in evoked potentials to auditory stimuli in normal human subjects. *Electroencephalogr. Clin. Neurophysiol., 44,* 447–458.

Goodglass, H., and Kaplan, E. (1972). *The Assessment of Aphasia and Related Disorders.* Philadelphia: Lea and Febiger.

Gordon, B. (1984, February). Perceptual repetition memory spared by medial temporal lesions but not by Alzheimer's disease. Presented at the Annual Metting of the International Neuropsychological Society, Houston, Texas.

Grufferman, S. (1978). Alzheimer's disease and senile dementia: One disease or two? In: R. Katzman, R. D. Terry, and K. L. Bick, eds., *Aging,* vol. 7, *Alzheimer's Disease: Senile Dementia and Related Disorders,* New York: Raven, pp. 35–41.

Gurland, B. J., Copeland, J., Sharpe, L., and Kelleher, M. (1976). The Geriatric Mental Status Interview (GMS). *Int. J. Aging Human Dev., 7,* 303–311.

Gurland, B. J., Fleiss, J. L., Goldberg, K., Sharpe, L., Copeland, J. R. M., Kelleher, M. J., and Kellet, J. M. (1976). A semi-structured clinical interview for the assessment of diagnosis and mental state in the elderly: The Geriatric Mental State Schedule II, A factor analysis. *Psychol. Med., 6,* 451–459.

Gurland, B., Golden, K., and Challop, J. (1982). Unidimensional and multidimensional approaches to the differentiation of depression and dementia in the elderly. In: S. Corkin, K. L. Davis, J. H. Growdon, E. Usdin, and R. L. Wurtman, eds., *Aging,* vol. 19, *Alzheimer's Disease: A Report of Progress* New York: Raven, pp. 119–125.

Gurland, B., Kuriansky, T., Sharpe, L., Simon, R., Stiller, P., and Birkett, P. (1977–78). The Comprehensive Assessment and Referral Evaluation (CARE): Rationale, development and reliability. *Int. J. Aging Human Dev., 8,* 9–42.

Gurland, B, and Toner, J. (1983). Differentiating dementia from nondementing conditions. In: R. Mayeux and W. G. Rosen, eds., *The Dementias,* New York: Raven, pp. 1–17.

Gustafson, L., Hagberg, B., and Ingvar, D. H. (1978). Speech disturbances in presenile dementia related to local cerebral blood flow abnormalities in the dominant hemisphere. *Brain and Lang., 5,* 103–118.

Gustafson, L., Risberg, J., and Silverskjold, P. (1981). Cerebral blood flow in dementia and depression (letter). *Lancet, 1(8214),* 275.

Haaland, K. Y., Linn, R. T., Hunt, W. C., and Goodwin, J. S. (1983). A normative study of Russell's variant of the Wechsler Memory Scale in a healthy elderly population. *J. Consult. Clin. Psychol., 51,* 878–881.

Hachinski, V. C., Lassen, N. A., and Marshall, J. (1974). Multi-infarct dementia, a cause of mental deterioration in the elderly. *Lancet, 2,* 207–210.

Hagberg, B. (1978). Defects of immediate memory related to the cerebral blood flow distribution. *Brain and Lang., 5,* 366–377.

Hagberg, B., and Ingvar, D. H. (1976). Cognitive reduction in presenile dementia related to regional abnormalities of the cerebral blood flow. *Br. J. Psychiat., 128,* 209–222.

Haglund, R. M. J., and Schuckit, M. A. (1976). A clinical comparison of tests of organicity in elderly patients. *J. Gerontol., 31,* 654–659.

Hansch, E. C., Syndulko, K. Pirozzolo, F. J., Cohen, S. N., Tourtellotte, W. W., and Potvin, A. R. (1980). Electrophysiological measurement in aging and dementia. In: F.J. Pirozzolo and G. J. Maletta, eds., *Advances in Neurogerontology,* vol. 1, *The Aging Nervous System* New York: Praeger, pp. 187–210.

Harris, R. (1982). Genetics of Alzheimer's disease. *Br. Med. J., 284,* 1065–1066.

Hartley, J. T., Harker, J. O., and Walsh, D. A. (1980). Contemporary issues and new directions in adult development of learning and memory. In: L. W. Poon, ed., *Aging in the 1980s: Psychological Issues,* Washington, D.C.: American Psychological Association, pp. 239–252.

Hasher, L., and Zacks, R. T. (1979). Automatic and effortful processes in memory. *J. Exp. Psychol.: General,* 108, 356–388.

Hendrickson, E., Levy, R., and Post, F. (1979). Averaged evoked responses in relation to cognitive and affective state of elderly psychiatric patienst. *Br. J. Psychiat., 134,* 494–501.

Hersch, E. L. (1979). Development and application of the extended scale for dementia. *J. Am. Geriatric Soc., 27,* 348–354.

Hersch, E. L., Kral, V. A., and Palmer, R. B. (1978). Clinical value of the London Psychogeriatric Rating Scale. *J. Am. Geriatrics Soc., 26,* 348–354.

Hersch, E. L., Merskey, H., and Palmer, R. B. (1980). Prediction of discharge from a psychogeriatric unit: development and evaluation of the LPRS prognosis index. *Canad. J. Psychiat., 25,* 234–241.

Heston, L. L., Mastri, A. R., Anderson, V. E., and White, J. (1981). Dementia of the Alzheimer type. Clinical genetics, natural history and associated conditions. *Arch. General Psychiat., 38,* 1085–1090.

Hirst, W. (1982). The amnesic syndrome: descriptions and explanations. *Psychol. Bull., 91,* 435–460.

Hounsfield, G. N. (1973). Computerized transverse axial scanning (tomography): Part I. Description of a system. *Br. J. Radiol., 46,* 1016–1022.

Hughes, J. R., and Cayaffa, J. J. (1977). The EEG in patients at different ages without organic cerebral disease. *Electroencephalogr. Clin. Neurophysiol., 42,* 776–784.

Hutton, J. T. (1980). Clincal nosology of the dementing illnesses. In: F. J. Pirozzolo and G. J. Maletta, eds., *Advances in Neurogerontology,* vol. 1, *The Aging Nervous System* New York: Praeger, pp. 149–174.

Inglis, J. (1959). A paired associate learning test for use with elderly psychiatric patients. *J. Mental Sci., 105,* 440–448.

Inglis, J., and Caird, W. K. (1963). Modified-digit spans and memory disorder. *Dis. Nervous System, 24,* 46–50.

Ishii, T. (1966). Distribution of Alzheimer's neurofibrillary changes in the brain stem and hypothalamus of senile dementia. *Acta Neuropathol., 6,* 181–187.

Jacobson, P. L., and Farmer, T. W. (1979). The "hypernormal" CT scan in dementia: bilateral isodense subdural hematomas. *Neurology, 29,* 1522–1524.

Jacoby, R. J., Levy, R., and Dawson, J.M. (1980). Computed tomography in the elderly: 1. The normal population. *Br. J. Psychiat., 136,* 244–255.

James, A. E., Partain, C. L., Holland, G. N., Gore, D., Rollo, F., Harms, A., and Price, D. (1982). Nuclear magnetic resonance imaging: the current state. *Am. J. Neuroradiol., 138,* 201–210.

Jenkyn, L. R., Walsh, D. B., Culver, C. M. and Reeves, A. G. (1977). Clinical signs in diffuse cerebral dysfunction. *J. Neurol., Neurosurg., Psychiat., 40,* 956–966.

Johannesson, G., Hagberg, B., Gustafson, L., and Ingvar, D. H. (1979). EEG and cognitive impairment in presenile dementia. *Acta Neurol. Scand., 59,* 225–240.

Kahn R., Goldfarb, A., Pollack, M., Peck, A. (1960). Brief objective measures for the determination of mental status in the aged. *Am. J. Psychiat., 117,* 326–328.

Kaplan, E., Goodglass, H., and Weintraub, S. (1978). *The Boston Naming Test.* Boston: E. Kaplan and H. Goodglass.

Kaszniak, A. W., and Allender, J. A. (1985). Psychological assessment of depression in older adults. In: G. M. Chaisson-Stewart, ed., *Depression in the Elderly: An Interdisciplinary Approach,* New York: Wiley, pp. 107–106.

Kaszniak, A. W., Fox, J., Gandell, D. L., Garron, D. C., Huckman, M. S. and Ramsey, R. G. (1978). Predictors of mortality in presenile and senile dementia. *Ann. Neurol., 3,* 246–252.

Kaszniak, A. W., Garron, D. C., and Fox, J. H. (1979). Differential effects of age and cerebral atrophy upon span of immediate recall and paired-associate learning in older patients suspected of dementia. *Cortex, 15,* 285–295.

Kaszniak, A. W., Garron, D. C., Fox, J. H., Bergen, D., and Huckman, M. (1979). Cerebral atrophy, EEG slowing, age, education, and cognitive functioning in suspected dementia. *Neurology, 29,* 1273–1279.

Kaszniak, A. W., Poon, L. W., and Riege, W. (in press). Information processing assessment of memory deficit. In: L. W. Poon et al., eds., *Handbook of Clincal Memory Assessment of the Older Adult*. Washington, D.C.: American Psychological Association.

Kaszniak, A. W., Sadeh, M., and Stern, L. Z. (in press). Differentiating depression from Organic Brain Syndromes in older age. In: G. M. Chaisson-Stewart, ed., *Depression in the Elderly: An Interdisciplinary Approach*, New York: Wiley, pp. 161–189.

Kaszniak, A. W., Wilson, R. S., and Fox, J. H. (1981). Effects of imagery and meaningfulness on free recall and recognition memory in presenile and senile dementia. *Int. J. Neurosci., 12*, 264.

Kaszniak, A. W., Wilson, R. S., Lazarus, L., Lessor, J., and Fox, J. H. (1981, February). Memory and depression in dementia. Presented at the Ninth Annual Meeting of the International Neuropsychological Society, Atlanta, Georgia.

Katzman, R. (1976). The prevalence and malignancy of Alzheimer disease. *Arch. Neurol., 33*, 217–218.

Katzman, R. (1981). Early detection of senile dementia. *Hospital Practice, 16*, 61–76.

Kendrick, D. C., and Post, F. (1967). Differences in cognitive status between healthy, psychiatrically ill, and diffusely brain-damaged elderly subjects. *Br. J. Psychiat., 113*, 75–81.

Kiloh, L. G. (1961). Pseudo-dementia. *Acta Psychiatr. Scand., 37*, 336–351.

Kinsbourne, M., and George, J. (1974). The mechanism of the word-frequency effect on recognition memory. *J. Verbal Learning and Verbal Behav., 13*, 63–69.

Kirshner, H. S., Webb, W. G., and Kelly, M. P. (1984). The naming disorder of dementia. *Neuropsychologia, 22*, 23–30.

Klisz, D. (1978). Neuropsychological evaluation in older persons. In: M. Storandt, I. Siegler, and M. Elias, eds., *The Clinical Psychology of Aging*, New York: Plenum, pp. 71–96.

Knight, R. G., and Wooles, I. M. (1980). Experimental investigation of chronic organic amnesia: a review. *Psychol. Bull., 88*, 753–771.

Koller, W. C., Glatt, S. L., Fox, J. H., Kaszniak, A. W., Wilson, R.. and Huckman, M. S. (1981). Cerebellar atrophy: Relationship to aging and cerebral atrophy. *Neurology, 31*, 1486–1488.

Koss, B., Friedland, R. P., and Ober, B. A. (1984, February). Lateral asymmetry in cerebral metabolism: a prominent feature of Alzheimer-type dementia. Presented at the Annual Meeting of the International Neuropsychological Society, Houston, Texas.

Kral, V. A. (1962). Senescent forgetfulness, benign and malignant. *Canad. Med. Assoc. J., 86*, 257–260.

Ladurner, G., Iliff, L. D.,, and Lechner, H. (1982). Clinical factors associated with dementia in ischaemic stroke. *J. Neurol., Neurosurg. Psychiat., 45*, 97–101.

Larner, S. (1977). Encoding in senile dementia and elderly depressives: a preliminary study. *Br. J. Soc. Clin. Psychol., 16*, 379–390.

Larsson, T., Sjogren, T., and Jacobson, G. (1963). Senile dementia. A clinical, sociomedical and genetic study. *Acta Psychiatr. Scand., 39*, (Suppl. 167), 1–259.

Lawson, J. S., Rodenburg, M., and Dykes, J. A. (1977). A dementia rating scale for use with psychogeriatric patients. *J. Gerontol., 32*, 153–159.

Lawton, M. P. (1980). Psychosocial and environmental approaches to the care of senile dementia patients. In: J. O. Cole and J. E. Barrett, eds., *Psychopathology in the Aged*, New York: Raven, pp. 265–280.

Lawton, M. P., and Brody, E. M. (1969). Assessment of older people. Self-maintaining and instrumental activities of daily living. *Gerontologist, 9*, 179–186.

Lawton, M. P. Moss, M., Fulcomer, M., and Kleban, M. H. (1982). A research and service oriented multilevel assessment instrument. *J. Gerontol., 37*, 91–99.

Levin, H. S., and Peters, B. H. (1982). Appendix: Report of the ad hoc committee for the classification of the severity of Alzheimer's disease. In: S. Corkin, K. L. Davis, J. H. Growdon, E. Usdin, and R. L. Wurtman, eds., *Aging*, vol. 19, *Alzheimer's Disease: A Report of Progress* New York: Raven, pp. 501–506.

Lewis, R., and Kupke, T. (1977). The Lafayette Clinic repeatable neuropsychological test battery: its development and research applications. Presented at the annual meeting of the Southeastern Psychological Association, Hollywood, Florida.

Logue, P., and Wyrick, L. (1979). Initial validation of Russell's revised Wechsler Memory Scale: A comparison of normal aging versus dementia. *J. Consult. Clin. Psychol., 47,* 176–178.

Loring, D. W., and Largen, J. W. (1984, February). Presenile versus senile dementia of the Alzheimer type: a neuropsychological perspective. Presented at the Annual Meeting of the International Neuropsychological Society, Houston, Texas.

Maletta, G. J., Pirozzolo, F. J., Thompson, G., and Mortimer, J. A. (1982). Organic mental disorders in a geriatric outpatient population. *Amer. J. Psychiat., 139,* 521–523.

Marcer, D. (1979). Measuring memory change in Alzheimer's disease. In: A. I. M. Glen and L. J. Whalley, eds., *Alzheimer's Disease: Early Recognition of Potentially Reversible Deficits,* London: Churchill Livingstone, pp. 117–121.

Martin, A., and Fedio, P. (1983). Word production and comprehension in Alzheimer's disease: the breakdown of semantic knowledge. *Brain and Language, 19,* 124–141.

Matsuyama, H., and Nakamura, S. (1968). Senile changes in the brain in the Japanese: incidence of Alzheimer's neurofibrillary change and senile plaques. In: R. Katzman, R. D. Terry, and K. L. Bick, eds., *Alzheimer's Disease: Senile Dementia and Related Disorders,* New York: Raven, pp. 287–297.

Mattis, S. (1976). Mental Status examination for organic mental syndrome in the elderly patient. In: R. Bellack and B. Karasu, eds., *Geriatric Psychiatry* New York: Grune & Stratton, pp. 77–121.

Mayes, A., and Meudell, P. (1981). How similar is the effect of cueing in amnesics and in normal subjects following forgetting? *Cortex, 17,* 113–124.

Mayeux, R. (1982). Depression and dementia in Parkinson's disease. In: C. C. Marsden and S. Fahn, eds., *Movement Disorders,* London: Butterworth Scientific, pp. 75–95.

Mazziotta, J. C., Phelps, M. E., Carson, R. E., and Kuhl, D. E. (1982). Tomographic mapping of human cerebral metabolism: auditory stimulation. *Neurology, 32,* 921–937.

McAllister, T. W. (1981). Cognitive functioning in the affective disorders. *Comp. Psychiat., 22,* 572–586.

McAllister, T. W. (1983). Overview: pseudodementia. *Am. J. Psychiat., 140,* 528–533.

McAllister, T. W., Ferrell, R. B., Price, T. R., and Neville, M. B. (1982). The dexamethasone suppression test in two patients with severe depressive pseudodementia. *Am. J. Psychiat., 139,* 479–481.

McAllister, T. W., and Price, T. R. P. (1982). Severe depressive pseudodementia with and without dementia. *Am. J. Psychiat., 139,* 626–629.

McCarthy, M., Ferris, S. H., Clark, E., and Crook, T. (1981). Acquisition and retention of categorized material in normal aging and senile dementia. *Exp. Aging Res., 7,* 127–135.

McCarty, S. M., Logue, P. E., Power, D. G., Ziesat, H. A., and Rosenstiel, A. K. (1980). Alternate-form reliability and age-related scores for Russell's revised Wechsler Memory Scale. *J. Consult. Clin. Psychol., 48,* 296–298.

McCarty, S. M., Siegler, I. C., and Logue, P. E. (1982). Cross-sectional and longitudinal patterns of three Wechsler Memory Scale subtests. *J. Gerontol., 37,* 169–175.

Meudell, P., and Mayes, A. (1981). A similarity between weak normal memory and amnesia with two and eight choice word recognition: a signal detection analysis. *Cortex, 17,* 19–29.

Meer, B., and Baker, J. A. (1966). The Stockton Geriatric Rating Scale. *J. Gerontol., 21,* 392–403.

Miller, E. (1971). On the nature of the memory disorder in presenile dementia. *Neuropsychologia, 9,* 75–78.

Miller, E. (1972). Efficiency of coding and the short-term memory defect in presenile dementia. *Neuropsychologia, 10,* 133–136.

Miller, E. (1973). Short-and long-term memory in presenile dementia (Alzheimer's Disease). *Psychol. Med.*, *3*, 221–224.

Miller, E. (1975). Impaired recall and the memory disturbance in presenile dementia. *Br. J. Soc. Clin. Psychol.*, *14*, 73–79.

Miller, E. (1977a). *Abnormal Ageing: The Psychology of Senile and Presenile Dementia*. New York: Wiley.

Miller, E. (1977b). Visual information processing in presenile dementia. *Br. J. Soc. Clin. Psychol.*, *16*, 99–100.

Miller, E. (1978). Retrieval from long-term memory in presenile dementia: two tests of an hypothesis. *Br. J. Soc Clin. Psychol.*, *17*, 143–148.

Miller, E. (1981a). The nature of the cognitive deficit in senile dementia. In: N. E. Miller and G. D. Cohen, eds., *Aging*, vol. 15, *Clinical Aspects of Alzheimer's Disease and Senile Dementia*, New York: Raven, pp. 103–120.

Miller, E. (1981b). The differential psychological evaluation. In: N. E. Miller and G. D. Cohen, eds., *Aging*, vol. 15, *Clinical Aspects of Alzheimer's Disease and Senile Dementia*, New York: Raven, pp. 121–138.

Miller, E. and Lewis, P. (1977). Recognition memory in elderly patients with depression and dementia: a signal detection analysis. *J. Abnorm. Psychol.*, *86*, 84–86.

Miller, N. E. (1980). The measurement of mood in senile brain disease: examiner ratings and self-reports. In: J. O. Cole and J. E. Barrett, eds., *Psychopathology in the Aged*, New York: Raven, pp. 97–122.

Miller, W. R. (1975). Psychological deficit in depression. *Psychol. Bull.*, *82*, 238–260.

Milner, B. (1971). Interhemispheric differences in the localization of psychological processes in man. *Br. Med. Bull.*, *27*, 272–277.

Montgomery, K., and Costa, L. (1983, February). Neuropsychological test performance of a normal elderly sample. Presented at the annual meeting of the International Neuropsychological Society, Mexico City, Mexico.

Morley, G. K., Haxby, J. V., and Lundgren, S. L. (1980). Memory, aging, and dementia. In: F. J. Pirozzolo and G. J. Maletta, eds., *Advances in Neurogerontology*, vol. 1, *The Aging Nervous System*, New York: Praeger, pp. 211–240.

Mortimer, J. A., Schuman, L. M., and French, L. R. (1981). Epidemiology of dementing illness. In: J. A. Mortimer and L. M. Schuman, eds., *The Epidemiology of Dementia*, New York: Oxford University Press, pp. 3–23.

Moscovitch, M. (1982). Multiple dissociations of function in amnesia. In L. S. Cermak (ed.), *Human Memory and Amnesia* (pp. 337–370). Hillsdale, N.J.: Lawrence Erlbaum.

Müller, H. F., and Schwartz, G. (1978). Electroencephalograms and autopsy findings in geropsychiatry. *J. Gerontol.*, *33*, 504–513.

Naeser, M. A., Gebhardt, C., and Levine, H. L. (1980). Decreased computerized tomography numbers in patients with presenile dementia. *Arch. Neurol.*, *37*, 401–409.

Nielsen, J., Homma, A., and Diorn-Henriksen, T. (1977). Follow-up 15 years after a gerontopsychiatric prevalence study: Conditions concerning death, cause of death and life expectancy in relation to psychiatric diagnosis. *J. Gerontol.*, *32*, 554–561.

O'Connor, K P., Shaw, J. C., and Ongley, C. O. (1979). The EEG and differential diagnosis in psychogeriatrics. *Br. J. Psychiat.*, *135*, 156–162.

Osborne, D. P., Brown, E. R., and Randt, C. T. (1982). Qualitative changes in memory function: aging and dementia. In: S. Corkin, K. L. David, J. H. Growdon, E. Usdin, and R. L. Wurtman, eds., *Aging*, vol. 19, *Alzheimers Disease: A Report of Progress* New York: Raven, pp. 165–169.

Pavio, A. (1971). *Imagery and Verbal Processes*. New York: Holt, Reinhart and Winston.

Perez, F. I. (1980). Behavioral studies of dementia: methods of investigation and analysis. In: J. O. Cole and J. E. Barrett, eds., *Psychopathology in the Aged*, New York: Raven, pp. 81–95.

Perez, F. I., Gay, J. R. A., Taylor, R. L., and Rivera, V. M. (1975). Patterns of memory performance in the neurologically impaired aged. *Canad. J. Neurol. Sci.*, *2*, 347–355.

Perez, F. I., Rivera, V. M., Meyer, J. S., Gay, J. R. A., Taylor, R. L., and Mathew, N. T. (1975). Analysis of intellectual and cognitive performance in patients with multi-infarct dementia, vertebrobasilar insuddiciency with dementia, and Alzheimer's disease. *J. Neurol., Neurosurg. Psychiat., 38,* 533–540.

Perez, F. I., Stump, D. A., Gay, J. R., and Hart, V. R. (1976). Intellectual performance in multi-infarct dementia and Alzheimer's disease: A replication study. *Cana. J. Neurol. Sci., 3,* 181–187.

Perry, E. K., Perry, R. H., Blessed, G., and Tomlinson, B. E. (1977). Necropsy evidence of central cholinergic deficits in dementia. *Lancet, 1,* 189.

Perry, E. K., Tomlinson, B. E., Blessed, G., Bergman, K., Gibson, P. H., and Perry, R. H. (1978). Correlation of cholinergic abnormalities with senile plaques and mental test scores in senile dementia. *Br. Med. J., 2,* 1457–1459.

Peterson, L. R., and Peterson, M. J. (1959). Short-term retention of individual items. *J. Exp. Psychol., 58,* 193–198.

Pfeffer, R. I. (in press). Degenerative neurologic disease: Alzheimer's disease, senile dementia of the Alzheimer's type, and related disorders. In: D. Holland, ed., *Textbook of Public Health,* New York: Oxford University Press.

Pfeffer, R. I., Kurosaki, T. T., Harrah, C. H., Chance, J. M., Bates, D., Detels, R., Filos, S., and Butzke, C. (1981). A survey diagnostic tool for senile dementia. *Am. J. Epidemiol., 114,* 515–527.

Pfeffer, R. I., Kurosaki, T. T., Harrah, C. H., Chance, J. M., and Filos, S. (1982). Measurement of functional activities in older adults in the community. *J. Gerontol., 37,* 323–329.

Pfefferbaum, A., Ford, J. M., Wenegrat, B., Tinklenberg, J. R., and Koppel, B. S. (1982). Electrophysiological approaches to the study of aging and dementia. In: S. Corkin, K. L. Davis, J. H. Growdon, E. Usdin, and R. L. Wurtman, eds., *Aging,* vol. 19, *Alzheimer's Disease: A Report of Progress* New York: Raven, pp. 83–91.

Pfeiffer, E. (1975). A short portable mental staus questionnaire for the assessment of organic brain deficit in elderly patients. *J. Am. Geriatrics Soc., 23,* 433–441.

Pfeiffer, E. (1976). *Multidimensional functional assessment: the OARS methodology.* Durham, N.C.: Duke University Center for the Study of Aging and Human Development.

Pfeiffer, E. (1977). Psychopathology and social pathology. In: J. E. Birren and K. W. Schaie, eds., *Handbook of the Psychology of Aging,* New York: Van Nostrand-Reinhold, pp. 650–671.

Pirozzolo, F. J., and Lawson-Kerr, K. (1980). Neuropsychological assessment of dementia. In: F. J. Pirozzolo and G. J. Maletta, eds., *Advances in Neurogerontology,* vol. 1, *The Aging Nervous System,* New York: Praeger, pp. 175–186.

Plutchik, R., and Conte, H. (1972). Change in social and physical functioning of geriatric patients over a one-year period. *Gerontologist, 12,* 181–184.

Plutchik, R., Conte, H., Lieberman, M., Bakur, M., Grossman, J., and Lehrman, N. (1970). Reliability and validty of a scale for assessing the function of geriatric patients. *J. Am. Geriatrics Soc., 18,* 491–500.

Poon, L. W. (in press). Differences in human memory with aging: nature, causes and clinical implications. In: J. E. Birren and K. W. Schaie, eds., *Handbook of the Psychology of Aging.* New York: Van Nostrand Reinhold.

Poon, L. W., and Fozard, J. L. (1980). Age and word frequency effects in continuous recognition memory. *J. Gerontol., 35,* 77–86.

Power, D. E., Logue, P. E., McCarty, S. M., Rosenstiel, A. K., and Ziesat, H. A. (1979). Interrater reliability of the Russell revision of the Wechsler Memory Scale: an attempt to clarify some ambiguities in scoring. *J. Clin. Neuropsychol., 1,* 343–345.

Prigatano, G. P. (1978). Wechsler Memory Scale: A selective review of the literature. *J. Clin. Psychol., 34,* 816–832.

Rabins, P. V., Mace, N. L., and Lucas, M. J. (1982). The impact of dementia on the family. *J. Am. Med. Assoc., 248,* 333–335.

Radue, E. W., du Boulay, G. H., Harrison, M. T. G., and Thomas, D. J. (1978). Comparison of angiographic and CT findings between patients with multi-infarct dementia and those with dementia due to primary neuronal degeneration. *Neuroradiology, 16,* 113–115.

Randt, C. T., Brown, E. R., and Osborne, D. P. (1980). A memory test for longitudinal measurement of mild to moderate deficits. *Clin. Neuropsychol., 2,* 184–194.

Raskind, M., Peskind, E., and Rivard, M. F. (1982). Dexamethasone suppression test and cortisol circadian rhythm in primary degenerative dementia. *Am. J. Psychiat., 139,* 1468–1471.

Reifler, B. V., Larson, E. and Hanley, R. (1982). Coexistence of cognitive impairment and depression in geriatric outpatients. *Am. J. Psychiat., 139,* 623–626.

Reisberg, B., Ferris, S. H., and Crook, T. (1982). Signs, symptoms, and course of age-associated cognitive decline. In: S. Corkin, K.L. Davis, J.H. Growdon, E. Usdin, and R. L. Wurtman, eds., *Alzheimer's Disease: A Report of Progress (Aging, Volume 19)* (pp. 177–181). New York: Raven.

Reisberg, B., Ferris, S. H., Schneck, M. K., deLeon, M. J., Crook, T. H., and Gershon, S. (1981). The relationship between psychiatric assessments and cognitive test measures in mild to moderately cognitively impaired elderly. *Psychopharmacol. Bull., 17,* 99–101.

Reitan, R. M. (1979). *Neuropsychology and Aging.* Tucson: Ralph M. Reitan and Associates.

Reitan, R. M., and Davison, L. A., eds. (1974). *Clinical Neuropsychology: Current Status and Applications.* New York: Wiley.

Reynolds, A. F., Villar, H. V., and Kaszniak, A. W. (1981). Jejunoileal bypass: a reversible cause of dementia. *Neurosurgery, 9,* 153–156.

Risberg, J., Gustafson, L., Johanson, M., Brun, A., and Silfverskiold, R. (1983, February). Differential diagnosis of organic dementia by regional cerebral blood flow measurements. Presented at the Annual Meeting of the International Neuropsychological Society, Mexico City, Mexico.

Roberts, M. A., McGeorge, A. P., and Caird, F. I. (1978). Electroencephalography and computerized tomography in vascular and non-vascular dementia in old age. *J. Neurol., Neurosurg. Psychiat., 41,* 903–906.

Robinson, R. A. (1979). Some applications of rating scales in dementia. In: A. I. M. Glen and L. J. Whalley, eds., *Alzheimer's Disease: Early Recognition of Potentially Reversible Deficits,* New York: Churchill-Livingstone, pp. 108–114.

Ron, M. A., Toone, B. K., Garralda, M. E., and Lishman, W. A. (1979). Diagnostic accuracy in presenile dementia. *B. J. Psychiat., 134,* 161–168.

Rosen, W. G. (1983). Clinical and neuropsychological assessment of Alzheimer's disease. In: R. Mayeux and W. G. Rosen, eds., *The Dementias,* New York: Raven, pp. 51–63.

Rosen, W. G., and Mohs, R. C. (1982). Evolution of cognitive decline in dementia. In: S. Corkin, K. L. Davis, J. H. Growdon, E. Usdin, and R. L. Wurtman, eds., (Aging, vol. 19, *Alzheimer's Disease: A Report of Progress* New York: Raven, pp. 183–188.

Rosen, W. G., Terry, R. D., Fuld, P. A., Katzman, R., and Peck, A. (1980). Pathological verification of ischemic score in differentiation of dementias. *Ann. Neurol., 7,* 486–488.

Roth, M. (1980). Senile dementia and its borderlands. In: J. O. Cole and J. E. Barrett, eds., *Psychopathology in the Aged,* New York: Raven, pp. 205–232.

Roth, M., and Hopkins, B. (1953). Psychological test performance in patients over 60: I. Senile psychosis and the affective disorders of old age. *J. Mental Sci., 99,* 439–450.

Russell, E. W. (1975). A multiple scoring method for the assessment of complex memory functions. *J. Consult. Clin. Psychol., 43,* 800–809.

Salzman, C., Shader, R. I., Kochansky, G. E., and Cronin, D. M. (1972). Rating scales for psychotropic drug research with geriatric patients: I. Behavior ratings. *J. Am. Geriatrics Soc., 20,* 209–214.

Schneck, M. K., Reisberg, B., and Ferris, S. H. (1982). An overview of current concepts of Alzheimer's disease. *Am. J. Psychiat., 139,* 165–173.

Seltzer, B., and Sherwin, I. (1983). A comparison of clinical features in early-and late-onset primary degenerative dementia. *Arch. Neurol., 40,* 143–146.

Shepard, R. N. (1967). Recognition memory for words, sentences and pictures. *J. Verbal Learning and Verbal Behav., 6,* 156–163.

Shore, D., Overman, C. A., and Wyatt, R. J. (1983). Improving accuracy in the diagnosis of Alzheimer's disease. *J. Clin. Psychiat., 44,* 207–212.

Sim, M. (1979). Early diagnosis of Alzheimer's disease. In: A. I. M. Glen and L. J. Whalley, eds., *Alzheimer's Disease: Early Recognition of Potentially Reversible Deficits,* New York: Churchill-Livingstone, pp. 78–85.

Sluss, T. K., Gruenberg, E. M., Rabins, P., and Kramer, M. (1982). Distribution of focal signs in a group of demented men. *Neuropsychobiology, 8,* 109–112.

Smith, J. M., Bright, B., and McCloskey, J. (1977). Factor analytic composition of the Geriatric Rating Scale (GRS). *J. Gerontol., 32,* 58–62.

Spar, J. E., and Gerner, R. (1982). Does the dexamethasone suppression test distinguish dementia from depression? *Amer. J. Psychiat., 139,* 238–240.

Sperling, G. (1963). A model for visual memory tasks. *Human Factors, 5,* 19–31.

Squire, L.R. (1982). The neuropsychology of human memory. *Ann. Rev. Neurosci., 5,* 241–273.

Sternberg, S. (1966). High speed scanning in human memory. *Science, 153,* 652–654.

Storandt, M., Botwinick, J., and Danziger, W. L. (in press). Longitudinal changes: mild SDAT and matched healthy controls. In: L. W. Poon et al., eds., *Handbook of Clinical Memory Assessment of the Older Adult.* Washington, D.C.: American Psychological Association.

Sulkava, R. (1982). Alzheimer's disease and senile dementia of the Alzheimer type. A comparative study. *Acta Neurol. Scand., 65,* 636–650.

Sulkava, R., and Amberla, K. (1982). Alzheimer's disease and senile dementia of the Alzheimer type. A neuropsychological study. *Acta Neurol. Scand., 65,* 651–660.

Swets, J. A. (1973). The relative operating characteristic in psychology. *Science, 182,* 990–1000.

Talland, G. A., and Schwab, R. S. (1964). Performance with multiple sets in Parkinson's disease. *Neuropsychologia, 2,* 45–53.

Taylor, H. G., and Bloom, L. M. (1974). Cross-validation and methodological extension of the Stockton Geriatric Rating Scale. *J. Gerontol., 29,* 190–193.

Terman, L. M., and Merrill, M. A. (1973). *Stanford-Binet Intelligence Scale. Manual for the Third Revision, Form L-M.* Boston: Houghton Mifflin.

Terry, R. D., and Davies, P. (1980). Dementia of the Alzheimer type. *Ann. Rev. Neurosci., 3,* 77–95.

Terry, R., and Katzman, R. (1983). Senile dementia of the Alzheimer type: defining a disease. In: R. Katzman and R. Terry, eds., *The Neurology of Aging,* Philadelphia: F. A. Davis, pp. 51–84.

Terry, R. D., Peck, A., DeTeresa, R., Schecter, R., and Horoupian, D. S. (1981). Some morphometric aspects of the brain in senile dementia of the Alzheimer type. *Ann. Neurol., 10,* 184–192.

Tomlinson, B. E. (1977). The pathology of dementia. In: C. E. Wells, ed., *Dementia,* Philadelphia: F. A. Davis, pp. 113–153.

Tomlinson, B. E. (1982) Plaques, tangles and Alzheimer's disease. *Psychol. Med., 12,* 449–459.

Tomlinson, B. E., Blessed, G., and Roth, M. (1968). Observations on the brain in non-demented old people. *J. Neurol. Sci., 7,* 331–356.

Tomlinson, B. E., Blessed, G., and Roth, M. (1970). Observations on the brains of demented old people. *J. Neurol. Sci., 11,* 205–242.

Trier, T. R. (1966). Characteristics of mentally ill aged: a comparison of patients with psychogenic disorders and patients with organic brain syndromes. *J. Gerontol., 21,* 354–364.

Tulving, E. (1972). Episodic and semantic memory. In: E. Tulving and W. Donaldson, eds., *Organization of Memory*, New York: Academic Press, pp. 381–403.

Tulving, E., and Colotla, V. A. (1970). Free recall of trilingual lists. *Cognitive Psychol.*, *1*, 86–98.

Underwood, B. J. (1957). Interference and forgetting. *Psychol. Rev.*, *64*, 49–60.

Vitaliano, P. P., Breen, A. R., Albert, M. S., Russo, J., and Prinz, P. N. (1984). Memory, attention, and functional status in community-residing Alzheimer type dementia patients and optimally healthy aged individuals. *J. Gerontol.*, *39*, 58–64.

Wang, H. S. (1978). Prognosis in dementia and related disorders in the aged. In: R. Katzman, R. D. Terry, and K. L. Bick, eds., *Alzheimer's Disease: Senile Dementia and Related Disorders*, New York: Raven, pp. 309–313.

Warrington, E. K. (1982). The double dissociation of short-and long-term memory deficits. In: L. S. Cermak, ed., *Human Memory and Amnesia*, Hillsdale, N.J.: Lawrence Erlbaum, pp. 61–76.

Watkins, M. J. (1974). Concept and measurement of primary memory. *Psychol. Bull.*, *81*, 695–711.

Waugh, N. C., and Norman, D. A. (1965). Primary memory. *Psychol. Rev.*, *72*, 89–104.

Wechsler, A. F. (1977). Presenile dementia presenting as aphasia. *J. Neurol., Neurosurg., Psychiat.*, *40*, 303–305.

Wechsler, D. (1945). A standardized memory scale for clinical use. *J. Psychol.*, *19*, 87–95.

Wechsler, D. (1958). *The Measurement and Appraisal of Adult Intelligence*, 4th ed. Baltimore: Williams and Wilkins.

Wechsler, D. (1981). *Wechsler Adult Intelligence Scale-Revised Manual*. New York: The Psychological Corporation.

Weingartner, H., Kaye, W., Smallberg, S., Cohen, R., Ebert, M. H., Gillin, J. C., and Gold, P. (1982). Determinants of memory failures in dementia. In: S. Corkin, K. L. Davis, J. H. Crowdon, E. Usdin, and R. L. Wurtman, eds., *Aging*, vol. 19, *Alzheimer's Disease: A Report of Progress*, New York: Raven, pp. 171–176.

Weingartner, H., Kaye, W., Smallberg, S. A., Ebert, M. H., Gillin, J. C., and Sitaram, N. (1981). Memory failures in progressive idiopathic dementia. *J. Abnor. Psychol.*, *90*, 187–196.

Wells, C. E. (1977). Diagnostic evaluation and treatment in dementia. In: C. E. Wells, ed., *Dementia* 2d ed., Philadelphia: F. A. Davis, pp. 247–276.

Wells, C. E. (1979). Pseudodementia. *Am. J. Psychiat.*, *136*, 895–900.

Wells, C. E. (1982). Pseudodementia and the recognition of organicity. In: D. F. Benson and D. Blumer, eds., *Psychiatric Aspects of Neurologic Disease*, vol. II, New York: Grune & Stratton, pp. 167–178.

Wells, C., and Duncan, G. W. (1977). Danger of over-reliance on computerized cranial tomography. *Am. J. Psychiat.*, *34*, 811–813.

Whitehead, A. (1973). The pattern of WAIS performance in elderly psychiatric patients. *Br. J. Soc. Clin. Psychol.*, *12*, 435–436.

Whitehouse, P. J., Price, D. L., Struble, R. G., Clark, A. W., Coyle, J. T., and DeLong, M. R. (1982). Alzheimer's disease and senile dementia loss of neurons in the basal forebrain. *Science*, *215*, 1237–1239.

Willis, S. L., and Baltes, P. B. (1980). Intelligence in adulthood and aging: contemporary issues. In: L. W. Poon, ed., *Aging in the 1980's: Psychological Issues*, Washington, D.C.: American Psychological Association, pp. 266–272.

Wilson, R. S., Bacon, L. D., Fox, J. H., and Kaszniak, A. W. (1983a). Primary memory and secondary memory in dementia of the Alzheimer Type. *J. Clin. Neuropsychol.*, *5*, 337–344.

Wilson, R. S., Bacon, L. D., Kaszniak, A. W., and Fox, J. H. (1982). The episodic-semantic memory distinction and paired associate learning. *J. Consult. Clin. Psychol.*, *50*, 154–155.

Wilson, R. S., Bacon, L. S., Kramer, R. L., Fox, J. H., and Kaszniak, A. W. (1983*b*). Word frequency effect and recognition memory in dementia of the Alzheimer Type. *J. Clin. Neuropsychol., 5*, 97–104.

Wilson, R. S., Fox, J. H., Huckman, M. S., Bacon, L. D., and Lobick, J. J. (1982). Computed tomography in dementia. *Neurology (Ny), 32*, 1054–1057.

Wilson, R. S., and Kaszniak, A. W. (in press). Longitudinal changes: Progressive idiopathic dementia. In: L. W. Poon et al., eds., *Handbook of Clinical Memory Assessment of the Older Adult.* Washington, D.C.: American Psychological Association.

Wilson, R. S., Kaszniak, A. W., Bacon, L. D., Fox, J. H., and Kelly, M. P. (1982). Facial recognition memory in dementia. *Cortex, 18*, 329–336.

Wilson, R. S., Kaszniak, A. W., and Fox, J. H. (1981). Remote memory in senile dementia. *Cortex, 17*, 41–48.

Wilson, R. S., Kaszniak, A. W., Fox, J. H., Garron, D. C., and Ratusnik, D. L. (1981, February). Language deterioration in dementia. *Presented at the Annual Meeting of the International Neuropsychological Society,* Atlanta, Georgia.

Wilson, R. S., Kaszniak, A. W., Klawans, H. L., and Garron, D. C. (1980). High speed memory scanning in Parkinsonism. *Cortex, 16*, 67–72.

Wilson, R., Rosenbaum, G., and Brown, G. (1979). The problem of premorbid intelligence in neuropsychological assessment. *J. Clin. Neuropsychol., 1*, 49–53.

Yamaguchi, F., Meyer, J. S., Yamamoto, M., Sakai, F., and Shaw, T. (1980). Noninvasive regional cerebral blood flow measured in dementia. *Arch. Neurol., 37*, 410–418.

Yamaura, H., Ito, M., Kubata, K., and Matsuzawa, T. (1980). Brain atrophy during aging: a quantitative study with computed tomography. *J. Gerontol., 4*, 492–498.

10

The Neuropsychology of Depression: The Pseudodementia Syndrome

ERIC D. CAINE

Background and Definition

Major depression is thought to be a reversible disorder when treated appropriately. However, epidemiological studies in the United Kingdom (Kay, 1962; Roth, 1955) indicate that the natural history of late onset depression is not benign, with a mortality experience which is intermediate between that of demented patients and individuals without psychopathology. This impression is also supported by the findings of Cole and Hicking (1976), who noted that elderly depressives with "minor organic signs" had less likelihood of being discharged following admission than those without such signs. This group was characterized by older age, later onset, and few discernible precipitating events leading to admission. Among the "minor organic signs," memory impairment was prominent.

Recent work with neuropsychiatric disorders suggests that there are some "final common pathways" for the symptomatic behavioral expression of such disordered CNS function (Caine, 1981a, 1981b; Caine and Shoulson, 1981; Reifler, 1982). These "pathways" include abnormalities of (1) arousal, attention, and concentration; (2) mood and affect; (3) perception (both ideational and physical, internal and external); (4) specific intellectual functions (e.g., memory, language); and (5) personality (e.g., "He's not the same person he used to be.").

The major psychiatric disorders have proven remarkably difficult to distinguish from behavioral disorders resulting from neuropathology despite our attempts to define homogeneous clusters of patients. Notwithstanding advances in biological psychiatry and increased understanding of neuropharmacology, we are still confronted by an apparent lack of specificity with regard to pathogenesis, pathophysiology, and disordered behavior in these disorders. Tertiary syphilis, a disorder with a precisely defined infectious agent, has protean manifestations (Lishman, 1978). Huntington's disease has manifestations throughout a range of psychopathology (Caine and Shoulson, 1983) despite its discrete mode of genetic transmission. Conversely, a wide variety of neuropathological states may lead to expression of a schizophrenic syndrome (Davison and Baggley, 1969).

The clinician evaluating a patient with progressive cognitive impairment must answer several questions. What is the nature of this disorder? What is the course of this disorder? Is this an unremitting dementing process, or a pseudodementia which will be allayed if it is treated adequately? To understand all that these questions imply, wider issues concerning depression and aging must be examined. In addition, one must develop a differential diagnosis that includes both those diseases causing continuous, gradual CNS degeneration and those which are reversible. Though not well discussed in the psychiatric literature, "reversible dementias" have been described which are curable if detected and treated adequately (Benson, 1982; Cummings, Benson, and LoVerme, 1980). "Pseudodementia" has become the designation for those psychiatric dementing disorders which are persistent if left unattended.

In this chapter, the clinical and research evidence for pseudodementia and its neuropsychological manifestations will be presented, and the disorder will be viewed in the context of progressive neuropathological conditions, aging, and depression.

Descriptive Studies of Pseudodementia: Neurological and Psychiatric Perspectives

Criticism of the concept of pseudodementia rightly grows from the inconsistency with which the term is used in publications. Kiloh (1961) suggested that "pseudo-dementia" be a descriptive label for patients in whom "the diagnosis of dementia is entertained but has to be abandoned because of the subsequent course of the illness."

Two elements were inherent in this definition: that the patient looked demented and that the course was nonprogressive. Kiloh raised our 'index of suspicion' about those confusing psychiatric patients for whom clinicians too often withheld treatment, falsely assuming a hopeless diagnosis of "senility" or "hardening of the arteries." He also alerted us to the fact that patients with Ganser syndrome, malingering, hysteria, depression, paraphrenia, bipolar disorder, and other ill-defined psychiatric disorders can look extremely—and convincingly—impaired.

This 1961 description did not exclude the possibility that pseudodementia might be related indirectly to neuropathology. Though one may use reversibility of the mental status impairment following treatment as an empirical criterion for establishing the diagnosis of pseudodementia, these patients may be suffering from neurological disorders. Such conditions as seizures, small infarctions, and nutritional deficiencies may lead to treatable reversible mental status abnormalities, so inferences concerning etiology cannot be uncritically drawn from the response to treatment.

Much of the inconsistency in the pseudodementia literature reflects the different types of physicians presenting clinical data and the sources of their pa-

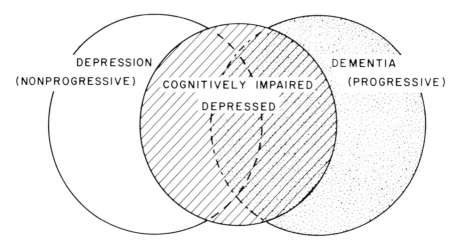

Fig. 1. Relationship of depression and dementia in the elderly.

tient examples. Neurologists typically examine referred patients with an admitting diagnosis of "dementia" or "organic brain syndrome." Many of these patients ultimately receive a primary psychiatric diagnosis. Marsden and Harrison (1972), Freemon (1976), and Smith and associates (1976) reviewed the results of thorough clinical evaluations of patients suffering progressive intellectual deterioration and confirmed this finding. Seltzer and Sherwin (1978) carefully assessed a stable V.A. population in which "organic brain syndrome" has been used as a catch-all label for various forms of intellectual impairment. Of the 346 patients described in these reports, 30 (8.7%) showed no evidence of a primary neuropathological disease. By inference, they had psychiatric disorders. Depression, schizophrenia, bipolar disease, hysteria, inadequate personality, and "no apparent abnormality of the mental state" were their presumptive psychiatric diagnoses. This type of data offers one perspective on "pseudodementia," that of the neurologist, or the consultation psychiatrist who sees patients after the initial neurological evaluation.

Nott and Fleminger (1975) and Ron and coworkers (1979) retrospectively analyzed groups of patients who were initially diagnosed as having idiopathic dementing disorders. Figure 1 places their work in context. Among the initial patients coming for neurological evaulation, and described in the previously noted studies, 47% (110 of a possible 233) were said to have a dementia without a specific etiology, or in the terminology of DSM-III, primary degenerative dementia. Presumably this group has been thoroughly evaluated, showing abnormalities of mental status with no focal neurological deficits, and demonstrating findings on ancillary examinations which are thought to reflect "organic disease." It is these types of individuals that Nott and Fleminger and Ron et al. studied.

Nott and Fleminger (1975) assessed the course of 35 patients who had been initially diagnosed at the Guys' Hospital from 1950–1969. Forty-three percent of the group (15 patients) had suffered the progressive decline which would have been predicted on the basis of their diagnosis. Surprisingly, 18 had maintained a stable condition and two had improved. Three of them were said to be depressed, another three suffered anxiety states, six experienced "somatic symptoms without organic basis," one had an hysterical reaction, and another suffered paranoid ideation associated with respiratory failure. Of the five people who showed no disorder during the followup period, one evidently developed a hemiplegia 20 years after the original diagnosis of presenile dementia.

Nott and Fleminger (1975) also did a retrospective analysis of their patient's admitting mental status and clinical evaluations. They found that memory disturbance was prominent in both those who had progressive disease and those who didn't. Disorientation was not a distinguishing sign, and at most, results from psychometric, EEG, and pneumoencephalographic studies showed modest differences between the groups, with substantial overlap among individuals. It was significant that the authors found that only their demented patients experienced problems with naming, writing, calculation, or motor praxis. This would suggest that this group of patients was the only one to suffer "higher cortical dysfunctions."

Ron et al. (1979) had similar results, although a higher proportion of their patients, 35 of 51 (69%), had progressive disease. Of the 16 misidentified individuals, seven had "functional psychiatric illness only," with five cases of primary affective disturbance, one of paranoid psychosis, and one "schizophrenic defect state." Three individuals suffered depression and "possible organic disorder," with alcoholism, seizures, and atypical facial pain providing the confounding findings. Another six patients clearly had neuropathological disturbances; four of these showed significant behavioral symptoms.

Whether one wants to label the patients with "organic disease" as having pseudodementia becomes a point of argument, as noted previously. These individuals did not decline progressively. Given their failure to demonstrate progressive disease, and their frequent manifestation of major psychopathological symptoms, it would seem most appropriate to consider them under the pseudodementia rubric. Moreover, it is essential to distinguish patients with a favorable prognosis for treatment from those unlikely to improve.

Identifying the Treatable Pseudodementia Patient

An initial approach to defining the limits of "treatable" must be based on clinicians' needs, for whom developing an effective differential diagnosis is vital. When a clinician shifts to research, however, the focus must narrow. Homogeneity becomes the aim, and excluding potential false positive subjects is of paramount importance. Clinical thinking requires an over-inclusive methodology: Ideally, the uncertain clinician will initially consider the depressed, dementing patient as having "pseudodementia" (where there is hope for recovery) and begin antidepressant therapy. He must guard against fatalistically diagnosing the cognitively impaired depressed as irretrievably "demented" and withholding treatment as a result.

In an attempt to identify diagnostic clues, Ron et al. (1979) reexamined their initial clinical assessments to determine what factors might separate the progressive from the nonprogressive patients. Through consolidation of (1) clinical history (with particular attention to previous affective disorders), (2) current mental status assessment, (3) results from neuropsychological testing, (4) penumoencephalographic findings (most of these patients were admitted before the age of computerized tomography), and (5) EEG, they developed a statistical method for distinguishing the two groups. Unfortunately, although these separations were statistically meaningful, close scrutiny of their findings demonstrated a substantial overlap between the two populations, where the practicing physician would have extreme difficulty prognosticating with confidence for a particular individual.

For example, though their nondemented patients showed no statistically significant difference between Wechsler verbal I.Q. and performance I.Q. (while their demented patients had a large discrepancy between the two), the mean verbal and performance I.Q. scores of the nonprogressive patients were at the low end of the normal range, consistent with the findings that some were suffering from CNS diseases. (Further complicating the matter, dementing patients can present a mild, equal decline of verbal and performance I.Q. scores early in the course of the progressive dementia.)

Although many neuropsychologists have indicated that sophisticated cognitive assessments can distinguish patients with "organic impairment" from those suffering primary psychopathology, it is notable that Smith et al. (1976) commented, "Overall, psychometric testing was of very limited value in distinguishing pseudodemented from demented patients." This coincides with the impressions gained from the work of Nott and Fleminger (1975).

However, Wells (1979) noted in describing his series of pseudodementia patients that, "all of these patients [nine in his study who were evaluated neuropsychologically] perform poorly on one or more tests usually used to measure organic dysfunction." He went on to state: "it was their inconsistent performance from test to test that argues most strongly against attributing their clinical dysfunction primarily to organic disease" (as it was in part their inconsistency in clinical performance that led clinicians to question the diagnosis of dementia), but his patients were qualitatively different from those seen by Nott and Fleminger (1975) or Ron et al. (1979).

Wells (1979) described a series of patients who confounded straightforward medical diagnosis, akin in many respects to the series initially described by Kiloh (1961). His population, more of the kind one would see in a referral practice, provided a very different impression of what constituted "pseudodementia." Although a number of his patients had depression or depressed affect, the interplay between personality disturbance and functional impairment was evident. Wells detailed his patients' inconsistent performance, evidenced both in their behavior and their neuropsychological test performances. He stressed that the nature of onset, course, and clinical phenomenology may be sufficient to discriminate the demented from the nondemented.

Folstein, Folstein, and McHugh (1975) acquired patients with pseudodementia in another fashion, screening a population of depressed patients with their Mini-Mental Status Examination (Folstein et al., 1975). They defined cognitive impairment as performance falling below a cutoff score of 24 points out of a possible 30 on the examination. They delineated a group of impaired depressives whose performance overlapped with that of patients diagnosed as having idiopathic dementia. From this they described an intellectual disorder they termed the "dementia syndrome of depression" (McHugh and Folstein, 1979).

Their method has the advantage of using a consistent criterion for inclusion in their patient group, at least in terms of cognitive performance, which reduces the chance of falsely including individuals who are not sufficiently intellectually impaired to be called demented. On the other hand, their approach requires the initial identification of patients having depression. When considering this work, as well as that of previous authors, it is worth noting that no defined diagnostic criteria were utilized for psychiatric diagnoses.

Detailed Case Studies

Attempting to overcome some of these design difficulties, Caine (1981) described a series of cases where pseudodementia was defined prospectively, and DSM-III diagnoses were established for those patients who fulfilled the requisite criteria. The definition included (1) an intellectual impairment in a patient with a primary psychiatric disorder; (2) features of the neuropsychological abnormality resembling, at least in part, the presentation of a neuropathologically induced cognitive deficit; (3) reversible intellectual disorder; and (4) no apparent primary neuropathological process that led to the genesis of the disturbance. The final criterion required lengthy followup in some cases to determine whether a disease process was progressive, and as will become clear, the separation between neuropathological and "functional" disturbances was often difficult to establish.

Eleven patients were evaluated and treated who fit the descriptive criteria for pseudodementia. All were followed for a sufficient period of time to discuss their findings with a high level of confidence, and patients who were not observed long enough to establish their course definitely were excluded. DSM-III diagnoses included the following: major depression (cases 3,6,7,8,9,11); bipolar affective disorder (case 5); schizophrenic disorder (case 4); atypical psychosis (cases 2 and 10); and somatization disorder (case 1). Cases 1 and 10 also showed major depressive features, whereas case 2 demonstrated multiple conversion symptoms. Cases 1 and 7 were thought to have severe, contributing personality disorders.

The diagnoses were distributed in an age-related pattern (Mann-Whitney U Test, $p<.05$). All patients with unipolar depressive disorders were 52 years or older (52,57,65,67, and 77 years) whereas the other, younger cases (15,23,42,49, and 52 years) fell into a more varied diagnostic grouping. Four of the depressed patients (cases 3,6,8,9) had the onset of symptoms after age 50.

The relationship between psychopathology and underlying neuropathology remained in question, despite efforts to establish a clear distinction between neurological and psychiatric syndromes. Indeed, the findings from this series suggested that such a distinction may not be possible in all cases. In six of the patients in the study (cases 1,3,4,5,7,8) there was no evidence of any neuropathological or neurophysiological abnormality. Five had findings indicative of structural brain changes, however, although clinical evaluation, response to pharmacotherapy, and prolonged followup suggested that they did not contribute specifically to the genesis of their psychiatric conditions. In two cases (patients 2 and 10) a progressive neuropathological disorder could not be excluded beyond doubt, but there was no deterioration during the first 2 years following discharge. Patient 2 had small areas of focal, frontal lobe atrophy demonstrated by computed tomography and EEG findings suggestive of an epileptic disorder. She never manifested symptoms consistent with a seizure disorder, and failed to demonstrate any substantial clinical improvement during two separate anticonvulsant trials. In contrast, case 10 had mild, left peri-sylvian atrophy detected by computed tomography, and neuropsychological testing showed subtle but definite signs of language dysfunction. Nonetheless, she remained stable neurologically and neuropsychologically during the 2 years following discharge despite having continued, fluctuating affective symptoms. Case 6 showed a "possible small, focal infarct, adjacent to the right frontal horn," and Case 9, an 85-year-old man, was found to have "generalized sulcal prominences," with ventricles that were normal in size for his age. Should these patients be said to have "underlying neuropathological disturbances"?

All of these patients had complaints or evidence of a memory disorder, although it was mild in some instances (cases 3,7,11). There were a variety of other findings, including multiple Ganser answers (case 1) and repeated responses of a psychotic nature (case 2). Patients would often avoid evaluation with answers such as, "I don't know," or "I can't remember." Prodding or persistence on the part of the examiner would often elicit a more productive response. Another patient complained of "confusion," but showed no clinical evidence of altered mental state during his "episodes." A number of patients (cases 3,5,6,10) would respond to the questions that were relatively easy to answer, but avoided "effortful" tasks which demanded attention and concentration. Although most patients had no evidence of higher cortical dysfunction, case 6 did manifest deficits in praxis and gnosis, and case 4 initially had selectively depressed verbal I.Q. scores on the Wechsler Intelligence Scale for Children—Revised (Wechsler, 1974). His verbal function improved remarkably as his psychosis remitted.

This series demonstrates the difficulty the physician faces establishing clinical diagnoses in the pseudodementia population. Some patients demonstrated "organic" findings on neuropsychological testing which remitted completely following successful therapeutic intervention. In contrast, others who also improved continued to show some residual deficits. It may be impossible to determine where a psychiatric disorder leaves off and a neurological disorder begins. *Indeed, such a distinction may not be necessary, as long as one establishes that the course is nonprogressive.* Therapeutic interventions are based on the presence of responsive target symptoms, and although a diagnosis is important to determine, it may not be essential for initiating effective treatment measures.

Coexistence of Psychiatric and Neurologic Impairments

Recent papers point to the coexistence of depressive pseudodementia and structurally based intellectual impairments in elderly patients (McAllister and Price, 1982; Reifler, Larson, and Hanley, 1982; Snow and Wells, 1981). Reifler et al. (1982) diagnosed depression in 27 of 103 geriatric outpatients who conformed to a DSM-II diagnosis of dementia (American Psychiatric Association, 1968); 20 of the 27 demonstrated intellectual impairment as detected by the Mental Status Questionnaire. In their overall study population, depression occurred with decreasing frequency as the cognitive impairment became more severe: the difference in frequency of depression in the mild, moderate, and severe cognitive impairment groups was statistically significant. Nearly half of the patients who had no demonstrable intellectual impairment showed depression, while 33% of the mildly impaired group, 23% of the moderately impaired group, and only 12% of the severely deficient group received a diagnosis of depression. The study was confounded, perhaps, by combining probable and definite RDC diagnoses, and primary and secondary depression to establish the diagnosed "depression" group. Additionally, 15 of the 103 clinically "demented" outpatients showed no cognitive impairment. Despite the relationship demonstrated between less intellectual dysfunction and more frequent depression, it is difficult to assess whether the cognitive impairment was in any way related to the depression etiologically, as the authors did not report on changes which occurred following treatment.

In contrast, McAllister and Price (1982), and Snow and Wells (1981) described individuals whose mixed depression-dementia picture was seemingly clarified by vigorous therapeutic intervention. The former authors presented two individuals whose condition markedly improved both clinically and cognitively with ECT. Both investigations also described patients whose affective state benefitted from treatment, but who failed to show a rebound in neuropsychological functioning.

These findings reinforce the notion that there may be relatively few "final common pathways" for manifesting behavioral symptoms of central nervous system disease. Certainly, part of the difficulty in defining pseudodementia clinically stems from the common occurrence of significant depressive symptoms in patients with developing progressive dementia (Miller, 1980; Sim and Sussman, 1962). Another major source of this difficulty is the prominent neuropsychological impairment that is now known to occur in patients with depressive disorders. These clinical studies give an indication of the variety of clinical syndromes which may, as part of their symptom picture, manifest pseudodementia. "Depressive pseudodementia" appears to occur more commonly in elderly patients, while the younger intellectually impaired have symptoms of a greater variety of psychiatric disease states.

The problem of depressive pseudodementia in the elderly will be increasing in coming years, as our population ages. Moreover, difficult diagnostic dilemmas are posed by these patients, who by virtue of presentation and age are at risk for progressive neuropathological disease. Unfortunately, we have no sound method for demarcating the boundaries between (1) intellectually intact depressed elderly individuals; (2) others who have significant affective symptoms and substantial cognitive impairment, where the intellectual deficits are reversible following vigorous therapeutic intervention; and (3) those who suffer a progressing neurological disease which manifests itself with both behavioral symptoms (see Fig. 1). Clinically, one can take the optimistic approach of initiating treatment for all, given the judicious use of diagnostic methods and sensitivity to drug side effects. While this pragmatic view prevents potentially devastating errors where one pessimistically assumes that all "dementia" is irreversible, we are left in an unsatisfactory position.

How shall we begin to understand the psychobiological bases of depressive pseudodementia in the elderly? One approach would be to examine the neuropsychological deficits of their younger depressed counterparts, as we have scant information regarding intellectual disturbances arising from geriatic psychiatric syndromes *per se*. In principle, we can develop new hypotheses for focused inquiry by understanding the "psychophysiological meaning" of cognitive impairment in younger depressives. We turn now to a survey of the evidence from studies of younger depressed and elderly depressed patients.

Neuropsychological Studies of Depressed Patients

There are relatively few carefully controlled neuropsychological studies of nongeriatric patients with major depressive disorders, and they have tended to focus on only one or a few aspects of cognitive dysfunction in affected patients. Comprehensive neuropsychological studies that assess a broad array of gnostic, praxic, and mnemonic functions are nonexistent at this time. Moreover, many of the investigations have reflected in some ways the dichotomy which now exists in neuropsychology between qualitative and quantitative traditions. Psychiatrists wanting to do neuropsychological or cognitive studies of large groups of psychiatric patients have often employed instruments developed by the "psychometricians," as these were more readily administered to substantial numbers of patients and controls. Experimental psychologists who evaluate psychiatric patients used more focused tests designed to illuminate a specific psychological process or failing. These procedures were derived from the college campus setting, where undergraduate volunteers were recruited for studies of normal cognitive processing in the learning laboratory.

Thus, most neuropsychological studies of depression have utilized procedures which have given us a view of elements of disordered cognitive processing in depressives, but did not develop inferences regarding the neuroanatomical substrate of these impairments. There have been no studies that have effectively combined the separate neuropsychological traditions. Such studies could conceivably benefit from some amalgam of qualitative and quantitative analytic approaches, yielding results about neuropsychological mechanisms of dysfunction, and pointing, at least tentatively, to their underlying neurobiological bases (see the methodological chapters in part 1 for a sampling of such approaches).

DISORDERED ATTENTION IN DEPRESSION. Many clinicians have noted that depressed patients are inattentive, but there are few investigations documenting this in an objective manner. Byrne (1977) studied 10 patients with neurotic depression (dysthymic disorder), 10 psychotic depressive patients, and 10 normal controls. He demonstrated that there was a significant negative relationship between severity of depression and performance on a signal detection task. Byrne asked subjects to participate in a auditory vigilance task of 30 minutes' duration. The background consisted of random digits spoken at a rate of one per second: Subjects had to identify strings of three odd digits in sequence. Although Byrne found a correlation with diagnosis, he failed to demonstrate a significant relationship between self-rated affective state and vigilance performance.

Malone and Hemsley (1977) studied 10 depressed patients with an auditory signal detection task, and repeated this procedure following remission. No chronically depressed patients were tested, as the authors wished to assess the effects of antidepressants. Subjects were required to detect a tone against a white noise background, a task where the volume of the tone was gradually increased or decreased, and a subject's "threshhold" was recorded as the mean intensity level at which he could detect the stimulus tone. The authors found that depressives demonstrated a lowered motor responsiveness during their symptomatic state. The overall mean reaction time was substantially longer during depression, and patients had a lower degree of sensitivity for signal detection. Sensitivity improved while patients were receiving antidepressant medications, but it was not possible using this paradigm to assess whether the increased responsivity associated with this treatment reflected true sensory differences or differences in attentional functioning.

Frith and colleagues recently reported on the effects of depression and ECT on a variety of intellectual tasks (Frith, Stevens, and Johnstone, 1983). They utilized, for example, a continuous performance task administered over 15 minutes to assess attention. Randomly selected letters from the alphabet appeared every second, and the subject was required to press a button every time the letter "A" appeared. This signal was presented randomly at a rate of three per minute (approximately one per 20 presentations), and the total number of missed signals and false positive responses was recorded. It is unfortunate that the authors did not employ a control group for this task, unlike their design for other test procedures conducted in this careful research. Nonetheless, their findings are of interest. The mean number of errors (misses and false positives) improved following both sham and real ECT. The authors state that their patients "were performing very badly prior to treatment."

MEMORY STUDIES. Investigators have documented clearly that memory and learning functions are impaired in depressed patients, confirming what has been known for several decades. Remembering is the final product of multiple central nervous system functions. Sustained arousal, attention, concentration, and motivation are essential; intact stimulus perception and decoding provide a foundation for memory formation. Three essential psychological processes must be completed in order to learn and later recall new information. They can be subsumed under the following: acquisition—getting new information into memory; retention—maintaining or keeping that information in memory for a prolonged period of time; and retrieval—recalling the information at a specified later time. Failure to remember can be caused by a defect in one or more of these steps. Various terms have been used to describe these fundamental tasks, with a lack of uniformity among authors about their meanings (see Squire, this volume). (Additionally, designations such as short-term memory, long-term memory, encoding, storage, etc., have very different implications for experimental psychologists, clinical neuropsychologists, and medical practitioners.)

Cronholm and Ottosson (1961) demonstrated more than two decades ago that endogenously depressed patients suffered significant memory dysfunction. They gave patients and matched controls three tests, a 30-word-pair task, a 20-figure test, and a 30-item personal data test. The latter consisted of six drawn fictitious persons, and five items of data (e.g., age, profession) were presented for each figure. For all tasks, recall was assessed immediately following presentation ("immediate reproduction") and three hours later ("delayed reproduction"). The difference between these performances was inferred to be a measure of "forgetting." Depressives suffered significantly impaired immediate and delayed performance, but their derived "forgetting" scores were the same as those of controls. (ECT later specifically depressed forgetting scores.) The authors suggested that their depressed subjects had impaired initial learning, but once an item was acquired, it would be retained as efficiently as normal.

Stromgren (1977) took a slightly different tack and utilized the Wechsler

Memory Scale (WMS), a standardized test instrument, to examine the effects of depression and ECT on memory. She did not use a control group, unlike Cronholm and Ottosson (1961), as her study focused on comparing bilateral vs. unilateral ECT and their effects on memory and symptoms outcome. She divided the WMS into three major subfunctions, defined as "mental control," "verbal learning," and "visual reproduction." The "mental control" item included the orientation, mental control, and digit span forwards subtests of the WMS, while "verbal learning" included logical memory, associate learning, and digit span backwards, and "visual reproduction" included the visual reproduction subtest. Stromgren defined "mental control" as "simple, readily accessible material which can be reproduced almost automatically, whereas verbal learning and visual reproduction represent complex tasks for the solution of which more elaboration and structuration (sic) are required." She also employed concepts of "delayed reproduction" and "forgetting" from earlier work by Cronholm and Ottosson (1961), in which delayed reproduction was defined by the amount of previously learned material from the logical memory and visual reproduction subtests which could be reproduced 20 minutes after learning. "Forgetting" was again defined as the difference between immediate reproduction and delayed reproduction. Forgetting and delayed reproduction were combined as a measure of the hypothetical variable "retention."

Stromgren used 100 patient subjects to find that endogenous depression clearly impaired memory functioning as measured by the WMS and the derived scores of retention; recovery was associated with marked improvement. The "mental control" cluster of tests was found to be slightly more sensitive than the other memory tests. The degree of depression was inversely related to immediate and delayed reproduction, and positively correlated with the forgetting measure, both as assessed in the logical memory and visual retention subtests. Interestingly, there were no correlations between age, the severity of depression, and the degree of memory dysfunction. However, since the study used subjects 19–65-years-old, one would be hard-pressed to consider its implications for the geriatric population.

It is clear that depressed patients have substantial difficulty with "mental control," although it was not possible to define from this paper which of the subtests (orientation, mental control, or digit repetition forwards) contributed most to the overall finding. Stromgren viewed this task as a relatively automatic, effortless process. It is notable that one cannot infer from her study whether memory acquisition processes are impaired, as the failure on the "retention" task could have been due to either a deficit in acquisition or retention, or both. Moreover, the "forgetting" and "retention" tasks may also have tapped what we can define as retrieval deficits, or instances when an individual has an item in memory, but cannot produce it at the time requested. Less demanding retrieval circumstances (such as a recognition test) can show the presence of an item in memory even when it is not reproduced spontaneously. Thus, it seems certain from Stromgren's investigation that depressed patients are indeed impaired, but little specific information is presented about either the neuropsychological or neurobiological mechanisms underlying it.

Breslow, Kocsis, and Belkin (1980) repeated Stromgren's (1977) study, examining 21 hospitalized depressed patients, and an equal number of matched controls. Patients were diagnosed using the Research Diagnostic Criteria (Spitzer, Edicott, and Robins, 1978) and required a minimum score of 20 on the Hamilton Depression Scale to be included in the study. Unfortunately, five patients were already undergoing antidepressant pharmacotherapy while tested. The findings from this study were strikingly similar to those of Stromgren, and the authors presented their data in such a fashion to allow further assessment of the Wechsler Memory Scale subtests which were most impaired. No deficits ware discerned on the orientation (part of "mental control") and paired associate learning (part of "verbal learning") subtests. The latter subtest is most interesting, as it is one of the "purer" memory tasks included on the Wechsler Memory Scale. Indeed, the WMS examines far more than one would define as memory, and the sparing of associate learning raises questions about the true nature of the depressive's "memory" impairment. (Cronholm and Ottosson's paired associate test involved three sets of 10 pairs each, given one after the other. Theirs was significantly more taxing than the WMS subtest, perhaps accounting for the discrepancy of results.) Patients' performances on digit span forwards, digit span backwards, mental control, and logical memory subtests were all deficient when compared with controls'. These findings reinforced those of Stromgren, especially since a control group was included to ensure confidence in the significance of these findings.

A number of investigations provide the opportunity to further disentangle the mechanisms behind learning-memory deficits in depressed patients. Frith et al. (1983) undertook a number of well-designed cognitive procedures in an effort to disentangle the effects of depression and ECT on memory. The results of their vigilance tests were noted previously. They found, as well, that patients showed no preference for pleasant or unpleasant words while undertaking memory/learning procedures. Recall deficits were noted, but they were mild. More strikingly, their patients demonstrated a significantly increased number of errors (misses plus false positives) compared to controls when undertaking a recognition task where old words were mixed with new distractor items. The authors also found that depressed individuals had difficulty learning to tag verbal labels (name, town of residence, and occupation) to new faces, a finding akin to Cronholm and Ottosson's (1961). Additionally, Frith et al. are one of the few sets of investigators to have examined remote memories: they presented patients with a large number of names, some of well-known personalities and others fictitious. Most of the famous personalities had been well known in the past, but were no longer prominent (an additional control study had shown that normal subjects in their 20s did not typically recognize the famous names). The 70 depressed patients in this study (mean age, 49.4 years; range, 30–69 years) performed significantly worse than controls on this task. This difference disappeared 6 months after treatment had been completed.

Few studies have examined recall of previously learned information. Frith et al. demonstrated that depressed patients have problems remembering names they once knew, which is evidently a reflection of their depressed state at the time of initial testing. This conclusion is justified by the improved performance 6 months later, when the clinical effects of depression had remitted. These data suggested that depressed patients have difficulty learning new information, as demonstrated by the naturalistic face labelling task. This impairment is not absolute, as demonstrated by the word list learning test where deficits were not substantial. Though earlier investigators inferred from "forgetting" scores that retention is intact in depression, their results indicate that it too is not spared. These findings suggest that patients may have deficits in all of the stages of learning/remembering, including acquisition, retention, and retrieval (cf. results on Korsakoff's patients, Brandt and Butters, Chapter 19).

The findings of Sternberg and Jarvik (1976) appear to conflict with those of Frith et al. (1983), but problems with design vitiate their conclusions. Sternberg and Jarvik examined 26 endogenously depressed patients and 26 control subjects matched for age, education, and sex. They used the same memory tests as Cronholm and Ottosson (1961), looking at paired associate learning, figure recall, and memory for personal data. These authors presented tests in a different order, though they too undertook delayed recall tasks to infer whether deficits were detected primarily after initial learning (which Sternberg and Jarvik called "short-term memory") or following retention of 3 hours (which they called "long-term memory"). They found that patients suffered particular decrements on a "registration" score they developed (derived from the difference between delayed recall of a previously rehearsed task and delayed recall of a task where rehearsal was prevented), but not on a measure of "retention" which was calculated using the same method as Cronholm and Ottosson's "forgetting" score.

Unfortunately, the design of this study was one which allowed for interference effects which could not be adequately explained by the data analysis. That is, Sternberg and Jarvik (1976) intermingled the administration of two word lists in a manner that learning the second could interfere with recalling the first. Additionally, trying to remember the first could impair attempts to learn the second. Furthermore, the authors inferred that "registration" could be ascertained by examining the difference between two equivalent delayed recall tasks, one where rehearsal was allowed and the other where practice was prevented. Given a significant delay period, conclusions regarding initial acquisition processes are potentially unreliable. Thus, the most interesting finding of these authors, that the retention processes of depressed patients are intact, must be considered cautiously.

Perhaps the most comprehensive series of experimental psychological studies of depressed patients has come from Weingartner and colleagues. Henry et al. (1973) demonstrated that 25 depressed patients showed decreased performance on a serial learning task, when subjects were required to learn words in the exact order of list presentation. Patients also experienced impaired free recall when serial order was not constrained. Notably, depressed subjects' word association patterns were no different from normals, when using standardized word association lists.

Weingartner et al. (1981) examined further how patients process and remember words. They asked one group of depressed subjects to remember words that were processed for either their sound or their meaning. Patients were far less effective than controls in remembering semantically processed words, whereas there was no difference when freely remembering acoustically processed information. Normals showed the expected advantage in remembering semantically processed vs. acoustically processed words, while the recall for the two types of words was equivalent in the depressed patients. Both groups showed robust increases in recall when retrieval cues were given.

A second group of patients was required to sort unrelated words into categories and then asked to recall them. The normal controls formed the equivalent of six equal-sized categories from the 32 stimulus items that were originally presented, while the depressed patients formed the equivalent of four equal-sized categories. The depressed patients were deficient in recalling the random words after sorting. In contrast, there was no difference between patients and controls when sorting related words that came from well-defined categories, and both groups recalled these words equally. This finding suggested that the memory deficit for random words reflected ineffective initial processing.

Weingartner and associates evaluated this lead in a third test, in which depressed patients and matched controls were given a series of 32-item word lists, and the number of categories varied from none (random words) to 8 categories (4 words each) per list. The categorical words were presented together in one type of test condition, while in others they were presented in less clustered fashions. Overall, depressed patients recalled slightly fewer words, and although this effect was statistically significant, it was the least pronounced finding. More importantly, there was an interaction between presentation format (clustered vs. unclustered), list organization, and groups. Depressed patients did not differ from controls in their recall after presentation of highly organized lists with overt clustering. When there were fewer categories and the ordering was random, patients' word recall was diminished. The largest differences were seen when random words were utilized.

This group of researchers continued its investigations by looking at the effects of effort and of the emotional properties of words on memory functioning. Cohen et al. (1982) found a strong positive correlation between performing a motor task (dynamometer squeezing) and recalling nonsense consonant trigrams, the latter an often used procedure to assess initial memory processing and decay. Cohen et al. used a format where recall was assessed at 0, 3, 6, 9 or 18 seconds. They found that there was a significant negative correlation between mood state and motor performance, and mood and trigram memory.

Silberman and coinvestigators (1983) looked at the learning and remembering of words that varied in their degree of emotionality or associated imagery. They found that their depressive subjects showed impaired spontaneous retrieval of high imagery and high emotion words as compared to controls, and impaired recognition of low imagery and low emotion words. There was no interaction between depression and the degree of emotionality of stimulus items, a finding which matches results of Frith et al. Thus, depressed patients appear not to use verbal stimulus properties which usually enhance initial acquisition and later recall.

OTHER NEUROPSYCHOLOGICAL STUDIES. Raskin, Friedman, and DiMascio (1982) examined 277 depressed patients and 112 normal controls matched for age, sex, and education in a multicenter research project. Diagnoses were made using DSM-II criteria. The investigators found that the depressed subjects performed poorly on a number of motor performance tasks, including tapping, aiming, and circle tracing. They were also impaired on nonsense syllable learning, the Stroop Color Word Interference Test (Stroop, 1935), and the Clock Reversal Test. These investigators demonstrated a substantial negative effect of depression on skills requiring sustained effort, concentration, perceptual flexibility, abstract thinking, and performance accuracy. They also found an age effect, though their data was analyzed by comparing patients under 40 with those over 40. It is not possible to discern whether or not there were deficits specific to their geriatric population that were not found among middle-aged patients.

Caine (1981) did a preliminary examination of the neuropsychological functioning of 17 patients with major depressive disorder (6 men, 11 women; mean age, 46.1 years; range, 24–79 years). Qualitative assessment included level of consciousness, attention, and orientation. The following were assessed quantitatively: repetition; reading comprehension; confrontation naming; picture identification (nonverbal output); spontaneous word generation; Presidents (information); verbal learning (immediate and delayed recall, and recognition); visual recall (immediate and delayed recall); copying; clock drawing; verbal description, mathematics; finger tapping); proverb interpretation; trail-making (Armitage, 1946) and motor praxis. There was a robust negative correlation between age and performance on the neuropsychological test procedures. Specific intellectual functions such as repetition, reading, naming, mathematics, and motor praxis were spared. Most impaired were tasks dependent on attention, mental processing speed, spontaneous elaboration, and analysis of detail. This was most prominently seen in the first verbal learning trial, written description (where there was a paucity of output), proverb interpretation (with concrete interpretations), and trail testing, where there were problems with scanning speed, set changing, and occasionally, maintenence of the number or letter sequence. Taken together, these findings were consistent with the interpretation that cortically mediated intellectual functions are spared, while deficits dependent on arousal-attention-concentration are more prominently impaired. No control subjects were included in this preliminary investigation, however, precluding efforts to disentangle the effects of age and depression.

Neuropsychological Studies of Nongeriatric Depressive Patients

Given the prominent place of cognitive impairment in the clinical picture of major depressive disorder, it is remarkable that there have been so few studies examining the neuropsychology of depression. Investigators have tended to focus on specific psychological functions and have not undertaken the type of study necessary to infer both the overall pattern of neuropsychological failure and its related neuroanatomical substrate. Nonetheless, careful investigations have assessed the memory deficits of depressed patients, and have reached several conclusions regarding the nature of memory failure in depression.

(1) Depressed patients suffer deficits in attention on tasks requiring "effort." Though some investigators have concluded that depressed patients may have "motivational" disorders (Cohen et al., 1982), it is difficult to jump from impaired vigilance or dynamometer squeezing to disordered "motivation," since the latter concept involves altered arousal, state-related depressive phenomena, and persisting personality traits. In any event, depressed patients are evidently less "with it" than unimpaired controls. Their deficit impedes the reception of new information as well as its initial processing.

(2) Ineffective initial acquisition appears to be central to later recall failures. When information is presented in a structured format, as shown by Weingartner et al. (1981), memory deficits are not apparent. As the presentation structure is disrupted, problems develop. Patients also fail to benefit from word properties or processing strategies which are used to enhance encoding and remembering, including verbal imagery, the degree of emotionality, and semantic association. These types of encoding deficiencies are not alone in explaining patients' overall acquisition failure, as evidenced by their poor performance with trigram recall, where rapid memory decay was apparent.

(3) Once information is remembered, it appears that depressed patients will retain it (viz. Cronholm and Ottosson, 1961), although the extent to which this is done effectively remains to be fully clarified. Silberman et al. (1983), for example, demonstrated poor recognition of low imagery and low emotion items, indicating that a retention failure was at least in part in evidence. These results concur with those of Frith and coworkers (1983).

(4) Retrieval deficits are quite apparent in depressives. Part of their failure may be explained by poor initial processing, but it is evident that patients fail to produce items in a spontaneous fashion, only to show increased remembering with less stringent recall testing (e.g., recognition). The data from Frith and colleagues (1983) indicate that recall for information learned early in life is reduced before treatment, but the same "forgotten" information is available 6 months after therapy has been concluded. In sum, depressed patients fail to pull forth from memory information which was learned long before their

depressive episode, and new items acquired in the midst of their dysphoric state.

There appears to be a high correlation between being depressed and suffering cognitive impairment, and the data from Cohen et al. point to a convincing correlation between effort, memory performance, and mood state. Are the two causally linked, with cognitive impairment reflecting disordered mood, or is there a third process which underlies both? Data from Weingartner and associates would indicate that cognitive impairment and mood state are separable components of some greater constellation of symptomatic impairments.

Henry et al. (1973) gave L-dopa to depressed subjects, while others (Gold et al., 1979; Weingartner et al., 1981) gave desamino-8-D-arginine-vasopressin (DDAVP) to their patients, and Reus and others (1979) administered d-amphetamine. The investigators used similar tests to those cited previously. They found that the drugs were able to enhance cognitive functioning, either without altering mood or when mood changed in a fashion which was unrelated to intellectual performance. It was striking that these investigators, who have tended to look for links between disordered mood state and cognitive dysfunction, consistently teased the two apart, showing rather convincingly that disordered memory may be a distinctive symptom which stands beside disturbed affect as one of the principal manifestations of the major depression syndrome.

It is not yet possible to make specific inferences regarding the anatomical substrate of the neuropsychological failures in depressed patients. Although Caine's data suggest that there are few higher cortical deficits in the depressed patients he studied, his preliminary investigation suffered from a lack of control subjects, a design failing which is particularly crucial given the broad age range examined. The neuropsychology of depression thus remains an incomplete picture, one where we can speak with some confidence regarding attentional and memory deficits, have suspicions that gnostic and praxic functions are spared, and know that effort-related performance skills are impaired. Additionally, few of the present results would seem to link these younger individuals readily with the emerging picture of depressive pseudodementia in the elderly on a structural, causative basis.

Cognitive Studies in the Elderly Depressed

Despite the large number of studies of neuropsychological and intellectual changes associated with normal aging (Caine, 1981; Poon, Fozard, and Cermak, 1980), there have been few controlled, prospective studies of the elderly depressed. This deficiency limits our ability to tie together the phenomenological observations described earlier with the detailed neuropsychological findings seen in younger depressed patients.

Findings from the few studies available have been inconclusive and conflicting. Cavanaugh and Wettstein (1983) administered the Beck Depression Inventory (Beck et al., 1961) and the Mini-Mental State Examination (Folstein et al., 1975) to 289 randomly selected medical in-patients. For the entire population, there was a positive, but not strong, correlation between the two assessments. Interaction between age and the Beck score approached significance. Interestingly, when broken down by age, there was no significant relationship between the severity of self-rated depression and cognitive dysfunction for the younger group under 65 years, and a nearly significant relationship for those 65 and older. Given the design of this study, with its use of medical in-patients and no diagnostic criteria for the assessment of depression, these findings are not surprising.

Reisberg et al. (1982) recently examined the relationship between cognition and mood in 22 older out-patients who had subjective complaints of depression. Diagnostic criteria were drawn from DSM-III. A number of standardized procedures were used, including the Guild Memory Scale, digit span repetition (forwards and backwards), memory for faces, and a series of perceptual motor tasks, including perceptual speed, simple and dysjunctive reaction time, and finger tapping. Unfortunately the authors did not include a control group. They found that the performances of their patients varied widely, with nine subjects in the above average range, seven below average, and six one standard deviation or more below average. "There were no statistically significant correlations between total Hamilton scores and any of the psychometric test scores." Reisberg and collaborators did find a strong relationship between slowing of simple reaction time and a single depression rating. Though the nature and direction of the statistical interaction between the two was consistent with previous findings, a solitary positive result in a study of this magnitude leaves one to question whether it was a chance finding.

The study of Reisberg et al. (1982) points out a number of methodological difficulties apparent in assessing geriatric individuals. The subjects were outpatients, necessarily a less severely impaired population despite using the Hamilton Rating Scale as a selection tool. The Hamilton Rating Scale, with its somatic orientation, may overestimate the severity of depression in the elderly, who often demonstrate significant somatic complaints without any evidence of a major affective disorder. The study had no matched elderly controls, making interpretation most difficult. Standardized tests can be used in descriptive studies, as in Stromgren's (1977) study of the effects of ECT on memory, but one must avoid a research design that ultimately assesses the performance of study subjects against the standard developed for a hypothetical "normal" population.

Hilbert, Niederehe, and Kahn (1976) and Miller and Lewis (1977) compared depressed patients with individuals that had "organic" brain disorders or dementia. The former used the Sternberg paradigm (Sternberg and Jarvik, 1976) to assess the speed and accuracy of memory scanning. They found that depressed subjects performed less accurately and more slowly than controls, particularly on negative trials, but did not differ in their rate of memory scanning. Depression was associated with reduced memory efficiency, and interestingly, depressed subjects demonstrated greater tolerance for false positive errors. In contrast, Miller and Lewis (1977), who used a word recognition assessment technique, found that their patients adopted a very conservative response strategy, tending to downplay the number of false positive errors. Both sets of investigators were able to distinguish results from depressed patients from those of dementing individuals with little difficulty.

These two investigations appear to conflict substantially. The first study involves rapid presentation on a display scope of a subspan list of digits for memorization. A "probe" digit is then flashed on the scope, and the subject must decide as quickly as possible whether the digit was among the prior stimuli. Miller and Lewis (1977) showed each participant a sequence of 160 cards, one every three seconds, with each card presenting a simple geometric design. After presenting an initial block of 20 cards with different designs, subsequent blocks of 20 were shown that contained 12 new designs and 8 that were in the original block. The subject is required to indicate whether he has seen the design before. Thus, it is quite plausible that the apparent difference in response strategies may be a reflection of the requirements of each examination, the modality of the test stimuli (numbers vs. designs), the rate at which the test is undertaken (fast-paced vs. slow), and the diagnostic characteristics of each group.

These latter two studies utilize carefully conceived experimental psychological approaches, but they are not similar to those used to investigate younger depressed patients. If we hope to learn more about the neuropsychological mechanisms of cognitive impairments in the elderly depressed, compare these findings with those from younger subjects, and begin to understand the neuroanatomical substrates of these disorders, we will have to standardize our clinical-experimental approaches to these problems.

Conclusion

Though pseudodementia occurs in a wide variety of psychopathological disorders, future studies should be directed at the most common syndromes and the most confusing clinically. Investigators will require relatively homogeneous groups of patients, knowing that their efforts to reduce variance will inevitably exclude some potential subjects. As noted earlier, it is in the elderly, with their declining intellectual abilities, disturbances in day-to-day functioning, and evident depression, that the differential diagnosis between neuropathology and psychopathology becomes most difficult. We must begin our efforts with these individuals.

Both depression and aging lead to a similar set of "symptoms." Growing old is not a disease, of course, but quantitative studies of intellectual performance show age-related declines (Caine, 1981; Poon et al., 1980). There have yet to be any studies which attempt to disentangle the effects of age and depression as they contribute to intellectual performance decrements among hospitalized geriatric patients. Both lead to less effective verbal processing, impaired attentional functioning, and apparent deficits in memory acquisition (Caine, 1981). Although both result in similar output failures, no data suggest that they reflect similar underlying neurobiological processes. It is plausible that the two interact and lead to a more serious, though reversible, neuropsychological decline which presents itself in its most malignant form as "pseudodementia."

Future clinical history studies of depression in the elderly must include thorough psychopathological assessments, extensive neuropsychological testing, careful documentation of therapeutic interventions and responses, and assessments with the newly developed dynamic electrophysiological and radiological measures of active cerebral processes. Our ability to clinically differentiate depression, pseudodementia, and progressive dementia will remain imperfect using present descriptive and diagnostic tools. By relating new measures of cerebral activity with neuropsychological assessments and later measures of outcome, we may be able to develop the clinical skills necessary to prospectively determine which late onset depressive patients have a more rapidly progressive course. Indeed, we may learn that despite an initial favorable response of some to antidepressants, many late onset patients continue to show a functional decline which leads to an early death. Efforts to discriminate "malignant depression" will also help effectively identify nonprogressing, impaired individuals whose symptoms reflect physiological reversible CNS alterations. A therapeutic approach of giving treatment when in doubt is a poor substitute for knowing when to prescribe a specific therapeutic intervention.

In closing, it is worth reviewing the evidence presented here. As a clinical phenomenon, pseudodementia exists and has been the subject of considerable description and definition. However, its etiology and relationship to aspects of aging, depression, and other major psychiatric disorders is unclear. Studies of patients with pseudodementia, depression, and geriatric patients with depression have produced some initial findings that will be of use in designing more focused studies. The objective of such studies will be to understand the nonprogressive course of the disease and yet identify necessary and appropriate treatment for accurately identified cases. To accomplish this, researchers and clinicians will need to employ neuropsychological tools that have greater anatomic and systematic precision without sacrificing the fundamental underpinings of reliability and validity.

REFERENCES

American Psychiatric Association (1968). *Diagnostic and Statistical Manual of Mental Disorders,* 2d ed. Washington, D.C.: American Psychiatric Association.
American Psychiatric Association (1980). *Diagnostic and Statistical Manual of Mental Disorders* 3rd ed. Washington, D.C.: American Psychiatric Association.
Armitage, S. G. (1946). An analysis of certain psychological tests for the evaluation of brain injury. *Psychol. Monographs, 60* (Whole No. 277).
Beck, A. T., Ward, C. H., Mendelson, M., and Erbaugh, J. K. (1961). An inventory for measuring depression. *Arch. General Psychiat. 4,* 561–571.

Benson, D. F. The treatable dementias. In: Benson, D. F., Blumer, D., eds., *Psychiatric Aspects of Neurologic Disease,* vol. II. New York: Grune and Stratton, 1982, pp. 123–148.

Breslow, R., Kocsis, J., and Belkin B. (1980). Memory deficits in depression: Evidence utilizing the Wechsler Memory Scale. *Percept. Motor Skills, 51,* 541–542.

Byrne, D. C. (1977). Affect and vigilance performance in depressive illness. *J. Psychiat. Res. 13,* 185–191.

Caine, E. D. (1981a). Mental status changes with aging. *Seminars in Neurology, 1,* 36–42.

Caine, E. D. (1981b). Pseudodementia: Current concepts and future directions. *Arch. General Psychiat, 38,* 1359–1364.

Caine, E. D., and Shoulson, I. (1983). Psychiatric syndromes in Huntington's disease. *Amer. J. Psychiat., 140,* 728–733.

Cavanaugh, S., and Wettstein, R. M. (1983). The relationship between severity of depression, cognitive dysfunction, and age in medical inpatients. *Amer. J. Psychiat., 140,* 495–496.

Cohen, R. M., Weingartner, H., Smallberg, S. A., and Murphy, D. L. (1982). Effort and cognition in depression. *Arch. Gen. Psychiatr., 39,* 593–597.

Cole, M., and Hicking, T. (1976). Frequency and significance of minor organic signs in elderly depressives. *Canad. Psychiat. Assoc. J., 21,* 7–12.

Cronholm, B., and Ottosson, J. (1961). Memory functions in endogenous depression. *Arch. General Psychiat., 5,* 193–197.

Cummings, J., Benson, D. F., and LoVerme, S., Jr. (1980). Reversible dementia. *J. Am. Med. Assoc., 243,* 2434–2439.

Davison, K., and Baggley, C. R. (1969). Schizophrenic-like psychoses associated with organic disorders of the central nervous system. A review of the literature. *Br. J. Psychiat.* (Special Publ. No. 4), 113–184.

Folstein, M. F., Folstein, S. E., and McHugh, P. R. (1975). "Mini-Mental State." *J. Psychiat. Res., 12,* 189–198.

Freemon, F. R. (1976). Evaluation of patients with progressive intellectual deterioration. *Arch. General Neurol., 33,* 658–659.

Frith, C. D., Stevens, M., Johnstone, E. C., et al. (1983). Effects of ECT and depression on various aspects of memory. *Br. J. Psychiat., 142,* 610–617.

Gold, F. W., Weingartner, H., Ballenger, J. C., et al. (1979). Effects of I-desamino-8-D-arginine vasopressin on behaviour and cognition in primary affective disorder. *Lancet, 2,* 992–994.

Henry, G. M., Weingartner, H., and Murphy, D. L. (1973). Influence of affective states and psychoactive drugs on verbal learning and memory. *Am. J. Psychiat., 130,* 966–971.

Hilbert, N. M., Niederehe, G., and Kahn, R. L. (1976). Accuracy and speed of memory in depressed and organic aged. *Educ. Gerontol. Int. Quart., 1,* 131–146.

Kay, D. W. K. (1962). Outcome and cause of death in mental disorders of old age: A long-term follow-up of functional and organic psychosis. *Acta Psychiat. Scand., 38,* 249–276.

Kiloh, L. G. (1961). Pseudo-dementia. *Acta Psychia. Scand., 37,* 336–351.

Lishman, W. A. (1978). *Organic Psychiatry.* Oxford: Blackwell Scientific, 527–594.

Malone, J. R. L., and Hemsley, D. R. (1977). Lowered responsiveness and auditory signal detectability during depression. *Psychol. Med., 7,* 717–722.

Marsden, C. D., and Harrison, M. J. B. (1972). Outcome of investigation of patients with progressive intellectual deterioration. *Br. Med. J., 2,* 249–252.

McAllister, T. W., and Price, T. R. P. (1982). Severe depressive pseudodementia with and without dementia. *Am. J. Psychiat., 139,* 626–629.

McHugh, P. R., and Folstein, M. F. (1979). Psychopathology of dementia: Implications for neuropathology. In: Katzman, R., ed. *Congenital and Acquired Cognitive Defects.* New York: Raven Press.

Miller, N. E. (1980). The measurement of mood in senile brain disease: Examiner ratings and self-reports. In: Cole, J. and Barret, J., eds. *Psychopathology in the Aged.* New York: Raven Press, pp. 97–118.

Miller, E., and Lewis, P. (1977). Recognition memory in elderly patients with depression and dementia: A signal detection analysis. *J. Abnorm. Psychol., 86,* 84–86.

Nott, P. N., and Fleminger, J. J. (1975). Presenile dementia: The difficulties of early diagnosis. *Acta Psychiat. Scand., 51,* 210–217.

Poon, L. W., Fozard, J. L., Cermak, L. S., et al. (1980). *New Directions in Memory and Aging.* Hillsdale, New Jersey: Lawrence Erlbaum Associates.

Raskin, A., Friedman, A. S., and DiMascio, A. (1982). Cognitive and performance deficits in depression. *Psychopharmacol. Bull., 18,* 196–202.

Reifler, B. V. (1982). Arguments for abandoning the term pseudodementia. *J. Amer. Gerontol. Soc., 1982, 30,* 665–668.

Reifler, B. V., Larson, E., and Hanley, R. (1982). Coexistence of cognitive impairment and depression in geriatric outpatients. *Amer. J. Psychiat., 139,* 623–626.

Reisberg, B., Ferris, S. H., Georgotas, A. et al. (1982). Relationship between cognition and mood in geriatric depression. *Psychopharmacol. Bull., 18,* 191–193.

Reus, V. I., Silberman, E., Post, R. M., et al. (1979). d-Amphetamine: Effects on memory in a depressed population. *Biol. Psychiat., 14,* 345–356.

Ron, M. A., Toone, B. K., Garralda, M. E., (1979). et al. Diagnostic accuracy in presenile dementia. *Br. J. Psychiat., 134,* 161–168.

Roth, M. (1955). The natural history of mental disorder in old age. *J. Ment., Sci., 101,* 281–301.

Seltzer, B., and Sherwin, I. (1978). Organic brain syndromes: An empirical study and critical review. *Am. J. Psychiat., 135,* 13–21.

Silberman, E. K., Weingartner, H., Laraia, M., et al. (1983). Processing of emotional properties of stimuli by depressed and normal subjects. *J. Nerv. Ment. Dis., 171,* 10–14.

Sim, M., and Sussman, I. (1962). Alzheimer's disease: Its natural history and differential diagnosis. *J. Nerv. Ment. Dis., 135,* 489–499.

Smith, J. B., Kiloh, G. L., Ratnavale, G. S., et al. (1976). The investigation of dementia: The results of 100 consecutive admissions. *Med. J. Australia, 2,* 403–405.

Snow, S. S., and Wells, C. E. (1981). Case studies in neuropsychiatry: Diagnosis and treatment of coexistent dementia and depression. *J. Clin. Psychol., 42,* 439–441.

Spitzer, P., Endicott, J., and Robins, E. (1978). Research diagnostic criteria; Rationale and reliability. *Arch. Gen. Psychiatr., 35,* 773–782.

Sternberg, D. E., and Jarvik, M. E. (1976). Memory functions in depression. *Arch. General Psychiat., 33,* 219–224.

Stromgren, L. S. (1977). The influence of depression on memory. *Acta Psychiat. Scand., 56,* 109–128.

Stroop, J. R. (1935). Studies of interference in serial verbal reactions. *J. Exp. Psychol., 18,* 643–662.

Wechsler, D. (1974). *WISC-R manual. Wechsler Intelligence Scale for Children—Revised.* New York: Psychological Corporation.

Wechsler, D. (1955). *Wechsler Adult Intelligence Scale. Manual.* New York: Psychological Corporation.

Wechsler, D. (1945). A standardized memory test for clinical use. *J. Psychol., 19,* 87–95.

Weingartner, H., Gold, P., Ballenger, J. D., et al. (1981). Effects of vasopressin on human memory functions. *Science, 211,* 601–603.

Wells, C. E. (1979). Pseudodementia. *Amer. J. Psychiat., 136,* 895–900.
  memory functions. *Science, 211,* 601–603.

Wells, C. E. (1979). Pseudodementia. *Amer. J. Psychiat., 136,* 895–900.

11

Adult Outcomes of
Childhood Central Processing Deficiencies

BYRON P. ROURKE / GERALD C. YOUNG / JOHN D. STRANG /
DIANE L. RUSSELL

This chapter provides neuropsychological assessment information on a group
of persons whom we have found to be at considerable risk for the development of serious socio-emotional problems as an apparent result of deficiencies
in the analysis, organization, and synthesis of nonverbal information. We
compare the assessment findings of two individuals who underwent neuropsychological examinations as children (because they were thought to be
"learning disabled") and again as young adults. As children, these individuals
exhibited distinct patterns of central processing abilities and deficits which we
have found to be associated with different and predictable adaptive outcomes
in adulthood. Then we examine the neuropsychological protocols of eight individuals seen for assessment as adults who presented with socio-emotional
difficulties that had occasioned intervention by psychiatrists and other mental
health professionals. These protocols bear a striking resemblance to one another and to the pattern of abilities and deficits exhibited by children who
present with the particular pattern of nonverbal learning disability that is the
focus of this chapter. As a framework for our discussion, we begin with an
overview of long-term follow-up studies of children who present with problems processing information. This is followed by a brief examination of the
empirical and theoretical underpinnings of our work in this area.

Summary of Long-term Followup Studies

Learning disabilities in children have been defined in a variety of ways, which
has posed a series of problems in the evaluation of research findings in this
area. Issues relating to this definitional problem have been dealt with elsewhere (Rourke and Gates, 1981), and the discussion will not be repeated here.
However, it is important to note that we choose to view this group of clinical
disorders as manifestations of distinct patterns of central processing abilities
and deficiencies. Thus, our working hypothesis is that the subtypes of learn-

ing disabilities which have been identified in various neuropsychological investigations (e.g., Bakker, Licht, Kok, and Bouma, 1980; Doehring, Hoshko, and Bryans, 1979; Fisk and Rourke, 1979; Lyon, Stewart, and Freedman, 1982; Morris, Blashfield, and Satz, 1981; Petrauskas and Rourke, 1979) are manifestations of distinct patterns of such abilities and deficits; that is, we maintain that there are several definable subtypes of learning disabilities which have specific neuropsychological patterns associated with them. This view will become more salient as we discuss the two subtypes of learning disabled children that are of particular interest to us in this chapter. First, however, it is necessary to review the main findings of the six major long-term followup studies of learning disabled children that have appeared in the recent neuropsychological literature.

Muehl and Forrell (1973) followed 43 disabled readers from elementary school through junior high school to high school for a total of 5 years. They found that poor readers in elementary and junior high school, as a group, continued to be poor readers in high school 5 years after the initial diagnosis of reading disability. Only 4% of the group read at average or above-average levels at followup. Early diagnosis was predictive of positive consequences, but the subsequent reading levels did not even approximate the levels expected for the chronological age and grade of the subjects.

Trites and Fiedorowicz (1976) studied two groups of children who had been diagnosed as having a primary reading disability. One group consisted of 27 boys, the other, of 10 girls. A third group of 10 boys who had a reading disability presumed to be secondary to a neurological disorder was also studied. Upon initial examination, all of the children had problems on three achievement tasks, doing only slightly better on arithmetic than on reading and spelling. All three groups improved in reading, spelling, and arithmetic, but not enough to keep pace with the time interval. For all groups on all three achievement measures the discrepancy between their grade placement and their actual achievement level increased with age. This occurred despite remedial help in all cases. This was true for both sexes and for both groups of reading disabled children. The authors caution researchers against using high school completion as a criterion for reading proficiency: Many students can complete high school with as low as fourth grade scores on achievement tests such as those used in this investigation.

Yule and Rutter (1976) conducted a study in which they compared two groups of children with reading problems. One group of children displayed "reading backwardness" which was defined as reading accuracy or reading comprehension, as measured by the Neale Analysis of Reading Ability Test (Neale, 1958), which was 2 years, 4 months or more below the child's chronological age. The second group of children displayed "specific reading retardation," which was defined as reading accuracy or reading comprehension which was 2 years, 4 months or more below the level predicted on the basis of the child's age and pro-rated WISC full scale I.Q. Children in the group of retarded readers displayed higher I.Q.s and more neurological disorders, constructional apraxia, clumsiness, motor impersistence, and problems in right–left discrimination than did children in the group of backward readers. In addition, there were more boys in the group of retarded readers than in the group of backward readers.

These children were tested initially at ages 9 and 10, and followed over a period of 4–5 years. In spite of much higher intelligence levels, the group with specific reading retardation made significantly less progress in both reading and spelling during this period than the group of backward readers did. In both groups, the children's spelling performance was even more impaired than their reading performance. In contrast, the children with specific reading retardation made more progress in arithmetic than did the backward readers. Even so, both groups still performed well below age level on arithmetic tests.

Followup studies into adolescence revealed some disturbing findings about the reading habits and vocational aspirations of the retarded readers. Despite average intelligence, few of these youths read a morning newspaper or read books for pleasure. Approximately 70% of the retarded readers expected to leave school at the earliest opportunity, and none anticipated going on to professional or university training. It should be emphasized that this group of children exhibited at least average levels of psychometric intelligence, had had 10 years of schooling, and still emerged at young adulthood with major handicaps in reading and spelling.

In another longitudinal study, Rourke and Orr (1977) reported results from a 4-year followup investigation of normal and disabled readers. These children all had average WISC full scale I.Q.s and were not suffering from any visual or auditory acuity deficits or socio-emotional problems. On both initial and followup testing, the normal readers performed at significantly higher levels than did the disabled readers on all measures of achievement. Only 5 of the 19 children originally classified as disabled readers made substantial gains in reading achievement over the 4-year period; only 3 of the 19 made substantial gains in spelling. Approximately three-quarters of the group of disabled readers made little, if any, progress on all measures of achievement, and at the time of followup testing they were still performing well below the levels that would be expected for their chronological age and full scale I.Q.

Satz et al. (1978) reported the results of a 6-year followup study of 497 white male kindergarten children in a public school system in Florida. At the end of second grade, the children were divided into four groups based on classroom reading level as indicated by the teacher. The groups were labelled as (a) severely disabled (no readiness), (b) mildly disabled (first reader), (c) average (second reader), (d) superior (above second reader). When these children were assessed 6 years after the initial testing, the severe group significantly lagged behind the other three groups on achievement measures such as hand-writing, mathematics, and the Wide Range Achievement Test (WRAT; Jastak and Jastak, 1965) Reading, Spelling, and Arithmetic subtests. By this time, the incidence of severe cases was approximately 20%. Of the children originally classified within the severely disabled reading group, 95% were still having problems in reading at the end of fifth grade.

Prognostic figures indicated that only 6.1% of the severe cases improved, while 17.7% of the mild cases showed improvement from grades 2 to 5. Approximately 30% of the average readers and 3.2% of the superior readers became problem readers. The only optimistic prognosis was for the superior readers. All other groups showed little or no improvement and many actually got worse.

Finally, Peter and Spreen (1979) have reported the results of a followup study of 177 learning handicapped children seen for neuropsychological testing and educational counselling between the ages of 8 and 12. These subjects were followed for periods ranging from 4 to 12 years. Originally, the subjects were divided into the following three groups on the basis of data from a neuropsychological examination: brain damaged, minimally brain damaged, and learning handicapped with no neurological signs. These subjects were compared to 67 normal adolescents and young adults with no history of learning problems or brain damage. The results indicated that there was a significant relationship between a previous diagnosis of neurological impairment and behavioral deviance (reported by the parents in a rating scale) at followup. These findings remained statistically significant when the effects of sex, age, and level of psychometric intelligence were taken into account. The subjects with learning handicaps demonstrated deviant behaviors and more personal maladjustment than did those in the normal control group at followup.

Level of psychometric intelligence and sex were also important factors in the outcome of this study. Subjects with higher levels of intelligence showed less overall behavioral pathology and better personal adjustment than the subjects with lower levels of intelligence did. Females showed significantly more maladaptive behaviors and signs of personal maladjustment than did males. The control group did not exhibit these sex differences.

Peter and Spreen (1979) conclude that "in summary, this study has indicated a significant relationship between the presence of a learning handicap in childhood and later personal maladjustment. It has also demonstrated that where there is evidence of neurological handicap certain behaviors associated with that condition persist into adulthood" (p. 89). It therefore appears that the presence of a learning handicap in children is a chronic disorder, and that it may affect many or all aspects of everyday life.

Several general conclusions can be drawn from the results of these six followup studies. (1) Children identified as reading disabled early in school generally continue to have problems in reading, spelling, and other related subjects as they progress through school; the vast majority of them do not "catch up" academically. (2) The academic problems continue to exist, despite what seems to be adequate remedial instruction. (3) Many socio-emotional and behavioral difficulties have been shown to accompany these learning disabilities and they seem to persist into adolescence and young adulthood.

These conclusions are based upon the results of studies that have focussed on children with "learning disabilities" broadly defined or, more often, on children chosen for study because they exhibited a reading disability. In the following section, we turn our attention to followup studies that have focussed on learning disabled children who have been classified into subtypes on the basis of their patterns of performance on several measures of academic performance. It is our contention that this level of subtype specification is necessary if we are to draw valid conclusions regarding the adult outcomes of the central processing deficiencies that we infer give rise to learning disabilities in childhood.

Variations in Patterns of Reading, Spelling, and Arithmetic Abilities and Disabilities

For the past several years, we have been examining the neuropsychological significance of variations in patterns of reading, spelling, and arithmetic abilities and disabilities as part of a more general approach to the neuropsychological study of central processing deficiencies in children. Three groups of children have been studied in considerable detail in our Windsor laboratory. The subjects were selected from over 2,000 children who had received an extensive battery of neuropsychological tests administered in the recommended standardized manner (see Rourke, 1976) by technicians trained specifically for that purpose. In all cases, the children had been referred for neuropsychological assessment because of learning, "perceptual," or other types of behavioral problems to which it was thought cerebral dysfunction might contribute. The subjects in each of the three groups were between the ages of 9 and 14 years, were right-handed, and their WISC full scale I.Q.s fell within the range of 86–114. All had attended school regularly since they ware 6 years of age. On the basis of their social and medical histories and school records, none of the children were (a) considered to be "culturally deprived," (b) hampered by defective vision or hearing, or (c) reported to be in need of psychiatric treatment for an emotional disorder.

Group 1 was composed of children who were uniformly deficient in reading, spelling, and arithmetic; children in Group 2 were relatively adept (though still impaired relative to age norms) at arithmetic compared to reading and spelling; Group 3 was composed of children whose reading (word-recognition) and spelling performances were average or above, but whose arithmetic performance was quite deficient. We have noted frequently in our everyday clinical practice that children who exhibit specific and outstanding impairments on the WRAT Arithmetic subtest (such as those in Group 3) are particularly "at risk" for the development of socio-emotional problems. Furthermore, compared to other types of learning impaired children, they are much less likely (1) to be identified as in need of specialized educational and other forms of intervention, particularly during the early years of their elementary school

career, and (2) to receive treatment that is tailored to meet their special neurodevelopmental and general behavioral needs. With these observations as
background, we have completed three investigations that were designed to determine the neuropsychological dimensions of this particular subtype of learning
disabled child, compared to the two other subtypes of children who present
with outstanding difficulties in reading and spelling. There have also been a
number of followup studies concerning, in particular, the behavioral characteristics of Group 3 children.

In the first investigation in this series, Rourke and Finlayson (1978) compared the three groups of children on a number of auditory-perceptual, verbal, and visual-perceptual-organizational variables that in previous research (e.g.,
Boll, 1974; Rourke, 1975) have been shown to be sensitive to the relative integrity and primary functional capabilities of the two cerebral hemispheres in
children. The results of this study indicated that children who perform relatively poorly on WRAT Arithmetic tests compared with their levels of achievement on WRAT Reading and Spelling tests (Group 3) also exhibit generally
well-developed auditory-perceptual and verbal skills and somewhat deficient
visual-perceptual-organizational skills. On the other hand, children who were
relatively adept at arithmetic, compared with their level of proficiency in reading and spelling (Group 2), scored well on tests of visual-perceptual-
organizational abilities and performed relatively poorly on measures of verbal
and, in particular, auditory-perceptual abilities.

A second study (Rourke and Strang, 1978) compared these same three groups
on measures of motor, psychomotor, and tactile-perceptual abilities. While there
were no significant differences between the groups on tests of simple motor
skills, Group 2 children performed at quite different levels on measures of
complex psychomotor abilities and on a composite measure of fine tactile-
perceptual skills. Specifically, Group 2 children performed at average or above-
average levels on measures of more complex psychomotor abilities, although
they exhibited relatively poor right-hand compared to left-hand performance
on the Tactual Performance Test (TPT; Reitan and Davison, 1974). Children
in Group 3 exhibited normal right-hand and impaired left-hand TPT performance. Performance with both hands together for Group 3 children on the
TPT was particularly impaired, as were their performances on other tests involving complex psychomotor skills. Furthermore, Group 3 children exhibited evidence of bilateral impairment on a composite measure of tactile-
perceptual abilities; the tactile-perceptual impairment was more marked on the
left side of the body. Group 2 children performed significantly better than did
Group 3 children on this composite measure of tactile-perceptual abilities with
the left hand.

The results of the Rourke and Finlayson (1978) and Rourke and Strang
(1978) studies indicated that learning disabled children who were relatively
adept at arithmetic compared with their performances on the WRAT Reading
and Spelling subtests (Group 2) scored lower than expected (vis-a-vis developmental norms) on measures of abilities ordinarily thought to be subserved

primarily by the left cerebral hemisphere. These Group 2 children performed much better (in an age-appropriate fashion) on measures of abilities ordinarily thought to be subserved primarily by the right cerebral hemisphere. The opposite was true of the learning disabled children who performed satisfactorily on the WRAT Reading and Spelling subtests and scored outstandingly low on the WRAT Arithmetic subtest. These Group 3 children scored lower on measures of abilities ordinarily thought to be subserved primarily by the right cerebral hemisphere and much higher (in an age-appropriate fashion) on measures of abilities ordinarily thought to be subserved primarily by the left cerebral hemisphere.

In a third study (Strang and Rourke, 1983), the possible difference in the nonverbal concept-formation capacities of Group 2 and Group 3 children were investigated. This study examined only two (Groups 2 and 3) of the three groups because the neuropsychological ability structure of these two groups appeared to be of particular theoretical interest (Rourke, 1982a). Furthermore, it had been demonstrated previously that learning disabled children who are selected on the basis of uniform deficiencies in all three subjects (Group 1) do not constitute a homogeneous group (Fisk and Rourke, 1979).

The performances of Group 2 and Group 3 children on the Halstead Category Test (Reitan and Davison, 1974) were compared. The Category Test is designed to measure nonverbal concept-formation and problem-solving abilities; it also involves hypothesis testing, strategy generation, and the ability to benefit from positive and negative informational feedback. In this investigation, it was found that the group of children who exhibited relatively poor WRAT Reading and Spelling abilities and somewhat better WRAT Arithmetic abilities (Group 2) performed in an age-appropriate fashion on this complex nonverbal problem-solving test. The Category Test performances of those who concern us most in this chapter (Group 3 children) were found to be significantly inferior to those of Group 2 children. Furthermore, it was found that children with outstanding difficulties in arithmetic performed most poorly on the subtests of the Category Test that are least amenable to solutions using a verbal strategy and that require substantial shifting of psychological set to arrive at satisfactory solutions.

In summary, children who exhibit outstanding and rather specific deficiencies on WRAT Arithmetic tests (as compared to their performances on WRAT Reading and Spelling tests) were found to exhibit evidence of bilateral tactile-perceptual impairment (particularly on the left side of the body) and bilateral psychomotor impairment, except on the TPT. On the latter test, Group 3 children exhibited normal right-hand performance, impaired left-hand performance, and markedly impaired performance when both hands were used conjointly on a third trial. They also exhibited evidence of poorly developed visual-perceptual-organizational abilities and their nonverbal concept-formation abilities were found to be impaired as well. As a group, their neuropsychological strengths were most directly associated with language-related skills of the "automatic," rote (overlearned) variety. A summary of the results of our studies of Group 2 and Group 3 children is displayed in Fig. 1.

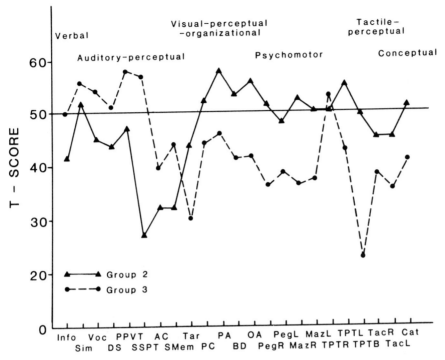

Fig. 1. Mean *T* scores for Groups 2 and 3. Good performance: above 50; poor performance: below 50. Abbreviations: Info, WISC information; Sim, WISC Similarities; Voc, WISC Vocabulary; DS, WISC Digit Span; PPVT, Peabody Picture Vocabulary Test; SSPT, Speech Sounds Perception Test; AC, Auditory Closure Test; SMem, Sentence Memory Test; Tar, Target Test; PC, WISC Picture Completion; PA, WISC Picture Arrangement; BD, WISC Block Design; OA, WISC Object Assembly; PegR, Grooved Pegboard–Right Hand; PegL, Grooved Pegboard–Left Hand; Maz R, Maze Test–Right Hand; Maz L, Maze Test–Left Hand; TPT R, Tactual Performance Test–Right Hand; TPT L, Tactual Performance Test–Left Hand; TPT B, Tactual Performance Test–Both Hands; TacR, Tactual-perceptual abilities–Right Hand; TacL, Tactual-perceptual abilities–Left Hand; Cat, Category Test.

(The *T* score means are structured in such a way that average performance for the particular age-group in question is represented by *T* = 50, with a standard deviation (S.D.) of 10. Thus, a *T* score of 60 represents a level of performance that is one S.D. above the mean, whereas a *T* score of 40 represents a score that is one S.D. below the mean for the particular age group. This use of *T* scores allows direct comparisons to be made among the various tests in this type of profile analysis. Such comparisons would not be possible if raw scores were used.)

We have also completed a number of in-depth followups of the Group 3 type of child concerning (a) their mechanical arithmetic deficiencies and (b) their personality status. Strang and Rourke (1985b) noted that the mechanical arithmetic difficulties exhibited by Group 3 children were in some ways quite unlike those exhibited by other subgroups of arithmetically-impaired children. In general, it was found that Group 3 children tended to make more errors and a wider range of "types" of mechanical arithmetic errors. In addition, it was clear that their understanding of mathematical concepts was particularly deficient.

Similarly, the personality status and adaptive behavior characteristics of the Group 3 type of child have also been dealt with in detail (Strang and Rourke, 1985a). The latter work was based on short- and long-term longitudinal studies of individual children; comparisons of the adaptive behaviors and other characteristics of the Group 3 type of child with those of other subtypes of neuropsychologically-impaired children; perusals of historical records of Group 3 children; and accounts of the children's behavior, given by their parents and teachers, which were remarkably uniform. Some of the behavior was alarmingly deviant.

In general, the Group 3 type of child was not often thought to be "at risk" for educational or socio-emotional difficulties during early and middle childhood. For the most part, educators were particularly convinced that the children's abilities were at least adequate, primarily because of their well-developed language skills. It should be noted that most of these children tend to be quite talkative and to exhibit a well-developed vocabulary. Furthermore, older children of this type exhibit outstanding efficiency at decoding words. Although most tend to be somewhat clumsy and to participate quite inadequately with their peers in play situations, the possibility that such children had some actively debilitating cognitive deficiencies was rarely even considered before our neuropsychological assessment of them had been completed. Even when the children had received a complete neuropsychological assessment and appropriate feedback had been given, some professional persons and parents held quite fervently to the notion that the child in question was simply immature and that he/she only required more social and educational experience.

We have found that, although these children are quite loquacious, their verbiage may not often coincide with the events at hand. In the academic realm, their well-developed word-recognition skills stand in marked contrast to their obviously inferior and often quite impaired reading comprehension abilities. In addition to problems with mechanical arithmetic, their hand-writing and the general organization of their work are often found to be particularly poor. Socially, their inadequacies are quite serious. Indeed, we have noted that these children almost always fare quite poorly in novel or otherwise complex (e.g., unstructured) social situations. Friendships are typically struck up with children much younger than themselves, and some of the children are virtually friendless.

With this information as background, Strang and Rourke (in preparation) investigated the personality status of the Group 3 type of child from a psychometric point of view. In this study, the Personality Inventory for Children (PIC; Wirt et al., 1977) profiles of the Group 3 type of child were compared with those of two other subtypes of learning impaired children who bore some resemblance to those employed in the Rourke and Finlayson (1978), Rourke and

Strang (1978), and Strang and Rourke (1983) studies. For example, one of the groups exhibited evidence of poorly developed auditory-perceptual and verbal skills, compared to their well developed visual-perceptual-organizational abilities (similar to Group 2); the other group (similar to Group 1) did not exhibit any particularly well-developed skills as measured by the control variables which served to define the groups.

In this study, it was found that the children who most closely resembled the Group 3 type of child exhibited a (mean) PIC profile which was most suggestive of the presence of psychopathology. The PIC Psychosis scale and, in general, those scales that are associated with the psychopathology-internalization factor—Depression, Withdrawal, Anxiety, and Social Skills (Lachar, 1975)—best characterized and distinguished the PIC profile of the Group 3 type of child. On the other hand, the children who exhibit evidence of specific auditory-perceptual and verbal handicaps (similar to Group 2) were, as a group, found to exhibit a normal personality profile on the PIC.

When the degree of discrepancy between auditory-perceptual and verbal skills on the one hand and visual-perceptual-organizational skills on the other for the two groups which exhibited particular strengths or weaknesses in these areas (i.e., those similar to Group 2 and 3) were maximized through a reselection procedure, the PIC results became even more pronounced (in the direction of increased psychopathology) for the Group 3 type of child, while they failed to change in any significant way for the children who exhibited outstanding auditory-perceptual and verbal deficiencies (Group 2 type).

Theoretical Considerations

This pattern of markedly impaired visual-spatial-órganizational, tactile-perceptual, psychomotor, and problem-solving/concept-formation abilities accompanying some quite well-developed psycholinguistic skills has been interpreted according to a neurodevelopmental theory which emphasizes the differential contributions and dynamic interplay of left and right hemispheral systems in the acquisition, integration, and deployment of descriptive systems and adaptive behavior (Rourke, 1982a). Of particular importance are the aspects of this model which have to do with the individual's capacity to adapt to novel situations. Specifically, it is postulated that right hemispheral systems play an important role in the normal individual's attempts to orient himself and deal effectively with the novel features of new situations. In addition, it is postulated that left hemispheral systems are involved in the programmatic elaboration of acquired descriptive systems and their associated behaviors. A noteworthy example of the latter set of skills is natural language. Within this theoretical framework, the initial acquisition of various linguistic codes and associated skills is seen as involving right hemispheral systems primarily, whereas the subsequent stereotypic application of the natural language code (which presumes that it has been overlearned and amenable to rote application) is seen as a function that is mediated primarily by systems within the left hemisphere.

Thus, in terms of this model, it would be expected that Group 3 children (and later adults) would have particular difficulty in adapting to situations which require systematic orientation to and analysis of novel situations when there exist no overlearned descriptive systems and/or patterns of adaptation for coping with them. For example, it would be expected that it would be very difficult for such individuals to adapt to social situations in which changing patterns of relationships, discourse, modes of communication and interaction are likely to be the rule rather than the exception. Rather than orient successfully to such circumstances, plan and execute adequate coping strategies, and deal flexibly with changing patterns of interaction, we expect that such individuals would attempt to apply previously overlearned strategies in a stereotypic fashion. Needless to say, such inflexible approaches are likely to meet with resistance from others involved in the interaction. The predicament becomes even worse for such individuals when, as is very likely to be the case, they attempt to deal with every situation verbally when some other mode of interaction (e.g., touching, psychomotor expression, appropriate gesturing) is demanded. As the inevitable rebuffs that such persons experience are multiplied many times over, it is reasonable to expect that they will begin to withdraw from such contacts after brief encounters with them, and that they may eventually become seriously withdrawn and avoid social encounters.

Of course, it would stand to reason that the social difficulties of these individuals would be minimized if they could adopt a life style in which they could largely cope by the programmatic application of overlearned verbal formulae. An example would be an individual of this type gravitating toward a best friend or constant companion who exhibits similar tendencies—i.e., a preference for social interactions that depend almost exclusively upon verbal intercourse without the necessity to appreciate fully the nonverbal messages of others involved in the interaction. A very frequently observed pattern of relationship that often transpires in our waiting rooms is a parent (usually the mother) and her/his child (usually a daughter) who both exhibit this pattern of abilities and deficits and carry on a verbal interaction almost indefinitely, the content of which is reminiscent of two adjacent motorized sidewalks in an airport moving in opposite directions. That is, what one says bears little or no relationship to what the other is saying—almost as though they were oblivious to virtually every aspect of the relationship except for the comfort that each rather obviously feels in rattling on with verbiage that can twist and turn in any direction so long as the air remains filled with words. It is not uncommon to observe both parties talking about different things at the very same time, and seeming completely oblivious to the communicative intent or content of each other's discourse.

Another characteristic of these individuals that is addressed in the model under consideration is their problem in inter-modal integration. Within the model, the systems of the left hemisphere are viewed as being particularly geared to intra-model integration, whereas right hemispheral systems are thought to be particularly suited for handling inter-modal integration. Since Group 3 individuals are thought to be particularly deficient in the abilities thought to be subserved primarily by right hemispheral systems, it would be expected that situations that call for inter-modal integration would be particularly difficult for them. Assessing another's emotional state by integrating information gleaned from his/her facial expressions, tone of voice, posture, psychomotor patterns, and so on is only one of the many obvious situations that arise in everyday social intercourse that would be particularly difficult for the Group 3 child, and later adult, to handle.

The end result of repeated failures in coping with deficiencies in information processing—especially when aggravated by other sources of stress (including the confusion and frustration often experienced by the child's parents and teachers)—usually is loss of self esteem, feelings of inferiority, emotional confusion and distress, and any number of other strains within the personality that render the likelihood of developing significant socio-emotional problems all but certain.

To illustrate this, we present in the next section an example of a Group 3 person who underwent neuropsychological assessment at the age of 11 and again when she was approximately 21 years old. This set of neuropsychological test results is compared with those of a Group 2 person who was examined three times over approximately the same developmental interval. Both of these individuals were referred for neuropsychological assessment initially because they were thought to be learning disabled. The very different socio-emotional difficulties they faced in early adulthood are predictable from the model under discussion and serve to illustrate the sorts of prognostic statements that we feel are quite justifiably made when one takes into consideration the adaptive implications of the different patterns of central processing abilities and deficits exhibited by these two types of individuals.

Initial and Followup Comparisons: F.V. and T.A.

F.V. (a Group 2 individual) is a male who was first referred for neuropsychological assessment at the age of 9 years and 3 months primarily because of difficulty reading and spelling. The results of his second (followup) neuropsychological assessment at age 10 years, 9 months and his third (final) assessment at age 23 years, 11 months are presented in Fig. 2 since these ages correspond best with those at which T.A. was tested. T.A. (a Group 3 individual) was referred initially at age 11 years and 4 months (approximately two years later than was F.V.) because of some academic and behavioral difficulties. Some of the results of this assessment and her followup assessment at age 20 years, 9 months are shown in Figs. 2 and 3.

As can be seen in Figs. 2 and 3, the general configuration of neuropsychological test results for T.A. and F.V. are somewhat remarkable on two counts:

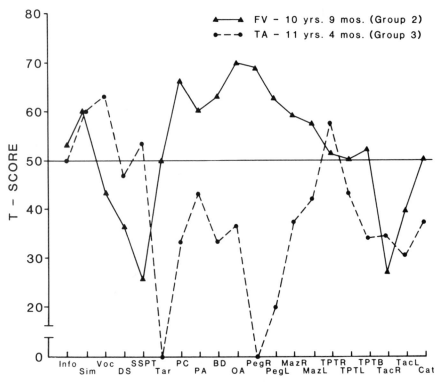

Fig. 2. T scores for the initial neuropsychological assessments of F.V. and T.A. Good performance: above 50; poor performance: below 50. Abbreviations as in Fig. 1.

(1) T.A. exhibited better developed language-related abilities within the context of difficulties in nonverbal (including problem-solving) areas, while F.V. exhibited an almost entirely opposite pattern of abilities and deficits: (2) the general configuration of neuropsychological test results did not change substantially over time (approximately 10 years for T.A. and 13 years for F.V.) for either individual.

A closer examination of Figs. 2 and 3 reveals that, on two verbal measures (WISC Information and Similarities), F.V. and T.A. performed at similar levels relative to age-based norms. However, on the WISC Vocabulary and Digit Span subtests and the Speech-Sounds Perception Test, T.A.'s performance was considerably better than the performance of F.V. (The considerable gains made by F.V. on the latter test between the two assessments is quite typical of persons who, like F.V., continue to have severe difficulty in translating graphemes to phonemes, as demanded in oral reading, but who eventually learn to recognize the graphic equivalents of speech-sounds, as required on this test.) On the visual-perceptual-organizational measures (Target Test, WISC Picture Completion, Picture Arrangement, Block Design, and Object Assembly) F.V.

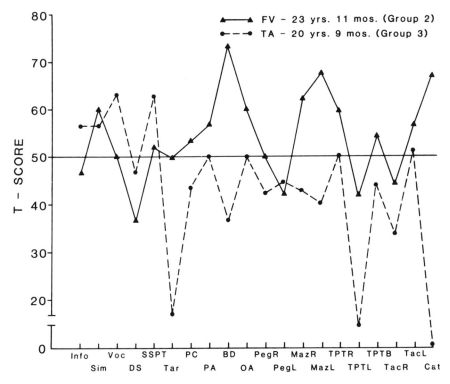

Fig. 3. *T* scores for the followup neuropsychological assessments of F.V. and T.A. Good performance: above 50; poor performance: below 50. Abbreviations as in Fig. 1.

performed better. This was also the case on four tests of complex psychomotor abilities (Grooved Pegboard Test, right- and left-hand scores, and the Maze Test, right- and left-hand scores). On the Tactual Performance Test (TPT) F. V. and T.A. were equally proficient (with scores within the average range) when using the right hand. With the left hand, T.A.'s performance declined markedly, while F.V.'s score remained within the average range. Using both hands proved to be very difficult for T.A., while F.V. again performed within normal limits on this task. Both F.V. and T.A. experienced difficulty on the tactile-perceptual tasks with the right hand. F.V. exhibited slightly less difficulty than did T.A. on these tasks with the left hand. Finally, on the Category Test, F.V. exhibited average or above-average scores, while T.A.'s performances were well below average. A comparison of Fig. 1 with Figs. 2 and 3 reveals the similarities, in terms of both patterns and levels of performance, between F.V. and the Group 2 cases and between T.A. and Group 3 cases.

The initial referring complaints (reading difficulties for F.V. and some specific learning and behavioral difficulties for T.A.) remained essentially the same at the time of followup for both. In fact, F.V. referred himself for neuropsychological reassessment as an adult to provide information that would perhaps lead to a furthering of his education. At present, he is still unable to read and he is receiving intensive remedial educational assistance. He felt that, after having gone through and essentially not benefitted from numerous special educational treatments and programs, he was now once again motivated to learn to read. His prognosis in this respect remains guarded.

Despite his reading handicap, F.V. is gainfully employed as a "large rig" truck driver. He is responsible and is generally considered to be a well-adjusted and pleasant person. However, his inability to read has continued to be a source of concern to him and he becomes somewhat anxious and disconcerted when it is discussed.

T.A., on the other hand, was referred as an adult for neuropsychological reassessment by a governmental agency that is involved with vocational rehabilitation. Although she was cooperative in the testing situation (as she had been when she was younger), she did not appear to be particularly reflective about or deeply concerned with the quality of her performances. Rather, she seemed to be somewhat unaware of her shortcomings. Moreover, her social interactional style, even in the highly structured testing situation, was rather stilted and lacking in spontaneity.

This young woman had been employed as a housekeeper in a hospital but was laid off. It is noteworthy that this job was not in keeping with her level of academic achievement or educational experience. Furthermore, she reported that she had "flunked out" of some sort of retraining program offered by a governmental service. The professionals who were trying to place her in a job were quite confused by her evident inability to adapt, and they were in a quandary as to how to meet her short- and long-term vocational needs.

While the prognosis for substantial gains being made by F.V. in reading and related subjects is not particularly encouraging, there is every indication that he will manage quite well in other aspects of his adult life: He is an adaptive problem-solver who is quick to discern the relevant aspects of social situations, and he is quite capable of procuring and maintaining gainful employment in a wide variety of occupations. The prognostic picture for T.A., on the other hand, is quite bleak. In this connection, it should be noted that many individuals who exhibit a similar pattern of neuropsychological strengths and weaknesses have been referred to us by job placement agencies. In general, it has been the case that long-standing, meaningful employment is not usually found for them. Instead, what appears to be a job that is well within their capabilities (e.g., serving at a snackbar) becomes problematic for them and for those with whom they work because of their inadequate social judgment and inappropriate social behavior, in addition to apparent insensitivity and inconsistent emotional reactivity. In order to illustrate the relationship of this Group 3 pattern of neuropsychological abilities and deficits to disordered socio-emotional behavior, we present next a brief description of eight adults, all of whom exhibit this particular neuropsychological profile.

Adults Exhibiting the Group 3 Pattern (Syndrome)

This group of patients comprised 5 females and 3 males whose ages at the time of testing ranged from 17 to 48 years. The sex distribution of this adult sample corresponds well with the sex distribution in the sample of children who have similar neuropsychological characteristics. In the Windsor laboratory, for example, at least 50% of children who exhibit this particular pattern of neuropsychological strengths and weaknesses are female. This sex distribution is markedly different than is the case for other types of (primarily psycholinguistic) "learning disabilities" where males outnumber females by at least a 6-to-1 ratio.

The social and cultural backgrounds of the adult group varied considerably. Six were from various parts of Canada, while one was from India and one was from Guyana. Socio-economic status ranged from working class (1 case) to upper or privileged class (1 case); the other six patients came from what could be best described as middle-class backgrounds. Nevertheless, there was a remarkable degree of homogeneity in many aspects of their early development, educational experience, social and emotional development, and particularly in their neuropsychological profiles, as is illustrated in Fig. 4. The T score means for this group were derived from norms for these tests that were taken from a number of sources.

Also presented in Fig. 4 for comparison purposes are the mean T scores for Group 3 children (as contained in Fig. 1). The remarkable resemblance between this group of adults and the Group 3 children can be seen. Both the patterns and levels of performance on the verbal, auditory-perceptual, visual-perceptual-organizational, and tactile-perceptual measures are virtually identical. Slight discrepancies are evident on the psychomotor measures. On the Grooved Pegboard Test (PegR and PegL) the Group 3 children performed at a higher level compared to age-based norms than the adults did, although their performances were clearly below average. Also of note are the performances of the two groups on the Tactual Performance Test (TPT). When using the right hand, the Group 3 children performed at an average level, while the adults performed well below average. With the left hand, the Group 3 children exhibited a decline in performance but still performed at a relatively higher level than did the adults. However, it should be noted that the *pattern* of relatively better right-hand than left-hand performance on the TPT was evident in both groups. When both hands were used together, the performances of the two groups were well below average, but the Group 3 children scored relatively higher than did the adults on this task.

The data relating to summary measures on the Wechsler scales and the Wide Range Achievement Test scores for both groups are not represented in Fig. 4. In all cases for individuals in both groups their verbal I.Q.s were notably higher than their performance I.Q.s on the Wechsler scales, and their Reading and Spelling subtest performances exceeded their Arithmetic subtest per-

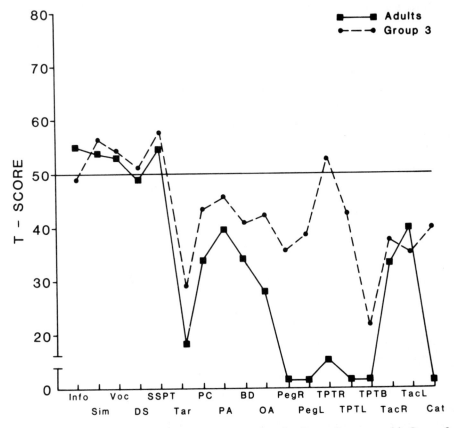

Fig. 4. Mean *T* scores for the eight adults exhibiting the Group 3 pattern with Group 3 performances included for comparison purposes. Good performance: above 50; poor performance: below 50. Abbreviations as in Fig. 1.

formances on the Wide Range Achievement Test. In general, therefore, it can be concluded that adults and Group 3 children exhibit a great degree of similarity in their neuropsychological ability structures, both with respect to developmentally appropriate levels and configurational patterns of performance.

It is important to note that, even as infants and young children, this group of adults were typically described as awkward and poorly coordinated. Until their neuropsychological examination was carried out, no clear or characteristic neurological picture of this group of patients had emerged apart from the recognition of their clumsiness and poor coordination. This was so in spite of the raised incidence of positive neurological signs and radiological evidence in this group of patients. Two of the eight had a seizure disorder (idiopathic epilepsy) controlled by medication. A third had an abnormal CT scan indicative of cerebral atrophy. In the fourth case, the possibility of arrested hydrocephalus at birth was raised and, in another case, the possibility of hypoxic cerebral damage during the perinatal period was mentioned. So, in three of the eight cases, there was clear evidence of neurological disorder and in two others there were suggestive "soft" signs. In the remaining three cases, no neurological opinion was available.

With respect to Group 3 children in the Rourke and Finlayson (1978), Rourke and Strang (1978), and Strang and Rourke (1983) studies, even though subjects were chosen for study who had no known or obvious neurological problems, it was found that 10 of the 14 subjects who were administered EEGs had recordings that were considered to be "abnormal." This is a higher incidence of abnormal EEGs than is typical of the general population of learning disabled children. In addition, there was a higher incidence of primary ocular problems (e.g., "lazy eye") and mixed eye dominance among this group of children than was the case for the other two groups in the studies carried out by Rourke and his colleagues.

In most cases, the academic problems of the adults examined related to difficulties in perceptual-motor and visual-spatial functioning and marked deficiencies in complex concept-formation and problem-solving. These problems were manifested in poor writing and drawing skills, difficulty in mathematics, geometry, geography, and science, and an inability to participate in sports and games. These patients were never able to make sense out of graphs, charts, or maps, and they tended to require lengthy explanations or repetition of instructions and directions. On the other hand, they were relatively successful in subjects in which language was paramount (e.g., civics and history). Even so, most of these patients seldom expressed an opinion in class and they exhibited an inability to make inferences or draw conclusions. This was so despite the fact that most of them spent long hours doing their homework. Much of their study time consisted of committing the material to memory and, despite the long hours of study, exams were always extremely stressful for them and they were likely to obtain barely passing grades.

The extent to which a learning disability was identified during the early school years in this group of patients is unclear from their histories. In most cases, it appears that the motor and psychomotor difficulties (e.g., poor graphomotor skills and general motoric clumsiness) were identified, but in only three of the eight cases was it reported that a "learning disability" was in evidence. Even then, there was no indication that any of these patients ever received remedial help during their school career. In one case, a "vocational school" placement was arranged, in spite of the fact that this patient's motor coordination was obviously impaired. In most cases, the patients themselves were essentially unaware of the nature and severity of their learning disability until the neuropsychological assessment was completed. By that time, most had completed their formal education.

A recurring theme in the histories of these patients was their seriously deficient social skills. They were typically described as being socially inept and often inappropriate and as having few, if any, friends. Furthermore, they were said to have a very low level of self-esteem and usually showed a tendency to become withdrawn and isolated. Their peers saw them as being "different," and they were sometimes the victims of ridicule. In six of eight cases, the principal problem and reason for referral for complete neuropsychological assessment had to do with serious occupational maladjustment. In the other two cases, psychiatric problems were primary, both having "schizophrenia" as part of the diagnostic picture.

All of these patients exhibited some psychological difficulties. Such problems, in fact, constituted the second major reason for referral: Four of the eight (including the two who carried a diagnosis of schizophrenia) were treated within a psychiatric service, three as in-patients and one in an out-patient day treatment program. In these four cases, the principal presenting problem was said to be depression. At least two of the four (the two who were not diagnosed as schizophrenic) were thought to be seriously suicidal. Of the four patients who were not under psychiatric treatment at the time of referral, three were also prone to severe, chronic depression.

At the time these patients were seen for neuropsychological assessment, all eight had completed high school, four had received Bachelor of Arts degrees (one in economics, one in psychology, one in social work, and one in general arts). Two others had completed two years of community college, and another had completed one year of university. Nevertheless, none of these eight patients had ever worked at an occupation (or at a level) that was commensurate with their educational experience. The vocational history of H.S. is in many ways quite typical of adults who exhibit the pattern of neuropsychological abilities and deficits under consideration.

CASE H.S.

H.S., a 31-year-old woman, was referred by her family physician for complete neuropsychological assessment. She had a history of being unable to obtain and/or hold jobs which were in keeping with her level of educational achievement. In addition, she exhibited signs of depression and had many questions about herself and her situation. Her father felt that these could best be answered by professionals. After completing secondary school, she worked as a waitress, but had to quit because of her poor coordination. Thereafter, she tried to be a saleswoman, but she failed because she made too many errors using a cash register. Following this, she obtained a job that involved key punching. Her employers found that she was too slow and made too many errors so she was dismissed.

On the advice of a psychologist who had given her an Interest Inventory, she enrolled in a social work program at a university. With considerable help, including remedial reading (for comprehension) and writing, as well as supportive counselling, she managed to obtain a degree in this field. Her supervisors reported that she continues to have difficulty conducting interviews because of her strict, inflexible adherence to prescribed interview techniques. She also experienced marked problems in summarizing and organizing interview material to write reports, and in making critical judgments. Because of these difficulties, in addition to her inability to tolerate the stress of carrying a normal caseload, she has yet to find suitable employment five years after graduation. She recently attempted to obtain further remedial help in a reputable private learning clinic and was able to obtain government assistance for it. However, she was eventually dropped from the program because, in the view of the director (who had initially demonstrated some optimism), her goal of obtaining a full-time position as a social worker was unreasonable, given the severity of her deficits.

In most cases, the efforts of these patients to pursue their chosen professions were unsuccessful or were forsaken for a "less demanding" job. Even then, they were often ill-suited for the so-called "less demanding" jobs. Apparently many of them involved "thinking on one's feet", and, as has been mentioned throughout this chapter, dealing adaptively with the demands of new or otherwise complex situations is particularly problematic for this group of children and adults.

In general, we have found that patients who exhibit this pattern of adaptive abilities and deficits are doubly handicapped occupationally. While they are able to succeed in many academic courses and programs (presumably because of their relatively adequate verbal skills), their social ineptness and cognitive limitations (in concept-formation, hypothesis testing, strategy generation, and the capacity to benefit from nonverbal information, including feedback) preclude working as teachers, counsellors, salespersons, etc., for which their verbal skills initially make them appear suitable. Furthermore, their nonverbal (visual-spatial and perceptual-motor) skills are so seriously deficient that they are unable to work in trades or even do factory work. A similar type of "bind" could cause serious (at least short-term) emotional adjustment difficulties even for the normal adult—that is, someone who has the adaptive resources to cope with the problem. When one considers the virtual inability of these patients to reflect on the nature and seriousness of their problems, their outstanding difficulties in generating adequate solutions for them, and the misunderstandings of various professionals and others concerning the significance of their adaptive difficulties, the psychiatric problems they have should not be surprising.

Their typical psychiatric profile includes low self-esteem, loneliness, depression, isolation, and withdrawal. Also, it is often noted that there is a sense of urgency, and in some instances panic, even in relatively innocuous problem-solving situations; it is typical for minor annoyances (from an objective standpoint) to become major crises. Psychotherapy with such patients progresses extremely slowly and consists, for the most part, of continual crisis intervention. A typical crisis might revolve around an off-hand remark of some acquaintance who intended nothing more than mild disagreement, but the "crisis" may last for weeks. As such times, the "therapy" session might consist mainly of an exhaustive recapitulation of the incident by the patient, after which the therapist offers a detailed explanation and integration of the incident. The "crisis" may appear to be resolved, only to come up in the very next session, at which time the entire procedure is repeated. (It is at such times that the probability of counter-transference on the part of the therapist is particularly great!) This inability to grasp the objective significance of situations and the marked difficulty in gaining insight, despite lengthy discussions and explanations, is characteristic. Helping such patients to understand the nature of their difficulties through "verbal, insight-oriented" psychotherapeutic approaches is extremely difficult if not impossible. Although they may benefit from a more "concrete" task-oriented approach, it usually requires an unreasonable amount of the therapist's time and such programs prove to be extremely expensive.

Similar problems occur when attempts are made to improve patients' social skills. Typically, in their relationships with peers, friends, and relatives, they consistently misread and misinterpret the nuances of ordinary social interactions, particularly such nonverbal intricacies as gestures, facial expressions, laughter, and so on. Therapeutic efforts to help them understand and alter their interpretations and responses usually require lengthy (verbal) recapitulations and repetitions of typical incidents. Even when these attempts are relatively successful, their "altered" behavior most often lacks the "naturalness" of the average person, appearing stilted and "programmed." Moreover, their virtually complete dependence on explicit verbal feedback mitigates against benefitting from positive and negative feedback in social situations (which is mostly nonverbal). Hence, they experience considerable difficulty in modifying their behavior even to suit some very common social circumstances.

The picture that we have painted of these individuals as adults may seem to be overly bleak and hopeless. This is certainly the case, in our experience, when no treatment or inappropriate treatment is provided for them. Even when such patients are "understood," they are typically thought to be inappropriate candidates for the sort of psychotherapy in which most therapists are prepared to engage (i.e., some variation of the "talking cure"). Note that this is likely to occur only after the therapist has "seen through" the camouflaging efforts of the patient's excessive and irrelevant verbiage, and has gained an appreciation of his/her extreme difficulties in concept formation, problem solving, judgment, and reasoning.

Were this a work on psychotherapy, we would outline our views on how such patients should be treated. Since it is not, we will refrain from so doing. However, the interested reader may wish to consult a recent work (Rourke et al., 1983) on therapy with Group 3 type children. We feel that a similar approach would be quite beneficial for this group of adults.

Summary and Conclusions

In this chapter, we have focussed on a particular type of individual whom we originally identified through our studies of children who exhibit different subtypes of learning disabilities. This type of child exhibits an easily identifiable pattern of abilities and deficits on neuropsychological examination. In addition, he/she exhibits a form of socio-emotional disturbance that is equally as discernible and quite predictable. We infer that the adults discussed in this chapter are virtually identical to Group 3 children, whom we described at some length, and we presented one longitudinal followup case to demonstrate that this disturbance can, in fact, occur. In contrast, the longitudinal followup of an individual who exhibited the virtually opposite pattern of neuropsychological abilities and deficits (Group 2 type) served to illustrate the vastly different educational, social, and emotional outcomes that we have found to be quite typical in such cases. Finally, with respect to the purpose and thrust of this book, we should point out, as we have elsewhere (Rourke, 1982b; Rourke and Fisk, 1981; Strang and Rourke, 1985a), that we feel that this type of evidence tends to support the view that the individual's (neuropsychological) pattern of central processing abilities and deficits can and does play a crucial role in all aspects of both academic learning and socio-emotional/adaptational proficiencies and difficulties.

REFERENCES

Bakker, D. J., Licht, R., Kok, A., and Bouma, A. (1980). Cortical responses to word reading by right- and left-eared normal and reading-disturbed children. *J. Clin. Neuropsychol.*, 2, 1–12.

Boll, T. J. (1974). Behavioral correlates of cerebral damage in children aged 9 through 14. In: R. M. Reitan and L. A. Davison, eds., *Clinical Neuropsychology: Current Status and Applications*. Washington, D.C.: V. H. Winston & Sons.

Doehring, D. G., Hoshko, I. M., and Bryans, B. N. (1979). Statistical classification of children with reading problems. *J. Clin. Neuropsychol., 1,* 5–16.

Fisk, J. L., and Rourke, B. P. (1979). Identification of subtypes of learning-disabled children at three age levels: A neuropsychological, multivariate approach. *J. Clin. Neuropsychol., 1,* 289–310.

Jastak, J. F., and Jastak, S. R. (1965). *The Wide Range Achievement Test*. Wilmington, Delaware: Guidance Associates.

Kløve, H. (1963). Clinical neuropsychology. In: F. M. Forster, ed., *The Medical Clinics of North America*. New York: Saunders.

Lachar, D. (1975). Factor analysis of PIC scales. In: R. D. Wirt, D. Lachar, J. K. Klinedinst, and P. D. Seat, *Multidimensional Description of Child Personality. A Manual for the Personality Inventory for Children*. Los Angeles: Western Psychological Services.

Lyon, R., Stewart, N., and Freedman, D. (1982). Neuropsychological characteristics of empirically derived subgroups of learning disabled readers. *J. Clin. Neuropsychol., 4,* 343–365.

Morris, R., Blashfield, R., and Satz, P. (1981). Neuropsychology and cluster analysis: Potentials and problems. *J. Clin. Neuropsychol., 3,* 79–99.

Muehl, S., and Forrell, E. R. (1973). A follow-up study of disabled readers: Variables related to high school reading performance. *Reading Res. Quart., 9,* 110–123.

Neale, M. D. (1958). *Neale analysis of reading ability manual*. London: MacMillan.

Ozols, E. J., and Rourke, B. P. (1985). Dimensions of social sensitivity in two types of learning disabled children. In: B. P. Rourke, ed., *Neuropsychology of Learning Disibilities: Essentials of Subtype Analysis.*New York: Guilford.

Peter, B. M., and Spreen, O. (1979). Behavior rating and personal adjustment scales of neuropsychologically and learning handicapped children during adolescence and early adulthood: Results of a follow-up study. *J. Clin. Neuropsychol., 1*, 75–91.

Petrauskas, R., and Rourke, B. P. (1979). Identification of subgroups of retarded readers: A neuropsychological, multivariate approach. *J. Clin. Neuropsychol., 1*, 17–37.

Porter, J., and Rourke, B. P. (1984). Empirically derived personality subtypes of learning disabled children. In: B. P. Rourke, ed., *Learning Disabilities in Children: Advances in Subtype Analysis*. New York: Guilford.

Reitan, R. M., and Davison, L. A., eds. (1974). *Clinical Neuropsychology: Current Status and applications*. Washington, D.C.: V. H. Winston & Sons.

Rourke, B. P. (1975). Brain-behavior relationships in children with learning disabilities: A research program. *Am. Psychol., 30*, 911–920.

Rourke, B. P. (1976). Issues in the neuropsychological assessment of children with learning disabilities. *Canad. Psychol. Rev., 17*, 89–102.

Rourke, B. P. (1978a). Neuropsychological research in reading retardation: A review. In: A. L. Benton and D. Pearl, eds., *Dyslexia: An Appraisal of Current Knowledge*. New York: Oxford University Press.

Rourke, B. P. (1978b). Reading, spelling, arithmetic disabilities: A neuropsychologic perspective. In: H. R. Myklebust, ed., *Progress in Learning Disabilities*, vol. IV. New York: Grune & Stratton.

Rourke, B. P. (1981). Neuropsychological assessment of children with learning disabilities. In: S. B. Filskov and T. J. Boll, eds., *Handbook of Clinical Neuropsychology*. New York: Wiley-Interscience.

Rourke, B. P. (1982a). Central processing deficiencies in children: Toward a developmental neuropsychological model. *J. Clin. Neuropsychol., 4*, 1–18.

Rourke, B. P. (1982b). Child-clinical neuropsychology: Assessment and intervention with the disabled child. In: J. de Wit and A. L. Benton, eds., *Perspectives in Child Study: Integration of theory and Practice*. Lisse, The Netherlands: Swets & Zeitlinger.

Rourke, B. P. (1983). Reading and spelling disabilities: A developmental neuropsychological perspective. In: U. Kirk, ed., *Neuropsychology of Language, Reading, and Spelling*. New York: Academic Press.

Rourke, B. P., Bakker, D. J., Fisk, J. L., and Strang, J. D. (1983). *Child Neuropsychology.: An Introduction to Theory, Research, and Clinical Practice*. New York: Guilford.

Rourke, B. P., and Finlayson, M. A. J. (1978). Neuropsychological significance of variations in patterns of academic performance: Verbal and visual-spatial abilities. *J. Abnorm. Child Psychol., 6*, 121–133.

Rourke, B. P., and Fisk, J. L. (1981). Socio-emotional disturbances of learning disabled children: The role of central processing deficits. *Bull. Orton Soc., 31*, 77–88.

Rourke, B. P., and Gates, R. D. (1981). Neuropsychological research and school psychology. In: G. W. Hynd and J. E. Orbzut, eds., *Neuropsychological Assessment and the School-aged Child: Issues and Procedures*. New York: Grune & Stratton.

Rourke, B. P., and Orr, R. R. (1977). Prediction of the reading and spelling performances of normal and retarded readers: A four-year follow-up. *J. Abnorm. Child Psychol., 5*, 9–20.

Rourke, B. P., and Strang, J. D. (1978). Neuropsychological significance of variations in patterns of academic performance: Motor, psychomotor, and tactile-perceptual abilities. *J. Pediatr. Psychol., 3*, 62–66.

Rourke, B. P., and Strang, J. D. (1983). Subtypes of reading and arithmetical disabilities: A neuropsychological analysis. In M. Rutter, ed., *Developmental Neuropsychiatry*. New York: Guilford.

Satz, P., Taylor, H. G., Friel, J., and Fletcher, J. M. (1978). Some developmental and predictive precursors of reading disabilities: A six-year follow-up. In: A. L. Benton and D. Pearl, eds., *Dyslexia: An Appraisal of Current Knowledge*. New York: Oxford University Press.

Strang, J. D., and Rourke, B. P. (1983). Concept-formation/non-verbal reasoning abilities of children who exhibit specific academic problems with arithmetic. *J. Clin. Child Psychol.*, *12*, 33–39.

Strang, J. D., and Rourke, B. P. (1985a). Adaptive behavior of children with specific arithmetic disabilities and associated neuropsychological abilities and deficits. In: B. P. Rourke, ed., *Neuropsychology of Learning Disabilities: Essentials of Subtype Analysis.* New York: Guilford.

Strang, J. D., and Rourke, B. P. (1985b). Arithmetic disability subtypes. In: B. P. Rourke, ed., *Neuropsychology of Learning Disabilities: Essentials of Subtype Analysis.* New York: Guilford.

Strang, J. D., and Rourke, B. P. (in preparation). Personality correlates of children with learning disabilities.

Trites, R. L., and Fiedorowicz, C. (1976). Follow-up study of children with specific (or primary) reading disability. In: R. M. Knights and D. J. Bakker, eds., *The Neuropsychology of Learning Disorders: Theoretical Approaches.* Baltimore: University Park Press.

Wechsler, D. (1949). *Wechsler Intelligence Scale for Children.* New York: Psychological Corp.

Wirt, R. D., Lachar, D., Klinedinst, J. K., and Seat, P. D. (1977). *Multidimensional Description of Child Personality: A Manual for the Personality Inventory for Children.* Los Angeles: Western Psychological Services.

Yule, W., and Rutter, M. (1976). Epidemiology and social implications of specific reading retardation. In: R. M. Knights and D. J. Bakker, eds., *The Neuropsychology of Learning Disorders: Theoretical Approaches.* Baltimore: University Park Press.

12

The Neuropsychology of Memory Dysfunction and its Assessment

LARRY R. SQUIRE

Memory disorders merit separate attention in a volume on clinical neuropsychology because complaints about memory are very common, particularly among neurological and psychiatric patients. Among neurological patients with organic illness, memory problems are considered to be the most common initial complaint (Strub and Black, 1977). Among psychiatric patients, memory problems are commonly reported in association with affective disorder (Sternberg and Jarvik, 1976; Stromgren, 1977) and schizophrenia (Chapman, 1966, Chapter 8). Memory functions are also of special interest in cases of psychogenic amnesia (Nemiah, 1980), and in considerations of the possible side effects of treatments such as psychotropic drugs and electroconvulsive therapy (ECT).

Evaluation of memory disorders with quantitative methods makes it possible to identify the various disorders that can occur, to understand the similarities and differences between them, and to follow their course reliably in individual patients. Several books and articles have appeared in recent years that consider the subject of memory disorders and memory testing (Barbizet, 1970; Butters and Cermak, 1980; Erickson and Scott, 1977; Russell, 1981; Squire and Butters, 1984; Talland, 1965). The purpose of this chapter is to identify components of memory testing and to develop a rationale for the neuropsychological evaluation of memory functions.

Of the higher cortical functions (e.g., perception, language, memory, and action), memory is perhaps the most studied and the best understood. Although our understanding is still very primitive, there is optimism among neuroscientists that memory will be among the first of the higher brain functions to be explained—both at the cellular level, in terms of cellular events and synaptic change, and at the systems (or neuropsychological) level, in terms of brain regions and brain organization. Accordingly, when one turns to the topic of memory disorders from the perspective of clinical neuropsychology, one can bring to the subject a good deal of relevant information from cognitive psychology and the neurosciences about normal memory and how it is organized in the brain. Readers may wish to consult any of several recent reviews and monographs that address these issues (Cermak, 1982; Kandel, 1977; Klatzky, 1975; McGaugh, 1982; Lynch, McGaugh, and Weinberger, 1984; Mishkin, 1982; Norman, 1982; Squire, 1982a; Squire and Cohen, 1984; Squire and Davis, 1981; Thompson, Berger, and Madden, 1983; Weiskrantz, 1982).

Memory dysfunction most often occurs in association with other disorders of intellectual function, as in depression or dementia. If attention is impaired, acquisition of memory will be deficient. If language is impaired, it may be difficult to remember words or to call them to mind with the usual facility. In this sense, it might seem unfruitful, or even misleading, to speak about memory and memory disorders in isolation from other cognitive functions. However, there is an important reason for considering memory as a distinct neurological function. Disorders of memory can sometimes occur as a relatively pure entity. Although such disorders are rather uncommon, by studying them one can hope to recognize and understand memory disorders when they occur in a web of other disorders.

Functional Amnesia

Disorders of memory have many causes and can take many forms. A first step in their classification is to distinguish disorders of functional or psychogenic origin from disorders that result from a direct perturbation of brain function, i.e., from neurological injury or disease. Functional amnesias may be the best known, having been the subject of frequent treatment in films and literature. They are not nearly as common, however, as the so-called "organic" amnesias, and with proper testing these two general types of memory impairment are rather easy to distinguish.

A recently published case of functional amnesia is particularly instructive (Schacter et al., 1982). A 21-year-old man approached a policeman in downtown Toronto complaining of back pain. When brought to hospital, it was discovered that he did not know his own name or anything about his past, except for an isolated period 1 to 2 years earlier when he had worked for a courier service. He also gave a nickname Lumberjack (this was the pseudonym used in the published report to protect the patient's identity), but did not know how he had come by that name. During 4 days of testing in the hospital, he exhibited a good capacity for learning new material and in informal conversation he also demonstrated a continuing awareness of what had occurred since his admission.

On a formal test of remote memory using photographs of famous persons who had come into the news at different times in the past, he obtained a normal score. In contrast, his performance on a test of past autobiographical memory was quite abnormal. This test asked for recall of past personal events in response to cue words (Crovitz and Schiffman, 1974). For example, he was given the word "box" and asked to recall a specific episode from his past that involved a box. Only 14% of his recalled episodes were dated by him as having occurred more than 4 days earlier, prior to hospitalization. By contrast, 91% of the episodes recalled by a control subject came from more than 4 days earlier. In addition, when the patient's amnesia subsequently cleared, he was given a second form of the test and now dated 92% of his episodes from the period prior to hospitalization. Thus, during his period of amnesia, his past was nearly barren of personal memories; yet his store of general information about past public events was good.

On the fourth day in the hospital, while watching a climactic funeral scene in the television version of *Shogun,* his personal past began to return to him. The recent death of a favorite grandfather had provoked his memory loss. Lumberjack had been a nickname given him during his time at the courier service, which had been a particularly happy time of his life. In the end his past memory fully recovered, except for a 12-hour period preceding his hospital admission. This case illustrates the essential features of functional disorders of memory. There is often loss of personal identity. Anterograde amnesia (loss of new learning capacity) does not usually occur. Retrograde amnesia (loss of memory for events that occurred before the onset of amnesia) is extensive but it can be limited to autobiographical memory.

Amnesia Due to Neurological Injury or Disease

The "organic" amnesias have quite a different character. Amnesia can occur for a number of reasons (e.g., temporal lobe surgery, chronic alcohol abuse, head injury, hypotensive episode, encephalitis, epilepsy, tumor, or vascular accident). In addition, memory dysfunction is often a prominent and early sign of dementia, including Alzheimer's disease. Patients with memory dysfunction due to neurological injury or disease can appear normal to casual observation, even when the deficit is severe. These patients can have normal intelligence, as measured by conventional I.Q. tests, and normal ability to hold information in immediate memory, as measured by digit span tests. In conversation, they can exhibit appropriate social skills, have insight into their condition, and exhibit normal language ability.

The noted case H.M., for example, was able to detect various kinds of linguistic ambiguity [e.g., "Racing cars can be dangerous"; "Charging tigers should be avoided" (Lackner, 1974)]. In an often quoted passage, H.M. expresses his own experience of his memory disorder.

Right now, I'm wondering. Have I done or said anything amiss? You see, at this moment everything looks clear to me, but what happened just before? That's what worries me. It's like waking from a dream; I just don't remember. (Milner, 1970, p. 37)

Case N.A. also has clear and continuing insight into his condition. The failure of insight, or outright denial of illness, seems to occur for two reasons. First, when memory problems have a gradual onset, as with dementia or a slowly growing tumor, memory loss is often underappreciated. Second, when memory problems occur as part of a confused and disoriented state, as in acute conditions like Wernicke-Korsakoff syndrome, patients can be unaware of their memory impairment.

The Brain Regions Affected in Amnesia

It has been known for almost 100 years that amnesia depends on the disruption of normal function in one of two brain regions, the medial surface of the temporal lobes and the diencephalic midline of the brain. In the case of the medial temporal region, it has usually been supposed that amnesia depends on bilateral damage to the hippocampal formation, but the evidence on this point is by no means decisive. The idea that amnesia depends on hippocampal damage is based largely on a famous series of epileptic and psychotic patients. Some of these patients had sustained bilateral resection of amygdala and did not exhibit amnesia. Two others (including the well-known case H.M.), who sustained more radical excisions of both amygdala and hippocampus, developed profound amnesia (Scoville and Milner, 1957). Yet, it is also possible, based on the same evidence, to suppose that severe amnesia requires damage to both amygdala and hippocampus, and the findings of a series of studies with monkeys are consistent with this idea (Mishkin, 1978; Mishkin, 1982). Further studies of memory and amnesia in the monkey are needed to settle this issue and to evaluate the possible contribution of damage to the cortical tissue surrounding hippocampus and amygdala, which is necessarily damaged during surgery (cf. Mahut, Moss, and Zola-Morgan, 1981; Mahut, 1984; Murray and Mishkin, 1984; Squire and Zola-Morgan, 1983; Zola-Morgan, 1984; Zola-Morgan and Squire, *in press.*

In the case of diencephalic damage, a large body of neuropathological data has associated amnesia with damage to the mammillary bodies and to the dorsomedial thalamic nucleus (Brierley, 1977; Victor, Adams, and Collins, 1971; Mair, Warrington, and Weiskrantz, 1979). Damage to these structures is prominent in the neuropathology of the alcoholic Korsakoff syndrome, perhaps the best-studied example of amnesia, but there is disagreement as to whether separate damage to one structure or the other can cause amnesia, and disagreement as to which structure deserves the greater emphasis. The region of the left dorsomedial nucleus of the thalamus is damaged in case N.A. (Squire and Moore, 1979), a well-studied single case. N.A. became amnesic in 1960, primarily for verbal material, as the result of an accidental stab wound to the brain with a miniature fencing foil (Kaushall, Zetin, and Squire, 1981; Teuber, Milner, and Vaughan, 1968). In addition, individual cases of amnesia have been reported with vascular damage to the region of the dorsomedial nucleus due to occlusion of the paramedian artery (Michel et al., 1982; Mills and Swanson, 1978; Speedie and Heilman, 1982). Nevertheless, the relative importance of the dorsomedial nucleus and the mammillary bodies in amnesia is not yet clear. Studies with monkeys with circumscribed surgical lesions of these structures, alone and in combination, will be needed to address these issues in a decisive way (see Zola-Morgan and Squire, 1985).

Similarities and Differences among the Amnesias: A First Approximation

Korsakoff patients are sometimes taken as typical of amnesia in general, because this syndrome is the most thoroughly studied amnesic disorder. But the Korsakoff syndrome differs in several ways from other types of amnesia. For example, Talland (1965) wrote that the memory disorder in patients with Korsakoff's syndrome "does not present simply a derangement in memory" (p. 108), and Zangwill (1977) contended that

other and more extensive psychological dysfunction must co-exist with amnesia for the classic picture of Korsakoff's syndrome to emerge. (p. 113)

Some of these other deficits may derive from frontal lobe dysfunction. Neuropsychological signs of frontal lobe impairment are commonly present in these patients and can influence neuropsychological test performance (Moscovitch, 1982; Squire, 1982b).

It is also worth noting that the confabulation sometimes exhibited by Korsakoff patients is by no means a common feature of either amnesia in general or of the Korsakoff syndrome itself. Confabulation is the misstatement of fact, often in an amusing, bizarre, and self-contradictory way, which occurs as short-latency responses to questions (Mercer et al., 1977). Confabulation is seen most often in the acute phase of the disease, particularly in association with denial of illness, and is seen much less often in the chronic phase. Neuropsychological examination patients with memory dysfunction must take into account this idea that etiologically distinct forms of amnesia may present with particular deficits superimposed on amnesia. In addition, the nature of the disorder itself may depend to some extent on the locus of the effective lesions (Squire and Cohen, 1984).

Neuropsychological Assessment of Memory Dysfunction

Time-line Measurements: Anterograde and Retrograde Amnesia

Because many patients have insight into their conditions, one useful way to obtain information about memory loss is to construct a time-line of the deficit. This technique was used to good advantage by Barbizet (1970) as a way of identifying what past time periods were affected (Figure 1). This method can reveal in an approximate way the duration of both anterograde and retrograde amnesia, and can show how the deficit changes with the passage of time. In the case of Barbizet's patient, who had suffered a severe closed head injury, anterograde amnesia remained fixed at about 3½ months, even after memory capacities had largely recovered. This presumably occurred because

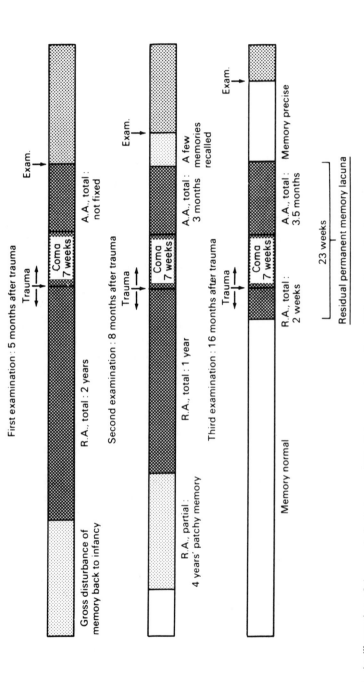

Fig. 1. An illustration of time periods that were difficult to remember at three different intervals after a severe head injury. (From Barbizet, 1970.)

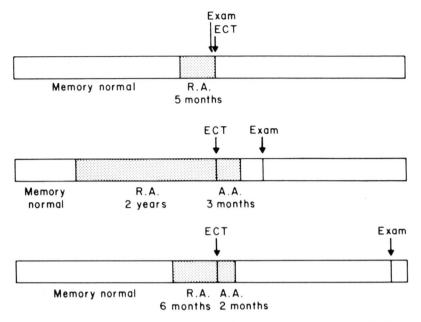

Fig. 2. Estimates of time periods that were difficult to remember obtained before *(top bar)*, 7 months after *(middle bar)*, and 3 years after *(bottom bar)* bilateral ECT (*N* = 31). Shaded areas represent the median time period perceived as affected both from the period before ECT (i.e., R.A., retrograde amnesia) and after ECT (i.e., A.A., anterograde amnesia). Since the first time estimate was obtained just prior to ECT *(top bar)*, the 5 months perceived as affected at that time presumably reflected memory problems associated with depressive illness. (From Squire and Slater, 1983.)

the anterograde amnesia reflected a time when memories could not be formed in the normal way. Accordingly, even though the capacity to form new memories eventually recovered, memories did not return for those events that had occurred during the period of anterograde amnesia. Retrograde amnesia was initially severe and extensive, but gradually shrank to 2 weeks. Oldest memories recovered first.

A similar relationship between anterograde and retrograde amnesia holds for psychiatric patients undergoing a prescribed course of bilateral ECT (Figure 2). Thirty-one patients were interviewed before, 7 months after, and 3 years after ECT. Before treatment, patients on average reported having difficulty remembering the 5 months prior to ECT, presumably because of their depressive illness. Seven months later, patients reported difficulty remembering events that occurred during the 3 months after treatment and during the 2 years preceding. Three years later, retrograde amnesia had shrunk to about the pre-ECT level, and anterograde amnesia remained fixed at 2 months (Squire and Slater, 1983).

The largest study of disorders of this type, which occur without penetration

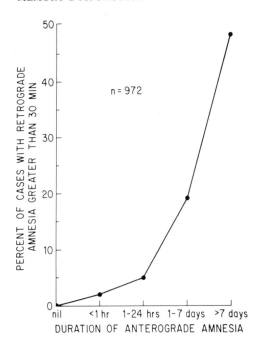

Fig. 3. The relationship between anterograde and retrograde amnesia in a large series of head injury patients. (Reconstructed from Russell and Nathan, 1946.)

of brain tissue, comes from the classic work of Russell and Nathan (1946) on traumatic amnesia. Their study of 1031 consecutive cases makes several points about the relationship between anterograde and retrograde amnesia. First, based on 972 of these cases where information was available about memory loss, retrograde amnesia was typically brief, covering a period of less than 30 minutes in 90% of the cases. Second, the longer the anterograde amnesia, the longer the retrograde amnesia (Figure 3). Third, retrograde amnesia was more severe in closed (concussive) head injury than in gunshot wounds or other cases of penetrating brain injury. Fourth, during the period of amnesia, neither the anterograde or retrograde component of memory loss could be infuenced significantly by hypnosis or barbiturate drugs.

Quantitative Measurement: Standardized Tests and Batteries

Though the time-line technique can be of considerable help in diagnosis and in obtaining a rough idea of the temporal dimensions of the memory deficit, it is of less help in judging the severity of the deficit because it provides no quantitative information. Formal tests are needed to obtain reliable quantitative data. Because of the rich tradition of basic research on problems of memory during the past few decades, many good tests are available.

One of the advantages of formal neuropsychological testing is that it permits one to compare objectively the scores of a given patient to a known group average. This protects us from a natural tendency to rationalize, minimize, or forget clinical observations when they do not conform to expectation. These tendencies are, of course, not confined to clinical observers. In his autobiography, Charles Darwin (1892) wrote:

I had also, during many years, followed a golden rule, namely, that whenever a published fact, a new observation or thought came across me, which was opposed to my general results, to make a memorandum of it without fail and at once; for I had found by experience that such facts and thoughts were far more likely to escape from the memory than favorable ones. (p. 42)

It is also true that we have been so influenced by literature and film to look for psychological explanations of behavior that, in the absence of formal neuropsychological testing, we often tend to develop psychological explanations for "organic" memory disorders. A few years ago, I received a letter from a woman telling me of her son's memory problems, which had resulted from a traumatic head injury sustained in an auto accident. Feeling that his memory problems seemed greater sometimes than others, she had said to him, "You only remember what you want to." Whereupon, he had replied, "Don't we all?" Her son was probably right. Persons with memory dysfunction, so long as it is not so severe as to be absolute, have the same tendencies that we all have to remember more reliably things that seem important, compared to things that seem trivial, and in general to exercise the same denial, repression, and selection that we all are heir to while learning or remembering. In amnesia these normal selective factors operate on an overall reduced retentive capacity.

The best known and most often used neuropsychological batteries provide for only limited testing of memory functions (Golden, Hammeke, and Purisch, 1980; Reitan and Davison, 1974). Further, the well-known Wechsler Memory Scale (WMS) (Wechsler, 1945) is inadequate to the task of detecting circumscribed memory problems, especially when they are mild. Twenty-four hours after the fifth treatment, patients receiving bilateral ECT were reliably impaired only on the paired-associate subtest of the WMS (Small, 1974), despite the fact that specialized tests of memory functions show clear defects at this time. In addition, because the WMS contains questions about contemporary facts (e.g., who is President? Governor of your State? Mayor of your City?), the WMS will yield lower scores for patients who have been amnesic for a long time than for patients who have become amnesic only recently. Russell (1975) has greatly improved the usefulness of the WMS by revising it to include delayed recall measures. Delayed recall tasks are critical to the task of bringing out an amnesic deficit, and they are discussed more fully below.

Another standardized battery, the N.Y.U. Memory Test (Randt, Brown, and Osbourne, 1980) was constructed specifically to detect memory dysfunction of the organic type. It contains delayed recall measures, a test of paired associate learning (see next section), and a sensitive test of incidental learning. This group of tests has been used extensively to evaluate memory in aging subjects (Osbourne, Brown, and Randt, 1982). Because five alternate forms are available, it can be used in longitudinal studies.

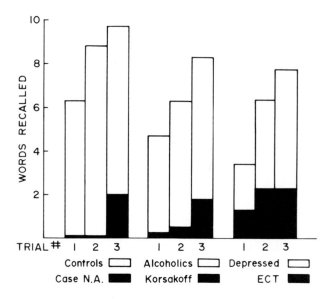

Fig. 4. Impairment in paired-associate learning by three kinds of amnesic patients and separate control groups: case N.A., patients with alcoholic Korsakoff syndrome, and patients receiving bilateral ECT. Subjects were presented with 10 noun–noun pairs on each of three trials. After each presentation they tried to recall the second word of each pair upon seeing the first word.

Those who prefer to use one of the popular, general purpose neuropsychological batteries could include an explicit test of memory dysfunction by adding a simple procedure at the conclusion of testing. Give the patient a test form that includes simple phrases describing several of the tests that he has taken, together with phrases describing bogus tests that were not taken. Ask the patient to indicate for each description whether he recognizes having taken such a test. The sensitivity of this recognition measure could be increased by (1) preceding it with a recall test, i.e., ask patients to describe by unaided recall the tests that they have taken; (2) following the recognition test with a request to place the descriptions of the subtests in their correct chronological order.

PAIRED ASSOCIATE LEARNING. Among tests specialized for the detection and quantification of memory dysfunction, perhaps the most sensitive is paired associate learning. Figure 4 shows the performance of three kinds of patients with memory problems who attempted to learn 10 noun–noun word pairs (e.g., army–table, door–sky). In this case, three consecutive presentations of the word pairs were given, and after each presentation subjects were asked to try to produce the second word of the pair upon hearing the first. Case N.A., patients with alcoholic Korsakoff syndrome, and psychiatric patients tested 1–2 hours after their fifth bilateral ECT all performed poorly on this test, obtaining an average score of less than 3 correct responses out of 10 on the third learning trial. Control subjects for each kind of patient performed much better. In this same test, case H.M. was unable to produce any correct responses after three trials, even when he was instructed in the use of imagery techniques for associating the words in each pair (Jones, 1974).

Though paired associate learning is a sensitive technique for detecting memory impairment, it is limited by the fact that poor performance could result from factors other than circumscribed memory loss, e.g., depression, inattention, or dementia. Accordingly, perhaps the greatest value of the test is to rule out memory impairment in persons who perform well. If performance is poor, then further tests are needed to interpret the poor score.

FREE RECALL AND REMINDING TECHNIQUES. Another useful single test, which can generate a good deal of information for individual subjects, is to assess the free recall of words using a method of selective reminding or restricted reminding (Buschke and Fuld, 1974). In both cases, 10 words from a single category, e.g., animal names, are presented and subjects are asked to recall as many of them as possible after each of several presentations. In selective reminding, each successive presentation of the list includes only words not recalled on the preceding trial. Trials continue until the subject succeeds in recalling all of the words on a single trial. In restricted reminding, each successive presentation of the list includes only words that have not been recalled on any trial. Trials continue until the subject has succeeded in recalling each word once. These techniques can yield useful data from single subjects regarding both their ability to acquire new information and their consistency of performance.

EXCEEDING IMMEDIATE MEMORY CAPACITY. The critical feature of both paired associate learning tasks and selective or restricted reminding tasks that accounts for their sensitivity to amnesia is that the information presented to the patient exceeds the immediate memory capacity. Even severely amnesic patients can have normal digit spans and a normal ability to report back the relatively small amount of information that can be maintained in "conscious awareness". William James (1890) termed this capacity "primary memory":

an object in primary memory . . . was never lost; its date was never cut off in consciousness from that of the immediately present moment. In fact it comes to us as belonging to the rearward portion of the present space of time, and not to the genuine past . . . Secondary memory, as it might be styled, is the knowledge of a former state of mind after it had already once dropped from consciousness . . . It is brought back, recalled, fished up, so to speak, from a reservoir in which, with countless other objects, it lay buried and lost from view. (pp. 646–648)

This concept of primary memory remains quite useful in understanding the nature of the memory impairment in amnesia. An interesting study of five amnesic patients, including the noted surgical case H.M. (Drachman and Arbit,

1966) illustrates this point in a formal way. Patients and control subjects were given digit strings of increasing length until an error occurred. An error was defined as failing three times in succession on three different digit strings of the same length. At that point a different string of digits of the same length was given repeatedly until it was reproduced correctly, or until 25 repetitions of the same digit string had been given. Each time a correct response was given, a new string of digits was presented that was one digit longer than the preceding string. With this procedure, normal subjects were able to increase their digit span to at least 20 digits. Amnesic patients, however, had great difficulty once their digit span capacity had been reached, i.e., at the digit string length when their first error had occurred. H.M. was unable, even after 25 repetitions of the same digit string, to increase his digit span by one digit beyond his premorbid level of six digits.

Thus for amnesic patients, performance on tests involving immediate recall depends on whether the amount of information to be remembered exceeds a finite processing capacity, termed "primary memory" or "immediate memory capacity". It is also true that memory performance will be poor, even when the amount of information to be remembered is within the limits of that capacity, whenever a delay filled with distraction is interposed between learning and retention testing in order to prevent active rehearsal. If the delay is very long, e.g., an hour or more, the natural distraction of ongoing activity is sufficient to prevent rehearsal and to reveal a deficit, if one is present. If the delay is short, e.g., seconds or minutes, a formal distraction procedure is needed to prevent rehearsal. The following observation of case H.M. makes this point.

Forgetting occurred the instant his focus of attention shifted, but in the absence of distraction his capacity for sustained attention was remarkable. Thus he was able to retain the number 584 for at least 15 minutes, by continuously working out mnemonic schemes. When asked how he had been able to retain the number for so long, he replied: "It's easy. You just remember 8. You see, 5, 8, and 4, add to 17. You remember 8, subtract it from 17 and it leaves 9. Divide 9 in half and you get 5 and 4, and there you are: 584. Easy." (Milner, 1970, p. 37)

The Importance of Delayed Recall Measures

With these considerations in mind, it is easy to understand that the hallmark of the organic amnesias is considered to be impaired performance on tests of delayed recall (with interpolated distraction). These tests form the cornerstone of any thorough neuropsychological assessment of memory functions. Tests of delayed recall are simply formal versions of the familial bedside examination used by neurologists. Typically, the names of three objects are presented to the patient with the instruction to repeat them in order to demonstrate comprehension and attention. Then after a delay of several minutes, which is filled with the continuing mental status examination, the patient is asked to recall the words. This informal method can be expanded to yield even more information by first asking patients at the time of recall how many words they had been asked to remember, by cueing them with synonyms or rhymes for any words that could not be produced in unaided recall, and finally by offering several words to patients and asking them to pick out the ones that had been presented earlier. Failure to recognize words as having been previously presented is a more reliable sign of memory disorder than failure to recall, and recognition failure denotes a more severe disorder as well. The use of recall and recognition tests together makes it possible to detect subtle, early signs of impairment.

Since in many medical settings, patients are tested repeatedly by different physicians and students, it would be useful if the number of words given for memorization were sometimes four, not always three, and of course the words themselves should be different on each test session. Patients with memory problems, like the rest of us, may forget unique events but still retain information about events that are repeated. This sometimes enables them to defeat the purpose of mental status examinations by rehearsing the answers. My colleague tells the story of encountering a neurological patient one day in the hospital outside a room where the patient was about to be presented at Rounds. As my colleague passed by, the patient approached him, asking anxiously, "Say, doc, who's the President of the United States?"

DELAYED RECALL OF PROSE MATERIAL. There are several formal neuropsychological tests of delayed recall that can be used to good advantage. One useful test of this kind uses connected prose, such as the logical memory subtest of the Wechsler Memory Scale, and asks patients to repeat back the story immediately after hearing it and then again after some delay (Milner, 1958). Figure 5 shows the performance of 15 patients prescribed bilateral ECT on a test of this type (not the Wechsler Memory Scale), using a delay of 24 hours. Both immediate and delayed recall were assessed before ECT and then again, with an alternate form, 6–10 hours after the fifth treatment of the series. ECT had no effect on immediate recall of the prose passage, and by this measure one might have supposed memory functions to be very good. Indeed, by 6–10 hours after the fifth treatment, patients can score normally on tests of verbal I.Q., show no signs of confusion or disorientation, and can carry on conversations in a normal and appropriate way. It is not uncommon at this time to hear comments from hospital staff not familiar with ECT that the patient's memory is all right or that the patient can remember what he/she wants to. Yet, delayed recall tests show that memory functions are not normal at this time. Whereas patients tested before their prescribed series of ECT showed considerable retention 24 hours after hearing the prose passage, only two of 15 patients could recall any part of the prose passage after ECT, and some could not remember having heard any passage or having seen the experimenter previously. Figure 5 also shows the performance of another group of subjects tested 6 to 9 months after the completion of treatment. The ability to learn and retain prose material has considerably recovered by this time after treatment.

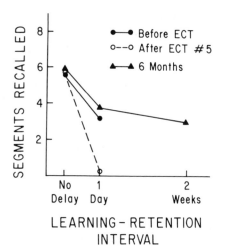

Fig. 5. Delayed recall of a short prose passage by 15 patients prescribed bilateral ECT. Testing occurred before treatment, 6–10 hours after the fifth treatment, and for a different group of 16 patients 6–9 months after bilateral treatment.

This pattern of deficit, i.e., impaired recall at a delayed test but not at an immediate test, helps to distinguish the so-called "organic" memory disorders from memory disorders due to depression. Indeed, delayed recall tests are sensitive measures of neurological dysfunction and can detect early signs of progressive impairment. By contrast, depression affects immediate memory, presumably because patients are preoccupied or inattentive, but does not affect delayed recall beyond what would be expected from the level of recall achieved at immediate testing (Cronholm and Ottoson, 1961; Sternberg and Jarvik, 1976).

MATERIAL-SPECIFIC MEMORY DYSFUNCTION AND ITS ASSESSMENT. In addition to addressing the issue of severity, neuropsychological testing of memory must also address the fact that memory dysfunction can be different, depending on whether the neurological injury or disease is bilateral, or whether it affects structures in the left or right cerebral hemisphere. The effect on memory follows from the asymmetry of hemispheric function with respect to language: verbal impairment from left-sided damage, nonverbal impairment from right-sided damage, "global" impairment from bilateral damage. This point has been best demonstrated in the thorough work of Brenda Milner on temporal lobe function (Milner, 1958, 1971). Patients with left medial temporal lobe resections complain, for example, that they cannot remember what they have read and they do poorly on verbal memory tests. Delayed recall tests of short prose passages, as just described, are useful in bringing out this deficit. Patients who have sustained right medial temporal lobe resections complain, for example, that they do not remember where they have put things, and they do poorly on tests of memory for faces, spatial relationships, and other things that are not ordinarily encoded in words.

These disorders of memory, which arise from unilateral brain injury or disease, were termed material-specific disorders (Milner, 1968a) to signify that the side of the brain affected determines the kind of material that is difficult to learn and remember. The sensory modality through which material is learned (e.g., auditory, visual, or tactile) is ordinarily not important. For example, in the case of left medial temporal injury, a short prose passage will be difficult to remember regardless of whether the patient reads the story or hears it read. These material-specific effects have been demonstrated for left or right temporal lobe surgical lesions (Milner, 1971); epileptic foci of the left or right temporal lobe (Delaney, Rosen, Mattson, and Novelly, 1980); left or right unilateral ECT (in which the two electrodes are applied to the same side of the head, in contrast to bilateral ECT in which one electrode is applied to each temple)(Squire, 1982c); unilateral diencephalic lesions (Michel, et al., 1982; Speedie and Heilman, 1982; Squire and Slater, 1978; Teuber, Milner, and Vaughan, 1968); and unilateral diencephalic brain stimulation (Ojemann, 1971).

Ross (1980a, 1980b) has described five patients with medial temporal dysfunction who provided evidence for the existence of "fractional", modality-specific memory disorders. The deficit affected the tactile or visual modality and in three of the five cases did not affect memory functions in other modalities. In addition, three patients with acute unilateral lesions of the medial temporal region were reported to have "tactile recent memory loss" for stimuli applied to the hand opposite the lesion, but not for stimuli applied to the ipsilateral hand. These observations raise the possibility that left or right medial temporal lesions need not always cause equally severe deficits in all modalities, as has been believed traditionally. Moreover, even deficits following unilateral lesions that affect all modalities might sometimes be more severe when information is presented to the visual field or body half contralateral to the lesion. Additional systematic comparisons of modality (e.g., visual vs. auditory vs. tactile), side of presentation (left vs. right), and kind of material (verbal vs. nonverbal) are needed before the relative importance of all three factors can be appreciated.

DELAYED RECALL OF NONVERBAL MATERIAL. Of the tests that have been used to assess delayed recall of nonverbal material, perhaps the best known is the Rey-Osterreith figure (Fig. 6). The subject is asked to copy the figure and then after a delay is asked to reconstruct it from memory without forewarning. An immediate test of reconstruction can be used as well. Milner and her colleagues have developed an alternate form for this figure and a standardized 36-point scoring system for both figures (Milner and Teuber, 1968). Another method for testing delayed recall of nonverbal memory, suggested by Russell (1975), is to use the figures from the Wechsler Memory Scale. The ability to reconstruct these figures is tested in the normal way, immediately after presentation, and again 30 minutes later. When patients have constructive deficits or other problems that preclude using memory tests that involve drawing, then other tests can be used, e.g., recognition after a delay of previously presented faces (Milner, 1968b) recollection of the position of a dot on an 8-inch hori-

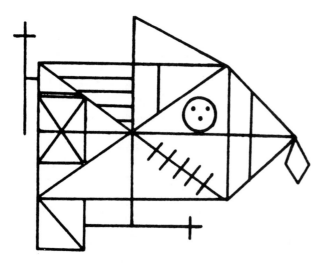

Fig. 6. The Rey-Osterreith figure, used to assess delayed recall of nonverbal material. (From Osterreith, 1944; also see Milner and Teuber, 1968.)

zontal line (Milner, 1973), or recognition by touch of wire shapes or other objects that are not easily remembered by verbal labels (Milner and Teuber, 1968).

PRESERVED LEARNING. Although the deficit exhibited by amnesic patients with bilateral brain damage has often been described as global, as if it affects the learning and memory of any or all material, it is now clear that the memory impairment in fact is quite selective. Perceptuo-motor skills, such as the eye–hand coordination skills involved in certain tracking tasks and in mirror-drawing can be acquired by amnesic patients (Corkin, 1968; Milner, 1962). Acquisition of such skills can occur at a normal rate over a period of days, though patients may deny having worked at the task before. More recently this observation has been extended to cognitive skills, like mirror-reading and the solutions to certain puzzles (Cohen and Corkin, 1981; Cohen and Squire, 1980).

Figure 7 shows the Tower of Hanoi problem, which has been studied extensively by cognitive psychologists (Anzai and Simon, 1979). The task is to move the five blocks to the right-most peg, observing two rules: move one block

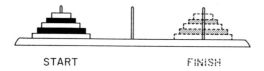

START   FINISH

Fig. 7. The Tower of Hanoi puzzle used to demonstrate intact skill learning in amnesic patients (Cohen and Corkin, 1981). Subjects must move all five blocks from A to C, but must move one block at a time without ever placing a larger block on a small one. The puzzle can be solved in 31 moves.

at a time and never put a larger block on a smaller one. The puzzle can eventually be solved in a minimum of 31 moves. When given multiple opportunities to solve the puzzle on different days, case H.M. reduced progressively the number of moves needed to attain the solution, and eventually was able to solve the task in 31 moves (Cohen and Corkin, 1981). At no time did H.M. recognize that he had worked on the problem previously. These observations have suggested a distinction between information based on skills or procedures (procedural knowledge), which is intact in amnesia, and information based on facts or data (declarative knowledge), which is impaired.

The capacity for acquiring skills apparently does not require the integrity of the medial temporal or diencephalic brain regions damaged in amnesia, whereas the capacity to acquire facts about the world, e.g., the ability to recognize the words that have been read in a mirror-reading task, appears to depend on the integrity of these brain regions. These ideas have been developed in more detail elsewhere, with the suggestion that the nervous system honors the distinction between two different kinds of memory systems (Cohen, 1981; Cohen, 1984; Squire, 1982a; Squire and Cohen, 1984).

This idea is reminiscent of other classical distinctions concerning the representation of knowledge (e.g., knowing-how vs. knowing-that when [Ryle, 1949], and procedural vs. declarative knowledge [Winograd, 1975]). These distinctions seem to capture the difference between what amnesic patients can and cannot do, as we presently understand them. Other terminologies have also been suggested, based on findings that amnesic patients (or experimental animals with presumably similar lesions) can successfully accomplish some kinds of learning and memory, but not other kinds: conscious recollection vs. skills (Moscovitch, 1982), memory vs. habits (Mishkin, 1984), mediational vs. semantic memory (Warrington and Weiskrantz, 1982), episodic vs. semantic memory (Kinsbourne and Wood, 1975), taxon vs. locale (O'Keefe and Nadel, 1978); reference vs. working memory (Olton, Becker, and Handelmann, 1979), vertical vs. horizontal associative memory (Wickelgren, 1979). Whatever language is used, there now seems to be good reason to suppose that there is more than one kind of memory. The notion of two (or more) kinds of memory or memory systems has interesting implications for a variety of issues, such as infantile amnesia, phylogeny of memory, and psychoanalytic theory (Nadel and Zola-Morgan, 1984; Schacter and Moscovitch, 1984; Squire, in press).

Recent work with amnesic patients suggests that the domain of learning and memory that is spared includes not only skills but also classical conditioning (Weiskrantz and Warrington, 1979) and what have been termed repetition effects (Warrington and Weiskrantz, 1982), priming effects (Graf, Squire, and Mandler, 1984) or perceptual fluency (Jacoby, 1982). It has been suggested (Cohen, 1984; Squire and Cohen, 1984) that what is spared in amnesia depends on changes in already existing knowledge structures, changes that influence performance in an unconscious way without affording access to previous events. By contrast, the domain of learning and memory that is affected in amnesia appears to provide additional information, i.e., directly accessible information about individual events, then time and place of occurrence, facts about the world derived from the events, and the awareness and sense of familiarity that a particular event has previously occurred.

Preserved learning should be demonstrable in amnesic patients to the extent that amnesia occurs relatively free from other cognitive deficits. For example, the presence of frontal lobe signs, a common feature of Korsakoff syndrome, or the presence of dementing illness may interfere with the capacity for skill learning. It remains to be seen whether the preserved capacity for learning and memory in amnesic patients has any implications for rehabilitation.

ASSESSMENT OF REMOTE MEMORY. One of the striking features of amnesia is that it commonly involves some loss of information for events that occurred before the onset of amnesia. Before considering the retrograde aspect of memory dysfunction, it is important to note that in memory disorders that have a gradual onset the distinction between anterograde and retrograde amnesia is blurred. It is not always possible to determine if information has been 'lost' because it was not acquired in the first place, or if information has been lost because it was first acquired and then later lost as the result of the onset of amnesia.

Several techniques have been developed to assess memory for remote events in a formal quantitative way. When amnesia has a very recent onset, or a known time of onset, one can know which test questions access retrograde amnesia. Of the tests available for clinical neuropsychological testing, most ask for information about public events that occurred at specified times in the past. This insures that the information is verifiable and accessible to all subjects. The first remote memory tests to explore the nature of memory disorders in amnesic patients consisted of multiple-choice questions about persons or events that had been in the news in Great Britain, or faces of famous people who had been prominent in Great Britain at different times in the past (Sanders and Warrington, 1970). By asking questions that covered the past several decades, it was possible to obtain a sampling of an individual's knowledge of past events. Subsequently, similar tests based on public events or famous faces were developed for use in the United States (Albert, Butters, and Levin, 1979; Seltzer and Benson, 1975; Squire, 1974). In addition to multiple-choice techniques, these tests can all be given in a free-recall format prior to recognition testing, and many of them can be given in a "detailed-recall" format, in which subjects are asked to tell all they can about a previous event (Cohen and Squire, 1981; Squire and Cohen, 1982). In this case, the responses are recorded, transcribed, and then scored for number of details produced.

Another remote memory test that has found useful application in the study of memory disorders is a test of former one-season television programs (Squire and Fox, 1980; Squire and Slater, 1975). It was designed to overcome an important limitation of all other available remote memory tests, i.e., the difficulty of comparing scores from different past time periods. To make valid comparisons across time periods, the items selected must satisfy the criterion

Fig. 8. Items from the Famous Faces Test of the Boston Retrograde Amnesia Battery (Albert et al., 1979). Top row, from left to right: John L. Lewis (1930s), Fulton Sheen (1940s), Joe McCarthy (1950s). Bottom row: Jimmy Hoffa (1960s), H.R. Haldeman (1970s).

of equivalence, i.e., they must sample past time periods in an equivalent way so that the events from different time periods are likely to have been learned about to the same extent and then forgotten at similar rates. The television test appears to satisfy this criterion, as demonstrated by tests with updated versions of the test during a 7-year period (Squire and Fox, 1980).

Remote memory tests cannot be assumed to satisfy the criterion of equivalence just because normal subjects obtain the same score (e.g., 75% correct) across all time periods sampled by the test. As discussed in detail elsewhere (Squire and Cohen, 1982), it is possible that the events selected from more remote time periods were initially more salient and more widely known than the events selected from more recent time periods. In addition, the events from more remote periods could have been forgotten more slowly. Accordingly, findings from patients taking these tests will necessarily be ambiguous, to the extent that the point of testing is to compare performance across time periods.

These issues notwithstanding, all the remote memory tests have some useful application to the quantitative examination of memory disorders. As with any neurological instrument, the appropriateness of these tests depends on the particular question being asked. Thus, the television test, though advantageous in some respects, is limited by the relatively short time span that it can reliably cover (about 20 years), and by the fact that it yields variable results when used clinically to explore the memory capacity of a single patient. Indeed, many of the tests available for assessing memory, including the TV test, were originally designed to investigate specific research questions in groups of patients, and they are not always as useful when trying to understand the nature of an individual patient's memory impairment. For this reason it is advisable to use several different tests when studying a single patient.

An important general point about remote memory tests for public events is the issue of test sensitivity. Unfortunately, multiple-choice tests and recall tests that ask for a single word or phrase do not appear to be sufficiently sensitive to rule out definitively the presence of remote memory impairment. Case N.A., who has a circumscribed diencephalic lesion involving the region of the left dorsomedial thalamic nucleus, performed six such tests normally but was impaired on two tests that assessed his detailed recall for past events (Cohen and Squire, 1981; Zola-Morgan et al., 1983). Until detailed recall tests are given to other patients with dorsomedial thalamic damage, the status of retrograde amnesia in this group remains uncertain. Despite these uncertainties about patients with focal diencephalic lesions, remote memory tests have been useful in characterizing and differentiating clinical groups (Butters and Albert, 1982; Cohen and Squire, 1981).

All the remote memory tests just described share the advantage of being based on verifiable and publicly accessible information. A final remote memory test should be mentioned here that does not have this feature, but that nevertheless can be of considerable value in the neuropsychological assessment of memory disorders. It derives from early quantitative studies by Galton (1879) and was recently modified and applied to the study of memory by Crovitz (Crovitz and Schiffman, 1974). The test is designed to obtain autobiographical remote memory about specific past episodes of a patient's life. Patients are given standard cue words (e.g., window, tree, ticket, bird) and are asked in each case to recall a specific memory from the past that involves the word. Various scoring procedures can be used, a 0 or 1 method that can be done during the testing session, or a 0 to 3 method, where the responses are recorded, then later transcribed and then scored according to some predetermined system of partial credits. After recalling a memory for a given cue word, subjects are asked to date the memory as best they can. This test can provide useful information about the quality and quantity of recalled information, as well as vital information about the time periods from which recall is possible. Even amnesic patients who obtain normal scores for recall may draw their memories from different time periods than normal subjects. This was true in the case of the patient with functional amnesia, described above, who atypically drew most of his memories from the immediately preceding four days— after the onset of his amnesic disturbance (Schacter et al., 1982). Patients with alcoholic Korsakoff syndrome, though they could obtain normal or near normal scores on the recall test, drew their memories from 10 years earlier than their alcoholic control subjects (Zola-Morgan et al., 1983).

The material obtained in an autobiographical test, of course, is not easily corroborated. One way to check against outright fabrication is to ask subjects

Table 1. Self-rating scale of memory functions

	(−4 to +4)
1. My ability to search through my mind and recall names or memories I know are there is	——
2. I think my relatives and acquaintances now judge my memory to be	——
3. My ability to recall things when I really try is	——
4. My ability to hold in my memory things that I have learned is	——
5. If I were asked about it a month from now, my ability to remember facts about this form I am filling out would be	——
6. The tendency for a past memory to be "on the tip of my tongue," but not available to me is	——
7. My ability to recall things that happened a long time age is	——
8. My ability to remember the names and faces of people I meet is	——
9. My ability to remember what I was doing after I have taken my mind off it for a few minutes is	——
10. My ability now to remember things that have happened more than a year ago is	——
11. My ability to remember what I read and what I watch on television is	——
12. My ability to recall things that happened during my childhood is	——
13. My ability to know when the things I am paying attention to are going to stick in my memory is	——
14. My ability to make sense out of what people explain to me is	——
15. My ability to reach back in my memory and recall what happened a few minutes ago is	———
16. My ability to pay attention to what goes on around me is	——
17. My general alertness to things happening around me is	——
18. My ability to follow what people are saying is	——

a second time, some time after initial testing, to date the memories they had recalled (Schacter et al., 1982). This procedure typically yields close agreement between the dates produced in the two sessions.

SELF-RATINGS OF MEMORY. This chapter began by pointing out how much can be learned about memory disorders by constructing a time-line of the disorder, based in part on what patients themselves report about their impairment. This section shows how quantitative and qualitative information can be obtained with formal tests, which take advantage of patients' own sense of their memory problems. Of course, self-reports of memory function can be misleading. For example, in depressed elderly patients memory complaints appeared to be related more to depression than to performance on memory tests (Kahn et al., 1975). Conversely, patients receiving ECT who were clinically improved often denied memory impairment despite the fact that memory impairment could be documented by formal tests (Cronholm and Ottoson, 1963). Nevertheless, correlations between memory self-ratings and objective measures of performance can be demonstrated (Baddeley, Sunderland, and Harris, 1982; Zelinski, Gilewski, and Thompson, 1980).

Table 1 shows an 18-item self-rating scale that has been used with patients

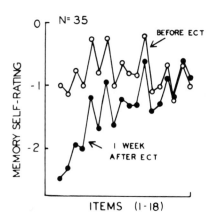

Fig. 9. Memory self-ratings before and 1 week after a course of bilateral ECT. Items have been ordered from the one yielding the largest before–after difference (item 1 to left) to the one yielding the smallest difference (item 18 to right). The results show that ECT both increased memory complaints and changed their character. The test items (1–18) are shown in Table 1. (From Squire, Wetzel, and Slater, 1979.)

receiving ECT (Squire, Wetzel, and Slater, 1979). This scale takes advantage of the fact that memory problems due to depression are different from memory problems due to amnesia (Cronholm and Ottoson, 1961). The former impairs immediate recall but has no special effect on delayed recall. The latter impairs delayed recall, but has little or no effect on immediate recall—especially if the amount of material to be remembered is small and can be held in immediate memory (see earlier discussion of delayed recall of prose material). The scale was designed with the idea that patients might reflect this difference in their own assessments of their memory abilities. Patients given the scale were asked to rate each item from −4 (worse than ever before) through zero (same as before) to +4 (better than ever before).

Figure 9 shows the findings for 35 patients prescribed bilateral ECT who were tested before and one week after treatment (mean = 11.1 treatments, range = 5–21). Before ECT, memory self-ratings were below the zero level, and parallel to the horizontal axis. Thus depression itself, for which ECT had been prescribed, impairs patients' self-ratings of memory to a measurable degree and to an equivalent extent across all items. One week after ECT, overall self-ratings were worse than before ECT, but now some items were rated worse than others. That is, the profiles of self-ratings obtained before and after ECT were different, indicating that ECT changed the patients' own experience of memory functions. Whereas reports of poor memory before ECT can probably be attributed to depression, we suppose that after ECT reports of poor memory are influenced largely by the amnesic effects of the treatment.

This finding makes it possible to study patients long after ECT and to ask whether persisting complaints about memory functions are influenced by depression or by amnesia. The results shown in Fig. 10, for the same 35 patients, answer this question. First, self-ratings of memory functions have improved between 1 week and 7 months after the completion of treatment, corresponding to the findings from objective tests given at these times (Price, 1982; Squire, 1982c). Second, self-ratings retain the form that they had 1 week after

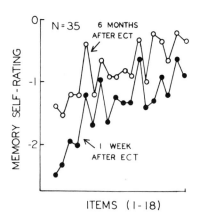

Fig. 10. Memory self-ratings 1 week after and 7 months after bilateral ECT. Items are arranged as in Fig. 9. The results show that passage of time diminished the severity of memory complaints, but did not alter the pattern observed 1 week after ECT. (From Squire, Wetzel, and Slater, 1979.)

ECT, when patients were amnesic, and they differ from the form before ECT, when patients were depressed. These findings suggest that persisting memory complaints long after ECT reflect an experience of amnesia rather than an experience of depression, or some other condition that was present both before and after ECT. In an additional followup of these same patients 3 years later (Squire and Slater, 1983), self-ratings remained about the same as they were at 6 months after ECT. It was suggested that the experience of memory impairment is in part veridical, insofar as it is related to the gap in memory that patients experience for events that occurred close to the time of treatment, and in part related to a natural tendency to attribute normal memory problems to the ECT experience. So far, formal memory testing in patients 6 months or more after ECT has not provided any evidence for a permanent impairment in new learning capacity following a typical course of ECT (i.e., 6 to 12 treatments) (Price, 1982; Squire, 1982a; Weeks, Freeman, and Kendell, 1980).

Self-rating scales could be useful in a variety of settings where there is interest in understanding memory complaints and relating them to objective test performance. For example, they might be useful in distinguishing depression in the elderly from incipient brain disease. In addition, they could be of use in assessing patients with memory disorders who are given pharmacological treatments to improve their memory functions. Some of these treatments might work in part by improving mood, rather than by affecting memory mechanisms directly, and such effects might be teased apart by self-rating scales.

Head Injury and Dementia

Memory dysfunction is commonly encountered by the clinical neuropsychologist in cases of traumatic head injury and cases of dementia, especially Alzheimer's disease. In both circumstances, memory loss occurs in a constellation of other disorders. The specific testing of memory functions, however, can follow the same guidelines that have been developed here for more circumscribed disorders.

The neuropsychology of head injury has been reviewed thoroughly (Newcombe, 1983; Levin, Benton, and Grossman, 1982). Though memory dysfunction may be the most ubiquitous sign of closed head injury, it commonly occurs together with a reduction in general intellectual capacity, disorders of language and visual perception, apraxias, impairment of attention, and personality change. These multiple disorders are consistent with the variable and widespread pattern of cerebral damage that can result from severe head injury.

Whereas the great majority of patients admitted to hospitals with a head injury eventually make a good recovery, Newcombe (1983) notes that perhaps 1% have persisting signs of impairment. This impairment is now recognized in most cases to have a neurological basis, not a functional basis (e.g., compensation neurosis) as once believed. The neuropsychologist must address questions about the severity and nature of the deficit, the predicted rate of recovery, as well as questions about possible rehabilitation.

The memory deficits themselves have been carefully reviewed by Schacter and Crovitz (1977). Interestingly, tests of immediate and delayed prose recall, considered above, correlate better with judgments by relatives of a patient's memory abilities than do other formal laboratory tests of memory (Baddeley et al., 1981). In addition to specialized memory tests, assessment might be facilitated by the use of one or more scales that have been developed especially for head-injured patients (Jennett et al., 1981; Teasdale and Jennett, 1974). The Galveston Orientation and Amnesia Test (Levin, O'Donnell, and Grossman, 1979) can be used repeatedly and yields estimates of retrograde amnesia and of the duration of post-traumatic amnesia. The duration of post-traumatic amnesia is the best available index of severity of injury and is a good predictor of recovery (Jennett, 1976).

In general, techniques that improve memory functions in normal subjects can be expected to improve memory functions in head injury patients (and other amnesic patients as well). Accordingly, the techniques most often mentioned in the context of rehabilitation or retraining are elaborate note-keeping, imagery, and rehearsal. Imagery may be of special value in working with patients with memory impairment due to left hemispheric dysfunction (Patten, 1972). However, for a balanced perspective on the difficulties of making simple generalizations about rehabilitation, see Newcombe (1983).

Dementia is estimated to affect 4%–5% of the population over 65 years of age. Alzheimer's disease, the most common form of dementia, accounts for at least 50% of the cases (Katzman, 1976; Terry and Davies, 1980). Memory problems are perhaps the most common and often the earliest sign of the disease, but disorders of language (especially anomia) and visuo-spatial disorders can also occur early. The disease is progressive, eventually involving most or all intellectual functions. It typically develops over a period of 5–10 years. At present, the diagnosis of Alzheimer's disease cannot be made definitively without neuropathological data. A primary question for the neuropsychologist, then, is to what extent the disease can be detected early and differentiated from the benign forgetfulness of normal aging (Kral, 1978), from depression or pseudodementia (McAllister, 1983; Wells, 1979), and from other sometimes treatable forms of dementia.

There is insufficient information to identify Alzheimer's disease in a consistent way on the basis of neuropsychological data, but progress is being made (for recent reviews, see Fuld, 1978; Kaplan, 1979; Miller, 1981; Corkin et al., 1982). In many respects, the memory loss exhibited by patients diagnosed as having Alzheimer's disease seems to resemble the memory loss exhibited by patients with more circumscribed amnesias. This conclusion is consistent with the finding that neuropathological changes in Alzheimer's disease are prominent in the medial temporal region (Corsellis, 1970), Hyman, et al., 1984). However, two features of memory dysfunction in Alzheimer's disease have been identified that are not observed in the circumscribed amnesias. First, patients with even mild Alzheimer's disease have impaired digit span scores, whereas amnesic patients are usually normal at digit span tasks (Corkin, 1982). Second, patients with Alzheimer's disease have been reported to exhibit an extensive deficit in remote memory without any sign of temporal gradient (Wilson, Kaszniak, and Fox, 1981). With additional work, it should be possible to determine, the typical sequence of the disease, what brain regions become affected at particular times, and to what extent good memory testing can succeed at making early diagnoses.

A Recommended Selection of Memory Tests

The preceding sections considered some of the issues involved in undertaking a clinical neuropsychological evaluation of memory functions. Specialized techniques are available for assessing memory dysfunction, and they can be used to distinguish functional from "organic" disorders, to identify material-specific disorders, to assess both anterograde and retrograde amnesia, to assess skill learning, and to explore patients' self-reports of memory functions. Table 2 lists a minimal selection of tests that should serve most clinical needs. More than one test of each type can be used if the findings in any one area are ambiguous. Additional tests can be used as needed, once the clinician becomes familiar with the status of the patient's memory functions.

Neuropsychological testing of memory is most informative when memory tests are supplemented with some additional tests. Additional tests can establish valuable reference points that help in interpreting memory test scores. They can also identify or rule out other kinds of impairment, which if present would influence memory test scores. The Wechsler Adult Intelligence Scale is probably the most helpful, since it can define the general test-taking ability of the patient and, in conjunction with the Wechsler Memory Scale, give a rough in-

Table 2. A recommended selection of tests for the neuropsychological assessment of memory

---

1. Construction of Time-line (Barbizet, 1970; Squire and Slater, 1983)
2. Immediate recall of prose passage (Milner, 1958)
3. Copy of Rey-Osterreith figure (Milner and Teuber, 1968)
4. Paired associate learning (Jones, 1974)
5. Delayed recall of prose passage
6. Delayed reconstruction of Rey-Osterreith figure
7. Remote memory for famous faces (Albert, Butters, and Levin, 1979)
8. Cued recall of autobiographical memory (Crovitz and Schiffman, 1974)
9. Self-rating scale (Squire, Wetzel, and Slater, 1979)

---

dication of whether or not memory problems are present. A naming test (Goodglass and Kaplan, 1972) can also be valuable, because patients with anomia will perform poorly on some memory tests (e.g., recall tests of remote memory). Anomia is not always detectable by casual bedside examination. A formal quantitative method, which includes many low-frequency object names (protractor, trellis, paddle) will often reveal impairment that is missed by a briefer, more casual exam. Finally, tests of frontal lobe function are often helpful, since frontal lobe dysfunction can influence scores on many memory tests (Moscovitch, 1982; Squire, 1982b).

Conclusion

Having considered the available methods for testing memory, and various clinical settings where these methods can be usefully applied, it is worth noting that much of this progress has become possible because of basic research. An enormous amount has been learned in recent years about how the brain accomplishes memory storage, and an inventory of memory tests has been one of the fruits of this enterprise.

The neuropsychological study of memory is part of a broader program of research aimed at understanding the biology of memory at all levels of analysis—from cellular and synaptic events to the whole behavior of complex animals like man. It seems certain that a broad, basic research approach to problems of memory and the brain will continue to inform us about mechanism and organization, and at the same time will produce improved methods for neuropsychological assessment of patients with memory dysfunction. Ultimately, perhaps, these same research efforts may result in methods for the treatment of memory dysfunction.

REFERENCES

Albert, M. S., Butters, N., and Levin, J. (1979). Temporal gradients in the retrograde amnesia of patients with alcoholic Korsakoff's disease. *Arch. Neurol., 36,* 211–216.

Anzai, Y., and Simon, H. A. (1979). The theory of learning by doing. *Psychol. Rev., 86,* 124–140.

Baddeley, A., Sunderland, A., and Harris, J. (1982). How well do laboratory-based psychological tests predict patients' performance outside the laboratory? In: S. Corkin, K. L. Davis, J. H. Growden, E. Usdin, and R. J. Wurtman, eds., *Alzheimer's Disease: A Report of Progress in Research,* New York: Raven Press, pp. 141–148.

Barbizet, J. (1970). *Human Memory and Its Pathology.* San Francisco: W. H. Freeman and Company.

Brierley, J. B. (1977). Neuropathology of amnesic states. In: C. W. M. Whitty and O. L. Zangwill, eds., *Amnesia,* 2d ed. London: Buttersworths, pp. 199–223.

Buschke, H. and Fuld, P. A. (1974). Evaluating storage, retention, and retrieval in disordered memory and learning. *Neurology, 24,* 1019–1025.

Butters, N., and Albert, M. (1982). Processes underlying failures to recall remote events. In: L. Cermak, ed., *Human Memory and Amnesia.* Hillsdale, New Jersey: Lawrence Erlbaum, pp. 257–273.

Butters, N., and Cermak, L. S. (1980). *Alcoholic Korsakoff's Syndrome: An Information Processing Approach to Amnesia.* New York: Academic Press.

Cermak, L. S., ed. (1982). *Human Memory and Amnesia.* Hillsdale, New Jersey: Lawrence Erlbaum.

Chapman, J. (1966). The early symptoms of schizophrenia. *Br. J. Psychiat., 112,* 225–251.

Cohen, N. J. (1981). Neuropsychological evidence for a distinction between procedural and declarative knowledge in human memory and amnesia. Unpublished doctoral dissertation, University of California, San Diego.

Cohen, N. J. (1984) Preserved learning capacity in amnesia: Evidence for multiple memory systems. In: L. R. Squire and N. Butters, eds. *Neuropsychology of Memory.* New York: Guilford Press, pp. 83–103.

Cohen, N. J., and Corkin, S. (1981). The amnesic patient H. M.: Learning and retention of a cognitive skill. *Soc. Neurosci. Abstr., 7,* 235.

Cohen, N. J., and Squire, L. R. (1980). Preserved learning and retention of pattern-analyzing skill in amnesia: Dissociation of knowing how and knowing that. *Science, 210,* 207–210.

Cohen, N. J., and Squire, L. R. (1981). Retrograde amnesia and remote memory impairment. *Neuropsychologia, 19,* 337–356.

Corkin, S. (1968). Acquisition of motor skill after bilateral medial temporal lobe excision. *Neuropsychologia, 6,* 255–265.

Corkin, S. (1982). Some relationships between global amnesias and the memory impairments in Alzheimer's disease. In: S. Corkin, K. L. Davis, J. H. Growdon, E. Usdin, and R. J. Wurtman, eds., *Alzheimer's Disease: A Report of Progress in Research.* New York: Raven Press, pp. 149–164.

Corkin, S., Davis, K. L., Growdon, J. H., Usdin, E., and Wurtman, R. J., eds. (1982). *Alzheimer's Disease: A Report of Progress in Research.* New York: Raven Press.

Corsellis, J. A. N. (1970). The limbic areas in Alzheimer's disease and in other conditions associated with dementia. In: G. E. W. Wolstenholme, and M. O'Connor, eds., *Alzheimer's Disease and Related Conditions.* London: Churchill, pp. 37–50.

Cronholm, B., and Ottosson, J. O. (1961). Memory functions in endogenous depression. *Arch. General Psychiat., 5,* 101–107.

Cronholm, B., and Ottosson, J. O. (1963). The experience of memory function after electroconvulsive therapy. *Br. J. Psychiat., 109,* 251–258.

Crovitz, H. F., and Schiffman, H. (1974). Frequency of episodic memories as a function of their age. *Bull. Psychonomic Soc., 4,* 517–518.

Darwin, F., (1892). *Life of Charles Darwin.* London: John Murray.

Delaney, R. C., Rosen, A. J., Mattson, R. H., and Novelly, R. A. (1980). Memory function in focal epilepsy: A comparison of non-surgical, unilateral temporal lobe and frontal lobe samples. *Cortex, 16,* 103–117.

Drachman, D. A., and Arbit, J. (1966). Memory and the hippocampal complex. *Arch. Neurol.,* *15,* 52–61.

Erickson, R. C., and Scott, M. L. (1977). Clinical memory testing: A review. *Psychol. Bull., 84,* 1130–1149.

Fuld, P. A. (1978). Psychological testing in the differential diagnosis of the dementias. In: R. Katzman, R. D. Terry, and K. L. Bick, eds., *Alzheimer's Disease: Senila Dementia and Related Disorders.* New York: Raven Press, pp. 185–193.

Galton, F. (1879). Psychometric experiments. *Brain, 2,* 148–162.

Golden, C. J., Hammeke, T. A., and Purisch, A. D. (1980). *The Luria-Nebraska Neuropsychological Battery: Manual.* Los Angeles: Western Psychological Services.

Goodglass, H., and Kaplan, E. (1972). *The Assessment of Aphasia and Related Disorders.* London: Henry Kimpton.

Graf, P., Squire, L. R., and Mandler, G. (1984). The Information that amnesic patients do not forget. *J. Exp. Psychol.: Learning, Memory, and Cognition, 10,* 164–178.

Hyman, B. T., Van Hoesen, G. T., Damasio, A. R., Barnes, C. L. (1984). Alzheimer's disease: cell-specific pathology isolates the hippocampal formation. *Science, 225,* 1168–1170.

Jacoby, L. L. (1982). Knowing and remembering: Some parallels in the behavior of Korsakoff patients and normals. In: L. S. Cermak, ed., *Human Memory and Amnesia.* Hillsdale, New Jersey: Lawrence Erlbaum, pp. 97–122.

James, W. (1890). *Principles of Psychology,* vol. 1. New York: Dover.

Jennett, B. (1976). Assessment of severe head injury. *J. Neurol., Neurosurg., Psychiat., 39,* 647–655.

Jennett, B., Snoek, J., Bond, M. R., and Brooks, D. N. (1981). Disability after severe head injury: Observations on the use of the Glasgow Outcome Scale. *J. Neurol., Neurosurg., Psychiat., 44,* 285–293.

Jones, M. K. (1974). Imagery as a mnemonic aid after left temporal lobectomy: Contrast between material-specific and generalized memory disorders. *Neuropsychologia, 12,* 21–30.

Kahn, R. L., Zarit, S. H., Hilbert, N. M., and Niederehe, G. (1975). Memory complaints and impairment in the aged. *Arch. General Psychiat., 32,* 1560–1573.

Kandel, E. (1977). Neuronal plasticity and the modification of behavior. In: J. M. Brookhart, V. B. Mountcastle, E. R. Kandel, and S. R. Geiger, eds., *Handbook of Physiology.* Bethesda, Maryland: American Physiological Society, pp. 1137–1182.

Kaplan, O. J. (1979). Psychological testing of seniles. In: O. J. Kaplan, ed., *Psychopathology of Aging.* New York: Academic Press, pp. 45–78.

Katzman, R. (1976). The prevalence and malignancy of Alzheimer's disease. *Arch. Neurol., 33,* 217–218.

Kaushall, P. I., Zetin, M., and Squire, L. R. (1981). A psychosocial study of chronic, circumscribed amnesia. *J. Nerv. Ment. Dis., 169,* 383–389.

Kinsbourne, M., and Wood, F. (1975). Short-term memory processes and the amnesic syndrome. In: D. Deutsch and J. A. Deutsch, eds., *Short-Term Memory.* New York: Academic Press, pp. 258–291.

Klatzky, R. L. (1975). *Human Memory: Structures and Processes,* San Francisco: W. H. Freeman.

Kral, V. A. (1978). Benign senescent forgetfulness. In: R. Katzman, R. D. Terry, and K. L. Bick, eds., *Alzheimer's Disease: Senile Dementia and Related Disorders.* New York: Raven Press, pp. 47–52.

Lackner, J. R. (1974). Observations on the speech processing capabilities of an amnesic patient: Several aspects of H. M.'s language function. *Neuropsychologia, 12,* 199–207.

Levin, H. S., Benton, A. L., and Grossman, R. G. (1982). *Neurobehavioral Consequences of Closed Head Injury.* New York: Oxford University Press.

Levin, H. S., O'Donnell, V. M., and Grossman, R. G. (1979). The Galveston Orientation and Amnesia Test: A practical scale to assess cognition after head injury. *J. Nerv. Ment. Dis., 167,* 575–684.

Lynch, G., McGaugh, J., and Weinberger, N., eds. (1984). *Neurobiology of Learning and Memory*. New York: Guilford Press.

Mahut, H. (1984). Consolidation of memory—The hippocampus revisited. In: L. R. Squire and N. Butters, eds., *Neuropsychology of Memory*. New York: Guilford Press.

Mahut, H., Moss, M., and Zola-Morgan, S. (1981). Retention deficits after combined amygdalo-hippocampal and selective hippocampal resections in the monkey. *Neuropsychologia, 19*, 201–225.

Mair, W. G. P., Warrington, E. K., and Weiskrantz, L. (1979). Memory disorder in Korsakoff's psychosis: A neuropathological and neuropsychological investigation of two cases. *Brain, 102*, 749–783.

McAllister, T. W. (1983). Overview: Pseudodementia. *Am. J. Psychiat., 140*, 528–533.

McGaugh, J. L. (1982). Hormonal influences on memory. *Ann. Rev. Psychol., 24*, 297–323.

Mercer, B., Wagner, W., Gardner, H., and Benson, F. (1977). A study of confabulation. *Arch. Neurol., 34*, 429–433.

Michel, D., Laurent, B., Foyatier, N., Blanc, A., and Portafaix, M. (1982). Infarctus thalamique paramedian gauche. *Rev. Neurol., 138*, 533–550.

Miller, E. (1981). The nature of the cognitive deficit in senile dementia. In: N. E. Miller and G. D. Cohen, eds., *Clinical Aspects of Alzheimer's Disease and Senile Dementia*. New York: Raven Press.

Mills, R. P., and Swanson, P. D. (1978). Vertical oculomotor apraxia and memory loss. *Ann. Neurol., 4*, 149–153.

Milner, B. (1958). Psychological defects produced by temporal lobe excision. *Res. Proc. Assoc. Res. Nerv. Ment. Dis., 36*, 244–257.

Milner, B. (1962). Les troubles de la memoire accompagnant des lesions hippocampiques bilaterales. In: *Physiologie de l'hippocampe*. Paris: Centre National de la Recherche Scientifique.

Milner, B. (1968a). Disorders of memory after brain lesions in man. Preface: Material-specific and generalized memory loss. *Neuropsychologia, 6*, 175–179.

Milner, B. (1968b). Visual recognition and recall after right temporal lobe excision in man. *Neuropsychologia, 6*, 191–209.

Milner, B. (1970). Memory and the medial temporal regions of the brain. In: K. H. Pribram and D. E. Broadbent, eds., *Biology of Memory*. New York: Academic Press, pp. 29–50.

Milner, B. (1971). Interhemispheric differences in the localization of psychological processes in man. *Br. Med. Bull., 27*, 272–277.

Milner, B. (1974). Hemispheric specialization: Scope and limits. In: F. O. Schmitt and F. G. Worden, eds., *The Neurosciences Third Study Program*. Cambridge, Massachusetts: MIT Press, pp. 75–89.

Milner, B., and Teuber, H.-L. (1968). Alteration of perception and memory in man: Reflection on methods. In: L. Weiskrantz, ed., *Analysis of Behavioral Change*. New York: Harper and Row, pp. 268–375.

Milner, B., Corkin, S., and Teuber, H.-L. (1968). Further analysis of the hippocampal amnesic syndrome: 14-year follow-up study of H. M. *Neuropsychologia, 6*, 215–234.

Mishkin, M. (1978). Memory in monkeys severely impaired by combined but not by separate removal of amygdala and hippocampus. *Nature, 273*, 297–298.

Mishkin, M. (1982). A memory system in the monkey. In: D. E. Broadbent and L. Weiskrantz, eds., *Philosophical Transactions of the Royal Society of London, 298*, 85–96.

Mishkin, M. (1984). Memories and habits: Two neural systems. In: G. Lynch, J. L. McGaugh, and N. M. Weinberger, eds., *Neurobiology of Learning and Memory*. New York: Guilford Press, pp. 65–77.

Moscovitch, M. (1982). Multiple dissociations of function in amnesia. In: L. Cermak, ed., *Human Memory and Amnesia*. Hillsdale, New Jersey: Lawrence Erlbaum, pp. 337–370.

Murray, E. and Mishkin, M. (1984). Severe factual as well as visual memory deficits follow combined removal of the amygdala and hippocampus in monkeys. *J. Neurosci., 4*, 2565–2580.

Nadel, L., and Zola-Morgan, S. (1984). Infant memory: A perspective from animal research. In: M. Moscovitch, ed., *Infant Memory*. New York: Plenum Press, pp. 145–172.

Nemiah, J. C. (1980). Dissociative disorders. In: H. Kaplan, A. Freedman, and B. Sadock, eds., *Comprehensive Textbook of Psychiatry*. Baltimore: Williams ‡ Wilkins, pp. 1544–1561.

Newcombe, F. (1983). The psychological consequences of closed head injury: Assessment and rehabilitation. *Injury, 14,* 111–136.

Norman, D. A. (1982). *Learning and Memory*. San Francisco: W. H. Freeman.

Ojemann, G. A. (1971). Alteration in nonverbal short term memory with stimulation in the region of the mammillothalamic tract in man. *Neuropsychologia, 9,* 195–201.

O'Keefe, J., and Nadel, L. (1978). *The Hippocampus as a Cognitive Map*. London: Oxford University Press.

Olton, D. S., Becker, J. T., and Handelmann, G. E. (1979). Hippocampus, space, and memory. *Behav. Brain Sci., 2,* 313–365.

Osbourne, D. P., Brown, E. R., and Randt, C. T. (1982). Qualitative changes in memory function: Aging and dementia. In: S. Corkin, K. L. Davis, J. H. Growdon, E. Usdin, and R. J. Wurtman, eds., *Alzheimer's Disease: A Report of Progress in Research*. New York: Raven Press, pp. 165–170.

Osterreith, P. (1944). Le test de copie d'une figure complexe. *Arch. Psychol., 30,* 206–356.

Patten, B. M. (1972). The ancient art of memory. *Arch. Neurol., 26,* 25–31.

Price, T. R. P. (1982). Short- and long-term cognitive effects of ECT: Part 1—Effects on memory. *Psychopharmacol. Bull., 18,* 81–91.

Randt, C. T., Brown, E. R., and Osbourne, D. P. (1980). A memory test for longitudinal measurement of mild to moderate deficits. *Clin. Neuropsychol., 2,* 184–194.

Reitan, R. M., and Davison, L. A. (1974). *Clinical Neuropsychology: Current Status and Applications*. Washington, D.C.: V. A. Winston.

Ross, E. D. (1980A). Sensory-specific and fractional disorders of recent memory in man. I. Isolated loss of visual recent memory. *Arch. Neurol., 37,* 193–200.

Ross, E. D. (1980B). Sensory-specific and fractional disorders of recent memory in man. II. Unilateral loss of tactile recent memory. *Arch. Neurol., 37,* 267–272.

Russell, E. W. (1975). A multiple scoring method for assessment of complex memory functions. *J. Consult. Clin. Psychol., 43,* 800–809.

Russell, E. W. (1981). The pathology and clinical examination of memory. In: S. B. Filskov and T. J. Boll, eds., *Handbook of Clinical Neuropsychology*. New York: John Wiley, pp. 287–319.

Russell, W. R., and Nathan, P. W. (1946). Traumatic amnesia. *Brain, 69,* 280–300.

Ryle, G. (1949). *The Concept of Mind*. London: Hutchinson.

Sanders, H. I., and Warrington, D. K. (1971). Memory for remote events in amnesic patients. *Brain, 94,* 661–668.

Schacter, D., and Crovitz, H. F. (1977). Memory function after closed head injury: A review of the quantitative research. *Cortex, 13,* 150–176.

Schacter, D. L., and Moscovitch, M. (1984). Infants, amnesics, and dissociable memory systems. In: M. Moscovitch, ed., *Infant Memory*. New York: Plenum Press, pp. 173–216.

Schacter, D., Wang, P. L., Tulving, E., and Freedman, P. C. (1982). Functional retrograde amnesia: A quantitative case study. *Neuropsychologia, 20,* 523–532.

Scoville, W. B., and Milner, B. (1957). Loss of recent memory after bilateral hippocampal lesions. *J. Neurol., Neurosurg., Psychiat., 20,* 11–21.

Seltzer, B., and Benson, D. F. (1974). The temporal pattern of retrograde amnesia in Korsakoff's disease. *Neurology, 24,* 527–530.

Small, I. F. (1974). Inhalent convulsive therapy. In: M. Fink, S. Kety, J. McGaugh, and T. A. Williams, eds., *Psychobiology of Convulsive Therapy*. New York: John Wiley, pp. 65–77.

Speedie, L. J., and Heilman, K. M. (1982). Amnesic disturbance following infarction of the left dorsomedial nucleus of the thalamus. *Neuropsychologia, 20,* 597–604.

Squire, L. R. (1974). Remote memory as affected by aging. *Neuropsychologia, 112,* 429–435.

Squire, L. R. (1982A). The neuropsychology of human memory. *Ann. Rev. Neurosci.*, 5, 241–273.

Squire, L. R. (1982B). Comparisons between forms of amnesia: Some deficits are unique to Korsakoff syndrome. *J. Exp. Psychol.: Learning Memory and Cognition*, 8, 560–571.

Squire, L. R. (1982C). Neuropsychological effects of ECT. In: W. B. Essman and R. Abrams, eds., *Electroconvulsive Therapy*. New York: Spectrum, pp. 169–186.

Squire, L. R. Memory and the brain. In: S. Friedman, K. Klivington, and R. Peterson, eds., *Brain, Cognition, and Education*. New York: Academic Press, *in press*.

Squire, L. R., and Butters, N. M., eds. (1984). *Neuropsychology of Memory*. New York: Guilford Press.

Squire, L. R., and Cohen, N. J. (1982). Remote memory, retrograde amnesia, and the neuropsychology of memory. In: L. Cermak, ed., *Human Memory and Amnesia*. Hillsdale, New Jersey: Lawrence Erlbaum, pp. 275–303.

Squire, L. R., and Cohen, N. J. (1984). Human memory and amnesia. In: G. Lynch, J. McGaugh, and N. M. Weinberger, eds., *Neurobiology of Learning and Memory*. New York: Guilford Press, pp. 3–64.

Squire, L. R., and Davis, H. P. (1981). The pharmacology of memory: A neurobiological perspective. *Ann. Rev. Pharmacol. Toxicol.*, 21, 323–356.

Squire, L. R., and Fox, M. M. (1980). Assessment of remote memory: Validation of the television test by repeated testing during a seven-year period. *Behav. Res. Methods Instrum.*, 12, 583–586.

Squire, L. R., and Moore, R. Y. (1979). Dorsal thalamic lesion in a noted case of chronic memory dysfunction. *Ann. Neurol.*, 6, 503–506.

Squire, L. R., and Slater, P. C. (1975). Forgetting in very long-term memory as assessed by an improved questionnaire technique. *J. Exp. Psychol.: Human Learning and Memory*, 104, 50–54.

Squire, L. R., and Slater, P. C. (1978). Anterograde and retrograde memory impairment in chronic amnesia. *Neuropsychologia*, 16, 313–322.

Squire, L. R., and Slater, P. C. (1983). Electroconvulsive therapy and complaints of memory dysfunction: A prospective three-year follow-up study. *Br. J. Psychiat.*, 142, 1–8.

Squire, L. R., Wetzel, C. D., and Slater, P. C. (1979). Memory complaint after electroconvulsive therapy: Assessment with a new self-rating instrument. *Biol. Psychiat.*, 14, 791–801.

Squire, L. R., and Zola-Morgan, S. (1983). The neurology of memory: The case for correspondence between the findings for man and non-human primate. In: J. A. Deutsch, ed., *The Physiological Basis of Memory*, 2d ed. New York: Academic Press, pp. 200–268.

Sternberg, D. E., and Jarvik, M. E. (1976). Memory functions in depression. *Arch. General Psychiat.*, 33, 219–224.

Stromgren, L. S. (1977). The influence of depression on memory. *Acta Psychiatr. Scand.*, 56, 109–128.

Strub, R. L., and Black, F. W. (1977). *The Mental Status Examination in Neurology*. Philadelphia, Pennsylvania: F. A. Davis.

Talland, G. A. (1965). *Deranged Memory*. New York: Academic Press.

Teasdale, G., and Jennett, B. (1974). Assessment of coma and impaired consciousness. A practical scale. *Lancet*, 2, 81–84.

Terry, R. D., and Davies, P. (1980). Dementia of the Alzheimer type. *Ann. Rev. Neurosci.*, 3, 77–95.

Teuber, H.-L., Milner, B., and Vaughan, H. G. (1968). Persistent anterograde amnesia after stab wound of the basal brain. *Neuropsychologia*, 6, 267–282.

Thompson, R., Berger, T., and Madden, J. (1983). Cellular processes of learning and memory in the mammalian CNS. *Ann. Rev. Neurosci.*, 6, 447–491.

Victor, M., Adams, R. D., and Collins, G. H. (1971). *The Wernicke-Korsakoff Syndrome*. Philadelphia: F. A. Davis.

Warrington, E. K., and Weiskrantz, L. (1982). Amnesia: A disconnection syndrome? *Neuropsychologia, 20,* 233–248.

Wechsler, D. (1945). A standardized memory scale for clinical use. *J. Psychol., 9,* 87–93.

Weeks, D., Freeman, C. P. L., and Kendell, R. E. (1980). ECT: III: Enduring cognitive deficits? *Br. J. Psychiat., 137,* 26–37.

Weiskrantz, L. (1982). Comparative aspects of studies of amnesia. In: D. E. Broadbent and L. Weiskrantz, eds., *Philo. Trans. Roy. Soc. London, 298,* 97–109.

Weiskrantz, L., and Warrington, E. K. (1979). Conditioning in amnesic patients. *Neuropsychologia, 17,* 187–194.

Wells, C. E. (1979). Pseudodementia. *Am. J. Psychiat., 136,* 895–900.

Wickelgren, W. A. (1979). Chunking and consolidation: A theoretical synthesis of semantic networks, configuring in conditioning, S-R v. cognitive learning, normal forgetting, the amnesic syndrome and the hippocampal arousal system. *Psychol. Rev., 86,* 44–60.

Wilson, R. S., Kaszniak, A. W., and Fox, J. H. (1981). Remote memory in senile dementia. *Cortex, 17,* 41–48.

Winograd, T. (1975). Understanding natural language. In: D. Bobrow and A. Collins, eds., *Representation and Understanding.* New York: Academic Press.

Zangwill, O. L. (1977). The amnesic syndrome. In: C. W. M. Whitty and O. L. Zangwill, eds., *Amnesia: Clinical, psychological, and medicolegal aspects.* London: Buttersworths.

Zelinski, E. M., Gilewski, M. K., and Thompson, L. W. (1980). Do laboratory tests relate to self-assessment of memory ability in the young and old? In: L. W. Poon, J. L. Fozard, L. S. Cermak, D. Arenberg, and L. W. Thompson, eds., *New Directions in Memory and Aging.* Hillsdale, New Jersey: Lawrence Erlbaum, pp. 519–544.

Zola-Morgan, S. (1984). Toward an animal model of human amnesia: Some critical issues. In: L. R. Squire and N. Butters, eds., *Neuropsychology of Memory.* New York: Guilford Press, pp. 316–329.

Zola-Morgan, S., Cohen, N. J., and Squire, L. R. (1983). Recall of remote episodic memory in amnesia. *Neuropsychologia, 21,* 487–500.

Zola-Morgan, S., and Squire, L. R., Memory impairment and monkeys following lesions of the hippocampus. *Behavioral Neuroscience, in press.*

Zola-Morgan, S., and Squire, L. R. (1985). Complementary approaches to the study of memory: human amnesia and animal models. In N. Weinberger, J. McGaugh, G. Lynch, eds., *Memory Systems of the Brain: Animal and Human Cognitive Processes.* New York: Guilford Press.

13

Clinical and Neuropsychological Outcome Following Psychosurgery

MICHAEL JOSCHKO

Traditionally, psychosurgery has referred to neurosurgical operations on the frontal lobes of the brain intended to alter the behavior of psychiatric patients who have no demonstrable brain disease. With the use of stereotaxic procedures, however, modern psychosurgery is no longer limited to the frontal lobes *per se;* limbic-hypothalmic brain regions previously considered almost inaccessible are now reached with great precision. Common synonyms for psychosurgery are psychiatric surgery, mental surgery, sedative neurosurgery, psychiatric neurosurgery, behavioral neurosurgery, and functional neurosurgery.

All of these terms allude to surgical intervention in the brain as a means of affecting the thought patterns, emotional tone, personality characteristics, or the social interaction patterns of psychiatric patients. The British term leucotomy, which means the cutting of the white matter, has been applied to a number of different psychosurgical procedures and is generally equivalent to the American term, lobotomy. Both terms refer to psychosurgical operations on the frontal lobes and will be used interchangeably in this chapter to preserve consistency with the older literature.

Behavior change through psychosurgery has engendered much controversy. The report of the National Commission for the Protection of Human Subjects of Biomedical and Behavioral Research (Department of Health Education and Welfare, 1977) provides a review of the issues involved.

The purpose of this chapter is not to fuel the controversy, but to help fill the need for a systematic and impartial collection of data on both past and present psychosurgical procedures. The clinical nature of most of the published reports and the lack of sophistication in their behavioral research strategies have resulted in confusing and often conflicting findings and a paucity of consistent, scientifically sound conclusions regarding the effects of psychosurgery.

Thus, this chapter attempts to integrate the heterogeneous published findings concerning the effects of psychosurgical interventions on the behavior and higher cognitive functions of individuals with psychiatric disorders. It deals primarily with two questions. Does psychosurgery produce desired behavioral changes in psychiatric patients? What are the neuropsychological sequelae of psychosurgery?

A review of the history of psychosurgery would be in order, but because of space limitations the reader is referred to the historical overviews published by Greenblatt (1950), Kalinowsky and Hippius (1969), and Valenstein and Heilman (1979). In addition, Valenstein (1977) has provided a review of the literature published during the 1971–1976 period, which is helpful in understanding the more recent trends in this field.

For the neuroscientist or clinician interested in the behavioral, emotional, or cognitive effects of psychosurgery, the above reviews will likely give some pause for thought. Clearly, the term refers to a wide variety of neurosurgical techniques for disconnecting or destroying various brain regions in heterogeneous populations of psychiatric patients. Psychosurgery has evolved from very crude procedures which were quite variable in their neuroanatomical and behavioral effects to much more refined and precise stereotaxic procedures.

Different psychosurgical procedures generally entail differences in the location and nature of the lesion (e.g., lesions might have been produced by a surgical cut, a gross removal of brain tissue, a freezing probe, or focussed ultrasonic energy), as well as differences in the quantity of brain tissue destroyed. Likewise, the same psychosurgical procedure has often been varied as a function of the severity of the patient's symptoms (e.g., unilateral vs. bilateral leucotomies or standard vs. radical lobotomies for more seriously disturbed patients). These considerations must be taken into account when evaluating the outcome of psychosurgery. Much of the published literature, however, is quite poor in controlling, or even acknowledging, these potentially confounding influences. Heterogeneous groups of psychiatric patients who have undergone very different psychosurgical procedures often have been lumped together in the outcome literature. This limitation marks most of the reports reviewed in this chapter.

Outcome of Psychosurgery: Clinical Effects

The clinical goal of psychosurgery has generally been to change the maladaptive behavior of psychiatric patients who have proven to be unresponsive to other treatment approaches. In this section, the question of whether or not psychosurgery produces the desired behavioral changes in psychiatric patients is considered by reviewing the clinical lore and empirical findings available in the published literature.

Clinical Impressions

The gross, empirical, standard lobotomy of Freeman and Watts (1942), produced clinically dramatic results, which helps to explain the subsequent popularization of lobotomy. Psychiatric patients suffering from schizophrenic disorders, who for years had been chronically disturbed, became calmer and less of a management problem (Freeman and Watts, 1942; Moore et al., 1947). The suffering of anxiety-debilitated patients of all types was substantially reduced (Rylander, 1973). These relatively positive results, however, were accompanied by the severe, undesirable sequelae of the well-known "Frontal Syndrome" (Rylander, 1948). Usually, the immediate postoperative effects were apathy, disorientation, and clouded sensorium, while the more permanent effects were the disruption of abstract thought and foresight, emotional flattening concomitant with a later tendency towards euphoria, and a loss of initiative.

Clinically, the overall positive effect of psychosurgery was frequently viewed as a "diminished reaction and vigilance of the brain to unpleasant sensations" (Kalinowsky, 1973). Unfortunately, it was generally conceded that this "diminished reaction" also applied to pleasant sensations. In addition to reducing the concern over obsessions, hallucinations, delusions, etc., early psychosurgery also tended to cause an overall decrease in the drive and interest of the patient. The recognition of these defects which accompanied a standard lobotomy prompted psychosurgeons to try new and improved methods to produce maximal benefit with minimal side effects.

The clinical literature indicates the gyrectomies (Penfield, 1948), topectomies (Pool, 1949), and inferior, partial, and unilateral lobotomies (Freeman and Watts, 1942) were not as therapeutically effective as lobotomies, and were still accompanied by undesirable sequelae. Superior undercutting (Scoville, 1949) produced good results but interfered with intellectual functioning. Generally, only orbital and restricted orbital undercutting (Hirose, 1965; Knight, 1960; Scoville, 1949), cingulate operations (Livingston, 1953; Whitty et al., 1952), and bimedial leucotomies (Falconer and Schurr, 1959) were considered to have produced good results with limited or slight undesirable side effects. According to Kalinowsky (1973) these procedures produced fewer undesirable sequelae because they left part of the frontothalamic fibers intact.

In summary, the overall clinical results stemming from early psychosurgery seem to have been basically similar regardless of the locus of the lesion produced. The vast majority of psychosurgery patients would seem to have exhibited a substantial reduction in their symptomatology to the point that they were significantly less of a management problem to those charged with their care (Boyd, Weber, and McKenzie, 1958; Moore et al., 1947). Only the relative balance between the desired and undesired sequelae appears to be related to the location of the lesion and the quantity of brain tissue destroyed (Kalinowsky, 1973). However, many neurosurgeons and neuropsychiatrists believe that the personality structure of the patient significantly interacts with the effects of the psychosurgery (Kalinowsky and Hippius, 1969). Therefore, according to psychosurgery lore, the response to psychosurgery depends greatly upon the patient's personality structure.

The aforementioned clinical impressions are characteristic of the early psychosurgery literature. Modern neurosurgeons and neuropsychiatrists, however, are in strong disagreement with the notion that "different mental illnesses do not need different operative procedures" and that the results of psychosurgery are largely the same regardless of the lesion site (see Valenstein (1977) for an extended discussion of this point). The general quality of the research in this area is currently so poor that drawing any firm conclusions about the possible differential effects of common lesion sites is not possible.

Efficacy of Psychosurgery: Empirical Findings

A brief review is given here of the variables and research strategies used to evaluate the effectiveness of psychosurgery. No attempt, however, is made to review specifically the heterogeneous and often equivocal results of many reports in the literature.

Type of operation and diagnosis of the patient are the two primary independent variables which have been used in the psychosurgery outcome literature. Even though both variables are of necessity part of every study in this domain, the results of psychosurgery have not always been analyzed in terms of these variables. Many reports have considered specifically diagnosis (e.g., Fleming and Baker, 1972; Freeman, 1961; Knight, 1972). Other reports have considered symptomatology regardless of diagnosis (Laitinen and Vilkki, 1972), age (Strom-Olsen and Carlisle, 1972), and the duration of illness and hospitalization before psychosurgery (Lindstrom, 1972).

Other less frequently investigated variables are response to ECT (Hetherington, Haden, and Craig, 1972); premorbid personality (Hirose, 1972); general vs. mental hospital patient; race; sex; marital status; level of education; and type of occupation (Freeman, 1961). Some attempts have also been made to investigate the predictive efficiency of standardized preoperative ratings of social adjustment (Fleming and Baker, 1972; Miller, 1954) or psychometric testing (Choppy, Zimbacca, and LeBeau, 1973) on outcome after psychosurgery.

Global, subjective, clinical ratings, e.g., "good," "fair," "poor" (Mingrino and Schergna, 1972), "unchanged," "improved," "markedly improved," "no treatment needed" (Ballantine et al., 1967), have been used almost exclusively in assessments of the outcome of psychosurgery. The difficulties with such subjective dependent variables are self-evident and will not be dealt with here.

Some authors have used more specific, less global assessments either alone or in combination with clinical ratings. For example, ratings of the patient's ability to work and to function in society have been used in a number of studies (Freeman, 1961; Hetherington et al., 1972; Strom-Olsen and Carlisle, 1972). Ratings of personality defects and relief of symptoms (Hetherington et al., 1972; Knight, 1972; Lindstrom, 1972), discharge and readmission rates (Freeman, 1961; Hetherington et al., 1972; Hirose, 1961), and number of months in hospital after surgery (Hetherington et al., 1972) have been used by some researchers. Objective, operationally defined rating scales (Boyd, Weber, and McKenzie, 1958; Fleming and Baker, 1972; Miller, 1967), psychometric test scores, and personality test data (Laitinen and Vilkki, 1972; Meyer et al., 1973; Walsh, 1976) have also been used to evaluate psychosurgery's clinical effectiveness. The great variation in the descriptive information accompanying clinical and work ratings makes comparisons between many studies relatively meaningless. Only research strategies that use operationally defined rating scales, psychometric test scores, and discharge and readmission rates, etc., provide useful, quantitative data that can be meaningfully compared between studies and the cross-validation of results.

Relatively few controlled studies of the clinical effects of psychosurgery have been attempted. In a review of the earlier published reports, Robin (1958) concluded that many of the so-called controlled studies lacked adequate matching of the treatment and control groups or suffered from two short a followup period. The findings of these reports were generally equivocal. One report (Livingston, 1953), however, deserves special mention. It is probably the only study reported in the literature that used sham-operated patients. Livingston finds evidence in his study for the positive effect of the surgery per se, with the treatment group improving more than the sham-operated controls. These results are tempered by the short period of followup and preoperative differences between the two groups.

Robin (1958) compared leucotomy patients and controls matched for chronicity, age on admission, sex, and length of treatment, and found no significant differences between the treatment and control groups on a number of outcome measures. However, Robin did not attempt to match his groups on preoperative diagnoses. McKenzie and Kaczanowski (1964) also found no differences between their leucotomy and control subjects matched on overall prognosis, tendency to spontaneous remission, period and place of hospitalization, and length of followup. This study matched groups and did not attempt to match for diagnoses. Also, McKenzie and Kaczanowski used a very short period of followup (5 years). Other controlled studies (Marks, Birley, and Gelder, 1966; Tan, Marks, and Marset, 1971) have reported favorable results for the treatment groups as compared to the controls. Different proportions of the treatment groups in these latter two studies were not adequately matched.

In an attempt to overcome some of the methodological limitations of earlier outcome studies utilizing controls, Joschko (1979) conducted an archival study of a complete hospital sample consisting of 377 mixed psychiatric patients who underwent bimedial prefrontal leucotomy during the period 1952–1967. In addition to studying an entire leucotomy clinic in which 99% of the psychosurgery was conducted in a standard fashion by the same neurosurgeon, this investigation used objective measures, temporally and emotionally removed from the data, acceptable control groups (including 100 individually matched psychiatric patients and a small group of patients considered for psychosurgery who were subsequently rejected for leucotomy because of medical, legal, or clinical reasons), a relatively long followup, and appropriate statistical analyses. Overall, the results of this investigation indicated that prefrontal leucotomy was generally not effective in the treatment of psychiatric problems. The data, however, suggested that leucotomy was effective in a considerable proportion of the patients afflicted with affective disorders.

Conclusions

There is a dearth of objective data and appropriate statistical analyses in the psychosurgery outcome literature. Studies which have utilized statistical procedures generally have relied on univariate designs which do not adequately take into consideration the multiple influences of interacting variables on the outcome of psychosurgery. The psychosurgery literature is also overrun by studies using widely different criteria for success, varying subject populations, and different operative procedures. In addition, the majority of the studies in the literature are quite limited in their descriptions of the variables necessary to scientifically evaluate psychosurgery outcome.

Psychosurgery research has generally neglected the use of appropriate control groups and the role of "spontaneous recovery" in large groups of psychotics. The confounding effects of deriving indications for psychosurgery from improved cases and thereby only selecting patients with good prognoses, comparing patients treated decades apart, or not reporting the acute vs. chronic nature of the psychiatric problems are also neglected in most studies. Almost all investigations of psychosurgery outcome neglect to attempt to isolate the effect of prepsychosurgery treatments (e.g., the number of ECT treatments, trials of psychotropic medications, length of institutionalization, etc.).

Another major problem with the clinical outcome literature is the subjective nature of the researchers' evaluation tools. Most of the articles in the literature consist of largely subjective reports by persons closely involved in the actual decisions to perform psychosurgery on the patients described. Valenstein (1973) has outlined the difficulties inherent in studies conducted by such "ego-involved" personnel relying on subjective impressions for psychosurgical evaluation. These include the subtleties of nonconscious distortion or selective attention to data supportive of individual research biases, and the effects of attitudinal changes and expectations on the part of the involved treatment—research personnel, relatives, and the psychosurgery patient.

In summary, although there is sufficient consistency in the literature to suggest that psychiatric patients become more sedate and less difficult to manage following psychosurgery, and that patients with affective disorders in particular are helped by psychosurgery (e.g., see Joschko, 1979; Mirsky and Orzack, 1977; Valenstein, 1977), it is not clear whether the changes brought about by psychosurgery necessarily lead to permanent gains in the patients' social adaptation. Whether chemotherapy may provide the same function today that psychosurgery seems to have provided many of the early psychosurgery patients is debatable.

Outcome of Psychosurgery: Neuropsychological Effects

The neuropsychologist, rather than being interested in the clinical efficacy of psychosurgery per se, is more likely to be concerned with defining the cognitive changes correlated with the well-defined lesions produced by psychosurgery. This section reviews the neuropsychological effects of psychosurgery.

As is the case in the literature describing the clinical effects of psychosurgery, outcome studies reporting the use of objective tests that might contribute to the understanding of the neuropsychological effects of psychosurgery are generally replete with methodological problems and deficiencies in data reporting. The final section of this chapter discusses some of these methodological problems with special reference to neuropsychological research strategies. Because of space limitations and these methodological problems, no attempt has been made to provide an exhaustive review of the literature relevant to the cognitive correlates of psychosurgery. Nonetheless, there are some clear consistencies in the findings reported in the literature which allow some reasonable, tentative conclusions to be made regarding the neuropsychological effects of psychosurgery. In the following discussion, representative studies are briefly described. The research has been grouped into areas which have some fairly clear significance for the clinician and researcher.

The Effects of Psychosurgery on Measures of Psychometric Intelligence

Many researchers have been concerned with the effect of psychosurgery on "intelligence" as measured by standard psychometric instruments such as the Wechsler-Bellevue Scales (WBS) or the Wechsler Adult Intelligence Scale (WAIS). The research strategies used have included (1) comparisons of psychometric scores with the normative sample, (2) comparisons of pre- and postpsychosurgery measures, and (3) comparisons of psychosurgery and control patients. Overall, the bulk of the evidence reported in the literature suggests that significant reductions in psychometric intelligence do not permanently accompany psychosurgery and that psychosurgery patients generally obtain scores on psychometric instruments similar to the normative population (Andy and Jurko, 1972; Bailey, Dowling, and Davies, 1973; Cochrane and Kljacic, 1979; Gaches, LeBeau, and Choppy, 1972; Hitchcock et al., 1973; Mitchell-Heggs, Kelly, and Richardson, 1976; Mingrino and Schergna, 1972; Scoville and Bettis, 1977; Teuber, Corkin, and Twitchell, 1977; Vilkki, 1977).

Generally, postpsychosurgery comparisons of matched lobotomized and control psychiatric patients suggest that psychosurgery does not lead to significant decrements in psychometric intelligence. For example, a comparison of matched lobotomized and nonlobotomized institutionalized schizophrenic patients (Wehler and Hoffman, 1978) revealed no significant WAIS I.Q. of subtest differences. Similar findings have been reported by Finlayson (1979) and Mirsky and Orzack (1977). Stuss et al. (1981), however, found differences between their leucotomy and control patients when the psychosurgery group was divided on the basis of clinical recovery. The "good" recovery group in this study had significantly higher WAIS full scale I.Q. scores than the schizophrenic control group. Significant differences in WAIS full scale I.Q. favoring the normal control group, were also found when the "no recovery" group was compared with the control group.

A few studies (Hamlin, 1970; Smith and Kinder, 1959) have reported significant decrements in psychometric intelligence following psychosurgery. These findings would seem to be related to the location of the lesion produced by the psychosurgery. Hamlin's (1970) followup over 14 years indicates clearly the differential effects of orbital and superior frontal lobe lesion sites on intellectual functions such as those measured by the subtests of the WBS. Although patients who had undergone orbital topectomy showed some intellectual deterioration shortly after psychosurgery, they did not differ from control subjects on any of the Wechsler subtests 14 years after psychosurgery. The superior topectomy group, on the other hand, demonstrated permanent decrements in the order of 10 I.Q. points. The importance of taking into consideration the site of the lesion (or the brain tracts disrupted) in assessing the cognitive effects of psychosurgery cannot be overemphasized, but has not always been recognized in the psychosurgery literature. This point will be discussed further later in this chapter.

Although there are clear methodological limitations in many of the studies which report psychometric test data, it is clear that the majority of the studies in the literature indicate that there is no permanent deterioration in psychometric intelligence following psychosurgery. A number of investigators, however, have reported improved postpsychosurgery scores (e.g., see Mitchell-Heggs et al., 1976; Mingrino and Schergna, 1972; Mirsky and Orzack, 1977; Smith, Kiloh, and Boots, 1977; Teuber et al., 1977). The length of time between surgery and testing would seem to be an important variable. Teuber et al. (1977) have shown that there are no pre/post changes in psychometric intelligence scores if cingulotomy patients are tested within a few months of their psychosurgery; significant increases in test performance, however, were evident if the patients were tested more than four months after surgery.

Since it is generally agreed that psychosurgery reduces anxiety and "emotionality", improvements in test performance following psychosurgery must be evaluated conservatively. It is self-evident that reduced anxiety levels might lead to better performance on tasks such as intelligence tests which require substantial concentration. This suggests an obvious difficulty with the presurgery baseline. (See chapters 7 and 8 for a detailed discussion of neuropsychological assessment in the psychiatric patient.)

Psychiatric patients referred for psychosurgery generally could be expected to be quite disturbed and to be functioning well below their optimum potential prior to surgery. Whether or not the accumulative effects of the electroconvulsive and drug treatments administered to many patients prior to psychosurgery further confound presurgery measures is currently moot, but worthy of consideration by psychosurgery researchers. The "wearing off" of these hypothesized effects when the presurgery treatments are discontinued following psychosurgery is a possible confounding influence on postpsychosurgery test results.

When studies which demonstrate no postpsychosurgery deterioration in intelligence are considered in light of the aforementioned problems, one is still forced to consider the possible detrimental effects of psychosurgery on premorbid intelligence. Once again, however, the effects of prepsychosurgery treatments would have to be dissociated from the effects of the neurosurgery per se.

The Effects of Psychosurgery on Measures of Abstract Thinking

Neuropsychologists and others have long been interested in the "riddle of the frontal lobes" (Teuber, 1964). Halstead's (1947) studies indicated that the frontal lobes are particularly important for "biological intelligence." Since psychosurgery has generally been done on areas within the frontal lobes or on brain sites with a strong anatomical connection to the frontal lobes, many tests thought to be sensitive specifically to frontal lobe dysfunction have been administered to psychosurgery patients. These "frontal tests" have included measures of abstraction (categorization), foresight, and planning, based on the commonly held idea that the higher cognitive functions are mediated by the anterior regions of the brain.

Unlike the results on measures of psychometric intelligence after psychosurgery, there are frequent reports in the literature (e.g., see Drewe, 1974; Faillace et al., 1971; Halstead, 1947; Jurko and Andy, 1973; Mirsky and Orzack, 1977; Walsh, 1976) of deficits on tests of abstract thinking. The measures commonly used in psychosurgery studies have been the Porteus Maze Test (a measure of planning and visuo-spatial abilities), the Wisconsin Card Sorting Test (a measure of the capacity to sort and categorize stimuli and to shift psychological set), the Halstead Category Test (a measure of concept formation, nonverbal problem-solving, planning, and the ability to shift psychological set), the Trail Making Test (a measure of visual conceptual and visuomotor tracking), and the Wechsler and Kohs block design tests (measures of planning, problem-solving, and two-dimensional visuo-construction). It must be emphasized, however, that deficits on measures of abstract thinking are not consistently reported in the literature (e.g., see Bailey et al., 1973; Kelly and Mitchell-Heggs, 1973; Teuber et al., 1977).

PORTEUS MAZE TEST (PMT). Riddle and Roberts (1978) have reviewed much of the data available on the effects of early psychosurgical procedures (e.g., topectomy and Freeman and Watts-style prefrontal lobotomies) upon PMT performance. When practice effects are taken into consideration, these authors report that there are significant immediate postoperative losses in PMT performance followed by *partial* recovery within 3 months. In addition, these authors conclude that more posterior lesions produce a greater, and likely permanent, loss in PMT ability than do more anterior psychosurgical lesions; they report no data with respect to the permanence of losses following anterior surgery. There is some evidence (Mirsky and Orzack, 1977; Teuber et al., 1977) that permanent PMT deficits do not accompany lesions produced by more modern psychosurgical procedures.

WISCONSIN CARD SORTING TEST (WCST). In a study of a group of 26 psychosurgery patients (who had been operated on by one of three different neurosurgeons using vastly different neurosurgical techniques), Mirsky and Orzack (1977) report that their psychosurgery group made significantly more perseverative errors on the WCST than their psychiatric control group. The selection of an appropriate control group in psychosurgery research is a difficult but vital task. [See Joschko (1979) for one approach to this problem.] Since Mirsky and Orzack's control group consisted of only eight subjects who were comparable to some of the psychosurgery patients only in terms of general psychiatric diagnosis, and because of other methodological problems, the interpretation of the differences in WCST performance in their study is quite problematical.

Teuber et al. (1977) report no consistent deficiencies in WCST performance following psychosurgery in a group of 34 patients who underwent bilateral cingulotomy for the relief of persistent pain ($N = 11$) or psychiatric illness. No preoperative differences between the scores of the psychosurgery group and the mean for the normal control subjects were eivdent. Only four of 12 patients for whom the data were available obtained lower WCST scores when tested within 4 months of their psychosurgery; when two of those patients were retested later they obtained scores equal to their preoperative performance.

OTHER MEASURES OF ABSTRACT REASONING. Deficiencies on the Trail Making Test and the Wechsler Block Design and Similarities subtests following thalamotomy have been reported by Jurko and Andy (1973). Walsh (1977) reports some deficiencies in his psychosurgery group on the Goldstein and Scheerer (1941) version of the Kohs block design tests. Finlayson (1979) compared a small group of patients who had undergone bilateral inferior prefrontal leucotomy with control groups of psychiatric patients with and without evidence of cerebral dysfunction. He found that the leucotomy patients were more like the psychiatric patients than the brain-damaged patients in their performance on an expanded Halstead-Reitan test battery. Nonetheless, the leucotomy group was clearly impaired relative to normal subjects on a number of measures including the Halstead Category Test; borderline performances were evident on the Trail Making Test.

In summary, the published evidence about the effect of psychosurgery on abstract thinking does not lead to any straightforward conclusions. It would appear that deficits in abstract thinking following psychosurgery either are not permanent or cannot be dissociated from factors related to long-term psychiatric illness. Future research in this area would seem to require careful consideration of possible confounding influences and more detailed qualitative analyses of the neuropsychological performances of psychosurgery patients.

The Effects of Psychosurgery on Measures of Attention, Memory, and Verbal Fluency

Deficiencies in attention have frequently been associated with frontal lobe pathology (Buffery, 1967; Luria, 1964). Because the Wechsler Digit Span subtest (DS) has been considered to be a measure of attention and "freedom from distractibility", and because DS is easily administered, it has frequently been used in attempts to evaluate the attentional abilities of psychosurgery patients. Hamlin (1970), for example, reports that an impairment in DS performance was particularly characteristic of the long-term effects of superior topectomy. Inferior topectomy, however, did not produce any long-term DS deficiencies. These latter findings are consistent with the long-term followup studies on Finlayson (1979) and Stuss et al. (1981) for psychiatric patients who had undergone prefrontal leucotomy.

The results of a number of studies (Cochrane and Kljajic, 1979; Mirsky and Orzack, 1977; Stuss et al., 1981; Teuber et al., 1977) indicate that mnemonic abilities, such as those measured by the Wechsler Memory Scale (WMS) are not affected adversely by a variety of psychosurgical procedures. Since the WMS is composed of a heterogeneous group of subtests, further qualitative analyses of the mnemonic abilities of psychosurgery patients would seem to be warranted. Other measures of mnemonic abilities (e.g., learning of associations, face recognition, memory for designs, etc.) also have generally produced negative results with respect to the effects of psychosurgery (Jurko and Andy, 1973; Teuber et al., 1977; Vilkki and Laitinen, 1974). For the present, therefore, it seems necessary to conclude that consistent mnemonic deficiencies are not produced by psychosurgical procedures.

There is some evidence that deficits in verbal fluency are associated with frontal lobe dysfunction, particularly when the measures involve a written response (Milner, 1964). In a study which assessed the verbal fluency abilities in cingulotomy patients, Teuber et al. (1977) found no deficiencies in either written or verbal fluency which were attributable to psychosurgery per se.

The Effects of Psychosurgery as Measured by Comprehensive Neuropsychological Test Batteries

To date, much of the literature describing the cognitive effects of psychosurgery has consisted of studies using a barely minimal neuropsychological examination frequently involving only the Wechsler scales and one or two "frontal lobe tests." One of the exceptions to this in the early psychosurgery literature is the Columbia-Greystone battery (Landis, 1952) for studying the cognitive effects of topectomy in a small group of psychiatric patients; many of the tests included in the battery, however, were not standardized for a brain-damaged population or were shown in other studies to be insensitive to frontal lobe dysfunction. The results of the Columbia-Greystone study indicate that no parmanent deficits were evident on the tests used.

More recent investigations which have used comprehensive neuropsychological test batteries consisting of standardized tests known to be sensitive to brain damage in general and frontal lobe dysfunction in particular have also produced negative results not unlike those of the Columbia-Greystone project. For example, Teuber et al. (1977) report that there were "no lasting effects of the cingulotomy *per se* on the 24 behavioral tasks sampled in our study, though there were significant effects associated with chronological age and the number of ECT". Similarly, Mirsky and Orzack (1977) state that "there was no evidence of overall cognitive or intellectual deficit attributable to the psychosurgery" performed on their subjects.

Finlayson's (1979) findings using an expanded Halstead-Reitan test battery are also consistent with the aforementioned studies. Although Finlayson's leucotomy group performed quite poorly on most of the neuropsychological tests relative to what is known about normal performances on these measures, as a group, their neuropsychological test performance was more like a psychiatric control group than a brain-damaged control group. While clinical interpretation of the neuropsychological test profiles of Finlayson's leucotomy patients point to some frontal lobe dysfunction, the similarity of the leucotomy and nonleucotomized psychiatric patients cautions against the interpretation that deficits shown by the leucotomy group are attributable to the psychosurgery per se. Since many of Finlayson's patients had undergone extensive ECT and psychopharmacological treatments before psychosurgery (Joschko, 1979), it is possible that the neuropsychological deficits were, in part, due to these factors.

In summary, the literature relevant to the neuropsychological effects of psychosurgery does not indicate that any permanent changes in cognitive abilities consistently follow any of the modern psychosurgical procedures. Older topectomy and lobotomy procedures, however, seem to have produced some permanent neuropsychological deficits. Whether more sophisticated neuropsychological research strategies will consistently elicit as of yet undetected deficits in modern psychosurgery patients awaits to be seen.

General Conclusions: The Neurobiology of Psychosurgery and Future Research Strategies

This section presents conclusions which appear warranted on the basis of the psychosurgery literature and of my own followup of a large series of psychiatric patients who had undergone bilateral inferior prefrontal leucotomy. Methodological problems that bear heavily on the results of psychosurgery research are emphasized and suggestions regarding fruitful avenues of research are offered.

With the exception of some of the older psychosurgery procedures, consistent neuropsychological changes have not been detected following psychosurgery. That is, there do not appear to be specific neuropsychological patterns that are typical of psychosurgical lesions. These deficits following psychosurgery that have been reported in the literature seem to be either transient or the result of factors which are not directly related to the psychosurgery. With respect to the older procedures, there appears to be a strong, positive correlation between the severity and permanence of the neuropsychological sequelae and the location and size of the lesion within the frontal lobes.

The failure to find consistent neuropsychological correlates of the lesions produced by psychosurgery is at first glance quite perplexing. Psychosurgery patients clearly have documented cerebral lesions in areas of the brain thought by many to subserve important higher-order cognitive functions (Banna et al., 1978). The extensive theoretical and empirical data base of human neuropsychology would lead one to expect some measurable cognitive deficits following psychosurgery. Why then are there no consistent effects reported? In my view, there seem to be three general answers to this question.

(1) Small, carefully placed psychosurgical lesions do not produce any significant cognitive changes because the brain areas disrupted are involved primarily in the mediation of emotion rather than cognition. This position is most likely to be held by neurosurgeons and neuropsychiatrists who believe that psychosurgical techniques have gone beyond the experimental stage and are specifically indicated for certain patients (e.g., Hirose, 1972; Kalinowsky, 1973; Knight, 1972; Lewin, 1973; Scoville, 1973). Support for this notion is easily drawn from the empirical findings available. Theoretical support is more strained, but can be gleaned from the role of the limbic system and anatomically related structures in regulating emotional behavior (Valenstein and Heilman, 1979). Findings of serious cognitive deficits following certain lesions of the limbic system (Butters, 1979), however, have to be reconciled with any "limbic" theory of the effects of psychosurgery. Other hypothesized physiological explanations of the brain mechanisms involved in psychosurgery effects have been reviewed by Valenstein (1977) and have been found to be without much substance. On the whole, this first explanation of the lack of neuropsychological sequelae following psychosurgery is not very satisfying.

(2) Because of the "plasticity" of the CNS, there is substantial recovery of function following psychosurgery. As research progresses, the concepts of plasticity (Stein, Rosen, and Butters, 1974), redundancy, multiple control, functional substitution, and diaschisis (Laurence and Stein, 1978) will undoubtedly emerge as important variables in understanding the failure to find consistent neuropsychological changes following psychosurgery. At least one article in the psychosurgery literature (Sweet, 1973) has suggested the possibility of recovery of function in psychosurgery patients. Future research in this

area, however, will have to address the dissociation between the effects of psychosurgery and cerebral plasticity on emotional and cognitive functioning.

(3) Methodological problems in psychosurgery research have limited the ability of neuropsychological measures to detect cognitive changes following psychosurgery. There are a number of specific methodological problems which could lead to false negatives in neuropsychological studies of psychosurgery outcome. These relate to variables associated with the psychosurgery procedure, the psychosurgery patient, and the neuropsychological evaluation procedures.

Psychosurgery outcome studies generally have not considered the differential effects of lesion size and location, even though both of these variables are known to affect patterns of neuropsychological impairment (Chapman and Wolff, 1959; Luria, 1966; Reitan, 1966). Patients who have undergone even dramatically different psychosurgery procedures have frequently been grouped together by investigators. Such practices may have served to blur the neuropsychological deficits produced by psychosurgery and may have given rise to misleading generalizations. The effect of the nature of the lesion (e.g., surgical cut vs. tissue removal) is another potentially important variable which deserves some consideration in future research.

Probably the most confounding influences in psychosurgery outcome studies have been variables associated with the psychotherapy patients themselves. Not only have researchers frequently neglected to consider separately the results for patients of different sex, age, and socioeconomic level, level of education, or level of intelligence, but they have made little if any effort to dissociate the effects of psychosurgery from the seriously confounding influences of prepsychosurgery treatments and pre-existing psychiatric symtomatology. Parsons and Prigatano (1978) have reviewed the importance of these former variables in neuropsychological research, and Finlayson, Johnson, and Reitan (1977) have investigated this topic; they will be dealt with no further here.

Although the short-term effects of ECT treatments on mnemonic abilities have been well documented (Heaton and Crowley, 1981), there does not appear to be any consistent evidence relating ECT treatments to persistent neuropsychological deficits. However, given the large numbers of ECT treatments received by some psychosurgery patients—e.g., some of the patients studied by Joschko (1979) had received over 500 ECT treatments—the possibility of permanent neuropsychological sequelae in some psychosurgery patients cannot be ruled out. In this regard, Teuber et al. (1977) have reported neuropsychological deficits associated with the number of ECT's received by their cingulotomy patients. The effects of psychotropic drugs on neuropsychological test performance have been reviewed by Heaton and Crowley (1981). Almost without exception, drug effects seem not to have been taken into consideration in psychosurgery outcome research (Adams, 1977). It is self-evident that psychiatric patients who differ on this variable from psychosurgery patients would not be valid control subjects for assessing the neuropsychological correlates of psychosurgery.

Numerous studies (reviewed by Davison, 1974) have demonstrated the difficulty in distinguishing brain-damaged patients from chronic schizophrenic patients on group comparisons of neuropsychological measures. Whether these studies support the hypothesis that cerebral impairment underlies chronic psychiatric disease is moot. Nonetheless, these findings make it difficult to interpret results which indicate that there are no neuropsychological differences between psychosurgery patients and control patients with chronic psychiatric disorders. The long-term institutionalization of many psychosurgery patients may have some effects on their cognitive functioning which confound the neuropsychological results of psychosurgery. Finger (1978) presents some intriguing data in support of the hypothesis that environmental factors can influence brain-lesion symptoms in rats. Regardless of whether this hypothesis is ever supported with data from human research, the common practice of combining psychosurgery patients with relatively short- or long-term psychiatric hospitalization would seem to be questionable. Overall, it is clear that the effects of somatic treatments and the related variables of severity and length of illness are of considerable importance and need to be evaluated in future investigations.

Variables associated with the neuropsychological evaluation procedures used in psychosurgery research deserve some mention. Some of these variables have been dealt with by Parsons and Prigatano (1978) and will not be described further here. Other variables such as the length of postoperative recovery prior to evaluation, subject selection, and the measures utilized in psychosurgery outcome research require some specific attention. The studies by Hamlin (1970) and Teuber et al. (1977) have demonstrated clearly that neuropsychological sequelae following psychosurgery, in some instances, can be related to the time of assessment. Some of the current confusion in psychosurgery research may result from the researchers' failure to take into consideration the length of postoperative recovery.

The selection of psychosurgery and control subjects definitely needs more attention in psychosurgery research. It is axiomatic that outpatient psychosurgery patients who volunteer for study and who can travel to a university or hospital clinic for assessment may differ in important ways from psychosurgery patients who have remained institutionalized. To provide generalizable findings, the researcher must try to ensure that psychosurgery patients selected for study are representative of other patients who have undergone the same procedure, and control patients must be carefully selected to minimize the confounding effects of psychiatric illness, somatic treatments, age, level of intelligence, etc.

The nature of the neuropsychological measure used in psychosurgery research is crucial to the research findings obtained. Obviously, tests which are insensitive to the cognitive effects of psychosurgery will lead to negative results. The researcher need only be reminded of Sperry and Gazzaniga's (Gazzaniga, 1978; Sperry and Gazzaniga, 1967) work with split-brain patients to see the problems inherent in concluding that a psychosurgical procedure has no effect when one cannot be sure appropriately sensitive testing procedures have been used.

In this regard, qualitative analyses in neuropsychological outcome studies of psychosurgery may hold great promise. It is possible that current testing procedures are not refined enough to detect a qualitative loss in neuropsychological abilities following psychosurgery (see Chapters 2, 3, and 4). It is also possible that the cognitive effects of psychosurgery are subtle and may only emerge under certain conditions of stress (see Ewing et al., 1980, for support of such a hypothesis for a minor head injury population).

Three other methodological issues should be considered in future research. (1) Multivariate research strategies which can take into account the cumulative and interactive effects of large numbers of variables would likely provide more scientifically useful information than earlier univariate designs. (2) Subgroup analyses as well as case studies employing qualitative, intra-individual analyses hold considerable promise in the study of the neuropsychological correlates of psychosurgical interventions. Individual or subgroup differences before and after psychosurgery are probably obscured by group means, yet these differences likely affect the response to psychosurgery, and they may reflect some of the significant neuropsychological effects of psychosurgery. (3) Much of the current psychosurgery research consists of one-shot studies whose contributions to knowledge are limited because of idiosyncrasies in research design and subject selection. Collaborative, programmatic models for neuropsychological research projects, such as the Collaborative Neuropsychological Study of Polydrug Users (Grant et al., 1978), may help to overcome many of the problems inherent in psychosurgery outcome research due to small samples, different lesion and patient types, and different research protocols.

Neuropsychological research presumably can provide a theoretical framework within which the nature of the higher cortical functions affected by psychosurgical procedures can be elucidated. Whether neuropsychological research with psychosurgery patients can also provide useful scientific information about the effects of frontal lobe lesions on human behavior in general, or the normal functions subserved by the frontal lobes of the brain, is at present questionable because of the pre-existing psychiatric disorders and the attendant effects of other treatment conditions in patients who have undergone psychosurgery. Similar operations performed in healthy brains would very likely produce different neuropsychological effects than those seen in psychosurgery patients.

ACKNOWLEDGMENT

The support of Mr. N. John Scholten, Director of the Sarnia-Lambton Centre for Children and Youth and Mr. Gerry F. Fisher, Executive Director of Queen Alexandra Hospital for Children, and the assistance of Mrs. Eleanor Sloot is gratefully acknowledged.

REFERENCES

Adams, K. M. (1977, September). The long-term effects of prefrontal leucotomy. Paper presented at the annual meeting of the American Psychological Association.

Andy, O. J., and Jurko, M. F. (1972). Hyperresponsive syndrome. In: E. Hitchcock, L. Laitiner, and K. Vaernet, eds., *Psychosurgery*. Springfield, Illinois: Charles C. Thomas, pp. 117–126.

Bailey, H. R., Dowling, J. L., and Davies, E. (1973). Studies in depression: III. The control of affective illness by cingulotractotomy: A review of 150 cases. *Med. J. Australia, 2,* 366–371.

Ballantine, H. T., Cassidy, W. L., Flanagan, N. B., and Marino, R. (1967). Stereotaxic anterior cingulotomy for neuropsychiatric illness and intractable pain. *J. Neurosurg., 26,* 488–495.

Banna, M., Adams, K. M., Finlayson, M. A. J., and Tunks, E. (1978). Computed tomography after psychosurgery. *J. Comput. Tomog., 12,* 98–99.

Boyd, B. A., Weber, W. H., and McKenzie, K. G. (1958). Leucotomy—Its therapeutic value on the disturbed wards of a mental hospital. *Can. Psychiat. Assoc. J., 3,* 170–179.

Buffery, A. W. H. (1967). Learning and memory in baboons with bilateral lesions of frontal or inferotemporal cortex. *Nature, 214,* 1054–1056.

Butters, N. (1979). Amnesic disorders. In: K. M. Heilman and E. Valenstein, eds., *Clinical Neuropsychology*. New York: Oxford University Press, pp. 439–474.

Chapman, L. F., and Wolff, H. G. (1959). The cerebral hemispheres and the highest integrative functions of man. *Arch. Neurol., 1,* 19–35.

Choppy, M., Zimbacca, N., and LeBeau, J. (1973). Psychological changes after selective frontal surgery (especially cingulotomy) and after stereotactic surgery of the basal ganglia. In: L. V. Laitinen and K. E. Livingston, eds., *Surgical Approaches in Psychiatry*. Baltimore: University Park Press, pp. 174–181.

Cochrane, N., and Kljacic, I. (1979). The effects on intellectual functioning of open prefrontal leucotomy. *Med. J. Australia, 7,* 258–260.

Davison, L. A. (1974). Current status of clinical neuropsychology. In: R. M. Reitan and L. A. Davison, eds., *Clinical Neuropsychology: Current Status and Applications*. Washington, D.C.: Winston, pp. 325–361.

Department of Health, Education and Welfare. (1977). *Psychosurgery: Report and recommendations of the national commission for the protection of human subjects of biomedical and behavioral research.* (DHEW Publication No. 05-77-001), Washington, D.C.: U.S. Government Printing Office.

Drewe, E. A. (1974). The effect of type and area of brain lesion on Wisconsin card sorting test performance. *Cortex, 10,* 159–170.

Ewing, R., McCarthy, D., Cronwall, D., and Wrightson, P. (1980). Persisting effects of minor head injury observable during hypoxic stress. *J. Clin. Neuropsychol., 2,* 147–155.

Falconer, M. A., and Schurr, R. P. (1959). Surgical treatment of mental illness. In: C. W. T. H. Fleming, A. Walk, J. London, and A. Churchill, eds., *Recent Progress in Psychiatry*, pp. 352–367.

Faillace, L. A., Allen, R. P., McQueen, J. D., and Northrup, B. (1971). Cognitive deficits from bilateral cingulotomy for intractable pain in man. *Diseases of the Nervous System, 32,* 171–175.

Finger, S. (1978). Environmental attenuation of brain-lesion symptoms. In: S. Finger, ed., *Recovery from Brain Damage, Research and Theory*. New York: Plenum Press, pp. 297–329.

Finlayson, M. A. J. (1979, June). Prefrontal leucotomy. Neuropsychological functioning 15 years later. Paper presented at the annual meeting of the Canadian Psychological Association, Quebec City, 1979.

Finlayson, M. A. J., Johnson, K., and Reitan, R. M. (1977). Relationship of level of education to neuropsychological measures in brain-damaged and non-brain-damaged adults. *J. Consult. Clin. Psychol., 45,* 536–542.

Fleming, J. F. R., and Baker, E. F. W. (1972). Bimedial prefrontal leucotomy. In: E. Hitchcock, L. Laitinen, and K. Vaernet, eds., *Psychosurgery*. Springfield, Illinois: Charles C. Thomas, pp. 322–331.

Freeman, W. (1961). Psychosurgery: A quarter of a century later. In: *Proceedings, Third World Congress of Psychiatry,* vol. 1. Toronto: University of Toronto Press, pp. 141–148.

Freeman, W., and Watts, J. W. (1942). *Psychosurgery,* 1st ed. Springfield, Illinois: Charles C. Thomas.

Gaches, J., LeBeau, J., and Choppy, M. (1972). Psychosurgery in severe obsessive syndromes. In: E. Hitchcock, L. Laitinen, and K. Vaernet, eds., *Psychosurgery.* Springfield, Illinois: Charles C. Thomas, pp. 230–241.

Gazzaniga, M. S. (1978). Is seeing believing: Notes on clinical recovery. In: S. Finger, ed., *Recovery from Brain Damage, Research and Theory.* New York: Plenum Press, pp. 409–414.

Goldstein, K., and Scheerer, M. (1941). Abstract and concrete behavior: An experimental study with special tests. *Psychological Monographs, 43,* 1–151.

Greenblatt, M. (1950). Psychosurgery: A review of recent literature. In: M. Greenblatt, A. Arrot, and H. C. Solomon, eds., *Studies in Lobotomy.* New York: Grune and Stratton, Inc.

Grant, I., Adams, K. M., Carlin, A. S., Rennick, P. M., Judd, L. L., and Schooff, K. (1978). The collaborative neuropsychological study of polydrug users. *Arch. General Psychiat., 35,* 1063–1074.

Halstead, W. C. (1947). *Brain and Intelligence: A Qualitative study of the Frontal Lobes,* Chicago: University of Chicago Press.

Hamlin, R. M. (1970). Intellectual function 14 years after frontal lobe surgery. *Cortex, 6, 3,* 311–318.

Heaton, R. K., and Crowley, T. J. (1981). Effects of psychiatric disorders and their somatic treatments on neuropsychological test results. In: S. B. Filshov and T. J. Boll, eds., *Handbook of clinical Neuropsychology.* New York: John Wiley and Sons, pp. 481–525.

Hetherington, R. F., Haden, P., and Craig, W. J. (1972). Neurosurgery in affective disorder: Criteria for selection of patients. In: E. Hitchcock, L. Laitinen, and K. Vaernet, eds., *Psychosurgery.* Springfield, Illinois: Charles C. Thomas, pp. 332–345.

Hirose, S. (1961). Psychosurgery 1947–60: Evaluation of 450 patients treated by prefrontal lobotomy and a new method of orbito-ventromedial undercutting. In: *Proceedings, Third World Congress of Psychiatry,* vol. 1. Toronto: University of Toronto Press, pp. 138–141.

Hirose, S. (1965). Orbito-ventromedial undercutting 1957–63. Follow-up of 77 cases. *Am. J. Psychiat., 121,* 1194.

Hirose, S. (1972). The case selection of mental disorder for orbitoventromedial undercutting. In: E. Hitchcock, L. Laitinen, and K. Vaernet, eds., *Psychosurgery.* Springfield, Illinois: Charles C. Thomas, pp. 291–303.

Hitchcock, E. R., Ashcroft, G. W., Cairns, V. M., and Murray, L. G. (1973). Observations on the development of an assessment scheme for amygdalotomy. In: L. V. Laitinen, and K. E. Livingston, eds., *Surgical Approaches in Psychiatry.* Baltimore: University Park Press, pp. 142–155.

Joschko, M. (1979). Bilateral prefrontal leucotomy: An ex post facto archival study of a complete hospital sample. *J. Clin. Neuropsychol., 1,* 167–182.

Jurko, M. F., and Andy, O. J. (1973). Psychological changes correlated with thalamotomy site. *J. Neurol., Neurosurg. Psychiat., 36,* 846–852.

Kalinowsky, L. B. (1973). Attempt at localization of psychological manifestations observed in various psychosurgical procedures. In: L. V. Laitinen and K. E. Livingston, eds., *Surgical Approaches in Psychiatry.* Baltimore: University Park Press, pp. 18–21.

Kalinowsky, L. B., and Hippius, H. (1969). *Pharmacological, Convulsive and Other Somatic Treatments in Psychiatry.* New York: Grune and Stratton.

Kelly, D., and Mitchell-Heggs, N. (1973). Stereotactic limbic leucotomy—A follow-up study of thirty patients. *Postgrad. Med. J., 49,* 865–882.

Knight, G. C. (1960). 330 cases of restricted orbital undercutting. *Proc. R. Soc. Med., 53,* 728.

Knight, G. C. (1972). Neurosurgical aspects of psychosurgery. *Proc. R. Soc. Med.*, *65*, 1099–1204.

Laitinen, L. V., and Vilkki, J. (1972). Stereotaxic ventral anterior cingulotomy in some psychological disorders. In: E. Hitchcock, L. Laitinen, and K. Vaernet, eds., *Psychosurgery*. Springfield, Illinois: Charles C. Thomas, pp. 242–252.

Landis, C. (1952). Remarks on psychological findings attendant on psychosurgery. In: *The Biology of Mental Health and Disease*. New York: Hoeber.

Laurence, S., and Stein, D. G. (1978). Recovery after brain damage and the concept of localization of function. In: S. Finger, ed., *Recovery from Brain Damage, Research and Theory*. New York: Plenum Press, pp. 369–407.

Lewin, W. (1973). Selective leucotomy: A review. In: L. V. Laitinen and K. W. Livingston, eds., *Surgical Approaches in Psychiatry*. Baltimore: University Park Press, pp. 69–73.

Lindstrom, P. A. (1972). Prefrontal sonic treatment—sixteen years' experience. In: E. Hitchcock, L. Laitinen, and K. Vaernet, eds., *Psychosurgery*. Springfield, Illinois: Charles C. Thomas, pp. 357–376.

Livingston, K. E. (1953). Angulate cortex isolation for the treatment of psychoses and psychoneuroses. *Assoc. Res. Nerv. Ment. Dis.*, *31*, 374–378.

Luria, A. R. and Homskay, E.D. (1964). Disturbance in the regulative role of speech with frontal lobe lesions. In: J. M. Warren and K. Akert, eds., *The Frontal Granular Cortex and Behavior*. New York: McGraw-Hill, pp. 353–371.

Luria, A. R. (1966). *Higher Cortical Functions in Man*, B. Haigh, Trans. New York: Basic Books.

Marks, I. M., Birley, J. L. T., and Gelder, M. G. (1966). Modified leucotomy in severe agoraphobia: A controlled serial inquiry. *Br. J. Psychiat.*, *112*, 757–769.

McKenzie, K. G., and Kaczanowski, G. (1964). Prefrontal leucotomy: A five-year controlled study. *Canadian Med. Assoc. J.*, *91*, 1193–1196.

Meyer, G., McElhaney, M., Martin, W., and McGraw, C. P. (1973). Stereotactic cingulotomy with results of acute stimulation and serial psychological testing. In: L. V. Laitinen and K. E. Livingston, eds., *Surgical Approaches in Psychiatry*. Baltimore: University Park Press, pp. 39–58.

Miller, A. (1954). *Lobotomy, a clinical study*. Monograph No. 1, Ontario Department of Health. Toronto: Queen's Printer.

Miller, A. (1967). The lobotomy patient—a decade later: A follow-up study of a research project started in 1948. *Canadian Med. Assoc. J.*, *96*, 1095–1103.

Milner, B. (1964). Some effects of frontal lobectomy in man. In: J. M. Warren and K. Akert, eds., *The Frontal Granular Cortex and Behavior*. New York: McGraw-Hill, pp. 313–334.

Mingrino, S., and Schergna, E. (1972). Stereotaxic anterior cingulotomy in the treatment of severe behavior disorders. In: E. Hitchcock, L. Laitinen, and K. Vaernet, eds., *Psychosurgery*. Springfield, Illinois, Charles C. Thomas, pp. 258–263.

Mirsky, A. F., and Orzack, M. H. (1977). Final report on psychosurgery pilot study. In: *Psychosurgery. report and recommendations. The national commission for the protection of human subjects of biomedical and behavioral research:* Appendix, Psychosurgery (DHEW Publication No. (05) 77–0002). Washington, D.C.: U.S. Government Printing Office.

Mitchell-Heggs, N., Kelly, D., and Richardson, A. (1976). Stereotactic limbic leucotomy—A follow-up at 16 months. *Br. J. Psychiat.*, *128*, 228–240.

Moore, B. E., Friedman, S., Simon, B., and Farmer, J. (1947). A cooperative clinical study of lobotomy. *Assoc. Res. Nerv. Ment. Dis.*, *27*, 769–794.

Parsons, O. A., and Prigatano, G. P. (1978). Methodological considerations in clinical neuropsychological research. *J. Consult. Clin. Psychol.*, *46*, 608–619.

Penfield, W. (1948). Symposium on gyrectomy. In: J. K. Fulton, ed., *Frontal Lobes*. Baltimore: Williams and Wilkins.

Pool, J. L. (1949). Topectomy. *Proc. R. Soc. Med.*, *42*, 1–3.

Reitan, R. M. (1966). A research program on the psychological effects of brain lesions in human beings. In: N. R. Ellis, eds., *International Review of Research in Mental Retardation*, vol. 1. New York: Academic Press.

Riddle, M., and Roberts, A. H. (1978). Psychosurgery and the Porteus Maze Tests: Review and reanalysis of data. *Arch. General Psychiat.*, *35*, 493–497.

Robin, A. A. (1958). A controlled study of the effects of leucotomy. *J. Neurol., Neurosurg., Psychiat.*, *21*, 262–269.

Rylander, G. (1948). Personality analysis before and after frontal lobotomy. *Assoc. Res. Nerv. Ment. Dis.*, *27*, 691–705.

Rylander, G. (1973). The renaissance of psychosurgery. In: L. V. Laitinen and K. E. Livingston, eds., *Surgical Approaches in Psychiatry.* Baltimore: University Park Press, pp. 3–12.

Scoville, W. B. (1949). Selective cortical undercutting as a means of modifying and studying frontal lobe function in man. *J. Neurosurg.*, *6*, 65–73.

Scoville, W. B. (1973). Surgical locations for psychiatric surgery with special reference to orbital and cingulate operations. In: L. V. Laitinen and K. E. Livingston, eds., *Surgical Approaches in Psychiatry.* Baltimore: University Park Press, pp. 29–36.

Scoville, W. B., and Bettis, D. B. (1977). Results of orbital undercutting today: A personal series. In: W. H. Sweet, eds., *Neurosurgical Treatment in Psychiatry.* Baltimore: University Park Press, pp. 189–202.

Smith, A., and Kinder, E. F. (1959). Changes in psychological test performances of brain-operated schizophrenics after eight years. *Science, 129,* 149.

Smith, J. S., Kiloh, L. B., and Boots, J. A. (1977). A prospective evaluation of prefrontal leucotomy. The results at 30 months follow-up. In: W. H. Sweet, ed., *Neurosurgical Treatment in Psychiatry.* Baltimore: University Park Press, pp. 217–224.

Sperry, R. W., and Gazzaniga, M. S. (1967). Language following surgical disconnection of the hemispheres. In: C. Millikan and F. Darley, eds., *Brain Mechanisms Underlying Speech and Language.* New York: Grune and Stratton, pp. 108–121.

Stein, D. G., Rosen, J. J., and Butters, N. (1974). *Plasticity and Recovery of Function in the Central Nervous System.* New York: Academic Press.

Strom-Olsen, R., and Carlisle, S. (1972). Bifrontal stereotaxic tractotomy. A follow-up study. In: E. Hitchcock, L. Laitinen, and K. Vaernet, eds., *Psychosurgery.* Springfield, Illinois: Charles C. Thomas, pp. 278–288.

Stuss, D. T., Kaplan, E. F., Benson, D. F., Weir, W. S., Naeser, M. A., and Levine, H. L. (1981). Long-term effects of prefrontal leucotomy—An overview of neuropsychologic residuals. *J. Clin. Neuropsychol.*, *3,* 13–32.

Sweet, W. H. (1973). Treatment of medically intractable mental disease by limited frontal leucotomy—justifiable? *N. Engl. J. Med.,* 289(21), 1117–1125.

Tan, E., Marks, I. M., and Marset, P. (1971). Bimedial leucotomy in obsessive-compulsive neurosis: A controlled serial enquire. *Br. J. Psychiat.*, *118,* 115–164.

Teuber, H. L. (1964). The riddle of frontal lobe function in man. In: J. M. Warren and K. Akert, eds., *The Frontal Granular Cortex and Behavior.* New York: McGraw-Hill, pp. 410–444.

Teuber, H. L., Corkin, S., and Twitchell, T. E. (1977). A study of cingulotomy in man. In *Psychosurgery: Report and recommendations of the national commission for the protection of human subjects of biomedical and behavioral research.* Appendix (DHEW Publication No. 05 77-0002. Washington, DC: U.S. Government Printing Office.

Valenstein, E. S. (1973). *Brain control.* New York: John Wiley and Sons.

Valenstein, E. S. (1977). The practice of psychosurgery: A survey of the literature (1971–1976). In: *Psychosurgery: Report and recommendations of the national commission for the protection of human subjects of biomedical and behavioral research.* Appendix (DHEW Publication No. 05-77-0002). Washington, DC: U. S. Government Printing Office.

Valenstein, E., and Heilman, K. M. (1979). Emotional disorders resulting from lesions of the central nervous system. In: K. M. Heilman and E. Valenstein, eds., *Clinical Neuropsychology.* New York: Oxford University Press, 413–438.

Vilkki, J. (1977). Effects of pulvinotomy and ventrolateral thalamotomy on some cognitive functions. In: W. H. Sweet, eds., *Neurosurgical Treatment in Psychiatry.* Baltimore: University Park Press, pp. 673–677.

Vilkki, J., and Laitinen, L. V. (1974). Differential effects of left and right ventrolateral thalamotomy on receptive and expressive verbal performances and face-matching. *Neuropsychologia, 12,* 11–19.

Walsh, K. W. (1977). Neuropsychological aspects of modified leucotomy. In: W. H. Sweet, ed., *Neuropsychological Treatment in Psychiatry.* Baltimore: University Park Press, pp. 163–174.

Wehler, R., and Hoffman, H. (1978). Intellectual functioning in lobotomized and nonlobotomized long term chronic schizophrenic patients. *J. Clin. Psychol., 34,* 449–451.

Whitty, C. W. M., Duffield, J. E., Tow, P. M., and Cairns, H. (1952). Anterior cingulectomy in the treatment of mental disease. *Lancet,* 1:475.

14

Neuropsychological Aspects of Epilepsy

M. R. TRIMBLE / PAMELA J. THOMPSON

Epilepsy is a clinical definition of a group of central nervous system disorders that have, as their common symptom, seizures. The latter arise from disturbed electrical activity within the brain and take a variety of forms including episodes of disturbed movement, sensation, perception, and behavior, which are usually but not inevitably accompanied by alteration of the level of consciousness. As such, it is a common disorder, and an acceptably quoted prevalence rate is around 5/1,000 of the population (Neugebauer and Susser, 1979).

In discussing the etiology of the condition it is usual to divide epilepsy into idiopathic and symptomatic groupings. In the former there is thought to be some form of inherited mechanism which leads to a low seizure threshold, whereas in the latter there are more clearly defined and identifiable causes that lead to the seizures. These include tumors, infections, vascular lesions, anoxia and head trauma.

Classification of epilepsy is complicated, not the least because it is a chronic condition with variable etiology, the symptom pattern of which may change over time. At present it is somewhat easier to classify seizure type, based on the clinical description and underlying electrophysiological abnormalities associated with the episode. An abbreviated version of the classification recommended by the International League Against Epilepsy (1970) is shown in Table 1.

Partial seizures are those of focal origin which either remain focal or become generalized. Their symtomatology is described as simple or complex—the latter referring to interference with high-level cerebral activity in which disturbance of consciousness occurs. Such patients present with a variety of experiences including hallucinations, affective disturbances, and thought disorder, and they usually have electroencephalographic, radiological, or neuropsychological evidence of temporal lobe abnormalities.

Generalized seizures are due to bilateral disturbances which are usually symmetrical from the outset. There is always loss of consciousness. Classical tonic–clonic seizures have a sudden onset with loss of consciousness, tonic muscular contractions followed by clonic ones, after which the patient is unarousable for a short period of time. Absence attacks are sudden transient lapses

Table 1. An abbreviated classification of seizures

I. Generalized Seizures
    (A) Absences with or without 3 c/s spike and wave
    (B) Complex absences
    (C) Bilateral massive myoclonus
    (D) Clonic, tonic or clonic–tonic seizures
    (E) Atonic seizures
II. Partial Seizures
    (A) With elementary symptomatology: motor, sensory, other
    (B) With complex symptomatology
    (C) Partial seizures, followed by secondary generalized seizures
III. Unilateral Seizures

---

of consciousness which may be so slight as to be scarcely perceptible to an on-looker. Myoclonic and akinetic seizures are also associated with momentary lapses of consciousness and in addition, brief bilateral clonic jerking of the face, limbs and/or trunk, or a sudden loss of postural tone.

The treatment of epilepsy is directed first towards removing any possible cause or precipitating factor, after which the prime aim is to control the main symptoms, namely the seizures. Pharmacological agents have become the standard form of treatment; Table 2 displays some of the anticonvulsant drugs currently available.

Experience has demonstrated that some seizure types respond better to certain anticonvulsant drugs than others. For absence episodes, the drugs of choice are ethosuximide and sodium valproate. For generalized and partial seizures there is a wider choice. Phenytoin, carbamazepine, primidone and phenobarbital are the most widely prescribed; but other drugs such as the benzodiazepines (e.g., clonazepam), A.C.T.H., dextroamphetamine, and acetazolamide are also sometimes used in the management of epilepsy.

An important advance in the management of epilepsy was the introduction of techniques for measuring serum anticonvulsant levels. Evidence has now accumulated demonstrating that the drugs' anticonvulsant properties and the occurrence of neuro-toxic side effects, such as ataxia and nystagmus, are better correlated to the concentration of the drug in the serum rather than to the dosage. From research in this area, the concept of the therapeutic range emerged—the range of serum levels within which maximum seizure control can be expected with the minimum incidence of side effects. Commonly quoted upper values for therapeutic ranges are given in Table 2.

In a small proportion of patients, seizure control is achieved following surgery. Thus, if epilepsy originates in a clearly demonstrable area of the brain that is accessible to surgery, and removal of it will not produce significant neuropsychological or physical problems, surgery is indicated if seizure control by medication has failed.

In recent years there has been a growing interest in nonpharmacological treatments for epilepsy, including biofeedback and techniques based on learn-

Table 2. Serum concentrations and related drug effects of commonly used anticonvulsants

Drug	Average daily maintenance dose		Usual therapeutic serum concentration range (mcg/ml)	Signs and symptoms usually associated with elevated serum concentrations or toxicity
	Adults (mg/kg)	Children (mg/kg)		
Carbamazepine (Tegretol)	10–20	20–30	4–12	Vertigo, lethargy, nystagmus, blurred vision, diplopia, confusion, ataxia, stupor
Clonazepam (Clonopin)	0.05–0.2	0.10–0.2	0.02–0.08	Sedation, confusion, slurred speech, somnolence, respiratory depression, coma, hypotension
Ethosuximide (Zarontin)	20–40	20–30	40–100	Nausea, vomiting, gastric distress, drowsiness, ataxia
Phenobarbital	2–3	3–5	15–40	Sedation, drowsiness, slurred speech, nystagmus, confusion, somnolence, ataxia, respiratory depression, coma, hypotention
Primidone (Mysoline)	10–25	10–25	5–12	Same as phenobarbital
Phenytoin (Dilantin)	3–5	4–7	10–20	Vertigo, ataxia, slurred speech, nystagmus, diplopia, somnolence, coma (arrhythmias with rapid intravenous administration)
Valproic Acid (Depakene)	30–60	30–60	50–100	Sedation, gastric disturbance, diarrhea, ataxia, somnolence, coma

Adapted from American Medical Association (1983). *AMA Drug Evaluations*, 5th ed., Chicago, Illinois: American Medical Association, pp. 310, 312. Reprinted with permission.

ing theories (see Lubar and Deering, 1981). To date, few controlled studies have been carried out, and their usefulness must, at present, be confined to individual cases.

Neuropsychological Aspects of Epilepsy

Alteration of cognitive function in epilepsy has been noted for several centuries. Willis, for example, in his seventeenth century Oxford Lectures stated: "It often happens that epileptic patients, during their paroxysm and afterwards, suffer a severe loss of memory, intellect and phantasy . . ." (Dewhurst, 1980). This aspect of epilepsy received prominent attention during the nineteenth century from physicians, who, invoking a genetic theory influenced by the ideas of degeneracy introduced by Morel and others, implied that intellectual and moral deterioration was an inevitable part of the epileptic process.

Since that time, and especially since the 1950s, there has been fairly extensive discussion of intellectual changes in epilepsy, although only a few groups have approached the subject in a systematic way, many authors reiterating views noted in earlier textbooks. The progression from global clinical impressions to the more sophisticated use of psychological tests will be briefly reviewed before discussing the impact of epileptic and neurological variables and anticonvulsant drugs on the mental state.

Methodologies Used to Assess Intellectual Function in Epilepsy

Until the quantification of intellectual function using standardized intelligence tests was introduced in the first decade of this century, the reports of cognitive deterioration in the literature were entirely clinical, and few authors gave precise figures for evaluation. Reynolds (1861) noted that 61% of his patients had some degree of deterioration of mental function; slightly higher figures were given by Turner (1907), who estimated 86% of the patients at the Chalfont Colony had abnormalities, some 30% showing a most pronounced degree of dementia.

These early reports, and many others which could be quoted, clearly came from highly selected groups of patients, and used purely clinical impressions to estimate the mental state. One of the earliest reports that employed standardized tests to evaluate cognition in epilepsy was that of Fox (1924), who found the mean I.Q. of 150 institutionalized children to be 71 in males and 65 in females. Although several other authors confirmed such findings, again they were mainly investigating patients in institutions, and as others examined different groups of patients, lack of deterioration began to be stressed (Keating, 1960). Lennox (Lennox and Lennox, 1960) provided data on 1905 epileptics, and came to the conclusion that two-thirds were mentally normal, and only one-seventh were unmistakably subnormal. In a study on "office patients", one-quarter were found to have I.Q.s of greater than 120, again reflecting referral patterns (vol. 2, pp. 669–672).

Two of the many problems encountered in some earlier studies were the poor documentation of epileptic variables that are clearly important in assessing deterioration, and the absence of a longitudinal design whereby alteration of cognitive function could be evaluated relative to the course of the disease. Barnes and Fetterman (1938) noted little tendency for scores on I.Q. tests to decline in 23 patients tested over a period of 1 or 2 years, and Arieff and Yacorzynski (1942), in taking into account etiology, suggested that brain damage rather than the seizures themselves was the most significant cause of ensuing psychological deficits.

A summary of the data from studies using straightforward I.Q. tests would thus suggest that in unselected groups the mean I.Q. of epileptic patients is probably within or just below the normal range, unless epilepsy is associated with overt neurological disease or brain damage, although there is a tendency for the lower ranges of I.Q. to be overrepresented.

An important step in the evaluation of cognitive abilities in epilepsy came with the further development of techniques such as the Halstead-Reitan Neuropsychological Battery (Reitan, 1974). This protocol, fully discussed in Chapter 1, provided a much more complete evaluation of the various facets of the mental state and has been used by several investigators in patients with epilepsy. Kløve and Matthews (1966) examined four groups of patients: (1) normal controls, (2) patients with epilepsy plus identifiable brain pathology, (3) patients with epilepsy and no brain damage and, (4) patients with brain damage but no epilepsy. In the majority of comparisons, normal subjects were superior to the other three groups, and scoring was worse in the groups with brain damage.

Dikmen and co-workers (Dikmen and Matthews, 1977; Dikmen, Matthews, and Harley, 1977) looked at specific epileptic variables in relation to such tests and noted poorer test profiles with higher seizure frequency, and more severe cognitive deficits in relation to an early age of onset and long seizure duration.

A major drawback, however, in the use of such standardized tests in the evaluation of this condition, is that they were not designed to dissect out the problems of patients with epilepsy, being validated and standardized on different population groups such as patients with structural brain lesions. This has led several groups to alter their approach and to develop test batteries especially for use in patients with epilepsy. Dodrill (1982), based on his experience with the Halstead-Reitan Battery, selected a series of tests specifically designed to evaluate neuropsychological deficits in epilepsy. His "Neuropsychological Battery for Epilepsy" was selected from approximately 100 psychological test variables, based on their ability to discriminate epileptic from nonepileptic patients, and their "non-overlap," or excessive correlation between tests that may have led to a duplication of measures. He performed cross-validation studies, and the final battery emerged employing 16 measures. These were 11 from the Halstead/Reitan Battery (including the Tactual Performance Test-TPT Total Time, Memory and Localization; Tapping Test; Trail-Making Tests; Aphasia Screening Test; and perceptual examination error tests) plus the Stroop test, the logical and visual reproduction portions of the Wechsler Memory Scale, and the Seashore Tonal Memory Test. This battery is used clinically to evaluate patients at an epilepsy center, but has also been used to assess the effect of seizures or drugs on cognitive function. In one study (Dodrill and Troupin, 1977), which compared the psychotropic properties of carbamazepine with phenytoin, use of the standardized Halstead-Reitan tests showed no statistically significant findings. However, using the specially selected neuropsychological battery, several important differences between phenytoin and carbamazepine emerged. Dodrill has moreover now extended the use of this battery further by evaluating, in addition, the psychological and social problems with which epileptic patients have to contend. Their Washington Psychosocial Seizure Inventory has 132 items which cover family background, emotional adjustment, interpersonal adjustment, vocational adjustment, financial status, adjustment to seizures, and medical management. Coupled with the Neuropsychological Battery for Epilepsy, this inventory represents a forward step in providing a comprehensive evaluation of the cognitive, emotional, and psychosocial status of epileptic patients.

A different approach has been adopted in our focused studies on epilepsy at the National Hospital, Queen Square. In particular, it was considered necessary to develop a series of neuropsychological tests that could be used to evaluate the impact of anticonvulsant drug effects on cognitive function, taking into account the following important considerations. First, it was appreciated that the tests must be maximally sensitive to changes in psychological function, since those which accompany the administration of anticonvulsant drugs might well be subtle, and hence difficult to detect with standard neuropsychological measures. Second, it was important to adopt a longitudinal design for the studies, and therefore tests had to be minimally sensitive to the effects of practice. Third, the tests selected needed to have relevance to epilepsy. This meant that they had to address common complaints of epileptic patients and be sensitive to previously established neuropsychological deficits. Fourth, tests needed to be interesting and meaningful for the patients so they would be motivated and would cooperate in followup assessments. For the same reason it was considered important that the entire battery not take too long to administer, many neuropsychological batteries being considered inappropriate on account of their excessive length. Finally, the measures chosen had to have wide application so that they could be used across a broad spectrum of intellectual levels. Many drug-sensitive measures in the literature seemed to be too sophisticated for use in some patients with epilepsy, and there was evidence to suggest that drug effects are not infrequently overlooked in those of limited intelligence because they do not always present with the classical clinical signs of drug toxicity, and are unable to express, in a clinical setting, the difficulties they are experiencing.

The series of neuropsychological tests we developed included measures of attention, retention of new information, speed and accuracy of perceptual registration, decision-making and manual speed (for details see Thompson, Huppert, and Trimble, 1981). We emphasized time-based measures of performance since the literature on the effects of other drugs on cognitive function suggested that they were particularly sensitive to drug administration. Our results with the use of this battery are described below.

Selective Neuropsychological Deficits in Epilepsy

Apart from evaluating overall impairments (e.g., I.Q. decrements), a number of investigators have examined specific deficits in patients with epilepsy including abnormalities of memory, perceptuo-motor skills, speed of mental processing and attention. These will be considered briefly.

Memory deficits in association with epilepsy have been reported for more than a hundred years. In the last century, clinicians variously described the memory of patients with epilepsy as "defective," "more or less treacherous," and "impoverished". In 1942 Lennox, considering the nature of these memory difficulties wrote, "The patient finds it hard to recall events and names particularly those learned recently." Only a few studies, however, have been undertaken to assess memory functions in epilepsy. Deutsch (1953) assessed the memory skills of 30 patients with epilepsy and brain damage, 30 with epilepsy and no brain damage, and 30 with brain damage and no epilepsy. Both groups with epilepsy showed a similar pattern of deficits on tests of learning and memory, including impairments in tactile learning and auditory perceptual tasks, which were different from those observed in the brain damaged group. Deutsch claimed that the impairments were attributable to some epileptic factor, although she did not go on to elaborate what that might be. Mohan et al. (1976) administered the Boston Memory Scale to 50 patients with generalized epilepsy and 50 nonepileptic controls matched for age and level of education. The average performance of the epileptic group was inferior to that of the control group, but this was not significant. Loiseau (1979) reported a study in which he evaluated the memory skills of 100 epileptics with 100 controls matched for age, sex, education, and social status. Retention of both verbal and nonverbal material was assessed. Memory was found to be impaired in the epileptic group, particularly the ability to remember lists of words and simple geometric patterns.

Evidence has accumulated associating memory deficits with temporal lobe foci. Most studies, however, have been based on patients with intractable epilepsy who were undergoing lobectomy. Considerable agreement exists that the side of the excision determines the kind of material that will be more difficult for the individual to remember, left-sided lesions yielding memory deficits for verbal material and right-sided lesions for nonverbal material (for review see Milner, 1975; Iverson, 1977). Little attention has been devoted to patients with temporal lobe epilepsy who do not require surgical intervention; and findings from existing studies have not been entirely consistent.

Glowinski (1973) compared the performance of 30 patients with chronic generalized epilepsy with 30 that had chronic unilateral temporal lobe epilepsy, and he found the latter to display greater deficits on the Wechsler Memory Scale. Other studies have reported similar findings with both children and adults (Fedio and Mirsky, 1969; Quadfasel and Pruyser, 1955). On the other hand, Mirsky and associates failed to differentiate between patients with focal and generalized epilepsy on the Wechsler Memory Scale (Mirsky et al., 1960). Their failure might have been due to the inclusion of patients other than those with temporal lobe foci in the focal group.

Demonstrations of laterality effects have been less convincing. Fedio and Mirsky (1969) found that children with left temporal lobe foci displayed memory deficits for verbal material while their retention of nonverbal material was unaffected. The converse was true for children with right temporal foci. Similarly, Ladavas et al. (1979) reported that his left temporal group were impaired on verbal retention tests, whereas the right-sided group were more impaired on a spatial memory test. Delaney et al. (1980) compared the test performance of right and left temporal lobe epileptics matched for age of onset, duration of epilepsy, and seizure frequency. The tests they used included the logical memory and visual reproduction of the Wechsler Memory Scale and word list learning. Their results revealed significant impairment of verbal memory in left temporal epileptic subjects and significant impairment of nonverbal, visual memory in those with right-sided abnormalities. Agnetti et al. (1979) were able to demonstrate verbal learning deficits in patients with left-sided foci, but they observed no significant difference between right and left temporal lobe groups on nonverbal retention tests. Others have also failed to find impairments of nonverbal memory in patients with a right temporal focus (Berent et al., 1979), and some investigations have been unable to clearly demonstrate laterality effects at all (Glowinski et al., 1973).

An interesting interpretation of these findings of memory difficulties in patients with epilepsy has come from the work of Mayeux et al. (1980). They have postulated that the interictal memory impairment may be an anomia. Thus, impaired word usage has been a frequently mentioned complication of epilepsy, although there are few studies. Mayeux and colleagues examined 29 patients with epilepsy (14 with left-sided, and seven with right-sided temporal lobe epilepsy, and a third group with generalized tonic-clonic seizures), who were given the WAIS, the Wechsler Memory Scale, the Benton Visual Retention Test, the Rey-Osterreith Complex Figure Test, and two naming tests: the Controlled Word Association Test and the Boston Naming Test. No differences on the memory tests were noted between the groups, but the left temporal patients performed much worse on the confrontation naming tasks. Several measures of verbal intelligence, learning, and memory were highly correlated with the naming test performance. The authors, from these findings, suggested that "the relative anomia demonstrated in temporal lobe epilepsy patients may have been interpreted by these patients and their relatives as poor memory" (Mayeux et al., p. 123). This study emphasizes some of the many problems of evaluating cognitive deficits in epilepsy.

Impairments of attention in the absence of overt clinical seizures have been described by several writers. Holdsworth and Whitmore (1974) found that 42% of their sample of epileptic children were rated by their teachers as markedly inattentive. Little research involving more objective neuropsychological assessment has been undertaken. In one study Stores et al. (1978) compared the performance of 71 children with epilepsy and 35 nonepileptic controls on a series of specially designed tests of attention. Epileptic boys were found to be significantly less attentive than nonepileptic boys. No comparable differences, however, were found for girls with epilepsy.

Some researchers have proposed that the attentional difficulties in epilepsy are related to seizure type, patients with generalized seizures displaying greater impairments than those with focal seizures. Mirsky et al. (1960) assessed the performance of groups of patients with generalized seizures and with focal seizures on their Continuous Performance Test (CPT), a measure of sustained attention. In this task, subjects had to detect a critical stimulus from a random sequence of letters presented at a constant rate. The authors found, as predicted, that the generalized group displayed greater impairments on this measure than the focal group. Using the same test of attentional capacity, Fedio and Mirsky (1969) reported similar findings for epileptic children. Kimura (1964) compared the scores of patients with generalized and partial epilepsy on a sustained attention task, in which patients had to report aloud letters that were briefly flashed onto a screen, in any order on some trials and in alphabetical order on others. When patients with myoclonic epilepsy were excluded from the analysis, the scores of the generalized subjects were significantly inferior to patients with localized epileptogenic foci. In contrast, Glowinski (1973) was unable to demonstrate differences in attentional capacity relating to seizure type. However, in his study, all groups of patients were significantly impaired on a test of divided attention in comparison with a nonepileptic control group. Similar findings were reported by Remschmidt (1973).

Inconsistencies in the findings of studies looking at the relationship of cognitive impairments to seizure type may reflect differential sensitivity of the psychological tests employed. Furthermore, many measures of memory were not devoid of attentional components, and the converse seems true for measures of attention. At the present time it seems that the memory and attentional difficulties noted in epilepsy are not solely the consequences of seizure type.

Disturbances of perceptuo-motor skills have also been reported in epilepsy. Gastaut (1964) found that more than one-third of the epileptic children in his study displayed considerable handicaps which he felt were sufficient to interfere with learning to read and write. At a special school for epilepsy, 215 children were reported to be slow and clumsy. Several studies using the Bender Gestalt Test have demonstrated that children with seizures perform less well than control groups (Schwarz and Dennerll, 1970; Tymchuk, 1974). A study of visual perception of young children with epilepsy using the Frostig Test revealed impairments that were more marked in patients with partial seizures than in those with generalized seizures (Morgan and Groh, 1980).

Speed of mental processing, although not a distinct domain of abilities, is often of critical importance in the execution of psychological tests. References to mental slowing in people with epilepsy have been made since antiquity, investigators using such terms as "slowness of mental reaction," "slowness of thought and language," "stickiness of thought," "mental viscosity," "slowness of ideation," and "prolonged speed of cerebration." McGuckin (1980) suggests that lack of speed is one of the four barriers for patients with epilepsy when seeking employment. Bruhn and Parsons (1972) studied the reaction times of epileptics, brain damaged, and normal individuals, and found slowing was common in the two patient groups. Arena et al. (1979) reported slower simple and complex reaction times in patients with epilepsy than in matched controls.

Poor arithmetical ability was mentioned in the study of Fox (1924) of children attending a special school for epilepsy. This particular psychological deficit has been commented on by others, including Bradley (1947) and Bagley (1971). The latter author noted that the 31 epileptic children he studied were an average of 23.1 months behind in arithmetic compared to the expected attainment level. He believed the observed retardation was due to a specific epileptic factor. Green and Hartledge (1971) found even when children with epilepsy were at an appropriate academic placement they were often performing below expectancy in a variety of areas, computational abilities, in particular. In another study, only 17% of epileptic children were rated high in mathematical ability in contrast to 31% of nonepileptic controls (Ross and West, 1978).

Difficulty learning to read is another specific deficit mentioned frequently in studies on epilepsy. Tizard et al. (1969) claimed that 25% of their sample of 9 to 12 year olds with epilepsy were more than 28 months behind in reading and comprehension in comparison with 4% of the general population. Rutter, in his Isle of Wight study (Rutter et al., 1970), found that children with epilepsy were reading an average of 12 months behind their chronological age. Similar impairments in reading have been noted by Bagley (1971) and Long and Moore (1979).

Before discussing other possible reasons for the occurrence of cognitive deficits in epilepsy we would like to underscore an important but sometimes overlooked feature of neuropsychological performance among epileptic patients, namely, the marked fluctuation in performance level that can occur. While this is perhaps not surprising, in view of the constant alteration of electrical activity of the brain, and perhaps also of serum anticonvulsant levels, it does emphasize the importance of selecting correct controls in such studies, and highlights the difficulties of selecting appropriate tests.

Factors Underlying Neuropsychological Handicaps in Epilepsy

Brain Damage

Patients with epilepsy with known brain pathology have frequently been reported to be intellectually inferior to patients with epilepsy of unknown etiology (for a review see Keating, 1960; Tarter, 1972). Kløve and Matthews (1966) noted normal subjects to be superior to the epileptic and brain damaged groups in their study. Further, the performance of those with epilepsy and brain damage was generally inferior to those who had epilepsy without brain damage. Finally, the performance of a brain damaged group without epilepsy was inferior to that of the brain damaged group with epilepsy. The groups had been matched for age and level of education. Chaudhry and Pond (1961) reported on two groups of children with epilepsy; one group had deteriorated intellectually and the other had not. The two groups had been matched among other variables for the extent of brain damage.

Thus, pre-existing brain damage, although a factor, does not seem to completely explain the neuropsychological deficits observed in some patients with epilepsy. When patients with brain damage are excluded from analyses, or brain damage effects are controlled, neuropsychological deficits are still found.

Age of Onset

The majority of investigations suggest that an early onset of seizures carries a poor prognosis for neuropsychological functioning (for review see Keating, 1960; Tarter, 1972). Few of the early studies made a distinction between age of onset and duration of epilepsy. Dikmen et al. (1977) compared the performance of two groups of patients matched for duration and frequency of tonic–clonic seizures, but differing with regard to age of onset. They used the WAIS and the Halstead-Reitan test battery. Patients with epilepsy that commenced before the age of 5 were more impaired on the majority of the tests than patients with epilepsy of later onset, usually between the ages of 10 and 15. O'Leary et al. (1981) administered a battery of tests to 48 children aged 9 to 15 who had tonic–clonic seizures. The children with seizures of early onset (before the age of 5) were significantly impaired relative to the children with later onset on 8 of the 14 measures. The deficits were seen on tasks whose requirements included the repetition of a simple motor act, attention and concentration, memory, and complex problem solving. The authors made statistical adjustments in an attempt to control for the effect of disease duration.

Seizure Type

Research on the association between seizure type and cognitive function has not been entirely consistent. Many authors have reported that generalized absence (petit-mal) seizures had a less damaging effect than generalized tonic–clonic (major) seizures (Collins, 1951; Zimmerman et al., 1951). On the other hand, Halstead (1957) found that children with absence seizures had lower I.Q.s and poorer reading and arithmetic skills than children with tonic–clonic attacks. More recently, investigators have drawn attention to the potentially damaging effect of the "absence" in the classroom. Williams (1963) wrote of the epileptic child, "In his work his efficiency may be lower, particularly through the occurrence of petit mal, and it must be remembered that even two absences may prevent a child from maintaining the understanding of the theme of the lecturer, as we well know when our minds wander."

Comparisons between patients with generalized and partial seizures are difficult to interpret. Kløve and Matthews (1966) reported that patients with generalized seizure types performed less well than patients with partial seizures on the WAIS and the Halstead Neuropsychological Test Battery. The scores of patients with mixed seizure types fell somewhere between the two. However, the opposite has also been found, that is, that patients with partial seizures perform less well on neuropsychological tests (Glowinski, 1973). To complicate the picture further, some authors claim to find no consistent differences in psychological test performance between patients with partial and generalized seizures (Mirsky et al., 1960).

These contradictory findings have their bases in the variety of measures of neuropsychological function that have been used in individual studies. In addition, the reliability of seizure classification, particularly in older studies, may be questioned. It seems likely that the pattern of neuropsychological deficits may differ between seizure types, rather than that certain types produce less damaging effects overall than others. Indeed, this becomes clear in the more recent research, as discussed above with regard to memory in temporal lobe epilepsy.

In this regard, the age of onset of seizures may also be expected to have consequences for the pattern of cognitive abilities observed in a particular individual. For instance, a left-sided focus may have a different impact depending on whether it becomes active at the age of 1, 6, 16, or 60.

Seizure Frequency

If seizures themselves can produce neuronal damage, as some have suggested (Dam, 1980), then their increased frequency might be expected to have an adverse effect on neuropsychological function. Some investigators have found that frequent seizures are associated with more marked impairments of cognitive abilities (Dikmen et al., 1977; Rodin, 1968), but this has not been consistently demonstrated (Zimmerman et al., 1951; Delaney, 1980; Loiseau, 1981). In one recent study, Seidenberg and associates (1981) attempted to explore the influence of seizure frequency using a longitudinal design. They compared the test-retest performance on the WAIS of two groups of adult epileptics. For one group, seizure frequency had lessened during the test–retest interval, and in the other it had increased or remained unchanged. The former group showed significant improvements on WAIS full scale I.Q., performance I.Q., verbal I.Q. and on eight of the eleven subtests. In comparison, the latter group showed significant improvements only on the performance I.Q. and the Object Assembly subtest. The results, therefore, suggest that seizure frequency is likely to be one of the factors associated with fluctuations in test performance of epileptic patients. Whether the actual "cause" is more seizures *per se,* increased medication, or other related factors, remains unclear at this time.

Electroencephalographic (EEG) Findings

Investigators have also explored the possible relationship between neuropsychological functions and various EEG patterns. Much work has centered on the classical three-per-second spike-wave activity that accompanies absence seizures. The prevailing view is that this activity is associated with decrements in test performance which appear most marked on measures of reaction time and vigilance, particularly if the task is experimenter-paced (Browne et al., 1974). Some authors have demonstrated that alterations in the frequency of spike and wave bursts seem dependent on the meaning of the task for the individual, with a reduction in this abnormal activity occurring during periods of alertness and interest and an increase during periods of boredom (Guey et al., 1969). Interestingly, in some studies the observed behavioral effects precede the spike-bursts by 1–1.5 seconds (for review see Fenwick, 1982).

Other forms of epileptic activity in the EEG trace have been associated with neuropsychological dysfunction. In one study, patients with frequent epileptiform activity present in their EEG traces were found to be more impaired on a series of neuropsychological tests than patients for whom such epileptiform activity was either infrequent or absent (Wilkus and Dodrill, 1976). Not all investigators have detected impairments of psychological test performance in relation to epileptic activity on the EEG. This might be due to the relative insensitivity of scalp recordings. Studies involving in-depth recordings are infrequent, but they would seem to support the view that subclinical epileptic discharges can interfere with cognitive processes (Rausch et al., 1978). Many studies suffer from there being a gap of several days or weeks between the EEG recordings and the neuropsychological assessment.

It has also been suggested that nonepileptic abnormal electrical activity, for instance slowing of the background rhythm, might be related to neuropsychological disturbance. Dodrill and Wilkus (1978) found that a dominant posterior frequency of less than 7.5–8.0 was associated with poorer neuropsychological test performance. Performance seemed particularly impaired on tests involving attention and "complex mental manipulation." Combinations of slow waves and epileptiform activity were accompanied by greater impairments on the psychological measures than either slow waves or epileptiform activity in isolation. In an extension of this work, Dodrill and Wilkus (1978) reported the presence of large amounts of theta activity in the EEG trace to be the best predictor of impaired neuropsychological test performance. However, EEG irregularities are not a cause *per se,* and it is important to question what underlies the slowing of these rhythms in patients with epilepsy. One factor could be the administration of anticonvulsant medication.

Social and Psychological Factors

The factors outlined so far may be described as physical or illness factors. The influence of environmental factors upon neuropsychological functioning has been little investigated, perhaps because they are less amenable to objective measurement. Institutionalization (Halstead, 1957), nonattendance at school (Ross and West, 1978) and parental attitudes (Long and Moore, 1979) could all, theoretically, affect cognitive performance. Research suggests that the epileptic child at school can suffer discrimination by his peers, and even his teachers (Pazzaglia and Frank-Pazzaglia, 1976). When seeking employment, the patient with epilepsy may encounter repeated rejections which are likely to have a detrimental effect upon his motivation and morale. Depressive illness is not uncommon in epilepsy (Robertson and Trimble, 1982), and this may be an additional factor associated with deficits in neuropsychological test performance. Suurmeijer and associates (1973), in a series of studies of the contribution of social and psychological factors versus illness factors in epilepsy, claimed that the former may have a more devastating effect on the cognitive state of the individual than the latter does.

Neuropsychological Aspects of Treatment

The majority of patients with epilepsy will be maintained on anticonvulsant drugs for many years. Despite their wide application, little is known of the possible effects of these drugs upon cognition. Reviews of the literature reveal mainly the paucity of research in this field (e.g., Trimble and Reynolds, 1976). Only a few drugs have been investigated in any systematic way, and the results of studies on the same drug are often contradictory and inconclusive, such that only a few rather tentative conclusions may be drawn.

For most anticonvulsants, favorable reports, based mainly on subjective impressions, are noted soon after their introduction, but with more widespread and prolonged use, adverse effects usually emerge. Detrimental effects on neuropsychological abilities have now been reported for the majority of existing drugs (for review see Trimble, 1981). Although the nature of the deficits observed tends to vary between studies, they are generally sufficient to expect reduction in peak efficiency at work, school or other demanding daily activities. Phenobarbital has been most implicated (Macleod et al., 1978; Ozdirim et al., 1978; Oxley et al., 1979) and carbamazepine the least.

Another finding that is emerging from more recent studies is that a relationship exists between anticonvulsant serum concentration and cognitive functioning, with high but not necessarily toxic levels being associated with neuropsychological impairments (Diehl, 1978; Dodrill, 1975; Macleod et al., 1978; Matthews and Harley, 1975; Reynolds and Travers, 1974; Trimble et al., 1980).

More definitive conclusions are difficult to draw, since individual studies vary in fundamental ways, including the amount and duration of medication intake, and the populations studied vary with regard to the type, duration, and severity of epilepsy. In addition, many investigators have adopted cross-sectional designs, comparing groups of epileptic patients matched supposedly for all but drug related variables. However, as noted previously, patients with epilepsy are not a homogeneous group, and may vary along a vast number of variables, especially epilepsy-related ones which themselves are suspected of influencing neuropsychological functions. For this reason the matching of groups of patients with epilepsy is very difficult when investigating drug effects. A more appropriate design for such studies would seem to be intra-subject longitudinal comparisons, although these are not without their design problems.

Recent Studies on Cognitive Effects of Anticonvulsants, Conducted at the National Hospital

OBSERVATIONS OF NON-EPILEPTIC VOLUNTEERS. In some of our initial investigations, drug-induced changes in cognitive function were examined in nonepileptic volunteers. These trials had the advantage of allowing for a carefully controlled and balanced design including the use of placebos, which is generally not possible in patients with epilepsy for treatment and ethical reasons. In addition, the findings were not contaminated by the influence of other epileptic variables as discussed.

Subjects were administered anticonvulsants and matching placebo tablets on a daily basis each for a period of two weeks in a double-blind cross-over design. Psychological testing took place on three occasions before and on completion of each of the treatment phases. At the end of the second and third sessions, a blood sample was taken to analyze anticonvulsant serum concentrations and to check subject compliance.

Four different drug trials were undertaken in which different groups from a homogeneous subject pool were administered anticonvulsant doses of phenytoin, carbamazepine, sodium valproate, and clobazam (Thompson et al., 1981; Thompson and Trimble, 1981a, 1981b). Significant deficits in test performance were recorded in association with all of these four drugs (Fig. 1). Impairments were most marked following phenytoin, and occurred on measures of memory and mental and motor speed. The recorded deficits were observed at a mean anticonvulsant serum level that was well within the commonly quoted therapeutic range.

Significant correlations were observed between individual serum levels and the degree of deterioration in test performance on five measures. With sodium valproate and carbamazepine, significant deficits in test performance occurred on four and two measures respectively, with the mean anticonvulsant levels for both drugs falling within their respective therapeutic ranges. For clobazam two deficits were recorded and significant correlations were observed between individual clobazam serum levels and test performance, with deficits being most marked at the higher serum concentrations. On sodium valproate and clobazam the pattern of deficits suggested a slowing down of mental processing speed, which reached significance only when the demands of the task increased. In contrast, deficits in association with carbamazepine occurred in motor rather than mental speed. Indeed, on one measure of processing speed, perceptual registration, the administration of this drug was associated with significant improvement in performance.

These studies demonstrated that many of our selected measures were sen-

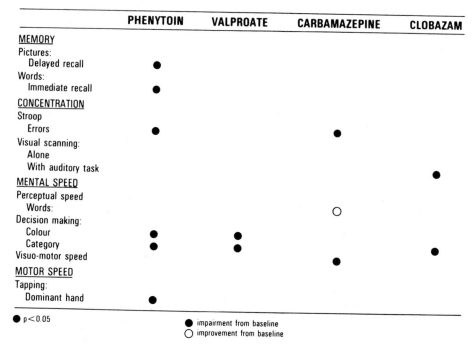

Fig. 1. Neuropsychological effects of four anticonvulsant drugs administered to nonepileptic volunteers to achieve serum levels in the therapeutic range.

sitive to the administration of anticonvulsants, and thus they were also adopted in investigations assessing drug effects in patients with epilepsy.

EFFECTS OF REDUCING ANTICONVULSANT LEVELS OR OF CHANGING TO A SINGLE ANTICONVULSANT. The first group of studies (Thompson and Trimble, 1982a, 1982b) assessed possible changes in the performance on the test battery of three groups of patients with epilepsy whose anticonvulsant regimens were altered in various ways. The first group consisted of 20 patients who had a reduction made in the number of different anticonvulsants they were prescribed, but no alternative medication was administered. The second group had 15 patients whose original medication was withdrawn or reduced and who were then prescribed carbamazepine. (Seven patients were prescribed carbamazepine monotherapy). There was no consistency in either group regarding the type of anticonvulsant that was withdrawn or reduced. The third group consisted of ten patients who did not have any anticonvulsant drug changes made, neither was there any marked fluctuation in their serum anticonvulsant concentration during the study.

Patients were seen on three occasions, at three monthly intervals, and following the first session medication changes were initiated in the first two groups. On each session patients performed the neuropsychological tests and completed subjective ratings of mood, on completion of which a blood sample was taken for the analysis of anticonvulsant serum concentrations. The number and type of seizures which had been recorded by the patients in the three months prior to each session were documented and, for as many patients as possible, a routine EEG was recorded.

The overall findings suggested that the drug changes made in both groups of patients resulted in improvements in the performance of the psychological tests, and since comparable changes were not seen in patients on stable therapy, the findings did not seem to be a consequence of practice effects (Fig. 2). In the first group, patients undergoing a reduction in polypharmacy towards monotherapy, improvements in performance were most marked on measures of concentration and motor speed and least marked on measures of memory, occurring on only one of the six measures. These observed benefits were generally not observed to be significant until the third assessment session, six months after the drug changes. This suggests that considerable time may need to elapse before it is advisable to evaluate the consequences of drug manipulations. The improvements in neuropsychological functioning took place in the absence of any marked changes in seizure frequency.

Patients changing to carbamazepine either alone, or in combination with some existing medication, displayed more widespread improvements in test performance, particularly on measures of memory, the latter occurring on all six tests (see Fig. 2). Changes in test performance were generally apparent three months following the drug change and were maintained with no further improvement to the six-month session, a different pattern from that observed in the first group. In these patients there was a consistent trend towards improved seizure control across the sessions which was significant in the case of tonic–clonic attacks by the third session. Since the changes were more marked than in the first group, there is some suggestion, considering the smaller sample size, that factors other than the withdrawal of polytherapy might be responsible for this. It seems likely that better seizure control, and perhaps an independent beneficial effect of carbamazepine, may underly the improvements. These studies confirmed clinical impressions that reduction of anticonvulsant drugs in patients on polytherapy is followed by beneficial effects on the mental state, and highlighted the possible psychotropic benefits of carbamazepine substitution, discussed widely elsewhere (e.g., Dalby, 1975).

HIGH VERSUS LOW SERUM ANTICONVULSANT LEVELS. The next studies explored the possible relationship between anticonvulsant serum levels and neuropsychological functioning. While previous investigators and our studies in volunteers have suggested such a relationship exists, interpretation of their findings is often difficult because of the experimental design adopted. The majority of clinical studies have either compared the neuropsychological test performance of two groups of patients divided about some arbitrary cutoff value into high and low serum level groups, or have correlated individual test scores with the patients' serum concentrations. Unfortunately, it is often not clear

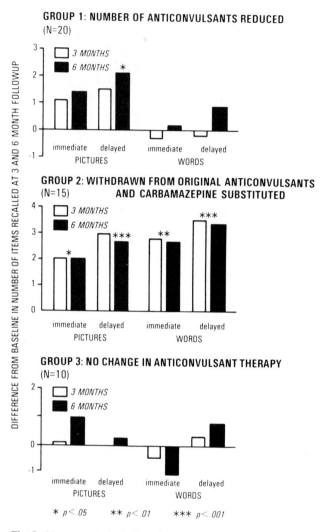

Fig. 2. Neuropsychological performance change of three groups of epileptic patients, three and six months after entering experimental protocols.

whether their findings are attributable to differences in serum level *per se* or to the influence of other epileptic variables that might distinguish patients with high serum levels from those with lower concentrations.

To explore further whether adverse effects on neuropsychological test performance do occur at high but perhaps even therapeutic concentrations, we undertook a study involving 28 patients with a diagnosis of epilepsy (Thompson and Trimble, 1984). Patients were seen on two occasions separated by an interval of three months. Following the first session patients had their dosage changed, in either direction, thus on one session the patient's serum level was high, and on the other it was low. For half the patients the high serum level session preceded the low one by three months, and for the others the reverse was the case. The format of the assessment was the same as in the previous study. Administration of psychological tests was followed by a blood sample, documentation of seizure frequency, and, in many cases an EEG recording. It was predicted that deficits in test performance would be most evident in association with high serum levels. The overall findings confirmed the prediction, since the mean scores of all 28 patients were worse on all but three measures in the high versus the low serum level session. Significant differences occurred on six measures, including tests of concentration, mental speed, and retention of new information. Impairments in performance seemed related to the demands of the task: as the level of difficulty increased so the extent of the impairment at high levels worsened.

Of the 28 patients, 12 were biochemically intoxicated in the high serum level session and accordingly the results obtained might merely reflect the value of keeping within the therapeutic range in order to avoid adverse effects on neuropsychological functioning. A second analysis, excluding these 12 patients, was undertaken, and the findings suggested that deficits in performance could still occur at subtoxic serum concentrations, but that they were less marked. Poorer scores in association with high concentrations were observed on eleven measures, but of these, only four were significant. As in the previous analysis, deficits were observed on the more demanding tasks. In these studies there were no statistically significant differences in the seizure frequency for the three months prior to each session.

Our findings were, therefore, consistent with those of other investigators in that deficits were found at high but not necessarily toxic levels, although the frequency of neuropsychological deficits was reduced when patients' serum concentrations were maintained within the therapeutic range. Impairments of concentration and mental processing speed associated with high concentrations deserve consideration, since they are likely to interfere with more complex mental abilities such as memory and decision making skills which are part of many daily activities. These may have particular consequences for school-age children. It also seemed important that deficits in performance in association with higher serum levels increased as the tests became more demanding. It appears likely that such impairments could easily be overlooked in a standard out-patient interview, using only a brief clinical evaluation of the mental state of the patient, and points towards the possible value of some form of more exacting neuropsychological assessment in monitoring anticonvulsant drug therapy.

HIGH VERSUS LOW SERUM LEVEL OF PHENYTOIN, CARBAMAZEPINE, OR VALPROATE. In the last group of studies, an attempt was made to look at individual anticonvulsants (Thompson and Trimble, 1982a, 1982b). Although the numbers of patients treated monotherapeutically were small (a maximum of nine pa-

	PHENYTOIN	VALPROATE	CARBAMAZEPINE
<u>MEMORY</u>			
Pictures:			
Immediate recall	●	●	
<u>CONCENTRATION</u>			
Stroop:			
Naming speed			●
Visual scanning:			
Alone		●	
With auditory task	●	●	
Auditory task:			
Part 3	●	●	
<u>MENTAL SPEED</u>			
Decision making:			
Category	●	●	
<u>MOTOR SPEED</u>			
Tapping:			
Dominant hand	●		
Both			●

● significant (p<.05) performance decrement in high vs. low concentration

Fig. 3. Decrement in neuropsychological performance of epileptic patients associated with high vs. low serum concentrations of three anticonvulsants.

tients per drug), patients were available to examine the effects of changes in serum levels of phenytoin, carbamazepine, and sodium valproate. As in the previous study, patients were seen on two occasions, at high and low drug concentrations, at an interval of three months. Deficits in performance were observed in association with the high serum level session, which were most marked for patients on phenytoin and sodium valproate (Fig. 3). One of the most striking features of the results was the degree of similarity in the profile of impairments at high levels of phenytoin and sodium valproate. For each drug, five significant differences occurred between the sessions with deficits occurring at high concentrations. Four of these were observed on the same measure, two on tests of concentration, one on a measure of decision making speed and one on retention of new information. In contrast, carbamazepine-treated patients showed no changes in performance between the sessions. Indeed, on the four measures which recorded significant impairments for the other two drugs, the trend at high levels of carbamazepine was towards improved performance, although this was not statistically significant. Impairments with high levels of this drug were recorded on two measures, one a measure of the speed of manual movements, and the other, the Stroop test. No significant changes in seizure frequency were recorded between the two sessions.

The findings indicate that certain patients may function better on neuropsychological testing at lower serum concentrations, and that this is not necessarily accompanied by any marked increase in seizure frequency. Most interestingly, the results suggest that carbamazepine may have a different pattern of effects on neuropsychological abilities than the other two drugs examined. Although the available data must be interpreted with caution because of the small sample size investigated, there is a suggestion that phenytoin and sodium valproate lead to a general slowing of mental processes, which, if severe enough, might be expected to result in impaired performance of many daily activities. Carbamazepine, on the other hand, appeared to have less widespread effects on cognitive functioning and did not seem to relate clearly to mental speed. The results of these investigations on patients treated monotherapeutically bear a marked resemblance to the results obtained in the studies with volunteers outlined above. In those studies, phenytoin led to a widespread disruption of cognitive ability, which, while much less with sodium valproate, was not of the more selective nature seen following carbamazepine. Such studies emphasize the value of examining both volunteer and patient groups, and allow us to conclude that some neuropsychological changes in epileptics occur as a direct result of anticonvulsant drugs rather than as a secondary consequence of the many other epileptic variables that can alter cognitive function in these patient groups.

SURGICAL INTERVENTION. Patients for whom anticonvulsant treatment has not succeeded in adequately controlling seizures, may be considered for surgery. Neuropsychological investigations of this patient group have contributed greatly to our understanding of brain–behavior relationships. From patients undergoing temporal lobectomies we have gained knowledge of the role of this area of the brain, particularly its association with memory functions (Milner, 1975; Iverson, 1977). Other patients have undergone surgery on the corpus callosum, and from them knowledge of the differential neuropsychological properties of the two hemispheres has emerged (Gazzaniga and Sperry, 1967). More recently, pre-operative neuropsychological assessment has been reported to be of value in predicting post-surgical outcome. Wannamaker and Matthews (1976) looked at cognitive performance on the Halstead-Reitan Neuropsychological Battery, and measures of motor proficiency and sensory discrimination, pre- and post-operatively in 14 patients with epilepsy. They found that improvement in seizure frequency following surgery was more likely to be seen in those with the least neuropsychological impairment pre-operatively. In addition, those patients who were most impaired pre-operatively were inclined to develop even greater neuropsychological deficits post-operatively. Their study also demonstrated that patients with right hemisphere resection fared better than those with left hemisphere surgery, both with regard to neuropsychological outcome and seizure control, although they made the important point that their chosen measures were weighted more to the assessment of dominant hemisphere functions.

The Contribution of Neuropsychological Assessment in Epilepsy

From this review, it seems that the neuropsychological assessment of patients with epilepsy is unlikely to contribute greatly to the diagnosis of epilepsy since no neuropsychological profile distinctive of this group of disorders has been established or seems likely to be. On the other hand, because patients with epilepsy frequently present with a variety of cognitive and motor deficits, neuropsychological assessment is valuable in baseline assessment and monitoring of treatment. Furthermore, knowledge of the nature and extent of neuropsychological difficulties may be useful in devising remedial programs which might help an individual overcome or minimize the effects of such deficits.

Recent research suggests that a relationship exists between neuropsychological performance, social functioning, and employability, and thus testing may be useful with regard to prognosis and management in these areas. Dikmen (1980) found highly significant neuropsychological differences between groups of patients with epilepsy differing in occupational status. Patients who were employed and who held higher jobs had better neuropsychological performance than those who held lower level jobs or were unemployed. Unemployed and low occupational status groups demonstrated more consistent impairments on measures of quickness, alertness, flexibility, and memory. Dikmen suggested that "these general skills may be a prerequisite for the effective utilization of other abilities as well as for learning new job skills."

An important application of neuropsychology is in the monitoring of the progress of epilepsy, especially the effects of treatment with anticonvulsant medication. The studies discussed in this chapter with regard to drug effects, although of a preliminary nature, demonstrate the potential usefulness of such monitoring. Neuropsychological assessment before and after the initiation of treatment, and before and after major drug changes, could be used to provide a more complete picture of the efficacy of such changes, and to a treatment regime for individuals that would exert the maximal effect of seizures while having minimal effects on cognitive processes.

Neuropsychology also can help determine the possible differences between anticonvulsant drugs in their cognitive effects. We have suggested that several drugs have somewhat different neuropsychological profiles. Other anticonvulsants in use need to be examined, and their different profiles explored. This will allow further rational selection of specific drugs for certain patients, taking their initial level of cognitive deficit into account. Since various anticonvulsant drugs appear to possess differential action on neurotransmitters, neuropsychological research also can lead to a greater understanding of the relationship between various neurochemical systems within the brain and neurocognitive performance.

REFERENCES

Agnetti, V., Ganga, M., Murrigaile, M., Piras, M. R., and Ticca, A. (1979). Memory assessment in temporal lobe epilepsy. Presented at the XIth Epilepsy International Symposium, Florence, Italy.

Arena, R., Menchetti, G., Tassinari, G., and Tognetti, M. (1979). Simple and complex reaction time to lateralised visual stimuli in groups of epileptic patients. Presented at the XIth Epilepsy International Symposium, Florence, Italy.

Arieff, A.J., and Yacorzinski, G. K. (1942). Absence of deterioration in patients with nonorganic epilepsy. *Journal of Nervous and Mental Diseases, 95,* 687–697.

Bagley, C. (1971). *The Social Psychology of the Child with Epilepsy.* London: Routledge Kegan & Paul Ltd.

Barnes, M. R., and Fetterman, J. (1938). Mentality of dispensary epileptic patients. *Arch Neurol., 40,* 903–910.

Berent, S., Boll, T. J., and Giordani, B. (1980). Hemispheric site of epileptogenic focus: Cognitive, perceptual and psychosocial implications for children and adults. In: R. Canger, F. Angeleri, and J. K. Penry, eds., *Advances in Epileptology.* New York: Raven Press.

Bradley, C. (1947). Treatment of the convulsive child in a children's psychiatric hospital. *The Nervous Child, 6,* 76–85.

Browne, T. R., Penry, J. K., Porter, R. J., and Dreifuss, F. E. (1974). Responsiveness before, during and after spike-wave paroxysms. *Neurology, 24,* 659–665.

Bruhn, P., and Parsons, O. A. (1977). Reaction time variability in epileptic and brain-damaged patients. *Cortex, 13,* 373–384.

Chaudhry, M. R., and Pond, D. A. (1961). Mental deterioration in epileptic children. *J. Neurol., Neurosurg. Psychiat., 24,* 213–219.

Collins, A. L. (1951). Epileptic intelligence. *J. Consult. Psychol., 15,* 392–399.

Dalby, M. A. (1975). Behavioural effects of carbamazepine. In: J. K. Penry and D. D. Daly, eds., *Complex Partial Seizures and Their Treatment. Advances in Neurology, vol 11.* New York: Raven Press, pp. 331–344.

Dam, A. M. (1980). Epilepsy and neuron loss in the hippocampus. *Epilepsia, 21,* 617–630.

Delaney, R. C., Rosen, A. J., Mattson, R. H., and Novelly, R. A. (1980). Memory function in focal epilepsy. A comparison of non-surgical unilateral temporal lobe and frontal lobe samples. *Cortex, 16,* 103–117.

Deutsch, C. P. (1953). Differences among epileptics and between epileptics and non-epileptics in terms of some learning and memory variables. *Arch. Neurol. Psychiat., 70,* 474–482.

Dewhurst, K. (1980). *Thomas Willis' Oxford Lectures.* Oxford: Sanford.

Diehl, L. W. (1979). *Treatment of Complicated Epilepsies in Adults. A Clinical-Statistical Study.* Basel, Switzerland: S. Karger A. G.

Dikmen, S. (1980). Neuropsychological aspects of epilepsy. In: B. P. Hermann, ed., *A Multidisciplinary Handbook of Epilepsy.* Springfield, Illinois: Charles C. Thomas, pp. 36–73.

Dikmen, S., and Matthews, C. G. (1977). Effect of major motor seizure frequency upon cognitive-intellectual functions in adults. *Epilepsia, 18,* 21–30.

Dikmen, S., Matthews, C. G., and Harley, J. P. (1975). The effect of early versus late onset of major motor epilepsy upon cognitive intellectual function. *Epilepsia, 16,* 73–81.

Dodrill, C. B. (1975). Diphenylhydantoin serum levels, toxicity and neuropsychological performance in patients with epilepsy. *Epilepsy, 16,* 593–600.

Dodrill, C. B. (1982). Neuropsychology. In: J. Laidlaw and A. Richens, *A Textbook of Epilepsy.* Edinburgh: Churchill Livingstone, pp. 282–291.

Dodrill, D. B., and Troupin, A. S. (1977). Psychotropic effects of carbamazepine in epilepsy: A double-blind comparison with phenytoin. *Neurology, 27,* 1023–1028.

Dodrill, C. B., and Wilkus, R. J. (1978). Neuropsychological correlates of the EEG in epileptics: III. Generalised non-epileptiform abnormalities. *Epilepsia, 19,* 453–462.

Fedio, P., and Mirsky, A. F. (1969). Selective intellectual deficits in children with temporal lobe or centrecephalic epilepsy. *Neuropsychologia, 7,* 287–300.

Fenwick, P. (1982). EEG Studies. In: E. H. Reynolds and M. R. Trimble, *Epilepsy and Psychiatry.* Edinburgh: Churchill-Livingstone, pp. 242–263.

Fox, J. T. (1924). Response of epileptic children to mental and educational tests. *Br. J. Med. Psychol., 4,* 235–248.

Gastaut, H. (1964, April). Enquiry into the education of epileptic children. In British Epilepsy Association and International Bureau for Epilepsy, *Epilepsy and Education, a Report of a Seminar in Marseilles.*

Gazzaniga, M. S., and Sperry, R. W. (1967). Language after section of the cerebral commissures. *Brain, 90,* 131–148.

Glowinski, H. (1973). Cognitive deficits in temporal lobe epilepsy: An investigation of memory functioning. *J. Nerv. Ment. Dis., 157,* 129–137.

Green, J. B., and Hartlage, L. G. (1971). Comparative performance of epileptic and nonepileptic children and adolescents. *Dis. Nerv. System, 32,* 418–421.

Guey, T., Charles, C., Coquilery, C., Roger, J., and Soulayrol, R. (1967). Study of psychological effects of ethosuximide (Zarontin) on 25 children suffering from petit mal epilepsy. *Epilepsia, 8,* 129–141.

Halstead, H. (1957). Abilities and behaviour of epileptic children. *J. Mental Science, 103,* 28–47.

Holdsworth, L., and Whitmore, K. (1974). A study of children with epilepsy attending ordinary schools. I. Their seizure patterns, progress and behaviour in school. *Dev. med. Child Neurol., 16,* 746–758.

International League Against Epilepsy (1970). Clinical and electroencephalographical classification of epileptic seizures. *Epilepsia, II,* 2–13.

Iverson, S. (1977). Temporal lobe amnesia. In: C. W. M. Whitty and O. L. Zangwill, *Amnesia.* London: Butterworths.

Keating, L. E. (1960). A review of the literature on the relationship of epilepsy and intelligence in school children. *J. Mental Science, 106,* 1042–1059.

Kimura, D. (1964). Cognitive deficit related to seizure patterns in centrecephalic epilepsy. *J. Neurol., Neurosurg. Psychiat., 27,* 291–295.

Kløve, H., and Matthews, C. G. (1966). Psychometric and adaptive abilities in epilepsy with different aetiology. *Epilepsia, 7,* 330–338.

Ladavas, E., Umilta, C., and Provinciali, L. (1979). Hemispheric-dependent cognitive performances in epileptic patients. *Epilepsia, 20,* 493–502.

Lennox, W. G. (1942). Brain injury, drugs and environment as a cause of mental decay in epilepsy. *Am. J. Psychiat., 99,* 174–180.

Lennox, W. G., and Lennox, M. A. (1960). *Epilepsy and Related Disorders.* Boston: Little, Brown.

Loiseau, P., Stube, E., Broustet, D., Battelleochi, S., Gomeni, C., and Morselli, P. D. (1980). Evaluation of memory function in a population of epileptic patients and matched controls. *Acta Neurologica Scandinavica, 62:80,* 58–61.

Long, C. G., and Moore, J. R. (1979). Parental expectations for their epileptic children. *J. Child Psychol. Psychiat., 20,* 313–324.

Lubar, J. F., and Deering, W. M. (1981). *Behavioral Approaches to Neurology.* London: Academic Press.

Macleod, C. M., Dekaban, A. S., and Hunt, E. (1978). Memory impairment in epileptic patients: Selective effects of phenobarbitone concentration. *Science, 202,* 1102–1104.

Matthews, C. G., and Harley, J. P. (1975). Cognitive and motor sensory performances in toxic and non-toxic epileptic subjects. *Neurology, 25,* 184–188.

Mayeux, J., Brandt, J., Rosen, J., and Benson, F. (1980). Interictal memory and language in temporal lobe epilepsy. *Neurology, 30,* 120–125.

McGuckin, H. M. (1980). Changing the world view of those with epilepsy. In: R. Canger, F. Angeleri, and J. K. Penry, eds., *Advances in Epileptology, XIth Epilepsy International Symposium, 1980.* New York: Raven Press, pp. 205–208.

Milner, B. (1975). Psychological aspects of focal epilepsy and its neurosurgical management. *Adv. Neurol., 8,* 299–321.

Mirsky, A. F., Primac, D. W., Marsan, C. A., Rosvold, H. E., and Stevens, J. R. (1960). A comparison of the psychological test performance of patients with focal and non-focal epilepsy. *Exp. Neurol., 2,* 75–89.

Mohan, V., Varma, V. K., and Sawhney, B. B. (1976). Intellectual and memory functions in epileptics. *India Neurol., 24,* 110.

Morgan, A., and Groh, C. (1980). Changes in visual perception in children with epilepsy. In: B. Kulig, H. Meinardi, and G. Stores, eds., *Epilepsy and Behaviour '79.* Lisse: Swets & Zeitlinger.

Neugebauer, R., and Susser, M. (1979). Some epidemiological aspects of epilepsy. *Psychol. Med., 9,* 207–215.

O'Leary, D. S., Seidenberg, M., Berent, S., and Boll, T. J. (1981). Effect of age of onset on tonic-clonic seizures on neuropsychological performance in children. *Epilepsia, 22,* 197–204.

Oxley, J., Rechens, A., and Wadsworth, J. (1979). Improvement in memory function in epileptic patients following a reduction in serum phenobarbitone levels. *Abstr., 11th Epilepsy Int. Symp.,* Florence, Italy.

Ozidrim, E., Renda, Y., and Epir, S. (1977). Effects of phenobarbitone and phenytoin on the behaviour of epileptic children. In: *Advances in Epileptology: Psychology and New Diagnostic Approaches.* Lisse: Swets and Zeitlingeer.

Pazzaglia, P., and Frank-Pazzaglia, L. (1976). Record in grade school of pupils with epilepsy: An epidemiological study. *Epilepsia,* 361–366.

Quadfasel, A. F., and Pruyser, P. W. (1955). Cognitive deficit in patients with psychomotor epilepsy. *Epilepsia, 4,* 80–90.

Rausch, R., Lieb, J. P., and Crandall, P. H. (1978). Neuropsychologic correlates of depth spike activity in epileptic patients. *Arch. Neurol., 35,* 699–705.

Reitan, R. M. (1974). Psychological testing of epileptic patients. In P. J. Vinken and G. W. Bruyn, eds., *A Handbook of Clinical Neurology, vol. 15.* N. Holland: Elsevier, pp. 559–575.

Remschmidt, H. (1973). Psychological studies of patients with epilepsy and popular prejudice. *Epilepsia, 14,* 347–356.

Reynolds, E. H., and Travers, R. D. (1974). Serum anticonvulsant concentrations in epileptic patients with mental symptoms. *Br. J. Psychiat., 124,* 440–445.

Reynolds, J. R. (1861). *Epilepsy: Its Symptoms, Treatment, and Relation to Other Chronic Convulsive Diseases.* London: J. Churchill.

Robertson, N. M., and Trimble, M. R. (1982). Flupenthixol in depression. A review. *Br. J. Clin. Practice,* Suppl. 18, 48–51.

Rodin, E. A. (1968). *The Prognosis of Patients with Epilepsy.* Springfield, Illinois: Charles C. Thomas.

Ross, E., and West, P. B. (1978). Achievements and problems of British 11 year olds with epilepsy. In: H. Meinardi and A. J. Rowan, eds., *Advances in Epileptology—1977. Psychology and New Diagnostic Approaches.* Amsterdam: Swets & Zeitlinger.

Rutter, M., Graham, P., and Uyle, W. (1970). A neuropsychological study in childhood. *Clinics in Developmental Medicine 35/36.* London: S.I.M.P. with Heineman.

Schwartz, M. L., and Dennerll, R. D. (1970). Neuropsychological assessment of children with and without questionable epileptogenic dysfunction. *Percept. Motor Skills, 30,* 111–121.

Seidenberg, M., O'Leary, D. S., Berent, S., and Boll, T. (1981). Changes in seizure frequency and test-retest scores on the Wechsler Adult Intelligence Scale. *Epilepsia, 22,* 75–83.

Stores, G., Hart, J., and Piran, N. (1978). Inattentiveness in school children with epilepsy. *Epilepsia, 19,* 169–175.

Suumeijer, J.P.B.M., Van Dam, A., and Blijham, M. (1978). Children with epilepsy; education, future orientation and school achievement level. *Tijdschr. Soc. Ganeesk.,* 342–348.

Tarter, R. E. (1972). Intellectual and adaptive functioning in epilepsy: A review of fifty years of research. *Dis. Nerv. System, 33,* 763–770.

Thompson, P. J., and Trimble, M. R. (1981a). Sodium valproate and cognitive functioning in normal volunteers. *Br. J. Clin. Pharmacy, 12,* 819–824.

Thompson, P. J., and Trimble, M. R. (1981b). Clobazam and cognitive functions. Effects in healthy volunteers. In: *Royal Society of Medicine International Congress and Symposium Series.* London: Academic Press, pp. 33–38.

Thompson, P. J., and Trimble, M. R. (1982a). Comparative effects of anticonvulsant drugs on cognitive functioning. *Br. J. Clin. Practice,* Suppl. 18, 154–156.

Thompson, P. J., and Trimble, M. R. (1982b). Anticonvulsant drugs and cognitive functions. *Epilepsia, 23,* 531–544.

Thompson, P. J., and Trimble, M. R. (1984). The effect of anticonvulsant drugs on cognitive function: Relation to serum levels. (Unpublished.)

Thompson, P. J., Huppert, F. A., and Trimble, M. R. (1981). Phenytoin and cognitive functions: Effects on normal volunteers and implications for epilepsy. *Br. J. Clin. Psychol., 20,* 155–162.

Tizard, J., Rutter, M., and Whitmore, K. (1969). *Education, Health and Behaviour.* London: Longmans.

Trimble, M. R. (1981). Anticonvulsant drugs, behaviour and cognitive abilities. In: W. Essman and L. Valzelli, eds., *Current Developments in Psychopharmacology, vol. 6.* New York: Spectrum Publications, pp. 65–91.

Trimble, M. R., and Reynolds, E. H. (1976). Anticonvulsant drugs and mental symptoms: A review. *Psychol. Med., 6,* 169–178.

Trimble, M. R., Thompson, P. J., and Huppert, F. (1980). Anticonvulsant drugs and cognitive abilities. In: R. Canger, F. Angeleri, and J. K. Penry, eds., *Advances in Epileptology: 11th International Epilepsy Symposium.* New York: Raven Press, pp. 199–204.

Turner, W. A. (1907). *Epilepsy.* London: MacMillan.

Tymchuk, A. J. (1974). Comparison of Bender error and time scores for groups of epileptic, retarded and behaviour problem children. *Percept. Motor Skills, 38,* 71–74.

Wannamaker, B. B., and Matthews, C. G. (1976). Prognostic implications of neuropsychological test performance for surgical treatment of epilepsy. *J. Nerv. Mental Dis., 163,* 29–34.

Wilkus, R. J., and Dodrill, C. B. (1976). Neuropsychological correlates of the electroencephalogram in epileptics. In: Topographic distribution and average rate of epileptiform activity. *Epilepsia, 17,* 89–100.

Williams, D. (1963). The psychiatry of the epileptic. *Proc. Roy. Soc. Med., 56,* 701–710.

Yacorzinski, G. K., and Arieff, A. J. (1942). Absence of deterioration in patients with nonorganic epilepsy. *J. Nerv. Mental Dis., 95,* 687–697.

Zimmerman, F. T., Burgemeister, B. B., and Putnam, T. J. (1951). Intellectual and emotional make up of the epileptic. *Arch. Neurol. Psychiat., 65,* 545–556.

15

Neurobehavioral Sequelae of Closed Head Injury

MICHAEL R. BOND

The Nature of Closed Head Injuries

Closed head injuries produce brain damage as a result of abrupt acceleration or deceleration of the head, and/or sharp rotational movements which cause loss of consciousness. The sufferer has a history of a blow to the head and will almost always exhibit bruising or laceration of the scalp or forehead; in a proportion of cases, the skull will be fractured but not breached. Interestingly, Adams and others (1977) reported that fractures are least common in cases coming to postmortem with the greatest amount of diffuse brain injury. Closed head injuries are distinguished from open injuries in which the skull is breached—wounds that are common during war or civil commotion and relatively uncommon in normal civilian life.

It is not possible to say how frequently head injuries occur since many minor injuries go unreported or are dealt with by family doctors. In Scotland the majority of injuries resulting in hospital stays or admission for treatment in those aged between 16 and 64 years are caused by motor vehicle accidents, whereas falls and domestic and sports' accidents account for the largest proportion of head injuries in younger victims, with a slightly different pattern for those aged 65 and over (Table 1). Similar figures have been obtained in other Westernized countries. The largest number of those injured are aged between 10 and 30 years (Table 2) with males outnumbering females by 2 or 3 to 1 in this age group. Usually there is a second peak of injuries among the elderly. Jennett (1983) reports that there are 22 to 23 fatal closed head injuries per hundred thousand population in the United States—twice as many as in Britain, Sweden, or Japan. In fact, 7 million head injuries are estimated to occur annually in the United States with some half million hospital admissions. In one of the few studies that includes all head injuries attending a hospital for a large semi-rural area Rimel and Jane (1983) found an overall incidence of 24 injuries per ten thousand population. In the age group 15–19 years it was 42 per ten thousand population and lower at 30 per ten thousand for those aged 75 years or more. Finally, it has been estimated that 150 per

Table 1. Causes of head injuries attending accident and emergency departments (Scottish study)

	Age			Sex	
	<15 years (N = 1516)	15–64 years (N = 1826)	>65 years (N = 217)	Males (N = 2501)	Females (N = 1067)
Road accidents	9%	24%	24%	16%	21%
Assault	3%	24%	1%	16%	9%
Falls	16%	13%	28%	14%	14%
Domestic accidents	27%	8%	29%	14%	26%
Sport/leisure	21%	6%	1%	13%	10%
Accidents at work or school	4%	12%	2%	10%	4%

From Jennett and Teasdale, 1981, p. 10, with permission.

100 thousand population in Britain are substantially disabled by closed head injury, which emphasizes Jennett and MacMillan's statement (1981) that "head injury is a major health problem in Westernized nations."

The majority of younger men admitted to hospital with closed head injuries are from the lower socioeconomic groups in society (Selecki, 1967) and, compared with similar individuals who do not suffer injuries, they take more risks and have a higher incidence of previous head injury and of contacts with judicial authorities (Jamieson, 1971). There are exceptions to these general characteristics, relating to marital and social status. For example, Rimel and Jane (1983) demonstrated the effect of having a population heavily loaded with university undergraduates. They reported that 59% of their population was single, compared with 39% of the population base as a whole, and that 24% of the injured were students. By comparison, in Glasgow, Scotland, approximately 50% of those who are injured are married. Consumption of alcohol is a frequent precursor of closed head injuries. Jennett and Teasdale (1981) re-

Table 2. Age distribution for brain damage due to head injury

Age (years)	Percentage
0–9	8
10–19	34
20–29	28
30–39	12
40–49	8
50–59	6
60–69	2
70+	2

Adapted from R. W. Rimel and J. A. Jane, 1983.

Table 3. Percentage of head injury victims who had consumed alcohol
(Scottish adults)

	Sent home after visit to emergency ward	Primary surgical ward admission	Neurosurgical unit admission
Male	20%	46%	42%
Female	8%	19%	17%
Total	17%	38%	37%

From Jennett and Teasdale, 1981, p. 10.

ported that in a Scottish study alcohol use was recorded more frequently in patients admitted to hospital than among those who attended the emergency room and were sent home (Table 3). Interestingly they also found that alcohol was more often detected in pedestrians than in motorists involved in accidents, and that injuries caused by assaults or falls were more often associated with alcohol than motor vehicle accidents were.

With regard to outcome, the fate of a large population of brain injured patients admitted to hospital, was examined by Rimel and Jane (1983) who demonstrated that over two-thirds made a good recovery at 3 months after injury using the Glasgow Outcome Scale of Jennett and Bond (1975), Table 4. However, this figure should be interpreted with care because in some of the patients recorded as having made a good recovery they detected subtle deficits, both neurological and neuropsychological, which they tentatively coupled with an unexpectedly high level of failure to return to work on leaving hospital. Whether this is truly cause and effect remains to be seen (Rimel et al., 1981). Jennett et al. (1981) examined outcome using the same form of assessment in severely brain injured patients 6 months after admission, and even in this group 47% of patients made a good recovery in terms of their ability to live independently (Table 5), a figure which is unlikely to change appreciably even a year after injury (Bond and Brooks, 1976).

Table 4. Outcome of head injured patients 3 months after injury, as assessed by the Glasgow Outcome Scale

Dead	7%
Vegetative	4%
Severely disabled	8%
Moderately disabled	12%
Recovered	69%

From R. W. Rimel and J. A. Jane, 1983, p. 19, with permission.

Table 5. Conscious survivors 6 months after severe brain injury

	All Glasgow cases[a]
Severely disabled	19%
Moderately disabled	34%
Good recovery	47%

From B. Jennett, J. Snoek, M. R. Bond, and D. N. Brooks, 1981.

[a]$N = 314$.

Definition of Severity of Injury

There is evidence that relatively trivial injuries to the head resulting in unconsciousness cause some structural brain damage (Adams et al., 1977). It is well known that the repeated blows to the head that boxers sustain cause substantial brain injuries and eventually lead to the "punch drunk syndrome" or, more properly, traumatic encephalopathy, yet the periods of unconsciousness sustained by an individual boxer may have been relatively few and short. In clinical practice there has been an increasing awareness that minor injuries do produce brain damage (Rimel et al., 1981), and evidence of both intellectual and disturbed neurological function—for example vision, hearing and balance—has accumulated. For many years there were two main criteria of severity, (1) the period of post-traumatic amnesia, or the time it takes continuous memory for day to day events to be restored, and (2) the duration of the period of unconsciousness.

That time taken to recover full consciousness is a measure of the quality of brain tissue destroyed was first noticed by Professor Ritchie Russell in England in 1932. In his original paper (Russell, 1932) he proposed the following relationship between post-traumatic amnesia (PTA) and severity of injury:

PTA < 1 hour = mild injury;
PTA 1–24 hours = moderate injury;
PTA 1–7 days = severe injury;
PTA > 7 days = very severe injury.

According to these criteria, most patients referred for neuropsychological assessment by neurosurgeons are severely or very severely injured, as the following figures from Glasgow reveal. Of 1,000 head injured patients, all had a post-traumatic amnesia greater than 2 days, 94% greater than 1 week, 80% greater than 2 weeks, and 60% greater than 4 weeks. All severely injured patients have a period of post-traumatic amnesia exceeding 1 day and it is not necessary to be very accurate when measuring post-traumatic amnesia in the very severely injured. In fact it may be impossible to estimate its duration exactly.

Those interested in the mild to moderate injuries may use a modified scale devised by Fortuny and others (1980):

PTA < 10 minutes = very mild injury;
PTA 10–60 minutes = mild injury;
PTA 1–24 hours = moderate injury.

This group studied patients admitted to hospital in Oxford, England, over a period of 6 months and found that 46.7% had very minor injuries, 17.3% mild injuries, and 20.8% moderate injuries. Only 6.6% had post-traumatic amnesia that exceeded 24 hours.

Although post-traumatic amnesia is generally used as a retrospective method of estimating the severity of injury, there are two techniques available for es-

Table 6. Glasgow Coma Scale

	Examiner's test	Patient's response	Assigned score
Eye opening	Spontaneous	Opens eyes on own	E4
	Speech	Opens eyes when asked to in a loud voice	3
	Pain	Opens eyes when pinched	2
	Pain	Does not open eyes	1
Best motor response	Commands	Follows simple commands	M6
	Pain	Pulls examiner's hand away when pinched	5
	Pain	Pulls a part of body away when examiner pinches him	4
	Pain	Flexes body inappropriately to pain (decorticate posturing)	3
	Pain	Body becomes rigid in an extended position when examiner pinches victim (decerebrate posturing)	2
	Pain	Has no motor response to pinch	1
Verbal response (talking)	Speech	Carries on a conversation correctly and tells examiner where he is, who he is, and the month and year	V5
	Speech	Seems confused or disoriented	4
	Speech	Talks so examiner can understand victim but makes no sense	3
	Speech	Makes sounds that examiner can't understand	2
	Speech	Makes no noise	1

Coma score $(E + M + V) = 3-15$.

timating its end-point as it occurs, which are based on the published methods of Levin, O'Donnell, and Grossman (1979) from the United States, and the British group of Fortuny and others (1980).

Clearly it is of fundamental importance to be able to determine the severity of injury in as short a time as possible after the brain injured patient has been admitted to hospital because knowing the severity is extremely important in determining management strategy, and of value for giving a short-term prognosis to relatives and others. For this purpose post-traumatic amnesia is useless of course, and for many years duration of unconsciousness was regarded as the main method of measuring severity of injury. Assessing levels of consciousness is difficult, however, and results vary from center to center. In fact, close examination of the technique proved it to be quite unreliable. It was for this reason that workers in Glasgow devised a reliable and valid scale that may be used from the moment of admission onwards by doctors or others closely involved in patient care with equal accuracy (Teasdale and Jennett, 1974). The Glasgow Coma Scale (GCS), which is used in many countries, is based on the principle that certain easily elicited neurological signs (Table 6) signify victims' chances of life or death, and can be used to calculate the probability of the immediate outcome within days of injury and, with a lower degree of certainty, the later level of survivors' overall disability. The Glasgow Coma Scale is relatively unaffected by differences in language and has high inter-rater and cross-cultural reliability. It defines coma in descriptive terms without reference to supposed anatomical sites of dysfunction, or to levels that depend on the concurrence of certain degrees of responsiveness with features such as pupil reactions or respiration abnormalities. The three neurological signs which have proved to be the most sensitive to severity of injury and are used to predict outcome are eye opening, best motor response, and verbal response (talking), each of which is graded separately. Coma is defined as (1) not opening the eyes, (2) not obeying commands, and (3) not uttering understandable words. The responses to testing are scored and patients are given a total score (E + M + V) with a range of 3–15 points. More recent modifications of the scale have rated poorest performances as zero giving a range of scores of 0–12 points.

Conscious patients score highest on the Coma Scale: 90% of those with scores of 8 or less are in coma, whereas none of those scoring 9 or more are in coma. Those with a coma score of 8 or less for a period of 6 hours or more from the time of impact are regarded as having severe brain damage. Fifty percent of these patients die, and among survivors the range of disability later during recovery varies widely. The grading of patients into severely injured (0–8), moderately injured (9–11) and mildly injured (12–15) provides a good framework for experimental studies of the mental, physical, and social consequences of brain injury, and is a basis for later practical measures of the outcome of various methods of rehabilitation early during recovery. Clearly there is no absolute measure of any particular grade of severity of injury, but the convention quoted is widely accepted—an important fact if results of work in different centers and countries are to be compared with confidence.

The Natural History of Recovery from Severe Closed Head Injury

Writing about recovery from lesions of the central nervous system in 1938 Karl Lashley stated "we cannot understand the process of recovery fully until we know the nature of the defects. . . ." He wrote at length about the physiological mechanisms that might be responsible for the many variations in the final levels of neuropsychological and physiological recovery seen in clinical practice and remarked that certain mental defects seemed to show little improvement with time; he included a reduced capacity for organization, lowered level of abstraction, slower learning, reduced retentiveness, and loss of interest and spontaneous motivation, concluding rather gloomily that earlier optimism about the brain's ability to recover from a serious physical insult must be tempered. In fact his observations proved broadly correct and have been made by various workers since that time. Although not quoted in Lashley's paper, the work of another psychologist, R. C. Conkey, published in the same year (1938), revealed evidence about the time sequence of recovery of cognitive skills in brain injured individuals—an issue not discussed by Lashley. Conkey observed that the greater part of recovery of basic cognitive skills takes place within 6 months of brain injury. This discovery, which did not arouse much interest at the time, was reestablished 40 years later during the early stages of a recent increase in the number of studies of the physical, mental, and social consequences of severe traumatic brain injury and methods of rehabilitating the brain injured. Until quite recently, most clinicians were uncertain about the nature of the process of recovery and usually indicated to a patient or his relatives that improvements of all types could continue for at least 2 years after injury. In an often quoted paper, Miller and Stern (1965), commented that full recovery takes even longer and argued that cases involving compensation should not be settled with undue haste, that is for at least 2 to 3 years, unless of course full recovery has already occurred. They commented that "in general the outcome in these cases of severe head injury (their sample) has proved to be much more favourable than was expected or predicted." They also commented "we have confirmed Russell's observation (1934) that functional complaints tend to be incapacitating for longer than all except the most severe organic sequelae of head injury." Finally, Miller and Stern made it clear that more detailed knowledge about the natural history of recovery from closed head injury was needed—in other words that studies of the effect of brain damage upon cognitive function, personality and behavior, and upon the relation of deficits in these areas to neurological deficits and the social consequences of injury were needed to improve the methods of management and of prognosis.

In 1977 Mandleberg and Brooks were the first to reproduce in general terms Conkey's report of 1938. They administered the Wechsler Adult Intelligence Scale serially to 40 severely brain injured adults and demonstrated that scores on verbal subtests were less impaired initially and recovered more quickly than nonverbal subtest scores. The former appeared to have reached their final plateau within a year of injury while nonverbal I.Q. showed recovery over 3 years. These observations were in keeping with earlier results of Vigouroux and others (1971) and with reports on the process of recovery following other forms of organic brain disorder (Morrow and Mark, 1955; Kløve and Reitan, 1958; Kløve, 1959; and Ladd, 1964). In view of the widespread nature of their patients' brain injuries the authors came to the confident conclusion that the differences in recovery that they had detected were genuine and not the result of greater damage to the right hemisphere than to the left. Attempting to explain the differences, Mandleberg and Brooks concluded that performance tests are more complex than verbal items, which can often be answered by simple readily elicited responses and which are structurally simpler than performance subtests that require the individual to integrate a number of complex functions including perception, learning, manual dexterity, speed, and attention. Finally, Newcombe and Fortuny (1979) made the important point that the differences also may have been due to the fact that most performance tests are timed. Concurrently with the work of Mandleberg and Brooks, Bond

(1975) published the results of a psychosocial study of outcome after severe head injury and reached the following conclusions:

1. The degree of social handicap present was significantly related to levels of neurological and physical deficits and the degree of mental impairment.

2. The duration of post-traumatic amnesia was related to levels of mental, physical, and social disability, and patients with a period of post-traumatic amnesia greater than 4 weeks were disabled in all three areas to some extent.

3. Impaired social functioning was chiefly attributed to disorders of memory, personality, and to physical handicap.

4. Family stress and breakdown was attributable more to mental than to physical disabilities with memory impairment and personality change being identified as the most stressful factors.

5. Post-traumatic psychiatric illness was chiefly related to premorbid psychosocial factors rather than to brain injury.

6. In terms of dependency, measured by means of the Glasgow Outcome Scale, the final level for more than three quarters of the patients was established within 6–9 months of injury.

The work of Bond and Brooks (1976) and Brooks (1983a, 1983b) demonstrates that the greater part of recovery of physical and mental functions of a primary nature, those attributable directly to brain function, occurs within 6 months of injury, slowing noticeably thereafter. They concluded that it is possible to produce recovery curves for very specific functions, for example verbal or nonverbal intelligence, using the Mill Hill Vocabulary Scale and Raven's Progressive Matrices tests respectively (Fig. 1). This observation has been supported by the results of other workers, including Roberts (1979), who studied the pattern of recovery of neurological deficits, and Newcombe and others (1975), who reported the process of recovery of speech following brain damage. Bond and Brooks also suggested that later recovery is primarily the gradual adaptation to primary mental and physical deficits that improve only slowly, if at all, and that this recovery depends on both the nature of the primary deficits, especially changes in personality, and on the interactions between patients and those who care for them. The latter also undergo emotional changes which, in their turn, influence the recovery of the injured person. In short, they suggested that recovery may be a two-stage process. First 'primary recovery' of simple functions, which parallels the recovery of brain function that occurs mainly in the first 6 months after injury, and second, late recovery, which is a process of adaptation to primary deficits. Dikmen and Reitan (1976) made an interesting observation which has been commented upon by others that greater recovery takes place in patients with more severe deficits initially, although they continue to show greater deficits 18 months after injury. They also noted that most neuropsychological recovery occurs in the first year after injury.

From the results of these studies it may be concluded that recovery has several aspects: (1) neurological recovery, (2) a more general adaptive process,

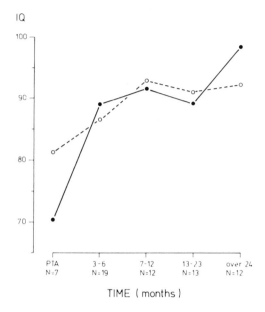

Fig. 1. Changes in verbal and non-verbal intelligence in severely brain damaged men up to 2 years after injury. (———) Raven's Progressive Matrices; (----) Mill Hill Vocabulary Scale (Reproduced from Bond and Brooks, 1976, with permission.)

and (3) a social process involving the interactions of the injured with those closest to them and any resultant changes in social status. All three aspects of recovery are linked and show definite changes with time; all have been investigated, although information is far from complete, especially about the third aspect of recovery. However, it is now possible to make a number of predictions about the eventual outcome for an injured person and his family, using information gained by assessing all three aspects of recovery.

Neuropsychological Outcome

Tests of mental function for the assessment of brain damage have evolved steadily over a period of many years. In the field of traumatic brain injury most interest was focussed initially on the consequences of missile injuries from the two World Wars, especially the second; it is only in the past 20 years that work has concentrated more upon closed head injuries. Missile injuries and damage to the brain caused by local abnormalities of brain function, resulting from tumor growth, cerebrovascular, or other types of pathology, aroused considerable interest and led to the development of neuropsychological tests that enabled the tester to relate the performance and behavior of the individual to the known or presumed region of the injury or defect. Goldstein from the United States, Milner from Canada, Luria from the USSR, and Russell et al. from England, are household names to all neuropsychologists as the pioneers in developing methods to assess focal brain injury in their respective countries.

At first those who studied the effects of closed injuries tended to use the batteries developed for examining subjects with focal brain injuries. With increasing experience, however, they began to appreciate that a wider range of tests was needed: first to assess more general changes of mental function (for example mental slowness), second to assess behavior, and third, to assess functional mental capacity in everyday life (Brooks and Aughton, 1979; Brooks, 1983a; Sunderland et al., 1983). The last need is based on an awareness that results of laboratory tests of mental function do not necessarily give a true indication of the way any given individual will perform in, and cope with, his day to day existence at home or at work. Consequently, those involved in neuropsychological testing of the victims of closed head injury are now extending both their psychobehavioral concepts and the means of assessing them. For example, a multicenter study of the neuropsychological and social consequences of severe closed head injury is currently underway, funded by the National Institute of Health, Washington DC. Despite what has been said, great reliance continues to be placed upon well-established batteries as the central core of neuropsychological testing, with the Halsteid-Reitan battery often favored in the United States. There is less adherence to specific batteries in the United Kingdom and in Europe, where the Wechsler Adult Intelligence Scale is used wholly or in part, accompanied by selected tests of learning, memory, language, perception, and constructional skills. Some of the difficulties encountered in the neuropsychological assessment of the victims of closed head injury are discussed by Levin, Benton, and Grossman (1982), Newcombe and Fortuny (1979), Bond (1983), Lynch (1983), McKinlay and Brooks (1984), and Brooks (1984). For a general consideration of methods used in neuropsychological research relating to closed head injury the reader also should consult the papers of Parsons and Prigitano (1978) and McKinlay and Brooks (1984).

The chief aim of most neuropsychologists engaged in routine clinical, as opposed to experimental, work is to give a broad view of the brain damaged person's cognitive function to be used as a basis for rehabilitation, including family counselling, and perhaps also for legal purposes. Their work is usually considered together with the results of neurological examination and laboratory tests, of which the most common is a CAT scan (computerized axial tomography) or NMR scan (nuclear magnetic resonance). If possible, personality change, behavior and daily activities are assessed, though these measures are usually carried out only in larger centers with a special interest in investigating and rehabilitating the brain injured because they require a longer period of study, preferably in an in-patient unit, or during a period of day attendance.

General Intelligence

Almost all test batteries aim to provide an overall picture of the level of an individual's post-traumatic intelligence. In the recent literature related to closed head injuries, Mandleberg and Brooks (1975) were among the first to examine the effects of injury upon general intelligence as measured by the Wechsler Adult Intelligence Scale. Using serial testing they found to their surprise that the cognitive abilities of their group of 40 patients eventually returned to normal levels despite the fact that all were severely injured initially, as defined by the Glasgow criteria mentioned previously. Later examination of the data indicated that the final scores achieved were unusually high and almost certainly attributable to a "learning effect" among patients who had been tested on several occasions. Miller (1979), commenting upon this paper, made the point that it is important to gauge the level of a subject's pretraumatic cognitive abilities before interpreting the significance of post-traumatic test results. Levin and others (1979) examined the long-term neuropsychological outcome of closed head injury also and reemphasized the point made previously by Mandleberg and Brooks (1975) and later by Bond and Brooks (1976), that levels of intelligence vary considerably on recovery from brain injury, despite the fact that all patients in their study and in others were severely injured, whether assessed using the Glasgow Coma Scale initially, the duration of post-traumatic amnesia, or a later rating on the Glasgow Outcome Scale (Table 7). Specifically, Levin and his coworkers found that patients who had made a good recovery as assessed by the Glasgow Outcome Scale usually functioned within the normal range of intelligence, whereas those with severe disabilities exhibited marked intellectual deficits. Further figures supporting this view were produced by Jennett and others (1981), who examined a group of 150 patients between 1 and 14 years (mean, 5.2 years; S.D., 2.6) after severe brain injury. In a sample of 61 patients from this group they found that seven of the nine patients who had severe cognitive deficits on formal psychological testing with the Wechsler Adult Intelligent Scale were severely disabled when assessed independently by a neurologist using the Glasgow Outcome Scale, and only two were graded higher, that is as moderately disabled. Of 45 who made a good cognitive recovery none were severely disabled as graded on the Glasgow Outcome Scale, and of seven patients with moderate cognitive disability, four were clinically moderately disabled also. These findings raise the question of the value of the two main measures of initial severity of injury as predictors of long-term cognitive function. Levin and others (1979) state "a low Glasgow Coma Scale score at the time of admission and a prolonged period of unresponsiveness were not necessarily incompatible with a good recovery and restitution of cognitive functioning." Brooks and others (1980) in a study of 89 severely brain injured patients, studied within 2 years of injury, demonstrated that the Glasgow Coma Scale bore little relation to cognitive outcome, whereas the duration of post-traumatic amnesia did significantly predict certain later cognitive problems. They measured intelligence, learning and memory, language, perceptual and constructional skills and found that the association of post-traumatic amnesia was greatest with tests of learning and memory.

In a review of the neuropsychological evaluation of mental deficits after brain

Table 7. The Glasgow Outcome Scale including methods of expanding and contracting the scale

Dead	Dead/Vegetative	Dead/Vegetative	Dead	Dead	Dead	Vegetative
						Disability:
		Severely disabled			Severely disabled	5
						4
	conscious		Dependent		Moderately disabled	3
Survivors						2
		Independent	Independent			2
					Good	1
					recovery	0
Number of categories	2	3		5[a]		8

[a]The original scale had five categories.

injury Newcombe and Fortuny (1979) are very critical of the use of intelligence tests, stating that they are "flagrantly inadequate as measures of intellectual handicaps following brain injury", and again, that "intelligence tests tend to measure well-practised skills in a highly structured setting." They do not, however, dismiss the use of certain tests, for example Raven's Progressive Matrices, a highly valid test of general ability, as measures of intellectual competence and for general screening purposes, as long as patients are allowed adequate time to solve the problems irrespective of the time usually allocated. Finally, they make the point that some patients do not perform nearly as well at home as might be predicted from the results of intelligence tests, and suggest that further examination of problems which might contribute to such failures; for example, defects in perceptual skills, attentional control, and fatigue must be explored. Some of these issues were reviewed by Lezak (1978a, 1978b), who concluded that such problems are common and often overlooked. It is also appreciated that their interference in test performance is a significant cause of misleading test results in the hands of inexperienced psychologists or psychometric technicians. Thus, because the major part of handicap due to head injury is not in intelligence but in attention, memory, and a broad range of information-processing skills, it is essential that psychological examination not be based solely on I.Q. measures.

Memory

Of all the possible defects patients may have, a disturbance of memory is the one that they and their relatives report most often and most readily. As Milner (1969) pointed out, however, the reports of patients cannot be taken at face value because a complaint of a poor memory, which as forgetfulness is reasonably acceptable socially, may represent a more general impairment of intellect, an attentional deficit, or heightened distractability. In a single chapter it is not possible to cover the large volume of papers on memory assessment; the reader may usefully consult the reviews of Schacter and Crovitz (1977), Brooks (1983), and Teasdale and Brooks (1985) for an account of the methodological difficulties associated with assessing memory function following closed head injury.

Studies of memory disorder during the period of post-traumatic amnesia are few in number and reveal that the injured person probably does store some information but it is limited in quantity and there is doubt about its accessibility for retrieval (Brooks 1983).

Once post-traumatic amnesia is over, the probability of a severely brain damaged individual having memory impairment is high, and the diffuse widespread subcortical damage of the type associated with closed injuries is particularly liable to impair memory function. Various studies dating back to Conkey's paper of 1938 on the late results of injury in patients with post-traumatic amnesia lasting over a week reveal that they suffer severe and persistent disorders of memory. There is general agreement that patients have marked difficulties in learning new material as, for example, was reported by Brooks (1976) who used the Wechsler Memory Scale. There is also evidence that information stored before injury is more readily recalled. The question of whether the problem is one of storing new information, or recalling what has been stored, or some combination of the two, has been the subject of various studies which favor, first, far less impairment of short-term memory (less than 60 seconds) than of long-term memory (Brooks 1975) and, second, that recall of stored material is the major handicap of everyday life. Interestingly, at a clinical level it is not uncommon to meet patients who may not remember some fact from everyday life but will say "give me a few minutes," or, "give me half an hour, and it will come back." Brooks (1975) also studied the question of the frequency of intrusions—that is the occasions during memory testing on a given word list, when words from a quite separate list learned previously are recalled. Fewer intrusions were recorded with head injury patients than controls, a result which Brooks regards as evidence of faulty storage. Levin and others (1979) graded severely brain injured patients using the Glasgow Outcome Scale and found that using the Selective Reminding Technique of Buschke and Fuld, defective storage was least in patients who made a good recovery (10%), slightly greater in the moderately disabled (33%), and universal in severely disabled patients. A similar pattern of results was obtained on tests of retrieval of material from long-term stores.

The correlation between evidence of focal brain injury and deficits in cognitive function has been examined many times in many ways. With regard to memory, Levin and others (1979) reported that acute hemiparesis in brain injured patients who had been in coma was significantly associated with a residual deficit in the Wechsler Adult Intelligence Scale performance I.Q., and with a disturbance of the retrieval memory process, but not of memory storage. They were not able to show that patients spared acute aphasia showed greater recovery of memory. Finally, they noted that patients who had occulo-vestibular abnormalities, and therefore brain stem damage, had greater cognitive impairment than others and that they had more profound disturbances of both memory storage and retrieval. Brooks and others (1980) examined the relationship of skull fracture, often associated with hematoma formation, and memory deficits but found no significant differences between patients with and without fractures. However, examination of patients with and without hematomas did reveal that subjects who had had hematomas, which had been removed surgically, performed better on at least one test of learning (significantly, of recall of stored information) and argued that this was due to less severe diffuse injury in the group. Thus to summarize, diffuse brain injury of the type caused by severe closed head injury causes more severe deficits of memory than focal brain damage. There is also evidence that, generally, the greater the damage the more profound the memory disorder, and that impairment of both storage and recall occur, with the latter deficit being most obvious in everyday life.

To what extent and over what period does recovery of memory take place?

Brooks (1983) stated that final levels of recovery vary considerably, as does the time it takes to reach those levels. He concludes that, contrary to a widely held belief, recovery of memory tends to be slower than that of many other cognitive functions, such as perception, intelligence, or language (Brooks and Aughton, 1979), and that the final level of recovery tends to be much lower. The severity of injury is related to the final level of deficit, but not to the rate of recovery. Similar general conclusions were reported by Levin and others (1979) and Groher (1977) who stated also that the relationship between scores on language and memory tests and the number of days of unconsciousness (his measure of severity) is strongest when the period of coma has been short or very long, and that it is less obvious with coma of an intermediate length (between 2–4 weeks).

To conclude, caution must be shown when reporting results of laboratory-based memory tests, because in everyday life, except for the most diffuse injuries, complaints of poor memory on the one hand and actual performance in the everyday world, do not always match test results (Sunderland et al., 1983). For several reasons, some of which have been mentioned, it is possible for a post-traumatic neurosis, or a depressive disorder, to contribute to a patient's difficulties with memory, even to the extent of producing a pseudodementia (Bond, 1984; McKinlay, Brooks, and Bond, 1983).

Language and Communication

Substantial disturbances of speech are said to be uncommon after closed head injuries and when present they tend to recover well (Thomsen, 1975). Heilman and others (1971) screened all adult patients with closed head injuries admitted to a Boston Hospital in the United States during one year. Of 750 cases examined, only 2% were judged to have residual aphasia. Groher (1983) makes the very important point that aphasic patients with brain damage caused by closed head injury tend to have multiple deficits of mental function and that aphasia does not therefore occur alone but in the presence of other cognitive deficits, for example, of memory, perception, orientation, judgement, and reasoning. Therefore, it is more correct to discuss problems of speech and communication—a more complex process involving both cognition and speech. If this is done the prevalence of disturbance rises to a figure of 15%–25% depending upon the source quoted. The complexity of communication difficulties is exposed when the use of language is examined; the combined deficits produce more problems for patients and are more apparent in free conversation compared with the demands made by carefully structured and conducted tests of language in a laboratory. Thus language and communication difficulties are a facet of underlying cognitive disorganization and are, therefore, different from the problems found among patients with aphasia due to more focal lesions, for example after strokes (Hagen, Malkmus, and Burditt, 1979), the victims of which tend to recover their language and communication skills more completely and more quickly than the head injured person (Kertesz and McCabe, 1977). This difference is probably the result of widespread injury following trauma.

The time taken to recover and the extent of recovery varies considerably from patient to patient according to Newcombe and Fortuny (1979), who agreed with Heilman and others (1971) that most recovery from aphasia takes place in the first 6 to 9 months. However, this does not mean that the use of language has recovered fully. In fact, in terms of standarized aphasia test batteries, intact language skills are present but a patient's capabilities may not extend beyond the performance of simple concrete tasks. Najenson (1978), using the Functional Communication Profile test (FCP), demonstrated that visual and auditory comprehension skills returned first, followed by expression and writing. These changes took place within 6 months; at a later stage the patients' main problems were with higher level reading and narrative writing. Groher (1977) using the Porch Index of Communication Ability examined patterns of communication in a small group of men who had had closed head injuries, and found that verbal expression, visual and auditory comprehension were largely adequate by the fourth month after injury but it was not until this point that patients' abilities to write began to improve. Interestingly, he also found that there was a close relationship between levels of behavioral disturbance and the extent of deficits in language and communication. Hagen and others (1979) demonstrated a close relationship between cognitive recovery and impairment of language and communication skills. This group commented that "recovery is hierarchical beginning with a recovery of attention mechanisms (both internal and external), discrimination, seriation, recovery of memory, categorisation, association and, finally, skills involving the synthesis of input and output."

Regarding later recovery, Kertesz and McCabe (1977) report that the pattern is one of "spurts and plateaux" which, in some cases, is still discernible 2 years after injury. There is work by Malkmus quoted by Groher (1983) confirming that most patients have intact language skills at 6 months as tested by aphasia batteries, but that retention and integration, or auditory and written abilities, deteriorate directly in relation to the complexity of the material given. She also observed that use of language for expression at a basic level in daily life is mostly adequate but that when patients are asked to formulate specific responses they often fail because they have ideational perservation (they cannot move from topic to topic), have difficulty retrieving words, have disorganized thought patterns, and impaired abstract reasoning capacity. Thus Malkmus provides further evidence of the importance of general cognitive functioning in communication.

In a prospective study of 55 severely brain damaged men McKinlay and others (1981) studied the patients' relatives' reports of post-traumatic language difficulties. They found that the most frequent problems were difficulties in expression (for example word finding or fluency) which was present in 47%, 44%, and 44% of cases at 3, 6, and 12 months respectively, and dysarthria in 33%, 26%, and 29% of cases at the same time intervals. Receptive difficulties were less common (no more than 15% of cases attending followup).

In a more recent prospective followup study on patients 10–15 years after injury Thomsen (1984) reports that of 19 patients who were aphasic immediately after injury 16 remained so at 2½ years and the number fell to 4 between 10 and 15 years. In sharp contrast, all 15 patients who were initially dysarthric remained so, even 10 to 15 years later. She commented that this is one of the most disabling and persistent of all causes of difficulties in speech and communication. Thomsen writes "at the second followup (10 to 15 years) many patients, whether originally aphasic or not, responded slowly and some needed repetition of questions. Subnormal rate of speaking, impaired word-finding and sporadic verbal paraphasia of the semantic type, frequent pauses and use of many set phrases and perseveration of words and subjects were common. Aposiopesis, a condition in which a sentence is left unfinished, was often observed."

Thus the passage of time after injury appears to leave deficits of memory and concentration, and mental slowness as prominent features, with language and communication difficulties as aspects of general cognitive impairment which, with the exception of dysarthria, show improvement over a long period.

Several important points emerge from the facts quoted. First, the use of an aphasia scale in the laboratory (for example the Boston Diagnostic Aphasic Examination, the Multilingual Aphasic Examination, or the Porch Index of Communication Ability) will provide a guide to the level of initial aphasia and the changes in it that occur with time. There is no obvious theoretical reason for choosing between the scales mentioned and nothing to be gained by increasing the number of tests of this type. Next it is clear that laboratory-based tests are of limited value in predicting a patient's performance in a very different outside world. As Newcombe and Fortuny (1979) commented, "experimental conditions rarely reflect the 'buzzing and booming confusion' of the busy world where several events and different strands of conversation have to be processed simultaneously." Last, in view of the important contribution made by various cognitive deficits to communicative difficulties, no assessment of speech and communication in brain damaged patients should be based solely on a test of aphasia.

Changes in Personality and Behavior

In 1967 Fahy and others made the point that mental handicap, and especially psychiatric disturbances following closed brain injury, are more often the cause of family disharmony, failure to adapt to social needs and difficulties in rehabilitation, than physical disabilities, most of which tend to recover to a variable extent. At that time, however, most rehabilitation centered upon physical deficits and neuropsychological assessments tended to be chiefly concerned with disorders of cognitive function, seldom included assessments of personality, abnormal behavior or psychiatric illness. Bond (1975) reported the results of a clinical study of 56 patients with closed head injury whose physical and psychosocial handicaps were assessed. He concluded also that mental deficits cause more disruption in the family of leisure and working life than do physical problems, and that changes in personality and behavior, together with impairment of memory, were the main sources of difficulty and stress. While not disagreeing with this general conclusion, Oddy and others (1978), reported results of a similar study of the effects of brain injury upon family life, work and leisure, as "encouraging." Of the 50 young men they assessed, most had returned to their social activities only 4 months after injury. Only those with a post-traumatic amnesia greater than 7 days did not do so, and social isolation was most marked in this group. However, a third of the total group had failed to return to work at this point. The authors concluded that the social problems of their patients were due chiefly to personality changes, such as restlessness, irritability, and impatience. Compared to populations studied by others (McKinlay and others, 1981; Levin and others, 1979), the group investigated by Oddy and his colleagues differed in several important ways. They were younger (80% were less than 25 years old), half had a post-traumatic amnesia of less than 7 days, and a high proportion came from upper socioeconomic groups—all factors which make a good outcome more likely.

From these brief observations it is clear that the assessment of problems resulting from changes in personality and behavior is based upon a dual approach. First, the patient's cognitive state is assessed using a formal psychometric battery. Second, by means of carefully constructed symptom check lists, questionnaires (Oddy et al., 1978), and (Levin et al., 1979) structured interviews (Bond, 1975; McKinlay et al., 1981), and perhaps the use of semantic differential type scales (Brooks and McKinlay, 1983; Brooks and Lincoln, 1984) behavior and personality change is measured. Frequently the instruments are administered to both the disabled person and his relatives, or to the relatives alone in order to test the reliability of the patient's responses, to determine differences in opinion between the patient and his closest relative, and also to establish the burden, that the consequences of the injury place upon the relative.

The task of analyzing behavior disturbances using a conventional psychometric test is exemplified by a study of 27 severely brain injured patients by Levin and others (1979) who used the Brief Psychiatric Rating Scale (BPRS), which they subsequently analysed on the basis of four factors.

Factor 1. Thinking Disturbance: Conceptual disorganization, unusual thought content and hallucinations.

Factor 2. Hostile Suspiciousness: Hostility, suspiciousness, and uncooperativeness.

Factor 3. Withdrawal/Retardation: Emotional withdrawal, motor retardation, and blunted affect.

Factor 4. Anxiety/Depression; Anxiety, guilt feelings, and depression.

Dividing each factor into three grades of severity the group found that behavioral disturbance was common in both moderately and severely disabled patients using the Glasgow Outcome Scale as the index of disability. The main difficulties were reflected in high scores on the thinking, disturbance, and withdrawal/retardation factors. The former were reflected in tangential, fragmented speech, due to aphasia and deficient filtering of irrelevant material from cognitive processes. Those with moderate or severe thinking disturbances tended to lack insight into their deficits and to concentrate their complaints on minor physical problems. Ratings of withdrawal/retardation chiefly revealed slowness or lack of spontaneous gross movements, or of speech. It is important to note that none of the patients who made a good recovery showed evidence of either a thinking disorder or hostile-suspicious symptoms. Most patients experienced mild levels of anxiety, depression or both, but only 15% of the population had a serious psychiatric disorder.

With time it has become clear that tests of mental function devised for psychiatric patients without organic brain dysfunction are not entirely suitable for assessing the brain injured, who present a constellation of symptoms quite different from those of functional or neurotic mental illnesses, an issue discussed recently by Bond (1984). Lezak (1978a, 1978b) illustrates one approach to defining the emotional and behavioral characteristics of the head injury victim that are most likely to give rise to adjustment problems for them and their families by suggesting five categories.

1. Emotional Change: Characterized by apathy, silliness, lability of mood, irritability, and an increased or (more often) reduced or absent libido.

2. Impaired Social Perceptiveness: Characterized by selfishness in which feelings for others, self-criticism, and an ability to reflect, are greatly diminished or absent.

3. Impaired Self-Control: Characterized by impulsivity, random restlessness, and impatience.

4. Increased Dependency: Characterized by lack of initiative despite talk of action, and by impaired judgement and planning ability.

5. Behavioral Rigidity: Characterized by inability to learn from experience even when the ability to learn new information is retained.

The question of how to assess these aspects of personality and behavior other than by description is not addressed and, so far, others have not published methods of assessing patients using similar descriptive criteria. In contrast, elements of personality, mood, and behavior that are included by implication in Lezak's dimensions have been the subject of study and assessment. The chief problem encountered by those involved has been to establish the validity of their measures. On the one hand the injured do not always have an objective view of their own emotional and behavioral characteristics, and, on the other, reports of relatives may be biased by their feelings about the accident and its personal or social consequences (Brooks and McKinlay, 1983). That the injured and their relatives do have a similar but not identical view of the frequency of symptoms was first shown by Oddy and others (1978). Information

Table 8. The 10 problems most frequently reported by relatives as being present in the patient (percent reporting)

	3 months after injury	6 months after injury	12 months after injury
Slowness	86	69	67
Tiredness	82	69	69
Irritability	63	69	71
Poor memory	73	59	69
Impatience	60	64	71
Tension and anxiety	57	66	58
Bad temper	48	56	67
Personality change	49	58	60
Depressed mood	57	52	57
Headaches	54	46	53

From McKinlay et al., 1981, with permission.

gained from 48 patients and their close relatives revealed that both groups regarded memory difficulties as the major problem, and there was reasonably close agreement regarding the frequency of troublesome temper tantrums, irritability, levels of energy, and restlessness. However, recent work in Glasgow has shown clearly that relatives and patients differ in their reporting of behavioral but not of physical symptoms, which reflects obvious differences of insight in the two groups (Brooks and McKinlay, 1983).

In a more detailed prospective study of problems generated by 55 more severely brain injured men, McKinlay and others (1981) reported not only symptoms giving rise to difficulty, but also the way in which they changed with time up to 1 year after injury (Table 8). The most frequently reported changes were mental rather than physical, with slowness, tiredness, irritability, and poor memory, being reported in the majority of cases. An analysis of seven problem groups (Table 9) namely those relating to emotion and to disturbances of behavior, are relevant to this discussion. Emotional changes, including poor temper control, irritability, and loss of mood stability, were reported quite often. It is important to note that whereas problems relating to language and physical symptoms lessened with time, half the items in the emotional group were reported with increasing frequency at consecutive interviews. Disturbed behavior was defined as bizarre or puzzling conduct, including violent or inappropriate social behavior. The most frequent changes in this category with time were the onset of excessive talking in 33%, 26%, and 27%, and childishness in 35%, 35%, and 46% at 3, 6, and 12 months. Violence and inappropriate behavior were reported in less than 20% at each interview, but if appearing in the family for the first time since injury, they were shown to be very stressful.

In a subsequent 5-year study of the cohort of severely brain injured men just described, the Glasgow group found that certain negative specific personality characteristics, for example irritability, and the more general factor of

Table 9. Mean number of difficulties (out of 10) reported by relatives

	3 months after injury	6 months after injury	12 months after injury
Physical	1.8	1.6	1.5
Subjective	4.5	4.3	4.5
Language	2.4	2.2	2.1
Emotional	4.6	5.1	5.4
Dependence	1.8	1.5	1.4
Disturbed behavior	1.4	1.6	1.9
Memory	2.7	2.3	2.7

From McKinlay et al., 1981, with permission.

personality change, both of which increased in prominence over the first year after injury (Table 9), persisted at high levels or were reported even more often. For example, by 5 years 64% of relatives continued to report irritability as a problem and 74% now described personality change as being present.

In the only very long-term prospective study in the literature 40 patients were followed for a minimum of 10 years (Thomsen, 1984). A structured interview technique was used and revealed that permanent changes of personality and emotion occurred in two-thirds of those studied and were especially frequent amongst the younger patients. Emotional and behavioral problems that lessened with time from 2 years after injury included childishness, sensitivity to stress, and change and general levels of interest. Those which did not included emotional lability, irritability, listlessness, and disturbed behavior. The latter, though the least frequent, were regarded by relatives as serious sequelae. Thus one-fifth were unduly aggressive and/or were sexually disinhibited. It may be of significance that all patients in this group were aged 15 to 21 when injured; in other words they suffered injury before personality maturity had taken place.

The specific issue of assessing personality following severe head injuries by psychometric rather than purely descriptive means remains a relatively untouched area of research. As Brooks and McKinlay (1983) state, "one reason for the paucity of studies may be the conceptual and methodological problems. . . . even the selection of an appropriate measuring instrument is a major problem here as there are many personality theories which generate a great variety of measures but these often seem singularly inappropriate when judged against the clinical realities of the head injured population." In order to overcome these difficulties, they chose to assess personality change rather than regard it as a fixed concept and obtained judgements from close relatives rather than the patient himself who they felt would show far less insight into any changes that had occurred. Their method used the semantic differential technique and multiple analogue scales, each being composed of one of 18 pairs of adjectives previously shown to be descriptive of head injured patients as a group, for example, irritable–easygoing and mature–childish. The popula-

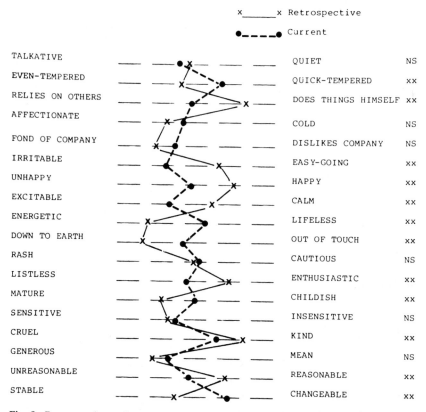

Fig. 2. Retrospective and current assessments at 6 months in cases with personality change (27 cases).

tion studied consisted of severely brain injured men who were assessed 3, 6, and 12 months after injury. A relative was asked to fill in the personality check list, first as the patient was *before* his injury and, second, (without referring to the "before" assessment) as the patient is *now*, i.e., at the time of interview. The results were presented as three adjective profiles of personality before and after injury (Fig. 2). The proportion of relatives describing personality change increased from half at 3 months to two-thirds at 6 months and 12 months, but the pattern of retrospective vs. current differences was established firmly at 3 months from injury and appeared to persist over the following 9 months. The changes reported were mostly of the negative type, and of the 18 items on the check list, 11 showed negative change by 3 months and 14 by 12 months. Items which appeared between the two dates were emotional coldness, disliking company, and cruelty. By 12 months, the following adjectives showed a significant negative change; even-tempered–quick-tempered*, irritable–easygoing*, unhappy–happy, excitable–calm*, mature–childish, unreasonable–reasonable, stable–changeable*. The adjectives marked with an asterisk reflect difficulties in emotional control, while the remaining two items reflect increased unhappiness and immature behavior. Two further important points emerged from the paper. First, increasing negative scores on the personality check list were significantly associated with high levels of perceived burden or stress in the relatives reporting the changes. Second, the severity of injury assessed by the duration of post-traumatic amnesia was of no significance in predicting the extent or pattern of personality change, although the two were weakly related.

Conclusion

Neuropsychological and neurobehavioral consequences of closed head injuries have been the subject of considerable empirical research in the past decade (c.f. Brooks, 1983b; Levin et al., 1982). As a result, much is known about the natural history of cognitive deficits and of changes in personality and behavior from the termination of post-traumatic amnesia onwards. The most prominent features of cognitive dysfunction are in learning, memory, and speed of information processing. The deficits are the result of structural damage within the brain and are established within 6–9 months of injury, after which they persist for many years with little change. In general the more severe the injury the greater the deficits, but there is wide variation among individuals. It is certain, however, that if a patient has a period of post-traumatic amnesia exceeding 4 weeks he or she will have evidence of cognitive impairment; and there is no guarantee that if post-traumatic amnesia is only a few days in duration he or she will not have impaired cognition. Thus, methods for predicting cognitive outcome at a late stage in recovery are not precise. It is important to note that the basic cognitive deficits mentioned represent only a proportion of those that may be present and that collectively they have a variable effect upon each individual's ability to cope with practical day to day needs. Since, unfortunately, results of laboratory tests do not always accurately forecast a person's likely performance in everyday life, interest in assessing cognitive function using the activities of daily life is being developed in a small number of centers.

Little attention has been paid to the question of why patients should have persistent cognitive deficits, and there have been few attempts to relate empirical observations to current neuropsychological theories of brain function. Therefore, there remains a need to analyze the nature of processes leading to deficits in terms of models of normal cognitive processes.

Methods of assessing personality change and associated behavior have not yet been developed on any scale, being hampered by the lack of both a single acceptable theory of personality and of measurement techniques relevant to the problems of the brain-injured. As a result, most work in this area has been descriptive and idiosyncratic, with few attempts to develop reliable and valid quantative measures (Brooks and McKinlay, 1983; McKinlay and Brooks, 1984).

Furthermore, the relationship of the changes observed to theoretical work on the neuropsychological basis of personality and behavior has yet to be examined, although Roberts (1979) ventured into this area briefly and Bond (1983) has drawn attention to the central importance of mechanisms controlling behavior and emotion and those which underpin the phenomenon of "insight."

Among therapists the implications of empirical research have aroused great interest and activity, resulting in the development of many centers for rehabilitation of the brain-injured, especially in the United States. Although their work is fired by great enthusiasm and marked by devotion to patients' needs, frequently it lacks the critical scientific approach needed to evaluate any cognitive behavioral rehabilitation techniques currently in use. In addition, relatively little attention is given to identifying and selecting patients who, on the basis of current knowledge about the process of recovery, might be expected to respond.

Finally, there is no doubt that the steady increase in the number of brain damaged young people entering the community each year poses serious social and economic problems. Until now research into the physical, mental, and social consequences of injury have been primarily clinical, but the time has come for a more fundamental approach to mechanisms underlying mental deficits and for scientific developments in the field of rehabilitation.

REFERENCES

Adams, J. H. (1975). The neuropathology of head injuries. In: *Handbook of Clinical Neurology*, vol. 23. P. J. Vinken and G. W. Bruyn, eds. Amsterdam: North-Holland Publishing Co., pp. 35–65.

Adams, J. H., Mitchell, D. E., and Graham, D. I. (1977). Diffuse brain damage of immediate impact type. *Brain, 100,* 489–502.

Bond, M. R. (1975). Assessment of the psychosocial outcome after severe head injury. In: *Outcome of Severe Damage to the Central Nervous System.* Ciba Foundation Symposium 34 (new series). Amsterdam: Elsevier-Excerpta Medica, p. 141–157.

Bond, M. R. (1983). In: *Rehabilitation of the Head-Injured Adult.* M. Rosenthal, E. R. Griffith, M. R. Bond, and J. D. Miller, eds. Philadelphia: F. A. Davis Company, p. 97.

Bond, M. R. (1984). The psychiatry of closed head injury. In: *Closed Head Injury: Psychological, Social and Family Consequences.* D. N. Brooks, ed. Oxford: Oxford University Press, pp. 148–178.

Bond, M. R., and Brooks, D. N. (1976). Understanding the process of recovery as a basis for the investigation of rehabilitation for the brain injured. *Scand. J. Rehab. Med., 8,* 127–133.

Brooks, D. N. (1975). Long and short term memory in head injured patients. *Cortex, 11,* 329–340.

Brooks, D. N. (1976). Wechsler Memory Scale performance and its relationship to brain damage after severe closed head injury. *J. Neurol., Neurosurg. Psychiat., 39,* 593–598.

Brooks, D. N. (1983). Disorders of memory. In: *Rehabilitation of the Head Injured Adult.* M. Rosenthal, E. R. Griffith, M. R. Bond, and J. D. Miller, eds. Philadelphia: F. A. Davis Company, pp. 185–196.

Brooks, D. N. (1984). *Closed Head Injury: Psychological, Social and Family Consequences.* D. N. Brooks, ed. Oxford: Oxford University Press, pp. 123–147.

Brooks, D. N., and Aughton, M. E. (1979). Psychological consequences of blunt head injury. *Int. Rehab. Med., 1,* 160–165.

Brooks, D. N., Aughton, M. E., Bond, M. R., Jones, P., and Rizvi, S. (1980). Cognitive sequelae in relationship to the early indices of severity of brain damage after severe blunt head injury. *J. Neurol., Neurosurg. Psychiat., 43,* 529–534.

Brooks, D. N., and Lincoln, N. B. (1983). Assessment for rehabilitation. In: *Clinical Management of Memory Problems.* B. Wilson and N. Moffatt, eds. London: Croome Helm, pp. 28–45.

Brooks, D. N., and McKinlay, W. W. (1983). Personality and behavioural change after severe blunt injury—a relative's view. *J. Neurol., Neurosurg. Psychiat., 46,* 336–344.

Conkey, R. C. (1938). Psychological changes associated with head injuries. *Arch. Psychol., 232,* 1–62.

Dikmen, S., and Reitan, R. M. (1976). Psychological deficits and recovery of functions after head injury. *Trans. Am. Neurol. Assoc.,* 72–77, 101–108. (sic)

Fahy, T. J., Irving, M. H., and Millac, P. (1967). Severe head injuries: A six year follow-up. *Lancet, i,* 475–479.

Fortuny, L. A. I., Briggs, M., Newcombe, F., Ratcliffe, G., and Thomas, C. (1980). Measuring the duration of post-traumatic amnesia. *J. Neurol., Neurosurg. Psychiat., 43,* 377–379.

Groher, M. (1977). Psychological consequences of blunt head injury. *Int. Rehab. Med., 1,* 160–166.

Groher, M. (1983). Communication Disorders. In: *Rehabilitation of the Head Injured Adult.* M. Rosenthal, E. R. Griffith, M. R. Bond, and J. D. Miller, ed. Philadelphia: F. A. Davis Company, pp. 155–165.

Hagen, C., Malkmus, D., and Durham, P. (1979). Levels of cognitive functioning. In: *Rehabilitation of the Head Injured Adult.* Professional Staff Association, ed. Douney, California.

Hagen, C., Malkmus, D., and Burditt, G. (1979). Quoted by Groher, M. (1983).

Heilman, K. M., Safran, A., and Geschwind, N. (1971). Closed head injury and aphasia. *J. Neurol., Neurosurg. Psychiat., 34,* 265–271.

Jamieson, K. G. (1971). Prevention of head injury. In: *Head Injuries.* W. Caveness and E. Walker, eds. Edinburgh: Churchill Livingstone, pp. 12–15.

Jennett, B. (1983). Scale and scope of the problem. In: *Rehabilitation of the Head Injured Adult.* M. Rosenthal, E. R. Griffith, M. R. Bond, and J. D. Miller, eds. Philadelphia: F. A. Davis Company, pp. 3–8.

Jennett, B., and Bond, M. R. (1975). Assessment of outcome after severe brain injury: A practical scale. *Lancet, i,* 480–484.

Jennett, B., and Macmillan, R. (1981). Epidemiology of head injury. *Br. Med. J., 282,* 101–103.

Jennett, B., Snoek, J., Bond, M. R., and Brooks, D. N. (1981). Disability after severe head injury: Observation on the use of the Glasgow Outcome Scale. *J. Neurol., Neurosurg. Psychiat., 44,* 285–293.

Jennett, B., and Teasdale, G. (1981). *Management of Head Injuries.* Contemporary Neurology Series, vol. 20. F. Plum, ed. Philadelphia: F. A. Davis Company, pp. 10–11.

Kertesz, A., and McCabe, P. (1977). Recovery patterns and prognosis in aphasia. *Brain, 100,* 1–6.

Kløve, H., and Reitan, R. (1958). The effects of dysphasia and spatial distortion on Wechsler-Bellevue results. Am. Med. Assoc., *Arch. Neurol. Psychiat., 80,* 708–713.

Kløve, H. (1959). Relationship of differential electroencephalographic patterns to distribution of Wechsler-Bellevue scores. *Neurology (Minneap.), 9,* 871–878.

Ladd, C. E. (1964). WAIS performance of brain damaged and neurotic patients. *J. Clin. Psychol., 20,* 114–121.

Lashley, K. (1938). Factors limiting recovery after central nervous lesions. *J. Nerv. Ment. Dis., 88,* 733–755.

Levin, H. S., Benton, A. L., and Grossman, R. G. (1982). *Neuropsychological consequences of closed head injury.* New York: Oxford University Press.

Levin, H. S., Grossman, R. G., Rose, J. E., and Teasdale, G. (1979). Long-term neuropsychological outcome of closed head injury. *J. Neurosurg., 50,* 412–422.

Levin, H. S., O'Donnell, V. M., and Grossman, R. G. (1979). The Galveston orientation and amnesia test: A practical scale to assess cognition after head injury. *J. Nerv. Ment. Dis., 167,* 675–684.

Lezak, M. D. (1978a). Subtle sequelae of brain damage. *Am. J. Phys. Med., 57,* 9–15.

Lezak, M. D. (1978b). Living with the characterologically altered brain injured patient. *J. Clin. Psychiat., 39,* 592–598.

Lynch, W. J. (1983). Neuropsychologic assessment. In: *Rehabilitation of the Head-Injured Adult.* M. Rosenthal, E. R. Griffith, M. R. Bond, and J. D. Miller, eds. Philadelphia: F. A. Davis Company, p. 291–308.

Mandleberg, I. A., and Brooks, D. N. (1975). Cognitive recovery after severe head injury: 1. Serial testing on the Wechsler Adult Intelligence Scale. *J. Neurol., Neurosurg. Psychiat., 38,* 1121–1126.

McKinlay, W. W., and Brooks, D. N. (1984). Methodological problems in assessing psychosocial recovery following severe head injury. *J. Clin. Neuropsychol., 6,* 87–99.

McKinlay, W. W., Brooks, D. N., and Bond, M. R. (1983). Post-concussional symptoms, financial compensation and outcome of severe blunt head injury. *J. Neurol., Neurosurg. Psychiat., 46,* 1084–1091.

McKinlay, W. W., Brooks, D. N., Bond, M. R., Martinage, D. P., and Marshall, M. M. (1981). The short-term outcome of severe blunt head injury as reported by relatives of the injured person. *J. Neurol., Neurosurg. Psychiat., 44,* 527–533.

Miller, E. (1979). The long-term consequences of head injury: A discussion of the evidence with special reference to preparation of legal reports. *Br. J. Soc. Clin. Psychol., 18,* 87–98.

Miller, H., and Stern, G. (1965). The long-term prognosis of severe head injury. *Lancet, i,* 225–229.

Milner, B. (1969). Residual intellectual and memory deficits after head injury. In: *The Late Effects of Head Injury.* E. Walker, W. F. Caveness, M. Critchley, eds. Spingfield, Illinois: Charles C. Thomas, p. 84.

Morrow, R. S., and Mark, J. C. (1955). The correlation of intelligence and neurological findings on 22 patients autopsied for brain damage. *J. Consult. Psychol., 19,* 283–290.

Najenson, T. (1978). Recovery of communicative functions after prolonged traumatic coma. *Scand. J. Rehab. Med., 10,* 15–23.

Newcombe, F., and Fortuny, L. A. I. (1979). Problems and perspectives in the evaluation of psychological deficits after cerebral lesions. *Int. Rehab. med., 1,* 182–192.

Newcombe, F., Hiorns, R. W., Marshall, J. C., and Adams, C. B. T. (1975). Acquired dyslexia: Patterns of deficit and recovery. In: *Outcome of Severe Damage to the Central Nervous System.* Ciba Foundation Symposium 34 (new series). Amsterdam: Elsevier-Excerpta Medica, pp. 227–244.

Oddy, M., Humphrey, M., and Uttley, D. (1978). Subjective impairment and social recovery after closed head injury. *J. Neurol., Neurosurg. Psychiat., 41,* 611–616.

Parsons, O. A., and Prigitano, G. P. (1978). Methodological considerations in clinical neuropsychological research. *J. Consult. Clin. Psychol., 4,* 608–614.

Rimel, R. W., Giordani, B., Bartin, J. J., Boll, T. J., and Jane, J. A. (1981). Disability caused by minor head injury. *Neurosurgery, 9,* 221–235.

Rimel, R. W., and Jane, J. A. (1983). Characteristics of the head-injured patient. In: *Rehabilitation of the Head Injured Adult.* M. Rosenthal, E. R. Griffith, M. R. Bond, and J. D. Miller, eds. Philadelphia: F. A. Davis Company, pp. 9–21.

Roberts, A. H. (1979). *Severe Accidental Head Injury: An Assessment of Long-Term Prognosis.* London: Macmillan Press, pp. 55–89.

Russell, W. R. (1932). Cerebral involvement in head injury. *Brain, 55,* 549–603.

Russell, W. R. (1934). The after-effects of head injury. *Edinburgh Med. J., 41,* 129–141.

Schacter, D. L., and Crovitz, H. F. (1977). Memory function after closed head injury: A review of quantitative research. *Cortex, 13,* 150–176.

Selecki, B. R. (1967). A retrospective study of neuro-traumatic admission to a teaching hospital: Part 1, General aspects. *Med. J. Australia, 2,* 113–121.

Sunderland, A., Harris, J. E., and Baddeley, A. D. (1983). Do laboratory tests predict everyday memory? A neuropsychological study. *J. Verbal Learning Behav., 22,* 1–5.

Teasdale, S., and Brooks, D. N. (1986). Traumatic amnesia. In: *Handbook of Clinical Neurology,* vol. 1 (45): Clinical Neuropsychology. P. J. Vuik, and G. W. Bruyn, and H. L. Klawans, eds. Amsterdam: Elsevier, North-Holland Publishing Co.

Teasdale, G., and Jennett, B. (1974). Assessment of coma and impaired consciousness. *Lancet, ii,* 81–84.

Thomsen, I. V. (1974). Evaluation and outcome of aphasia in patients with severe closed head injury. *J. Neurol., Neurosurg. Psychiat., 38,* 713–718.

Thomsen, I. V. (1984). Late outcome of very severe blunt head trauma: A 10–15 year second follow-up. *J. Neurol., Neurosurg. Psychiat., 47,* 260–268.

Vigouroux, R. P, Baurand, C. Naquet, R., Chament, J. H., Choux, M., Benayoun, R., Bureau, M., Charpy, J. P., Clamen-Guey, M. J., and Guey, J. (1971). A series of patients with cranio-cerebral injuries studied neurologically, psychometrically, electro-encephalographically and socially. In: *Head Injuries.* Proceedings of an International Symposium. Ed. W. Caveness and S. Walker, eds. Edinburgh: Churchill-Livingstone, p. 335–410.

16

Neuropsychological Impairment in Patients with Parkinson's Disease

DOMENICO PASSAFIUME / FRANCOIS BOLLER / NANCI C. KEEFE

Involuntary tremulous motion, with lessened muscular power, in parts not in action and even when supported; with a propensity to bend the trunk forward, and to pass from a walking to a running pace: The senses and intellects being uninjured.

The above quotation from James Parkinson's "Essay of the Shaking Palsy" (1817) defines most of the characteristics of the disease known today as idiopathic Parkinson's disease. This chapter will show, however, that in many instances the last sentence of Dr. Parkinson's statement is incorrect and that neuropsychological changes are quite often, if not universally, found in patients with Parkinson's disease.

Description of Parkinson's Disease

Idiopathic Parkinson's disease (PD) is a disease of the central nervous system primarily characterized by (1) tremor, (2) a movement difficulty known as akinesia or bradykinesia, (3) rigidity (increased muscle tone), and (4) loss of normal postural reflexes. The tremor most commonly affects the distal part of the extremities, especially the hands. It is usually bilateral, although it is not uncommon to see an asymmetrical form—especially in the early stage of the disease. Tremor is due to alternate contraction of antagonistic muscles. The tremor of Parkinson's disease is classically referred to as a "resting" tremor, but it is typically absent during sleep and while patients are completely relaxed. Tremor appears most often when the patient is under some stress or decides to initiate an act. It often disappears when the patient actually initiates a voluntary action but tends to reappear during the continuation of that action, thus making some daily tasks very difficult (for example, drinking from a full glass or cup).

Akinesia or bradykinesia is difficulty initiating voluntary movement, which often produces a lack of dexterity with a loss of normal associated movements. The facial muscles are also affected, which flattens the face and gives patients what has been called a "mask-like" appearance, or *amimia*.

The rigidity appears as an increased resistance to passive movements of all joints, particularly prominent in the upper limbs. On occasion, passive stretching of these hypertonic muscles produces an irregular jerkiness known as cogwheel rigidity. It is often overlooked that rigidity of the axial muscles (particularly those of the back) contributes in a major fashion to the impairment, creating postural changes that in turn make walking very difficult. The loss of normal postural reflexes also contributes to a disorder of equilibrium and righting reactions, as shown by the fact that when PD patients are standing, they tend to fall following a simple shove on the chest and, in a more advanced stage, even spontaneously.

The etiology of PD is unknown, even though (as will be seen below) there are many factors and diseases that may produce a condition similar to Parkinson's disease. Essentially, its diagnosis is based on the constellation of symptoms and signs mentioned above. Its pathology and biochemistry have been extensively studied and there is now convincing evidence that the most constant finding in PD is a loss of pigmented cells in the substantia nigra and other pigmented subcortical nuclei (e.g., locus cereleus). The remaining cells of these structures contain characteristic eosinophilic cytoplasmic inclusion bodies known as Lewy bodies. The demonstrated depletion of dopamine that accompanies lesions of these structures (Hornykiewicz, 1966) has led to current treatment of PD by L-dopa (Cotzias, Van Woert, and Schiffer, 1967) a precursor of dopamine, as well as other drugs that affect the metabolism of catecholamines. It is a frequent disease affecting about 1% of the population over the age of 50 years, and one can therefore estimate that over one half-million persons have the disease in the United States alone (Adams and Victor, 1981, p. 807). Onset of the disease is rare before the age of 30, usually occuring between the ages of 50 and 70. Clough, Mendoza, and Yahr (1981), however, have recently reported a case with onset at age 15. In the United States it has been found to occur more often in whites than in blacks (Kessler, 1972), but it is observed in all countries and in all ethnic groups. Older studies found a high familial incidence of the disease, but a recent study (Duvoisin et al., 1981) showed that out of 12 monozygotic twin pairs, not one was concordant for Parkinson's disease. Other than aging, very few if any risk factors have been identified. Oddly, it appears that cigarette smoking tends to protect one from the disease (Baumann et al., 1980; Marttila and Rinne, 1980), a finding that may be related to older claims that patients with PD may have prior peculiar personality traits (Aring, 1962; Booth, 1948) that in turn may tend to reduce smoking. It has recently been shown that a condition resembling PD both clinically and pathologically can be induced in humans and primates by a product that chemically resembles the narcotic analgesic Meperidine (Ballard et al., 1983).

Symptom pictures resembling PD may result from other diseases. Following the epidemic of encephalitis lethargica (known as Von Economo's encephalitis) in the earlier part of this century, a large number of cases of so-called post-encephalitic Parkinsonism appeared. Parkinsonism was clinically different from

PD in that there was a more rapid progression, a higher incidence of dementia, a characteristic eye movement disorder (oculogyric crises) and often bizarre movements, posture, and gait. Pathologically, these patients showed neurofibrillary tangles (NFT) in the brain stem but no Lewy bodies. No new cases of Von Economo's encephalitis have occurred since 1930, thus postencephalitic Parkinsonism has practically disappeared. Other encephalitides, cerebrovascular disease, trauma, upper brain stem tumors and rare conditions such as progressive supernuclear palsy or striato nigral degeneration are to be separated from typical PD (see Selby, 1968a and 1968b, for a review). Since none of these conditions involve the appearance of Lewy bodies, idiopathic PD is also referred to as Lewy bodies Parkinson's disease. The relationship between PD and Alzheimer's disease (AD) will be discussed below. Modern treatment has increased the life expectancy of PD patients, although it is still lessened by the disease, especially in PD patients who develop dementia (Boller et al., 1980).

Neuropsychological Findings and Diagnostic Considerations

In his original description James Parkinson stated specifically that the mental status of his patients was normal. Almost a century and a half later, Charcot and Vulpian (1861, p. 819) stated that "in general, psychic faculties are definitely impaired". What is the true state of affairs?

There is little question that either on a bedside mental status examination or on formal neuropsychological tests, PD patients tend to show impairment when asked to perform some tasks. Many factors could conceivably explain this impairment. Besides the obvious effect of aging, it is evident that tests must be selected that do not depend on the often slowed motor and verbal responses of patients with PD. Also, we must keep in mind that depression is known to occur more often in PD than in normal individuals (Mayeux et al., 1983; Todes, 1983). Some authors think that no neuropsychological impairment can be found in PD patients once the above factors are taken into account. These authors—including Talland (1962), Diller and Riklan (1956), and Matthews and Haaland (1979)—range from neurologists who based their conclusion only on clinical impressions to contemporary neuropsychologists who have administered specifically designed neuropsychological tests. There are several explanations for these negative findings. A common feature of these papers is that they draw a comparison between the whole population of PD patients and controls, a method by which a fairly sizable number of demented patients might escape detection. Some of these papers, in fact, specifically mention that dementia is occasionally seen in PD. For example, Diller and Riklan (1956, p. 1294) point out that

in a small percentage [of PD patients], there is evidence of mental deterioration . . . [and] . . . overall functioning was markedly below what one would have been led to expect from the past education and vocational attainment.

Another characteristic of the papers stating that no dementia is found in Parkinson's disease is that the great majority are based on studies which were performed around or before 1970. Even the very recent study of Matthews and Haaland (1979) selected PD patients on the basis of no history of dopaminergic medication; thus the subjects had presumably been tested before L-dopa and similar drugs became widely available.

Many other authors, however, have found that there is a clearcut neuropsychological impairment in patients with PD, even when age and depression are taken into account and when the tests administered do not rely heavily on motor performance. It is important, however, to clearly separate two very different sets of symptoms in PD patients who have cognitive impairment: one is a specific neuropsychological deficit mainly affecting visuo-spatial behavior, and the second is a generalized decrement of intellectual functions with a pattern of dementia that tends to mimic that of Alzheimer's disease.

Visuo-spatial Impairment

The incidence of visuo-spatial deficits is considerably higher than that of any other cognitive changes found in PD and there are experimental data suggesting that the same deficits result from lesions of the basal ganglia in animals. For example, rodents with caudate lesions show a significant deficit on maze-solving tasks (Thompson, 1974) which seems to be due to the animal's inability to monitor its spatial orientation relative to its starting position. Also, after unilateral cooling of the globus pallidus, monkeys seem to have "spatial" difficulty in locating auditory stimuli and tracking stimuli in the field contralateral to the lesion (Caan and Stein, 1979).

Teuber and Proctor (1964) were probably the first to point out the presence of visuo-spatial disorders in PD using a rod and frame apparatus. They studied PD patients on the Aubert effect in the context of several experimental conditions: the subjects had to adjust a line to a vertical position when they were in an upright position and then while they themselves were tilted. In a third condition the subjects, blindfolded, were tilted and had to adjust themselves to an upright position. The results showed that PD patients were no different from normal controls in the first experimental situation; however, there were significant differences in both the second and third conditions, where PD patients made more errors than normal controls in adjusting the line to the vertical while they were in the tilted position and in setting their own body to the upright position. Similar results were reported by Proctor et al. (1964).

The spatial orientation of PD was further investigated by Bowen, Hoehn and Yahr (1972a, 1972b). In their experiment, PD patients were divided into three groups: (1) Those with symptoms lateralized prevalently to the right side of the body (neurological lesions presumably on the left side of the basal ganglia and substantia nigra); (2) symptoms lateralized to the left (neurological lesions on the right side); and (3) bilateral symptomatology. The results showed that PD patients with bilateral symptomatology were significantly impaired with respect to normal controls or those with right sided symptoms when they had to move through a room following a series of spots on the floor, according to a map. Impairment on a rotation task in which the subjects were required to point out on their own bodies the body parts indicated on a human figure presented, both from the front and from the back, has also been reported (Bowen, 1976).

Other more recent papers have brought out further evidence favoring the existence of visuo-spatial deficits in PD patients. Mayeux et al. (1981) found that PD patients were impaired when attempting to reproduce movements they saw through a translucent screen by moving their own arms and bodies. Villardita et al. (1982) found that PD patients had an impaired performance on the Benton Visual Retention Test and the Frostig Visual Perception Test (Frostig, Horne, and Miller, 1972) and that these visuo-perceptive disabilities were relatively independent of mental deterioration. Mortimer et al. (1982) on the other hand found that PD patients were impaired on a series of visuo-spatial tasks, especially Wepman's Visual Discrimination Test (VDT) (Wepman, Morency, and Seidl, 1975), in which subjects were required to match a "model" drawing with one of four alternatives by pointing. Because the motor response required in VDT is quite elementary and because the patients' intelligence was not impaired, the findings of Mortimer et al. (1982) are compatible with the conclusion that the PD subjects have an impairment in visual perceptual behavior, but it is not clear which possible component of visual perceptual behavior is specifically impaired in PD.

The majority of the tests used by researchers to diagnose visuo-spatial difficulties in PD subjects and in experimental animals, with the exceptions of Villardita et al. (1982) and Mortimer et al. (1982), required complex motor responses such as walking on a given route, making complex gestures, and drawing. Boller et al. (1982) therefore decided to undertake a more specific study of visuo-spatial functions of PD patients. They defined impairment of visuo-spatial perception as difficulty appreciating the relative position of stimulus-objects in space, difficulty integrating those objects into a coherent spatial framework, and difficulty performing mental operations involving spatial concepts.

Thirty PD patients and thirty normal controls (NC) were compared on visual perceptual task performances requiring a motor response (such as drawing). All the PD patients had idiopathic Parkinsonism and were in stages I to III (Hoehn & Yahr, 1967) of the disease. Age, education, and sex distributions were equal in both groups. Details of the tests used can be found in the paper by Boller et al. (1984). It was found that PD patients' performance was significantly impaired on several tasks. Figure 1 shows that following a transformation into Z scores, the pooled data suggest that the PD group performed significantly worse than the NC group on both "perceptual" and "motor" tasks. The tests that discriminated best between PD and NC turned out to be relatively simple visuo-spatial tests such as the angle perception test described by Benton, Hannay, and Varney (1975). The spatial deficit shown by the PD patients was independent of intellectual impairment.

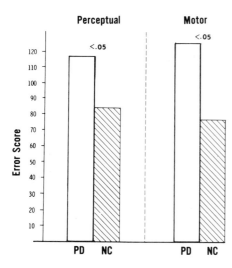

Fig. 1. Mean Error Score of the Parkinson's disease (PD) group and the normal control (NC) group on perceptual and motor tasks.

All the above papers strongly suggest that visuo-spatial impairment is universally present in patients with Parkinson's disease and must be clearly distinguished from generalized dementia.

The Relation of Parkinson's Disease to Generalized Dementias

Several authors contend that generalized mental impairment is found in PD patients considerably more often than in the general population. This conclusion is based on a variety of methodologies ranging from clinical impressions to application of standardized intelligence tests such as the Wechsler Adult Intelligence Scale (WAIS) or portions of neuropsychological test batteries such as the Halstead-Reitan. From a qualitative standpoint, the mental status changes of patients with generalized dementia appear to be rather nonspecific. Some authors have pointed out a tendency for a marked discrepancy to exist between the verbal and performance scales of the WAIS, with the verbal I.Q. being significantly higher than the performance I.Q. (Loranger et al., 1972). In a recent retrospective study based on chart reviews, Boller et al. (1980) found that PD patients with severe dementia had a rather standardized pattern of deficit, with orientation, construction, and memory particularly affected, while social behavior, language, praxis, and to some extent, manipulation of old information were relatively less impaired. This change is somewhat similar to what is found in Alzheimer's disease, and the progression in the course of the dementia also resembled that of Alzheimer's disease. Other patients in that study showed a mild dementia manifested by a decrease in their ability to learn new material as is seen in patients with "benign senescent forgetfulness" (Kral, 1978; Kral and Dorken, 1951). The percentage of demented PD patients found by authors after 1970 has varied from 33% to 81% (Boller, 1980).

Pathology of Dementia

Until recently, very little was known about the possible pathology of the dementia in PD. It has been known for some time that cortical atrophy is often found in PD, as demonstrated by pneumoencephalography (Gath et al., 1975; Selby, 1968a, 1968b; Svennilson et al., 1960), CT scan (Schneider et al., 1977), and autopsy data (Alvord, 1971). Alvord (1971) was probably the first to hypothesize that demented PD patients may also have AD. Recent studies (Alvord et al., 1974; Boller et al., 1980; Hakim and Mathieson, 1979; Sugimura, Yamasaki, and Ando, 1977) have established clearly that AD is found in PD patients in a much greater proportion than would be expected in a population of similar age. Boller et al. (1980) reported that 9 out of 9 PD patients with severe dementia and 3 out of 7 with mild dementia were found to have AD.

Conclusions

These clinical pathological correlations suggest that, in the majority of demented PD patients, the mental changes are probably not directly related to the classical subcortical pathology of PD, but rather to clearcut changes occurring in the cerebral cortex. The relationship between PD and AD has been reviewed recently by Boller et al. (1984). Although AD patients tend to show some extrapyramidal features, especially in the intermediate to late stage of the disease, (Parkes et al., 1974; Pearce, 1974), they do not usually show true Parkinson disease.

The reasons for this phenomenon are not clear. Only a few authors have reported Lewy bodies in AD (Forno, Barbour, and Norville, 1978; Woodard, 1962; Rosenblum and Ghatak, 1979). Whitehouse et al. (1983) found that demented PD patients show a selective loss of cells in the nucleus basalis of Meynert, a change that is typically found in AD.

It may be possible that changes in the substantia nigra and the rest of the dopaminergic system may account for some neuropsychological changes; such as the mild dementia found in some patients or the "specific" deficits such as the visuo-spatial disorders discussed above.

There appears to be a considerable rise in the incidence of dementia reported by various authors, which cannot be explained easily. It could be due simply to a greater awareness of dementia on the part of investigators and to the use of more discriminative and appropriate neuropsychological tests. It must be noted that the tendency toward an increase in reported incidence of dementia in connection with PD began with the studies that were performed after L-dopa became available.

The relationship between L-dopa and dementia is far from clear. Some authors have reported that L-dopa improves the mental status and neuropsychological test performance of PD patients (Drachman and Stahl, 1975; Meier and Martin, 1970). On the other hand, an impairment in the mental abilities of patients treated with dopaminergic drugs compared to the PD patients on anticholinergic drugs is reported by several authors (e.g., Botez and Barbeau, 1973).

Still other studies, however, showed that L-dopa does not produce any long-term difference in mental status of PD patients (Markham, Treciokas, and Diamond, 1974). It must be emphasized that many patients on L-dopa do not show dementia and that the presence of dementia in PD patients was reported by many authors long before the introduction of L-dopa. The specific role of dopaminergic drugs in the visuo-spatial behavior of PD patients has not been studied. Boller et al. (1984) found however, that anticholinergic drugs do not seem to effect the visuo-spatial performance of PD patients.

Why do some PD patients develop dementia when others do not? No clear explanation is available, but some researchers (Boller et al., 1980; Leiberman et al., 1979) have postulated the presence of two distinct forms of PD: one with pathology confined to the substantia nigra that does not produce dementia and in which the only cognitive change corresponds to the visuo-spatial impairment mentioned above, and the other with cortical pathology as well as subcortical pathology that produces dementia.

Further investigations are needed to establish the nature and etiology of specific neuropsychological deficits in PD. It seems clear that some patients do develop neurobehavioral problems beyond those observed by James Parkinson's in 1817.

ACKNOWLEDGMENT

Research supported in part by the Medical Research Council of the Veterans Administration and by a National Institute of Health (National Institute of Aging) Program Grant #P01 AG-03705.

REFERENCES

Adams, R. D., and Victor, M. (1981). *Principles of neurology*. New York: McGraw Hill, p. 807.
Alvord, E. C. (1971). The pathology of Parkinsonism. Part II: An interpretation with special reference to other changes in the aging brain. In: F. H. McDowell and C. H. Markham, eds., *Recent Advances in Parkinson's Disease*. Philadelphia: Davis, pp. 131–161.
Alvord, E. C., Forno, L. S., Kusske, J. A., Kauffman, R. J., Rhodes, J. S. and Goetowski, C. R. (1974). The pathology of Parkinsonism: A comparison of degenerations in cerebral cortex and brainstem. *Adv. Neurol.*, 5, 175–193.
Aring, C. D. (1962). The riddle of the Parkinson syndrome. *Arch. Neurol.*, 6, 1–4.
Ballard, P., Langston, J. W., Tetrud, J., and Burns, R. S. (1983). Chemically induced chronic Parkinsonism in young adults: Clinical and neuropharmacologic aspects. *Neurology, 33, (Suppl. 2)*, 90.
Baumann, R. J., Jameson, H. D., McKean, H. E., Haack, D. G., and Weisberg, L. M. (1980). Cigarette smoking and Parkinson's disease. *Neurology, 30*, 839–843.
Benton, A. L., Hannay, H. J., and Varney, N. R. (1975). Visual perception of line direction in patients with unilateral brain disease. *Neurology, 25*, (NY), 907–910.
Boller, F. (1980). Mental status of patients with Parkinson disease. *J. Clin. Neuropsychol., 2*, 157–172.

Boller, F., Mizutani, T., Roessmann, U., and Gambetti, P. (1980). Parkinson disease, dementia and Alzheimer disease: Clinicopathological correlations. *Ann. Neurol., 7,* 329–335.

Boller, F., Passafiume, D., Rogers, K., Morrow, L., and Kim, Y. (1982). Visuospatial impairment in Parkinson disease: Role of perceptual and motor factors and of disease stage. *Neurology, 32,* A189.

Boller, F., Passafiume, D., Keefe, M. C., Rogers, K., Morrow, L., and Kim, Y. (1984). Visuospatial impairment in Parkinson disease: Role of perceptual and motor factors. *Arch. Neurol., 41,* 485–490.

Booth, G. (1948). Psychodynamics in Parkinsonism. *Psychosomatic Med., 10,* 1–14.

Botez, M. I., and Barbeau, A. (1973). Long term mental changes in levodopa treated patients. *Lancet, 2,* 1028–1029.

Bowen, F. P. (1976). Behavioral attention in patients with basal ganglia lesions. In: M. D. Yahr, ed., *The Basal Ganglia.* New York: Raven Press, pp. 169–177.

Bowen, F. P., Hoehn, M. M., and Yahr, M.D. (1972a). Cerebral dominance in relation to tracking and tapping performance in patients with Parkinsonism. *Neurology, 22,* 32–40.

Bowen, F. P., Hoehn, M. M., and Yahr, M. D. (1972b). Parkinsonism: Alterations in spatial orientation as determined by a route-walking test. *Neuropsychologia, 10,* 355–361.

Caan, W., and Stein, J. F. (1979). The effects of cooling globus pallidus on manual tracking in trained rhesus monkeys. From the Proceedings of the Physiological Society, 20–21, April. *J. Physiol., 293,* 69P.

Charcot, J. M., and Vulpian, A. (1861). De la paralysie agitante: Part II. *Gazette Hebdomadaire de Medicine et de Chirurgie, 8,* 816–820.

Clough, C. G., Mendoza, M., and Yahr, M. D. (1981). A case of sporadic juvenile Parkinson's disease. *Arch. Neurol., 38,* 730–731.

Cotzias, G. C., Van Woert, M. H., and Schiffer, L. M. (1967). Aromatic amino acids and modification of Parkinsonism. *The New Engl. J. Med., 276,* 374–379.

Diller, L., and Riklan, M. (1956). Psychosocial factors in Parkinson's disease. *J. Am. Geriat. Soc., 4,* 1291–1300.

Drachman, D. A., and Stahl, S. (1975). Extrapyramidal dementia and levodopa. *Lancet, 1,* 809.

Duvoisin, R. C., Eldridge, R., Williams, A., Nutt, J., and Calne, D. (1981). Twin study of Parkinson disease. *Neurology, 31,* 77–80.

Forno, L. S., Barbour, P. J., and Norville, R. L. (1978). Presenile dementia with lewy bodies and neurofibrillary tangles. *Arch. Neurol., 35,* 818–822.

Frostig, M., Horne, M., and Miller, A. M. (1972). *The Frostig Program for the Development of Visual Perception.* Chicago: Follett Education.

Gath, I., Jorgensen, A., Sjaastad, O., and Berstad, J. (1975). Pneumoencephalographic findings in Parkinsonism. *Arch. Neurol., 32,* 769–773.

Hakim, A. M., and Mathieson, G. (1979). Dementia in Parkinson's disease: A neuropathological study. *Neurology, 29,* 1209–1214.

Hoehn, M. M., and Yahr, M. D. (1967). Parkinsonism: Onset, progression and mortality. *Neurology, 17,* 427–442.

Hornykiewicz, O. (1966). Dopamine (3-hydroxytyramine) and brain function. *Pharmacol. Rev., 18,* 925–964.

Kessler, I. (1972). Epidemiologic studies of Parkinson's disease. III: A community based survey. *Am. J. Epidemiol., 96,* 242–254.

Kral, V. A. (1978). Benign senescent forgetfulness. In: R. Katzman, R. D. Terry, and K. L. Bick, eds., *Alzheimer's Disease: Senile Dementia and Related Disorders.* New York: Raven Press, pp. 47–51.

Kral, V. A., and Dorken, H. (1951). Comparative psychological study of hyperkinetic and akinetic extrapyramidal disorders. *Arch. Neurol. Psychiat., 66,* 431–442.

Lieberman, A., Dziatolowski, M., Kupersmith, M., Serby, M., Goodgold, A., Korein, J., and Goldstein, M. (1979). Dementia in Parkinson disease. *Ann. Neurol., 6,* 355–359.

Loranger, A. W., Goodell, H., McDowell, F. H., Lee, J. E., and Sweet, R. D. (1972). Intellectual impairment in Parkinson's syndrome. *Brain, 95,* 405–412.

Markham, C. H., Treciokas, L. S., and Diamond, S. G. (1974). Parkinson's disease and levodopa: A five-year follow-up and review. *The Western Journal of Medicine, 121,* 188–206.

Marttila, R. J., and Rinne, V. K. (1980). Smoking and Parkinson's disease. *Acta Neurol. Scand., 62,* 322–325.

Matthews, C. G., and Haaland, K. Y. (1979). The effect of symptom duration on cognitive and motor performance in Parkinsonism. *Neurology, 29,* 951–956.

Mayeux, R., Cote, L., Stern, Y., and Williams, J. B. W. (1983). Depression in Parkinson's disease: Alterations in monoamine metabolism. *Neurology, 33, (Suppl. 2),* 103.

Mayeux, R., Stern, Y., Rosen, J., and Leventhal, J. (1981). Depression, intellectual impairment, and Parkinson disease. *Neurology, 31,* 645–650.

Meier, M. J., and Martin, W. E. (1970). Intellectual changes associated with levodopa therapy. *J. Am. Med. Assoc., 213,* 465–466.

Mortimer, J. A., Pirozzolo, F. J., Hansch, E. C., and Webster, D. D. (1982). Relationship of motor symptoms to intellectual deficits in Parkinson disease. *Neurology, 32,* 133–137.

Parkes, J. D., Marsden, C. D., Rees, J. E., Curzon, G., Kantamaneni, B. D., Knill-Jones, R., Akbar, A., Das, S., and Kataria, M. (1974). Parkinson's disease, cerebral arteriosclerosis and senile dementia. *Quart. J. Med., 43,* 49–61.

Parkinson, J. (1817). *An Essay on The Shaking Palsy.* London: Sherwood, Neely & Jones.

Pearce, J. (1974). The extrapyramidal disorder of Alzheimer's disease. *Eur. Neurol., 12,* 94–103.

Proctor, F., Riklan, M., Cooper, I. S., and Teuber, H. L. (1964). Judgement of visual and postural vertical by Parkinsonian patients. *Neurology, 14,* 287–293.

Rosenblum, W. I., and Ghatak, N. R. (1979). Lewy bodies in the presence of Alzheimer's disease. *Arch. Neurol., 36,* 170–171.

Schneider, E., Fischer, P. A., Becker, H., Hacker, H., Pencz, A., and Jacobi, P. (1977). Relationship between arteriosclerosis and cerebral atrophy in Parkinson's disease. *J. Neurol., 217,* 11–16.

Selby, G. (1968a). Cerebral atrophy in Parkinsonism. *J. Neurol. Sci., 6,* 517–559.

Selby, G. (1968b). Parkinson's disease. In: P. J. Vinken, G. W. Bruyn, eds., *Handbook of Clinical Neurology,* vol. 6. Amsterdam: Elsevier/North Holland, pp. 173–211.

Sugimura, K., Yamasaki, Y., and Ando, K. (1977). Parkinson's disease accompanied by dementia. A case of concurrent Parkinson's and Alzheimer's diseases (in Japanese). *Rinsho Shinkeigaku, 17,* 513–519.

Svennilson, E., Torvik, A., Lowe, R., and Leksell, L. (1960). Treatment of Parkinsonism by stereotactic thermolesions in the pallidal region. *Acta Psychiat. Scand., 35,* 358–377.

Talland, G. A. (1962). Cognitive function in Parkinson's disease. *J. Nerv. Ment. Dis., 135,* 196–205.

Teuber, H. L., and Proctor, F. (1964). Some effects of basal ganglia lesions in subhuman primates and man. *Neuropsychologia, 2,* 85–93.

Thompson, R. (1974). Localization of the "maze memory system" in the white rat. *Physiol. Psychol., 2,* 1–17.

Todes, C. (1983). Inside Parkinsonism. *Lancet, 1,* 977–978.

Villardita, C., Smirni, P., Le Pira, F., Zappala, G., and Nicoletti, F. (1982). Mental deterioration, visuoperceptive disabilities and constructional apraxia in Parkinson's disease. *Acta Neurol. Scand., 66,* 112–120.

Wepman, J. M., Morency, A., and Seidl, M. (1975). *Visual Discrimination Test.* Chicago: Language Research Associates.

Whitehouse, P. J., Hedreen, J. C., White, C. L. III, and Price, D. L. (1983). Basal forebrain neurons in the dementia of Parkinson disease. *Ann. Neurol., 13,* 243–248.

Woodard, J. S. (1962). Concentric hyaline inclusion body formation in mental disease, analysis of twenty-seven cases. *J. Neuropathol. Exp. Neurol., 21,* 442–449.

17

The Effects of Cerebral Vascular Disease and Its Treatment on Higher Cortical Functioning

GREGORY G. BROWN / ANNE DULL BAIRD / MARK W. SHATZ

Pathophysiology of Stroke

About 1 liter of blood—nearly one-fifth of cardiac output—passes through the brain each minute. Blood supplies the brain with glucose and oxygen, while dispersing the heat and metabolic products of cerebral activity (Toole and Patel, 1974, pp. 53–54). The brain can tolerate only a brief cessation in the delivery of glucose and oxygen, the removal of metabolites, or the dispersion of heat before neural functioning is disrupted. Diseases that clog or rupture vessels, reduce the content of glucose and oxygen in the blood, or affect the autoregulation of blood flow can cause severe neurologic and behavioral deficit.

Stroke is the third leading cause of death in the United States. Although the age-adjusted annual death rate from cerebrovascular disease has steadily declined in the United States, cerebrovascular disease still caused approximately 50 deaths per 100,000 people in 1976. Cerebrovascular disease is a major cause of disability, causing economic loss, in addition to the cost of medical care and treatment (Kurtzke, 1980). Since neuropsychological measures are sensitive to the brain changes associated with stroke and have implications for adaptive behavior outside the laboratory, they span the distance between the physiological changes associated with stroke and its effects on quality of life. This paper will review the consequences of cerebral vascular disease and its treatment as manifested on standardized neuropsychological tests.

Metabolic Effects of Complete Cerebral Ischemia

Stroke is the rapid onset of focal neurologic deficit. It is usually caused by cerebrovascular disease, but other diseases, such as neoplasm, may present with a stroke-like syndrome. Strokes may be due to cerebral hemorrhage or to cerebral ischemia. In the latter, blood flow to neural tissue is insufficient to maintain physiologic function. Cerebral infarction occurs when ischemia is severe enough to produce nerve cell death (Mohr, Fisher, and Adams, 1980).

The effects of total cerebral ischemia on cellular metabolism occur rapidly.

Within seconds after occlusion of blood flow, glucose metabolism declines, until it is 15% of its normal level 30 seconds later. Slowing of the electroencephalogram may be observed as soon as 5 seconds after the onset of ischemia. Twenty to 25 seconds later it becomes isoelectric. The alterations in glucose metabolism, as well as the abrupt termination in venous removal of lactic acid and other metabolites, causes acidic pH levels in the brain. This acidosis may alter the excitability of neural tissue (Reivich and Waltz, 1980). An excess of metabolites may dilate cerebral vessels and lead to a loss of autoregulation (Høedt-Rasmussen et al., 1967).

The ability of mitochondria to produce the high energy phosphates necessary to fuel the activities of a nerve cell declines rapidly in the first minute of total ischemia (Reivich and Waltz, 1980). Since the distribution of potassium and sodium across the cell membrane depends on active pumps that use high energy phosphates as fuel, these ionic channels collapse and the resting potential dissipates (Meyer, Deshmukh, and Welch, 1976).

Alteration and loss of presynaptic vesicles occur 3 to 4 minutes into the ischemic period (Williams and Grossman, 1969). These alterations are accompanied by the release of the neurotransmitters dopamine, serotonin, and norepinephrine into the extracellular space and cerebrospinal fluid (Meyer et al., 1974). Disordered cholinergic transmission following acute stroke may add a neurogenic component to metabolic factors causing a disruption of autoregulation (Ott et al., 1975).

Between the first and fourth hours after complete cerebral ischemia, the blood becomes stagnant, changes occur in the thin internal lining of the blood vessels, edema develops, and the regional collapse of autoregulation occurs. Histologic changes continue to develop over the hours and days following ischemia. Late changes include liquefaction and cavitation of the infarcted tissue, with a surrounding zone of astrocyte proliferation (Hudgins and Garcia, 1970).

The Distribution of Cerebral Vessels and Their Collaterals

Two anatomical facts in great part determine the focus and severity of cerebral ischemia: the topographies of the major arterial trees and their interconnectedness. Pairs of carotid and vertebral arteries bring blood to the major vessels of the brain. Figure 1 shows that the cerebral circulation divides into an anterior division, where the anterior and middle cerebral arteries form the rostral extension of the internal carotid artery, and a posterior division formed by the vertebral-basilar-posterior cerebral arterial network. Although the posterior communicating artery connects these two arterial divisions, little blood is exchanged in normals (Toole and Patel, 1974, pp. 17–18).

Several connections exist among the major arteries of the brain. The two anterior cerebral arteries are connected by the anterior communicating artery; the carotid and posterior cerebral arteries are joined by the posterior communicating arteries. Together these connections form the Circle of Willis. The major cerebral arteries are also joined at their ends by small vessels that

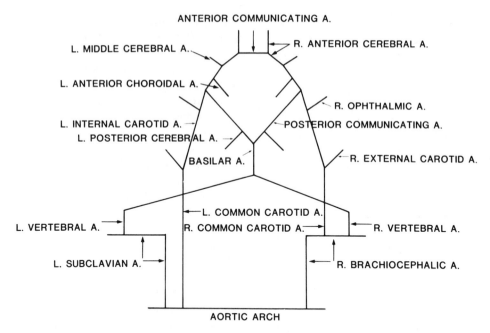

Fig. 1. A schematic diagram of the major vessels supplying blood to the brain.

pass through the leptomeninges. The pericallosal branch of the anterior cerebral artery may also communicate with the posterior cerebral artery, as it bends around the splenium of the corpus callosum (Van der Drift and Kok, 1972). The external carotid artery has connections with the internal carotid artery, primarily through the ophthalmic artery (Osborn, 1980, pp. 78–85). This complex of connections is a network available to provide a second or collateral source of blood flow when a major artery becomes occluded. Individual variability in this pattern of collateral supply is an important factor in determining the pattern and severity of damage in stroke. Nilsson, Cronqvist, and Ingvar (1979) have shown that patients with occlusion of an internal carotid artery but collateral flow through the Circle of Willis have normal regional blood flow values in the hemisphere ipsilateral to the occlusion, while those with collateral flow through the ophthalmic or leptomeningeal arteries had flow values 40%–60% below normal.

Neuropsychology of Stroke

The Behavioral Effects of Stroke in the Carotid Arterial System

Typically, strokes produce focal or multifocal deficits on neuropsychological batteries. Often there is evidence of generalized cerebral involvement in addition to focal dysfunction. Since each carotid artery supplies blood to one cerebral hemisphere, lateralized deficits are common among stroke victims.

MOTOR IMPAIRMENT. Reitan and Fitzhugh (1971) studied the effects of lateralized strokes on motor performance measured by Halstead's Finger Tapping Test, the Smedley Hand Dynamometer, and Halstead's Tactual Performance Test (TPT). These authors studied 15 triads of patients composed of one patient with a left hemisphere cerebrovascular lesion, one with a right hemisphere lesion, and one with diffuse cerebrovascular disease. The triads were matched on age, education, and duration of diagnosis. Diagnoses were made on the basis of a "complete neurological evaluation"; no patient was on any medication at the time of the study.

Reitan and Fitzhugh found that within-subject comparisons of left and right handed performance revealed a clearer picture of lateralized motor deficit than did between-group comparisons. As an example, patients with right or left hemisphere strokes did not differ on finger tapping or TPT performance with the right hand, even though they did differ on right-handed grip strength. But when difference scores between the two hands were calculated, the left and right hemisphere stroke patients did differ on each of the three measures of motor functioning.

Although the within group data of Reitan and Fitzhugh clearly demonstrated lateralized motor effects, the absence of a normal control group coupled with a dominance of the right hand for grip strength and finger tapping makes it difficult to decide if one hemisphere has greater bilateral control over those motor functions. If one hemisphere does have bilateral motor control, then one might falsely infer bilateral cerebral involvement from the effects of a unilateral lesion. Evidence for left hemisphere control of motor behaviors that involve "manual skill requiring several hand movements" has been reported by several authors (Liepmann, 1913; Kimura and Archibald, 1974; Kimura, 1977).

To pursue this laterality issue further, Haaland and Delaney (1981) studied the motor performance of 26 patients with left hemisphere strokes and 17 with right hemisphere strokes. Both groups were evaluated on grip strength, finger tapping, grooved pegboard, maze coordination, vertical groove steadiness, and static steadiness about 2 years after their stroke. Haaland and Delaney's analysis showed that the left hemisphere does not exercise greater bilateral control over the types of motor tasks they studied. They did find that their motor tasks were unequal in their sensitivity to the ipsilateral effects of stroke. The hand ipsilateral to the stroke differed from the performance of controls only on the grooved pegboard, maze coordination, and steadiness tests, while the hand contralateral to the stroke was impaired relative to controls on grip strength, finger tapping, grooved pegboard, and maze coordination.

Finlayson and Reitan (1980) also found no convincing evidence that cerebrovascular lesions, traumatic brain injuries, or neoplasms of the left hemisphere produce greater ipsilateral deficit on grip strength and finger tapping than the same type of lesion in the right hemisphere. They argued that some of the evidence for greater left hemispheric control of ipsilateral motor performance is explained by right hand dominance for these tasks. Since right handers perform better on grip strength tests with the right hand, it is not surprising that the left hand of patients with left hemisphere lesions is relatively worse than the right hand following right hemisphere lesions. Depending on how the research design is developed, one might confuse this dominant hand effect for greater bilateral control by the left hemisphere.

Actually, neither Kimura and Archibald (1974) nor Kimura (1977) found that the left hemisphere had more control over the left hand than the right hemisphere had over the right hand on tests of simple finger flexion, finger tapping, or grip strength. Instead, data from their stroke patients imply greater bilateral control of a series of skilled movements by the left hemisphere.

We may infer several generalizations about the motor performance of stroke patients from the studies in this section. In right handers, grip strength and finger tapping are selectively impaired on the hand contralateral to the hemisphere with the cerebrovascular lesion. Neither the right nor the left hemisphere predominates in the bilateral control of grip strength, finger flexion, or simple coordination. Tests that depend heavily on intact motor steadiness or coordination show greater ipsilateral effects than do finger tapping or grip strength. The left hemisphere may have greater bilateral control than the right over motor tests that involve a series of learned movements.

SENSORY DEFICITS. Reitan and Fitzhugh (1971) also studied the lateralization of deficits in single and double simultaneous visual, auditory, and tactile stimulation, finger gnosis, and finger graphesthesia. When comparing left and right hemisphere lesion patients, only one right-sided sensory test produced a significant group difference, while seven left-sided sensory measures differed by group. Only the comparison between the right and left hands during double simultaneous stimulation of the two hands produced a clear cross-over effect, suggesting a strong lateralizing sign. Overall, the patterns of between and within group comparisons suggested greater bilateral control of tactile processing by the right hemisphere, greater contralateral loss in visual functioning after right hemisphere lesions, and very little lateralization of simple auditory perception. Boll (1974) has shown that for a mixed group of lateralized trauma, stroke, and tumor patients, right hemisphere lesions are associated with a greater number of ipsilateral errors on tests of finger gnosis, finger graphesthesia, and tactile form recognition than are patients with left hemisphere lesions. He also reported a greater number of contralateral errors among right hemisphere lesion patients than left.

INTELLECTUAL FUNCTIONING. Reitan and Fitzhugh (1971) examined the effects of stroke on Wechsler-Bellevue I scores. Patients with left hemisphere strokes scored worse on verbal I.Q. than right hemisphere patients, while there was no difference between the two groups on performance I.Q. However, the within-group comparisons showed a more strongly lateralized pattern; left hemisphere stroke patients scored significantly worse on verbal I.Q. than performance I.Q., while right hemisphere patients scored significantly worse on performance than verbal I.Q. The between and within group findings together suggested that left hemisphere vascular lesions affect both verbal and performance I.Q.s, although verbal I.Q. is affected to a greater extent. Right hemisphere cerebrovascular lesions may leave verbal I.Q. relatively unaffected, while impairing performance I.Q. However, the absence of a nonpatient control group in the Reitan and Fitzhugh study makes it impossible to ascertain whether the verbal I.Q. of the right hemisphere lesion patients was truly normal.

DIASCHISIS. Von Monakow (1914) believed that focal damage to the brain might depress the functioning of brain regions distant from the damage. Without a method of measuring diaschisis that is independent of the evidence of focal dysfunction, diaschisis becomes a tautological explanation for the remote effects of a focal lesion. Measures of the metabolic activity of the noninfarcted hemisphere are one example of information that is logically independent of behavior and could form the basis of a noncircular explanation of bilateral, behavioral effects of stroke. Høedt-Rasmussen and Skinhøj (1964) found depression of cerebral blood flow and of oxygen and glucose utilization in the noninfarcted hemisphere as long as 3 weeks after stroke. Welch and Meyer (1975) suggested that the outflow of neurotransmitter substances into nonischemic brain regions might explain bilateral changes in cerebral metabolism after unilateral infarction. Further research that quantitatively relates lateralized behavioral deficits during the first 3 weeks of stroke to changes in regional energy metabolism, cerebral blood flow, and electrophysiological activity, should help to clarify the mechanisms of diaschisis.

Transient Ischemia

Some patients with cerebrovascular disease will develop focal neurological deficit that reverses within 24 hours. Although this one-day cutoff is commonly taken as significant in clinical research and practice, it is not soundly based on any pathological or metabolic model of ischemia. While patients with infarction often have dramatic lateralized deficits, Delaney, Wallace, and Egelko (1980) found that patients with TIAs differ from normals on tests of concept formation, perceptual-motor integration, verbal fluency, and memory, rather than tests of simple motor or sensory functioning.

Ponsford, Donnan, and Walsh (1980) have reported on ten patients who had a history of vertebrobasilar ischemia (VBI); four of the ten patients had symptoms on neurological examination and perhaps had infarction, rather than transient ischemia. In five cases angiography was performed to confirm the diagnosis of VBI. Patients with vertebrobasilar ischemic disease performed worse than matched controls primarily on memory tests, although there were no differences on tests of general orientation, prose recall (immediate or delayed), or Lhermitte and Signoret's (1972) tests of spatial and logical arrangement. Vertebrobasilar patients performed like controls on Benton's Facial Recognition Test and on the Block Design and Picture Completion subtests of the WAIS. Additionally, Ponsford et al. (1980) found that the Wechsler Memory Quotient was lower than the WAIS verbal I.Q. in 9 of 10 patients. The authors concluded that patients with vertebrobasilar ischemic disease have a specific problem with memory functioning, rather than a global dementia.

Research in our laboratory failed to confirm the consistent presence of memory deficit in patients with the symptoms and angiographic findings of vertebrobasilar ischemia (Baird et al., 1984). Five of 11 of our VBI patients had Wechsler Memory Quotients ten or more points higher than their full scale I.Q. Further, we could not distinguish patients with symptoms and angiographic findings associated with carotid disease from those with vertebrobasilar disease. Perez and associates also found nearly equal full scale I.Q.s (mean, 97.15) and Wechsler Memory Quotients (mean, 96.81) in 16 VBI patients (Perez et al., 1975a; Perez et al., 1975b). If most of the patients studied by Ponsford et al. (1980) had admitting complaints of memory loss, then they studied a more selective sample of VBI patients than did we or Perez et al. Given the variety of complaints with which VBI patients present (Futty et al., 1977) and the wide distribution of sites in the brain stem, cerebellum, midbrain, diencephalon and cerebrum that may be involved, it is unlikely that any one symptom would be present in most patients with VBI, unless it was a necessary criterion for the diagnosis.

Distinguishing the Effects of Stroke from the Effects of Other Brain Diseases

STROKE AND TUMORS. Distinguishing patients with rapidly growing tumors, from stroke patients is a challenging clinical problem, since patients from each group often have lateralized findings and moderate to severe impairment of general neuropsychological functioning. Finkelstein's (1977) BRAIN program, a set of automated rules for interpreting the Halstead-Reitan Neuropsychological Test Battery, includes an algorithm for making this distinction. It reaches the diagnosis "cerebrovascular accident" if the patient has evidence of brain dysfunction, with lateralized deficits characterized either by a severe deficit in finger tapping or a moderate finger tapping deficit coupled with disturbance in tactile functioning mediated by the cortex and lateralized to the same hand. The program relies on tests of finger gnosis, finger graphesthesia, and the single or double stimulation of face and hand as tactile-cortical tests. Finkelstein's program has other diagnostic rules for identifying vascular abnormalities with recent bleeding, and diffuse cerebral atherosclerosis. He also has separate rules for detecting metastatic carcinoma and slowly growing tumors. In the original validation study, Finkelstein's program correctly diagnosed 9 of 12 patients with cerebrovascular accidents and 8 of 12 with fast growing tumors. For only three patients were these two diagnoses confused.

DEMENTIA OF THE ALZHEIMER'S TYPE AND MULTI-INFARCT DEMENTIA. In two studies Perez and associates (Perez et al., 1975b; Perez et al., 1976) found that patients with dementia of the Alzheimer's type (DAT) may perform more poorly or the same as patients with multi-infarct dementia (MID) on the WAIS full scale I.Q. or on WAIS subtests. DAT patients did score worse than MID patients on the Wechsler Memory Quotient and on all the subtests of the WMS, other than information and logical memory (Perez et al., 1975a). Together, the research on the WAIS and on the WMS indicate that patients with DAT are more consistently impaired on tests of higher cognitive functioning than patients with MID. The variability in the level of performance of MID patients coupled with their greater prevalence of lateralized sensory or motor deficits are two useful signs for the differential diagnosis of the two common causes of dementia. Finkelstein's program uses presence or absence of lateralized deficits as a major criterion in distinguishing recent cerebrovascular disease from primary neuronal degenerative disease.

Stroke Risk Factors and Neuropsychological Correlates

The Framingham Study (Stroke Risk Handbook, 1974) identified a number of medical risk factors that increase the likelihood of stroke for an individual. There is a higher incidence of strokes with increased age and, within the same age cohort, the incidence of strokes is greater for males. Hypertension, elevated serum cholesterol, high blood and urine glucose levels, abnormal triglyceride levels, tobacco smoking and cardiovascular disease also correlate with increased probability of stroke.

Most of these eight factors also have correlations with neuropsychological test data. Since these factors are all prevalent in samples of stroke patients, it becomes important to be aware of these correlations to delineate the neuropsychological effects of the stroke as a specific neurovascular event.

We will consider these risk factors, excluding age and sex, since the effects of these two variables on neurobehavioral functioning are reviewed in Chapter 6 of this book. For the sake of brevity, we will also not consider personality variables.

HYPERTENSION. Early research (Apter, Halstead, and Heimburger, 1951; Reitan, 1954) indirectly suggested mild neuropsychological impairment in hypertensive individuals. These studies employed personality tests and work histories as criteria. In Reitan's study (1954), hypertensive patients scored at an intermediate level, between normal controls and frankly brain-damaged patients, on Piotrowski's signs of organicity and Beck's Rorschach scores.

More recently, Goldman et al. (1974) found a moderate but significant correlation between diastolic blood pressure and both Category Test scores and WAIS full scale I.Q.s in 14 male VA patients with untreated moderate to severe hypertension. Though these correlations remained significant when age was partialed out, they did not have an age-matched, nonhypertensive sample. While blood and urine analysis and neurological examination were used to exclude subjects with additional medical complaints, no neuroradiological results were reported that would allow one to judge the extent of cerebral atherosclerosis.

Using 11 of these 14 patients, Goldman et al. subsequently conducted a study to determine whether successful biofeedback training also could yield neuropsychological improvement (Goldman et al., 1975). Seven hypertensive patients underwent biofeedback training over 9 weeks, while four hypertensive patients simply had their blood pressure monitored. The subjects receiving biofeedback training obtained an average decrease in diastolic pressure of 14.7 mm Hg but there was no significant change in systolic blood pressure from first to last session. Five of the seven subjects also obtained significantly fewer errors on the post-training administration of the Category Test. The four untreated hypertensive patients showed no significant post-test change in either systolic or diastolic blood pressure. However, these four patients were not retested on the Category Test.

The small sample size and absence of a control group for practice effects make it impossible to draw firm conclusions from this interesting study. However, the experimental paradigm used by Goldman et al. (1974, 1975) is a worthwhile, underutilized one in this area of research, and their results are consistently suggestive of a negative correlation between blood pressure and cognitive functions.

Data collected by Light (1975; 1978) raises questions about whether obtained correlations between hypertension and cognitive functions might be due to their mutual associations with age and cerebral arteriosclerosis. In two studies with large samples, Light found no significant differences in serial-reaction time between untreated hypertensives and nonhypertensives of the same age range. However, Light did find a very mild decrement in subjects treated for hypertension and an independent trend for slower serial reaction time to be associated with higher plasma renin activity. She found no differences among the effects of five medication regimens and cardiac medications; related pharmacological treatment in some cases may be responsible for neuropsychological impairment rather than the medical disorder itself.

Schultz and associates also studied the cognitive performance of hypertensives and normotensives, but employed the WAIS rather than reaction-time as the criterion measure (Schultz et al., 1979). Shultz's findings contrast with each of Light's three major results. In Shultz's sample of 68 mild hypertensives, neither medication history nor plasma renin activity correlated significantly with WAIS scores. Though one group of normotensives received a potent diuretic before testing, this group performed no differently on the WAIS than the unmedicated normotensive group. Moreover, Schultz did obtain a negative relationship between hypertension and the WAIS, although this correlation was found only for subjects aged 21 to 39, and only for the verbal scale.

At least one other study reported no change in concentration and reaction time among 11 hypertensive patients taking part in a 6-day trial with atenolol, a beta-blocking agent (Schenk, Lang, and Anlauf, 1981). The authors did find a significant shift towards higher alpha frequencies in the centro-parietal EEG lead. They interpreted this as improvement of "electrophysiologically determined vigilance" (Schenk et al., 1981, p. S38). These results suggest that the question of drug effects on neuropsychological functions in hypertensives needs further exploration with large numbers of patients and thorough sampling of the antihypertensive agents in use.

CARDIAC DISEASE. Several studies have suggested that mild neuropsychological impairment is present in some patients with frank heart disease, even of mild degree. In a large study primarily involving past or present pilots and air-traffic controllers, Spieth (1964) found that 59 normotensive subjects with mild to moderate cardiovascular disease were impaired on a composite speed score relative to 560 subjects with neither hypertension nor vascular disease. The composite speed score was derived from reaction time tests, the WAIS Digit Symbol test, and the Trail Making Test. However, the impairment observed in the cardiovascular group was subtle. For example, subjects with either cardiovascular disease or hypertension obtained an age-scaled score of 11.1 on the WAIS Digit Symbol subtest, slightly higher than the mean of 10.0 in the WAIS standardization sample. Spieth notes that most of his subjects come from the top quarter of the population in terms of education and occupation. Thus, comparisons among the groups of air traffic controllers and pilots in the study are likely to be more valid and sensitive to impairment than comparisons with published norms drawn from the general population.

It seems plausible to assume that if patients show behavioral improvement after effective surgery for heart disease, then they must have had behavioral deficits related to cardiac disease preoperatively. Unfortunately, rather than focusing on this question, most studies have looked at the incidence and nature of postoperative test decrements, usually related to the presence of postoperative psychosis or neurological signs. An exception is the study recently reported by Juolasmaa and associates (Juolasmaa et al., 1981). They examined 69 consecutive patients who underwent open-heart surgery for cardiac valvular disease, and found a trend towards mild improvement on a battery including the WAIS, the Wechsler Memory Scale, the Bender-Gestalt, and Finger Tapping Test. Neuropsychological decrements were fairly well limited to patients with either frank postoperative psychosis or new neurological signs after surgery. The authors attribute the mild postoperative improvement in the remaining patients chiefly to practice effects. However, they note a trend for patients with more severe aortic valvular disease preoperatively to show more improvement postoperatively, if postpsychotic patients were excluded. Together, four hemodynamic variables accounted for 19% of the variance in a multiple stepwise regression analysis with an index of neurobehavioral improvement as the dependent variable. This suggests that at least in a subset of more severely diseased patients, there is significant partially reversible neurobehavioral impairment. The tests on which most improvement was shown were Digit Span, the Bender Gestalt, Picture Arrangement, Block Design, and tests of verbal reasoning (opposites), numerical ability, and psychomotor speed. The authors suggest that the tests showing most improvement related to "visual functions."

Three problems with the literature on the effects of hypertension and cardiac disease must be raised. First, longitudinal studies that examine neuropsychological performance before and after successful treatment of hypertension and heart disease are very scarce. Such quasi-experimental studies seem feasible and would help to delineate a causal rather than merely correlational relationship between these medical factors and neuropsychological performance. Secondly, these studies generally do not mention whether "silent" cerebral infarction or significant cerebral arteriosclerosis was ruled out in neuropsychologically impaired hypertensive and cardiac patients through history or imaging studies. Thirdly, Light (1978) suggested that for some patients antihypertensive medications may actually interfere with cognitive functions by lowering blood pressure in vascular systems which had adapted to hypertension. Her speculation seems plausible but needs further testing.

SERUM GLUCOSE AND DIABETES. Diabetes mellitus involves dysregulation of blood glucose. In principle, either excessive control (repeated hypoglycemia) or undercontrol (repeated ketoacidosis) could have adverse effects on brain function. Furthermore, microvascular disease (thickening of capillary basement membranes, microaneurysms) is associated with diabetes mellitus, although severity of microangiopathy is not necessarily correlated with the degree of metabolic disturbance. Thus, neuropsychological deficit in diabetes could be related to small vessel disease of the brain, as well as to glucose dysregulation.

Since examination of the retina can provide direct information on small vessel status, Rennick and associates decided to compare neuropsychological functioning in two groups of 15 diabetics, with and without retinopathy (Rennick et al., 1968). The two groups were matched on age and education and did not differ insofar as their functional vision and state of health were concerned. A general impairment rating, the Percentage of Scores in the Impaired Range (PSIR), was calculated from 12 tests—seven Halstead-Reitan tests, the WAIS Digit Symbol test, Trails B, and three scores derived from aphasia and perceptual tests. Rennick found that the group with retinopathy had a mean PSIR of 51.8, compared to 30.3 in the patients without retinopathy. Rennick observed that impaired scores occurred chiefly on complicated problem-solving tasks rather than on measures of crystallized verbal information or basic sensory and motor abilities.

Bale (1973) studied a sample of 100 adult-onset diabetics and an equal number of controls, matched on age, education, and socioeconomic status. The only measures used were the Walton-Black Modified New Word Learning Test and the WAIS. A significantly greater number of diabetics (17 vs. 6) scored in the impaired range on the Walton-Black Test. Within the diabetic group, there was an apparent relationship between the severity of past hypoglycemic episodes and an impaired score on the Walton-Black Test: 10 of 15 subjects who had required hospitalization for hypoglycemia needed an excessive number of study trials to learn a word list.

On the other hand, Bale (1973) found that history of stroke did not seem responsible for the impairment seen in his sample. Only one of six patients with a history of stroke scored in the impaired range on the learning task. Similarly, neither age nor duration of illness was related to an impaired learning score in this sample with a mean age of 47 and an average onset of illness at 25. There was no significant increase in verbal/performance I.Q. discrepancy among patients with below average learning scores.

Questions have been raised about the possibility that treatment of diabetes in itself might cause cognitive dysfunction. Multiple injections of insulin and insulin pumps (termed maximized metabolic control) can produce more frequent mild hypoglycemic episodes than standard injection of insulin once or twice daily. Hung and Barbosa (undated) reported preliminary results on a study of complications of clinical treatment. They found no differences between a sample of patients under maximized control and a matched sample under standard control on the Wechsler Memory Scale. All patients were in the normal range of performance except a subject with known traumatic brain damage and a subject with a history of severe insulin-induced hypoglycemic coma. Both groups were severe diabetics with juvenile onset of the disease an average of 20 years earlier.

Rather uniformly, neuropsychological researchers in diabetes have stressed the need for more studies with a wider array of neuropsychological tests and more carefully differentiated diabetic samples. The literature does suggest that neuropsychological impairment directly attributable to diabetes may be limited to patients with past hypoglycemic attacks severe enough to require hospitalization or induce seizures and possibly to patients with significant microvascular pathology. There is no firm evidence that patients with adequate control of their disease suffer lasting neuropsychological consequences from the mild hypoglycemic and hyperglycemic episodes that occur virtually on a daily basis.

SERUM CHOLESTEROL AND TRIGLYCERIDES. Hyperglycemia is known to be linked statistically with hypercholesterolemia. Shafrir (1975) estimated that a third to a half of diabetics have one variety or another of hyperlipidemia. There is preliminary evidence that cholesterol is correlated with neuropsychological functioning.

Reitan and Shipley (1963) studied 156 healthy men over a period of 18 months with serial determination of cholesterol levels and repeated testing on the Category Test, Trail Making Test, Finger Tapping Test, Tactual Performance Test, Rhythm Test, and Speech-Sounds Perception Test. In a partial preliminary analysis of the data, they compared the performance of 80 subjects who reduced their serum cholesterol levels by 10% or more with 76 subjects with less than 10% cholesterol reduction. Among the 113 subjects less than 45 years old, there was no difference in summary scaled score changes over 12 months between subjects with two levels of cholesterol reduction. All subjects, regardless of age, showed a tendency to improve on the repeated testing 12 months later. The improvement thus was attributed to practice effects. However, among the 43 subjects 45 years of age or older, there was a statistically significant relationship between cholesterol reduction and intraindividual changes on neuropsychological tests. Specifically, older subjects with less than 10% serum cholesterol reduction showed a milder practice effect on repeated testing when compared to subjects of similar ages who achieved cholesterol reductions of 10% or greater. The two older groups did not differ in initial neuropsychological performance.

These early findings are intriguing. Ideally, one would like to have angiographic information on these subjects and measures of cerebral metabolism, as well as serum lipid determinations. This might allow one to determine whether the results are attributable to the role of hyperlipidemia in atherogenesis, as theorized by Reitan and Shipley (1963), or whether disturbances in lipid metabolism affect brain function in other ways.

SMOKING. Tobacco smoking is probably the most complicated of the stroke risk factors, since it is the only factor that is behavioral. One of the byproducts of smoking is carbon monoxide, which interferes with oxygen transport to the brain by displacing oxygen from hemoglobin (Adams, Sawyer, and Kvale, 1980). Although it is plausible to argue that a smoking habit could thus interfere directly with neuropsychological functioning, results so far have been ambiguous.

Some studies have shown that smoking produces increments on certain tasks, such as delayed recall (Andersson, 1975; Williams, 1980) and choice reaction-time (Myrsten et al., 1972); other reports have shown decrements in smokers on tasks such as incidental memory (Andersson and Hockey, 1977), symbol-letter substitution (Carter, 1974), the Wisconsin Card Sorting Test (Stevens, 1976), auditory vigilance (Tong et al., 1977), and immediate and delayed recall (Houston, Schneider, and Jarvik, 1978); still other studies have failed to find significant differences between habitual smokers who were smoking and those who refrained from smoking during cognitive tests (Myrsten, Elgerot, and Edgren, 1977). Typically, theories of arousal, thought to be increased by nicotine, are invoked to explain these diverse results.

The literature thus far does not yield firm evidence of direct strong and lasting effects of smoking on neuropsychological performance. We would expect that the mild mixed effects which do appear to be present might be overridden in clinical studies by stronger risk factors and simply by individual differences. However, we note that the studies reported in the literature primarily use college students and young adults as subjects. Thus, we see justification for more research involving subjects who are older or who have other disorders that impinge on the central nervous system. In samples from such populations, subtle simple or interactive neuropsychological effects of smoking might emerge.

While at present there is no evidence for direct neuropsychological correlates of tobacco smoking, there is recent, fairly consistent evidence of significant neuropsychological impairment in patients with chronic obstructive pulmonary disease (COPD), an incurable disorder that usually becomes manifest only in older adults and has a known association with chronic smoking, as discussed by Adams, Sawyer, and Kvale (1980) and by the NOTT group (Nocturnal Oxygen Therapy Trial Group, 1980).

Typically, neuropsychological impairment occurs on measures of perceptual-motor integration, abstraction, and, less consistently, short-term memory (Grant et al., 1980, 1982; Krop et al., 1977; Prigatano et al., 1983). The impairment seen is pervasive. In a study involving 203 COPD patients with an average age of 65, the Nocturnal Oxygen Therapy Trial group (Grant et al., 1982) reported a mean Russell-Neuringer average impairment index in the moderately impaired range (2.28). Moderate to severe impairment, based on clinical ratings of Halstead-Reitan results, was found in 42% of patients vs. 14% of controls. There was an association between degree of hypoxemia and neuropsychological impairment.

Patients with frank COPD often have other central nervous system disorders and are usually in their older sixties. However, Krop, Block, and Cohen (1973) demonstrated partial improvement of neuropsychological functions in 10 COPD patients following a month of continuous oxygen therapy. The NOTT group reported that almost half of their oxygen-treated patients registered neuropsychological improvement after 6 months, a rate greatly exceeding practice effect found in retested nonpatient controls. By 12 months patients receiving continuous oxygen outperformed those receiving oxygen only at night (Heaton et al., 1984). The Intermittent Positive Pressure Breathing study (IPPB trial, Prigatano et al., 1983) examined COPD patients who had less severe disease (and less hypoxemia) than the NOTT patients. Neuropsychological deficits were correspondingly milder, but generally qualitatively similar to those reported by Grant et al. (1982). Although neither the IPPB nor the NOTT studies found direct links between smoking history and neuropsychological deficit in COPD patients, it seems plausible that in smokers a carbon-monoxide-induced reduction in oxygen availability might interact with established hypoxemia to produce greater neuropsychological impairment.

Smoking is also known to increase serum cholesterol, even in young subjects (Brackenridge and Bloch, 1972; Rustin et al., 1978). If hypercholesterolemia is correlated with neurobehavioral functions, as discussed earlier, this might indicate a second indirect route by which smoking can produce neuropsychological deficits.

SUMMARY. The existing literature does at least raise the question of direct effects of each of the medical risk factors discussed above on neuropsychological functioning, in addition to their known correlations with cerebrovascular occlusive disease. In the case of some factors, for example, smoking habit, consistent direct measurable effects may occur only with frank disease secondary to the risk factor, i.e., hyperlipidemia or chronic obstructive pulmonary disease. In others, possibly hypertension and cardiac disease, neuropsychological decrements may appear even at relatively mild levels of the risk variable.

Most of the factors considered have a general effect on higher cognitive-perceptual-motor functioning. Overall, effects seem strongest on difficult tasks, such as abstracting, vigilance, and reaction-time tasks, which require rapid, flexible information processing. In the absence of neuropsychological data in stroke patients for whom information on relevant medical risk factors is available, one can speculate that medical risk factors contribute relatively little to the lateralized sensorimotor findings seen in cases of frank infarction. However, in cases where neuropsychological impairment is milder and less lateralized, such as in TIAs, medical risk factors and their possible neurobehavioral effects may complicate the interpretation of neuropsychological data.

A review of the literature shows a surfeit of correlational studies involving the study of these risk factors and neuropsychological variables. There are very few studies that compare neuropsychological functioning before and after treatment of the risk factor in either a cross-sectional or longitudinal design. While Kelly, Garron, and Javid (1980) and Bornstein, Trites, and Benoit (1981b) suggested that medical risk factors may moderate neurobehavioral improvement after carotid endarterectomy, a procedure to prevent stroke, there are no studies which focus on medical risk factors and neuropsychological functioning in individuals who have had major strokes.

This lack of research seems surprising since almost all of the risk factors are experimentally treatable. Additionally, in centers seeing large numbers of patients with strokes or at risk for strokes, it would seem quite feasible to do prospective or retrospective studies of neuropsychological impairment in stroke patients with medical risk factors present. Such studies would allow us to answer questions such as the following. (1) How much do pre-existing risk factors influence the severity and nature of neuropsychological impairment in patients who subsequently have strokes? (2) How much do these factors influence the neuropsychological recovery of stroke victims? (3) Does treatment of risk factors reduce the neuropsychological deficits of patients who subsequently have strokes? (4) Does the presence of risk factors mitigate against the effectiveness of treatments, such as cerebral revascularization, and cognitive retraining, which otherwise might prevent or reduce neuropsychological deficits associated with stroke?

Recovery of Functioning

At some point in sustained cerebral ischemia, sufficient damage is done to a nerve cell that it can no longer rebuild itself after the ischemic event and it dies. Jones and associates have shown that even when ischemia of one hemisphere is not complete, cell death and contralateral hemiparesis can occur after 3 hours of reduced blood flow (Jones et al., 1981). After infarction, the process of recovery becomes complex, involving reduction in edema, restoration of normal neurotransmitter activity and metabolism, changes in regional cerebral blood flow, and the reorganization of brain systems. We will discuss several studies that are good examples of how neuropsychological tests may assist in measuring and predicting recovery of functioning.

Meier and associates (Meier and Resch, 1967; Meier and Okayama, 1969; Meier, 1970) have conducted a series of studies on recovery from stroke. Meier and Resch (1967) studied short-term change following stroke in 93 patients who had an infarction 1 month or less before admission. Patients with obvious hemorrhagic stroke were not included in the study. Neurological examinations of all patients were made on the day of admission and at discharge 7 to 10 days after admission. On the second day of hospitalization, patients also received the Porteus Maze Test, the Trail Making Test, a modified Sequin-Goddard Formboard test, and the Visual Space Rotation Test. The latter test required the patient to draw an X while viewing his effort through prisms that rotate the visual field. The authors developed a set of decision rules for using these tests to predict overall change in neurological status for the short hospitalization. Forty-four patients showed no improvement or regressed; 26 improved but had major residuals; and 23 patients improved with only minor residuals. The degree of improvement of neurological status was directly related to the success patients had when performing neuropsychological tests. The decision rules successfully identified those patients with no improvement, and successfully separated these patients who improved the most from the other groups.

Meier (1970) also reported the utility of these decision rules in predicting overall recovery after one year or more. The decision rules, based on the psychological data, were systematically related to the degree of neurological recovery. Additionally, patients who died had baseline test scores similar to those of patients who did not improve, but lived. The test scores successfully predicted recovery of functioning a year after stroke.

More recently Meier, Ettinger, and Arthur (1982) reported on the recovery of 60 patients with cerebral infarction, studied after their strokes. They divided their sample into four subgroups by separating patients with a dense hemiparesis from those with less weakness and by subdividing those two groups at a Porteus Maze age score of less than eight. The recovery of these four groups was monitored by the Grooved Pegboard Test, the Index Finger Tapping Test, the Ballistic Arm Tapping Test, the modified Tactual Performance Test, prorated Wechsler Full Scale I.Q. test, part V of the Token Test, and the abbreviated Reitan-Indiana Aphasia Screening Test. Patients with better Porteus performance improved on all eight motor tests at 6 months. Those patients with poorer Porteus scores showed less consistent recovery of motor functioning. They did have more consistent increases in their cognitive test scores. Even with these gains, patients with low Porteus scores performed worse on cognitive tests at 6 months than patients with better Porteus scores. Most of the recovery occurred within the first two months; the nonhemiplegic group with better Porteus scores showed the most consistent recovery of motor functioning for the 2-month period.

Hartman (1981) used the Porch Index of Communicative Ability (PICA) to measure short-term recovery of aphasia in 44 right-handed stroke patients. Each patient received the PICA 14 days after stroke and 13 to 16 days later. No patient received speech training; 42 of the 44 patients improved, suggesting considerable spontaneous improvement.

Kinsella and Ford (1980) reported on the neuropsychological performance of 31 patients with stroke who had disabling residuals for at least 6 weeks. Patients with subarachnoid hemorrhages or brainstem infarction were excluded. Neuropsychological tests were given an average of 4, 8, and 12 weeks after the stroke. The improvement reported below occurred during the 4 and 8 week assessment. No improvement was reported during the 8 to 12 week period. Seventy-six percent of the left hemisphere cases had some aphasia; both their aphasia and left-right orientation improved. Kinsella and Ford found no improvement for the entire group on tests of ideomotor dyspraxia; nor did the right hemisphere patients with unilateral spatial neglect improve. Finally, patients with unilateral spatial neglect showed less improvement on a scale rating activities in daily living, despite comparable functional movement.

Heaton and Pendleton (1981) reviewed five studies of the ability of psychological tests to predict everyday behavior following stroke (Lehmann et al., 1975; Lorenzo and Cancro, 1962; Bourestrom and Howard, 1968; Anderson et al., 1974; Ben-Yishay et al., 1970). These studies showed that neuropsychological tests could predict disposition from a rehabilitation program (home vs. institutional placement) and rehabilitation gains in self-care, ambulation, dressing, and mobility. Heaton and Pendleton note that these studies examined a very restricted set of everyday behaviors.

Considerable recovery of function occurs during the first 3 months after stroke. We need to learn more about the reorganization of brain and behavior during this relatively brief period. Improvement in neuropsychological functioning during recovery needs to be systematically related to changes in regional cerebral blood flow, cerebral metabolism, neurotransmitter levels, structural damage, and edema. Does the adequacy of collateral flow predict better recovery of neuropsychological functioning? How much recovery might be associated with the return of neurotransmitters to normal levels in the blood and cerebrospinal fluid? Does the pattern of metabolic change during recovery provide any evidence that intact brain regions take over the function of infarcted brain regions? In answering these questions, neuropsychological data will often serve as criteria rather than predictors, as in the early studies of recovery. Future research should also aim at developing metabolic-rCBF-behavioral profiles to identify those patients who do not recover.

Treatment

Cerebral Vasodilators

Cerebral vasodilators are intended to treat the decline in higher cognitive functioning among patients with cerebral vascular disease by increasing blood flow to the brain. Vasodilators might restore the functioning of marginally ischemic neurons by increasing the rate of oxygen and glucose delivery or by increasing the rate of removal of toxic metabolites.

Since vasodilators might steal blood from ischemic areas of patients with recent stroke (Cook and James, 1981), they have primarily been used to treat intellectual decline in patients with a chronic, slowly progressive course.

CYCLANDELATE. This drug relaxes smooth muscles, including those in blood vessels throughout the body. In animals it accelerates the development of collateral vessels, enhances resistance to hypoxia, and increases glucose uptake in the brain. It increases cerebral blood flow in patients with cerebral vascular disease (Hyams, 1978).

Several authors report improvement with cyclandelate treatment in the higher cognitive functioning of patients with "cerebral atherosclerosis." Smith and Lowrey (1971) and Smith, Lowrey, and Davis (1968) performed ten, two-tailed t-tests on change scores and found significant improvement on the Raven's Coloured Matrices and on the comprehension, similarities, and picture arrangement subtests of the WAIS. The improvement was unrelated to dosage level. The authors pointed to the need for a placebo control group to rule out nonspecific treatment effects. Fine et al. (1971) found that the Brief Psychiatric Rating Scale scores and Digit Span, but not the Bender-Gestalt, significantly improved in the treated group during the first 2 weeks of a double-blind, crossover study. Ball (1971) and Ball and Taylor (1967, 1969) found significant improvement on the Maudsley Hospital Mental Status Exam and on spatial, temporal, and personal orientation after 4 months of cyclandelate treatment. The placebo group showed no improvement. The improvement in orientation and mental status was unrelated to changes in cerebral blood flow. Stocker (1971) found consistent subject by subject improvement in auditory and visual simple reaction times with cyclandelate treatment. Improvement in reaction time scores was not systematically associated with changes in blood flow. Young, Hall, and Blakemore (1974) did not find any change in WAIS I.Q. in the cyclandelate condition, when compared with the initial baseline score. But they did find that the cyclandelate condition was associated with higher I.Q.s than the placebo condition. Young et al. (1974) suggested that cyclandelate may decelerate or stop intellectual decline among patients with arteriosclerotic dementia, even though it may not reverse the dementia.

Negative results have also appeared. In a well designed study, Westreich, Alter, and Lundgren (1975) found no convincing evidence that the cyclandelate condition produced more improvement than the placebo condition on a large battery of psychological tests.

PAPAVERINE HCL, NAFTIDROFURYL, ISOXSUPRINE HCL, AND BETAHISTINE HCL. When given intravenously, papaverine HCL acts directly on smooth muscle to dilate cerebral vessels and increase cerebral blood flow. Of the four double-blind studies of papaverine reviewed by Hyams (1978), three showed improvement in the EEGs of "elderly subjects." Naftidrofuryl dilates vessels, is an antagonist to serotonin and bradykinin, has antidepressant effects, and operates as an anesthetic. It may enhance tissue oxidative metabolism, increase glucose utilization, and produce a rise in the cerebral concentration of the energy source, adenosine triphosphate. Isoxsuprine is a derivative of adrenaline and dilates skin vessels as well as cerebral vessels. It may increase cerebral blood flow, but the evidence is conflicting (Hyams, 1978). Betahistine HCL is effective in increasing regional cerebral blood flow in the vertebrosbasilar circulation. It also dilates microvessels to the labyrinth of the inner ear. Hyams (1978) should be consulted for a more thorough discussion of the effects of these drugs.

Smith, Philippus, and Lowrey (1968) found that papaverine did not produce any significant improvement on their battery of neuropsychological tests. On post-hoc analyses, the authors did find significantly more positive changes than expected on the similarities and picture arrangement subtests of the WAIS, on Wechsler Memory Scale, and on critical flicker fusion. They suggest that papaverine might improve posterior frontal functioning. Ritter et al. (1971) found no significant difference between placebo and papaverine in their double-blind, placebo trial.

Bovier, Passeron, and Chupin (1974) found that naftidrofuryl did not improve performance on the Benton Visual Retention Test when compared with placebo. But scores on the Wechsler Memory Quotient improved in the treatment condition, while not changing in the placebo condition. In a preliminary statement, Smith (1970) reported some promising improvement on the similarities subtest of the WAIS and the visual reproduction subtest of the Wechsler Memory Scale when patients were treated with isoxsuprine HCL in a double blind, cross-over trial.

Rivera et al. (1976) reported that betahistine-HCL produced a significant improvement in their measures of verbal cognition, memory, language, and perceptual-motor coordination, among patients with vertebrobasilar ischemia. But inspection of Fig. 4 of their paper indicates that the betahistine condition was more efficacious than placebo for only three comparisons, while placebo produced better performance for two comparisons and no difference was found between treatment and placebo on 15 comparisons.

The principal difficulty with these studies is that cerebral arteriosclerosis is no longer believed to be a frequent cause of dementia. Most of the patients in these studies had histories of a slowly progressive dementia. But this course is not due to narrowing of cerebral vessels by atherosclerosis; it is usually associated with dementia of the Alzheimer's type (Hachinski, Lassen and Marshall, 1974). Young et al. (1974) did use inclusion criteria that were apparently validated at autopsy by Hall and Harcup (1969). But the latter study reported on less than 20% of a sample that met the admission criteria of Young et al. (1974). The autopsy study also failed to report clear descriptions of the autopsied brains. These brains might have had Alzheimer changes or areas of infarction.

Reports in the literature are also frequently flawed by the use of multiple statistical tests. It is axiomatic that one expects 5% of a large number of independent, statistical tests to be significant under the null hypothesis, when the critical value of the statistic is set at 0.05. If the statistical tests are correlated, as they usually are when repeated on the same sample, one expects some studies to find more than 5% of the statistical tests significant, while others to find fewer than 5%, even when there are no population differences. So the high yield of significant statistical tests in an occasional study does not argue against the null hypothesis.

Several other shortcomings were evident. One-shot, pre-post studies confound specific and nonspecific treatment effects. Since many subjects were patients from chronic care institutions, participation in these studies might have provided an extra source of stimulation that increased their activity level and their interest in their environment. Some vasodilators might have antipsychotic or antidepressant effects. Either psychotropic effect could produce small improvements in cognitive functioning without affecting the underlying disease. Complete drug regimens should be published, since the cerebral effects of drugs that treat diseases of organs other than the brain and the interactions of such drugs with drugs that affect cerebral functioning is not well understood. The use of cross-over designs does not separate beneficial interactions from the primary effect of the experimental drug, since the drug's primary effect and its interaction with other drugs are both present in the treatment conditions and both absent in the placebo conditions. Treatment studies should publish at least the means and variances of each treatment condition so that clinicians can judge the size of the treatment effect. Preferably the data for all subjects should be provided, permitting one to judge the generality of the treatment (Matarazzo et al., 1979).

Since the effects of vasodilators on cerebral functioning were small or nonsignificant, and in view of the methodological problems raised above, we believe that the potential for vasodilators to reverse the primary cognitive symptoms of dementia in patients with cerebrovascular disease is unproven.

Surgery

CAROTID ENDARTERECTOMY. It is now nearly three decades since DeBakey performed the first carotid endarterectomy (CE) in 1953 and since Eastcott, Pickering, and Rob (1954) published their pioneering study on this procedure. Its value in reducing the incidence of stroke in patients with transient ischemic attacks is widely accepted (Thompson and Talkington, 1976). However, the issue of whether it has any restorative effect on higher cortical functioning remains unresolved. We now present a review of the research on the restoration of function with carotid endarterectomy, and we attempt to synthesize the rather chaotic results.

While the degree of stenosis necessary to reduce arterial flow and perfusion pressure is open to debate (Archie and Feldtman, 1981), there is no disagreement about the fact that a sufficiently severe stenotic lesion of the carotid artery does reduce both flow and perfusion pressure. In many cases, collateral circulation can compensate for flow reductions. The cerebral circulation is, at least to some extent, set up to allow both intra- and interhemispheric compensation for changes in blood supply. However, factors such as the presence of bilateral disease, anatomic variability, and low cardiac output can, in some cases, reduce the effectiveness of natural compensatory mechanisms. It is hypothesized that in patients who are unable to compensate for reduced blood flow, a significant stenotic lesion in the carotid artery can produce a region of chronic marginal ischemia. That is, there may be tissue in which flow and perfusion pressure are sufficient to prevent ischemic infarction yet not sufficient to maintain normal neuronal function. The hypothesized mechanism for improvements in higher cognitive function with endarterectomy posits that improved cerebral blood flow, after endarterectomy, perfuses these marginally ischemic tissues and restores them to normal function. We must point out here that this hypothetical model has never been proven experimentally.

As endarterectomy gained popularity in the prophylaxis of stroke, some patients were noted to show marked improvements in cognitive functioning postoperatively. This clinical observation raised the possibility that CE might lead to restoration of function in patients with carotid artery stenosis. The first study to employ standardized psychological tests to investigate this possibility was that of Williams and McGee (1964). At postoperative followup three of six patients were said to show slight gains, two patients no change, and one patient slight overall loss.

Duke et al. (1968), in one of the better early studies of neurobehavioral change with CE, found significant gains in I.Q. in both the operated ($N = 16$) and the small vessel disease control group ($N = 19$) but not in the large vessel disease nonoperated control group ($N = 12$). No significant retest changes were shown for any group on the Trail Making or Finger Tapping tests.

Drake, Baker, Blumenkrantz, and Dallgren (1968) found seven of their 12 private hospital patients with bilateral occlusive disease to be significantly improved at followup, while their VA hospital patient sample ($N = 11$) did not show any significant postoperative improvement. The authors noted that the private hospital patients had significantly higher socioeconomic status and significantly shorter mean chronicity of illness (7.2 months vs. 57.45 months) when compared to the VA patients.

Goldstein, Kleinknecht, and Gallo (1970) were the first to report on the use of the Halstead-Reitan Battery to evaluate postendarterectomy changes in neuropsychological function. These authors noted that the diseased group

($N = 6$) showed some improvements on sensitive Halstead neuropsychological measures. However, they felt that much of the improvement was due to practice effects.

Horne and Royle (1974) found statistically significant postoperative improvement on the WAIS performance subtest I.Q. scores of their endarterectomy patients ($N = 16$). However, the failure of these authors to report the postoperative followup interval makes it difficult to interpret these results.

Perry, Drinkwater, and Taylor (1975) noted overall improvement in their endarterectomy patients ($N = 20$), as measured by Halstead's Impairment Index, with the most improvement on the Category and Tactual Performance (Time) tests. Twelve of the 13 patients who were impaired preoperatively were found to be improved at the 3 month followup.

In the study of Haynes et al. (1976) we find the first use of a general surgical control group. The endarterectomy group ($N = 17$) showed significant improvement in Verbal Comprehension, Perceptual Organization factor scores, Trails A and B, and MMPI scales 5 and 7 (which appear to correspond to the paranoia and schizophrenia scales in the standard numbering system). The control group ($N = 9$) showed no significant gains on any of these measures.

Recent studies of postoperative recovery of function with carotid endarterectomy are more sound methodologically than many of the earlier studies, with larger samples of patients and more control groups. Kelly, Garron, and Javid (1980) evaluated 35 carotid endarterectomy patients with at least 70% carotid stenosis or a known ulcerated plaque. A comparison group of 20 patients, hospitalized for the surgical treatment of peripheral vascular disease, was also evaluated. These authors employed a battery of neuropsychological and personality tests. Postoperative testing took place 4 to 8 weeks following surgery with the mean postsurgical interval approximately 51 days in both the endarterectomy and control groups. Both the control and endarterectomy group showed significant postoperative improvements on a measure of left-right discrimination as well as perceptual analysis. Only the endarterectomy group showed improvements on the Wechsler Memory Scale and a test of expressive language fluency. Further analyses demonstrated that postendarterectomy improvements were most likely to be found in patients who were younger, better educated, and had lower systolic blood pressure on admission.

Matarazzo et al. (1979) studied 17 carotid endarterectomy patients preoperatively and again 20 weeks postoperatively. These test–retest results were compared with those of three comparison groups drawn from the literature (29 healthy normal young males, 35 chronic schizophrenic patients, 16 cerebrovascular disease patients). The results of this study showed slight gains on I.Q. and Halstead-Reitan tests in all four groups. Matarazzo et al. (1979) concluded that the small improvements seen in their sample of endarterectomy patients were most parsimoniously explained as practice effects, since these postsurgical changes did not differ in magnitude from those seen in the comparison groups. Unfortunately, the authors failed to note the lack of comparability of practice effects across the four different groups which their sample comprised (Shatz, 1981). They also omitted mention of WAIS retest data in the cerebrovascular disease comparison group. This group's retest data would have provided the most meaningful comparison to the CE patients.

Bornstein, Benoit, and Trites (1981a) evaluated the largest series of endarterectomy patients reported to date. Their sample included 55 carotid endarterectomy patients, 13 general surgical controls, and 14 patients with cerebrovascular disease, including those who were considered CE candidates but refused surgery. Patients in this study were evaluated 1 or 2 days preoperatively and again after 6 months. The test battery included the WAIS, WMS, and Halstead-Reitan Battery. Bornstein et al. (1981a) did not provide mean scores for any of the tests administered. This study reported a fairly complex and unusual data analysis. Chi square analysis of the number of significant matched pre-post t-tests in each group revealed that significantly more measures improved in the operated than in the nonoperated group. Further, breakdown by side of operation and side of stroke or TIA revealed that patients with right CE or right hemisphere pathology showed the greatest benefit from this procedure. Analysis of ipsilateral and contralateral effects led these authors to conclude that while there might be a partial restorative role for carotid endarterectomy, permanent left hemisphere damage might prevent this effect from emerging.

The brief review illustrates the difficulties in comparing studies on neuropsychological effects of carotid endarterectomy. These studies differ in terms of measures used, test-retest interval, and patient and control selection criteria. Given these differences, it is not surprising that researchers have reached different conclusions on the question of whether this surgical procedure has any restorative effect on neuropsychological function. The two key confounding variables which have not been addressed adequately are practice and nonspecific treatment effects. Obviously, a large-scale randomized study of this procedure could clearly answer these questions; unfortunately such a randomized study is, given the well-established therapeutic value of endarterectomy, not ethically acceptable.

Many different approaches to the problem of nonrandomization have been taken. Several authors have eschewed the use of control groups entirely. Others have used control groups which span the range of comparability to the operated group, from healthy young male policemen (Matarazzo et al. 1979) at the least comparable end, to a cerebrovascular group that included surgical candidates who refuse surgery (Bornstein, et al., 1981a) at the most comparable end. Unfortunately, it is not clear whether one can generalize from the performance of these "comparison" groups on retesting to that of endarterectomy patients. This issue is most salient with respect to an analysis of practice effects in that there is some evidence that the amount of practice effect expected in carotid endarterectomy patients might be significantly smaller than in nonneurologically impaired comparison groups (Shatz, 1981). The available data suggest that, given a sufficient retest interval, practice effects are likely to be small and may not be a significant problem in research on the neuro-psychological effects of carotid endarterectomy.

Several studies have administered personality and/or anxiety measures pre- and postoperatively. Kelly et al. (1980) did report statistically significant declines in level of state anxiety following carotid endarterectomy. In contrast, Haynes et al. (1975) failed to find any significant changes in State-Trait-Anxiety Index scores. In spite of the statistically significant reduction in state anxiety reported by Kelly et al. (1980), it does not appear likely that anxiety plays any meaningful role in artificially suppressing preoperative scores. For example the state anxiety scores reported by Kelly et al. (1980) were at about the 38th percentile preoperatively when compared to the male general medical and surgical standardization samples, and at about the 36th percentile postoperatively (Spielberger, Gorsuch, and Lushene, 1970). Thus, it does not appear that the statistically significant change in state-trait anxiety scores in the Kelly et al. (1980) study was meaningful clinically.

SUPERFICIAL TEMPORAL TO MIDDLE CEREBRAL ARTERY BYPASS SURGERY. Evans and Austin (1976) reported an early study of the effects of superficial temporal artery to middle cerebral artery (STA-MCA) bypass surgery on higher cortical functioning. This surgical technique, which is used to treat patients with transient ischemic attacks who have carotid occlusions or intracranial stenoses, involves connecting a scalp artery to branches of the middle cerebral artery. Evans and Austin gave 14 patients with TIAs eight subtests of the WAIS, the Bender-Gestalt Test, Goodenough's Draw-A-Man Test and a Proverb Interpretation Test before surgery and 2 to 4 weeks after surgery. Twelve of the 14 patients improved on a composite of test scores following surgery, a finding significant beyond the 0.05 level for a one-tailed, sign test. The improvement on psychological tests was correlated with the surgeon's judgment of improvement. The authors observed that practice effects might have played an important role in generating these results.

Ferguson and Peerless (1976) found that I.Q. improved after STA-MCA surgery in three of four cases with multiple extracranial arterial occlusion. One patient showed a dramatic improvement in intellectual functioning with surgery, after 3 years of intellectual decline.

Binder et al. (1982) compared the higher cortical functioning of 12 patients with TIAs or stroke, who were treated by STA-MCA bypass surgery, and seven patients treated with aspirin and dipyridamole. Both groups improved on the Purdue Pegboard, Tokens Test (part V). and the Wechsler Memory Quotient, as well as on the Paired Associate Learning and Logical Memory subtests of the Wechsler Memory Scale, after a 2-month interval. These authors attributed the improvement in both the medical and surgical groups either to spontaneous remission or to practice effects.

Dull et al. (1982) examined 40 ischemia patients who were neurosurgical candidates, with respect to relative levels of preoperative impairment. Duration of longest ischemic attack correlated with objective neuropsychological impairment. Initial level of neuropsychological impairment was held to have potential importance when considered with other symptom duration factors and historical data.

On another topic, Baird et al. (1984) did not find previously reported differences between neuropsychological impairment patterns of patients who eventually proved to have primarily anterior versus posterior cerebral circulation deficits (Ponsford et al., 1980). In another report, however, Baird and associates (*in press*) did find a useful but complex general concordance between angiographic and neuropsychological measures of impairment.

Hungerbuhler and associates studied the effects of STA-MCA bypass surgery on the regional cerebral blood flow and neuropsychological functioning of 31 patients with completed stroke (Hungerbuhler et al., 1981). The mean time between a patient's surgery and stroke was 6–8 months. An impairment index was calculated from each patient's performance on a lengthy battery of neuropsychology tests. The grey matter component of the two-compartment model of regional cerebral blood flow showed small but significant improvement 1 week and 3 months following surgery. Neuropsychological performance improved for patients studied at 3 months, but not at 1 week or 9 months. Hungerbuhler and associates did not report whether the patients with improved neuropsychological functioning also had increased regional cerebral blood flow.

SUMMARY. The evidence from studies of the neuropsychological effects of carotid endarterectomy suggests that this surgical procedure has a beneficial effect on behavior that cannot be accounted for by practice effect or presurgical anxiety. The literature for a similar effect of STA-MCA bypass surgery is less convincing. Since the mean improvement in higher cognitive functioning following these two surgical techniques is modest, it might be explained by natural recovery, concomitant treatment of stroke risk factors, or by medical treatment. Further, since the effect of increased cerebral blood flow is the proposed mechanism for improvement in behavior caused by these surgeries, future studies should correlate improvement in neuropsychological functioning with improvement in regional cerebral blood flow. The dramatic restoration of higher cortical functioning that has appeared in a few case reports indicates that some research efforts should be directed towards establishing a profile for patients most likely to show substantial benefits. They could then be identified on an a priori basis and managed in the most beneficial manner.

Final Comments

We began with the observation that neuropsychological evaluations could play a critical role in relating the anatomical and physiological effects of cerebrovascular disease to the capacity for self-care and independent living. None of the papers that we reviewed made such a direct connection. There is a considerable need to study the adjustment of patients with cerebrovascular disease in their homes, their neighborhoods, and their places of work. The number of studies predicting vocational adjustment, response to rehabilitation, and quality of life from neuropsychological data is embarrassingly small for an empirical science. Perhaps neuropsychologists have been so enchanted by the task of predicting brain dysfunction from behavioral variables that we have been distracted from the equally important task of predicting social and psychological competence at daily activities. We hope that future research will redress this imbalance.

REFERENCES

Adams, K. M., Sawyer, J. D., and Kvale, P. D. (1980). Cerebral oxygenation and neuropsychological adaptation. *J. Clin. Neuropsychol., 2,* 189–208.

Anderson, T. P., Bourestrom, N., Greenberg, F. R., and Hildyard, V. G. (1974). Predictive factors in stroke rehabilitation. *Arch. Phys. Med. Rehab., 55,* 545–553.

Andersson, K. (1975). Effects of cigarette smoking on learning and retention. *Psychopharmacologia, 41,* 1–5.

Andersson, K., and Hockey, G. R. (1977). Effects of cigarette smoking on incidental memory. *Psychopharmacology, 52,* 223–226.

Apter, N. S., Halstead, W. C., and Heimburger, R. F. (1951). Impaired cerebral functions in essential hypertention. *Am. J. Psychiat., 107,* 808–813.

Archie, J. P., and Feldtman, R. W. (1981). Critical stenosis of the internal carotid artery. *Surgery, 81,* 67–72.

Baird, A. D., Adams, K. M., Shatz, M. W., Brown, G. G., Diaz, F. G., and Ausman, J. I. (1984). Can neuropsychological tests detect the sites of cerebrovascular stenoses and occlusions? *Neurosurgery, 14,* 416–423.

Baird, A. D., Boulos, R., Mehta, B., Adams, K. M., Shatz. M. W., Ausman, J. I., Diaz, F. G., and Dujovney, M. *(in press).* Cerebral angiography and neuropsychological measurement: The twain shall meet. *Surgical Neurology.*

Bale, R. N. (1973). Brain damage in diabetes mellitus. *Br. J. Psychiat., 122,* 337–341.

Ball, J. A. C. (1971). Psychological tests in elderly patients with a note on the effect of cyclandelate on mental functions and cerebral blood flow. In G. Stocker, R. A. Kuhn, P. Hall, G. Becker, E. van der Veen, eds., *Assessement in Cerebrovascular Insufficiency.* Stuttgart: Georg Thieme Verlag, pp. 51–61.

Ball, J. A. C., and Taylor, A. R. (1967). Effect of cyclandelate on mental function and cerebral blood flow in elderly patients. *Br. Med. J., 3,* 525–528.

Ball, J. A. C., and Taylor. A. R. (1969). The effect of cyclandelate on mental function and cerebral blood flow in elderly patients. In: J. S. Meyer, H. Lechner, O. Eichhorn, eds., *Research on the Cerebral Circulation: Third International Salzburg Conference.* Springfield, Ill: Charles C. Thomas, pp. 347–363.

Ben-Yishay, Y., Gerstman, L., Diller, L., and Haas, A. (1970). Prediction of rehabilitation outcomes from psychometric parameters in left hemiplegics. *J. Consult. Clin. Psychol., 34,* 436–441.

Binder, L. M., Tanabe, C. T., Waller, F. T., and Wooster, N. E. (1982). Behavioral effects of superficial temporal artery to middle cerebral artery bypass surgery: Preliminary report. *Neurology, 32,* 422–424.

Boll, T. J. (1974). Right and left hemisphere damage and tactile perception: Performance of the ipsilateral and contralateral sides of the body. *Neuropsychologia, 12,* 235–238.

Bornstein, R. A., Benoit, B. G., and Trites, R. L. (1981a). Neuropsychological changes following carotid endarterectomy. *Canad. J. Neurol. Sci., 8,* 127–132.

Bornstein, R., Trites, R., Benoit, B. (1981b, February). *Effects of medical risk factors on extent of improvement following carotid endarterectomy.* Presented at the meeting of the International Neuropsychological Society, Atlanta, Georgia, February 1981.

Bourestrom, N. C., and Howard, M. T. (1968). Behavioral correlates of recovery of self-care in hemiplegic patients. *Arch. Phys. Med. Rehab., 49,* 449–454.

Bovier, J. B., Passeron, O., and Chupin, M. P. (1974). Psychometric study of Praxilene. *J. Int. Med. Res., 2,* 59–65.

Brackenridge, C. J., and Bloch, S. (1972). Smoking in medical students. *J. Psychosomatic Res., 16,* 35–40.

Carter, G. L. (1974). Effects of cigarette smoking on learning. *Percept. Motor Skills, 39,* 1344–1346.

Cook, P., and James, I. (1981). Drug therapy: Cerebral vasodilators. *New Engl. J. Med., 305,* 1508–1513.

Delaney, C., Wallace, J. D., and Egelko, S. (1980). Transient cerebral ischemic attacks and neuropsychological deficit. *J. Clin. Neuropsychol., 2,* 107–114.

Drake, W., Baker, M., Blumenkrantz, J., and Dallgren, H. (1968). The quality and duration of survival in bilateral carotid occlusive disease. A preliminary survey of the effects of thromboendarterectomy. In: J. Toole, R. Siekert, and J. Whisnant, eds., *Cerebral Vascular Disease.* New York: Grune and Stratton.

Duke, R., Bloor, B., Nujent, R., and Majzoub, H. (1968). Changes in performance on WAIS, Trail Making Test and Finger Tapping Test associated with carotid artery surgery. *Percept. Motor Skills, 26,* 399–404.

Dull, A., Brown, G. G., Adams, K. M., Shatz, M. W., Diaz, F. G., and Ausman, J. I. (1982). Preoperative neurobehavioral impairment in cerebral revascularization candidates. *J. Clin. Neuropsychol., 4,* 151–165.

Eastcott, H., Pickering, G., and Rob, C. (1954). Reconstruction of internal carotid artery in a patient with intermittent attacks of hemiplegia. *Lancet, 2,* 994.

Evans, R. B., and Austin, G. M. (1976). Psychological evaluation of patients undergoing microneurosurgical anastomoses for cerebral ischemia. In: G. M. Austin, ed., *Microneurosurgical Anastomoses for Cerebral Ischemia.* Springfield, Ill: Charles C. Thomas.

Ferguson, G. G., and Peerless, S. J. (1976). Extracranial-intracranial arterial bypass in the treatment of dementia and multiple extracranial arterial occlusion. *Stroke, 7,* 13.

Fine, E. W., Lewis, D., Villa-Landa, I., and Blakemore, C. B. (1971). the effect of cyclandelate on mental functioning in patients with arteriosclerotic disease. In: G. Stocker, R. A. Kuhn, P. Hall, G. Becker, E. van der Veen, eds., *Assessment in Cerebrovascular Insufficiency.* Stuttgart: Georg Thieme Verlag.

Finkelstein, J. N. (1977). BRAIN: A computer program for interpretation of the Halstead-Reitan Neuropsychological Test Battery (Doctoral Dissertation, Columbia University, 1976). *Dis. Abstr. Int., 37,* 5349B. (University Microfilms No. 77-8, 8864).

Finlayson, M. A. J., and Reitan, R. M. (1980). Effect of lateralized lesions on ipsilateral and contralateral motor functioning. *J. Clin. Neuropsychol., 2,* 237–243.

Futty, D. E., Conneally, P. M., Dyken, M. L., Price, T. R., Haerer, A. F., Postranzer, D. C., Swanson, P. D., Calanching, P. R., and Gotshall, R. A. (1977). Cooperative study of hospital frequency and character of transient ischemic attacks: V. Symptom analysis. *J. Am. Med. Assoc., 238,* 2386–2390.

Goldman, H., Kleinman, K. M., Snow, M. Y., Bidus, D. R., and Korol, B. (1974). Correlation of diastolic blood pressure and signs of cognitive dysfunction in essential hypertension. *Dis. Nerv. System, 35,* 571–572.

Goldman, H., Kleinman, K. M., Snow, M. Y., Bidus, D. R., and Korol, B. (1975). Relationship between essential hypertension and cognitive functioning: Effects of biofeedback. *Psychophysiology, 12,* 569–573.

Goldstein, S. G., Kleinknecht, R. A., and Gallo. A. E., Jr. (1970). Neuropsychological changes associated with carotid endarterectomy. *Cortex, 6,* 308–322.

Grant, I., Heaton, R. K., McSweeny, A. J., Adams, K. M., and Timms, R. M. (1980). Brain dysfunction in COPD. *Chest, 77 (Suppl.* 2), 308–309.

Grant, I., Heaton, R. K., McSweeny, A. J., Adams, K. M., and Timms, R. M. (1982). Neuropsychologic findings in hypoxemic chronic obstructive pulmonary disease. *Arch. Int. Med., 142,* 1470–1476.

Haaland, K. Y., and Delaney, H. D. (1981). Motor deficit after left or right hemisphere damage due to stroke or tumor. *Neuropsychologia, 19,* 17–27.

Hachinski, V. C., Lassen, N. A., and Marshall, J. (1974). Multi-infarct dementia—a cause of mental deterioration in the elderly. *Lancet, 2,* 207–209.

Hall, P., and Harcup, M. (1969). A trial of lipotropic enzymes in atheromatous ("arteriosclerotic") dementia. *Angiology, 20,* 287–300.

Hartman, J. (1981). Measurement of early spontaneous recovery from aphasia with stroke. *Ann. Neurol., 9,* 89–91.

Haynes, C. D., Gideon, D. A., King, G. D., and Dempsey, R. L. (1976). The improvement of cognition and personality after carotid endarterectomy. *Surgery, 80*(6), 699–704.

Heaton, R. K., Grant, I., McSweeny, A. J., Adams, K. M., and Petty, T. L. (1983). Psychologic effects of continuous and nocturnal oxygen therapy in hypoxic chronic obstructive pulmonary disease. *Arch. Int. Med. 143,* 1941–1947.

Heaton, R. K., and Pendleton, M. G. (1981). Use of neuropsychological tests to predict adult patients' everyday functioning. *J. Consult. Clin. Psychol., 49,* 807–821.

Høedt-Rasmussen, K., and Skinhøj, E. (1964). Transneural depression of the cerebral hemispheric metabolism in man. *Acta Neurol. Scand., 40,* 41–46.

Høedt-Rasmussen, K., Skinhøj, E., Paulson, O., Ewald, J., Bjerrum, J. K., Fahrenkrug, A., and Lassen, N. A. (1967). Regional cerebral blood flow in acute apoplexy: The "luxury perfusion syndrome" of brain tissue. *Arch. Neurol., 17,* 271–281.

Horne, D., and Royle, J. (1974). Cognitive changes after carotid endarterectomy. *Med. J. Australia, 1,* 316–317.

Houston, J. P., Schneider, N. G., and Jarvik, M. E. (1978). Effects of smoking on free recall and organization. *Am. J. Psychiat., 135,* 220–222.

Hudgins, W. R., and Garcia, J. H. (1970). Transorbital approach to the middle cerebral artery of the squirrel monkey: A technique for experimental cerebral infarction applicable to ultrastructural studies. *Stroke, 1,* 107–111.

Hung, J., and Barbosa, J. (undated). *The Minnesota Diabetes Clinical Trial. Cognitive functions under long-term maximized and standard metabolic control.* Publication #96 from the University of Minnesota Diabetes Research Group.

Hungerbuhler, J. P., Younkin, D., Reivich, M., Obrist, W. D., O'Conner, M., Goldberg, H., Gordon, J., Gur, R., Hurtig, G. and Amarnek, W. (1981). The effect of STA-MCA anastomosis on rCBF, neurologic, and neuropsychologic function in patients with completed stroke. In: J. S. Meyer, H. Lechner, M. Reivitch, E. Ott, and A. Aranilian, eds., *Cerebral Vascular Disease 3.* Princeton: Excerpta Medica, pp. 73–75.

Hyams, D. E. (1978). Cerebral function and drug therapy. In: J. C. Broklehurst, ed., *Textbook of Geriatric Medicine and Gerontology,* 2nd ed. Edinburgh: Churchill Livingston, pp. 670–711.

Jones, T. H., Morawetz, R. B., Crowell, R. M., Marcoux, F. W., FitzGibbon, S. J., De-Girolami, U., and Ojemann, R. G. (1981). Thresholds of focal cerebral ischemia in awake monkeys. *J. Neurosurg. 54,* 773–782.

Juolasmaa, A., Outakoski, J., Hirvenoja, R., Tienari, P., Sotaniemi, K., and Takkunen, J. (1981). Effect of open heart surgery on intellectual performance. *J. Clin. Neuropsychol., 3,* 181–197.

Kelly, M. P., Garron, D. C., and Javid, H. (1980). Carotid artery disease, carotid endarterectomy and behavior. *Arch. Neurol., 37,* 743–748.

Kimura, D. (1977). Acquisition of a motor skill after left-hemisphere damage. *Brain, 100,* 527–542.

Kimura, D., and Archibald, Y. (1974). Motor functions of the left hemisphere. *Brain, 97,* 337–350.

Kinsella, G., and Ford, B. (1980). Acute recovery patterns in stroke patients: Neuropsychological factors. *Med. J. Australia, 2,* 663–666.

Krop, H. D., Block, A. J., and Cohen, E. (1973). Neuropsychologic effects of continuous oxygen therapy in chronic obstructive pulmonary disease. *Chest, 64,* 317–322.

Krop, H. D., Block, A. J., Cohen, E., Cronchen, R., and Shuster, J. (1977). Neuropsychologic effects of continuous oxygen therapy in the aged. *Chest, 72,* 737–743.

Kurtzke, J. F. (1980). Epidemiology of cerebrovascular disease. In: *Cerebrovascular Survey Report* (NINCDS Monograph available from the NIH, Bldg. 31, Rm. 8A06). Bethesda: Office of Scientific and Health Reports, pp. 135–176.

Lehmann, J. F., DeLateur, B. J., Fowler, R. S., Warren, C. G., Arnhold, R., Schertzer, G., Hurka, R., Whitmore, J. J., Masock, A. J., and Chambers, K. H. (1975). Stroke rehabilitation: Outcome and prediction. *Arch. Phys. Med. Rehab., 56,* 383–389.

Lhermitte, F., and Signoret, J. L. (1972). Analyse neuropsychologique des syndrome amnesiques. *Rev. Neurol. (Paris), 126,* 161–178.

Liepmann, H. (1913). Motor aphasia, anarthria, and apraxia. In: *Transactions of the 17th International Congress of Medicine,* Sec. XI, part II, 97–106.

Light, K. A. (1975). Slowing of response time in young and middle-aged hypertensive patients. *Exp. Aging Res., 1,* 209–227.

Light, K. A. (1978). Effects of mild cardiovascular and cerebrovascular disorders on serial reaction time performance. *Exp. Aging Res., 4,* 3–22.

Lorenzo, E. J., and Cancro, R. (1962). Dysfunction in visual perception with hemiplegia: Its relation to activities of daily living. *Arch. Phys. Med. Rehab., 43,* 514–517.

Matarazzo, R. G., Matarazzo, J. D., Gallo, A. E., and Wiens, A. T. (1979). IQ and neuropsychological changes following carotid endaterectomy. *J. Clin. Neuropsychol., 1,* 97–116.

Meier, M. J. (1970). Objective behavioral assessment in diagnosis and prediction: Presentation 14. In: A. L. Benton, ed., *Behavioral Change in Cerebrovascular Disease.* New York: Harper & Row.

Meier, M. J., Ettinger, M. G., and Arthur, L. (1982). Recovery of neuropsychological functioning after cerebrovascular infarction. In: R. N. Malatesha and L. C. Hartlage, eds., *Neuropsychology and Cognition,* vol. II, Boston: Martinus Nijhoff, pp. 552–564.

Meier, M. J., and Okayama, M. (1969). Behavior assessment. *Geriatrics, 24,* 95–110.

Meier, M. J., and Resch, J. A. (1967). Behavioral prediction of short term neurologic change following acute onset of cerebrovascular symptoms. *Mayo Clinic Proc., 42,* 641–647.

Meyer, J. S., Deshmukh, U. D., and Welch, K. M. A. (1976). Experimental studies concerned with the pathogenesis of cerebral ischemia and infarction. In: R. W. Ross Russell, ed., *Cerebral Arterial Disease.* New York: Churchill Livingstone, pp. 57–84.

Meyer, J. S., Welch, K. M. A., Okamoto, S., and Shimazu, K. (1974). Disordered neurotransmitter function: Demonstration by measurement of norepinephrine and 5-hydroxytriptamine in CSF of patients with recent cerebral infarction. *Brain, 997,* 655–664.

Mohr, J. P., Fisher, C. M., and Adams, R. D. (1980). Cerebrovascular diseases. In: K. J. Isselbacher, R. D. Adams, E. Braunwald, R. G. Petersdorf, and J. D. Wilson, eds., *Harrison's Principles of Internal Medicine,* 9th ed. New York: McGraw-Hill, pp. 1911–1942.

Myrsten, A.-L., Elgerot, A., and Edgren, B. (1977). Effects of abstinence from tobacco smoking on physiological and psychological arousal levels in habitual smokers. *Psychosomatic Med., 39,* 25–38.

Myrsten, A.-L., Post, B., Frankenhaeuser, M., and Johansson, G. (1972). Changes in behavioral and physiological activation induced by cigarette smoking in habitual smokers. *Psychopharmacologia, 27,* 305–312.

Nilsson, B., Cronqvist, S., and Ingvar, D. H. (1979). Regional cerebral blood flow (rCBF) studies in patients to be considered for extracranial-intracranial bypass operations. In:

J. S. Meyer, H. Lechner, and M. Reivich, eds., *Cerebral Vascular Disease 2*. Amsterdam: Excerpta Medica, pp. 295–300.

Nocturnal Oxygen Therapy Trial Group (1980). Continuous or nocturnal oxygen therapy in hypoxemic chronic obstructive lung disease. *Ann. Int. Med., 93*, 391–398.

Osborn. A. G. (1980). *An Introduction to Cerebral Angiography*. New York: Harper & Row, pp. 78–85.

Ott, E. O., Abraham, J., Meyer, J. S., Achari, A. N., Chee, A. N. C., and Mathew, N. T. (1975). Disordered cholinergic neurotransmission and dysautoregulation after acute cerebral infarction. *Stroke, 6,* 172–180.

Perez, F. I., Gay, J. R. A., Taylor, R. L., and Rivera, V. M. (1975a). Patterns of memory performance in the neurologically impaired aged. *Canad. J. Neurol. Sci., 2,* 347–355.

Perez. F. I., Rivera. V. M., Meyer, J. S., Gay, J. R. A., Taylor, R. L., and Mathew, N. T. (1975b). Analysis of intellectual and cognitive performance in patients with multi-infarct dementia, vertebrobasilar insufficiency with dementia and Alzheimer's disease. *J. Neurol., Neurosurg. Psychiat., 38,* 533–540.

Perez, F. I., Stump, D. A., Gay, J. R., and Hart, V. R. (1976). Intellectual performance in multi-infarct dementia and Alzheimer's disease—A replication study. *Canad. J. Neurol. Sci., 3,* 181–187.

Perry, P. M., Drinkwater, J. E., and Taylor, G. W. (1975). Cerebral function before and after carotid endarterectomy. *Br. Med. J., 4,* 215–216.

Prigatano, G. P., Parsons, O., Wright, E., Levin, D. C., and Hawryluk, G. (1983). Neuropsychological test performance in mildly hypoxemic patients with chronic obstructive pulmonary disease. *J. Consult. Clin. Psychol., 51,* 108–116.

Ponsford, J. L., Donnan, G. A., and Walsh, K. W. (1980). Disorders of memory in vertebrobasilar disease. *J. Clin. Neuropsychol., 2,* 267–276.

Reitan, R. M. (1954). Intellectual and affective changes in essential hypertension. *Am. J. Psychiat., 110,* 817–824.

Reitan, R. M., and Fitzhugh, K. B. (1971). Behavioral deficits in groups with cerebral vascular lesions. *J. Consult. Clin. Psychol., 37,* 215–223.

Reitan, R. M., and Shipley, R. E. (1963). The relationship of serum cholesterol changes to psychological abilities. *J. Gerontol., 18,* 350–357.

Reivich, M., and Waltz. A. G. (1980). Circulatory and metabolic factors in cerebrovascular disease. In: *Cerebrovascular Survey Report* (NINCDS Monograph available from NIH, Bldg. 31, Rm. 8A06). Bethesda: Office of Scientific and Health Reports, pp. 55–134.

Rennick, P. H., Wilder, R. M., Sargent, J., and Ashley, B. J. (1968). Retinopathy as an indicator of cognitive-perceptual-motor impairment in diabetic adults. *Proceedings of the 76th Annual Convention APA,* 473–474. Washington: American Psychological Association.

Ritter, R. M., Nail, H. R., Tatum, P., and Blazi, M. (1971). The effect of papaverine on patients with cerebral arteriosclerosis. *Clin. Med., 78,* 18–22.

Rivera, V. M., Meyer, J. S., Baer, P. E., Faibish, G. M., and Mathew, N. T. (1976). Vertebrobasilar insufficiency as a cause of dementia. Controlled therapeutic trial with betahistine-HCL. In: J. S. Meyer, H. Lechner, and M. Reivich, eds., *Cerebral Vascular Disease.* Stuttgart: Georg Thieme, pp. 112–118.

Rustin, R. M., Kittel, F., Dramaix, M., Kornitzer, M., and DeBacker, G. (1978). Smoking habits and psycho-sociobiological factors. *J. Psychosomatic Res., 22,* 89–99.

Schenk, G. K., Lang, E., and Anlauf, M. (1981). Beta-receptor blocking therapy in hypertensive patients: Effects on vigilance and behavior. *Aviation, Space, & Environmental Med., 52,* S35–S39.

Schultz, N. R., Dineen, J. T., Elias, M. F., Pentz, C. A., and Wood, G. W. (1979). WAIS performance for different age groups of hypertensive and control subjects during the administration of a diuretic. *J. Gerontol., 34,* 246–253.

Shafrir, E. (1975). Hyperlipidemia in diabetes. In: K. E. Sussman and R. J. S. Metz, eds., *Diabetes Mellitus.* New York: American Diabetes Association, pp. 221–228.

Shatz, M. W. (1981). WAIS practice effects in clinical neuropsychology. *J. Clin. Neuropsychol.*, *3*, 171–179.

Smith, W. L. (1970). The effects of vasodilators on psychological test performance in patients with cerebral vascular insufficiency. In: W. L. Smith, ed., *Drugs and Cerebral Function.* Springfield, Illinois: Charles C. Thomas, pp. 252–260.

Smith, W. L., and Lowrey, J. B. Differential effects of cyclandelate on psychological test performance in patients with cerebral vascular insufficiency. In: G. Stocker, R. A. Kuhn, P. Hall, G. Becker, and E. van der Veen, eds., *Assessment in Cerebrovascular Insufficiency.* Stuttgart: Georg Thieme Verlag, pp. 69–73.

Smith, W. L., Lowrey, J. B., and Davis, J. A. The effects of cyclandelate on psychological test performance in patients with cerebral vascular insufficiency. *Curr. Therap. Res.*, *10*, 613–618.

Smith, W. L., Philippus, M. J., and Lowrey, J. B. (1968). A comparison of psychological and psychophysical test patterns before and after receiving papaverine HCL. *Curr. Therap. Res.*, *10*, 428–431.

Spielberger, C. D., Gorsuch, R. L., and Lushene, R. E. (1970). *State Trait Anxiety Inventory, (Marval).* Palo Alto: Consulting Psychologist Press.

Spieth, W. (1964). Cardiovascular health status, age and psychological performance. *J. Gerontol.*, *19*, 277–284.

Stevens, H. A. (1976). Evidence that suggests a negative association between cigarette smoking and learning performance. *J. Clin. Psychol.*, *32*, 896–898.

Stocker, G. Cerebral function and cerebral blood flow. In: G. Stocker, R. A. Kuhn, P. Hall, G. Becker, E. van der Veen, eds., *Assessment in Cerebrovascular Insufficiency.* Stuttgart: Georg Thieme Verlag, pp. 74–83.

Stroke Risk Handbook: Estimating risk of stroke in daily practice. (1974). (Prepared with the help of W. B. Kannel and T. R. Dawber). American Heart Association.

Thompson, J., and Talkington, C. (1976). Carotid endarterectomy. *Ann. Surg.*, *184*(1), 1–15.

Toole, J. F., and Patel, A. N. (1974). *Cerebrovascular Disorders*, 2d ed. New York: McGraw-Hill Book Company.

Tong, J. E., Leigh, G., Campbell, J., and Smith, D. (1977). Tobacco smoking, personality and sex factors in auditory vigilance performance. *Br. J. Psychol.*, *68*, 365–370.

Van der Drift, J. H. A., and Kok, K. D. (1972). Steal mechanisms between the carotid and vertebrobasilar systems. In: J. S. Meyer, M. Reivich, H. Lechner, and O. Eichhorn, eds., *Research on the Cerebral Circulation: Fifth International Salzburg Conference.* Springfield, Illinois: Charles C. Thomas.

Von Monakow, C. (1914). *Die Lokalisation im Grosshirn und der Abbau der Funktion durch & Kortikale.* Herde, Wiesbaden: J. F. Bergmann.

Welch, K. M. A., and Meyer, J. S. (1975). Disordered cerebral metabolism after cerebral ischemia and infarction—therapeutic implications. In: J. S. Meyer, ed., *Modern Concepts of Cerebrovascular Disease.* New York: Spectrum Publications, Inc.

Westreich, G., Alter, M., and Lundgren, S. (1975). Effect of cyclandelate on dementia. *Stroke*, *6*, 535–538.

Williams, D. G. (1980). Effects of cigarette smoking on immediate memory and performance in different kinds of smokers. *Br. J. Psychol.*, *71*, 83–90.

Williams, M., and McGee, T. F. (1964). Psychological study of carotid occlusion and endarterectomy. *Arch. Neurol.*, *10*, 293–297.

Williams, V., and Grossman, R. G. (1969). Ultrastructure of cortical synapses after failure of presynaptic activity in ischemia. *Anat. Records*, *166*, 131–141.

Young, J., Hall, P., and Blakemore, C. (1974). Treatment of the cerebral manifestations of arteriosclerosis with cyclandelate. *Br. J. Psychiat.*, *124*, 177–180.

18

Neuropsychological Findings in the Early and Middle Phases of Alcoholism

TOR LØBERG

When considering evidence for brain disorders in the early and middle phases of alcoholism, it is well to remember that alcohol dependency is associated with a broad range of disturbances of behavior and health. Alcoholics treated in inpatient units are regularly found to have difficulties in their family relationships, friendships, work, and finances, in addition to legal and health problems (Løberg, 1980a). More specifically, and complicating neuropsychological inquiry, alcohol abuse is related to diseases in several parts of the body, including the esophagus, the stomach, the small intestine, the pancreas, the liver, the heart, the muscles of the body and the endocrine system, and contributes to cancer in several of these organs. Further, alcohol intoxication contributes to serious accidents on the road, in the home, and in industry. With regard to traffic accidents causing serious injury to the driver, statistics from two hospitals in Norway showed that in one, 46% of those injured had been intoxicated and in the other, 62%. These findings correspond fairly well with those from several other countries, and of course brain damage can be a consequence of such accidents. Weighing the evidence for possible direct effects of alcohol on the central nervous system (CNS), we should keep in mind sources of neurological morbidity that are associated with the "alcoholism life style," beyond the specific neurotoxic effects of ethanol (Grant, Adams, and Reed, 1984).

A second point to consider in evaluating neuropsychological findings is the typical source of alcoholic subjects. Referrals for clinical neuropsychological evaluation in alcohol dependency most frequently come from alcoholism treatment facilities, although some suspected alcoholics will also be referred from neurological, neurosurgical, and general medical-surgical practices. There are usually some very good reasons for referring a patient, since the frequent limitation in neuropsychological service capacities makes it necessary to set priorities. Patients referred are often those who show a protracted withdrawal reaction, clinical evidence of reduced cognitive functioning or emotional disturbances, or a history or test results that may give reason to suspect a brain disorder. Accordingly, inferences about alcohol-brain relationships based on patients referred for neuropsychological evaluation will be biased in favor of finding morbidity. On the other hand, some alcoholics suffering from neurologic sequelae completely escape detection in medical practice. Recent findings from the pathological-anatomical laboratory at Ulleval Hospital, Norway, indicated that of 68 cases of Wernicke's encephalopathy diagnosed at autopsy, only three had been suspected or identified clinically before death (Torvik and Lindboe, 1982). This corresponds roughly to findings from Australia which showed that of 51 cases diagnosed as Wernicke's encephalopathy at autopsy, only 17 had been diagnosed during life (Harper, 1979).

The Diagnosis of Alcoholism

A further complication for neuropsychological research is the problematic nature of the diagnosis of alcoholism. Despite vigorous efforts to find a biomedical indicator of excessive alcohol consumption, as yet no marker with clinical applicability and general validity has been discovered. For instance, the value of gamma-glutamyl transferase (GGT) as a biological marker has been questioned recently in two studies (Garvin, Foy, and Alford, 1981; Gluud et al., 1981). Suspicion of alcohol problems can, of course, be raised simply by the general appearance of the patients, e.g., dermatological changes.

Absenteeism, sleep disturbances, or pathological jealousy may be present but obviously occur for other reasons as well.

Nevertheless, direct measures of alcohol misuse and related problems are available and have a much higher degree of validity than was once assumed (Miller, 1976). Several questionnaires for obtaining this information may be used for research as well as clinical practice. These include the ALCADD Test (Manson, 1949), the Michigan Alcoholism Screening Test (MAST) (Selzer, 1971), the Iowa Scale of Preoccupation with Alcohol (ISPA) (Mulford and Miller, 1960), the Alcohol Use Inventory (AUI) (Wanberg, Horn, and Foster, 1977), the Severity of Alcohol Dependence Questionnaire (SADQ) (Stockwell et al., 1979), the Drinking Profile (Marlatt, 1976), and questionnaires constructed by Cahalan and his colleagues (Cahalan, 1978). Of these, the AUI is very well validated, the Drinking Profile has good clinical utility, and the Cahalan questionnaire has been used successfully in national surveys of drinking habits. A new progressive diagnostic schema for alcoholism from the New York State Research Institute on Alcoholism in Buffalo, based on data from 1251 subjects, also has clinical utility (Brown and Lyons, 1981).

Ideally, the neuropsychologist establishes a positive diagnosis of alcohol dependence through anamnestic information, self-report measures, and independent biological and behavioral information. The next task is to determine if neuropsychological deficit is present, and to develop hypotheses as to its cause.

Neuropsychological Methods in Alcoholism Research

Why Neuropsychological Assessment?

Many strategies, of course, are available for the study of brain-behavior relationships. Much of the alcoholism literature is based on the Halstead-Reitan Battery (Reitan and Davison, 1974) and its derivatives, so my review will focus on this approach. There is extensive literature, as well, on specific techniques of assessing memory disorders in alcoholism; these are addressed in Chapter 19.

Studies in the Halstead-Reitan tradition typically include seven of Halstead's original ten tests: the Category Test, Tactual Performance Test (time, memory, and localization), Speech-Sounds Perception Test, Rhythm Test, and Tapping Test. Others are often added, such as the Trail Making Test, the Reitan-Kløve Sensory-Perceptual Examination, the Kløve-Matthews Motor Steadiness Battery and the Reitan-Kløve Lateral Dominance Examination. (For a description of these tests, see Reitan and Davison, 1974.) Also included frequently are psychometric tests of intelligence, such as the WAIS, and of memory, such as the Wechsler Memory Scale, as well as objective measures of personality, e.g., the MMPI. In our department the standard neuropsychological test battery includes all the tests mentioned above with additional clinical interviews or history taking, and in the case of alcohol and drug dependencies, a screening questionnaire as well.

The validity of the Halstead-Reitan Battery for assessing brain dysfunction is well established and its correspondence with several other measures of brain lesions has been documented (Kløve, 1974; Heaton et al., 1981). Agreement tends to be best for the presence of brain pathology, next best for lateralization, and least good for the precise nature and progression of lesions (Heaton et al., 1981; Chapter 1). Such disagreements need not necessarily invalidate the neuropsychological method, but point to the differential sensitivity and inherent limitations not only of testing, but also of the neurological examination, EEG, pneumoencephalography, computerized tomography, blood-flow measures, and arteriography.

General Findings and Approaches to the Impairment Issue

This chapter will focus on the neuropsychology of the early and middle phases of alcoholism. Readers are referred to Chapter 19, and to several general reviews and discussions of methodological issues (Acker, 1982; Goldstein, 1976; Grant and Mohns, 1975; Grant and Reed, 1984; Grant, Reed, and Adams, 1980; Kleinknecht and Goldstein, 1972; Miller and Saucedo, (in press); Parsons, 1975, 1977; Parsons and Farr, 1981; Ron, 1979; Ryan and Butters, 1983; Tarter, 1975a, 1975b, 1976a, 1976b, 1978; Tarter et al., 1977).

The findings in general are consistent across different samples and even in cross-national comparisons. When clinical samples are studied, and the diagnosis is one of alcohol dependency, usually with a prior history of excessive drinking for some ten or more years, excluding patients with primary neurological disorders as well as manifest thought disturbances, and when subjects are examined a few weeks after hospital admission or after having quit drinking, male alcoholics tend to show a similar cognitive profile. Though psychometric intelligence as measured by the WAIS or the Wechsler-Bellevue Test is in the normal range, as indicated by the full scale I.Q. and particularly the verbal I.Q., the performance I.Q. is frequently inferior. Memory, as indicated by a composite measure like the Wechsler Memory Scale (WMS) and the derived Memory Quotient (MQ), is usually only moderately impaired, the MQ requently being in the same range as the performance I.Q. More sensitive neuropsychological tests, however, show more severe impairment. Alcoholics are frequently reported to be impaired on the Category Test, the Trail Making Test, and the Tactual Performance Test (TPT) (total time and localization, in particular). Tests from the extended Halstead-Reitan Battery which have yielded negative or inconsistent findings include the Tapping Test, Speech Sounds Perception Test, Memory part of the TPT, and the Aphasia Screening and Sensory-Perceptual examinations. The composite Halstead Impairment Index is generally in the impaired range.

Our Neuropsychology Center in Bergen, Norway, includes the Klove-Matthews Motor Steadiness Battery in neuropsychological assessments. We have found that simple motor skills (speed and strength) are preserved, but impairment is increasingly evident as motor tasks become more complex and require more mental involvement (Fig. 1). (Though not included in this figure, our subjects were also impaired on tests of higher cognitive functions, like the Category Test and the Trail Making Test.)

It is important to be aware that there are four main approaches in determining whether an alcoholic sample is impaired or not, and that each approach may give somewhat different results.

The ideal experiment would, of course, randomize subjects into alcoholic and nonalcoholic groups. This being an unreachable ideal, the next best strategy involves a case-control design. The validity and generalizability of results from such an experiment will depend directly on how carefully subjects were matched for variables other than the one under investigation. Despite its power, the case control approach is always vulnerable to unaccountable sources of neuropsychological variability, as well as the possibility of "regression toward the mean" in test results. (For further discussion of this, see Grant and Reed, 1984; Adams, Brown, and Grant, 1985.)

Another approach is to compare the alcoholic group to established criteria of impairment, e.g., the Halstead Impairment Index (Reitan and Davison, 1974; also, see Reitan, Chapter 1), an Average Impairment Rating (Russell, Neuringer, and Goldstein, 1970), or using cutoff scores on the individual neuropsychological tests. A third approach is for clinicians to rate test protocols and categorize blindly into, for instance, "normal" and "brain dysfunction" by the use of an ad hoc set of criteria, usually after having established interrater con-

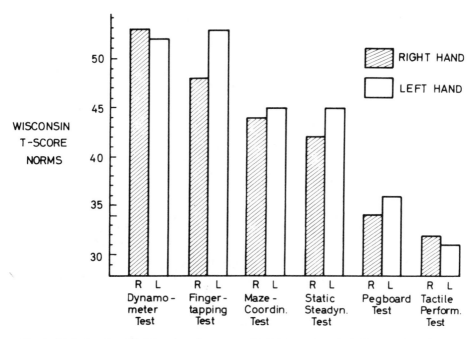

Fig. 1. Right-hand and left-hand performance of 111 Norwegian alcoholics on selected motor tests. Scores on tests have been converted to *T* scores. (Reprinted by permission from *Journal of Studies on Alcohol, 41*, 119–128, 1980. Copyright by *Journal of Studies on Alcohol*, Inc., New Brunswick, NJ 08903.)

sensus through a reliability measure (e.g., see Heaton et al., 1981). This approach is based on the researcher's best total frame of reference, and can be linked to a case-control design [e.g., see Grant, Adams and Reed, 1979; 1984].

A fourth approach is to compare the alcoholic group with a set of norms, for instance a T-score distribution of individual test scores. It is crucial that the researcher be familiar with how such sets of norms were derived and which population they represent. For instance, a T-score distribution from the Neuropsychological Laboratory in Madison, Wisconsin, is based on referrals that did not evidence any independent signs of brain dysfunction. The Ottawa, Ontario norms for children were derived in a similar way (Trites, 1981). Another T-score distribution for some of these neuropsychological tests was based on a random sampling from Swedish communities, and thus are representative of that population (Bergman et al., 1982).

Different strategies have yielded different findings. In their recent survey of neuropsychological studies in alcoholism, Miller and Saucedo looked at the results from cutoff score vs. case control studies. With few exceptions studies which used cutoff scores inferred alcoholics to have deficits more often than case control studies. Three studies revealed this discrepancy for the Trail Making Test, both parts A and B, one additional for part A only. Five studies reported the same findings for several measures from the TPT, time and location scores, in particular.

The problem with attempting to apply predetermined cutoff scores universally was well illustrated by a recent study by Bergman and associates (1982), who examined a normative group from the Karolinska Hospital in Sweden. Their sample consisted of 195 men and 192 women randomly drawn from the general population. Among men aged 50–65, even those who were better educated (i.e., above the median) scored in what would traditionally be considered the impaired range on Category Test (51 errors), TPT total time (18.9 minutes for 30 blocks), and Dominant Hand Tapping (50 taps for 10 seconds). The average Halstead Impairment Index for this group was also in the borderline area (0.4). Subjects with less education generally performed even less well on these tests and the index.

In Chapter 6, Heaton, Grant, and Matthews document further the need to develop age-education specific norms for various tests if the cutoff score strategy is to be applied in a meaningful way. Most importantly, Heaton et al. provide evidence for an age by education interaction for many test results. As an example, for a number of tests, age-related declines in performance were found to be more precipitous in the least educated than in the best-educated groups.

These findings indicate that carefully matched groups are essential in research on the neuropsychology of alcoholism, and also that groups should be rigorously matched on education and age variables as well as other sociodemographic variables. Such matching must attend not only to means, but also to possible differences in range and skewness of distribution.

Although I have focused on the problems of false positives arising from the uncritical use of cutoff scores, it must be emphasized that the converse problem of false negatives can also occur, particularly among groups in whom early or subtle forms of neuropsychological dysfunction might be expected—as in the early and middle phases of alcoholism. Reitan (1964) has emphasized the need to take the intraindividual neuropsychological pattern into account when considering the question of the possible presence of brain dysfunction. In their study of neurological and "pseudoneurological" subjects, Matthews and associates showed that Halstead's Impairment Index was a relatively inefficient "yes"/"no" discriminator; nevertheless, considering the *pattern* of neuropsychological test results, they were able to classify subjects appropriately in a high proportion of instances (Matthews, et al., 1966). In a similar vein, Heaton and associates (1981) were able to show that suitably trained clinicians achieved a higher "hit rate" than did a standard actuarial index (Average Impairment Rating of Russell et al., 1970). In studies on the neuropsychological consequences of substance abuse among younger subjects, Grant and associates were able to demonstrate that distribution of impairment was significantly higher in poly-substance-abusing groups when clinical ratings were used; in these same studies, individual test results were generally not strikingly different between substance abusers and controls (Grant et al., 1976; Grant et al., 1978).

Another effective way of identifying subtle changes in abilities earlier in the natural history of alcoholism is to identify tests that have common variance to develop composite ability area scores. Factor analysis represents one suitable way of creating such composites. Using this technique, and with an independent groups design, Fabian and Parsons (1983) were able to show that women alcoholics who were recently detoxified had impairments in perceptuomotor tasks, as was the case for long-term sober women alcoholics. Long-term sobriety, however, tended to normalize complex problem solving skills. Grant et al. (1984) also found that recently detoxified male alcoholics differed from those who had been abstinent an average of 4 years on problem solving and learning. Fabian and Parsons suggested that recovery of cognitive functioning in female alcoholics is similar to that reported for male alcoholics.

Issues in the Interpretation of Neuropsychological Findings

*Inconsistencies in Neuropsychological Findings in Samples
of Alcohol Dependence*

I stated above that most investigations of alcoholic samples have suggested intact psychometric intelligence but found evidence of some impairment in higher cognitive functions. There are, however, noteworthy disagreements. Two of the more comprehensive studies reached opposite conclusions, and an analysis of their source of disagreement may be instructive. One extreme is represented by Miller and Orr (1980), who reported very severe impairment in alcoholics; the other by the studies of Grant and coworkers (Grant, Adams, and Reed, 1979; Grant et al., 1979; Adams, Grant, and Reed, 1980) giving some alcoholics a neuropsychological "clean bill of health." In the Miller and Orr study the alcoholics' severe impairment is exemplified by a Category Test score of 90, a TPT Total Time score of 22.9, and an Impairment Index of 0.7. They were thus inseparable from a group with diagnosed brain syndromes (except for the Impairment Index), and clearly more impaired than a mixed psychiatric group. The alcoholics, however, were referred for neuropsychological evaluation and not randomly selected from the alcoholic in-patient population. The investigators were aware of this limitation in representativeness of this sample, and suggested that those with more apparent deficits might have been referred. I suspect that this was the case.

In the studies by Grant, Adams, and collaborators, samples consisted of recently detoxified male alcoholics who had been in a Veterans Administration Alcoholism Treatment Unit for 3 weeks and of alcoholic men who had been abstinent for 18 months or more (Grant et al., 1979a). A subsample of these subjects has been compared to polydrug abusers (Grant et al., 1979b) and the investigators also succeeded in obtaining retest data on many of the same subjects in a 1 year followup study (Adams et al., 1980). In all of these studies, alcoholics demonstrated average psychometric intelligence levels and no impairment in higher mental skills compared to cutoff scores and compared to a group of nonalcoholic subjects; indeed, alcoholics occasionally scored better on some tests than the nonalcoholic group. When compared to Bergman's T-score distribution, their performances are almost superior. These results also differ from those of other VA programs which have reported considerably more impairment in alcoholics, although the subjects in most VA studies are inpatients while those of Grant et al. were outpatients.

How are the findings of Grant and associates to be explained? Their estimate of total alcohol consumption seems to be typical for most samples where comparisons can be made. The number of years of excessive drinking (5.9 and 6.1 years) is lower than in most studies, yet similar to the studies of Fitzhugh, Fitzhugh, and Reitan (1965) and Jones and Parsons (1971). Similar to most studies, patients with a primary neurological diagnosis were excluded; however, even those who had received a specialized neurodiagnostic test were also excluded. Their criteria also excluded anyone who had ever received a diagnosis of schizophrenia or bipolar affective disorders, or had been treated in an inpatient or day treatment setting, or had been given antipsychotics, antidepressants or lithium regularly or had abused other drugs. Finally, those with a more persisting alcohol abstinence syndrome were excluded.

These exclusion criteria are, of course, very strict. The fact that one group had been abstaining for 18 months testifies to the alcoholics' adaptive resources, as does the fact that the clear majority of both groups were abstinent another year later in the followup study. Looking back to my own data for Norwegian alcoholics (Løberg, 1980a), I found that prior treatment for a psychiatric disorder other than alcoholism was not uncommon, in fact, 0.3 times for the average patient. Furthermore, when the MMPI data in the Grant et al. (1979a) study is inspected, it is evident that the group profile for each of the alcoholic groups is not very deviant, corresponding most closely to subtypes I and II in Fig. 2, and is distinctly less deviant than subtypes III and IV. It was these two last personality subtypes that were particularly related to severe neuropsychological impairment in my own study (Løberg, 1981). It is clear, however, that Grant, Adams and coworkers, applying very rigorous exclusion criteria, have established the important fact that even excessive alcohol consumption of some 6 years duration is not itself necessarily related to manifest neuropsychological impairment.

Predicting Neuropsychological Performance
from Drinking History Parameters

There are two main approaches to the issue of predicting neuropsychological performance from drinking history. One has been to compare neuropsychological performance of groups with different levels of alcohol consumption, e.g., social drinkers, problem drinkers, and alcoholics. Such studies can be said to be exploring the "continuity" notion, i.e., that there is progressive neuropsychological decline with amount of drinking, detectable even at the social drinking level. The other approach has been correlational, analyzing the relationship between drinking dimensions (e.g., years of excessive drinking, amount consumed at drinking occasion) and neuropsychological measures specifically in abusive drinkers.

In support of the continuity notion Parker and Noble have over the past several years investigated cognitive functioning in social drinkers, and recently a replication study was published (MacVane et al., 1982). Parsons and Fabian (1982) and Parker (1982) have provided valuable comments on this study and also on previous studies of social drinkers (Parker and Noble, 1977; Parker et al., 1980; Jones and Jones, 1980). The findings from the Parker group can be summarized quite simply: frequency of drinking in the past months or total amount of lifetime alcohol consumption are not related to cognitive performance when sober; however,average amount of alcohol consumed on recent drinking occasions shows a significant relationship. MacVane et al. (1982) replicated some of these findings, but they did not corroborate more impairment in heavy vs. light drinkers. On the other hand, Jones and Jones (1980) did find that female moderate social drinkers had significantly inferior sober memory compared to female light drinkers. Jones et al. (1971) and Tarter (1973) also found short-term alcoholics to perform better than long-term alcoholics. The work of Fine and Steer (1979) can be considered with the "continuity studies," as the subjects were 100 males consecutively referred for a drinking while intoxicated (DWI) evaluation. Since only nine had been treated for alcoholism previously, this sample, in general, may be said to be in an early stage of dependency. Tested on memory for designs, 33% were within the borderline range and 24% within the critical range. Interestingly, education predicted performance but length of current drinking pattern did not.

Correlational studies of alcoholics, relating length of excessive drinking to neuropsychological impairment, generally have found very weak correlations, in the 0.20–0.30 range, which accounts for a minimal part of the variance. For instance, although Eckardt et al. (1978) reported that several cognitive measures in alcoholics were predicted by various consumption scores on the basis of nonlinear regression models, the coefficients were usually low. Adams and Grant (1984) constructed analagous quadratic equations, but did not succeed in predicting performance from drinking history. Looking at our data from Bergen on inpatient alcoholics, the duration of excessive drinking in years was significantly ($r = 0.023$) related to Category Test Impairment. However, a measure of consumption during the last 6 months was somewhat more related to impaired Memory Quotient ($r = -0.31$), verbal I.Q. ($r = -0.33$), performance I.Q. ($r = -0.23$) and full scale I.Q. ($r = -0.32$). This measure was not significantly related to Category Test performance. Counting days of intoxication over the last two months before discontinuing drinking, roughly the same relationship was found; the correlation with performance I.Q., however, was not significant.

We also found that blackouts (over the last few months) clearly were significantly related to cognitive measures. The correlation with Memory Quotient was −0.37 with a verbal I.Q. −0.48, with a performance I.Q. −0.43, with a full scale I.Q. -0.50, Category Test errors 0.24, and Impairment Index 0.22. It is an important future task to try to clarify whether a drinking style associated with blackouts is an independent predictor of subsequent neuropsychological impairment, or whether the blackouts are a sign of pre-existing CNS vulnerability which manifests itself in neuropsychological deficits, as well.

Neuroradiological Evidence of Brain Damage in Alcoholics:
Neuropsychological Correlates

The neuroradiological findings in non-Korsakoff alcoholics have recently been reviewed by Ron (1983). Between 1955 and 1971 several pneumonencephalographic (PEG) studies showed that the majority of patients studied had signs of cerebral atrophy. With the advent of a noninvasive brain imaging technique—computerized tomography (CT)—it became practicable to examine larger and more representative groups of alcoholics. In reviewing the CT literature, Begleiter, Porjesz, and Tenner (1980) concluded that the majority of alcoholics studied (approximately two-thirds) showed cortical atrophy, particularly in the frontal parietal regions, while ventricular enlargements were reported in about one-third of the cases. It is interesting to note that as CT studies have moved away from examinations of alcoholics *referred* to neuroradiology because of neurological complaints to studies of subjects who did not have neurological complaints (i.e., the more "typical" alcoholic) the severity of CT-measured abnormalities has become less pronounced. Despite this, even among the better-controlled recent investigations, alcoholics are found to have CT scan abnormalities in 50% or more of the cases (Cala et al., 1980; Bergman et al., 1980a; Carlen and Wilkinson, 1980; Ron, 1983). Interestingly, whereas Ron (1983) reported that 64% of her alcoholics exceeded the criterion for ventricle brain ratio (V/B) set at the mean plus 1 standard deviation for her control sample, Hill and Mikhael (1979) found that only 1 of 15 of their alcoholics had V/B abnormality. Furthermore, as Ron (1983) has reviewed, attempts at correlating CT scan findings with drinking history have yielded results that have been remarkably disappointing. In most instances, correlations between indices of atrophy and drinking history are either insignificant or low order; and even when significant, these correlations tend to be markedly reduced when appropriate age corrections are introduced (Ron, 1983). The increasing variability in CT scan findings with alcoholics, coupled with difficulty in correlating CT to drinking history makes it likely that many as yet unappreciated sources of variance have contributed to CT findings reported to date. Progress in interpreting these CT findings will depend on progressively more careful characterization of alcoholic samples being studied along relevant dimensions—age, education, premorbid neuromedical history, nutrition, coexisting medical disease—to name a few.

The correlations between neuropsychological and CT measures have generally been low in investigations of chronic alcoholism. Age is the variable which explains most of the correlations. Studying a random sample from the general population, Bergman et al. (1980b) found significant but low correlations between several neuropsychological measures and the anterior horn index, the width of the third ventricle, and with cortical changes. With age partialed out, however, the correlations became nonsignificant. In a second report focusing specifically on alcoholics, Bergman and associates (1980a) found that the Impairment Index related to cortical changes, the Trail Making Test, Memory for Designs, and Claeson Dahl verbal learning were related to subcortical changes, while the Category Test results were associated both with cortical and subcortical changes. Most of the NP-CT correlations showed less than 10% shared variance, and these correlations were not age-adjusted as in Bergman et al.'s (1980b) general population study.

Generally speaking, NP changes have been found more frequently in alcoholics than CT changes. This was true of the Hill (1980) report, the Hill and Mikhael (1979) study, the study by Kroll et al. (1980), and Wilkinson and Carlen (1980).

This is not surprising, since NP techniques, which in many ways represent an extension and refinement of the clinical neurological examination, tend to be sensitive to changes in brain metabolism and to neurotransmitter abnormalities long before these are translated into visualizable structural abnormalities. With further advances in brain imaging techniques which are more sensitive to brain function [e.g., cerebral blood flow measures (rCBF), positron emission tomography (PET), and nuclear magnetic resonance (NMR) scanning], we can anticipate improved associations between neuropsychological and neuroradiological criterion measures in studies of alcoholics.

Reversibility of Alcoholism-Related Impairment

To what extent is alcoholic cerebral disorder reversible? Some workers have suggested that structural changes, as measured with the CT, normalize to a certain extent during abstinence (Carlen et al., 1978; Lishman, 1981; Ron, 1983). Regional cerebral blood flow (rCBF) determinations (Berglund and Risberg, 1980) have also been studied in alcoholics who have improved their drinking habits over the last three years, and in heavy "bender" drinkers. The improved alcoholics showed significantly better scores when retested with a block design test, which was related to normalization of rCBF in the inferior frontal region. These changes were more pronounced among continuous drinkers than among intermittent ones. On the basis of these findings, the authors suggested that reversible impairment in alcoholism is related to a defect in activation due to frontal lobe dysfunction at initial testing. The findings appeared not to be related to withdrawal reactions.

In another study of rCBF (Berglund et al., 1982) and using the [133]Xenon inhalation technique, recovery was studied in impaired and unimpaired alcoholics, defined as being above or below the median on the Trail Making Test, part B. The impaired alcoholics initially had significantly lower mean hemisphere blood flow during abstinence, increasing by 8% from the first to the seventh week, but still not reaching the level of the unimpaired group. Furthermore, for the impaired group, the regional blood flow was abnormal in the superior frontal and in the parietal regions of the right hemisphere, an asymmetry which tended to normalize at the seventh week.

Auditory brain stem response (ABR) would be of considerable interest here since the brain stem certainly is implicated in the modulation and maintenance of activation. The ABR of chronic alcoholic patients was recently studied by Chu, Squires, and Starr (1982). They found a clear relationship between ABR abnormalities and age and number of alcoholic neurological complications. When patients with the Wernicke-Korsakoff syndrome and cerebellar degeneration, which both affect the brain stem, were excluded, 30% still had abnormal ABRs. The authors failed to state when in the abstinence period the testing was done. It would be of considerable interest to see a followup of alcoholics over several weeks.

Several neuropsychological studies on reversibility in abstinent alcoholics have been published (Adams et al., 1980; Ayers et al., 1978; Berglund, Leijonquist, and Hørlèn, 1977; Clarke and Haughton, 1975; Hester, Smith, and Jackson, 1980; Kish et al., 1980; Long and McLachlan, 1974; O'Leary et al., 1977; Page and Linden, 1974; Page and Schaub, 1977; Prigatano, 1980; Schau, O'Leary, and Chaney, 1980; Sharp et al., 1977; Templer, Ruff, and Simpson, 1975). The studies are not easy to compare, since two different designs frequently are used: repeated measures or matched group.

In repeated testing (without controls) the influence of the practice effect is difficult to ascertain. Attrition rate may also bias the composition of the groups. The results are, however, consistent overall, regardless of design, and confirm that improvement occurs parallel with cessation of drinking. Hester et al. (1980) found a better Category Test performance in alcoholics abstinent for 90 days than in a group abstinent for 8–10 days. Kish et al. (1980) found improvement from the third week and little further change over the next 13 weeks, improvement being most evident on Digit Span, Block Design, Raven, Similarities, Memory for Designs, and Trail Making Test, part B. O'Leary et al. (1977b) reported Trail Making Test, part A and B, to be better for controls at both administrations than for alcoholics over a 1-year interval, though alcoholics did improve. They found no clear relationship between drinking episodes and cognitive improvement. McLachlan and Levinson (1974) found improved Block Design performance 1 year after treatment for those who stopped drinking, whereas those who continued drinking were unimproved. Templer et al. (1975) found no difference between subjects who had been abstinent for 1–18 years and controls on a Trail Making Test. Long and McLachlan (1974) seem to be the only ones who did not find any significant improvement on this test one year later.

Schau et al. (1980) found improved problem-solving abilities over a 1-year period, yet alcoholics performed somewhat worse than controls. Improvement was more pronounced in left than right hand performance on the TPT and on the Finger Tapping Test; similarly, the Block Design was clearly the most improved intelligence subtest. Page and Schaub (1977) reported data for groups tested at 1, 3, and 25 weeks. They found most of the improvement to have occurred during the third week, but their only significant results were derived from the TPT. They also found nondominant hand performance on the TPT to be quantitatively improved in contrast to the dominant hand. If this cannot be explained by practice effects, these findings might be considered to be consistent with the Berglund et al.'s (1982) observations of an initially more disturbed right hemisphere, normalizing in the course of some several weeks (see further discussion of the right hemisphere hypotheses below).

In the 1-year followup study of Adams et al. (1980), in which alcoholic subjects initially were unimpaired, the group of recently detoxified men did not improve, and in some cases were even more impaired. This was found in spite of reportedly moderate alcohol consumption. The authors suggested that when tested the first time the alcoholics might have been in a "latent" phase of an alcohol-related brain disorder, and that over the year this disorder evolved to a point where deficits became more apparent. Such a speculation fit into their more general model of the natural history of substance-abuse-related cerebral disorder (Grant et al., 1980). Equally plausible, however, is that Adams and associates' subjects drank more in the interim than they admitted, and were, therefore, more impaired on that basis.

Localization of Brain Disorder in Alcoholism

RIGHT HEMISPHERE HYPOTHESES. It is now several years since Jones and Parsons (1972) suggested that the right hemisphere might be more vulnerable to long-term alcohol exposure than the left. In view of the gross structural similarity of the two hemispheres of the brain, this was a new as well as intriguing hypothesis. Research, particularly by Jones, Parsons, and collaborators, has emphasized the prominent difficulties in visuo-spatial integration, disproportionately worse performance I.Q. than verbal I.Q., and impaired motor regulation of the left hand (Parsons, Tarter, and Edelberg, 1972). Further experimental support for the right hemisphere hypothesis is found in the rCBF study of Berglund et al. (1982) and in the NP followup studies of Schau et al. (1980) and Page and Schaub (1977), as discussed above. Kostandov et al. (1982) studied differences in left and right visual field perception and lateral evoked potentials and found that both nonalcoholics given alcohol, and abstinent alcoholics evidenced a slower processing rate in the right than in the left hemisphere.

There are some problems with the right hemisphere hypothesis. Tasks generally thought to be "right hemispheric" are not all specific to that brain region. Further, many of these tasks are inherently harder or more novel than "left" tasks—thus, what we might be measuring is selective difficulty which alcoholics experience on more demanding tests. Recovery for such functions also might take more time. Sex differences could play a role in view of the findings of Inglis and Lawson (1981) who demonstrated, on the basis of 14 studies in general neuropsychology, that men with left and right-sided lesions showed the expected verbal I.Q. and performance I.Q. deficits, while women did not show such a pattern. Silberstein and Parsons (1979), who found less impairment in alcoholic women on visuo-spatial and tactile-spatial tests, suggested that less lateralization in brain organization in women might explain their findings. Depression, which occurs frequently in alcoholics, has been shown to relate significantly to impaired performance I.Q. in alcoholics (Løberg, 1980b). Since many "right hemisphere" tests are timed, depression-related lack of motivation and psychomotor retardation might contribute to poor performance. Depression seems to be reduced during abstinence (Bean and Karasievich, 1975), and might explain some NP improvement during this phase.

Several additional studies are inconsistent with the right hemisphere hypothesis. Prigatano (1980) reported that men tested before disulfiram treatment had higher performance I.Q. than verbal I.Q., and Smith and Smith (1977) found the same for noncirrhotic male alcoholics. Adams et al. (1980) found practically the same level on performance and verbal I.Q.'s at initial testing both for recently detoxified and long-term abstinent male alcoholics, and a quantitatively higher performance I.Q. than verbal I.Q. for both groups 1 years later. The latter, may, of course, be due to the effect of practice on timed performance tests. O'Leary, Donovan, and Chaney (1977a) found performance I.Q. and verbal I.Q. to be equal in field-independent alcoholics. Fitzhugh et al. (1960, 1965) found quantitatively higher performance than verbal I.Q. in both studies of alcoholic male subjects. Furthermore, in one study (Løberg, 1980), motor speed was found to be slower in the dominant as compared to the nondominant hand; significantly more pronounced static tremor was found in the right hand.

FRONTO-LIMBIC-DIENCEPHALIC HYPOTHESIS. The hypothesis of a fronto-limbic diencephalic dysfunction has been advanced by Tarter (1975a, 1975b, 1976a, 1976b), suggesting that brain damage in alcoholism occurs particularly in the anterior and basal regions of the brain. If this axis is extended to include fronto-parietal regions, the brain stem and the vermis of the cerebellum, it is certainly compatible with structural and functional evidence of alcohol-related findings in intermediate and long-term alcoholism. Yet it is distinct from the hypothesis of lateralized and also diffuse damage. Tarter's hypothesis does reconcile pneumoencephalographic, CT, and pathological findings which generally show symmetrical lesions. Only one study (Golden et al., 1981) has suggested structural asymmetries, in this case less density in the left hemisphere. The known variability of densitometric measurements is sufficiently high to be cautious about the reliability of the Golden et al. findings. On the other hand, lack of CT support for brain asymmetry in alcoholism need not reject the right hemisphere hypothesis, since functional asymmetry is possible despite symmetric CT findings (and, conversely, patients are sometimes functionally intact despite clear CT abnormalities; see Lewin, 1980). Tarter suggests that the commonly observed deficits of alcoholics in categorizing or abstraction (in the absence of other severe impairment) is very consistent with selective frontal lobe dysfunction. The finding of Berglund and others that frontal regional blood flow was most clearly related to Block Design performance, may also imply that of the different brain systems relevant for such a task, frontal lobes play a significant part at least in the early abstinence phase in alcoholics.

Diffuse Injury Hypothesis

Available findings offer less support for the hypothesis of diffuse brain damage in alcoholism, considering the frequent suggestions of asymmetric impairment in higher mental functions. It has never been clearly stated whether diffuse means disseminated focal lesions or a uniform and consistent damage to all neurons. Although verbal perception, learning, and memory can be impaired in alcoholics, the general preservation of verbal intelligence is difficult to reconcile with the diffuse injury hypothesis. It is possible, however, that the usual neuropsychological tests are not as sensitive to left hemispheric dysfunction as they are to the right.

PREMATURE AGING AND ALCOHOLISM. Several studies of alcoholics have concluded that premature aging describes the characteristic deficits found, that the brain changes which occur are the same as those which take place in normal aging (Parsons and Leber, 1981). Blusewicz et al. (1977) and Nichols-Hochla and Parsons (1982) have investigated both male and female alcoholics and their results are representative of several other studies. Both showed that recently detoxified young alcoholics and elderly controls performed at a lower level than young controls; severe alcoholics were more similar to elderly controls than was the nonsevere group.

In contrast, Grant and associates (1984) found that whereas both recently abstinent alcoholic status and growing older were related to a decline in learning and problem solving, aging but not alcoholism was associated with reduction in psychomotor speed and attention. Furthermore, there were no alcohol by age interactions. These data cast some doubt on the premature aging mechanism, and recall the caution articulated by Nichols-Hochla and Parsons: "These end results, i.e., similarities in specific test performance, could be the result of quite different impairment in the complex processes determining impairment" (Nichols-Hochla and Parsons, 1982, p. 245.) It is easy to share this reservation, and from a rather general point of view. In several diseases we find that symptoms, signs, and intellectual or sensorimotor impairment are manifested in a manner similar to what we observe in the natural aging process. Take for instance Parkinson's or Alzheimer's disease—even patient appearance might be suggestive of the aging process. There are, however, specific neuropathological changes which, though they may be found to some extent in normal aging, are specific enough to make the diagnosis of these distinctive diseases possible (see Chapters 10 and 16). Similar neuropathological overlaps and distinctions might well be true of alcohol-related brain disease and aging.

Possible Premorbid Neuropsychological Vulnerability in Alcoholics

Difficulties in adapting to new situations and inflexibility in choosing the adequate approach based on feedback given, may be said to be measured by tests like the Category Test. This is a test where alcoholics in early and intermediate phases of alcoholism show impairment in spite of intact psychometric intelligence. To what extent is this a characteristic cognitive style in individuals who eventually will develop a dependency problem, and to what degree is it a consequence of alcohol consumption? There are reasons to suspect that a subgroup of alcoholics has a prealcoholic CNS vulnerability that might predispose to alcohol abuse and dependency. Tarter (1978) reported that severe and "essential" alcoholics had a history of hyperactivity (minimal brain dysfunction) twice as frequently as less severe and "reactive" alcoholics. This overrepresentation has also been found in other retrospective investigations. Children with Attention Deficit Disorders and hyperactivity based on Minimal Brain Dysfunction seen at our department evidenced neuropsychological deficits of varying types and also appeared to have a hypoactivated CNS as indicated by the skin conductance level. Improvement in problem behavior was seen when stimulants were administered. This was parallelled by an increase or normalizing of the skin conductance level (Kløve and Hole, 1979). Since these symptoms might continue into adulthood for a majority (Tarter, 1978), it may well be that symptoms like impulsivity, low frustration tolerance, emotional lability, and diminished sensitivity to reinforcement may contribute to the development of a dependency. Since alcohol has some general stimulant properties during the ascending limb of the blood-alcohol curve, it is possible that it serves as a self-medication initially, enhancing or modulating low or unstable CNS arousal levels. On the descending limb of the curve, it seems possible that the combination of the depressant effects of alcohol and a hypoaroused CNS can serve to enhance pre-existing problems.

Studying belligerent behavior in intoxication, I found violent alcoholics to be the most neuropsychologically impaired. These same patients showed a very deviant MMPI profile typical of a personality disorder of paranoid type. They were younger, drank more aggressively, and had more blackouts. Of particular importance is that they very frequently reported behavior problems in school and gave evidence of impulsive acting-out during childhood, however, their home backgrounds were frequently also characterized by neglect and abuse (Løberg, 1984).

A Danish prospective study in development (Knop, 1982), which followed up 9006 pregnancies from 1959 to 1961 may provide answers to the relationship between early biological risk factors and subsequent drinking patterns. High-risk subjects (sons with paternal alcoholism) performed poorer on the

Halstead Category Test and were more impulsive and restless. A subsample of these showed decreased average EEG alpha-activity as compared to low-risk subjects when given alcohol. Since some of these several thousand subjects are certainly going to develop alcohol dependency over the years to come, a prospective study of this type should provide several answers regarding premorbid risk factors for alcohol dependency and related impairment. Although existence of prealcoholic brain dysfunction in some alcoholics seems probable, the extent is not established. This possibility should cause us to reexamine previous inferences about the cause of neuropsychological dysfunction in alcoholics.

The Relationship of Neuropsychological Disturbance to Personality in Alcoholics

It is commonly thought that whereas neuropsychological change is a sequel of alcoholism, personality change predates abusive drinking. There has been little research to link various personality disturbances seen among alcoholics to neuropsychological functions nor to examine their temporal relationships.

Our own research confirms the work of others (Hoffman, 1976) that there is no uniform "alcoholic personality." At the same time we have shown that personality subtypes can be uncovered across treatment facilities and nations when populations are demographically similar and tested at the same stage of treatment. Figure 2 shows the very close correspondence between three different populations, even when the subtypes were derived through independent cluster analysis in each sample. Subtypes I–IV in the Norwegian sample showed an increasing magnitude of alcohol-related problems and neuropsychological impairment (Løberg, 1981). These data suggest that empirically derived personality clusters, in association with specific neuropsychological deficits, might help define unique typologies of alcoholics.

Conclusions

Excessive drinking over several years seems to be related to cognitive deficits, and it may be that even social drinkers' neuropsychological performance is related to amount consumed per recent occasion. The majority of studies show moderate neuropsychological impairment even when the diagnosis is not one of "alcohol dementia" or Wernicke-Korsakoff syndrome. Computerized tomography, pneumoencephalography and EEG studies also provide evidence for brain changes, but the neuropsychologic-neuroradiologic overlaps are disappointing. Very few neuropsychological or other neurodiagnostic studies provide evidence of unimpaired functioning in intermediate stages of alcoholism. Yet the fact seems established that an excessive, but uncomplicated drinking career of some 6 years can be compatible with unimpaired neuropsychological functioning. Personality disturbances are common in alcoholic patients during

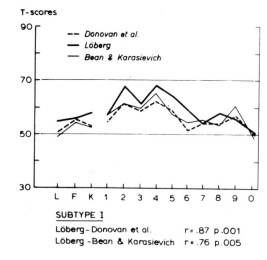

SUBTYPE I

Löberg - Donovan et al.   r = .87 p .001
Löberg - Bean & Karasievich   r = .76 p .005

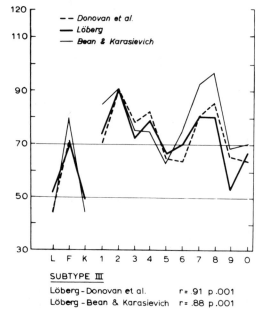

Fig. 2. MMPI subtypes: Comparison of the Donovan et al. four-cluster derived subtypes (program: UWBCL, iterative method, $N = 102$) and the Bean and Karasievich four-cluster derived subtypes (hierarchical grouping method, $N = 80$) with the Løberg four-cluster derived subtypes (program: CLUSTAN, hierarchical-agglomerative method, $N = 109$). Pearson correlation coefficients, two-tailed test of significance.

SUBTYPE III

Löberg - Donovan et al.   r = .91 p .001
Löberg - Bean & Karasievich   r = .88 p .001

treatment, and the degree and type of disorders may be related to neuropsychological performance. Based on evidence from blood flow studies and neuropsychological as well as CT studies, we may expect considerable recovery to occur. There is rapid NP improvement within 2–3 weeks and slower recovery thereafter. Blood flow studies further indicate that there is a period of at least 7 weeks when brain functions still are improving in the more impaired patients. CT studies suggest that there is a period of several months during which slight recovery takes place (Lishman, 1981). Some studies have reported a re-

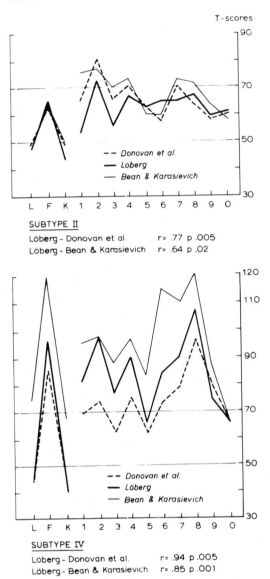

T-scores

SUBTYPE II

Löberg - Donovan et al.   r= .77 p .005
Löberg - Bean & Karasievich   r= .64 p .02

SUBTYPE IV

Löberg - Donovan et al.   r= .94 p .005
Löberg - Bean & Karasievich   r= .85 p .001

sidual impairment in neuropsychological followup of alcoholic patients after 1 year. One study noted decreased cognitive performance in a 1-year followup of patients who were initially unimpaired and who denied interim drinking. Subclinical or latent brain dysfunction has been suggested to account for this fact (Grant et al., 1980; Lishman, 1981). According to Lishman's hypothesis, a great number of alcoholics damage their brains quite early in their drinking career. With increasing age "this effect will couple readily with other pathologies—those of aging, trauma, vascular changes, hepatic dysfunction—and lead to more serious and irreversible change" (p. 51). Johanne-son, Berglund, and Ingvar (1982) found the most EEG abnormalities in the youngest and oldest alcoholics. They suggested that the adolescent brain is more sensitive to neurotoxic agents. An alternative explanation would be that these younger alcoholics are actually manifesting pre-existing Minimal Brain Dys-function, which appears to be associated with alcoholism in some cases. If this is the case, then some of the residual impairment found after years of absti-nence may be explained by a prealcoholic dysfunction.

That alcohol is neurotoxic is shown in laboratory animals (Riley and Walker, 1978; Walker et al., 1980). The existence of teratogenic effects of alcohol in humans as well as animals, and that these effects are dose-related, seem to be well documented (Streissguth et al., 1980), implying the vulnerability of the developing CNS. Not to implicate alcohol or its metabolites as neurotoxic agents in producing the brain lesions in adult alcoholics seems inappropriate. The mechanisms and agents through which damage occurs, however, may be mul-tiple. Greizerstein (1981) found a very high amount of congeners, or organic and inorganic compounds, other than ethanol in alcoholic beverages. This was true for wine, beer, and distilled spirits. Substances with very high toxicity, like acetaldehyde and methanol are abundant in wine, and both wine and beer can contain the toxic compound isopentanol. Findings like these indicate the need for further research on the effects of congeners on the brain.

The effects of head injuries related to intoxication may go unnoticed in se-vere alcoholics, being masked by, or mistaken for protracted abstinence reac-tions. On the other hand, statistics from several countries show the high inci-dence of intoxication in serious accidents. Presuming that quite a few of these individuals are excessive drinkers and that CNS damage frequently occurs, these individuals would then frequently be classified under a primarily neurological diagnosis. May this also be true of other brain disorders, to which alcohol may contribute? Hillbom and Kaste (1978) have described how alcohol intoxication may be a risk factor in ischemic brain infarction because cardiac arrhythmias during withdrawal can potentiate the formation of thrombi. Based on their findings, they suggested that ethanol intoxication increases the risk of brain infarction 2–3 times for men, 3–4 times for women. It has also been shown that even moderate doses of alcohol can produce increased sleep apnea with concurrent hypoxemia. This effect can persist two nights in some instances (Taasan et al., 1981). Chronic obstructive lung disease (COPD) also is related to breathing abnormalities and lowered blood oxygen during sleep. The com-bined effect of smoking and alcohol misuse certainly needs investigation, given recent evidence that COPD is itself associated with neuropsychological impair-ment (Grant et al., 1982).

Inpatient alcoholics frequently manifest emotional disturbances and have serious problems. In our own study, we found that problems with spouses, health, finances, work, friends, and the law were so extreme that the chance of finding similar problems in the general population was less than one in a thousand. In addition they are frequently neuropsychologically impaired.

The self-inflicted brain dysfunction that excessive long-term drinking may produce provides a good opportunity to study brain-behavior relations. Neuropsychologists are pursuing very interesting hypotheses about the anatomic and physiological substrates of this dysfunction, providing meaningful information on the individual patient in the process. Clinical neuropsychology posesses the tools to throw light on alcohol's effect on brain functions and may thus also contribute to our general understanding of brain and behavior.

REFERENCES

Acker, W. (1982). Objective psychological changes in alcoholics after the withdrawal of alcohol. *Br. Med. Bull.* 38; 95–98.

Adams, K. M., and Grant, I. (1984). Failure of nonlinear models of drinking history variables to predict neuropsychological performance in alcoholics. *Am. J. Psychiat., 141,* 663–667.

Adams, K. M., Brown, G. G., and Grant, I. (1985). Analysis of covariance as a remedy for demographic mismatch of research subject groups: Some sobering simulations. *J. Clin. and Experimental Neuropsychol., 1* 445–462.

Adams, K. M., Grant, I., and Reed, R., (1980). Neuropsychology of alcoholic men in their late thirties: One year follow-up. *Am. J. Psychiat., 137,* 928–931.

Ayers, J. L., Templer, D. I., Ruff, C. F., and Barthlow, V. L. (1978). Trail Making Test improvement in abstinent alcoholics. *J. Studies Alcohol, 39,* 1627–1629.

Bean, K. L; and Karasievich, G. O. (1975). Psychological test results at three stages of inpatient alcoholism treatment. *J. Studies Alcohol, 36,* 838–852.

Begleiter, H., Porjesz, B., and Tenner, M. (1980). Neuroradiological and neuropsychological evidence of brain deficits in chronic alcoholics. *Acta Psychiat. Scand., 62, (Suppl.)* 286, 3–13.

Berglund, M., Leijonquist, H., and Horlèn, M. (1977). Prognostic significance and reversibility of cerebral dysfunction in alcoholics. *J. Studies Alcohol, 38;* 1761–1770.

Berglund, M., and Risberg, J. (1980). Reversibility in alcohol dementia. In: H. Begleiter, ed. *Biological Effects of Alcohol.* New York: Plenum, pp. 787–796.

Berglund, M., Risberg, J., Bliding, A., Hagstadius, S., Johanson, M., and Mubrin, Z. (1982). Evidence of right hemisphere dysfunction in alcoholism. Presented at The First Nordic Neuropsychological Symposium. Helsinki, Finland.

Bergman, H., Bergman, I., Engelbrektson, K., Holm, L., Johanneson, K., and Lindberg, S. (1982). *Psykologhandboken (Handbook for Psychologists).* Stockholm: Magnus Huss Klinik, Karolinska Hospital.

Bergman, H., Borg, S., Hindmarsh, T., Idestrom, C. M., and Mutzell, S. (1980a). Computed tomography of the brain and neuropsychological assessment of alcoholic patients. In: H. Begleiter, ed. *Biological Effects of Alcohol.* New York: Plenum, p. 771–786.

Bergman, H., Borg, S., Hindmarsh, T., Idestrom, C. M., and Mutzell, S. (1980b). Computed tomography of the brain and neuropsychological assessment of male alcoholic patients and a random sample from the general male population. *Acta Psychiat. Scand., 62;* 77–88.

Blusewicz, M. J., Schenkenberg, T., Dustman, R. E., and Beck, E. C. (1977). WAIS performance in young alcoholic and elderly normal groups: An evaluation of organicity and mental aging indices. *J. Clin. Psychol. 33,* 1149–1153.

Brown, J., and Lyons, J. P. (1981). A progressive diagnostic schema for alcoholism with evidence for clinical efficacy. *Alcoholism: Clin. Exp. Res., 5;* 17–25.

Cahalan, D. (1978). Subcultural differences in drinking behavior in U.S. national surveys and selected European studies. In: P. E. Nathan, G. A. Marlatt, and T. Løberg, eds. *Alcoholism: New Directions in Behavioral Research and Treatment.* New York: Plenum.

Cala, L. A., Jones, B., Wiley, B., and Mastaglia, F. L. (1980). A computerized axial tomography (CAT) study of alcohol induced cerebral atrophy; in conjunction with other correlates. *Acta Psychiat. Scand., 62, (Suppl.)* 286, 31–40.

Carlen, P. L., and Wilkinson, D. A. (1980). Alcoholic brain damage and reversible deficits. *Acta Psychiat. Scand., 62,* 103–108.

Carlen, P. L., Wortzman, G., Holgate, R., Wilkinson, D. A., and Rankin, J. G. (1978). Reversible cerebral atrophy in recently abstinent chronic alcoholics measured by computed tomography scans. *Science, 200,* 1076–1078.

Chu, N. S., Squires, K. C., and Starr, A. (1982). Auditory brain stem responses in chronic alcoholic patients. *Electroencephalog. Clin. Neurophysiol., 54;* 418–425.

Clarke, J., and Haughton, H. (1975). A study of intellectual impairment and recovery rates in heavy drinkers in Ireland. *Br. J. Psychiat. 126;* 178–184.

Eckardt, M. J., Parker, E. S., Noble, E. P., Feldman, D. J., and Gottschalk, L. A. (1978). Relationship between neuropsychological performance and alcohol consumption in alcoholics. *Biol. Psychiat., 13,* 551–565.

Fabian, M. S., and Parsons, O. A. (1983). Differential improvement of cognitive functions in recovering alcoholic women. *J. Abnorm. Psychol., 92,* 87–95.

Fine, E. W., and Steer, R. A. (1979). Brain damage in early alcohol dependency. *Curr. Alcoholism, 5,* 251–256.

Fitzhugh, L. C., Fitzhugh, K. B., and Reitan, R. M. (1960). Adaptive abilities and intellectual functioning of hospitalized alcoholics. *Quart. J. Studies Alcohol, 21,* 414–423.

Fitzhugh, L. C., Fitzhugh, K. B., and Reitan, R. M. (1965). Adaptive abilities and intellectual functioning of hospitalized alcoholics: Further considerations. *Quart. J. Studies Alcohol, 26,* 402–411.

Garvin, R. B., Foy, D. W., and Alford, G. S. (1981). A critical examination of gamma glutamy, transpeptidase as a biochemical marker for alcohol abuse. *Addictive Behav., 6;* 377–383.

Gluud, C., Anderson, I., Dietrichson, O., Gluud, B., Jacobsen, A., and Juhl, E. (1981). Gamma-glutamyl transferase, asparate aminotransferase and alkaline phosphatase as markers of alcohol consumption in outpatient alcoholics. *Europ. J. Clin. Invest., 11,* 171–176.

Golden, C. J., Graber, B., Blose, I., Berg, R., Coffman, J., and Bloch, S. (1981). Differences in brain densities between chronic alcoholics and normal control patients. *Science, 211,* 508–510.

Goldstein, G. (1976). Perceptual and cognitive deficit in alcoholics. In: G. Goldstein and C. Neuringer, eds. *Empirical Studies of Alcoholism.* Cambridge, Mass.: Ballinger, p. 115–151.

Grant, I., Adams, K. M., Carlin, A. S., Rennick, P. M., Judd, L. L., and Schooff, K. (1978). The collaborative neuropsychological study of polydrug users. *Arch. General Psychiat., 35,* 1063–1074.

Grant, I., Adams, K., and Reed, R. (1979). Normal neuropsychological abilities of alcoholic men in their late thirties. *Am. J. Psychiat., 136,* 1263–1269. (a)

Grant, I., Adams, K. M., and Reed, R. (1984). Aging, abstinence and medical risk factors in the prediction of neuropsychological deficit amongst alcoholics. *Arch. General Psychiat., 41,* 710–718.

Grant, I., Heaton, R. K., McSweeny, J., Adams, K. M., and Timms, R. M. (1982). Neuropsychologic findings in hypoxemic chronic obstructive pulmonary disease. *Arch. Int. Med., 142,* 1470–1476.

Grant, I., and Mohns, L. (1975). Chronic cerebral effects of alcohol and drug abuse. *Int. J. Addictions, 10,* 883–920.

Grant, I., Mohns, L., Miller, M., and Reitan, R. M. (1976). A neuropsychological study of polydrug users. *Arch. General Psychiat., 33,* 973–978.

Grant, I., and Reed, R. (1985). Neuropsychology of alcohol and drug abuse. In: A. I. Alterman, ed. *Substance Abuse and Psychopathology.* New York: Plenum.

Grant, I., Reed, R., and Adams, K. M. (1980). Natural history of alcohol and drug-related brain disorder: Implications for neuropsychological research. *J. Clin. Neuropsychol.*, *2*, 321–331.

Grant, I., Reed, R., Adams, K. M., and Carlin, A. (1979). Neuropsychological functions in young alcoholics and polydrug abusers. *J. Clin. Neuropsychol.*, *1*, 39–47.

Greizerstein, H. (1981). Congener contents in alcoholic beverages. *J. Studies Alcohol*, *42*, 1030–1037.

Harper, C. (1979). Wernicke's encephalopathy) A more common disease than realized. A neuropathological study of 51 cases. *J. Neurol., Neurosurg. Psychiat.*, *42*, 226–231.

Heaton, R. K., Grant, I., Anthony, W. G., and Lehman, R. A. (1981). A comparison of clinical and automated interpretation of the Halstead-Reitan Battery. *J. Clin. Neuropsychol.*, *3*, 121–141.

Hester, R. K., Smith, J. W., and Jackson, T. R. (1980). Recovery of cognitive skills in alcoholics. *J. Studies Alcohol*, *41*, 363–367.

Hill, S. Y. (1980). Comprehensive assessment of brain dysfunction in alcoholic individuals. *Acta Psychiat. Scand.*, *60*, 57–75.

Hill, S. Y., and Mikhael, M. A. (1979). Computerized transaxial tomographic and neuropsychological evaluations in chronic alcoholics and heroin abusers. *Am. J. Psychiat.*, *136*, 598–602.

Hillbom, M., and Kaste, M. (1978). Does ethanol intoxication promote brain infarction in young adults? *Lancet*, 11:1181–1183.

Hoffman, H. (1976). Personality measurement for the evaluation and prediction of alcoholism. In: R. E. Tarter and A. A. Sugerman, eds. *Alcoholism: Interdisciplinary Approaches to an Enduring Problem*. Reading, Mass.: Addison-Wesley, pp. 309–358.

Inglis, J., and Lawson, J. S. (1981). Sex differences in the effects of unilateral brain damage on intelligence. *Science*, *212*, 693–695.

Johannesen, G., Berglund, M., and Ingvar, D. H. (1982). EEG abnormalities in chronic alcoholism related to age. *Acta Psychiat. Scand.*, *65*, 148–157.

Jones, M. K., and Jones, B. M. (1980). The relationship of age and drinking history to the effects of alcohol on memory in women. *J. Studies Alcohol*, *41*, 179–186.

Jones, B. M., and Parsons, O. A. (1971). Impaired abstracting ability in chronic alcoholics. *Arch. General Psychiat.*, *24*, 71–75.

Jones, B. M., and Parsons, O. A. (1972). Specific vs. generalized deficits of abstracting ability in chronic alcoholics. *Arch. General Psychiat.*, *26*, 380–384.

Kish, G. B., Hagen, J. M., Woody, M. M., and Harvey, H. L. (1980). Alcoholics' recovery from cerebral impairment as a function of duration of abstinence. *J. Clin. Psychol. 36*, 584–589.

Kleinknecht, R. A., and Goldstein, S. G. (1972). Neuropsychological deficits associated with alcoholism. *Quart. J. Studies Alcohol*, *33*, 999–1091.

Kløve, H. (1974). Validation studies in adult clinical neuropsychology. In: R. M. Reitan and L. A. Davison, eds. *Clinical Neuropsychology: Current Status and Applications*. New York: Wiley & Sons, pp. 211–235.

Kløve, H., and Hole, K. (1979). The hyperkinetic syndrome: Criteria for diagnosis. In: R. L. Trites, ed. *Hyperactivity in Children, Etiology Measurement and Treatment Implications*. Baltimore: University Park Press, pp. 121–137.

Knop, J. (1982). Biological variables in young males at high risk for alcoholism. *Acta Pharmacol. Toxicol.*, *51*, 31.

Kostandov, A., Arsumanov, Y. L., Genkina, O. A., Restchikova, T. N., and Shostakovich, G. S. (1982). The effects of alcohol on hemispheric functional asymmetry. *J. Studies Alcohol*, *43*, 411–426.

Kroll, P., Seigel, R., O'Neill, B., and Edwards, R. P. (1980). Cerebral cortical atrophy in alcoholic men. *J. Clin. Psychiat.*, *41*, 417–421.

Lewin, R. (1980). Is your brain really necessary? *Science*, *210*, 1232–1234.

Lishman, W. A. (1981). Cerebral disorder in alcoholism: Syndromes of impairment. *Brain*, *104*, 1–20.

Løberg, T. (1980a). Alcohol misuse and neuropsychological deficits in men. *J. Studies Alcohol,* *41,* 119–128.

Løberg, T. (1980b). Neuropsychological deficits in alcoholics: Lack of personality (MMPI) correlates. In: H. Begleiter, ed. *Biological Effects of Alcohol.* New York: Plenum, pp. 797–808.

Løberg, T. (1981). MMPI-based personality subtypes of alcoholics: Relationships to drinking history, psychometrics and neuropsychological deficits. *J. Studies Alcohol, 42,* 766–782.

Løberg, T. (1984). Belligerence in alcohol dependence. *Scand. J. Psychol., 51,* 32.

Long, J. A., and McLachlan, J. F. C. (1974). Abstract reasoning and perceptual-motor efficiency in alcoholics: Impairment and reversibility. *Quart. J. Studies Alcohol, 35,* 1220–1229.

MacVane, J., Butters, N., Montgomery, K., and Farber, J. (1982). Cognitive functioning in men social drinkers. *J. Studies Alcohol, 43,* 81–95.

Manson, M. P. (1949). The Alcadd Test. Beverly Hills: Western Psychological Service.

Marlatt, G. A. (1976). The Drinking Profile: A questionnaire for the behavioral assessment of alcoholism. In: E. J. Mash and L. G. Terdal, eds. *Behavioral Therapy Assessment: Design and Evaluation.* New York: Springer.

Matthews, C. G., Shaw, D. J., and Kløve, H. (1966). Psychological test performance in neurologic and "pseudoneurologic" subjects. *Cortex, 2,* 244–253.

McLachlan, J. F. C., and Levinson, T. (1974). Improvement in WAIS Block Design performance as a function of recovery from alcoholism. *J. Clin. Psychol., 30,* 65–66.

Miller, W. R. (1976). Alcoholism scales and objective assessment methods: A review. *Psychol. Bull., 83,* 649–674.

Miller, W. R., and Orr, J. (1980). Nature and sequence of neuropsychological deficits in alcoholics. *J. Studies Alcohol, 41,* 325–337.

Miller, W. R., and Saucedo, C. F. *(in press).* Neuropsychological impairment and brain damage in problem drinking. *J. Stud. Alcohol.*

Mulford, H. A., and Miller, D. E. (1960). Drinking in Iowa: Preoccupation with alcohol and definitions of alcohol, heavy drinking and trouble due to drinking. *Quart. J. Studies Alcohol, 21,* 279–291.

Nichols-Hochla, N. A., and Parsons, O. A. (1982). Premature aging in female alcoholics: A neuropsychological study. *J. Nerv. Ment. Dis., 170,* 241–245.

O'Leary, M. R., Donovan, D. M., and Chaney, E. F. (1977a). The relationship of perceptual field orientation to measures of cognitive functioning and current adaptive abilities in alcoholics and nonalcoholics. *J. Nerv. Ment. Dis., 165,* 275–282.

O'Leary, M. R., Radford, L. M., Chaney, E. F., and Schau, E. J. (1977b). Assessment of cognitive recovery in alcoholics by use of the Trail Making Test. *J. Clin. Psychol., 33,* 579–582.

Page, R. D., and Linden, J. D. (1974). "Reversible" organic brain syndrome in alcoholics: A psychometric evaluation. *Quart. J. Studies Alcohol, 35,* 98–107.

Page, R. D., and Schaub, L. H. (1977). Intellectual functioning in alcoholics during six months' abstinence. *J. Studies Alcohol, 38,* 1240–1246.

Parker, E. S. (1982). Comments on "Cognitive functioning in men social drinkers: A replication study." *J. Studies Alcohol, 43,* 170–177.

Parker, E. S., Birnbaum, I. M., Boyd, R., and Noble, E. P. (1980). Neuropsychological decrements as a function of alcohol intake in male students. *Alcoholism: Clin. Exp. Res., 4,* 330–334.

Parker, E. S., and Noble, E. P. (1977). Alcohol consumption and cognitive functioning in social drinkers. *J. Studies Alcohol, 38,* 1224–1232.

Parsons, O. A. (1975). Brain damage in alcoholics: Altered states of unconsciousness. In: M. M. Gross, ed. *Alcohol Intoxication and Withdrawal.* New York: Plenum, pp. 569–584.

Parsons, O. A. (1977). Neuropsychological deficits in alcoholics: Facts and fancies. *Alcoholism: Clin. Exp. Res., 1,* 51–56.

Parsons, O. A., and Fabian, M. S. (1982). Comments on "Cognitive functioning in men social drinkers: A replication study." *J. Studies Alcohol, 43*, 178–182.

Parsons, O. A., and Farr, S. D. (1981). The neuropsychology of alcohol and drug use. In: S. B. Filskov and T. J. Boll, eds., *Handbook of Clinical Neuropsychology.* New York: John Wiley and Sons, pp. 320–365.

Parsons, O. A., and Leber, W. R. (1981). The relationship between cognitive dysfunction and brain damage in alcoholics: Causal, interactive or epiphenomenal? *Alcoholism: Clin. Exp. Res., 5,* 326–343.

Parsons, O. A., Tarter, R. E., and Edelberg, R. (1972). Altered motor control in chronic alcoholics. *J. Abnorm. Psychol., 72,* 308–314.

Prigatano, G. P. (1980). Neuropsychological functioning of recidivist alcoholics treated with disulfiram: A followup report. *Int. J. Addictions, 15,* 287–294.

Reitan, R. (1964). Psychological deficits resulting from cerebral lesions in man. In: J. M. Warren and K. Akert, eds. *The Frontal Granular Cortex and Behavior.* New York: McGraw-Hill, pp. 295–312.

Reitan, R. M., and Davison, L. A. (1974). *Clinical Neuropsychology: Current Status and Applications.* New York: John Wiley and Sons.

Riley, J. N., and Walker, D. W. (1978). Morphological alterations in hippocampus after long-term alcohol consumption in mice. *Science, 201,* 646–648.

Ron, M. A. (1979). Organic psychosyndromes in chronic alcoholics. *Br. J. Addiction, 74,* 353–358.

Ron, M. A. (1983). The alcoholic brain: CT scan and psychological findings. *Psychological Medicine: Monograph Supplement 3.* Cambridge: Cambridge University Press.

Russell, E. W., Neuringer, C., and Goldstein, G. (1970). *Assessment of Brain Damage: A Neuropsychological Key Approach.* New York: Wiley-Interscience.

Ryan, C. J., and Butters, N. (1982). Cognitive effects in alcohol abuse. In: B. Kissin and H. Begleiter, eds., *Biology of Alcoholism, vol. VI: Biological Pathogenesis of Alcoholism.* New York: Plenum.

Schau, E. J., O'Leary, M. R., and Chaney, E. F. (1980). Reversibility of cognitive deficit in alcoholics. *J. Studies Alcohol, 41,* 733–740.

Selzer, M. L. (1971). The Michigan Alcoholism Screening Test: The quest for a new diagnostic instrument. *Am. J. Psychiat., 127,* 1653–1658.

Sharp, J. R., Rosenbaum, G., Goldman, M. S., and Whitman, R. D. (1977). Recoverability of psychological functioning following alcohol abuse: Acquisition of meaningful synonyms. *J. Consult. Clin. Psychol., 45,* 1023–1028.

Silberstein, J. A., and Parsons, O. A. (1979). Neuropsychological impairment in female alcoholics. *Curr. Alcohol., 7,* 481–495.

Smith, H. H., and Smith, L. S. (1977). WAIS functioning in cirrhotic and noncirrhotic alcoholics. *J. Clin. Psychol., 33,* 309–313.

Stockwell, T., Hodgson, R., Edwards, G., Taylor, C., and Rankin, H. (1979). The development of a questionnaire to measure severity of alcohol dependence. *Br. J. Addiction, 74,* 79–87.

Streissguth, A. P., Landesman-Dwyer, S., Martin, J. C., and Smith, D. W. (1980). Teratogenic effects of alcohol in humans and laboratory animals. *Science, 209,* 353–361.

Taasan, V. C., Block, A. J., Boysen, P. G., and Wynne, J. W. (1981). Alcohol increases sleep apnea and oxygen desaturation in asymptomatic men. *Am. J. Med., 71,* 240–245.

Tarter, R. E. (1973). An analysis of cognitive deficits in chronic alcoholics. *J. Nerv. Ment. Dis., 157,* 138–147.

Tarter, R. E. (1975a). Brain damage associated with chronic alcoholics. *Dis. Nerv. System, 36,* 185–187.

Tarter, R. E. (1975b). Psychological deficit in chronic alcoholics: A review. *Int. J. Addictions, 10,* 327–368.

Tarter, R. E. (1976a). Empirical investigations of psychological deficits. In: R. E. Tarter and

A. A. Sugerman, eds. *Alcoholism: Interdisciplinary Approaches to an Enduring Problem.* Reading, Mass.: Addison-Wesley, pp. 359–394.

Tarter, R. E. (1976b). Neuropsychological investigations of alcoholism. In: G. Goldstein and C. Neuringer, eds. *Empirical Studies of Alcoholism.* Cambridge, Mass.: Ballinger, pp. 231–256.

Tarter, R. E. (1978). Etiology of alcoholism: Interdisciplinary integration. In: P. E. Nathan, G. A. Marlatt, and T. Lorberg, eds. *Alcoholism: New Directions in Behavioral Research and Treatment.* New York: Plenum, pp. 41–70.

Tarter, R. E., McBride, H., Buonpane, N., and Schneider, D. U. (1977). Differentiation of alcoholics. *Arch. General Psychiat., 34,* 761–768.

Templer, D. I., Ruff, C. F., and Simpson, K. (1975). Trail Making Test performance of alcoholics abstinent at least a year. *Int. J. Addictions, 10,* 609–612.

Torvik, A., and Lindboe, C. F. (1982). Hjerneforandringer hos alkoholikere (Brain lesions in alcoholics). *J. Norwegian Med. Assoc., 102,* 638–642.

Trites, R. L. (1981). *Neuropsychological Manual.* Montreal: Technolab.

Walker, D. W., Barnes, D. E., Zornetzer, S. F., Hunter, B. E., and Kubanis, P. (1980). Neuronal loss in hippocampus induced by prolonged ethanol consumption in rats. *Science, 209,* 711–712.

Wanberg, K. W., Horn, J. L., and Foster, F. M. (1977). A differential assessment model for alcoholism: The scales of the Alcohol Use Inventory. *J. Studies Alcohol, 38,* 512–543.

Wilkinson, D. A., and Carlen, P. L. (1980). Relation of neuropsychological test performance in alcoholics to brain morphology measured by computed tomography. In: H. Begleiter, ed. *Biological Effects of Alcohol.* New York: Plenum, pp. 683–700.

19

The Alcoholic Wernicke-Korsakoff Syndrome and Its Relationship to Long-term Alcohol Abuse

JASON BRANDT / NELSON BUTTERS

Description of Wernicke's Disorder

In 1881, Carl Wernicke described in three patients (two male alcoholics and one woman with sulfuric acid poisoning) a neurolgical syndrome that included ataxia, optic abnormalities, and a confusional state. Postmortem examination of these three patients showed small punctate hemorrhages symmetrically located in the gray matter around the third and fourth ventricles of the brains. Wernicke characterized the disorder, which now bears his name, as an acute inflammatory disease of the ocular-motor nuclei, and noted that the symptoms were progressive and led to death in approximately 2 weeks. Six years after the publication of Wernicke's paper, S. S. Korsakoff published the first of a series of reports in which he detailed the amnesic and confabulatory symptoms that often accompanied disorders involving polyneuropathy. While long-term alcoholism often preceded these mental changes, Korsakoff noted that the symptoms also followed a number of other conditions, such as persistent vomiting, typhoid fever, and intestinal obstruction. On the basis of these observations, he concluded that the presence of a substance toxic to the peripheral and central nervous systems must have been the common denominator in his reported cases. Although neither Wernicke nor Korsakoff could be specific with regard to etiology, and both seemed unaware that their two syndromes often occurred sequentially in the same patients, their clinical descriptions of their patients' symptomatology were accurate and represented important initial steps in identifying and understanding the Wernicke-Korsakoff syndrome.

The major symptoms of the Wernicke stage include a global confusional state, opthalmoplegia, nystagmus, ataxia, and a polyneuropathy (e.g., pain, loss of sensation, weakness) of the legs and arms (Victor, Adams, and Collins, 1971). Of these neurological symptoms, the global confusional state is perhaps most germane to our interests. The patient is disoriented with regard to time and place, is unable to recognize familiar people, is apathetic, inattentive, and most significantly, is unable to maintain a coherent conversation.

If a patient with Wernicke's encephalopathy is not treated with large doses of thiamine, he is in danger of sustaining fatal midbrain hemorrhages. If, however, the patient does receive proper vitamin therapy, his neurological symptoms will evidence marked improvement. In most cases, the ocular problems will almost disappear, the ataxia and peripheral neuropathies will improve, and the confusional state will clear. That is, after 2 or 3 weeks of thiamine treatment, the patient will realize that he is in a hospital, recognize his wife and children, and be able to maintain an intelligible conversation with his physician. At this point, the patient has passed the acute Wernicke phase and has entered the chronic Korsakoff state. Very few (about 25%) Wernicke patients show a complete recovery to their premorbid intellectual state (Victor et al., 1971).

Anterograde Amnesia in Korsakoff's Syndrome

The alcoholic Korsakoff patient's anterograde amnesia is the most striking feature of his disorder. He is unable to learn new verbal and nonverbal information from the time of onset of his illness. Learning the name of his physician, nurses, the name of the hospital, and even the location of his bed, may require weeks or months of constant repetition and rehearsal. Events that occurred hours or even minutes before will be lost to the amnesic individual. Not only does he fail to learn the names of important people and places, often he will not remember previous encounters with them. If the patient spends 3 hours completing a number of psychometric tasks, he will fail to recall the entire test session 2 hours later. Experimentally, this severe anterograde problem is exemplified by the severe difficulty the Korsakoff patient has in learning even short lists of five or six paired-associates (Ryan and Butters, 1980a; Winocur and Weiskrantz, 1976). When the alcoholic Korsakoff patient is shown a list of word pairs (e.g., man–hammer) in which he must learn to associate the second word with the first, the acquisition of these associations may require 30 or 40 trials instead of the three or four presentations needed by intact subjects.

Since the publication of Talland's (1965) monograph, the vast majority of neuropsychological studies concerned with alcoholic Korsakoff's syndrome have centered upon the processes underlying this dense inability to learn new information. (For recent reviews, see Butters and Cermak, 1980, and Hirst, 1982.) With the exception of two studies (Baddeley and Warrington, 1970; Mair, Warrington, and Weiskrantz, 1979), investigators have consistently found that alcoholics with Korsakoff's syndrome are impaired in short-term memory or in the transfer of information from short- to long-term memory (see e.g., Butters and Cermak, 1974, 1975; Kinsbourne and Wood, 1975; Meudell, Butters, and Montgomery, 1978; Piercy, 1977). If the alcoholic Korsakoff patient is presented (visually or orally) with three words (e.g., apple, pen, roof) and then required to count backward from 100 by three's to prevent rehearsal (i.e., a distractor task), he will display impairments in the recall of the three words after only 9 or 18 seconds of interpolated activity. Similarly, the Korsakoff patient is unable to retain nonverbal materials (e.g., geometric patterns) for 18 seconds if a demanding distractor activity intervenes between presentation and recognition testing (DeLuca, Cermak, and Butters, 1975).

The inability of alcoholic Korsakoff patients to retain information when distractors are used to prevent rehearsal exemplifies one of the most prominent features of their anterograde amnesia, i.e., their increased sensitivity to interference. Numerous investigations have reported that alcoholics with Korsakoff's syndrome are unable to acquire new information because of interference from previously learned materials (i.e., proactive interference). The evidence for this interference phenomenon stems from three sources: (1) the nature of the Korsakoff patient's errors on learning tasks (Meudell et al., 1978), (2) demonstrations of normal performance when partial information is provided at the time of retrieval (Warrington and Weiskrantz, 1970), and (3) demonstrations of improved retention when the learning conditions are structured to reduce proactive interference (Butters and Cermak, 1975). As noted previously, Korsakoff patients are severely impaired on short-term memory tasks which limit rehearsal, but this impairment is not manifested in an equivalent manner throughout the test session. On early trials of the session, patients will often perform normally, but their recall will deteriorate very rapidly on subsequent trials. It has been shown that Korsakoff patients may recall as much as 90% of the presented materials on the first and second trials but may recall less than 50% of the information shown on the fifth trial of the session (Cermak, Butters, and Moreines, 1974). This rapid drop in performance seems related to a rapid increment in proactive interference. On trial 5 the patient is still recalling the material presented on trials 1 and 2. These intra-list intrusions suggest that the learning of material on trials 1 and 2 is hindering the attempt to recall the stimuli from trial 5. Meudell et al. (1978) compared the types of errors made by Korsakoff patients, demented patients with Huntington's disease, and normal control subjects on a short-term memory distractor task. Although both the Korsakoff and the demented patients made numerous errors on the test, they differed significantly in the types of errors they produced. The alcoholic Korsakoff patients' errors were primarily intrusions from prior list items, while the patients with Huntington's disease made many omission errors (that is, failures to respond).

With methods of retrieval that reduce interference, the performance of alcoholic Korsakoff patients may not differ from that of intact normal controls. Warrington and Weiskrantz (1970) have shown that while amnesics are severely impaired when unaided recall or recognition tests are employed, they do retrieve normally when partial information, such as the first two letters of to-be-remembered words, is provided. Warrington and Weiskrantz (1973) believe that the superiority of the partial information method stems from the limitations it places on interference from previously learned information. If the first two letters of the to-be-called word are "st", the number of words that can possibly interfere with the recall of the target word "stamp" are greatly limited. Apparently, free recall and recognition procedures do not limit proactive interference to the same degree that the method of partial information does.

It is well known from the literature on normal human memory that proactive interference may be reduced by specific manipulations of the conditions under which learning is attempted. For example, distributed practice results in less interference than does massed practice. Also, a consonant trigram (e.g., J-R-N) will interfere less with the retention of a word triad (e.g., rose-ship-camel) than will another word triad (e.g., tulip-car-horse). When the distractor task was administered with distributed (1 minute rests between successive trials) rather than massed (6 seconds between trials) presentation to alcoholic Korsakoff patients, patients with Huntington's disease, and alcoholic controls, the Korsakoff patients and the controls showed significant improvements in their performance (Butters et al., 1976). In fact, the Korsakoff patients recalled as many items with distributed practice as the controls did with massed practice. However, this reduction in interference (via distribution of trials) had no effect upon the memory deficits of the patients with Huntington's disease; they performed as poorly with distributed as with massed practice. Almost identical results have been found when a word triad was preceded by a consonant trigram rather than another word triad (Butters et al., 1976). Again, low interference conditions led to improvement in the short-term memory of alcoholic Korsakoff patients and normal controls but to no change in the poor performances of patients with Huntington's disease.

Warrington and Weiskrantz have been content to accept, and have indeed championed, an interference-retrieval model of amnesia (but cf. Warrington and Weiskrantz 1982). Other investigators, however, have viewed such retrieval-interference theories as primarily descriptive rather than explanatory (Piercy, 1977) and have offered specific hypotheses to account for both the patients' retention and interference problems. Butters and Cermak (1980) have suggested that the Korsakoff patient's verbal memory impairment is related to a failure to encode, at the time of storage, all of the attributes of the stimulus. Korsakoff patients may fully categorize verbal information according to phonemic and associative attributes, but they seem inadequate in their analyses of semantic features of the materials. Similarly, when confronted with photographs of unfamiliar faces, Korsakoff patients may analyze or focus upon some superficial feature (e.g., hair style or color) rather than upon the configurational aspects of the faces (i.e., the relationship among the eyes, nose, and mouth) (Biber et al., 1981; Dricker et al., 1978). Information that is not fully analyzed (encoded) may be stored in a degraded fashion and thus be more sensitive to interference and more difficult to retrieve. Some evidence supporting this conclusion stems from cueing studies in which phonemic (e.g., rhymes) and semantic (e.g., superordinate) cues were compared in terms of their ability to facilitate recall. In general, phonemic cues worked as well for alcoholic Korsakoff patients as for controls, but semantic cues only aided the recall of the control subjects (Butters and Cermak, 1980).

The most convincing evidence for the limited encoding theory has emanated from "orientation" studies which have attempted to induce Korsakoff patients to analyze more completely verbal stimuli (Cermak and Reale, 1978; McDowall, 1979) and nonverbal stimuli (Biber et al., 1981; Mayes, Meudell, and Neary, 1980) that must be recognized at a later time. Cermak and Reale (1978), utilizing a technique developed by Craik and Tulving (1975), attempted to ameliorate the alcoholic Korsakoff patient's verbal learning defect with orientation tasks that forced subjects to analyze and judge the semantic attributes of sequentially presented words. The basic premise was that the higher the level of encoding a subject is required to perform on a word, the greater the probability that he will remember the word on a subsequent unannounced recognition test. For each word presented, a question was asked which required the subjects to process on one of three levels: (1) a shallow orthographic level, e.g., "Is this (word) printed in upper case letters?"; (2) a phonemic level, e.g., "Does this (word) rhyme with fat?"; and (3) a semantic level, e.g., "Does this (word) fit into the following sentence_____?". Following the presentation of the entire series of questions, the patients were administered a recognition test to determine how many of the exposed words could be correctly identified.

In one experiment in which a 60-word stimulus list and a 180-word recognition test were divided into a series of short encoding and recognition tasks, Cermak and Reale (1978) found evidence that was at least partially consistent with the semantic encoding hypothesis. Although the alcoholic Korsakoff patients were still impaired under all encoding conditions, they did benefit from the semantic orientation task. The Korsakoff patients' best recognition occurred for the semantically encoded words, their poorest recognition for the words that had been associated with orthographic questions. Unfortunately, Cermak and Reale did not find that their semantic orientation task had a differentially greater effect upon alcoholic Korsakoff patients than upon their control subjects. In a more recent report, McDowall (1979) employed an orientation procedure similar to Cermak and Reale's and found that his Korsakoff patients did benefit more from a semantic orientation task than did his alcoholic control subjects.

Biber et al. (1981), using an orientation procedure in an attempt to improve face recognition, reported evidence that is consistent with the limited encoding hypothesis. Patients with alcoholic Korsakoff's syndrome, patients with a progressive dementia (Huntington's disease), patients with damage confined to the right cerebral hemisphere, and normal control subjects were administered a face recognition task under three experimental conditions that presumably induced different levels of facial analysis. The recognition scores of the Korsakoff patients, but not those of the other two patient groups, improved significantly following a "high-level" orientation task requiring the

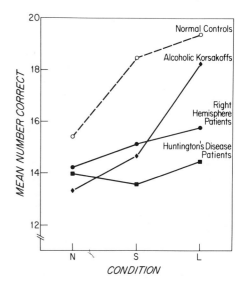

Fig. 1. Mean number of items correctly identified on the facial recognition test by each subject group. N = size-of-nose judgments; S = free study; L = likeability judgments. (From Biber et al., 1981.)

subjects to judge the likeability of the to-be-remembered faces. Under baseline conditions (i.e., no orientation task), normal controls appeared spontaneously to encode faces in a manner induced by the "high-level" task, whereas Korsakoff patients employed strategies consistent with the "low-level" orientation task (judgment of nose size). These findings, shown in Fig. 1, closely parallel those reported by McDowall (1979) using verbal materials and a semantic orientation task.

Although Biber et al.'s (1981) findings seem to support the limited encoding hypothesis, their data can also be explained by motivational-arousal concepts. Several investigators have remarked on the passivity and lack of initiative of alcoholic Korsakoff patients (Oscar-Berman, 1980; Talland, 1965; Victor et al., 1971) and have suggested that reduced motivation may contribute to the patients' severe learning and memory problems. Oscar-Berman and her collaborators (Oscar-Berman, Sahakian, and Wikmark, 1976; Oscar-Berman, 1980), who adapted methods borrowed from animal learning studies, have reported that alcoholic Korsakoff patients evidence reduced responsiveness to the effects of positive reinforcement. When confronted with a two-choice spatial probability learning test in which the two spatial alternatives were reinforced on a 70:30 or 30:70 ratio, normal controls altered their response tendencies to match the reinforcement contingencies. In marked contrast to the flexibility of the normals' behavior, the alcoholics with Korsakoff's syndrome continued to respond to each spatial alternative 50% of the time and seemed totally unaffected by the prevailing reinforcement contingencies (Oscar-Berman et al., 1976). In a second experiment (Oscar-Berman et al., 1980), alcoholic Korsakoff patients and normal controls were placed on a complex concurrent variable schedule of reinforcement. As with the spatial probability learning test, the responding of the normal controls, but not that of the Korsakoff patients, matched the reinforcement contingencies present in the experimental situation. In view of such demonstrations of motivational anomalies in alcoholic Korsakoff patients, Oscar-Berman (1980) has urged caution in explaining all of their memory deficits strictly from a cognitive perspective. For example, in Biber et al.'s (1981) study, the process of making a likeability judgment ("high-level" orientation task) may have motivational as well as cognitive consequences, and the significant improvement in the memory of Korsakoff patients following these judgments may reflect some form of affective-motivational arousal.

While interference-retrieval and limited encoding theories have dominated the alcoholic Korsakoff literature during the past 12 years, other investigators (Huppert and Piercy, 1976; Kinsbourne and Wood, 1975; Winocur and Kinsbourne, 1978; Winocur, Kinsbourne, and Moscovitch, 1981) have suggested that such memory deficits reflect a specific failure to encode the contextual attributes of new information. That is, alcoholic Korsakoff patients may be able to encode many specific physical or semantic attributes of a stimulus but fail to note the temporal and spatial contexts in which the stimulus was encountered. As a consequence of this deficit, these patients may later recognize the stimulus as familiar but be unable to "recall" when or where they experienced the stimulus. This hypothesis is consistent with the often-noted clinical observation that alcoholic Korsakoff patients can accurately select from a room full of people individuals they have seen before but are unable to recall under what circumstances the interaction occurred. Huppert and Piercy (1976) have provided some experimental evidence for this hypothesis. They presented Korsakoff patients and control subjects with a series of familiar and unfamiliar pictures and later asked them to select the ones that had been exposed previously. While the alcoholic Korsakoff patients were impaired for both familiar and unfamiliar pictures, their performance was much better with the unfamiliar pictures. The investigators believe that this disparity in performance was due to the fact that familiar, but not unfamiliar, pictures require the patients to make a contextual judgment. For the correct identification of an unfamiliar stimulus the Korsakoff patient only has to determine whether he has, or has not, seen the picture before. However, for correct identification of a familiar picture the patient must not only determine that he has seen the picture previously (i.e., that it is familiar) but also whether the familiar picture had been included in the series administered by the investigator. The patients' errors with the familiar pictures were largely false-positive responses, suggesting an inability to associate the pictures with the testing context.

Winocur and Kinsbourne (1978) have supplied additional evidence for this contextual encoding theory. Amnesic patients were required to learn lists of verbal paired-associates under conditions which maximized the interference between successive lists (e.g., both lists contained the same stimulus but different response elements). While this proactive interference made learning almost impossible for the Korsakoff patients, their performance could be greatly improved by increasing the saliency (e.g., use of different colored inks, background music) of the contextual cues in the learning environment.

Winocur et al. (1981) have suggested that the alcoholic Korsakoff patients' inability to discriminate contexts also results in their tendency not to demonstrate release from proactive interference (Cermak et al., 1974). Korsakoff patients and normal subjects were asked to recall successive lists of nine nouns drawn from the same taxonomic category (e.g., occupations, body parts, sports). In the non-shift (i.e., control) condition, the same category of nouns was used for five successive lists. In the shift (i.e., experimental) condition, a new taxonomic category (e.g., sports) was introduced on the fifth list after a single category (e.g., body parts) had been employed on the first four lists. Both the alcoholics with Korsakoff's syndrome and the control subjects demonstrated progressive decrements in performance over the five lists in the no-shift condition. When no effort was made to increase the contextual saliency between the fourth and fifth lists in the shift condition, only the normal control subjects evidenced a significant improvement in performance on the fifth (shift) list. However, if the subjects were provided with an instructional set warning them of the impending taxonomic change, or if the words comprising the fourth and fifth lists were printed in inks of different color, the alcoholic Korsakoff patients also recalled more words on the fifth than on the fourth list (i.e., release from proactive interference). On the basis of these findings, Winocur et al. (1981) concluded that the alcoholic Korsakoff patient's failure to release from proactive interference is not due to a deficit in semantic encoding (Cermak et al., 1974), but rather to an inability to contextually discriminate the words comprising the fourth and fifth lists.

At this point it is important to consider Moscovitch's (1982) contention that Korsakoff patients' failure to release from proactive interference may be an indicator of frontal lobe damage rather than a phenomenon closely linked to their anterograde amnesia. Like amnesic Korsakoff patients, nonamnesic patients with damage to the prefrontal cortex failed to release from proactive interference following taxonomic shifts (Moscovitch, 1982). When this finding is combined with Winocur et al.'s (1981) demonstration of the importance of contextual factors in release from proactive interference, it follows that impairment in the retrieval of contextual cues may be more pertinent to the Korsakoff patients' cognitive problems due to frontal lobe atrophy (see section on neuropathology) than to their anterograde amnesia. Milner's (1971) report that the left and right frontal lobes are involved in the "time-tagging" and temporal ordering of verbal and nonverbal materials, respectively, lends credence to this interpretation. Nonamnesic patients with unilateral frontal lobectomies were able to make successful identity (i.e., familiarity) judgments concerning verbal and nonverbal materials but were unable to judge which of two familiar (i.e., previously exposed) stimuli had been seen most recently.

In recent years there has been an increasing interest in exploring those memory capacities of Korsakoff patients that remain relatively intact despite the global amnesic state. One series of studies has focused upon the forgetting of newly acquired pictorial information by patients with diencephalic and hippocampal lesions. The diencephalic subjects have been patients with alcoholic Korsakoff's syndrome (see section on neuropathology) and patient N.A. who suffered a traumatic injury to the medial thalamus of the left hemisphere (Squire and Moore, 1979). The role of the hippocampus in forgetting has been evaluated by intensive study of Scoville and Milner's (1957) patient H.M. who developed a global amnesia following bilateral ablation of the mesial temporal region to treat a life-threatening epileptic condition (Milner, 1966, 1970).

Huppert and Piercy (1977, 1978, 1979) have reported that when patient H.M., patients with alcoholic Korsakoff's syndrome, and normal control subjects attain the same level of initial learning, important differences emerge in their rates of forgetting over a 7-day period. To insure that all subjects would attain approximately the same level of learning after a 10-minute delay period, exposure time during the initial presentation of the pictures was manipulated to insure a performance level of at least 75% correct. The results of these studies showed that although H.M., normal subjects, and alcoholic Korsakoff patients all performed more poorly on recognition tasks with increasing retention intervals (1 day, 7 days), H.M.'s performance revealed a much steeper rate of forgetting than did the scores of the other two groups. Indeed, the rates of forgetting of the alcoholic Korsakoff patients and the normal controls were indistinguishable. Based on these data, Huppert and Piercy suggest that the anterograde amnesias of H.M. and Korsakoff patients involve different deficits in information processing. While the Korsakoff patient's learning difficulties may emanate from a slowness in stimulus analysis, H.M.'s rapid forgetting of newly acquired materials may be an indicator of a problem with consolidation and storage.

Squire (1981) evaluated patient N.A., alcoholic Korsakoff patients, and depressed patients receiving bilateral ECT on pictorial (and verbal) forgetting tasks in which recognition was assessed after 10-minute, 2-hour, and 32-hour delays. His results are consistent with those of Huppert and Piercy. Patient N.A. and the alcoholic Korsakoff patients forgot at normal rates over the 32-hour period, whereas the patients receiving ECT evidenced an accelerated decay of pictorial (and verbal) material during the same period. Squire proposed that ECT affects memory by disrupting hippocampal mechanisms concerned with the consolidation process and concludes that amnesic symptoms associated with diencephalic and hippocampal dysfunction are dissociable in terms of the stage of information processing adversely affected.

Another investigation (Cohen and Squire, 1980) of some intact memory capacities of amnesic patients has reported that alcoholic Korsakoff patients can learn and retain over a 94-day period the general rules needed for mirror-reading despite severe amnesia for the previous training sessions and for the specific words they had read. Cohen and Squire propose that alcoholic Korsakoff patients, like all patients with amnesic conditions, are severely impaired in learning specific declarative knowledge but are capable of normal acquisition and retention of procedural knowledge and skills.

Retrograde Amnesia in Korsakoff's Syndrome

Retrograde amnesia is also a distinct and consistent feature of alcoholic Korsakoff's syndrome. The Korsakoff patient has trouble retrieving from long-term memory events that occurred prior to the onset of his illness. When asked who was President of the United States before Mr. Reagan, the patient might answer "Truman" or "Eisenhower." In 1975, we asked one of our then recently diagnosed Korsakoff patients if the United States was still at war. The patient replied, "I think they have that war in Korea all wrapped up." In general, this difficulty retrieving old memories is usually more pronounced for events just prior to the onset of the illness, while remote events from the patient's childhood and early adulthood are well remembered. Most alcoholic Korsakoff patients who served in World War II can describe their tours of duty with great detail and apparent accuracy but are unable to recall any of the major public events (e.g., the Kennedys' assassinations, Vietnam War protests) of the 1960s.

This temporal "gradient" is not only evident during a mental status examination but has been demonstrated in numerous experimental studies. Seltzer and Benson (1974) used a multiple-choice public events questionnaire and found that their alcoholic Korsakoff patients could remember famous events from the 1930s and 1940s better than events from the 1960s and 1970s. Marslen-Wilson and Teuber (1975) presented alcoholic Korsakoff patients with photographs of famous people and found that the patients had much more difficulty identifying famous faces from the 1960s than faces from the 1930s and 1940s.

Warrington and her associates have challenged the existence of this gradient and have presented evidence that amnesic patients have as much difficulty retrieving remote (e.g., childhood) events as recent events. Sanders and Warrington (1971) administered a "famous events" questionnaire and a test of famous faces to five patients with amnesia (mixed etiology). Their patients were impaired relative to the control group on all tests and for all periods of time. Unlike the impairment observed in the studies reviewed above, the impairment of the amnesics was of equal severity at all time periods. Warrington believes that the difference between her results and those of other studies is related to the relative difficulty and overexposure of the test items. That is, while Warrington attempted to insure that items from different decades were of equal difficulty and exposure (i.e., she chose people and events whose fame did not extend beyond a single decade), such controls were not evident in other studies of retrograde amnesia. It is entirely possible, according to Warrington, that the temporal gradients described by other investigators may be due to the fact that questions and faces from the 1930s and 1940s were easier to answer or recognize than those from the 1960s and 1970s.

Albert, Butters, and Levin (1979) reexamined retrograde amnesia in light of Warrington's criticisms of previous studies. Three tests were developed: a famous faces test, a recall questionnaire, and a multiple-choice recognition

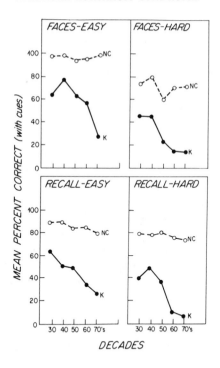

Fig. 2. Performance of alcoholic Korsakoff patients (K) and nonalcoholic control subjects (NC) on Albert et al.'s (1979) Famous Faces test and recall questionnaire. Results for easy and hard items are shown separately.

questionnaire. Each test consisted of items from the 1920s to the 1970s that had been evaluated with a large sample of normal controls before their inclusion in the final test battery. Half of the items were "easy" as determined by the performance of the standardization group; the other half were difficult or "hard" as determined by the same criterion. The "easy" items were all people or events whose fame spanned many decades (e.g., Charlie Chaplin, Charles Lindburgh) and the "hard" items were people or events whose fame was limited to one decade (e.g., Tiny Tim, Rosemary Clooney). In addition to the "easy–hard" dichotomy, the famous faces test included photographs of some individuals early and late in their careers. For example, photographs of Marlon Brando from the 1950s and 1970s were both included in the test battery. If a patient was initially unable to identify a famous face or recall a major public event, phonemic and/or semantic cues were provided to aid his retrieval.

When this retrograde battery was administered to a group of 11 alcoholic Korsakoff patients and a group of 15 normal controls matched to the amnesics for age and educational background, little evidence supporting Sanders and Warrington's conclusions were found. Rather, the classical gradient was evident regardless of the difficulty of the items. For both "easy" and "hard" items, the patients with alcoholic Korsakoff's syndrome identified more photographs from the 1930s and 1940s than from the 1960s. On the recall questionnaire the same gradients emerged. Figure 2 shows the results for the Famous Faces and Public Events Recall Questionnaire.

When Albert et al. assessed the patients' ability to identify photographs of famous people early and late in their careers, further evidence for the sparing of remote memories was found. While the normal controls were more accurate at identifying famous people later than earlier in their careers, the alcoholic Korsakoff patients performed in the opposite manner. Thus, the Korsakoff patients were more likely to identify Marlon Brando as he appeared in the 1950s than as he looked in the late 1960s or early 1970s.

Meudell et al. (1980) developed a retrograde amnesia test consisting of voices of famous people recorded in the last 50 years. When it was administered to patients with alcoholic Korsakoff's syndrome and control subjects, the results were similar to those reported with questionnaires and photographs of famous faces. The alcoholic Korsakoff patients showed a retrograde amnesia for voices extending over several decades and a relative preservation of memories for the more remote past. When subjects were asked to assign identified voices to their correct recorded decade, the alcoholic Korsakoff patients were significantly impaired in comparison to the normal control subjects.

Like Albert et al., Squire and his colleagues have attempted to develop a remote memory test that circumvents the overlearning and overexposure problems noted by Sanders and Warrington (1971). To insure limited but equivalent public exposure, Squire and Slater (1975) used the titles of television programs that had been aired for one season or less in the construction of their recall and recognition tests. The individual items on these tests were matched for public exposure on the basis of known viewing histories and, since each item had a brief exposure period, the time of learning could be specified.

In two extensive reports, Cohen and Squire (1981) and Squire and Cohen (1982) administered their television tests, several tests of public events, and Albert et al.'s (1979) Famous Faces Test to alcoholics with Korsakoff's syndrome, to long-term alcoholics with no clinical signs of amnesia, to depressed patients 1 hour after their fifth administration of bilateral ECT, and to the well-studied patient N.A. (Squire and Moore, 1979; Squire and Slater, 1978; Teuber, Milner, and Vaughn, 1968) described earlier in this chapter. The results of this testing showed a clear distinction between the remote memory losses of the Korsakoff patients and those of N.A. and the ECT patients. The alcoholic Korsakoff patients' loss of remote memories was severe, extended over several decades, and was characterized by a temporal gradient in which very remote memories (e.g., from the 1940s) were relatively spared, whereas both patient N.A. and the ECT patients had only mild-to-moderate retrograde amnesias that were limited on some tests to the 4-year period immediately preceding trauma or shock treatment. On the TV recognition test and the Famous Faces Test, the long-term alcoholics' (non-Korsakoff) retrieval of remote memories was mildly depressed, especially for events and people who were famous during the past 10 years.

It is also of some import to note that Milner's famous amnesic patient H.M. is also reported to have a retrograde amnesia limited to the 3 to 5 year period prior to his surgery (Milner, 1966, 1970). More recently, Butters et al. (1984) have described the chronic amnesia of an electrical engineer (patient R.B.) following the clipping of an aneurysm of the anterior communicating artery. Despite inordinate difficulty retaining life experiences and learning verbal and digit-symbol paired-associates, R.B.'s memory for events prior to his surgery seemed to be relatively intact.

The difference between the retrograde amnesias of alcoholic Korsakoff patients and of other amnesic populations has been addressed by Squire and Cohen (1982) and by Butters and Albert (1982). Both sets of investigators have suggested that the alcoholic Korsakoff patient's loss of remote memories may be secondary to a primary defect in establishing new memories (i.e., antero-grade amnesia) during the 20 years of alcohol abuse that preceded the diag-nosis of the amnesic syndrome. Although detoxified non-Korsakoff alcoholics have often been viewed as free of anterograde memory defects (for review, see Parsons and Prigatano, 1977), recent studies (Ryan and Butters, 1980a,b) using complex verbal and nonverbal stimuli have shown that detoxified alco-holics are impaired on short-term memory and paired-associate learning tasks and that these deficits are positively correlated with years of alcohol abuse. Consequently, if chronic alcoholics acquire less information each year due to a progressive anterograde memory deficit, then at the time an alcoholic pa-tient is diagnosed as having "Korsakoff's syndrome," one would expect to find a retrograde amnesia with a temporal gradient. From this viewpoint, the Kor-sakoff patients' loss of remote memories would be considered an artifact re-lated to a primary defect in establishing new memories and to a cognitive problem in locating memories that have been successfully stored. A corollary of this hypothesis is that true retrograde amnesias uncontaminated by defi-ciencies in original learning and cognitive retrieval strategies are temporally limited and are far less severe and devastating than the amnesic patients' an-terograde memory problems (Squire and Cohen, 1982).

In addition to Cohen and Squire's (1981) evidence of some deficiencies in the remote memories of long-term (non-Korsakoff) alcoholics, Albert, But-ters, and Brandt (1980) administered their remote memory battery to detox-ified long-term alcoholics (non-Korsakoff) and nonalcoholic control subjects to evaluate this "chronic" explanation of the Korsakoff patients' remote mem-ory problems. They reasoned that if the learning deficit related to alcoholism was responsible for the alcoholic Korsakoff patients' difficulties in recalling past events, two predictions could be made. One, the alcoholics should be impaired in their identification of famous faces and public events. Two, since the det-rimental effects of alcohol on the learning of new materials are related to years of alcohol abuse, the alcoholics' deficits in recalling past events should be most apparent for the years immediately preceding testing. The results partially confirmed these expectations. Although the alcoholics' mean recall scores for "hard" famous faces from the 1960s and 1970s were considerably lower than the scores of the nonalcoholic controls, the differences did not attain statistical significance. However, on the recall questionnaire the alcoholics had a mild but significant impairment in their recall of "hard" public events from the 1960s and 1970s with the greatest loss associated with the immediately preceding decade. It is also important that this deficit in the recall of remote events from the last two decades was consonant with the length of the patients' alcohol abuse (mean, 25.18 years).

Although the results of Albert et al.'s (1980) study are not of the magnitude to allow the alcoholic Korsakoff patients' retrograde amnesia to be reduced entirely to an anterograde problem, they do suggest that two separate etiological factors may be involved. One factor is the impact of chronic alcohol abuse on anterograde memory processes. Since long-term alcoholics may retain somewhat less information each year due to a chronic learning deficit, their store of remote memories for the recent past may be mildly or moderately deficient. The second factor may be a forgetting of, or a loss of access to, old memories that appears acutely during the Wernicke stage of the illness and results in a severe and equal loss for all time periods prior to the onset of the disease. When this acute loss of remote memories is superimposed on the patient's already deficient store, a severe retrograde amnesia with a temporal gradient would be expected. Patients should be impaired with respect to controls at all time periods, but memory for recent events should be most severely affected since less was learned initially during this period.

The most convincing evidence for this two-factor model of the alcoholic Korsakoff patients' retrograde amnesia comes from a single-case study (Butters, 1984) This patient (P.Z.), an eminent scientist and university professor who developed alcoholic Korsakoff's syndrome at the age of 65, had written and published an extensive autobiography three years before the acute onset of his Wernicke's encephalopathy in 1982. Like all alcoholics with Korsakoff's syndrome, P.Z. had severe anterograde and retrograde amnesias as assessed by clinical and formal psychometric techniques. On Albert et al.'s (1979) Famous Faces Test, he was severely impaired in his recall of famous people, but did evidence some sparing of faces from the 1930s and 1940s. To determine whether patient P.Z. had also lost access to autobiographical material which was well-known to him before his illness, a retrograde amnesia test based upon his autobiography was developed. The test consisted of questions about relatives, colleagues, collaborators, conferences, research assistants, research reports and books, all of which were prominently mentioned in the autobiography.

Patient P.Z.'s recall of these autobiographical facts is shown in Fig. 3. Two points are evident. First, P.Z. has a very severe retrograde amnesia for autobiographical events, with considerable sparing of information from the very remote past. Second, P.Z.'s retrograde amnesia for autobiographical material cannot be secondary to a deficiency in original learning. The fact that all the questions were taken from his own autobiography eliminates the possibility that he had never acquired the information. Just 3 years prior to the onset of his Wernicke-Korsakoff's syndrome, P.Z. obviously had retrieved this information, which he considered most prominent in his professional and personal

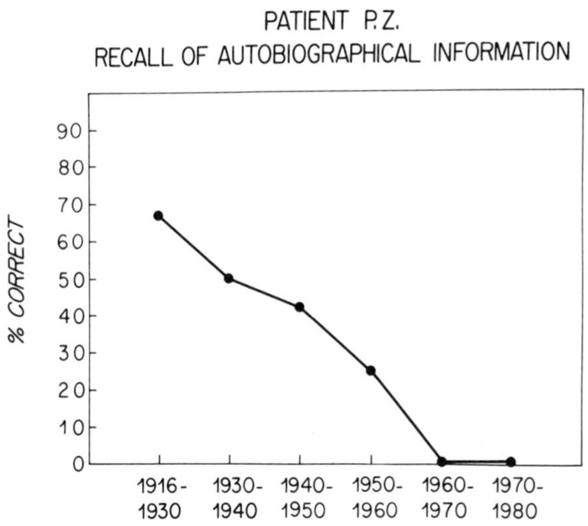

PATIENT P.Z.
RECALL OF AUTOBIOGRAPHICAL INFORMATION

Fig. 3. Patient P.Z.'s retrograde amnesia for information taken from his published autobiography.

life. Clearly, P.Z.'s illness marked the acute onset of his inability to access information that was once readily available to him. The relatively severe impairment for the most recent decades suggests that autobiographical information acquired during those time periods was not as stable (i.e., well-consolidated) as that acquired earlier in his lifetime.

The results of these remote memory studies also suggest that anterograde and retrograde amnesia can be dissociated from one another and may involve different neural circuits. Although alcoholic Korsakoff patients clearly demonstrate both types of amnesia, non-Korsakoff alcoholics can have substantial difficulty learning new information (Brandt et al., 1983; Ryan and Butters, 1980a, 1980b) but are often only mildly impaired in their recall of remote events (Albert et al., 1980). The fact that alcoholic Korsakoffs and other amnesic patients can be equally impaired in the learning of new information yet demonstrate retrograde amnesias of different duration and severity (Cohen and Squire, 1981; Butters et al., 1984) lends further support to the separability of anterograde and retrograde memory problems. It is not possible at this juncture to determine the exact neural circuits that mediate anterograde and retrograde memory processes, but a report based on stimulation studies with epileptic patients (Fedio and Van Buren, 1974) has produced evidence for such an anatomical separation within the temporal lobes. Since the amnesia of alcoholic Korsakoff patients is often attributed to damage to the dorsomedial nucleus of the thalamus and to the mamillary bodies (Victor et al., 1971), it is also of interest that patient N.A. who is severely amnesic with regard to learning new verbal material, but has a very limited retrograde amnesia, has now been reported to have unilateral destruction of the left dorsomedial nucleus of the thalamus and no other visible damage (Squire and Moore, 1979). Perhaps the Korsakoff patient's severe anterograde amnesia develops slowly due to the gradual atrophy of the dorsomedial nucleus of the thalamus, while his loss of remote memories appears suddenly with acute damage to other subcortical brain structures.

Confabulation of Alcoholic Patients with Korsakoff's Syndrome

The alcoholic Korsakoff patient's tendency to *confabulate* when faced with questions he cannot answer is an often cited characteristic of the disorder. When asked to recall his activities of the previous day, the Korsakoff patient may "fill in" the gap in his memory with a story about a trip to his home or to a sporting event that may actually have occurred many years ago. This confabulatory tendency is not a constant or necessarily permanent feature of amnesic patients, and there are marked individual differences among amnesic populations. In general, confabulation is most marked during the acute stages of the illness and becomes progressively less noticeable as the patient adjusts to his disorder. It is relatively easy to elicit confabulation from a patient in a Wernicke-Korsakoff confusional state, but such responses are rare in chronic Korsakoff patients who have had the disease for 5 years or more. Certainly the notion that confabulation is a cardinal symptom of Korsakoff's disorder is not consistent with most experiences with such patients.

Psychometric Features of Alcoholic Patients with Korsakoff's Syndrome

Despite the severity of the Korsakoff patients' memory impairments, their intellectual functions as measured by standardized I.Q. tests often remain relatively intact (Butters and Cermak, 1976, 1980). Thus, it is important to distinguish at this point the alcoholic Korsakoff patient from the patient with alcoholic dementia. The latter patient demonstrates a general and severe intellectual decline associated with decades of alcohol abuse, and his memory problems do not stand out as an especially noticeable and debilitating symptom (Lishman, 1981). When alcoholic Korsakoff patients and intact nonalcoholic controls are matched on relevant demographic variables (e.g., years of education, age, socioeconomic class), the two groups' verbal, performance, and full-scale I.Q.'s, as measured by the Wechsler Adult Intelligence Scale, are often indistinguishable (Butters and Cermak, 1976, 1980). Korsakoff patients have been found to be consistently impaired on the Digit Symbol subtest of the WAIS, but this task should not be considered a special marker because detoxified long-term alcoholics without any clinical signs of amnesia are usually impaired on the same substitution test (Glosser, Butters, and Kaplan, 1977; Kapur and Butters, 1977). Special note should be made of the alcoholic Korsakoffs' normal performance on the Digit Span subtest, a task that is often considered a measure of immediate memory.

In stark contrast to the normal performance of Korsakoff patients on the WAIS is their severely depressed memory quotient (M.Q.) as measured by the Wechsler Memory Scale (WMS). A 20–30 point spread between I.Q. (e.g., 100) and M.Q. (e.g., 75) is typical and serves as the psychometric hallmark of the amnesic syndrome of alcoholic Korsakoff patients (Butters and Cermak, 1976, 1980). Although the size of this discrepancy seems large, it probably represents an underestimation of the differences between the patients' general intelligence and their ability to learn new information. Most alcoholic Korsakoff patients perform within normal limits on the Digit Span and Mental Control sections of the WMS and thereby earn inflated M.Q. scores. When the Korsakoff patient's M.Q. is computed on the basis of the Associative Learning, Logical Memories, and Visual Reproduction subtests, all of which assess ability to learn and retain new materials, the discrepancy between I.Q. and M.Q. often exceeds 40 points.

Despite the alcoholic Korsakoff patient's normal I.Q., his cognitive performance is not completely intact. A full neuropsychological evaluation usually reveals a number of secondary defects that may or may not contribute to the patient's severe memory problems. The most common deficits involve visuo-perceptive and visuo-spatial capacities. Alcoholic Korsakoff patients are dramatically impaired on symbol-digit as well as on digit-symbol substitution tasks, on hidden or embedded figures tests (Glosser et al., 1977; Kapur and Butters, 1977; Talland, 1965), and on various concept formation tests that require the sorting and discrimination of complex visual stimuli (Oscar-Berman 1973; Oscar-Berman and Samuels, 1977). Such visuo-perceptive deficits should not be surprising, since chronic alcoholics who are not clinically amnesic have been reported to have the same perceptual problems. (For review, see Parsons and Farr, 1981; Parsons and Leber, 1981; Ryan and Butters, 1983). Although there are some indications that these visuo-perceptive deficits, like the memory disorders, may be due to atrophy of diencephalic structures surrounding the third ventricle (Jarho, 1973), many investigators have attributed these perceptual disorders to atrophy of cortical association areas (Parsons, 1975; Parsons, Tarter, and Jones, 1971).

Jones and her collaborators (Jones et al., 1978; Jones, Moskowitz, and Butters, 1975) have reported that alcoholic Korsakoff patients are significantly impaired in their senses of smell and taste, in addition to their visuo-perceptive and conceptual deficits. For both olfactory and gustatory stimuli, these investigators found that alcoholic Korsakoff patients have heightened intensity thresholds and noticeable difficulty in making qualitative discriminations. Mair and his colleagues (Mair, Capra, McEntee, and Engen, 1980) have also found patients with Korsakoff's syndrome to be impaired in their ability to discriminate among similar odorants, but concluded on the basis of a signal detection procedure that this deficit was not due to heightened intensity thresholds. Both groups of investigators agree that the patients' sensory problems can be traced to atrophy of several diencephalic structures anatomically associated with the olfactory and gustatory systems.

Personality Characteristics of Alcoholic Patients with Korsakoff's Syndrome

No description of the alcoholic Korsakoffs' major psychological symptoms would be complete without some mention of the patients' personality changes. Korsakoff patients often have premorbid histories of psychopathic behavior characterized by impulsive aggressive acts and petty crimes designed to support their chronic alcoholism. Many were "bar-room brawlers" who also violently attacked members of their immediate families. With the onset of Korsakoff's disease, a dramatic change occurs in these motivational-affective characteristics. Impulsivity, aggression, and severe alcohol abuse are replaced by apathy, passivity, a lack of initiative, and a virtual disinterest in alcohol. The patient is also unable to formulate or organize a series of plans. Left to his own devices, the Korsakoff patient is likely to remain seated before a television set or even in bed for long periods of time. He makes few demands or inquiries of hospital staff and will obey all instructions in a passive and indifferent manner. The apathy of the Korsakoff patient is not the consequence of institutionalization; his personality change is apparent shortly after he enters the Korsakoff phase of his illness, and occurs even in patients who return home.

One of the most perplexing and least investigated questions raised by the study of alcoholic Korsakoff patients concerns the relationship between their personality changes and their cognitive deficits. Talland (1965) has proposed that their difficulties in memory and perception are due to a faulty organization of cognitive strategies (i.e., a perseveration or rigidity of cognitive sets) resulting from a "premature closure" of activating mechanisms. That is, the patients' motivational and arousal deficits prevent thorough coding of new information (anterograde amnesia) and the organization of suitable search strategies for scanning stored information (retrograde amnesia). Since it is commonly believed that arousal and attentional processes are dependent upon the reticular activating system (RAS), Talland assumed that the alcoholic Korsakoff's midline diencephalic lesions interrupt the RAS's facilitative influence on cognitive (i.e., cortical) functions. Oscar-Berman's (1980) previously described report, as well as her more recent findings (Oscar-Berman et al., 1982), that positive reinforcement has less control over the operant responses of Korsakoff patients than of normal subjects lends some support to Talland's stress on motivational-attentional factors.

Granted that attentional and motivational factors may be responsible for some of the alcoholic Korsakoff's cognitive problems, it remains unlikely that most of the patient's amnesia can be explained by such concepts. Patients with frontal lobe lesions, including those who have had frontal lobotomies, develop personality characteristics similar to those of Korsakoff patients, yet fail to evidence the striking amnesic symptoms. If impairments in activation can occur without a concomitant change in memory functions, some skepticism must remain as to the extent to which the Korsakoff patients' personality changes influence their cognitive performance.

Neuropathology of Alcoholic Patients with Korsakoff's Syndrome

There have been several recent reviews of the neuropathology of the Wernicke-Korsakoff syndrome (Brierly, 1977; Mair et al., 1979; Victor et al., 1971), and only their major findings and conclusions will be outlined in this chapter. As Brierly (1977) notes, most of the literature supports the conclusion that the neurological symptoms of Wernicke's encephalopathy are related to lesions of the brain stem and cerebellum, while the amnesic symptoms of the chronic Korsakoff state involve damage to several thalamic and hypothalamic structures surrounding the third ventricle of the brain. The dorsomedial nucleus of the thalamus and the mammillary bodies of the hypothalamus are the specific structures most often associated with the alcoholic Korsakoff's amnesic symptoms.

Gamper (1928) studied the brains of 16 alcoholic Korsakoff patients and found that their lesions extended from the thalamus to the lower brainstem. He noted much variation from case to case, but concluded that the mammillary bodies were the crucial structure since all 16 Korsakoff patients had extensive atrophy of these nuclei. No correlations between brain pathology and clinical symptoms were reported.

Riggs and Boles (1944) examined 29 brains of patients who had "Wernicke's disease." While alcohol abuse was associated with nearly one-half of these cases, the remaining cases were due to a number of other causes (e.g., prolonged vomiting). The neuropathological findings showed that the mammillary bodies were affected in 21 of 23 cases, the dorsomedial nucleus of the thalamus in 23 out of 27, and the pulvinar of the thalamus in 10 out of 14.

Delay, Brion, and Elissalde (1958a, 1958b) described the neuropathology of eight alcoholic Korsakoff patients with both anterograde and retrograde memory deficits. Atrophy of the mammillary bodies was common to all cases, but significant thalamic involvement was noted in only one brain. These investigators stressed the lack of consistent cortical pathology, and pointed to the mammillary bodies as the most probable source of the patients' amnesic symptoms.

Adams, Collins, and Victor (1962) combined neuropathological findings with careful clinical and psychometric examinations of 300 Wernicke-Korsakoff patients. They found that the onset of the Wernicke stage was acute and subsided rapidly with the administration of large doses of thiamine. As the confusion, ataxia, nystagmus, and ocular palsies cleared, the patients' major remaining symptoms were severe anterograde and retrograde amnesia. Of the 300 cases, 54 brains were eventually studied. The investigators attributed the symptoms of Wernicke's disease to lesions in the brainstem (e.g., oculomotor nucleus) and cerebellum. The severe memory disorder of the Korsakoff stage of the illness was correlated with the presence of lesions in the mammillary bodies and several thalamic nuclei (dorsomedial, anteroventral, and pulvinar).

In a more recent report, Victor et al. (1971) examined the brains of 82 Wernicke-Korsakoff patients whose clinical symptomatology had been carefully studied premorbidly. The dorsomedial nucleus of the thalamus was systematically examined in 43 of these brains. In 38 of the 43 brains, extensive atrophy of the dorsomedial nucleus was noted, but in the five brains with no atrophy there had been no lasting memory disorder. Since all five of these "negative" cases (as well as the 38 remaining cases) showed severe atrophy of the mammillary bodies, Victor et al. concluded that the dorsomedial nucleus, and not the mammillary bodies, is the critical structure for the amnesic syndrome. It should be noted, however, that another interpretation can be drawn from the presented data. Since all 38 cases with amnesia had lesions in both the mammillary bodies and the dorsomedial nucleus of the thalamus, it is possible that this combined thalamic-hypothalamic lesion is the one that is both necessary and sufficient for Korsakoff's amnesia. To demonstrate the primacy of the dorsomedial nucleus, it would be necessary to have amnesic cases with atrophy limited to the dorsomedial nucleus. Victor et al. do not report any cases meeting this criterion.

Based upon the results of recent neurochemical studies (McEntee and Mair, 1978, 1980), it appears possible that the alcoholic Korsakoffs' diencephalic lesions are disrupting specific neural pathways dependent upon monoamine-containing neurons. These investigators (McEntee and Mair, 1978) demonstrated that the cerebrospinal fluid of nine Korsakoff patients contained significantly deficient levels of MHPG, the primary monoamine metabolite of norepinephrine. They also noted a significant correlation between the severity of the patients' memory impairments and the levels of MHPG in their cerebrospinal fluid. Further evidence linking damage to norepinephrine-containing neurons in subcortical centers with patients' memory disorders was provided in a second study by McEntee and Mair (1980). In this investigation, several drugs which potentiate central norepinephrine activity were administered to eight patients with Korsakoff's disease. Each patient was examined on a neuropsychological test battery, which included measures of memory and of perceptual and conceptual functions, before and after 2 weeks of drug administration. The results showed that the administration of one drug, clonidine, was associated with significant improvements on several measures of anterograde memory functions (e.g., short-term memory tests, specific subtests of the Wechsler Memory Scale). If these results are confirmed in future studies, they suggest that therapeutic strategies aimed at increasing norepinephrine levels in the brain may help reduce the Korsakoff patient's amnesic symptoms.

Although much of the neuropathological interest in Wernicke-Korsakoff's syndrome has focused on subcortical structures such as the mammillary bodies and the dorsomedial nucleus of the thalamus, studies examining the CT scans of living alcoholics (with and without Korsakoff's syndrome) have questioned whether the damage associated with long-term abuse is limited to a small number of subcortical structures and whether all of the symptoms associated with Korsakoff's syndrome should be attributed to atrophy of structures surrounding the third ventricle. All recent reviews of the CT scan literature with alcoholics (e.g., Cala and Mastaglia, 1981; Lishman, 1981; Wilkinson, 1982; Wilkinson and Carlen, 1981) conclude that the vast majority of all alcoholics who have been abusing alcohol for more than 10 years demonstrate significant cortical as well as subcortical atrophy. The changes are usually characterized as symmetrical shrinkage of the cortex of the cerebral hemispheres in addition to dilation of the lateral and third ventricles. Shrinkage of the vermis of the cerebellum and cerebellar hemispheres is also present in all advanced stages. Despite the diffuseness of this atrophy, the frontal lobes show the most marked shrinkage as indicated by a widening of the interhemispheric fissure and frontal horns of the lateral ventricles. This atrophic process of the frontal lobes has also been noted in young alcoholics with long-term histories of abuse. Some investigations have shown that this cortical atrophy is independent of the presence of liver disease, and others have reported moderate correlations (e.g., $r = 0.40$) between degree of atrophy and psychometric performance on various WAIS subtests and impairment indices derived from the Halstead-Reitan neuropsychological test battery.

If, as these CT scan results suggest, most long-term alcoholics have suffered considerable diffuse brain damage, how should the neuropsychological deficits of alcoholic Korsakoff patients be considered with regard to localization of function? Certainly the attribution of all of the alcoholic Korsakoffs' anterograde and retrograde memory problems, visuo-perceptual deficits, and changes in personality to atrophy of diencephalic structures is premature and probably incorrect. As noted previously, Moscovitch (1982) has already reported that failure to release from proactive interference is seen in nonamnesic patients with frontal lobe damage. Similarly, Milner's (1971) evidence that the ability to place a familiar word or pattern within a specific temporal context is dependent upon the integrity of the frontal lobes questions whether the Korsakoffs' context-retrieval deficits (Winocur and Kinsbourne, 1978) may not be related to some dysfunction of these cortical structures. For the present, it is perhaps appropriate to consider most cases of alcoholic Korsakoff's syndrome as involving both cortical and subcortical damage and to await further studies of patients with restricted localizable lesions before advancing further inferences concerning specific brain-behavior relationships in this syndrome.

Etiology of the Wernicke-Korsakoff Syndrome

Despite the numerous neuropathological studies, the etiology of the Korsakoff patients' brain damage remains obscure. Victor et al. (1971) and Dreyfus (1974) have gathered considerable data that point to thiamine (vitamin B_1) deficiency as the primary factor in this disease. Since chronic alcoholics often fail to eat nutritionally balanced diets, malnutrition and avitaminosis are common correlates of chronic alcohol abuse. According to this nutritional theory, the diencephalon, the brain stem, and the cerebellum are very sensitive to thiamine deficiencies and either atrophy or become prone to hemorrhagic lesions.

There are three principle forms of evidence to support this theory of avitaminosis. One, the symptoms of Wernicke's stage occur commonly in disorders that interfere with food metabolism and absorption. Protracted vomiting during pregnancy, carcinoma of the stomach, chronic gastritis, and intestinal obstruction are some of the disorders associated both with malnutrition and the previously described Wernicke's symptoms.

Two, treatment of Wernicke-Korsakoff patients with large amounts of thiamine alleviates some of the patients' symptoms. Opthalmoplegia and the confusional state begin to improve within a few hours after the administration of thiamine and usually clear within 7 days. The patients' nystagmus and ataxia show a slower and more limited improvement and may still be apparent in a mild form months or even years after the beginning of treatment. Of the various symptoms comprising the Wernicke-Korsakoff syndrome, the memory and personality changes remain the most refractory to thiamine therapy. Eighty percent of all Korsakoff patients show little, if any, improvement in their memory disorder and general apathy despite prolonged administration of vitamins. In fact, the amnesic disorder remains the chronic lifelong disability of the alcoholic Korsakoff patient. Victor et al. (1971) believe that this marked variability in the reversibility of symptoms with vitamin therapy reflects differences in the stages of pathology. They conclude that symptoms associated with the Wernicke stage are reversible because they are due to a "biochemical abnormality that has stopped short of significant structural change," while the memory disorders of the Korsakoff stage of the illness are irreversible because of the presence of permanent structural damage.

The third form of support for the thiamine hypothesis stems from experimental studies in which animals have been deprived of thiamine for varying periods of time. While these studies have employed a wide range of animals, including humans, monkeys, and rats, the overall results indicate that the major neurological symptoms of Wernicke's syndrome are associated with thiamine deficiency and that these symptoms are alleviated with the administration of thiamine (Dreyfus, 1974; Mesulam, Van Hoesen and Butters, 1977; Victor et al., 1971). Monkeys, cats, and rats maintained on thiamine-deficient diets usually develop diffuse lesions of the diencephalon, brain stem, cerebellum, and, in some cases, of the basal ganglia. However, it is important to note that none of these experimental studies has shown that thiamine deficiency leads to chronic irreversible memory problems.

Although most textbooks of neurology accept avitaminosis as the primary cause of the Wernicke-Korsakoff disorder, there is now impressive data that prolonged alcohol ingestion, unaccompanied by malnutrition, does result in permanent learning deficits and in significant brain pathology. Freund, Walker, and their colleagues (see Freund, 1973; Walker, Hunter, and Abraham, 1981) fed mice ethanol-containing liquid diets that were nutritionally controlled. After several months on this ethanol diet the mice were transferred to normal, ethanol-free laboratory diets for 2 months before the start of behavioral testing. Although these mice had never been fed a nutritionally unbalanced diet, they were impaired on a variety of behavioral tasks including avoidance and maze learning. In recent studies, Riley and Walker (1978) and Walker et al. (1980) have reported that mice maintained for 4 months on Freund's ethanol liquid diet show a significant loss of dendritic spines on hippocampal pyramidal cells and dentate granule cells as well as a significant loss of hippocampal neurons themselves.

The proposition that alcohol abuse has neurotoxic effects even in well-nourished humans finds some support in a recent study by Harper and Blumbergs (1982). These authors reported that the average brain weight of male alcoholics is less than that of age-matched nonalcoholics. Within the group of alcoholics, there was no difference between the mean brain weight of patients with histories of Wernicke's encephalopathy and those without such histories (rather, with macroscopically and microscopically normal brains). Both of these groups had abnormally low brain weights, suggesting that chronic alcohol consumption, not thiamine deficiency, is the major factor responsible for brain shrinkage.

This evidence that ethanol may have a direct toxic effect on the brain indicates the need to reevaluate the etiology of the Wernicke-Korsakoff syndrome. It is evident from our brief review that Wernicke's encephalopathy is closely linked to thiamine deficiency. Ocular palsies, nystagmus, and ataxia can be induced and then alleviated by controlling thiamine levels, and Victor et al.'s (1971) conclusion that these symptoms reflect brain stem and cerebellar abnormalities seem well-supported by the experimental literature. The major controversy concerning etiology focuses on the amnesic symptoms and the Korsakoff stage of the syndrome. Amnesic symptoms do not disappear with the administration of thiamine and, as Freund (1973) has noted, there is virtually no documented evidence of a *permanent* memory disorder in patients with thiamine deficiencies unaccompanied by alcohol abuse. In other words, thiamine deficiency appears to result in an amnesic syndrome only in alcoholic Korsakoff patients! It is possible then that the amnesic syndrome of the Korsakoff stage may result from the interaction of thiamine deficiency and the direct neurotoxic effects of alcohol. If this interaction hypothesis is valid, one would not necessarily expect a rapid onset of amnesic symptoms. Rather, the patient's difficulties in learning new material should slowly become more prominent over the course of many years of alcohol abuse. Our earlier discussion of possible mechanisms for the gradient of remote memory loss raised this very possibility. In the next section, we shall review some recent data demonstrating such memory disorders in chronic, non-Korsakoff alcoholics.

Memory Disorders in Non-Korsakoff Alcoholics

Attesting to the deleterious effects of alcohol ingestion on the central nervous system are a number of studies which have documented alcohol-related cognitive losses in non-Korsakoff patients. Detoxified long-term alcoholics display significant impairments, compared with their nonalcoholic, social-drinking peers, on tasks requiring visuo-perceptual abstraction such as in embedded-figures tests (Donovan, Queisser, and O'Leary, 1976; Kapur and Butters, 1977), concept learning as on the Wisconsin Card Sorting Test, (Tarter, 1973; Tarter and Parsons, 1971), and Halstead's Category Test (Fitzhugh, Fitzhugh, and Reitan, 1965; Jones and Parsons, 1971), and rapid encoding of novel stimuli as in symbol substitution tasks (Glosser, Butters, and Kaplan, 1977). All of these studies are consistent with the notion that cognitive changes seen in the Korsakoff patient have a gradual rather than precipitious onset.

While many of the cognitive changes associated with Korsakoff's syndrome are highly correlated with chronicity of alcoholism, the hallmark of this neuropsychiatric entity, a severe and lasting amnesia, has until very recently been refractory to such an analysis. This conclusion has been based on the frequent observation that long-term abusive drinkers were able to learn and retain new information as well as their nonalcoholic peers (Butters et al., 1977; Jonsson, Cronholm, and Izikowitz, 1962; Weingartner, Faillace, and Markley, 1971). In fact, as recently as 1977, Parsons and Prigatano concluded that "there is no evidence of lasting impairment of memory in detoxified alcoholic men." There are at least two possible explanations for failure to find anterograde memory deficits in detoxified chronic alcoholics. One is that, unlike the visuo-perceptual and abstract-conceptual difficulties of both the alcoholic and the Korsakoff patient, a significant memory loss emerges only when the diencephalic lesions of Korsakoff's disease are present. As stated earlier, these lesions have been linked most closely to chronic deficiency of thiamine. It may be that most chronic alcoholics consume enough thiamine to prevent these thalamic and hypothalamic lesions, and therefore escape significant memory impairment. A second possibility is that these early studies, which by and large relied on standard clinical tests such as the Wechsler Memory Scale (Wechsler, 1945), were simply not using the appropriate assessment techniques. If the chronic alcoholic does, in fact, have a mild-to-moderate defect in the ability to store, process, and retrieve new information, this may be evident only with carefully designed sensitive psychometric instruments.

In the first study from our laboratory to evaluate this latter possibility, Ryan and associates (Ryan, Butters, Montgomery, Adinolfi, and Didario, 1980) developed a battery of neuropsychological tests especially designed to uncover mild-to-moderate impairments in alcoholics. Among these tests were three memory tasks: a multitrial verbal paired-associate learning test, a symbol-digit paired-associate task, and a short-term memory task (distractor technique) using four words as the to-be-remembered material. Ryan and associates administered these tests to a group of 18 long-term alcoholic men (with at least 10-year histories of alcohol abuse and a minimum of 4 weeks of abstinence), a carefully-matched group of 18 nonalcoholic men, and 7 alcoholic Korsakoff patients. In spite of stringent subject selection criteria which eliminated from the study individuals with histories of other neurologic or psychiatric disease or polydrug abuse, the results of this investigation revealed striking memory deficits in the long-term alcoholic group. On all three memory tasks, the performance of the detoxified alcoholics fell part-way between the scores of the normal controls and the amnesic Korsakoff patients. Subsequent studies by Ryan and Butters (1980a,b) and a large-scale study by Brandt and coworkers (1983) have confirmed the existence of both short-term and long-term memory defects in detoxified alcoholics. The results of these studies have been interpreted as supporting the hypothesis, first proposed by Ryback (1971), of a continuum of cognitive impairment associated with alcohol use. That is, the Korsakoff patient may simply represent an endpoint of a continuum, with non-Korsakoff alcoholics representing milder forms of the same basic disorder.

A logical, though not intuitively obvious conclusion which may be deduced from the continuity model is that impairments of cognitive functioning are positively correlated with alcohol consumption and are not "reserved" for the chronically alcoholic individual. Therefore, even social drinkers might be expected to display subtle cognitive failings. Preliminary support for this conclusion has been provided by Parker and Noble (1977, 1980). They reported that scores on the Shipley-Hartford Institute of Living Scale (especially the Abstraction test) correlate negatively with total amount of alcohol consumed per drinking occasion. A very recent study by MacVane and associates (MacVane et al., 1982) obtained similar results. These data are consistent with the notion that alcohol is a behaviorally, as well as neurologically, noxious agent and affects cognition in a dose-related fashion.

The scenario outlined above, with the chronic alcoholic displaying incipient Korsakoff cognitive defects, is not, we should point out, without difficulty. The variety of mental ability changes seen in chronic alcoholics and the relatively subtle nature of the memory defects may indicate that they are experiencing a more generalized loss of cognitive abilities. Thus, the end state for these individuals may not be Korsakoff's syndrome, but rather alcoholic dementia. Lishman (1981) has suggested what while Korsakoff's syndrome may, in fact, develop insidiously, we have been "too far seduced" by the syndrome and have not paid sufficient attention to the syndrome of alcoholic dementia. The latter syndrome, Lishman maintains, is marked by pathology of the cerebral cortex, and may be seen on CT scans as sulcal widening and ventricular dilatation even in quite young alcoholics. In view of these considerations, we must not rule out the possibility that Ryback's proposed continuum of impairment should be revised to include the syndrome of alcoholic dementia as one of the endpoints of the continuum.

Alcoholism and Aging

The nature of the relationship between the neurobehavioral effects of alcoholism and normal aging has attracted considerable interest in the past decade (see Ryan, 1982, for a review). Many of the cognitive declines associated with chronic alcoholism are also seen in normally aging individuals (Bak and Green, 1980; Albert, 1981), and are especially conspicuous in abnormally aging individuals (Albert and Kaplan, 1980; Katzman, Terry, and Bick, 1978; Miller, 1977). Thus, on the surface, at least, alcohol-induced cognitive declines resemble premature aging. Early support for this hypothesis was found in the work of Parsons and associates (Bertera and Parsons, 1978; Jones and Parsons, 1971; Klisz and Parsons, 1977). These studies reported that when hypothesis testing and visual search tasks are administered to alcoholic and normal control subjects, only older alcoholics (typically men in their late 40's and early 50's) display impairments. This led Jones and Parsons (1971) to suggest that the "aging brain is differentially susceptible to the effects of alcohol." Other investigators (Adams, Grant, and Reed, 1980; Grant, Adams, and Reed, 1979) have also reported sparing of neuropsychological functions in young alcoholics (late 30s), but their initial results are limited by the fact that their alcoholics had relatively brief abuse histories (less than 10 years). In a sample of patients with longer histories, they have replicated these findings, however (Grant, Adams, and Reed, 1984).

Blusewicz and associates (Blusewicz et al., 1977) and Ryan and Butters (1980b) have reported a general cognitive dysfunction in both young and middle-aged alcoholics which mimics the deficits associated with the aging process. Blusewicz, utilizing portions of the Halstead-Reitan battery and other cognitive indices, found that young alcoholics (mean age, 33 years) perform these tests at a level between that of age-matched and elderly (mean age, 71 years) normal controls. Ryan and Butters (1980b) administered their Four-Word STM (Short-Term Memory) Test and Verbal and Symbol-Digit Paired-Associate Learning Tests to groups of young (mean age, 42 years) and old (mean age, 54 years) alcoholics and nonalcoholic control subjects. The authors reported that both young and old alcoholics display poorer memory abilities than nonalcoholics of the same ages. Furthermore, the performance of the young alcoholics was virtually identical to that of the old nonalcoholics. Likewise, the old alcoholics performed at a level which typifies that of elderly (60–65 year old) normals. Ryan and Butters interpreted these data as consistent with a premature aging hypothesis, since the alcohol abusers displayed age-related cognitive losses 5 to 10 years earlier than normal individuals.

Recently, Brandt and coworkers (Brandt et al., 1983) reexamined the issue of premature aging by administering visuo-perceptual tasks and portions of Ryan and Butters' memory battery to a large sample of alcoholic ($N = 134$) and nonalcoholic ($N = 76$) men. On both the Four-Word STM Test and the Symbol-Digit Paired-Associate Learning Test, there were highly significant main effects for both group and age. That is, alcoholics performed more poorly than nonalcoholics, and older individuals performed more poorly than younger individuals. (Early in this study, it became apparent that the Verbal Paired-Associate Learning Test was not as effective as the Symbol-Digit Paired-Associate Learning Test in illuminating long-term memory defects in alcoholics. Presumably, the abstraction and language skills of chronic alcoholics are sometimes sufficient to form mnemonics for word pairs, but are insufficient to form mnemonics for symbol-digit pairs.)

An important finding of the Brandt et al. (1983) study is that on none of the memory or visuo-perceptual tasks was there an age-by-group interaction, thereby indicating that young alcoholics are as vulnerable to the memory-impairing effects of ethanol as are older alcoholics. While it is true that young alcoholics obtain scores that are quantitatively similar to those of older control subjects, the lack of a significant interaction between age and history of alcohol abuse prevents us from attributing these findings purely to an increased vulnerability of the older brain. Thus, the concept of premature aging appears to be useful only at the *descriptive* level. It remains to be determined whether disruption of similar brain mechanisms underlies the performance deficits of the alcoholic and the aged individual. In fact, most recent electrophysiologic evidence suggests that quite different brain systems are involved. In a recent review article, Porjesz and Begleiter (1982) reported that there are major differences between alcoholics and aged normals in brain stem evoked responses and event-related auditory potentials. In addition, the recent findings of Becker et al. (1983) that only some cognitive tasks which are sensitive to aging are also sensitive to alcoholism indicate that the overlap between age- and alcohol-related cognitive impairments may be only partial.

Abstinence from Alcohol and Recovery of Function

It is relatively well established that little spontaneous recovery of cognitive function occurs in alcoholic Korsakoff patients (Victor et al., 1971). While the ataxia, optic abnormalities, and confusional state that are present during the Wernicke stage clear with the administration of thiamine, the memory disorder is a lasting feature of the chronic Korsakoff state. In fact, the few attempts to improve the verbal memories of Korsakoff patients have been relatively unsuccessful (Baddeley and Warrington, 1973; Cermak and Reale, 1978). (Note, however, Cermak, 1975.) The question remains, however, whether the chronic alcoholic who has not sustained acute lesions during an encephalopathic episode is able to recover cognitive skills lost during many years of alcohol abuse. Immediately upon cessation of drinking, most alcoholics begin a period of rapidly improving mental status (Burdick, Johnson, and Smith, 1970). Sharp and associates (Sharp et al., 1977), for example, reported that after 2 weeks of abstinence, the ability of alcoholics to acquire new verbal associations was entirely normal. Earlier, Page and Linden (1974) found significant recovery on a variety of cognitive tasks after 1 week of sobriety, while Cermak and Ryback (1976) found that the ability of young alcoholics to perform the STM distractor task was normal immediately upon sobriety (1 day after cessation of drinking). More recent studies of neuropsychological recovery after short periods of abstinence have examined the influence of a number of modifier variables (Guthrie, 1980), including lateralized psychological functions

(Ellenberg et al., 1980) and practice effects (Goldman, Klisz, and Williams, 1981).

Studies of longer-term recovery of function have indicated that significant improvement in memory and general neuropsychological status takes place during the first year of sobriety. Long and McLachlan (1974) administered the Wechsler-Bellevue Intelligence Scale and subtests of the Halstead-Reitan Battery to intelligent, middle-aged alcoholics at 1 to 2 weeks of sobriety and again at 1 year of abstinence. They reported improvement on several measures, though not to nonalcoholic levels. A similar finding was reported by Berglund, Leijonquist, and Horlan (1977), who found that alcoholics who had remained abstinent or who had greatly reduced their alcohol consumption for a 3-year period showed improvements over their performance at 1 to 2 weeks of detoxification. A limitation of both of these studies, however, is that the initial assessment of the patients was at a time when the acute effects of alcohol were still present. Therefore, the apparent long-term improvement might have all taken place within the first 2 to 3 weeks of abstinence, as the patients were recovering from the acute alcoholic brain syndrome. In a study designed to avoid confounding short-term improvement in performance with long-term recovery, Ryan, Didario, Butters, and Adinolfi (1980) studied two groups of alcoholics, all of whom had been sober at least 4 weeks. Short-term abstinent alcoholics (1 to 3 months of sobriety), long-term abstinent alcoholics (1 to 5 years) and normal controls were administered a STM distractor test, the Symbol-Digit Paired-Associate Learning Test, and two digit-symbol substitution tests. Although there was a tendency for the long-term abstinent group to perform better than the recently abstinent subjects on the substitution tests, there was no improvement whatsoever on the short-term memory or paired-associate learning tasks. The performance of the long-term abstinent group was essentially identical to that of the short-term abstinent group and both alcoholic groups performed more poorly than nonalcoholic controls.

The results of the study by Ryan et al. (1980) left open the possibility that more extensive alcohol-free periods are needed to document amelioration of alcohol-induced memory impairments. Brandt et al. (1983) studied three relatively large groups of abstinent alcoholics. Short-term abstinent (1 to 2 months), long-term abstinent (12 to 36 months) and prolonged abstinent (more than 60 months) alcoholics were administered a battery of memory and perceptual tasks which included Ryan's Four-Word STM Test and Symbol-Digit Paired-Associate Learning Test. With differences in mean-age and years of alcoholism among the groups statistically controlled, large and significant differences among the groups emerged on the short-term memory test (see Fig. 4). It is apparent (and statistical analyses confirm) that the short-term and long-term abstinent groups did not differ from each other, but both groups performed more poorly than did the prolonged abstainers. In fact, when the prolonged abstainers were later compared to a group of 50 nonalcoholic matched control subjects, no significant differences emerged.

In contrast, no significant improvement in performance associated with in-

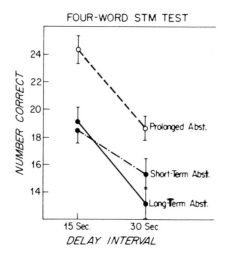

Fig. 4. Performance of short-term (1–2 months), long-term (12–36 months) and prolonged (≥60 months) abstinent alcoholics on Four-Word STM Test. (From Brandt et al., 1983.)

creasing length of abstinence was found on the Symbol-Digit Paired-Associate Learning Test (see Fig. 5). This is a task on which detoxified alcoholics have always been shown to be severely impaired (Brandt et al., 1983; Ryan and Butters, 1980a, 1980b).

The apparent improvement of short-term memory with prolonged abstinence from alcohol may be related to restitution of cortical functioning in these patients. It is well established that focal lesions of the posterior cerebral cortex may selectively impair short-term memory, while leaving long-term memory (e.g., paired-associate learning) intact (Butters et al., 1970; Samuels et al., 1971; Shallice and Warrington, 1970; Warrington and Shallice, 1969). While CT studies of the brains of chronic alcoholics have typically found generalized atrophy of the cerebral cortex to be most conspicuous (Cala and Mastaglia,

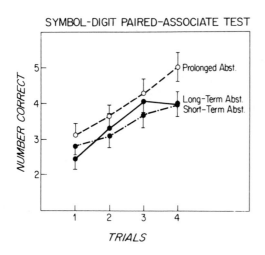

Fig. 5. Lack of improvement on Symbol-Digit Paired-Associate Learning Test with prolonged abstinence. (From Brandt et al., 1983.)

1981; Kroll et al., 1980; Wilkinson, 1982), at least three recent studies have documented a partial reversal of cerebral cortical shrinkage in some proportion of patients who remain abstinent for short periods of time (Artman, 1981; Carlen et al., 1978; Ron et al., 1982). The finding of Brandt et al. (1983) of improved performance on the Four-Word STM Test in prolonged abstinent alcoholics is consistent with the notion that this task requires intact cortical areas and further suggests that the mending of cortical tissues and the reinstatement of cortical functioning may continue for many years after cessation of drinking.

The refractory impairment on the Symbol-Digit Paired-Associate Learning task, a test of the ability to form and recollect novel associations, may indicate that alcohol has a relatively more permanent effect on brain mechanisms subserving long-memory. It appears to be the case that long-term memory requires the integrity of both limbic (i.e., hippocampal) and diencephalic (i.e., dorsomedial thalamic nucleus and mammillary bodies) structures (Milner, 1970; Scoville and Milner, 1957; Victor et al., 1971), and it has already been noted that alcoholic Korsakoff patients have their primary pathology in the diencephalic area. CT scan studies of non-Korsakoff chronic alcoholics have often found, in addition to generalized cortical atrophy, marked dilatation of the third ventricle, suggesting a degeneration of midline thalamic nuclei (Carlsson et al., 1979). Further evidence that the integrity of subcortical periventricular nuclei is essential for long-term memory in alcoholics is provided by recent studies by Gebhardt, Naeser, and Butters (1984). Both of these investigations, using computerized analyses of the CT scans of alcholics, found that the density of brain tissue surrounding the ventricular system is highly correlated with performance on paired-associate learning tasks. No such correlation has been found with short-term memory distractor tasks.

In summary, it appears that the dense anterograde and retrograde amnesia of the Korsakoff patient is relatively permanent and resistant to both spontaneous recovery and cognitive remediation (though, as pointed out earlier, pharmacologic treatment may hold some promise). The long-term alcoholic who has not experienced a Wernicke's encephalophy and has not suffered gross hemorrhagic lesions of the midbrain characteristic of Korsakoff's disease certainly displays impairments of memory and a variety of other cognitive deficits. However, at least some of them will spontaneously remit with prolonged abstinence from alcohol. Whether specific rehabilitative techniques can actually speed the restitution of functioning in the non-Korsakoff alcoholic is an area of ongoing research (e.g., Binder and Schreiber, 1980) and one of great theoretical and clinical importance.

ACKNOWLEDGMENT

The preparation of this chapter was supported in part by funds from the Medical Research Service of the Veterans Administration, grant AA00187 from NIAAA to Boston University, and grant BRS 2SO7RR07041–16 from NIH to the Johns Hopkins University.

REFERENCES

Adams, K. M., Grant, I., and Reed, R. (1980). Neuropsychology in alcoholic men in their late 30's: One year followup. *Am. J. Psychiat.*, *137*, 923–931.

Adams, R. D., Collins, G. H., and Victor, M. (1962). Troubles de la memoire et de l'apprentissage chez l'homme; leurs relations avec des lesions des lobes temporaux et du diencephale. In: *Physiologie de l'Hippocampe*. Paris: Centre National de la Recherche Scientifique.

Albert, M. S. (1981). Geriatric neuropsychology. *J. Consult Clin. Psychol.*, *49*, 835–850.

Albert, M. S., Butters, N., and Brandt, J. (1980). Memory for remote events in alcoholics. *J. Studies on Alcohol*, *41*, 1071–1081.

Albert, M. S., Butters, N., and Levin, J. (1979). Temporal gradients in the retrograde amnesia of patients with alcoholic Korsakoff's disease. *Arch. Neurol.*, *36*, 211–216.

Albert, M. S., and Kaplan, E. (1980). Organic implication of neuropsychological deficits in the elderly. In: L. W. Poon, J. L. Fozard, L. S. Cermak, D. L. Arenberg, and L. W. Thompson, eds., *New Directions in Memory and Aging*. Hillsdale, New Jersey: Erlbaum, pp. 403–432.

Artman, H. (1981). Reversible enlargement of cerebral spinal fluid spaces in alcoholics. *Am. J. Neuroradiol. 2*, 23–27.

Baddeley, A. D., and Warrington, E. K. (1970). Amnesia and the distinction between long- and short-term memory. *J. Verbal Learning Verbal Behav.*, *9*, 176–189.

Baddeley, A. D., and Warrington, E. K. (1973). Memory coding and amnesia. *Neuropsychologia, 11*, 159–165.

Bak, J. S., and Greene, R. L. (1980). Changes in neuropsychological functioning in an aging population. *J. Consult. Clin. Psychol.*, *48*, 395–399.

Becker, J. T., Butters, N., Hermann, A., and D'Angelo, N. (1983). A comparison of the effects of long-term alcohol abuse and aging on the performance of verbal and nonverbal divided attention tasks. *Alcoholism: Clin. Exp. Res.*, *7*, 213–219.

Berglund, M., Leijonquist, H., and Horlen, M. (1977). Prognostic significance and reversibility of cerebral dysfunction in alcoholics. *J. Studies on Alcohol*, *38*, 1761–1770.

Bertera, J. H., and Parsons, O. A. (1978). Impaired visual search in alcoholics. *Alcoholism: Clin. Exp. Res.*, *2*, 9–14.

Binder, L. M., and Schreiber, V. (1980). Visual imagery and verbal mediation as memory aids in recovering alcoholics. *J. Clin. Neuropsychol. 2*, 71–74.

Biber, C., Butters, N., Rosen, J., Gerstman, L., and Mattis, S. (1981). Encoding strategies and recognition of faces by alcoholic Korsakoff and other brain-damaged patients. *J. Clin. Neuropsychol.*, *3*, 315–330.

Blusewicz, M. J., Dustman, R. E., Schenkenberg, T., and Beck, E. C. (1977). Neuropsychological correlates of chronic alcoholism and aging. *J. Nerv. Ment. Dis.*, *165*, 348–355.

Brandt, J., Butters, N., Ryan, C., and Bayog, R. (1983). Cognitive loss and recovery in long-term alcohol abusers. *Arch. General Psychiat.*, *40*, 435–442.

Brierly, J. B. (1977) Neuropathology of amnesic states. In: C. W. M. Whitty and O. L. Zangwill, eds., *Amnesia*, 2d ed., London: Butterworths, pp. 199–223.

Burdick, J. A., Johnson, L. C., and Smith, J. W. (1970). Measurements of change during alcohol withdrawal in chronic alcoholics. *Br. J. Addiction*, *65*, 273–280.

Butters, N. (1984). Alcoholic Korsakoff's Syndrome: An Update. *Seminars in Neurology, 4*, 226–244.

Butters, N., and Albert, M. S. (1982). Processes underlying failures to recall remote events. In: L. S. Cermak, ed., *Human Memory and Amnesia*. Hillsdale, New Jersey: Lawrence Erlbaum Associates, pp. 237–273.

Butters, N., and Cermak, L. S. (1974). The role of cognitive factors in the memory disorder of alcoholic patients with the Korsakoff syndrome. *Ann. N.Y. Acad. Sci.*, *233*, 61–75.

Butters, N., and Cermak, L. S. (1975). Some analyses of amnesic syndromes in brain-damaged patients. In: R. Isaacson and K. Pribram, eds., *The Hippocampus*, vol. 2. New York: Plenum Press, pp. 377–409.

Butters, N., and Cermak, L. S. (1976). Neuropsychological studies of alcoholic Korsakoff patients. In: G. Goldstein and C. Neuringer, eds., *Empirical Studies of Alcoholism*. Cambridge, Mass.: Ballinger, pp. 153–195.

Butters, N., and Cermak, L. S. (1980). *Alcoholic Korsakoff's Syndrome: An Information Processing Approach to Amnesia*. New York: Academic Press.

Butters, N., Cermak, L. S., Montgomery, K., and Adinolfi, A. (1980). Some comparisons of the memory and visuoperceptive deficits of chronic alcoholics and patients with Korsakoff's disease. *Alcoholism, 1*, 73–80.

Butters, N., Miliotis, P., Albert, M. S., and Sax, D. S. (1984). Memory assessment: Evidence of the heterogeneity of amnesic symptoms. In: G. Goldstein, ed., *Advances in Clinical Neuropsychology, vol. 1*. New York: Plenum Press, pp. 127–159.

Butters, N., Samuels, I., Goodglass, H., and Brody, B. (1970). Short-term visual and auditory memory disorders after parietal and frontal lobe damage. *Cortex, 6*, 440–459.

Butters, N., Tarlow, S., Cermak, L. S., and Sax, D. (1976) A comparison of the information processing deficits of patients with Huntington's Chorea and Korsakoff's syndrome. *Cortex, 12*, 134–144.

Cala, L. A., and Mastaglia, F. L. (1981). Computerized tomography in chronic alcoholics. *Alcoholism: Clin. Exp. Res., 5*, 283–294.

Carlen, P. L., Wortzman, G., Holgate, T. C., Wilkinson, S. A., and Tankin, J. G. (1978). Reversible cerebral atrophy in recently abstinent chronic alcoholics measured by computed tomography scans. *Science, 200*, 1076–1078.

Carlsson, C., Claesson, L–E., Karlson, K–T., and Pettersson, L–E. (1979). Clinical psychometric and radiological signs of brain damage in chronic alcoholism. *Acta Neurol. Scand. 60*, 85–92.

Cermak, L. S. (1975). Imagery as an aid to retrieval for Korsakoff patients. *Cortex, 11*, 163–169.

Cermak, L. S., Butters, N., and Moreines, J. (1974). Some analyses of the verbal encoding deficit of alcoholic Korsakoff patients. *Brain and Language, 1*, 141–150.

Cermak, L. S., and Reale, L. (1978). Depth of processing and retention of words by alcoholic Korsakoff patients. *J. Exp. Psychol.: Human Learning and Memory, 4*, 165–174.

Cermak, L. S., Reale, L., and Baker, E. (1978). Alcoholic Korsakoff patients' retrieval from semantic memory. *Brain and Language, 5*, 215–226.

Cermak, L. S., and Ryback, R. S. (1976). Recovery of verbal short-term memory in alcoholics. *J. Studies on Alcohol, 37*, 46–52.

Cohen, N. J., and Squire, L. R. (1980). Preserved learning and retention of pattern analyzing skills in amnesia: Dissociation of knowing how and knowing that. *Science, 210*, 107–210.

Cohen, N. J., and Squire, L. R. (1981). Retrograde amnesia and remote memory impairment. *Neuropsychologia, 19*, 337–356.

Craik, F. I. M., and Tulving, E. (1975). Depth of processing and retention of words in episodic memory. *J. Exp. Psychol.: General, 104*, 268–294.

Delay, J., Brion, S., and Elissalde, B. (1958a). Corps mamillaires et syndrome Korsakoff. Etude anatomique de huit cas de syndrome de Korsakoff d'origine alcoolique sans alterations significative du cortex cerebral. I. Etude anatomo-clinique. *L'Presse Medicale, 66*, 1849–1852.

Delay, J., Brion, S., and Elissalde, B. (1958b). Corps mamillaires et syndrome Korsakoff. Etude anatomique de huit cas de syndrome de Korsakoff d'origine alcoolique sans alterations significative du cortex cerebral. II. Tubercules mamillaires et mécanisme de la memoire. *L'Presse Medicale, 66*, 1965–1968.

DeLuca, D., Cermak, L. S., and Butters, N. (1975). An analysis of Korsakoff patients' recall following varying types of distractor activity. *Neuropsychologia, 13*, 271–279.

Donovan, D. M., Queisser, H. R., and O'Leary, M. R. (1976). Group Embedded Figures Test performance as a predictor of cognitive impairment among alcoholics. *Int. J. Addictions, 11,* 725–739.

Dreyfus, P. M. (1974). Diseases of the nervous system in chronic alcoholics. In: B. Kissin and H. Begleiter, eds., *The Biology of Alcoholism: Clinical Pathology vol. 3.* New York: Plenum, pp. 265–290.

Dricker, J., Butters, N., Berman, G., Samuels, I., and Carey, S. (1978). Recognition and encoding of faces of alcoholic Korsakoff and right hemisphere patients. *Neuropsychologia, 16,* 683–695.

Ellenberg, L., Rosenbaum, G., Goldman, M. S., and Whitman, R. D. (1980). Recoverability of psychological functioning following alcohol abuse: Lateralization effects. *J. Consult. Clin. Psychol., 48,* 503–510.

Fedio, P., and Van Buren, J. M. (1974). Memory deficits during electrical stimulation in the speech cortex in conscious man. *Brain and Language, 1,* 29–42.

Fitzhugh, L. C., Fitzhugh, K. B., and Reitan, R. M. (1965). Adaptive abilities and intellectual functioning of hospitalized alcoholics: Further considerations. *Quart. J. Studies on Alcohol, 26,* 402–411.

Freund, G. (1973). Chronic central nervous system toxicity of alcohol. *Ann. Rev. Pharmacol., 13,* 217–227.

Gamper, E. (1928). Zur frage der Polioencephalitis haemorrhagic der chronischen Alkoholiker. Anatomische Befunde beim alkoholischen Korsakov und ihre Beziehungen zum klinischen Bild. *Deutsche Zeitschrift Fuer Nervenheilkunde, 102,* 122–129.

Gebhardt, C., Naeser, M. and Butters, N. (1984). Computerized measures of CT scans of alcoholics: Thalamic region related to memory. *Alcohol, 1,* 133–140.

Glosser, G., Butters, N., and Kaplan, E. (1977). Visuoperceptual processes in brain-damaged patients on the digit-symbol substitution tests. *Int. J. Neurosci., 7,* 59–66.

Goldman, M. S., Klisz, D. K., and Williams, D. L. (1981, February). Active and passive recovery of neuropsychological deficits in chronic alcoholics. Presented at the Ninth Annual Meeting of the International Neuropsychological Society.

Grant, I., Adams, K. M., and Reed, R. (1979). Normal neuropsychological abilities of alcoholic men in their late 30s. *Am. J. Psychiat., 136,* 1263–1269.

Grant, I., Adams, K. M., and Reed, R. (1984). Aging, abstinence and medical risk factors in the prediction of neuropsychological deficit amongst alcoholics. *Arch. Gen. Psychiat., 41,* 710–718.

Guthrie, A. (1980). The first year after treatment: Factors affecting time course of reversibility of memory and learning deficits in alcoholism. In: H. Begleiter, ed., *Biological Effects of Alcohol.* New York, Plenum Press, pp. 757–770.

Harper, C. G., and Blumbergs, P. C. (1982). Brain weights in alcoholics. *J. Neurol., Neurosurg., Psychiat., 45,* 838–840.

Hirst, W. (1982). The amnesic syndrome: Descriptions and explanations. *Psychological Bull., 91,* 435–460.

Huppert, F. A., and Piercy, M. (1976). Recognition memory in amnesic patients: Effect of temporal context and familiarity of material. *Cortex, 12,* 3–20.

Huppert, F. A., and Piercy, M. (1977). Recognition memory in amnesic patients: A defect of acquisition? *Neuropsychologia, 15,* 643–652.

Huppert, F. A., and Piercy, M. (1978). Dissociation between learning and remembering in organic aphasia. *Nature, 275,* 317–318.

Huppert, F. A., and Piercy, M. (1979). Normal and abnormal forgetting in organic amnesia: Effect of locus of lesion. *Cortex, 15,* 385–390.

Jarho, L. (1973). *Korsakoff-like Amnesic Syndrome in Penetrating Brain Inury.* Helsinki: Rehabilitation Institute for Brain Injured Veterans in Finland.

Jernigan, T. L. (1982, February). Computed tomographic findings in alcoholic vs. nonalcoholic dementia. Presented at the Tenth Annual Meeting of the International Neuropsychological Society.

Jones, B., and Parsons, O. A. (1971). Impaired abstracting ability in chronic alcoholics. *Arch. General Psychiat., 24,* 71–75.

Jones, B. P., Butters, N., Moskowitz, H. R., and Montgomery, K. (1978). Olfactory and gustatory capacities of alcoholic Korsakoff patients. *Neuropsychologia, 16,* 323–337.

Jones, B. P., Moskowitz, H. R., and Butters, N. (1975). Olfactory discrimination in alcoholic Korsakoff patients. *Neuropsychologia, 13,* 173–179.

Jonsson, C.-O., Cronholm, B., and Izikowitz, S. (1962). Intellectual changes in alcoholics: Psychometric studies of mental sequels of prolonged intensive abuse of alcohol. *Quart. J. Studies on Alcohol, 23,* 221–242.

Kapur, N., and Butters, N. (1977). Visuoperceptive deficits in long-term alcoholics with Korsakoff's psychosis. *J. Studies on Alcohol, 38,* 2025–2035.

Katzman, R., Terry, R. D., and Bick, K. C., (1978) eds. *Alzheimer's Disease: Senile Dementia and Related Disorders.* New York: Raven Press.

Klisz, D., and Parsons, O. A. (1977). Hypothesis testing in younger and older alcoholics. *J. Studies on Alcohol, 38,* 1718–1729.

Kinsbourne, M., and Wood, F. (1975). Short-term memory processes and the amnesic syndrome. In: D. Deutsch and J. A. Deutsch, eds., *Short-term Memory.* New York: Academic Press, pp. 287–291.

Kroll, P., Seigel, R., O'Neill, B., and Edwards, R. P. (1980). Cerebral cortical atrophy in alcoholic men. *J. Clin. Psychiat., 41,* 417–421.

Lishman, W. A. (1981). Cerebral disorder in alcoholism: Syndromes of impairment. *Brain, 104,* 1–20.

Long, J. A., and McLachlen, R. C. (1974). Abstract reasoning and perceptual-motor efficiency in alcoholics. *Quart. J. Studies on Alcohol, 35,* 1220–1229.

MacVane, J., Butters, N., Montgomery, K., and Farber, J. (1982). Cognitive functioning in men social drinkers: A replication study. *J. Studies on Alcohol, 43,* 81–95.

Mair, R., Capri, C., McEntee, W., and Engen, T. (1980). Odor discrimination and memory in Korsakoff's psychosis. *J. Exp. Psychol.; Hum. Percep. and Perf. 6(3),* 445–458.

Mair, G. P., Warrington, E. K., and Weiskrantz, L. (1979). Memory disorder in Korsakoff's psychosis. A neurological and neuropsychological investigation of two cases. *Brain, 102,* 749–783.

Marslen-Wilson, W. D., and Teuber, H. L. (1975). Memory for remote events in anterograde amnesia: Recognition of public figures from news photographs. *Neuropsychologia, 13,* 347–352.

Mayes, A., Meudell, P., and Neary, D. (1980). Do amnesics adopt inefficient encoding strategies with faces and random shapes? *Neuropsychologia, 18,* 527–540.

McDowall, J. (1979). Effects of encoding instructions and retrieval cueing on recall in Korsakoff patients. *Memory and Cognition, 7,* 232–239.

McEntee, W. J., and Mair, R. G. (1978). Memory impairments in Korsakoff's psychosis: A correlation with brain noradrenergic activity. *Science, 202,* 905–907.

McEntee, W. J., and Mair, R. G. (1980). Memory enhancement in Korsakoff's psychosis by clonidine: Further evidence for a noradrenergic deficit. *Ann. Neurol., 7,* 466–470.

Mesulam, M., Van Hoesen, G., and Butters, N. (1977). Clinical manifestations of chronic thiamine deficiency in the rhesus monkey. *Neurology, 27,* 239–245.

Meudell, P., Butters, N., and Montgomery, K. (1978). Role of rehearsal in the short-term memory performance of patients with Korsakoff's and Huntington's Disease. *Neuropsychologia, 16,* 507–510.

Meudell, P., Northern, B., Snowden, J. S., and Neary, D. (1980). Long-term memory for famous voices in amnesic and normal subjects. *Neuropsychologia, 18,* 133–139.

Miller, E. (1977). *Abnormal Aging: The Psychology of Senile and Presenile Dementia.* London, Wiley.

Milner, B. (1966). Amnesia following operation on the temporal lobe. In: C. W. M. Whitty and O. L. Zangwill, eds., *Amnesia.* London: Butterworths, pp. 109–133.

Milner, B. (1970). Memory and the medial temporal regions of the brain. In: K. H. Pribram and D. E. Broadbent, eds., *Biology of Memory.* New York: Academic Press, pp. 29–50.

Milner, B. (1971). Interhemispheric differences in the localization of psychological processes in man. *Br. Med. Bull., 27,* 272–275.

Moscovitch, M. (1982). Multiple dissociations of function in amnesia. In: L. S. Cermak, ed., *Human Memory and Amnesia.* Hillsdale, New Jersey: Lawrence Erlbaum Associates, pp. 337–365.

Oscar-Berman, M. (1973). Hypothesis testing and focusing behavior during concept formation for amnesic Korsakoff patients. *Neuropsychologia, 11,* 191–198.

Oscar-Berman, M. (1980). Neuropsychological consequences of long-term chronic alcoholism. *Am. Sci., 68,* 410–419.

Oscar-Berman, M., Heyman, G. M., Bonner, R. T., and Ryder, J. (1980). Human neuropsychology: Some differences between Korsakoff and normal operant performance. *Psychol. Res., 41,* 235–247.

Oscar-Berman, M., Sahakian, B. J., and Wikmark, G. (1976). Spatial probability learning by alcoholic Korsakoff patients. *J. Exp. Psychol.: Human Learning and Memory, 2,* 215–222.

Oscar-Berman, M., and Samuels, I. (1977). Stimulus preference and memory factors in Korsakoff's syndrome. *Neuropsychologia, 15,* 99–106.

Oscar-Berman, M., Zola-Morgan, S., Oberg, R. G. E., and Bonner, R. T. (1982). Comparative neuropsychology and Korsakoff's syndrome. III. Delayed response, delayed alternation and DRL performance. *Neuropsychologia, 20,* 187–202.

Page, R. D., and Linden, J. D. (1974). "Reversible" organic brain syndrome in alcoholics. *Quart. J. Studies on Alcohol, 35,* 98–107.

Parker, E. S., and Noble, E. P. (1977). Alcohol consumption and cognitive functioning in social drinkers. *J. Studies on Alcohol, 38,* 1224–1232.

Parker, E. S., and Noble, E. P. (1980). Alcohol and the aging process in social drinkers. *J. Studies on Alcohol, 41,* 170–178.

Parsons, O. A. (1975). Brain damage in alcoholics: Altered states of unconsciousness. In: M. Gross, ed., *Alcohol Intoxication and Withdrawal* vol. 2 New York: Plenum Press, pp. 564–584.

Parsons, O. A., and Farr, S. P. (1981). The neuropsychology of alcohol and drug abuse. In: S. B. Filskov and T. J. Boll, eds., *Handbook of Clinical Neuropsychology.* New York: Wiley, pp. 320–365.

Parsons, O. A., and Leber, W. R. (1981). The relationship between cognitive dysfunction and brain damage in alcoholics: Casual, interactive, or epiphenomenal? *Alcoholism: Clin. Exp. Res., 5,* 326–343.

Parsons, O. A., and Prigatano, G. P. (1977). Memory functioning in alcoholics. In: I. M. Birnbaum and E. S. Parker, eds., *Alcohol and Human Memory.* Hillsdale, New Jersey: Lawrence Erlbaum Associates.

Parsons, O. A., Tarter, R. E., and Jones, B. (1971). Cognitive deficits in chronic alcoholics. *Il Lavoro Neuro Psichiatrico, 49,* 5–14.

Piercy, M. F. (1977). Experimental studies of the organic amnesic syndrome In: C. W. M. Whitty and O. L. Zangwill, eds., *Amnesia,* 2d ed., London: Butterworths, pp. 1–51.

Porjesz, B., and Begleiter, H. (1982). Evoked brain potential deficits in alcoholism and aging. *Alcoholism: Clin. Exp. Res., 6,* 53–63.

Riggs, H. E., and Boles, H. S. (1944). Wernicke's disease: A clinical and pathological study of 42 cases. *Quart. J. Studies on Alcohol, 4,* 361–370.

Riley, J. N., and Walker, D. W. (1978). Morphological alterations in hippocampus after long-term alcohol consumption in mice. *Science, 201,* 646–648.

Ron, M. A., Acker, W., Shaw, G. K., and Lishman, W. A. (1982). Computerized tomography of the brain in chronic alcoholism. *Brain, 105,* 497–514.

Ryan, C. (1982). Alcoholism and premature aging: A neuropsychological perspective. *Alcoholism: Clin. Exp. Res., 6,* 22–30.

Ryan, C., and Butters, N. (1980a). Further evidence for a continuum-of-impairment encompassing male alcoholic Korsakoff patients and chronic alcoholic men. *Alcoholism: Clin. Exp. Res., 4,* 190–197.

Ryan, C., and Butters, N. (1980b). Learning and memory impairments in young and old alcoholics: evidence for the premature-aging hypothesis. *Alcoholism: Clin. Exp. Res., 4*, 288–293.

Ryan, C., and Butters, N. (1983). Cognitive deficits in alcohol abuse. In: B. Kissin and H. Begleiter, eds., *Biology of Alcoholism*, vol. 6. New York: Plenum Press, pp. 485–538.

Ryan, C., Butters, N., Montgomery, K., Adinolfi, A., and Didario, B. (1980). Memory deficits in chronic alcoholics: Continuities between the "intact" alcoholic and the alcoholic Korsakoff patient. In: H. Begleiter, ed., *Biological Effects of Alcohol*. New York: Plenum Press, pp. 701–717.

Ryan, C., Didario, B., Butters, N., and Adinolfi, A. (1980). The relationship between abstinence and recovery of function in male alcoholics. *J. Clin. Neuropsychol., 2*, 125–134.

Ryback, R. (1971). The continuum and specificity of the effects of alcohol on memory. *Quart. J. Studies on Alcohol, 32*, 995–1016.

Samuels, I., Butters, N., Goodglass, H., and Brody, B. (1971). A comparison of subcortical and cortical damage on short-term visual and auditory memory. *Neuropsychologia, 9*, 293–306.

Sanders, H. I., and Warrington, E. K. (1971). Memory for remote events in amnesic patients. *Brain, 94*, 661–668.

Scoville, W. B., and Milner, B. (1957). Loss of recent memory after bilateral hippocampal lesions. *Neuropsychologia, 20*, 11–21.

Seltzer, B., and Benson, D. F. (1974). The temporal pattern of retrograde amnesia in Korsakoff's disease. *Neurology, 24*, 527–530.

Shallice, T., and Warrington, E. K. (1970). Independent functioning of the verbal memory stores: A neuropsychological study. *Quart. J. Exp. Psychol., 22*, 261–273.

Sharp, J. R., Rosenbaum, G., Goldman, M. S., and Whitman, R. D. (1977). Recoverability of psychological functioning following alcohol abuse: Acquisition of meaningful synonyms. *J. Consult. Clin. Psychol., 45*, 1023–1028.

Squire, L. R. (1981), Two forms of human amnesia: An analysis of forgetting. *J. Neurosci., 1*, 635–640.

Squire, L. R., and Cohen, N. J. (1982). Remote memory, retrograde amnesia, and the neuropsychology of memory. In: L. S. Cermak, ed., *Human Memory and Amnesia*. Hillsdale, New Jersey: Lawrence Erlbaum Associates, pp. 275–301.

Squire, L. R., and Moore, R. Y. (1979). Dorsal thalamic lesions in a noted case of chronic memory dysfunction. *Ann. Neurol., 6*, 503–506.

Squire, L. R., and Slater, P. C. (1975). Forgetting in very long-term memory as assessed by an improved questionnaire technique. *J. Exp. Psychol.: Human Learning and Memory, 104*, 50–54.

Squire, L. R., and Slater, P. C. (1978). Anterograde and retrograde memory impairment in chronic amnesia. *Neuropsychologia, 16*, 313–322.

Talland, G. (1965). *Deranged Memory*. New York: Academic Press.

Tarter, R. E. (1973). An analysis of cognitive deficits in chronic alcoholics. *J. Nerv. Ment. Dis., 157*, 138–147.

Tarter, R. E., and Parsons, O. A. (1971). Conceptual shifting in chronic alcoholics. *J. Abnorm. Psychol., 77*, 71–75.

Teuber, H. L., Milner, B., and Vaughan, H. G. (1968). Persistent anterograde amnesia after stab wound of the basal brain. *Neuropsychologia, 6*, 267–282.

Victor, M., Adams, R. D., and Collins, G. H. (1971). *The Wernicke-Korsakoff Syndrome*. Philadelphia: F. A. Davis.

Walker, D. W., Barnes, D., Zornetzer, S., Hunter, B., and Kubanis, P. (1980). Neuronal loss in hippocampus induced by prolonged ethanol consumption in rats. *Science, 209*, 711–713.

Walker, D. W., Hunter, B., and Abraham, W. (1981). Neuroanatomical and functional deficits subsequent to chronic ethanol administration in animals. *Alcoholism: Clin. Exp. Res., 5*, 267–282.

Warrington, E. K., and Shallice, T. (1969). The selective impairment of auditory-verbal short-term memory. *Brain*, *92*, 885–896.

Warrington, E. K., and Weiskrantz, L. (1970). Amnesic syndrome: Consolidation or retrieval? *Nature*, *228*, 628–630.

Warrington, E. K., and Weiskrantz, L. (1973). An analysis of short-term and long-term memory defects in man. In: J. A. Deutsch, ed., *The Physiological Basis of Memory*. New York: Academic Press, pp. 365–395.

Warrington, E. K., and Weiskrantz, L. (1982). Amnesia: A disconnection syndrome? *Neuropsychologia*, *20*, 233–248.

Wechsler, D. (1945). A standardized memory scale for clinical use. *J. Psychol.*, *19*, 87–95.

Weingartner, H., Faillace, L. A., and Markley, H. G. (1971). Verbal information retention in alcoholics. *Quart. J. Studies on Alcohol*, *32*, 293–303.

Wilkinson, D. A. (1982). Examination of alcoholics by computer tomographic (CT) scans: A critical review. *Alcoholism: Clin. Exp. Res.*, *6*, 31–45.

Wilkinson, D. A., and Carlen, P. L. (1981). Chronic organic brain syndromes associated with alcoholism: Neuropsychological and other aspects. In: Y. Israel, F. Glaser, H. Kalant, R. Popham, W. Schmidt, and R. Smart, eds., *Research Advances in Alcohol and Drug Problems*, vol. 6. New York: Plenum Press, pp. 463–478.

Winocur, G., and Kinsbourne, M. (1978). Contextual cueing as an aid to Korsakoff amnesics. *Neuropsychologia*, *16*, 671–682.

Winocur, G., Kinsbourne, M., and Moscovitch, M. (1981). The effect of cueing on release from proactive interference in Korsakoff amnesic patients. *J. Exp. Psychol.: Human Learning and Memory*, *7*, 56–65.

Winocur, G., and Weiskrantz, L. (1976). An investigation of paired-associate learning in amnesic patients. *Neuropsychologia*, *14*, 97–110.

20

Neuropsychological Consequences of Drug Abuse

ALBERT S. CARLIN

So comes a reckoning when the banquet's o'er
The dreadful reckoning when men smile no more

John Gay, *The What D'ye Call It*, act II, scene 9

Neuropsychological consequences of drug abuse are of considerable importance in neuropsychiatric populations. Many patients consume licit or illicit psychoactive substances in prescribed or uncontrolled ways. This chapter reviews the evidence on various relationships between behavior and drug consumption, with particular reference to the long-term neurobehavioral impact of drug abuse.

It is commonly assumed that the abuse of most psychoactive substances results in neuropsychological deficit. Whether this attitude reflects a sense of moral retribution or the belief that repeated trips across the blood-brain barrier must exact their toll is an open question. Certainly, most psychoactive drugs affect neuropsychological functioning. The acute effects can be studied in a straightforward way by administering the drug under study in known dosage to subjects and then comparing either pre–post or drug–placebo performance.

The long-term consequences of chronic drug use are more difficult to assess. The problem arises not in the assessment of neuropsychological status, but in assigning any observed deficit to the appropriate cause. As will be seen, investigations of drug consequences are frequently cross-sectional; subjects have established drug-abuse careers so that it is difficult to differentiate premorbid impairment from drug-induced impairment. The accurate determination of past psychoactive drug use with regard to chronicity and frequency is vital but also difficult. Exposure to adulterants, the prevalence of multiple drug use, and the impact of route of administration all contribute to the uncertainties of attributing any observed impairment to the drug(s) under consideration. In addition, the neuropsychological status of drug users may be influenced by their medical or developmental history, independently or through interactions with drug use.

Neuropsychological consequences, as the term is used in this chapter, are relatively enduring deficits in behavior which presumably reflect changes in brain function. Actual structural changes may or may not be observed; physical procedures such as computerized axial tomography, EEG, or autopsy will be referred to where relevant. The chapter will focus on studies employing relatively systematic, objective behavioral assessments thought to reflect cortical integrity. For the most part, animal research will be omitted since the results are difficult to extrapolate to humans because of between-species differences in brain and behavior and in drug dose, pattern of use, and route of administration. For example, animal studies frequently involve much larger doses than humans take in a free situation; furthermore, it is unclear that dose per kg or M^2 is a valid translation from humans to animals of different species and size.

The entire gamut of psychoactive drugs has not received equal attention from those investigating neuropsychological consequences. Drug classes that were developed and marketed with therapeutic intent have been much less thoroughly studied than illicit and recreational drugs. Thus, LSD, marihuana and solvents have been the target of neuropsychological studies far more often than opiates, sedative hypnotics and minor tranquilizers.

The following review has been organized by drug class only for convenience of exposition, with full awareness that much drug abuse is, in fact, polydrug use. Often it is extremely difficult to classify people according to meaningful drug categories since heavy marihuana users may also drink heavily, opiate users may also use marihuana and amphetamines, and so on. With this caveat in mind, what are some of the neuropsychological findings related to drug abuse?

LSD

The long-term neuropsychological consequences of LSD use have been studied by several investigators. McGlothlin, Arnold, and Freedman (1969) examined a group of individuals who had initially received LSD as an adjunct to psychotherapy. Many of them continued using LSD in a nonmedical setting, resulting in a median of 75 LSD exposures (range, 20–1,l00). Other drug use was minimal in this somewhat older (mean age, 40), relatively well-educated group. Subjects were excluded who showed evidence of severe psychopathology before exposure to LSD or who had extensive drug abuse histories or pre-existing neurological pathology. Since the LSD-using subjects were initially psychotherapy patients, they were compared with other psychotherapy patients who had not been exposed to LSD or other hallucinogens. Both groups were given a selection of subtests of the Halstead-Reitan Battery including the Category Test, Trail Making Test, Rhythm test, and Finger Oscillation Test. In addition, the Shipley-Hartford, Porteus Maze, Witkin's Embedded Figures, Guilford's Associational Fluency Test, Minnesota Perceptuo-Diagnostic Test and a map-reading task were administered. A clinical interview was also carried out. The LSD group performed significantly worse on only one test, Category. However, no correlation was found between number of LSD ingestions and performance on this task. One of the two tests that did correlate with the number of LSD ingestions revealed better performance with greater use (Rhythm) while the other showed worse performance with greater use (Map Reading). The authors concluded that there was a possible association between LSD use and minimal brain dysfunction, but acknowledged the difficulty of establishing a causal relationship.

Illicit LSD users were studied by Cohen and Edwards (1969) with the complete Halstead-Reitan Battery as well as the Raven Progressive Matrices and the same test of spatial orientation (map reading) used by McGlothlin et al. (1969). These authors found that the LSD users differed from a comparison sample matched for age and education on Trails A and map following. On both tests, the LSD users scored worse than did the controls. Among the LSD users, a correlation was found between number of experiences and worse performance on Trails A and the Raven test. The authors concluded that "although no generalized neuropsychological deficit is associated with LSD use visual spatial orientation is impaired." The authors also provided the caveat that subject selection variables might have biased their results, since obviously impaired persons had been excluded as unable to complete the testing. Unfortunately, they provided no information about numbers of subjects excluded. It should also be noted that the drug users in this study had significant experience with a number of drugs other than LSD.

Wright and Hogan (1972) attempted to replicate the findings of Cohen and Edwards (1969) using similar subjects, although their LSD users had a lower exposure to LSD (median of 20 exposures vs. 50). Wright and Hogan also added the WAIS and the aphasia screening test to the battery used by Cohen and Edwards. They found that the LSD users performed better on the Information subtest of the WAIS and worse on the Comprehension subtest. No significant differences were found on other test scores nor on the Impairment Index. Aphasia screening scores were compared to a subgroup of college students, and although both groups evidenced a low rate of errors, they did not differ statistically. The authors concluded that they failed to replicate the findings of even mild impairment in LSD users. It is, of course, possible that the group studied by Wright and Hogan was not sufficiently exposed to LSD for impairment to emerge.

The most striking evidence of deleterious consequences of LSD use is provided by Acord (1972), who also had the most liberal definition of LSD abuse. His subjects were 40 inpatients and outpatients selected from the psychiatric services of a large military hospital who had used LSD at least once. He reported that their mean scores on the Category Test and the time, memory, and localization portions of the Tactual Performance Test (TPT) exceeded the usual cut-offs for impairment. Although striking, these results are difficult to interpret because there was no control group and because of the possibility that psychopathology or other factors inherent to being a psychiatric patient could affect neuropsychological performance. The importance of eliminating the contribution of uncontrolled variables is especially important in the light of the liberal inclusion criteria.

As a followup to this investigation, Acord and Barker (1973) compared 15 persons who had used hallucinogenic drugs at least once with 15 persons who denied use of drugs except for marihuana. In addition, all subjects were free of intracranial pathology, medically prescribed psychoactive drugs and psychopathology beyond character disorder or behavior disorder. Subjects were inpatients, outpatients and staff of a large military hospital. Subjects were essentially similar in age, education, and Navy General Classification test scores. All subjects received the Category Test, Trails B and TPT location (it is assumed that these subjects were administred the entire TPT, but only the location scores are reported). Hallucinogenic users scored significantly worse on Category and TPT location. The scores of the experimental group approached or exceeded cut-off scores proposed by Halstead (1947) and Reitan (1955). The authors did not indicate proportion of subjects who were patients or nonpatients in each group and also did not specify the extent of other drug involvement. Thus, it is not possible to determine whether the findings are related to hallucinogenic drug use, patient status, use of other drugs, or other selection factors. The rather liberal inclusion criterion, which lacks face validity, suggest that the last mentioned possibility must be entertained seriously.

Aside from problems in sample selection and inadequate consideration of obvious sources of neuropsychological variance, the studies above, and many to be reviewed below, lost power by relying wholly on univariate statistical comparisons to examine their hypotheses. Failure to employ multivariate statistical approaches, or at least to correct for use of multiple t or F tests by strategies such as the Bonferroni inequality method (Grove and Andreasen, 1982) open the findings to the criticism that they might be capitalizing on chance factors. At the same time exclusive reliance on measures of central tendency (avoiding clinical scoring and inference) assumes a uniformity of area of impairment which may not exist. Some users of the drugs in question may experience primarily spatial deficits, while others may demonstrate verbal impairment. Combining these subjects might well obscure their impairment through averaging of scores.

A study of phencyclidine (PCP) abusers by Carlin et al. (1979) provides a useful model of how possible contaminating variables can be isolated (if not controlled for) and how the more powerful reliance on clinical inference can be used to study the possible deleterious consequences of hallucinogenic drug abuse. The complete Halstead-Reitan Battery was administered to 12 chronic PCP abusers, 12 polydrug abusers who did not consume PCP and 12 normal controls who engaged in minimal drug use. A drug use history for the past 10 years preceding the study was conducted, as was a review of medical/neurological history. The drug use data were presented in milligrams of substance or occasions of use per week based on a 10 year average. They revealed that both drug-using groups used equivalent amounts of heroin and stimulants; the polydrug group consumed more depressants and opiates than did the PCP group who consumed more PCP and hallucinogens. Neuropsychological performance was rated on a six-point scale ranging from above average performance to severely impaired. The ratings were carried out by a clinician who was provided the protocols of all 36 subjects and who had no information regarding group membership. Both drug-using groups contained significantly more persons judged to be impaired, than did non-drug-using controls. Mean subtest score differences and appropriate statistical tests were also presented in this publication, but because of small sample size and variability, the differences were less dramatic. Medical-neurological risk was independent of neuropsychological status, as was recent drug consumption as reflected by positive urine tests. Because of the now common pattern of multiple drug abuse, only indirect evidence of the impact of PCP could be provided; but the fact that the PCP users consumed substantially less sedative-hypnotics (the class which previous research has associated with neuropsychological (NP) impairment) at least suggested that abuse of substances other than PCP or hallucinogens did not explain the PCP users' impairment.

Taken as an aggregate, the studies described above suggest that LSD has little enduring impact on higher level cognitive functioning. The studies of Acord and Acord and Barker are contaminated by mixing patients with "normals" and by an inclusion criterion so liberal it renders their results almost meaningless. It is also apparent from the results of Carlin et al. (1979) that the impact of the class of drugs, "hallucinogens," cannot be meaningfully considered. It is possible that some classes of hallucinogens might be implicated in the emergence of neuropsychological deficit while others might not be. It is also possible the impairment associated with LSD use requires greater exposure than experienced by subjects studied by Cohen and Edwards (1969), McGlothlin et al. (1969), and Wright and Hogan (1972), while the greater use of both LSD and PCP of subjects studied by Carlin et al. (1979) was sufficient to reveal a subtle relationship. It seems fair to conclude that if there are deleterious consequences of LSD, they are subtle, easily obscured by dose differences, and have a low prevalence among users.

Marihuana

The neuropsychology of marihuana use has also been studied extensively. Culver and King (1974) examined the neuropsychological performance of three groups of Dartmouth undergraduates from the 1971 and 1972 classes. The three groups were: marihuana users, marihuana plus LSD users, and non-drug users. The Halstead-Reitan Battery was administered. The data were analyzed separately for each year and then combined into a larger sample. Although of relatively small sample size, the cross-validation offered by this study is of great interest. Significant differences appeared, disappeared and reappeared among the groups and classes of different years. Consistent differences were found only for the Trail Making Test: the marihuana group performed significantly better than the LSD group. The marihuana group also drank more alcohol than the controls; the LSD group also used more marihuana and drank more than the marihuana group. The analysis was repeated with statistical control for amount of alcohol consumed with identical NP results.

The pattern of greater exposure to any one drug being related to more exposure to a greater variety of drugs was also reported by Rochford, Grant, and LaVigne (1977) who studied drug use among medical students. They found that marihuana smokers were a subset of those who used alcohol. Those who used hallucinogens, stimulants and opiates were a subset of the marihuana abusers. These authors also found that there were no differences between the marihuana smokers and the non-drug-using medical students on TPT, Trails A and B, the Hutt Adaptation of the Bender-Gestalt and the Minnesota Perceptuo-Diagnostic Test. This study replicates that of Grant et al. (1973) which used the complete Halstead-Reitan and found only one statistically significant difference, which the authors attributed to chance.

Carlin and Trupin (1977) studied persons who smoked daily for an average of 5 years and compared them to a group who were matched for age, education and intelligence. Their marihuana subjects, in contrast to those of Culver and King (1974), did worse on Trails B.

The lack of consistent findings from these empirical studies failed to support the clinical reports of Kolansky and Moore (1971, 1972) who observed organic-like impairment among a group of adolescent psychiatric patients who were heavy consumers of marihuana. It may be that Culver and King (1974), Grant et al. (1973), Rochford et al. (1977), and Carlin and Trupin (1977) studied biased samples of younger, brighter, and less impaired users. By focusing on college students the empirical studies might have been sampling from a population unlikely to contain many impaired persons. The empirically studied persons might have been the survivors while Kolansky and Moore (1971, 1972) reported on the casualties. Additionally, if one were to assume that impairment emerges with heavier daily use and longer exposure, then marihuana smoking in most Western countries has not existed long enough for the true casualty rate to surface.

A number of foreign cultures exist within which marihuana use has a longer tradition. Chronic cannabis users were studied in Egypt (Souief, 1976), Jamaica (Rubin and Comitas, 1975), and Costa Rica (Satz, Fletcher and Sutker, 1976). The Jamaican study is in many ways the more relevant as an investigation of persons who are functioning and who are also very long-term and very heavy users. This society has a tradition of cannabis use within which many view the drug as curative, benign, or even as a work enhancer. Rubin and Comitas (1975) reported no significant differences between users and non-users on an extensive battery of NP tests. Unfortunately, cross-cultural differences and attempts to cope with these confounded the interpretation of these results. The Information, Vocabulary and Picture Arrangement subtests of the WAIS were not used due to the subjects' unfamiliarity with the required knowledge and skills, and the authors acknowledged the questionable relevance of other subtests, but included them in an effort to have some metric of comparison of users and nonusers. Their report suggested that the child's version of the TPT was used, as was the child's version of the Category Test. Thus, the lack of significance on many test of the WAIS may be a function of a floor effect; that is, the absence of difference may reflect inapplicability of test items so that groups had little room to differ. Similarly, and perhaps of greater importance, use of the children's version of two of the most sensitive tests of higher level cognitive functioning (Category, TPT), might have created an artificial ceiling that obscured any drug effects.

Satz et al. (1971) carried out a more extensive evaluation with greater sensitivity to cross-cultural issues in their Costa Rica study. Pretesting was carried out to assure cultural compatibility of the Williams Memory Scale, Wechsler Memory Scale, Facial Recognition Memory Test, Benton Visual Retention Test, the IPAT Culture Fair Test and a short form of the Spanish version of the WAIS. Appropriate multivariate statistics failed to demonstrate differences between users, occasional users, and nonusers.

Souief (1976) is one of the few investigators to find marked differences between cannabis users and nonusers. His study, carried out among Egyptian prisoners, compared cannabis users and nonusers on a number of cognitive measures which do not have established neuropsychological validity. For this reason his results are difficult to interpret. A further problem is the educational differences between subjects.

Overall, controlled studies have failed to relate marihuana use to neuropsychological dysfunction. In the light of clinical reports such as those of Kolansky and Moore (1971, 1972), caution should be exercised in dismissing the drug as harmless. It is possible that the deficit is more subtle than can be detected by present tests or that the studies of users who were not patients systematically excluded impaired persons through biased sampling. It is also possible that users who have been studied have not smoked enough marihuana long enough to produce measurable impairment.

Solvents

In contrast to the preceding drugs of abuse whose long-term neuropsychological consequences have not been established, the deleterious consequences of chronic solvent abuse are clear and obvious. Many of the published reports are case histories documenting peripheral neuropathy and cerebellar dysfunction (Grabski, 1961; Knox and Nelson, 1966; Kelly, 1975; Lewis, Moritz, and Mellis, 1981; Malm and Lying-Tunell, 1980).

Turning to neuropsychological studies, Dodds and Santostefano (1964) compared teenage glue sniffers and nonsniffers on a variety of cognitive measures including the Benton Visual Retention Test and found no significant differences. Tsushima and Towne (1977) compared paint sniffers with nonsniffers equated for age, education, and SES on a number of tests which are subparts of the Halstead-Reitan Battery (Tapping, Rhythm, Trails A and B) and on the coding subtest of the WISC, the Stroop Color-Word test, the Graham-Kendall Memory for Designs, and the Peabody Picture Vocabulary Test. They found marked differences on 13 of 15 measures, the sniffers performing significantly worse. A possible artifact in their findings may be the result of presniffing differences. The sniffers differed on vocabulary-estimated I.Q. and thus it is possible that lower I.Q. functioning might account for both the glue sniffing and lower performance on other tests. The investigators explored this possibility by examining the relationship between length of abuse history and impairment and found a significant association. However, the nature of the relationship is puzzling: it is curvilinear, with relatively uniform performance until history of use exceeds 11 years, at which time a marked decrement appears. Either a threshold phenomenon exists or the results reflect a peculiar cohort difference.

A more clearcut finding is provided by Berry, Heaton and Kirby (1977) who examined glue sniffers and compared their performance on the Halstead-Reitan Battery with that of siblings and peers. They found significant differences (glue sniffers being worse) for verbal and full scale I.Q., TPT time and memory, and impairment in sensory-perceptual and motor functioning. The glue sniffers also had a higher Impairment Index and Average Impairment Rating. It is of interest that other measures of higher level functioning showed little or no differences.

One difficulty in research with solvents is that the concoctions that people inhale tend to contain a large variety of aldehydes, ketones, and aromatic compounds, each of which might have a different spectrum of neurotoxicity. So far, the weight of evidence from case reports suggest that toluene can cause cerebral and cerebellar atrophy, with lesser peripheral effects; some of the aldehydes and ketones (e.g., methylbutylketone), on the other hand, produce marked neuropathy but uncertain cerebral effects. The properties of many other aromatic compounds are largely unknown.

A second problem is that glue and paint sniffing tend to occur in older children and young adolescents, a time of active development of higher order cognitive capacities. Besides whatever direct toxicity solvents produce, they might also "stunt" cognitive growth by impairing learning at a critical developmental period. When one couples this possibility with common observations that glue and paint sniffing are most prevalent in socio-culturally disadvantaged youths, it becomes evident that results of neuropsychological study of these groups at some later time make it difficult to draw causal inferences.

Opiates

Considering the number of years opiates have been widely available and widely abused, the relative paucity of research on their neuropsychological consequences is surprising. Two early studies (Brown and Partington, 1942; Pfeffer and Ruble, 1946) failed to find any impairment which could be associated with opiate use. These two studies are more of historic than substantive interest at this time since their methodology is not comparable to the more recent studies with their more refined measures of neuropsychological functioning. A more recent example of the problem of unitary measures of "brain-damage" is provided by Korin (1974), who compared 27 Vietnam-era veterans who abused heroin with 17 who abused nonopiate drugs on a battery of tests which included the Bender-Gestalt, an instrument which has a reputation as a measure of brain damage. He found that heroin abusers performed worse on the Bender-Gestalt, but pointed out that personality traits are also likely to be reflected by the Bender-Gestalt and hence he wisely refrained from interpreting the results as suggesting neuropsychological impairment in the heroin abusers. Although the latter study differentiates between detoxified and currently using subjects, none of the studies provides any measures or estimates of chronicity or frequency of use of the drugs in question. A more elaborate study of neuropsychological assessment of Vietnam-era veteran heroin abusers was carried out by Fields and Fullerton (1974) who relied on the Halstead-Reitan Battery. A group of heroin abusers, addicted from 1 to 10 years (mean length of addiction, 4.9 years), was compared with a group of brain damaged subjects and a group of mixed nondrug abusing, non-brain-injured patients, all of whom were matched for education, age, and sex. They found that the heroin addicted sample tended to perform somewhat better than the control group and that both performed significantly better than the brain damaged comparison group. They concluded that their sample of heroin addicts failed to evidence deleterious consequences of heroin addiction. Although they administered the Halstead-Reitan Battery, which is readily amenable to clinical ratings and classification, Fields and Fullerton (1974) relied strictly on comparisons of group central tendencies for various tests. As discussed previously, such a strategy runs the risk of failing to identify drug effects that express themselves in different ways in different subjects.

The complexities of mode of examination of neuropsychological data is illustrated by two publications by the same group of authors which provide differing conclusions. Rounsaville, Novelly, and Kleber (1981) compared opiate addicts with epileptics using an impairment rating based on the sum of the number of tests on which each subject's score was one standard deviation from the mean in the direction of impairment on those tasks making up the Lafayette Clinic Neuropsychological Assessment Battery (Adams et al., 1975). These scores allowed the authors to classify subjects as demonstrating no impairment, mild impairment, and moderate to severe impairment. The two groups did not differ on either impairment rating or on mean individual test scores. They concluded that opiate abusers manifested neuropsychological impairment. In a later paper, using the same opiate abusing sample and the same epileptic comparison group, but with the addition of a CETA participant "normal" comparison group, Rounsaville et al. (1982) arrived at the opposite conclusion. Their data were unchanged, but their finding that the CETA participant group was as impaired as both the opiate abusers and the epilepsy comparison group caused them to re-evaluate the meaning of their findings.

Several possible conclusions can be drawn from this set of papers. Either the epilepsy group was not neuropsychologically impaired and, hence, neither were the opiate subjects; or, the CETA participants were impaired, as were the two original groups. It is also possible that the groups differed along some seemingly irrelevant dimension. For example, in both papers the addicts are described as predominately white while no ethnic or racial label was provided for the comparison groups. Could cultural differences beyond those of education and socioeconomic class account for the differences? The freedom to choose among these alternative explanations clearly indicates no conclusions can be drawn from these studies.

Hill et al. (1979) compared heroin abusers and alcohol abusers and normals on brain computerized tomographic (CT) and neuropsychological testing. Acquiring both a physical measure and a behavioral measure of cortical integrity provides a unique opportunity to explore the relationships among these measures. Overall, they found that alcoholics were most impaired compared to normals, with opiate addicts most often falling between these two groups on selected subtests of the Halstead-Reitan (TPT, Tapping and Category), the Raven Progressive Matrices, the Shipley-Hartford and the Peabody Picture Vocabulary Test. These authors found that length of opiate abuse career was associated with greater impairment. They also found that remission in opiate abusers was complexly related to impairment; those in remission performed somewhat better on Category and somewhat worse on TPT than current users. A small but significant correlation ($r = 0.27$) was found between CT measured ventricle/brain ratio and errors on Category and TPT total time. Interestingly, the investigators also found that opiate abusers had somewhat smaller ventricles and narrower sulci than controls (alcoholics had enlargement of both). The authors speculated that this might be the result of an allergic phenomenon that results in chronic swelling of brain tissue. The relatively weak relationship between CT scan and neuropsychological test findings is disappointing, but consistent with data emerging from comparisons of CT and NP measures in alcoholics (for discussions of this issue, see Ron, 1983; Grant and Reed, 1984; and Chapter 18, this volume).

Hendler et al. (1980) compared chronic pain patients who received only narcotics with those receiving only benzodiazepines using the WAIS, Wechsler Memory Scale, and Bender Gestalt tests, as well as on EEG measures. The subjects in this study were not "addicts" and no data were provided on length of use other than a history of drug use for 1 month prior to admission. They found chronic pain patients treated with narcotics to be less impaired than those treated with benzodiazepines. It may well be, as best can be determined from the publication, that they were measuring acute effects rather than consequences.

Although the relative paucity of neuropsychological research on the long-term consequences of opiate addiction dictates caution in arriving at conclusions, it appears that abuse of these drugs is not associated with easily detectable organicity—and even those studies which have provided suggestive evidence of mild impairment are contaminated by the inclusion of addicts receiving methadone maintenance. The opiates will be considered again later in this chapter in the discussion of polydrug research.

Sedative-Hypnotics

Despite the widespread use of barbiturates and other sedative hypnotics, including diazepam and other anxiolytics, relatively little research has been carried out on the neuropsychological consequences of these substances. Isbell et al. (1950) and Kornetsky (1950) studied the effects of short-term chronic administration of pentobarbital on five prison inmates using the Bender-Gestalt test, Koh's Block Test, and projective measures. They found impairment during intoxication and withdrawal, but none after 60 days of abstinence. Hill and Belleville (1953) and Wikler et al. (1955) employed similar techniques and found deficits associated with acute effects, but no long-term effects. These studies all examined relatively short-term use of these substances in persons whose cumulative lifetime use of barbiturates was actually quite low.

Bergman, Borg, and Holm (1980) studied 55 patients who were exclusive abusers of sedative and hypnotic drugs, most of whom had abused these substances for 5 years or less, but some of whom had used them for more than 10 years. Following withdrawal, they were tested using an intelligence battery developed in Sweden, the Trail-Making Test, and the Memory for Designs. This patient group was matched with a non-drug-using sample on the basis of age, education, sex, and level of employment. Comparisons were carried out on both separate test scores and on judgments of impairment which were performed by psychologists blind to group membership.

The investigators found that the drug-abusing sample was significantly more impaired as measured both by clinical judgments based on test protocols and on group comparison of test scores. Performance on tests which were believed to be resistant to intellectual impairment did not differ. The authors concluded that the observed impairment in exclusive abusers of sedative hypnotic drugs was the result of the use of these substances. They did not report a relationship between cumulative consumption and impairment nor did they address premorbid status. A number of observations of differences in leisure activities, living situation, and employment stability could have been either a function of drug-induced impairment, premorbid differences or sequelae of functional disorders, such as depression. Despite some shortcomings, by characterizing a group of abusers of a single class of substance, this study has taken an important step towards elucidating the longer-term effects of the sedative hypnotic drugs. The neuropsychological correlates of this drug class will be taken up again later in this chapter in the section on polydrug studies.

Stimulants

The neuropsychological consequences of the abuse of amphetamines, methylphenidate, cocaine, and related central stimulants have been studied hardly at all. Reports of deleterious consequences have been limited to observations of arteritis (Citron et al., 1970; Rumbaugh et al., 1971), vasculitis (Bostwick, 1981), and intracranial hemorrhage (Cahill, Knipp, and Mosser, 1981). The long-term effects of amphetamines on psychological performance have not been studied in populations of primary amphetamine abusers. Beyond the not infrequent observation of reversible paranoid psychosis, it seems likely that occasional abusers will experience cerebrovascular accidents with behavioral changes to match. Animal studies, such as those of Ellinwood et al. (1971), have found marked physical changes in the brains of cats exposed to high levels of amphetamines. The dosages given were extreme, and the animals did not have the opportunity to develop tolerance. It is possible that the observed deterioration in the cats' brains was a function of the pyrexic effects of amphetamine administered rapidly in large dosages rather than a long-term neuropsychopharmacological effect.

General Observations on Investigations Attempting to Study Effects of Single Drug Classes

Aside from the study by Bergman et al. (1980) and the early studies of marihuana and psychedelics, most of the studies reported above were carried out on multiple drug abusers. The authors chose to focus on a drug of interest or notoriety and either ignored use of other drugs or minimized their potential contaminating effects. A major difficulty in studying neuropsychological consequences among polydrug abusers is the inability to assign any observed consequences to any particular drug or combination of drugs. Bruhn and Maage (1975) studied four groups of Danish prisoners who varied in drug use from none to heavy use of several substances. They formed the groups based on interviews which explored the varieties of substances abused and the intensity of use. Based on a statistical analysis of WAIS and the Halstead-Reitan test battery, they found no differences among the four groups. The groups were formed based on frequency of use prior to incarceration; but in a correlated fashion, those who used drugs more frequently used a greater variety as well. As a result, the groups varied simultaneously in both frequency and extent of use. Based on statistical comparisons of individual subtests of the Halstead-Reitan, no differences were found in performance.

Many of the studies described above suffer from a number of common methodological deficiencies. Composition of relevant comparison groups is one issue. Are conclusions best drawn from comparing the performance of drug abusers to a normal (non-patient, non-drug-using) group? No doubt many drug abusers are suffering from serious psychopathology as well as the consequences of drug use and, therefore, it is not clear whether observed differences should be ascribed to psychopathology or drug use. Severe psychopathology (e.g., schizophrenia) does affect performance on tests of neuropsychological functioning (Heaton, 1980). If so, then a non-drug-abusing psychiatric comparison group might well be included in neuropsychological studies of drug abusers.

Although composition of the drug-abuse group itself seems straightforward, questions can be raised about the definitions of abuse and whether or not the groups studied are in fact sufficiently homogeneous. For example, Acord (1972) and Acord and Barker (1973) defined a group of psychedelic abusers as persons who used the substance under consideration "one or more times," a strategy which allows a larger study group, but one of doubtful validity. Even if history of use and measures of chronicity and frequency are taken into account, it is difficult to determine appropriate cutoff points to define group membership. Is an experimental user one who used a substance one, five, or ten times? Experimental, moderate and heavy use are arbitrary distinctions, and one investigator's moderate user may be another's heavy user.

Because all extant studies of the consequences of drug abuse are cross-sectional, it is difficult to ascribe differences to the drugs consumed and not to preexisting factors which might have produced impairment or produced increased vulnerability to drug effects. Examples include history of childhood illness, learning disabilities, brain trauma, or other neurological illness. One method of avoiding these potentially contaminating events of course is to exclude subjects who have such histories. However, excluding such subjects can influence the sampling procedures in an unknown fashion and lessen the validity and generalizability of the findings.

The difficulties faced by Rounsaville et al. (1981; 1982) in concluding whether or not their heroin addicts were neuropsychologically impaired were not only a function of what can be considered appropriate comparison groups, but also problems in defining what is impairment. Reitan (1974) describes the four methods of inference required to assess neuropsychological functioning and cautions that studies that rely only upon analysis of central tendency are likely to overlook impairment by averaging away the differences among subjects who have very different patterns of disability. Relying on the clinical method avoids this problem and allows a more powerful analysis. Using all available methods of inference, each protocol is judged by a clinician as to whether or not it represents impaired functioning, the nature of the impairment, and its severity. Heaton et al. (1981) recently showed that two suitably trained clinicians could achieve high reliability in clinical ratings of Halstead-Reitan battery results; furthermore, the clinicians were more accurate in identifying impairment than existing actuarial methods.

The Collaborative Neuropsychological Study of Polydrug Users (CNSP), carried out as part of a national study of polydrug abuse (Wesson et al., 1978) was designed to overcome many of the problems described above. The results of the CNSP have been described in detail in a number of publications (Grant et al., 1977; Grant et al., 1978a; Grant et al., 1978; Grant et al., 1978b; Carlin et al., 1978; 1980. The CNSP compared the Halstead-Reitan performance of abusers with that of groups of psychiatric patients and non-patient non-drug-users. Based on clinician ratings, protocols were dichotomized as impaired or normal. The study was cast into a 2×3 design in which group membership and neuropsychological status served as independent variables. Drug use, which was determined by querying 10-year history of frequency of use for seven categories of drugs (alcohol, marihuana, sedatives, stimulants, hallucinogens, opiates, and antipsychotics) formed the dependent variables in a multivariate analysis of variance (MANOVA). The resultant F was significant, and the significance was maintained when age and education were covaried out. These results were found both for 10-year cumulative use and for what was called peak week use. Peak week referred to amount consumed in the week of heaviest use of the drug in question in the preceding 10 years. Thus, drug use was found to be associated with impairment.

Associated significant univariate effects were found for two substances: opiates and sedatives. Followup evaluations carried out 3 months later found substantially similar results with only mild improvement in the polydrug sample. Neuropsychological status was once again associated with lifetime sedative and opiate use, but not with amount or frequency of drugs used during the followup interval.

In order to determine whether premorbid illnesses might account for observed differences, the results of the medical history questionnaire were examined. It was found that polydrug abusers reported more illness events than did psychiatric patients, who in turn reported more events than did normals. Medical history questionnaire score accounted for 20% of the variance in the Halstead Impairment Index. When the six medical history items which might possibly predict neuropsychological impairment but which predated drug use were examined, it was found that only one (learning disability) was associated with sedative and opiate use—a history of learning disability showed a weak *inverse* relationship with amount of sedative use. It appeared that health events occurring prior to or independent of drug use could be associated with impairment, independent of or in interaction with drug abuse.

The relatively large sample size allowed a factor analysis to be carried out on the neuropsychological test data. This was done to determine whether a specific pattern of disability was associated with the impairment found in the polydrug subjects. Four factors emerged: (1) a general verbal intelligence factor; (2) a perceptual-skills visual motor factor; (3) an attentional factor; (4) a trace factor which loaded primarily with motor strength. A multivariate analysis of variance (MANOVA) comparing group performance on the four factors reached significance. Associated univariate Fs were significant for the first, second, and fourth. When the effects of educational differences were removed via covariance analysis, the MANOVA maintained significance, but only the univariate F's for factor (2) and factor (4) contributed were significant. These data suggest the observed impairment associated with drug use was in the realm of observed visual-motor, spatial functioning. The re-evaluation of these subjects 3 months after the initial evaluation found that impairment was maintained despite little interim drug use. This would suggest that the observed impairment was relatively enduring or at best very slowly resolving.

The hypothesis that premorbid status and other factors interact to affect the relationship between drug use and impairment was examined via further analysis of the data provided by the CNSP. Earlier, Carlin and Stauss (1977, 1978) found it useful to characterize subgroups of polydrug abusing patients as either "streetwise" or "straight" and as either "social recreational" or "self-medicating" drug users. Sufficient data existed to allow 100 of the 151 members of the polydrug group used in the CNSP to be classified with this framework. Carlin et al. (1978) found that these dimensions predicted impairment better than did drug use history. "Straight", "self-medicating" drug abusers were far more likely to be impaired than "streetwise," "social recreational" users. Further analysis of these data revealed a complex relationship between drug use, streetwise status, and neuropsychological impairment (Carlin et al., 1980). A $2 \times 2 \times 2$ MANOVA was computed using streetwise status, self-medication, and impairment as independent variables and 10 year cumulative use of depressants, morphine, alcohol, stimulants, and marihuana as dependent variables. Of interest was the significant interaction between streetwise status and impairment. Associated univariate Fs were found significant for morphine, alcohol, opiates, and marihuana. "Streetwise" and "straight" users who were not impaired did not differ in their use of opiates, but impaired "streetwise" patients used more opiates and impaired "straight" subjects used less. A similar pattern was found for alcohol. With respect to marihuana, impaired users consumed less marihuana than did their unimpaired counterparts regardless of whether they were classified as "streetwise" or "straight". The results for sedatives differed from the opiate and alcohol interactions: "straight" impaired users tended to consume more sedatives than did impaired "streetwise" subjects and unimpaired users in either classification. Thus, it would appear as if "streetwise" subjects who are impaired consumed more opiates and alcohol, and "straight" impaired subjects consumed *less* of these substances, but more sedatives (the latter was a trend).

These findings gave rise to the question of what other factors could account for the impairment observed in the straight polydrug subjects who tended to use less drugs overall? In an effort to determine whether premorbid events may have contributed to the impairment of the straight subjects, an examination of the relationship between health events and impairment was carried out. Nine items from the health questionnaire were determined to represent a clear risk for impaired neuropsychological status. Subjects who endorsed any one of these items were classified as at risk allowing a dichotomy of subjects "at risk." Subjects were also classified as "high rate" and "low rate" drug users. High rate users were those whose use of opiates, alcohol, depressants, or stimulants fell into the upper quartile for that substance. Comparisons via chi-square revealed that risk status and impairment were associated for low rate users, but not for high rate users. Taken as a whole these data suggest that there exists a group of polydrug abusers whose extensive use of opiates and alcohol puts them at risk for neuropsychological impairment. In addition, there is another group of polydrug abusers whose health history contributes to their neuropsychological impairment either independently of drug use or through increasing their vulnerability to neurotoxic effects of drugs at lower levels of exposure. The former tend to be "streetwise" and the latter "straight".

What can be concluded from the CNSP findings? The foremost finding is that the relationship between consumption of psychoactive drugs of abuse and neuropsychological impairment is complex and precludes a simple answer to whether "drug abuse" is related to brain damage. It would appear that the answer must state that some impaired polydrug abusers have "done themselves in" through extensive use of opiates, alcohol, and perhaps sedative hypnotics. Another group either were impaired prior to drug use or were more vulnerable to the neurotoxic effects of drug abuse due to health events preceding or independent of drug use.

The implication of opiates as possible etiological agents in neuropsychological impairment is inconsistent with previous findings by Fields and Fullerton (1974) and consistent with the findings of Hill et al. (1979) and Rounsaville et al. (1981). It is possible that Fields and Fullerton's reliance on statistics which only compared central tendency might have obscured impairment among their patient subjects. It is also possible that their subjects had less exposure to opiates than did those in the CNSP, or that opiate use must be combined with sedatives and/or alcohol to produce neuropsychological dysfunction. Recent work by Bergman and associates with exclusive sedative abusers supports CNSP findings associating impairment with heavy use of these agents (Bergman, Borg, and Holm, 1980).

Once again marihuana emerges as a substance unlikely to be involved in "brain damage" in this CNSP population despite extensive use. Indeed, the CNSP reported a *negative* relationship, suggesting that impaired persons tended to avoid marihuana. Hallucinogens and solvents were little used by the CNSP study group, hence their failure to be implicated in impairment cannot be taken to mean absence of harmful effects. The lack of impairment related to amphetamines is of interest, being inconsistent with clinical reports of stroke and other neurological catastrophies associated with heavy use of these agents. It may be that amphetamine-related impairment occurs in an "all or none fashion", that is, impairment does not slowly accumulate, but rather a dramatic cerebral event (arterial spasm or hemorrhage) can result in relatively massive impairment. Such victims of amphetamine abuse are not likely to be common among the kinds of patients seen in the CNSP or other similar research populations.

The CNSP would appear to be one of the few studies that attempted to go beyond the global statement of whether or not "brain damage" exists and examine the nature of the deficit. It would appear as if visual-motor and spatial deficit can be most closely tied to misuse of opiates, sedatives, and alcohol.

Summary

In the face of methodological difficulties (discussed earlier) facing research on the neuropsychological consequences of drug abuse, it is not surprising that definitive statements which are empirically supported are difficult to come by. Rather than continue carrying out studies, which by their cross-sectional nature are limited, other strategies should be investigated. An obvious approach, but one unlikely to be carried out due to the relatively high cost, is a longitudinal study in which several cohorts at risk for drug misuse are followed over time.

It is also possible to carry out "meta-analysis" of the studies to date. This methodology attempts to estimate effect size in order to cumulate research findings across studies (Hunter, Schmidt, and Jackson, 1982). Superior to "vote counting" in which studies supporting or failing to support a relationship are tallied, this method might allow a reconciliation of the studies implicating or failing to implicate psychoactive substances in neuropsychological impairment. Adequacy of control groups, entry criteria, health factors and other possible contaminating variables, extensiveness and intensity of drug use, and other relevant variables can be coded and entered into the analysis. Appropriate computations could determine effect size. That is, an overall determination can be made of the extent of the relationship between consumption of a substance and measures of impairment which is relatively independent of traditional statistical significance. This determination is of particular importance if the impact of the drug on neuropsychological integrity is modest, as is likely for most substances. A modest or even small effect size does not suggest that the health implications are trivial. The example of cigarette smoking demonstrates that a small effect size can translate into a major public health problem.

Additional cross-sectional studies using small samples of subjects not rigorously selected are not likely to elucidate the issue of neuropsychological consequences, but may actually further the confusion. Small to moderate sample sizes and small to moderate effect sizes can be expected to increase the rate of nonreplication. Large samples and efforts to create more homogeneous subgroups of subject types will be required to clarify neuropsychological consequences of drugs of abuse and increase the meaningfulness of answers.

In neuropsychiatric settings, information about any significant drug abuse history and pattern must be seen as vital. The knowledge that a particular patient has a history of multiple substance abuse would potentially figure prominently in the construction of any model of behavioral deficit. In closing, we might offer that research in the neuropsychological effects of drug abuse may well advance into relevant health domains where other sources of impairment (e.g., cerebrovascular disease) may coexist with the likelihood of drug-modulated cerebral deficit.

REFERENCES

Acord, L. D. (1972). Hallucinogenic drugs and brain damage. *Military Med., 137*, 18–19.

Acord, L. D., and Barker, D. D. (1973). Hallucinogenic drugs and cerebral deficit. *J. Nerv. Mental Dis., 156*, 281–283.

Adams, K. M., Rennick, P., Schooff, K., and Keegan, J. (1975). Neuropsychological measurement of drug effects: Polydrug research. *J. Psychedelic Drugs, 7*, 151–160.

Bergman, H., Borg, S., and Holm, L. (1980). Neuropsychological impairment and exclusive abuse of sedatives or hypnotics. *Am. J. Psychiat., 137*, 215–217.

Berry, G. J., Heaton, R. K., and Kirby, M. W. (1977). Neuropsychological deficits of chronic inhalant abusers. In: B. Rumac and A. Temple, eds., *Management of the Poisoned Patient*. Princeton: Science Press, pp. 9–31.

Bostwick, D. G. (1981). Amphetamine induced cerebral vasculitis. *Human Pathol., 12*(11), 1031–1033.

Brown, R. R., and Partington, J. E. (1942). A psychometric comparison of narcotic addicts with hospital attendants. *J. General Psychol., 27*, 71–79.

Bruhn, P., and Maage, N. (1975). Intellectual and neuropsychological functions in young men with heavy and long-term patterns of drug abuse. *Am. J. Psychiat., 132*, 397–401.

Cahill, D. W., Knipp, H., and Mosser, J. (1981). Intracranial hemorrhage with amphetamine abuser (letter). *Neurology, 31*(8), 1058–1059.

Carlin, A. S., Grant, K., Adams, K. M., and Reed, R. (1979). Is phencyclidine (PCP) abuse associated with organic brain impairment? *Am. J. Drug Alcohol Abuse, 6*, 273–281.

Carlin, A. S., and Stauss, F. F. (1977). Descriptive and functional classifications of drug abuse. *J. Consult. Clin. Psychol., 45*, 222–227.

Carlin, A. S., and Stauss, F. F. (1978). Two typologies of polydrug abuses. In: D. R. Wesson, A. S. Carlin, K. M. Adams, and G. Beschner, eds., *Polydrug Abuse: The Results of a National Collaborative Study*. New York: Academic Press, pp. 97–127.

Carlin, A. S., Stauss, F. F., Grant, I., and Adams, K. M. (1978). Prediction of neuropsychological impairment in polydrug abuse patients. *Addictive Behav., 3*, 5–12.

Carlin, A. S., Stauss, F. F., Grant, I., and Adams, K. M. (1908). Role of streetwise status and drug use in neuropsychological impairment among polydrug abusers. *Addictive Behav., 5*, 229–234.

Carlin, A. S., and Trupin, E. (1977). The effects of long-term chronic cannabis use on neuropsychological functioning. *Int. J. Addictions, 12*, 617–624.

Citron, B. P., Halpern, M., McCarron, M., Lundberg, G. D., McCormick, R., Pincus, I. J., Tatter, D., and Haverback, B. J. (1962). Necrotizing angitis associated with drug abuse. *New Engl. J. Nerv. Mental Dis., 134*, 162–168.

Cohen, S., and Edwards, A. E. (1969). LSD and organic brain impairment. *Drug Dependence, 2*, 1–4.

Culver, C. M., and King, F. W. (1974). Neuropsychological assessment of undergraduate marihuana and LSD users. *Arch. General Psychiat., 31*, 707–711.

Dodds, J., and Santostefano, S. (1964). A comparison of the cognitive functioning of glue-sniffers and nonsniffers. *J. Pediatrics, 64*, 565–570.

Ellinwood, E. H., and Cohen, S. (1971). Amphetamine use. *Science, 171*, 420–421.

Fields, F. R. J., and Fullerton, J. R. (1974). The influence of heroin addiction on neuropsychological functioning. *Veterans Administration Newsletter for Research in Mental Health and Behavioral Sciences, 16*, 20–25. Washington, D.C., Department of Medicine and Surgery, Veterans Administration.

Grabski, D. A. (1921). Toluene sniffing producing cerebellar degeneration. *Am. J. Psychiat., 118*, 461–462.

Grant, I., Rochford, J., Fleming, T., and Stunkard, H. (1973). A neuropsychological assessment of the effects of moderate marihuana use. *J. Nerv. Mental Dis., 156*, 278–280.

Grant, I., Adams, K. M., Carlin, A. S., and Rennick, P. M. (1977). Neuropsychological deficit in polydrug abusers. *Drug and Alcohol Dependence, 2*, 91–108.

Grant, I., Adams, K. M., Carlin, A. S., Rennick, P. M., Judd, L. L., Schooff, K., and Reed, R. (1978). Organic impairment in polydrug abusers: Risk factors. *Am. J. Psychiat.*, *135*, 178–184.

Grant, I., Adams, K. M., Carlin, A. S., Rennick, P. M., Judd, L. L., and Schooff, K. (1978). The collaborative neuropsychological study of polydrug abusers. *Arch. General Psychiat.*, *35*, 1063–1073.

Grove, W. M., and Andreasen, N. C. (1982). Simultaneous tests of many hypotheses in exploratory research. *J. Nerv. Mental Dis. 170:*3–8.

Halstead, W. C. (1947). *Brain and Intelligence*. Chicago: University of Chicago Press.

Heaton, R. K., Baak, L. E., and Johnson, K. L. (1978). Neuropsychological test results associated with psychiatric disorders in adults. *Psychol. Bull.*, *85*, 141–162.

Heaton, R. K., Grant, I., Anthony, W. Z., and Lehman, R. A. (1981). A comparison of clinical and automated interpretation of the Halstead Reitan Battery. *J. Clin. Neuropsychol.*, *3*, 121–141.

Hendler, N., Cimini, C., Tra, T., and Lanz, D. (1980). A comparison of cognitive impairment due to benzodiazepines and to narcotics. *Am. J. Psychiat.*, *137*, 828–830.

Hill, H. E., and Belleville, R. E. (1953). Effects of chronic barbiturate intoxication on motivation and muscular coordination. *Arch. Neurol. Psychiat.*, *70*, 180–188.

Hill, S. Y., Reyes, R. B., Mikhael, M., and Ayre, F. (1979). A comparison of alcoholics and heroin abusers: Computerized transaxial tomography and neuropsychological functioning. *Currents in Alcoholism*, *5*, 187–205.

Hunter, J. E., Schmidt, F. L., and Jackson, G. B. (1982). *Meta-analysis: Cumulating Research Findings Across Studies*. Beverly Hills: Sage Publications.

Isbell, H., Altschul, S., Kornetsky, C. H., Eiseman, A. J., Flanery, H. G., and Fraser, H. F. (1950). Chronic barbiturate intoxication: An experimental study. *Arch. Neurol. Psychiat.*, *68*, 1–28.

Kelly, T. (1975). Prolonged cerebellar dysfunction associated with paint sniffing. *Pediatrics*, *56*, 605–606.

Knox, J., and Nelson, J. (1966). Permanent encephalopathy from toluene inhalation. *New Engl. J. Med.*, *275*, 1494–1496.

Kolansky, H., and Moore, W. T. (1971). Effects of marijuana on adolescents and young adults. *J.A.M.A.*, *216*, 486–492.

Kolansky, H., and Moore, W. T. (1972). Toxic effects of chronic marijuana use. *J.A.M.A.*, *222*, 35–41.

Korin, H. (1974). Comparison of psychometric measures in psychiatric patients using heroin and other drugs. *J. Abnorm. Psychol.*, *83*, 208–212.

Kornetsky, C. H. (1951). Psychological effects of chronic barbiturate intoxication. *Arch. Neurol. Psychiat.*, *65*, 557–567.

Lewis, J. D., Moritz, D., and Mellis, L. (1981). Long-term toluene abuse. *Am. J. Psychiat.*, *138*, 368–370.

Malm, G., and Lying-Tunell, U. (1980). Cerebellar dysfunction related to toluene sniffing. *Acta. Neurol. Scand.*, *62*, 188–190.

McGlothlin, W. H., Arnold, D. O., and Freedman, D. X. (1969). Organicity measures following repeated LSD ingestion. *Arch. General Psychiat.*, *21*, 704–709.

Pfeffer, A. Z., and Ruble, D. C. (1946). Chronic psychosis and addiction to morphine. *Arch. Neurol. Psychiat.*, *56*, 665–672.

Reitan, R. M. (1955). Investigation of the validity of Halstead's measure of biological intelligence. *AMA Arch. Neurol. Psychiat.*, *73*, 28–35.

Reitan, R. M., and Davison, L. A. (1974). *Clinical Neuropsychology: Current Status and Applications*. Washington, D.C.: V. H. Winston and Sons.

Rochford, J., Grant, I., and LaVigne, G. (1977). Medical students and drugs. Neuropsychological and use pattern considerations. *Int. J. Addictions*, *12*, 1057–1065.

Ron, M. A. (1983). The alcoholic brain: CT scan and psychological findings. *Psychological Medicine: Monograph Suppl. 3*. Cambridge: Cambridge University Press, pp. 1–33.

Rounsaville, B. J., Jones, C., Novelly, R. A., and Kleber, M. D. (1982). Neuropsychological functioning in opiate addicts. *J. Nerv. Mental Dis., 70*, 209–216.

Rounsaville, B. J., Novelly, R. A., and Kleber, M. D. (1981). Neuropsychology and impairment in opiate addicts: Risk factors. *Ann. New York Acad. Sci., 362*, 79–90.

Rubin, J., and Comitas, L. (1975). *Ganja in Jamaica: A Medical and Anthropological Study of Chronic Marihuana Use.* The Hague: Mouton.

Rumbaugh, C. L., and Fang, H. C. H. (1980). The effects of drug abuse on the brain. *Medical Times, 108*, 37s–52s.

Satz, P., Fletcher, J. M., and Sutker, L. S. (1976). Neuropsychologic, intellectual and personality correlates of chronic marihuana use in native Costa Ricans. In R. Dornbush, A. M. Freedman, and M. Fink, eds., *Chronic Cannabis Use. Ann. New York Acad. Sci., 282*, 266–306.

Souief, M. I. (1976). Differential association between chronic cannabis use and brain function deficits. In: R. Dornbush, A. M. Freedman, and M. Fink, eds., *Chronic Cannabis Use. Ann. New York Acad. Sci., 282*, 323–334.

Tsushima, W. T., and Towne, W. S. (1977). Effects of paint sniffing on neuropsychological test performance. *J. Abnorm. Psychol., 869*, 402–407.

Wesson, D. W., Carlin, A. S., Adams, K. M., and Beschner, G., eds. (1978). *Polydrug Abuse: The Results of a National Collaborative Study.* New York: Academic Press.

Wikler, A., Fraser, H. F., Isbell, H., and Pescor, F. T. (1955). Electroencephalograms during cycles of addiction to barbiturates in man. *Electroencephalogr. Clin. Neurophysiol., 7*(1), 1–13.

Wright, M., and Hogan, T. P. (1972). Repeated LSD ingestion and performance on neuropsychological tests. *J. Nerv. Ment. Dis., 154*, 432–438.

Author Index

510 AUTHOR INDEX

Test Index

Subject Index